**SEVENTH EDITION**

# Integrating Educational Technology into Teaching

## M. D. Roblyer
*Nova Southeastern University*

**PEARSON**

Boston   Columbus   Indianapolis   New York   San Francisco   Upper Saddle River
Amsterdam   Cape Town   Dubai   London   Madrid   Milan   Munich   Paris   Montréal   Toronto
Delhi   Mexico City   São Paulo   Sydney   Hong Kong   Seoul   Singapore   Taipei   Tokyo

**Vice President and Editorial Director:** Jeffery Johnston
**Executive Editor & Publisher:** Meredith Fossel
**Editorial Assistant:** Maria Feliberty
**Marketing Managers:** Christopher Barry and Krista Clark
**Senior Content Editor:** Maxine Effenson Chuck
**Program Manager:** Maren Beckman
**Project Manager:** Karen Mason
**Manufacturing Buyer:** Deidra Skahill
**Full-Service Project Management:** MPS North America LLC
**Compositor:** Jouve
**Rights and Permissions Research Project Manager:** Tania Zamora
**Manager, Cover Visual Research & Permissions:** Diane Lorenzo
**Cover Image Credits:** Courtesy of the Author and W. Wiencke
**Printer/Binder:** Courier Kendallville, Inc.

Photo Credits: Appear on the page with the image. Design credits: Technology Integration in Action header: Vs148/Shutterstock; Big Ideas icon: Floral_set/Fotolia; Footer watermark: Venimo/Fotolia; Open Source Options header: Scyther5/Shutterstock; Media callout screen: Rawpixel/Fotolia; Technology Integration Example image: Ra2 studio/Fotolia; Hot Topic Debate icon: Arcady/Fotolia; Hot Topic Debate header: Photo Lux/Shutterstock; Adapting for Special Needs icon: Zentilia/Fotolia; Adapting for Special needs background: Alphaspirit/Shutterstock; Summary watermark: Alexey Boldin/ Shutterstock; Collaborate, Discuss, Reflect header background: Artant/Fotolia

Text Credits: Credits and acknowledgments borrowed from other sources and reproduced, with permission, in this textbook appear on appropriate page within text.

**Library of Congress Cataloging-in-Publication Data**
Roblyer, M. D.
   Integrating educational technology into teaching / M.D. Roblyer. – Seventh edition.
     pages cm
   Includes bibliographical references and index.
   ISBN 978-0-13-379279-9 – ISBN 0-13-379279-X  1. Educational technology–United States.  2. Computer-assisted instruction–United States.  3. Curriculum planning–United States.  I. Title.
   LB1028.3.R595 2016
   371.33—dc23
                                        2014043396

10 9 8 7 6 5 4 3 2 1

ISBN-10: 0-13-379279-X
ISBN-13: 978-0-13-379279-9

For Bill and Paige Wiencke, whose love is,
as Arthur Clarke said of advanced technology,
indistinguishable from magic.

*—MDR*

Photo courtesy Paige Wiencke

**M. D. Roblyer** has been a technology-using professor and contributor to the field of educational technology for over 30 years and has authored or coauthored hundreds of books, monographs, articles, columns, and papers on educational technology research and practice. Her other books for Pearson Education include *Starting Out on the Internet: A Learning Journey for Teachers*; *Technology Tools for Teachers: A Microsoft Office Tutorial* (with Steven C. Mills); *Educational Technology in Action: Problem-Based Exercises for Technology Integration*; and the most recent text, *Introduction to Instructional Design for Traditional, Online, and Blended Environments* (2015).

She began her exploration of technology's benefits for teaching in 1971 as a graduate student at one of the country's first successful instructional computer training sites, Pennsylvania State University, where she helped write tutorial literacy lessons in the Coursewriter II authoring language on an IBM 1500 dedicated instructional mainframe computer. While obtaining a PhD in instructional systems at Florida State University, she worked on several major courseware development and training projects with Control Data Corporation's PLATO system. In 1981–1982, she designed one of the early microcomputer software series, *Grammar Problems for Practice*, in conjunction with the Milliken Publishing Company.

Currently, Dr. Roblyer is Adjunct Professor of Instructional Technology and Distance Education (ITDE) at Nova Southeastern University, chairing dissertations for ITDE doctoral students. She serves on editorial boards of various technology and research journals and is past-president of two AERA special interest groups. She is married to fellow FSU PhD William R. Wiencke and is the mother of a daughter, Paige.

# BRIEF CONTENTS

# CONTENTS

## PART 2 Technology Tools for 21st Century Teaching

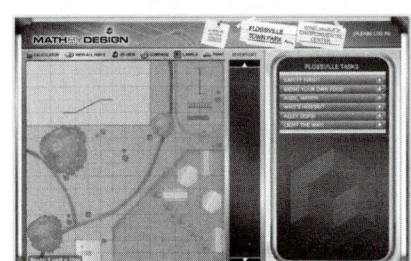

## PART 3   Linking to Learn: Technology Tools and Strategies

**8**   Online Models, Courses, and Programs  231

    LEARNING OUTCOMES  231

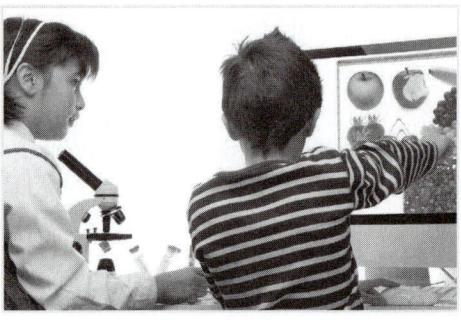

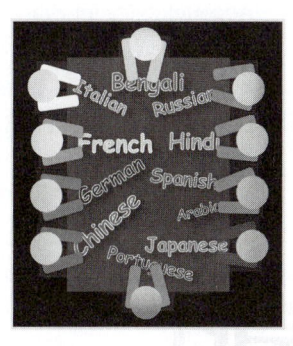

## 11 Teaching and Learning with Technology in Mathematics and Science  305

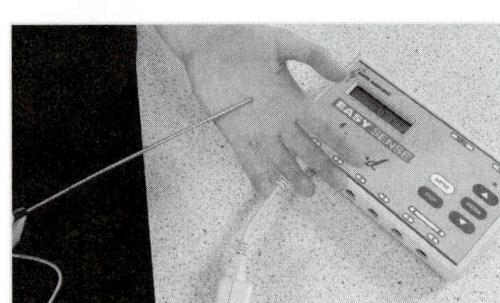

**14 Teaching and Learning with Technology in Health and Physical Education 378**

# SPECIAL FEATURES

# OPEN SOURCE OPTIONS

# TECHNOLOGY INTEGRATION EXAMPLES

After a three-year gestation, the first edition of this textbook emerged in 1996—and what a time to be born! Digital technology in education too, was an infant, on the threshold of becoming a very capable, very unpredictable child. It appeared to have potential, as any youngster does, but how could we have known how far it would go and how thoroughly and unexpectedly its transformation would transform us? This book has grown along with it, chronicling its advances and our responses to them over the years. In those early days of the Digital Age, educators, like the rest of the planet, were taking their fledgling first steps onto the World Wide Web; the first edition of this text was also the first to predict that the Internet would become a major distance education technology. Since then, the tools have become more capable, diverse, and ubiquitous, and societal interest in digital technologies has segued into obsession. But the greatest challenge remains as constant as a compass: deciding how best to make use of technology's prodigious possibilities. As Richard Florida (2013) said when describing the rise of robots in the workplace, it is not our technology that defines us. Rather it is how we choose to fit it to our needs.

In this seventh edition of *Integrating Educational Technology into Teaching*, as in past ones, I seek to go beyond describing the technical features and capabilities of 21st century technology tools to focus ever more on the teaching and learning strategies they can support. What have we learned so far that enables an enlightened view of technology in education? The following are some clearly defined guidelines on what works best when it comes to matching the needs of the educational community with technology's capabilities:

- **Good pedagogy comes first**—Advancements in distance education in the late 1990s and in knowledge sharing in the years afterward gave renewed support to those who predicted, as did their predecessors in the 1960s, that technology would decrease or eliminate the need for teachers. However, our experience with these very capable technologies has shown more clearly than ever that the interaction between teachers and students remains an essential quality of effective education. This textbook proposes that technologies are, above all, channels for helping teachers communicate better with students—ways of making their relationships more meaningful and productive. It can make good teaching even better; it cannot make bad teaching good. Consequently, technology-using teachers can never be a force for improved education unless they are first and foremost informed, knowledgeable shapers of their craft. Before integrating technology into their teaching, educators must know a great deal, for example, about why there are different views on appropriate teaching strategies, how societal factors and learning theories have shaped these views, and how each strategy can address differing needs.

- **Technology is us**—Rather than seeing technology as some foreign invader here to confuse and complicate the simple life of the past, we can recognize that technology is very much our own response to overcoming obstacles that stand in the way of a better, more productive way of life. As Walt Kelly's "profound 'possum" Pogo said, "We have met the enemy, and he is us." Technology is the tools we fashion and the ways we choose to use them to solve problems in our environment. Turmoil will accompany the transitions as we adapt to the new environment we ourselves have created. But technology is, by definition, intended to be part of our path to a better life, rather than an obstacle in its way.

- **We control how technology is used in education**—Finally, we must recognize the truth of Peter Drucker's statement: "The best way to predict the future is to create it." Both individual teachers and teaching organizations must see themselves as enlightened shapers of our future. Each teacher must help to articulate the vision for what the future of education should look like; each should acquire skills that will help realize that vision.

# WHAT'S NEW IN THE SEVENTH EDITION

Best known for its technology integration strategies grounded in strong research, the seventh edition of *Integrating Educational Technology into Teaching* offers a total technology integration package across all content areas that gives your students practice with technology tools as they learn how to incorporate technology into the curriculum to support and shape learning. This edition includes a number of additions that reflect changes in the field of educational technology.

- **NEW!** Chapter 1 has new coverage of issues that affect technology integration such as the need for digital literacy and digital citizenship, as well as information on new methods and technology formats such as Bring Your Own Device (BYOD) and Massive Open Online Courses (MOOCs), and expanded uses of access tools such as tablets.

- **NEW!** Chapter 2 has expanded coverage of each of the relevant behaviorist, cognitive, and constructivist learning theories that underlie technology integration strategies.

- **NEW!** Chapters 6 through 8 have been re-organized to emphasize the rapidly expanding role of online tools and strategies. New coverage includes methods to teach digital literacy and digital citizenship, new uses of social media, and design and use of online and blended learning formats such as flipped classrooms.

- **NEW!** Chapters 9 through 15 each offer strategies and a content-specific rubric that teachers can use to direct and self-assess their growth in technology integration.

- **UPDATED!** All chapters have updated research and examples for tools and/or strategies.

- **UPDATED!** Each chapter has been updated and new content has been added to document and illustrate major changes and trends in the field, such as the new emphasis on:
  - Blended learning (e.g., the flipped classroom)
  - Social media and networking
  - Virtual courses and virtual schools

- **NEW INTERACTIVE ETEXT FEATURES!** An all-new Pearson eText version includes the following interactive features in each chapter:
  - **Author-recorded BIG IDEAS OVERVIEWS (BIO)** on main chapter concepts and points to guide reading.
  - **Top Ten** (in Chapters 1 and 3–8) features highlight and describe the best software features, uses, and strategies for teachers to apply.
  - **Top Ten Must-Have Apps** (in Chapters 9–15) have been recommended by experts in the content area and present apps that are widely used in society; examples help educators see the role these tools are beginning to play in education.
  - **Links to video** illustrations and commentaries from practitioners in the field.
  - **Interactive Technology Learning Checks (TLCs)** at the end of each major section are matched to each chapter learning outcome. These help readers apply the concepts and ensure that they master each chapter outcome.
  - **End-of-chapter Technology Integration Workshops** now include links to a **Technology Application Activities** and a **Technology Lesson Plan Evaluation Checklist** that teachers can use to select most effective integration strategies.

# CORE PRINCIPLES AT THE CENTER OF THIS TEXT

The purpose of this book is to show how we are challenged to shape the future of technology in education. How we respond to this challenge is guided by how we see it helping us accomplish our own informed vision of what teaching and learning should be. Our approach to accomplishing this rests on four premises:

1. **Instructional technology methods should be based in both learning theory and teaching practice**—There is no shortage of innovative ideas in the field of instructional technology; new and interesting methods come forth about as often as new and improved gadgets. Those who would build on the knowledge of the past should know why they do what they do, as well as how to do it. Thus, various technology-based integration strategies are linked to well-researched theories of learning, and we have illustrated them with examples of successful practices based on these theories.

2. **Uses of technology should match specific teaching and learning needs**—Technology has the power to improve teaching and learning, but it can also make a teacher's life more complicated. Therefore, each resource should be examined for its unique qualities and its potential benefits for teachers and students. Teachers should not use a tool simply because it is new and available; each integration strategy should be matched to a recognized need. Do not oppose experimentation, but do advocate informed use.

3. **Old integration strategies are not necessarily bad; new strategies are not necessarily good**—As technologies change and evolve at lightning speed, there is a tendency to throw out older teaching methods with the older machines. Sometimes this is a good idea; sometimes it would be a shame. Each of the integration strategies recommended in this book is based on methods with proven usefulness to teachers and students. Some of the strategies are based on directed methods that have been used for some time; other strategies are based on the newer, constructivist learning models. Each is recommended on the basis of its usefulness rather than its age.

4. **A combination of technological, pedagogical, and content knowledge is necessary**—This textbook maintains that that teachers not only need to know the content they are teaching and good pedagogical strategies for connecting students with content, but must also recognize how to integrate technology into pedagogy to achieve greatest impact on desired outcomes. In other words, teachers need what the field now refers to as a combination of Technological Pedagogical Content Knowledge or Tech-PACK.

The goal of this edition is for teachers to see more clearly their role in shaping the future of technology in education. This book illustrates that great education means employing technologies to fulfill the vision they make possible: a worldwide social network and a global community that learns and grows together.

# FEATURES OF THIS TEXT

For the seventh edition, the author maintains a cohesive, comprehensive technology integration framework that builds on strong research and numerous integration strategies. This Technology Integration Framework achieves the following goals:

## Introduces Your Students to Technology Integration

**TECHNOLOGY INTEGRATION IN ACTION**
**SHARING A PASSION FOR POETRY**

GRADE LEVEL: Grades 4–5 • CONTENT AREA/TOPIC: Language arts, poetry • LENGTH OF TIME: An hour each day for 6 days

**PHASE 1** ANALYSIS OF LEARNING AND TEACHING NEEDS

**Step 1: Determine relative advantage.**

Mr. Lipe is a fifth grade teacher who has great difficulty getting his young students to share his passion for poetry. He tried various teaching approaches, but many students remained indifferent, and few are interested enough to read or write poems after the unit is over. When he taught mathematics activities, he had found that using his interactive whiteboard made it easier to engage students, especially if they played a part in illustrating and practicing concepts. He felt that with the right kinds of activities, he might also engage them in learning about and writing poetry. From a blog for teachers, he learned about some online materials to help teach poetry, some of which could be used with interactive whiteboards and allowed students to publish their work online. After reviewing the materials, he decided to restructure his poetry unit around these activities. He would display the online "poetry engine" on the whiteboard to illustrate several types of poems that kids can write, and it would also allow students some initial practice in writing poems. After more practice in pairs and small groups, each would have to write one poem of each kind, with or without the poetry engine, and each would be allowed to publish one poem on the website.

ZouZou/Shutterstock

**Step 2: Assess required resources and skills.**

Mr. Lipe felt he knew a great deal about writing poetry, since he had had good instructors in his undergraduate program and was a poet himself. But after three years of unsuccessful efforts to engage his students in poetry writing, he felt less confident in his ability to motivate young people on this topic. To improve his instructional approaches, he read through a variety of blogs and online materials looking for ideas on how to teach poetry better. After reading these materials and blogging with colleagues who gave him good leads, he felt more confident that the new approach would be much more motivating to students.

**PHASE 2** PLANNING FOR INTEGRATION

**Step 3: Decide on objectives and assessments.**

To help him see if students were achieving what he hoped in the poetry unit, Mr. Lipe created objectives and assessments to measure students' progress in poetry skills, as well as their attitudes toward poetry. The outcomes, objectives, and assessments were

Outcome: Write three different poems reflecting t...
Objective: After participating in the practice acti...
using either a poetry engine or writing on the wor...
Assessment: A rubric of criteria and points.

Outcome: Feel more positively about poetry.
Objective: At least 80% of students express inte...
comments to the teacher or poems they offer.
Assessment: Teacher observation.

**Step 4: Design integration strate...**

Mr. Lipe knew that the initial activities would be gr...
the following sequence of activities to be done in...

Day 1: **Introduce the unit.** Begin by reading two...
people (e.g., Shel Silverstein's *Where the Sidewalk*...
each poem from the book. Ask students to close...

CHAPTER 5 | Technology Tools for 21st C...

◀ **Technology Integration in Action** examples, located at the beginning of Chapters 2 through 15, are classroom-based scenarios that provide a classroom context for chapter content by focusing on the selection and use of specific technology within a classroom environment. Each walks the reader through the steps of the Technology Integration Lesson Planning exercise (TIP) Model and is tied to chapter objectives.

▼ **Hot Topics for Debate** help teachers address social issues that may present obstacles to effective technology integration.

**Hot Topic Debate**
**Can Students Learn as Well Online as Face-to-Face?**

Take a position for or against (based either on your own position or one assigned to you) on the following controversial statement. Discuss it in class or on an online discussion board, blog, or wiki, as assigned by your instructor. When the discussion is complete, write a summary of the main pros and cons that you and your classmates have stated, and not using various technologies. Similar studies have been done comparing distance learning and traditional learning (Bernard et al., 2009), yielding the same results: no significant differences. However, we also know that the dropout rate is higher in distance learning. Many recent studies report the quality and experiences [...] nt learning are impacted by issues ranging from [...] nteraction with the instructor to the type of media [...] hers are correct that the learning medium or dis- [...] akes no difference in learning outcomes, why is [...] e so high? Can you cite evidence to support or [...] on that all students are able to learn well online?

[...] students face-to-face for the first class meeting
[...] etter interaction throughout the course.

[...] dies show that students value and profit from
[...] d and logistical, during their course experiences,
[...] es and evaluation. DiPietro (2010) observed that
[...] ense of community among learners, resulting in
[...] on. McBrien, Cheng, and Jones (2009) find that
[...] rom the teacher and classmates, as well as frustra-
[...] egatively affect course satisfaction.

[...] nt evidence exists that technical problems can
[...] en, 2010; McBrien et al., 2009). Successful courses
[...] ms so that the student can focus on the learning
[...] issues. Not having to mediate technology prob-
[...] time on instruction and accommodating student

[...] stance learners. Some researchers have
[...] ctors that could predict whether a student might
[...] well in an online activity. A study conducted by
[...] at there is no single theory that can fully explain
[...] likely drop out due to a combination of variables.
[...] tance learners include self-motivation and ability
[...] ebba, 2010), previous experience with technology
[...] ude toward course subject matter (Hung, Chou,
[...] ntrol, or a personality characteristic of believing
[...] Vandewaetere & Clarebout, 2011). A study con-
[...] at spending more time online can predict whether
[...] environments. Some studies that support a cor-
[...] cacy and improved outcomes in online courses.
[...] (2011) found that students level of comfort with
[...] p. 437), or belief that they were good at using the
[...] line courses.

[...] ance instructors. Fish and Wickersham
[...] ctors need different skills than instructors for

**Adapting for Special Needs** ▶
features give your students alternative software and technology suggestions to consider for use in supporting students with special needs.

## Adapting for Special Needs

### Software Tools

As students enter middle school, the demands of changing classrooms and teachers each hour challenge the organizational abilities of even the best students. Suddenly, they have to do assignments in many different subjects and must have books and folders to keep track of each subject. Fortunately, most middle schools have a school-wide system (e.g., assignment notebooks, folders, homework-help Web pages) to help students get organized and keep track of all that they are supposed to know and do. However, by October each year some students are "organizationally failing," which makes it difficult for them to do well in their classes.

While staying organized and keeping track of important details is a lifelong challenge for everyone, difficulties with memory storage and retrieval is a fundamental characteristic of many individuals with learning disabilities. As a result, it is important to help these students find an information management system that is highly effective for them. Many of the following organizational tools have features that offer benefits to these students. However, please note that tools alone will not help students overcome deficits in organization and planning. Teachers and parents must commit to monitor the use of the tools and teaching new strategies so that the student can maximize the power of the tool.

- Evernote (at the Evernote website)—Encourages users to make artifacts (a note, image, or URL) of things they have to do, which are then indexed and made searchable.
- PocketMod (at the Pocketmod website)—Provides a way of creating a pocket guide of things to do and remember.
- Remember the Milk (at the Remember the Milk website)—Helps users create a system of reminders of tasks to do.
- Things 2 (at the Cultured Code website)—Lets users create an agenda and daily/weekly/monthly to-do lists.
- Toodledo (at the Toodledo website)—Helps users organize tasks they have to do into folders and subtasks.
- Todoist (at the To Do List website)—An online task manager to help users keep organized.
- Vitalist (at the Vitalist website)—A personal organization and productivity system.
- Voo2Do (at the Voo2do website)—An online system that helps users track priority, due dates, and time estimates for a number of different tasks.

—Contributed by Dave Edyburn

collect information from students, parents, or faculty or to implement surveys as part of research projects. Formatting even the simplest form can be time consuming on a word processor. These software tools structure the process and make the design simple to accomplish. As teachers create these forms, they can store them as templates for later use, perhaps with revisions.

 **TECHNOLOGY LEARNING CHECK**
Complete TLC 5.2 to review what you have learned from reading this section about materials generator features and uses.

### ◯ USING DATA COLLECTION AND ANALYSIS TOOLS

Data collection and analysis tools include database software, statistical software packages, online survey sites, student information systems, online and computer-based testing systems, and student response systems, or clickers. A summary of these tools, with sample products and classroom uses, is shown in Table 5.3.

### Database Software

**Databases** are computer programs that allow users to store, organize, and manipulate information, including both text and numerical data. Database software can perform some calculations, but its real power lies in allowing people to locate information through keyword searches. A database program is most often compared to a file cabinet or a Rolodex card file. Like these precomputer devices, the purpose of a database is to store important information in a way that makes it easy to locate later. This capability has become increasingly important as society's store of essential information grows in volume and complexity.

CHAPTER 5 | Technology Tools for 21st Century Teaching—Beyond the Basics | 149

# Helps Your Students Plan for Effective Technology Integration

**Technology Integration Examples (TIEs)** ▶ located in Chapters 3 through 15 offer numerous technology lesson ideas that can be incorporated into lesson planning across the curriculum. Each lesson suggestion is correlated to the ISTE National Educational Technology Standards for Students (ISTE Standards•S) and Common Core State Standards.

### TECHNOLOGY INTEGRATION

#### Example 5.1

TITLE: The Road to Revolution

CONTENT AREA/TOPIC: Social studies, history

GRADE LEVELS: 9–12

NETS FOR STUDENTS: Standard 1—Creativity and Innovation; Standard 2—Communication and Collaboration; Standard 6—Technology Operations and Concepts

CCSS: CCSS.ELA-LITERACY.RH.9-10.2, CSS.ELA-LITERACY. RH.9-10.3, CCSS.ELA-LITERACY.RH.11-12.6

NCSS THEMES: Thematic Standards: 1- Culture and Diversity; 3 - People, Places, and Environments; 6- Power, Authority, and

Governance; Disciplinary Standards:
1 - History

DESCRIPTION: Students listen to scenarios of events leading up to the Revolutionary War as the teacher displays information about the events on the whiteboard. As a whole group, students choose what they would do in response to each event. Each choice leads them to the next event where they see results of their choices. In the end, they reach the point where Britain closes Boston Harbor, and students must decide whether they identified most with Loyalists, Patriots, or Neutralists.

SOURCE: Based on a concept from the Smart Exchange lesson "The Road to Revolution" at http://exchange.smarttech.com.

### USING MATERIALS GENERATORS

Materials generators include desktop publishing software, Web page editors, whiteboard activity software, worksheet and puzzle generators, IEP generators, graphic document makers, and PDF and forms makers. A summary of these, with sample products and classroom uses, is shown in Table 5.2. Also see here a summary of free software tools in Open Source Options.

serve as blueprints for each special student's instructional activities, and teachers must provide documentation that such a plan is on file and that it governs classroom activities. **IEP generator** software assists teachers in preparing IEPs (Wilson, Michaels, & Margolis, 2005). Like test and worksheet generators, IEP generators provide on-screen prompts that remind users of the required components in the plan. When a teacher finishes entering all the necessary information, the program prints out the IEP in a standard format. Some IEP generation programs also accept data updates on each student's progress. See also the Adapting for Special Needs feature.

#### Graphic Document Makers

**Graphic document makers** are software tools that simplify the activity of making highly graphic materials, such as awards certificates and greeting cards. They offer sets of clip art and predesigned templates to which teachers and students can add their own content. For example, teachers have found certificates to be a useful kind of recognition. Certificates congratulate students for accomplishments, and the students can take them home and share them with parents and friends. Most certificate makers include numerous templates for various kinds of achievements, a feature that makes teachers prefer them over word processing software for these kinds of tasks. You can select the template that is appropriate for the kind of recognition intended (e.g., completing an activity, being a first-place winner) and enter the personal information for each recipient. Also, students frequently find it motivating to use these packages to design their own certificates, cards, and flyers. The most popular of these document makers is Printshop (Broderbund). This and similar software tools are listed in Table 5.2. Though graphic document makers are still being used, word processing and drawing software packages now offer many of the same advantages, including a variety of templates for various awards.

#### PDF and Forms Makers

**Portable Document Format (PDF)** file software, created by Adobe, permits the viewing and sending of documents as images. Since they are viewed as images, the PDF document displays all of the formatting and design elements (e.g., margins, graphics) of the original document without requiring access to the software used to create it. Adobe Acrobat Pro or a similar program is used to create these files, but Adobe also provides free software to read documents saved in PDF format. [PDF] is often used in conjunction with **forms makers** such as PDF [that] creates documents and Web pages with forms that can be filled [forms] makers useful because they make it easier to create forms to

## OPEN SOURCE
### OPTIONS *for Tool Software Sites*

| TYPES | FREE SOURCES |
|---|---|
| Materials generators | Scribus: scribus.net<br>NVu Web design software: nvu.com<br>Puzzle maker: discoveryeducation.com/free-puzzlemaker/<br>Certificate maker: certificatemaker.com<br>PDFforge PDF maker: pdfforge.org<br>PageBreeze forms maker: formbreeze.com |
| Data collection and analysis tools | Listing of free statistical software: freestatistica.info/en |
| Testing and grading tools | Gradebook (*Engrade*): engrade.com<br>Test generator: mytest.vocabtest.com<br>Rubric maker—*RubiStar* (use program to create a rubric or use pre-made rubrics): rubistar.4teachers.org |
| Graphics tools | Inkscape graphics editor<br>Tux Paint drawing softwa[re]<br>Gimp image editing soft[ware]<br>Charting/graphing tools:<br>Free WAV sound files: th[e]<br>Sourceforge font collecti[on]<br>Open font library: launch[pad]<br>Free animations: free-an[imations] |
| Planning and organizing tools | OpenSIS student informa[tion]<br>SchoolForge SIS: school[forge]<br>Parent-teacher conferen[ce] |
| Research and reference tools | GoldenDict: goldendict.[org]<br>Lingoes: lingoes.net/<br>Wikipedia: en.wikipedi[a] |
| Content-area tools | Archimedes *CAD* syste[m]<br>Audacity sound editor s[oftware]<br>Music Editor Free: music[...]<br>Free online readability ca[lculators.php]<br>Online graphing calcul[ator]<br>GPS education resource[s]<br>U.S. Census Bureau TIG[ER]<br>tiger.html<br>Language translators: ba[...] |

CHAPTER 5 | Techno[logy]

### COLLABORATE, DISCUSS, REFLECT

Monkey Business/Fotolia

The following questions may be used either for in-class, small-group discussions or may initiate discussions in blogs or online discussion boards.

1. Visit the Common Sense Media website and review its Digital Citizenship Curriculum (under the Education menu button). How could a grasp of these skills and attitudes help young people in learning and in their social contacts with other students?

2. In his 2012 editorial "Will MOOCs Destroy Academia?" from the *Communications of the ACM*, Vardi opines that "due to the seductive possibilities of lower costs . . . the very value of college education is being seriously questioned" (p. 5). What evidence can you cite to support or refute the idea that MOOCs will threaten education as we know it? Will it have any impact on K–12 schools?

3. Gene Glass, originator of meta-analysis techniques, said, "Experienced education leaders worry that something is lost when teachers are replaced by avatars and real life is replaced by Facebook . . . only a fool believes everything that can be gained from face-to-face teaching and learning also can be acquired online" (2010, p. 34). Give examples from research and practice to support or refute Glass's analysis.

4. Go to *Edutopia*'s website and do the following two activities:
   a. In *Edutopia*'s "Technology Integration Research Review" from February 5, 2013, there is evidence summarizing the impact of educational technologies; learn what research can teach us about effective uses of technology for learning. Read especially the studies by subject area, such as science or writing. Summarize what you learned about the overall benefits of technology-based strategies and of using technology to teach your subject.
   b. Also at the *Edutopia* website, click on the Video tab to access the video collection. In the Search by Topic window, use the menu to browse videos by topic, and select Technology Integration. Watch one of the videos. (i) Which of the perspectives that shaped educational technology is evident in the video? (ii) Refer to Figure 1.7 in the text, and list elements that show which reasons the technology in the video is being used.

5. Educational technology historian Paul Saettler (1990) said, "Computer information systems are not just objective recording devices. They also reflect concepts, hopes, beliefs, attitudes" (p. 539). Contrast the concepts, hopes, beliefs, and attitudes that our past versus current uses of technology in education reflect.

6. Richard Clark's now-famous comment about the impact of computers on learning was that the best current evidence is that media are mere vehicles that deliver instruction but do not influence student achievement any more than the truck that delivers our groceries causes change in our nutrition (Clark, 1983, p. 445). Why has this statement had such a dramatic (and, in some cases, emotional) impact on educational technology practitioners? What evidence could you cite to respond to it?

7. In their study of students' reasons for online plagiarism, Comas-Forgas and Sureda-Negre (2010) found that some students say it "is easier, simpler and more comfortable than doing the work yourself" (p. 223). Can you suggest arguments that would help persuade students that online plagiarism, while easy and quick, is not in their best interests?

### Chapter 1 Summary

The following is a summary of the main points covered in this chapter.

1. **Introduction: The "Big Picture" on Technology in Education**
   - This chapter's "big picture" review provides an important framework for viewing the field and consists of key terminology, reflections on the past, considerations about the present, and a look ahead to the future.
   - Four perspectives help define today's educational technology: educational technology as communications media (originally represented by AECT); educational technology as instructional systems and instructional design (originally represented by ISPI); educational technology as vocational training

◀ **Open Source Options** are free resources that help teachers stretch their limited budgets for educational materials.

◀ **Collaborate, Discuss, Reflect features** provide students with questions they can use either for in-class, small-group discussions or to initiate discussions in blogs or online discussion boards.

◀ **Summaries** at the end of each chapter tie back to the learning outcomes and act as study aids by summarizing and reviewing critical chapter content.

# Helps Your Students Practice Technology Integration

## TECHNOLOGY INTEGRATION **WORKSHOP**

### 1. APPLY WHAT YOU LEARNED

To apply the concepts and skills you've read about throughout this chapter, go to the Chapter 2 Technology Application Activity.

### 2. TECHNOLOGY INTEGRATION LESSON PLANNING: PART 1—EVALUATING AND CREATING LESSON PLANS

Complete the following exercise using the sample lesson plans found on any lesson planning site that you find on the Internet.

a. Locate lesson ideas—Identify three lesson plans that focus on any of the tools or strategies you learned about in this chapter. For example, select those that reflect:
* Directed integration strategies
* Constructivist integration strategies
* Integration strategies useful to support with directed or constructivist approaches

b. Evaluate the lessons—Use the Technology Lesson Plan Evaluation Checklist to evaluate each of the lessons you found.

c. Create your own lesson—After you have reviewed and evaluated some sample lessons, create one of your own using a lesson plan format of your choice (or one your instructor gives you). Be sure the lesson focuses on one of the strategies discussed in this chapter.

### 3. TECHNOLOGY INTEGRATION LESSON PLANNING: PART 2—IMPLEMENTING THE TIP MODEL

Review how to implement the TIP Model in your classroom by doing the following activities with the lesson you created in the Technology Integration Lesson Planning exercise above.

a. Describe the Phase 1—Planning activities you would do to use this lesson in your classroom:
* What is the relative advantage of using the technology(ies) in this lesson?
* Do you have resources and skills you need to carry it out?

b. Describe the Phase 2—Implementation activities you would do to use this lesson in your classroom:
* What are the objectives of the lesson plan?
* How will you assess your students' accomplishment of the objectives?
* What integration strategies are used in this lesson plan?
* How would you prepare the learning environment?

c. Describe the Phase 3—Evaluation/Revision activities you would do to use this lesson in your classroom: What strategies and/or instruments would you use to evaluate the success of this lesson in your classroom, in order to determine revision needs?

d. Add lesson descriptors—Create descriptors for your new lesson (e.g., grade level, content and topic areas, technologies used, NETS standards, 21st Century Learning standards).

e. Save your new lesson—Save your lesson plan with all its descriptors and TIP Model notes.

### 4. FOR YOUR TEACHING PORTFOLIO

* Lesson plan evaluations, lesson plans and products you created above
* Products of your group's Hot Topic Debates
* Products of your group's Collaborate, Discuss, Reflect online or in-class activities.

◀ **A Technology Integration Workshop,** located at the end of every chapter, includes hands-on, interactive activities that connect chapter content to real-life practice. Each Workshop contains the following:

* **Technology Integration Lesson Planning** exercises, which provide students the opportunity and resources to evaluate a set of technology integration lessons and to modify or create their own lesson plans to meet their classroom needs.

* **An Implementing the TIP Model** activity, which asks teachers to show how they would implement the TIP Model in their classrooms by doing activities with the lesson(s) they created in the Technology Integration Lesson Planning exercise.

* **For Your Teaching Portfolio** feature, which directs students to save the material they created in each chapter in a personal portfolio.

# NEW INTERACTIVE ETEXT FEATURES!

An all-new Pearson eText version includes the following interactive features in each chapter:

**Author-recorded BIG IDEAS OVERVIEW (BIO)** on main chapter concepts and points to guide reading. ▶

### CHAPTER 4 BIG IDEAS OVERVIEW

Before you begin reading the rest of this chapter, listen to the Chapter 4 Big Ideas Overview. It will give you a two-minute audio overview of main concepts to look for and help prepare you to work through information and exercises to achieve this chapter's outcomes.

### VIRTUAL REALITY ENVIRONMENTS

The potential of virtual reality (VR) systems to make cyberspace seem real has been talked about since William Gibson's 1984 novel, *Neuromancer*, in which people used **avatars**, or graphic icons, to represent themselves in virtual environments. Until recently, however, that potential has been tapped more for video games than for education. That is changing as better, more useful educational tools become available. Three types of environments are described here, along with integration strategies for them. Also, a sample of these virtual tools is shown in the Top Ten Virtual Education Environments.

◀ **Top Ten** (in Chapters 1, 3–8) pop up features highlight and describe the best software features, uses, and strategies for teachers to apply.

**Top Ten Must-Have Apps** (in Chapters 9–15) present apps that are widely used in society, and examples help educators see the role these tools are beginning to play in education. ▶

### A Changing Definition for Music Literacy

In music education, the term *music literacy* usually means an ability to read standard music notation. But the computer enables—if not encourages—experimentation with alternative ways to represent music. The earliest **music sequencers**, even those with notation capability, have always included a "graphic" or "matrix" editor, a window in which the user could edit music by dragging, deleting, or expanding small rectangles on a grid. Touchscreen interfaces such as those found on tablets have also led to apps that use similar drawing metaphors for creating music. These include apps such as Beatwave, Kaossilator, and Musyc, among others. See a list of the Top Ten Must-have Apps for Music.

Interactive Technology Learning Checks (TLCs) at the end of each major section matched to each chapter learning outcome. These help readers apply the concepts and ensure that they master each chapter outcome. ▶

**TECHNOLOGY LEARNING CHECK**
Complete TLC 2.5 to review what you have learned from reading this section about technology integration strategies based on both models.

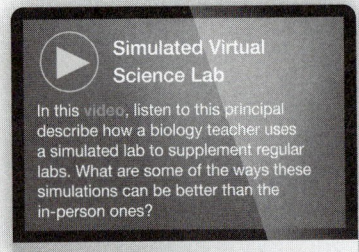

Simulated Virtual Science Lab

In this video, listen to this principal describe how a biology teacher uses a simulated lab to supplement regular labs. What are some of the ways these simulations can be better than the in-person ones?

◀ **Links to video** illustrations and commentaries from practitioners in the field.

**End-of-chapter Technology Integration Workshops** now include: Technology Application Activities and Technology Lesson Plan Evaluation Checklists ▶

## TECHNOLOGY INTEGRATION **WORKSHOP**

### 1. APPLY WHAT YOU LEARNED

To apply the concepts and skills you've read about throughout this chapter, go to the Chapter 7 Technology Application Activity.

### 2. TECHNOLOGY INTEGRATION LESSON PLANNING: PART 1—EVALUATING AND **CREATING LESSON PLANS**

Complete the following exercise using the sample lesson plans found on any lesson planning site that you find on the Internet.

**a.** Locate lesson ideas—Identify three lesson plans that focus on any of the tools or strategies you learned about in this chapter. For example:

- Web-based lessons and projects
- Podcasts and vodcasts
- Flipped classroom and other blended models

**b.** Evaluate the lessons—Use the Technology Lesson Plan Evaluation Checklist to evaluate each of the lessons you found.

**c.** Create your own lesson—After you have reviewed and evaluated some sample lessons, create one of your own using a lesson plan format of your choice (or one your instructor gives you). Be sure the lesson focuses on one of the technologies or strategies discussed in this chapter.

# SUPPORT MATERIALS FOR INSTRUCTORS

The following resources are available for instructors to download on www.pearsonhighered.com/educators. Instructors enter the author or title of this book, select this particular edition of the book, and then click on the "Resources" tab to log in and download textbook supplements.

## Instructor's Resource Manual and Test Bank (0133955389)

The *Instructor's Resource Manual and Test Bank* includes a wealth of interesting ideas and activities designed to help instructors teach the course. Each chapter contains learning outcomes, key terms, key concepts, and group activities, as well as a comprehensive test bank containing multiple choice, short answer and essay questions.

## PowerPoint Slides (0133971988)

Designed for teachers using the text, the *PowerPoint™ Presentation* consists of a series of slides that can be shown as is or used to make handouts or overhead transparencies. The presentation highlights key concepts and major topics for each chapter.

## TestGen (0133944859)

*TestGen* is a powerful test generator available exclusively from Pearson Education publishers. You install TestGen on your personal computer (Windows or Macintosh) and create your own tests for classroom testing and for other specialized delivery options, such as over a local area network or on the web. A test bank, which is also called a Test Item File (TIF), typically contains a large set of test items, organized by chapter and ready for your use in creating a test, based on the associated textbook material.

The tests can be downloaded in the following formats:

- TestGen Testbank file—PC
- TestGen Testbank file—MAC
- TestGen Testbank—Blackboard 9 TIF
- TestGen Testbank—Blackboard CE/Vista (WebCT) TIF
- Angel Test Bank (zip)
- D2L Test Bank (zip)
- Moodle Test Bank
- Sakai Test Bank (zip)

# ACKNOWLEDGMENTS

Both the goal and challenge of this book have been to provide the reader with the most up-to-date, yet foundational, theory, research, and practices in educational technology across the disciplines. I believe this goal has been achieved. As in any project, realizing this goal would not have been possible without the assistance of numerous individuals who helped sharpen the focus of this edition. These individuals include the reviewers for this edition: Li-Ling Chen, California State University at East Bay; Mary Jo Dondlinger, Texas A&M University, Commerce; Lynne M. Pachnowski, University of Akron; Karen M. McFerrin, Ed.D., Northwestern State University; Kevin Oliver, North Carolina State University.

Very special, heartfelt thanks go out to the school principals who agreed to share on video their invaluable perspectives on how current technologies are being used in their schools: Dr. Tony Donen, principal at the STEM School Chattanooga; Ms. Tammy Helton, Principal at East Ridge High School in Chattanooga; and Dr. Sonja Rich, Principal at the Hamilton County Virtual School. I learned so much from each of you! Thanks also to my two "in-house photographers," Bill Wiencke and Paige Wiencke, for all your work to capture the essence of this edition with their photos; and to the students at East Ridge High School and Dalewood Middle School in Chattanooga, who served as our model technology users. We appreciated the special assistance of Talley Caldwell and principal Christian Earl to make possible photos at Dalewood Middle School. Thanks also go out to Stacey Hill of the STEM School Chattanooga for her informed—and quick—work with CCSS labels.

I would also like to thank Aaron Doering, who contributed to the last two editions, and to our contributors for the current edition who include the following:

**Chapter 9**
Teaching and Learning with Technology in English and Language Arts

**Joan E. Hughes,** Professor
*University of Texas, Austin*
*College of Education*

**Chapter 13**
Teaching and Learning with Technology in Music and Art

**Jay Dorfman,** Assistant Professor
*Boston University*
*College of Fine Arts*

**Chapter 10**
Teaching and Learning with Technology in Foreign and Second Languages

**Phillip Hubbard,** Director, English for Foreign Students
*Stanford University*
*School of Humanities and Sciences*

**Chapter 14**
Teaching and Learning with Technology in Health and Physical Education

**Derrick Mears,** Program Coordinator, Ed.S. in Curriculum and Instruction
*University of Arkansas*
*College of Education*

**Chapter 11**
Teaching and Learning with Technology in Mathematics and Science

**Maggie Niess,** Professor Emeritus
*Oregon State University*
*College of Education*

**Chapter 15**
Teaching and Learning with Technology in Special Education and Adapting for Special Needs features

**Dave Edyburn,** Professor
*University of Wisconsin, Milwaukee*
*School of Education*

**Chapter 12**
Teaching and Learning with Technology in Social Studies

**Michael J. Berson,** Professor
*University of South Florida*
*College of Education*

And finally, the incredible support from the Pearson Education staff is impossible to measure. I could not have survived the massive amount of revision work and logistical challenges of this edition if it were not for the clear vision, high expertise, and caring support of our Senior Development Editor, Max Chuck. Max, you're still the best! I would also like to recognize the rest of the editorial and production team—Senior Acquisitions Editor, Meredith Fossel; Editorial Assistant, Maria Feliberty; Executive Field Marketer, Krista Clark; Senior Marketing Manager, Christopher Barry; Program Managers Janet Domingo and Karen Mason; Project Managers, Cynthia DeRocco and Jessica Sykes; Media Producer, Allison Longley; and Art Director, Diane Lorenzo—who made this version of the book useful, attractive, and meaningful. Thank you for your indispensable contributions to this text.

I would like to recognize the enduring love and patience of my family, Bill and Paige Wiencke, and the tenacious loyalty of all our friends in various parts of our global village. Also, I would like to continue to remember and acknowledge the incalculable contributions of those who are with us now only in memory: parents Servatius L. and P. Catherine Roblyer and Raymond and Marjorie Wiencke, and mentor and friend FJ King. Finally, I would like to acknowledge all the educators whose perseverance and commitment to their students remains a constant we can count on as we face the challenges of technological change.

—M. D. Roblyer

# Educational Technology in Context

## THE BIG PICTURE

## Learning Outcomes

After reading this chapter and completing the learning activities, you should be able to:

1. Analyze how the following work together to shape today's educational technology events and trends in schools: (a) different groups' historical perspectives on educational technology; and (b) current definitions for educational technology, instructional technology, and integrating educational technology. (ISTE Standards•T 5)

2. Identify periods in the history of digital technologies, and describe what we have learned from this history that can help us use educational technology effectively today. (ISTE Standards•T 5)

3. Place a given educational technology resource in one of the general hardware categories (microcomputer, handheld, display, imaging, peripheral, or external storage), software categories (instructional, productivity, and administrative), or media (e.g., flash drive, CD, DVD). (ISTE Standards•T 4, 5)

4. Identify and analyze the impact of societal, educational, cultural/equity, and legal/ethical issues on current uses of technology in education. (ISTE Standards•T 4, 5)

5. Identify examples of technology literacy and other 21st-century skills that teachers and their students need in order to be prepared for future learning and the world of work, and select a teaching portfolio format from available technology-based platforms to document your accomplishment of these skills and Tech-PACK growth. (ISTE Standards•T 5)

6. Generate a personal rationale for using technology in teaching based on research findings, popular teaching practices, and types of problems that technology applications can solve. (ISTE Standards•T 5)

7. Identify trends in emerging technologies and describe how they shape trends in teaching and learning. (ISTE Standards•T 5)

Vladgrin/Shutterstock

# TECHNOLOGY INTEGRATION IN ACTION: THEN AND NOW

## THEN . . .

Anna was almost as proud of her new classroom computers as she was of her new teaching degree. She had high hopes for the 1980–1981 school year in her first teaching position, especially since the principal had asked her if she could use two brand-new Apple computer systems that had been donated to the school. As a student teacher, she had helped children use **computer-assisted instruction (CAI)** on terminals that were located in the school's computer lab and connected by telephone lines to her university's big mainframe computer, but this would be much different. Now the computers would be located right in her classroom, and how she used them would be completely up to her. With her new skills and these marvelous devices at her disposal, she felt a heady sense of power and anticipation.

She found some shareware and other free drill-and-practice and instructional game software packages, and successfully lobbied the principal to buy others. She planned to buy yet more with money she would raise from bake sales. All the students wanted to use the computers, but with only two machines, Anna quickly devised activities that allowed everyone to have a turn. She had relay-race math practices to help students prepare for tests, and she created a computer workstation where they could play math games as a reward for completing other activities and where she could send students in pairs to practice basic skills.

As Anna used her new computers, she coped with a variety of technical problems. Some of the software was designed for an earlier version of the Apple operating system, and each disk required a format adjustment every time it was used. Programs would stall when students entered something the programmers had not anticipated; students had to either adjust the code or restart the programs. Despite these and other difficulties, by the end of the year Anna was still enthusiastic about her hopes, plans, and expectations. She felt she had seen a glimpse of a time when computers would be an integral part of everyday teaching activities. She planned to be ready for the future.

## NOW . . .

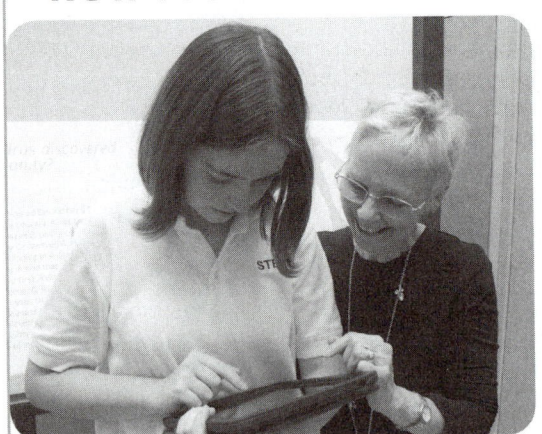

As she prepared to begin another school year, Anna found it difficult to believe it had been over 35 years since that first pioneering work with her Apple microcomputers. This school year, she had received a set of tablet computers, part of the district's one child-one computer initiative, and an **interactive whiteboard**, a device that would allow her to project information from a computer to a screen and then manipulate it either with special pens or hands. The school district had offered these tools to any teachers who proposed innovative ways to engage girls and minority students in math and science projects. With these devices, it would be so much easier for her students to access online math manipulatives and science simulations and collaborate with students in other locations. Her class's favorite activity this year was working with students around the state to gather and compare data on local environmental conditions, but they also liked the spreadsheet software's "Buy a Car" activity.

Anna also marveled at how most other teachers in the school were using technology in productive ways. Everyone communicated via email or online chats, and many, like herself, had their own, school-approved social network site so that students and parents could get up-to-date information on school and classroom activities. Students were using graphing calculators to solve problems, and they used online programs to practice foreign languages. She often heard them talking about webquests and virtual field trips they were doing in science and social studies. A video project to interview war veterans had drawn a lot of local attention, and the student projects displayed on school bulletin boards were ablaze with screen captures from websites and images students had taken with digital cameras.

There were still problems, of course. Computer viruses and spam sometimes slowed the district's network, and the firewall that had been put in place to prevent students from accessing undesirable Internet sites also prevented access to many other, perfectly good sites. Teachers reported intermittent problems with online bullying and inappropriate postings on social network sites, despite the schools Acceptable Use Policies. Some teachers complained that they had no time for innovative technology-based projects because they were too busy preparing students for the new state and national tests that would determine their schools' ratings and their own teacher effect scores.

Yet despite these concerns, Anna was amazed at how far educational technology had come from those first, hesitant steps in the classroom, and how much more there still was to try. She knew other teachers her age who had retired, but she was too interested in what she was doing to think about that. She was helping with a virtual program for homebound students and leading a funded project to develop curricula for the district's social media. Not a day went by that a teacher didn't come to her for help with a new project. She couldn't wait to see what challenges lay ahead. She looked forward to the future.

# CHAPTER 1 BIG IDEAS OVERVIEW

Before you begin reading the rest of this chapter, listen to the Chapter 1 Big Ideas Overview. It will give you a two-minute audio overview of main concepts to look for and help prepare you to work through information and exercises to achieve this chapter's outcomes.

# INTRODUCTION: THE "BIG PICTURE" ON TECHNOLOGY IN EDUCATION

Today's educators tend to think of educational or instructional technology as devices or equipment—particularly the more modern, digital devices, such as computers, cell phones, and tablets. But educational technology is not new at all, and it is by no means limited to the use of devices. Modern tools and techniques are simply the latest developments in a field that is as old as education itself. This chapter begins our exploration of educational technology with an overview of the field, from the early perspectives that shaped and defined it to the tools and conditions that determine the role it is able to play in today's society.

## Why We Need the "Big Picture"

The "big picture" review in this section serves an important purpose: It helps new learners develop mental pictures of the field, what Ausubel (1968) might call cognitive frameworks, through which to view all applications and consider best courses of action. This framework takes the following form.

- **Key terminology**. Talking about a topic requires knowing the vocabulary relevant to that topic. Educators who want to study the field must recognize that language used to describe technology reflects differing perspectives on the appropriate uses of educational technology.

- **Reflecting on the past**. Showing where the field began helps us understand where it is headed and why. Reflecting on changes in goals and methods in the field over time casts new light on the challenges and opportunities of today's technologies.

- **Considering the present**. The current role of educational technology is shaped primarily by two factors: available technology resources and our perspectives on how to use them. Available technologies dictate what is possible; a combination of social, instructional, cultural, and legal issues influence the directions we choose to take.

- **Looking ahead to the future**. Technology resources and societal conditions change so rapidly that today's choices are always influenced as much by emerging trends as by current conditions. To be informed citizens of an information society, teachers must be futurists.

## Perspectives That Define Educational Technology

Saettler (1990) says that the earliest references to the term *educational technology* were by radio instruction pioneer W. W. Charters in 1948, and *instructional technology* was first used by audiovisual expert James Finn in 1963. Even in those early days, definitions of these terms focused on more than just devices and materials. Saettler notes that the 1970 Commission on

Instructional Technology defined educational technology as both "the media born of the communication revolution which can be used for instructional purposes" (p. 6) and "a systematic way of designing, carrying out, and evaluating the total process of learning and teaching" (p. 6). As the 1970 commission concluded, a broader definition of educational technology that encompasses both tools and processes "belongs to the future" (Saettler, 1990, p. 6).

If educational technology is viewed as both processes and tools, it is important to begin by examining four different historical perspectives on these processes and tools, all of which have helped shape current practices in the field. These influences come to us from four areas of education and society, each with a unique outlook on what technology in education is and should be. Some of these views have merged over time, but each retains a focus that tends to shape integration practices. These four views and professional organizations that have represented them are summarized in Table 1.1.

### Perspective #1: Educational technology as communications media.
This perspective grew out of the audiovisual (AV) movement in the 1930s, when higher education instructors proposed that media such as slides and films delivered information in more concrete, and, therefore, more effective, ways than did lectures and books. This movement produced audiovisual communications, or the "branch of educational theory and practice concerned primarily with the design and use of messages that control the learning process" (Saettler, 1990, p. 9). The view of educational technology as delivery media has dominated areas of education and the communications industry.

### Perspective #2: Educational technology as instructional systems and instructional design.
This view originated with post–World War II military and industrial trainers who were faced with preparing large numbers of personnel quickly. Based on efficiency studies and learning theories from educational psychology, they advocated using more planned, systematic approaches to developing uniform, effective materials and training procedures. Their view was based on the belief that both human (teachers) and nonhuman (media) resources could be part of an efficient system for addressing any instructional need. Therefore, they equated "educational technology" with "educational problem solutions." This perspective has evolved into **human performance technology** or a systematic approach to improving human productivity and competence by using strategies for solving problems.

### Perspective #3: Educational technology as vocational training.
Also known as **technology education**, this perspective originated with industry trainers and vocational educators in the 1980s. They believed (1) that an important function of school learning

### TABLE 1.1 Organizations with Various Perspectives on Technology in Education

| Association for Educational Communications and Technology (AECT) | International Technology and Engineering Educators Association (ITEEA) | International Society for Performance Improvement (ISPI) | International Society for Technology in Education (ISTE) |
|---|---|---|---|
| **Perspectives on Technology in Education and Training** | | | |
| *Initial focus:* Audio-visual (AV) devices and media | *Initial focus:* Manufacturing and materials skills | *Initial focus:* Information concerned with programmed instruction | *Initial focus:* Computer systems |
| *Now:* Using any resources to improve teaching and learning | *Now:* STEM education and careers | *Now:* Improving human performance | *Now:* Digital devices and systems |
| **Current Definitions for Technology in Education/Training** | | | |
| *Educational technology* is facilitating learning and improving performance by creating and using technological processes and resources. | *Technology education* is problem-based learning using STEM principles. | *Human performance technology* is a systematic approach to improving productivity and competence. | *Educational technology* is the full range of digital hardware used to support teaching and learning. |

is to prepare students for the world of work in which they will use technology, and (2) that vocational training can be a practical means of teaching all content areas, such as math, science, and language. This view brought about a major paradigm shift in vocational training in K–12 schools away from industrial arts curricula centered in woodworking/metals and graphics/printing shops and toward technology education courses taught in labs equipped with technology stations, such as graphics production, robotics systems, and **computer-aided design (CAD) software**, a program used by architects and others to aid in the design of structures such as houses and cars.

**Perspective #4: Educational technology as computer systems (a.k.a., educational and instructional computing).** This view began in the 1950s with the advent of computers and gained momentum when they began to be used instructionally in the 1960s. As computers began to transform business and industry practices, both trainers and teachers began to see that computers also had the potential to aid instruction. From the time computers came into classrooms in the 1960s until about 1990, this perspective was known as educational computing and encompassed both instructional and administrative support applications.

At first, programmers and systems analysts created all applications. But by the 1970s, many of the same educators involved with media, AV communications, and instructional systems also were researching and developing computer applications. By the 1990s, educators began to see computers as part of a combination of technology resources, including media, instructional systems, and computer-based support systems. At that point, educational computing became known as **educational technology**.

## How This Textbook Defines Technology in Education

Each of these four perspectives on technology in education has contributed to the current body of knowledge about processes and tools to address educational needs. Since an informed use of educational technology must focus on all of these perspectives, this textbook attempts to merge them in the following ways:

- **Processes**—For the processes, or instructional procedures for applying tools, we look to (1) learning theories based on the sciences of human behavior, and (2) applications of technology that help prepare students for future jobs by teaching them skills in using current tools, as well as skills in "learning to learn" about tools of the future that have not yet been invented—or even imagined.

- **Tools**—This textbook looks at the roles technology tools play as delivery media, instructional systems, and technology support, and focuses primarily on those tools that play a current, high-profile role in furthering teaching and learning.

Figure 1.1 shows the framework in which to view these tools and processes. The terms shown in this figure have the following "evolving" definitions:

**FIGURE 1.1 A Framework for Viewing Educational Technology**

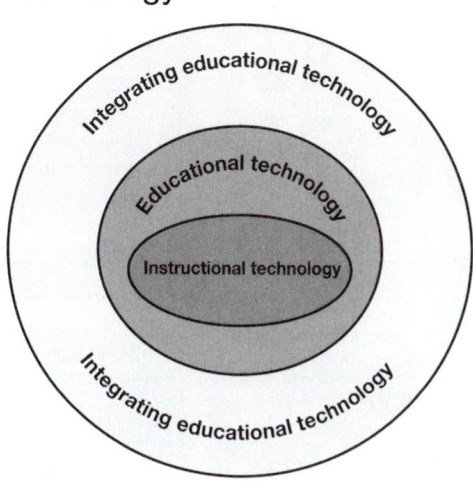

- **Educational technology** is a combination of the *processes* and *tools* involved in addressing educational needs and problems, with an emphasis on applying the most current digital and information tools.

- **Integrating educational technology** refers to the process of *matching digital tools and methods* to given educational needs and problems.

- **Instructional technology** is the *subset of educational technology* that deals directly with teaching and learning applications (rather than educational administrative ones).

**TECHNOLOGY LEARNING CHECK**

Complete TLC 1.1 to review what you have learned from reading this section about basic perspectives and definitions underlying technology integration.

# YESTERDAY'S EDUCATIONAL TECHNOLOGY: HOW THE PAST HAS SHAPED THE PRESENT

Though a "technology" can be anything from a pencil to a virtual environment, the modern history of technology in education has been shaped in large part by developments in digital technologies, such as computers. The four eras in the history of digital technologies, shown in Figure 1.2, are described in this section, followed by a summary of what we have learned from the past that can help us become more effective technology users today.

**FIGURE 1.2** Digital Technologies in Education: A Timeline of Events That Shaped the Field

## PRE-MICROCOMPUTER ERA

| **1950** | **1959** | **1960s** | **Early 1970s** | **Mid-to-late 1970s** | **Late 1970s** |
|---|---|---|---|---|---|
| First computers used for instruction: Computer-driven flight simulator trains MIT pilots | First computer used with school children: IBM 650 teaches binary arithmetic in NYC | University time-sharing movement: Mainframes used for programming and shared utilities | Computer-assisted instruction (CAI) movement: Schools use university-based mainframes/mini-computers | Schools begin using computers for instruction and administration: CDC's announces PLATO system | Arthur Luehrmann coins term *computer literacy*; Andrew Molnar warns: non-computer-literate students are at risk |

 © U.S. Air Force
 Studio 8/Pearson Education
 Eimantas Buzas/Shutterstock
 Weerapat1003/Fotolia
 Courtesy of Wikipedia
 John Foxx Collection/Imagestate

## MICROCOMPUTER ERA

## INTERNET ERA

| **1977** | **1980s** | **1980s–early 1990s** | **1993** | **1994** | **1995** |
|---|---|---|---|---|---|
| Microcomputers enter schools. Teachers begin to control instructional applications. | Microcomputer movements: software publishing, teacher authoring, Logo problem solving | ILS marks movement to networks, away from desktop systems | World Wide Web born: First browser (Mosaic) transforms Internet. Teachers enter Information Superhighway | Internet use explodes; distance learning increases in higher education | Virtual schooling (online courses in high school) begins |

 Pearson Education
 4tomania/Fotolia
 Monkey Business/Fotolia
 MaverickLEE/Shutterstock
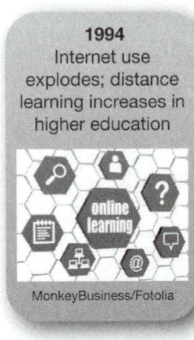 MonkeyBusiness/Fotolia
 Sophie Bluy/Pearson Education

## MOBILE TECHNOLOGIES, SOCIAL MEDIA, AND OPEN ACCESS ERA

| **2001** | **2005** | **2006** | **2007** | **2010** | **2010–2020** |
|---|---|---|---|---|---|
| Wikipedia begins; crowdsourcing movement gains momentum | Social networking sites such as Facebook are established | Twitter established; social media enter classrooms | Amazon releases first Kindle ebook reader) | Apple releases first iPad (handheld computer) | Mobile technologies spawn BYOD/BYOT movements; MOOCs offer schools new access possibilities |

 Arahan/Fotolia
 © Shutterstock
 Hackerkuper/Fotolia
 © Shutterstock
 Photo by W. Wiencke,
 Image 100/Corbis/Glow Images

# Era 1: The Pre-Microcomputer Era

Many of today's teachers began using computer systems only since microcomputers came into common use, but a thriving educational computing culture predated microcomputers by 20 years. The first computers were used instructionally as early as the 1950s. In the late 1960s, IBM pioneered the IBM 1500, the first instructional **mainframe**, or large-scale computer with many users connected to it with terminals. On the IBM 1500, these terminals were **multimedia learning stations** capable of displaying animation and video. By the time IBM discontinued it in 1975, some 25 universities were using this system to develop **computer-assisted instruction (CAI)** materials that schools used via long-distance connections. CAI was software designed to help teach information and/or skills related to a topic. The most prominent of these efforts was led by Stanford University professor and "Grandfather of CAI" Patrick Suppes, who developed the Coursewriter programming language to create reading and mathematics lessons. Companies such as the Computer Curriculum Corporation (CCC, founded by Suppes) and the Programmed Logic for Automatic Teaching Operations (PLATO) system (developed by the Control Data Corporation) dominated the field for about 15 years. Universities also developed CAI for these large-scale computers, as well as **computer-managed instruction (CMI)** applications, or programs that kept track of students' performance data based on mastery learning models. Even after smaller **minicomputer** systems, then a designation for systems smaller that mainframes that could support fewer users at a time, replaced mainframes to deliver CAI and CMI to schools, systems were expensive to buy and complex to operate and maintain, so school district offices controlled their purchase and use. But by the late 1970s, it was apparent that there was little support for computer-based curriculum controlled by district data processing and industry personnel; schools began to reject the business office model of using computers to revolutionize instruction.

# Era 2: The Microcomputer Era

Integrated circuits made computers both smaller and more portable beginning in 1975, and teachers began to bring small, stand-alone, desktop computers called **microcomputers**, or systems designed for use by only one person at a time, into their classrooms. This grassroots movement wrested control of educational computers from companies, universities, and school districts and placed them directly into the hands of teachers and schools. Several initiatives emerged to shape this new teacher-centered control: a software publishing movement that catered to teachers quickly sprang up; organizations emerged to review software and help teachers select quality products; and professional organizations, journals, and magazines began to publish software reviews and recommend "top products." Teachers clamored for more input into courseware design, so companies created authoring languages and systems (e.g., PILOT, SuperPILOT, GENIS, PASS). However, teacher authoring soon proved too time consuming, and interest faded. As schools searched for a way to make CAI more cost effective, districts began to purchase networked **integrated learning systems (ILSs)**, or networked systems that provide both CAI-based curriculum and CMI functions, to help teachers address required standards. Control of instructional computer resources moved once again to central servers in school district offices. Three other technology initiatives also became prominent in this era:

- **The computer literacy movement**. When author and researcher Arthur Luehrmann coined the term **computer literacy** to mean required levels of skills in using the computer, schools tried to implement computer literacy curriculum. However, these efforts were eventually dropped due to difficulties in defining and measuring skills.
- **Videodisc-based curriculum**. Companies such as ABC News and the Optical Data Corporation joined forces to offer curriculum on videodiscs, both standalone (level 1) and connected to microcomputers (level 3). But, when other forms of optical and digital storage replaced videodisc technology, curricula were not transferred.
- **The Logo movement**. A final focus during this period was teaching **Logo** programming, a high-level language originally designed as an **artificial intelligence (AI)** language designed to emulate decision-making capabilities of the human mind, but used by Seymour Papert (1980) to support his view that computers should be used as an aid to teach problem solving.

Logo began to replace CAI as the "best use" of computer technology. Despite its popularity and research showing it could be useful in some contexts, researchers could capture no Logo impact on mathematics or other curriculum skills, and interest in Logo, too, waned by the beginning of the 1990s.

## Era 3: The Internet Era

At the beginning of the 1990s, the **Internet**, a worldwide collection of university computer networks that could exchange information by using a common software standard had already been operating for many years. Then the **World Wide Web** was introduced in 1993. This was a system within the Internet that allowed graphic displays of Internet sites through hypertext links, or pieces of texts or images that allowed users to jump to other locations connected by the links. The first **browser** software (*Mosaic*) designed especially to allow users to use these links marked the beginning of the third era of educational technology. Teachers and students joined the throng of users on the "Information Superhighway," and interest in computer technology's potential for instruction once again sprang to life. By the beginning of the 2000s, email, online (i.e., Web-based) multimedia, and videoconferencing became standard tools of Internet users. Websites became a primary form of communication for educators, and distance education became a more prominent part of instructional delivery at all levels of education. The meaning of "online" changed from simply being on the computer to being connected to the Internet. **Virtual schools**, or schools in which "(K–12) students and teachers are separated by time and/or location and interact via computers and/or telecommunications technologies" (National Forum on Education Statistics, 2006, p. 1) began a steady growth that would see it become a mainstay of public education in the 2000s.

## Era 4: The Mobile Technologies, Social Media, and Open Access Era

The current era began the early 2000s, when portable devices such as smartphones and tablets made Internet access and computer power ubiquitous. As more and more individuals made texting and social networking sites like Facebook and Twitter part of their everyday lives, this constant connectedness transformed educational practice. The ease of access to online resources and communications drove several movements.

- **Distance learning**. A dramatic increase in the number and type of distance learning offerings came about, first in higher education and then in K–12 schools.
- **Electronic books** (**e-books** or **e-texts**). Texts in digital form on computers, e-book readers, and cell phones became increasingly popular alternatives to printed texts. Some school districts eschewed book adoptions in favor of allowing educators to choose their own digital materials.
- **Mobile access**. One-to-one laptop programs (and later tablet programs), as well as **Bring Your Own Device (or Technology, BYOD or BYOT) programs** were those that allowed students to use their own handheld devices for learning and accelerated the move to bring computer and Internet access into all classrooms. Another type of access that may be on the horizon is what some educators are calling **1:X Computing** or "one to many computing." This is when students have access to many different digital devices from which they may choose "depending on the task at hand" (Herold, 2013, p. s2).
- **Open access**. Around 2008, open-access university offerings called **Massive Open Online Courses (MOOCs)**, which allowed anyone anywhere in the world to participate in college courses for free, became available. By 2011, MOOC projects at MIT, Harvard, and Stanford popularized the concept, and MOOCs came into common use in other colleges and universities. The later part of the decade would see the MOOC concept evolve, as higher education began charging fees for MOOC credit.

As ubiquitous communications and social networking defined social practices in modern life, educators struggled to create appropriate policies and uses that could take advantage of this new power while minimizing its risks and problems.

# What We Have Learned from the Past

In no small part, developments in digital technologies have shaped the history of educational technology. However, knowing the history of educational technology is useful only if we apply what we know about the past to future decisions and actions. What have we learned from more than 60 years of applying technology to educational problems that can improve our strategies now? The following points are among the most important:

**No technology is a panacea for education.** Great expectations for products such as Logo and programs such as BYOD and MOOCs have taught us that even the most current, capable technology resources offer no quick, easy, or universal solutions. Computer-based materials and strategies are usually tools in a larger system and must be integrated carefully with other resources and with teacher activities. Planning must always begin with this question: What specific needs do my students and I have that (any given resources) can help meet?

**Teachers usually do not develop technology materials or curriculum.** In the microcomputer era, companies tried to market authoring systems so teachers could create their own materials, but such systems were never widely adopted. Teaching is one of the most time- and labor-intensive jobs in our society. With so many demands on their time, most teachers cannot be expected to develop software or create complex technology-based teaching materials. Publishers, school or district developers, or personnel in funded projects have traditionally provided the majority of this assistance; this seems unlikely to change in the future, even for distance education courses or digital instructional materials.

**"Technically possible" does not equal "desirable, feasible, or inevitable."** A popular saying is that today's technology is yesterday's science fiction. But science fiction also shows us that technology brings undesirable—as well as desirable—changes. For example, greater access to cell phones and tablets in classrooms means that online communications and information are increasingly available. But as recent events have shown, communications always come with caveats, and readily available information is not always reliable or helpful. New technological horizons make it clear that it is time to analyze carefully the implications of each implementation decision. Better technology demands that we become critical consumers of its power and capability. We are responsible for deciding just which science fiction becomes reality.

**Technologies change faster than teachers can keep up.** History in this field has shown that resources and accepted methods of applying them will change, often quickly and dramatically. This places a special burden on already overworked teachers to continue learning new resources and changing their teaching methods. Gone are the days—if, indeed, they ever existed—when a teacher could rely on the same handouts, homework, or lecture notes from year to year. Educators may not be able to predict the future of educational technology, but they know that it will be different from the present; that is, they must anticipate and accept the inevitability of change and the need for a continual investment of their time.

**Older technologies can be useful.** Technology in education is an area especially susceptible to fads. With so little time and resources dedicated to what actually works, anyone can propose dramatic improvements. When they fail to appear, educators move on to the next fad. This approach fails to solve real problems, and it draws attention away from the effort to find legitimate solutions. Worse, teachers sometimes throw out methods that had potential but were subject to unrealistic expectations. The past has shown that teachers must be careful, analytical consumers of technological innovation, looking to what has worked in the past to guide their decisions and measure their expectations in the present. Educational practice tends to move in cycles, and "new" methods often are old methods in new guise. In short, teachers must be as informed and analytical as they want their students to become.

**Teachers always will be more important than technology.** The developers of the first instructional computer systems in the 1960s foresaw them replacing many teacher positions; some advocates of today's distance learning methods envision a similar impact on future education. Yet good teachers are more essential now than ever. One reason for this was described in Naisbitt's (1984) *MegaTrends*: "whenever new technology is introduced into society, there must be a counterbalancing human response . . . the more high tech [it is], the more high touch [is needed]" (p. 35). We need more teachers who understand the role technology plays in society and in education, who are prepared to take advantage of its power, and who recognize its limitations. In an increasingly technological society, we need more teachers who are both technology savvy and child centered.

**TECHNOLOGY LEARNING CHECK**

Complete **TLC 1.2** to review what you have learned from reading this section about the history of digital technologies in education and what we have learned from it.

# TODAY'S EDUCATIONAL TECHNOLOGY RESOURCES: SYSTEMS AND APPLICATIONS

Digital technology may be thought of as systems, or combinations of hardware and software applications. The resources described in this section, along with current conditions in schools and society described in the next section, help define and shape the current climate for technology in education.

## An Overview of Digital Technology Tools

Technology integration strategies require a combination of **hardware**, or computing equipment, and **software**, or programs written to perform various functions. Even today's **mobile devices**, or portable, handheld computer equipment, such as cell phones or tablets, have this hardware/software combination. Sometimes software and data must be stored outside of the hardware using flash drives, CDs, or various types of DVDs. These are thought of as **storage media**, rather than hardware.

A growing trend is toward using online storage, referred to as **cloud computing**, a generic term for using a storage service accessed through the Internet. Sometimes this service is fee based, and sometimes sites such as Google make it available as a free service. The latter is referred to as Google Drive, though it is not really a hard drive device in the traditional sense. Users can send documents to this space, either as a backup copy or as an alternate to storing items on one's own computer system.

## Technology Facilities: Hardware and Configurations for Teaching

Figure 1.3 gives a visual overview of the six types of technology hardware in common use in today's classrooms. These include:

- **Microcomputers**—Though technologies are becoming increasingly smaller and more mobile, microcomputers, sometimes referred to as desktop or laptop computers, remain a mainstay of classroom computing.
- **Handheld technologies**—Even smaller, multipurpose devices, such as cell phones, tablets (e.g., iPads), e-books or e-texts, and "smart" pens, make it easier for teachers and students to view, communicate, and share information, regardless of location.
- **Display technologies**—These devices support whole-class or large-group demonstrations of information from a computer. They are sometimes used in combination with devices such as **clickers** (a.k.a., **student**

**FIGURE 1.3** The Teacher's Hardware Toolbox

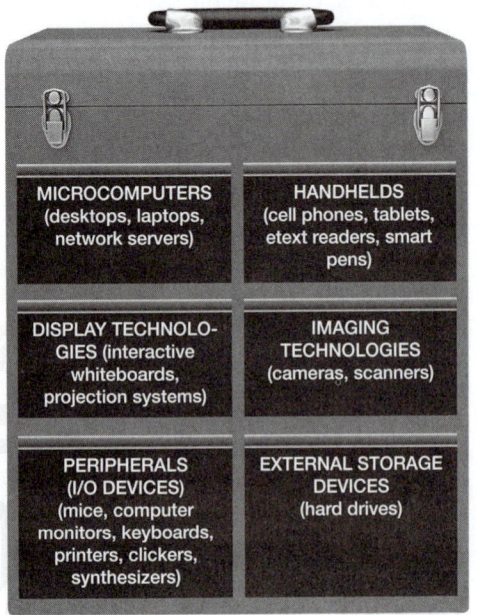

MICROCOMPUTERS (desktops, laptops, network servers)

HANDHELDS (cell phones, tablets, etext readers, smart pens)

DISPLAY TECHNOLOGIES (interactive whiteboards, projection systems)

IMAGING TECHNOLOGIES (cameras, scanners)

PERIPHERALS (I/O DEVICES) (mice, computer monitors, keyboards, printers, clickers, synthesizers)

EXTERNAL STORAGE DEVICES (hard drives)

**response systems**), which are wireless devices used for interactive polling of student answers to teacher questions in face-to-face classes.

- **Imaging technologies**—To make teaching and learning more visual, these devices allow the development and use of images ranging from still photos to full-motion videos.
- **Peripherals**—These are the input devices, such as keyboards and mice (to get information and requests into the computer for processing), and output devices, such as printers and synthesizers (to see or hear the results of the processing), that make microcomputers more functional.
- **External storage**—While most storage is either inside the computer itself or on storage media, sometimes a device is needed to hold large files that won't fit easily on storage media or to allow a backup copy of all files inside the computer.

As Tables 1.2 and 1.3 show, digital equipment can be arranged or configured in various ways, each of which is suited to supporting specific types of integration strategies. Configurations include:

- **Laboratories of networked computers**. As centralized resources, these are easier to maintain and secure; networking software can monitor individual performance in groups. However, students must leave their classrooms to use them.

## TABLE 1.2 Types of Technology Labs

| Types of Labs (20–30 computers) | Benefits | Limitations |
|---|---|---|
| Special-purpose labs:<br>• Programming or technical courses<br>• Technology education/vocational courses (e.g., with CAD, robotics, desktop publishing stations)<br>• MIDI music labs<br>• Labs dedicated to content area(s) (e.g., mathematics/science, foreign languages)<br>• For use by Chapter or Title III students<br>• Multimedia production work<br>• Teacher work labs | Permanent setups of group resources specific to the needs of certain content areas or types of students. | Usually excludes groups who do not meet the designated purpose. Tend to isolate resources by groups of students. |
| General-use labs | Accommodate all kinds of uses. | Must usually be scheduled for whole-class use. |
| Library/media centers | Usually permanent staff members are present to provide ready access to all materials to promote integration of computer and noncomputer resources. | Classes may not be able to do production or group work that might bother other users of the library/media center. |

## TABLE 1.3 Types of Classroom Arrangements

| Types of Arrangements | Benefits | Limitations |
|---|---|---|
| Mobile workstations (on carts) and mobile labs (sets of devices) | Can stretch resources by sharing among many users; supply on-demand access. | Sometimes difficult to get through doors or upstairs; can increase theft and breakage problems. |
| Classroom single computers or workstations | Enables teacher-productivity uses and integration strategies that require. whole-class demonstrations or a technology "learning station." | Limits number of students who can have hands-on use at one time. |
| Student-supplied handheld devices (BYOD) | Enables integration strategies that require a device for each student. | Requires infrastructure, policies, and strategies to limit access only to permitted content. |
| School-supplied devices (one-to-one programs) | Enables integration strategies that require a device for each student. | Expensive to purchase, maintain, and update. |

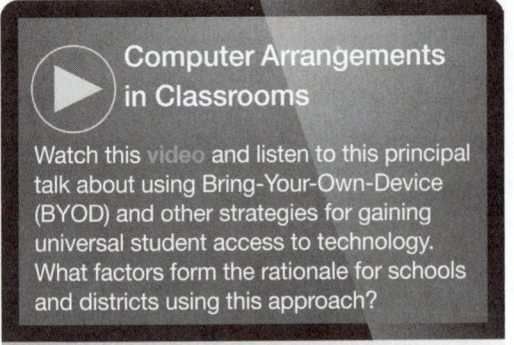

**Computer Arrangements in Classrooms**

Watch this video and listen to this principal talk about using Bring-Your-Own-Device (BYOD) and other strategies for gaining universal student access to technology. What factors form the rationale for schools and districts using this approach?

- **Computer arrangements in classrooms**. These are more convenient and accessible to both teachers and students, but teachers may have to use strategies to stretch available units when there are not enough for each student to have one. BYOD and one-to-one initiatives have tried to address this problem.

## Types of Software Applications in Schools

Schools carry out many types of activities in addition to teaching, and software has been designed to support each of these. Software to support educational technology applications in school settings include:

- **Instructional**—Programs designed to teach skills or information through demonstrations, examples, explanations, or problem solving. Examples are tutorials, drill-and-practice programs, and simulations.

- **Productivity**—Programs designed to help teachers and students plan, develop materials, communicate, and keep records. These include word processing, spreadsheet, database, and email programs, as well as a variety of other materials generators and data collection/analysis, graphics, and research and reference tools.

- **Administrative**—Programs that administrators at school, state, and district levels use to support record keeping and exchanges of information among various agencies. These include student records and payroll systems.

Technology integration strategies described in this textbook focus primarily on instructional and productivity applications that teachers implement. However, some administrative applications that both teachers and administrators use are also described.

**TECHNOLOGY LEARNING CHECK**
Complete TLC 1.3 to review what you have learned from reading this section about today's digital technology resources and skills.

## TODAY'S EDUCATIONAL TECHNOLOGY ISSUES: CONDITIONS THAT SHAPE PRACTICE

Teaching today is challenging because it occurs in an environment that mirrors—and sometimes magnifies—some of society's most problematic issues. Adding digital technologies to this mix continues to make the situation even more complex. Yet, to integrate technology successfully into their teaching, educators must recognize and be prepared to work in this environment with all of its subtleties and complexities. Some of today's important issues and their implications for technological trends in education are described in the following sections. Issues relevant to four areas—societal, educational, cultural/equity, and legal/ethical—are discussed here and summarized in Table 1.4.

### Social Issues

Technology uses have a way of both responding to societal needs and problems and creating a new set of issues with society-wide implications. School systems have recognized that social issues impact every school's mission and classroom climate and must be addressed by sound policies and a planned, ongoing education program to make teachers and students aware of these concerns and to limit possible negative impact. Social issues include the following:

**Privacy issues.** GPS technologies in combination with cell phone software features make it possible to pinpoint anyone's exact location and can communicate a great deal of personal information to others, usually without the user's knowledge. Some have decried schools'

# TABLE 1.4 Issues That Shape the Environment for Using Technology

| Issue | Implications for Educators and Students |
|---|---|
| **Social Issues** | |
| Privacy issues | • Technology-enabled tracking of user location, personal information<br>• Ability to photograph or record surreptitiously with wearable devices<br>• Private information made public on social networks |
| Health-related concerns | • Ailments resulting from technology overuse<br>• Obesity, fitness decline from physical inactivity |
| Fears about technology overuses, misuses | • Detrimental effects of multitasking<br>• Disruptions of cell phone uses in schools<br>• Dangers of sexting |
| Risks of being online | • Colleges monitoring of high school students social footprint<br>• Teachers faulted for social media uses<br>• Cyberbullying |
| Malware, viruses, spam, and hacking | • Harm to programs, data, and/or hardware<br>• Spam drains time, resources<br>• Identity theft from phishing schemes |
| **Educational Issues** | |
| Lack of technology funding | • Fewer funds available for technology hardware, software, and training force choice between technology and other education priorities |
| Teacher and student accountability needs | • Accountability emphases drive technology uses<br>• Decreased emphasis on innovative teaching strategies |
| Digital literacy /digital citizenship needs | • Students must become good digital citizens<br>• Responsibility falls on schools |
| Best practices with technologies | • Debate over teacher-directed methods versus inquiry-based methods |
| Reliance on distance education | • Not all students can learn well at a distance<br>• Some states and districts require an online course for graduation |
| **Cultural/Equity Issues** | |
| The digital divide | • Dropout rates from distance courses higher for already-underserved students |
| Racial and gender equity | • Females and some minorities use computers less and enter STEM at lower rates<br>• Uses by some underserved groups is often limited to remedial, rather than empowering, purposes |
| Students with special needs | • Devices and methods to allow equal access remain expensive, difficult to implement |
| **Legal/Ethical Issues** | |
| Hacking | • Students' personal data at risk from loss of privacy, identity theft<br>• Incumbent on schools to safeguard students |
| Safety issues | • Risks of predators, loss of privacy<br>• Acceptable Use Policies are required |
| The new plagiarism and academic dishonesty | • Online access enables cybercheating<br>• Online courses must safeguard against academic dishonesty, fraud |
| Illegal downloads/software piracy | • Ease of illegal access increases software and music piracy<br>• Students and others being prosecuted |

use of **radio frequency identification (RFID)** to track students' attendance and whereabouts as an attack on privacy. Also, social networks, mistakenly believed to be private, often make public users' personal information. New technologies such as Google Glass are wearable devices that make it possible to record video or images without others' awareness, continue to challenge our definitions of what is private.

## Hot Topic Debate
## Multitasking with Social Networking as Distraction?

*Take a position for or against (based either on your own position or one assigned to you) on the following controversial statement. Discuss it in class or on an online discussion board, blog, or wiki, as assigned by your instructor. When the discussion is complete, write a summary of the main pros and cons that you and your classmates have stated, and put the summary document in your Teacher Portfolio.*

In his essay "The End of Human Specialness," Lanier (2010), author of the book *You Are Not a Gadget*, said, "A post-Facebook generation is appearing, and its members are questioning the legacy of their predecessors. Recently, when I asked students not to tweet or blog during a lecture, they stood and cheered" (p. 7). In addition, research at Stanford University found that students who were multitaskers were more easily distracted and could not focus as well as others who multitasked less or not at all. Some educators view much of social networking as a form of multitasking and a distraction to learning, rather than a resource to support learning. What examples and research results (not opinions) could you use to either support or refute this position?

### Health-related concerns.

Potential problems such as hearing loss from headphone use or eye strain from gazing too long at digital screens have been posed and continue to be studied. Time spent at video games and computer work is time taken away from actual physical activity, which can lead to obesity and decline in fitness.

### Fears about technology misuses.

Young people feel that they excel at **multitasking**, or doing several (usually technology-enabled) activities at the same time. However, studies have shown that the practice negatively affects both accuracy and information retention, and texting while driving has proven a serious threat to public safety. Cell phone use during school can disrupt learning activities and may even be used for cheating on schoolwork or tests. Young people are often unaware that their cell phone uses are not private and, thus, may not hesitate to send out explicit photos or messages, a practice known as **sexting**. See one expert's opinion on technology overuse in this chapter's Hot Topic Debate.

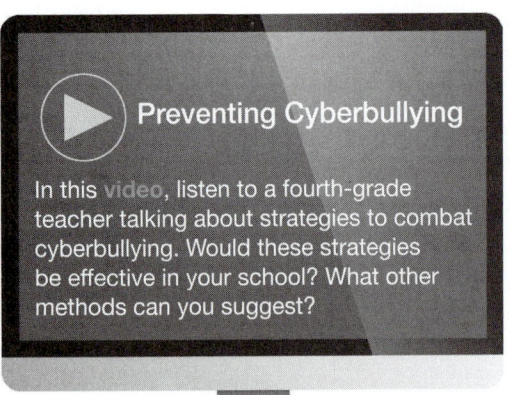

### Preventing Cyberbullying

In this video, listen to a fourth-grade teacher talking about strategies to combat cyberbullying. Would these strategies be effective in your school? What other methods can you suggest?

### Risks of online behaviors.

Time spent on social networking is often time taken away from schoolwork (Goodman, 2011). Students are often unaware that some colleges and universities admissions personnel review and consider information on students' social networking sites. Teachers who have their own social networking sites (e.g., Facebook) have encountered criticism for ill-advised personal posts and contacts with students. **Cyberbullying**, or online harassment in social networks, mirrors similar bullying on school campuses and can have as many negative consequences as in-person bullying (Cyberbullying Research Center website; Juvonen & Gross, 2008).

### Malware, viruses, spam, and hacking.

**Malware**, short for malicious software, can damage, destroy, disrupt operations, or spy on the operation of computers. **Viruses**, a type of **malware**, are programs written specifically to do harm or mischief to programs, data, and/or hardware, and include **logic bombs**, **worms**, and **Trojan horses**. **Spyware** is malware that secretly gathers information stored on a person's computer and can gather addresses, passwords, and credit card numbers to use for identity theft. Computers can be implanted with a program that enables outside control without the owner's knowledge. **Spam**, or unsolicited email messages or website postings, come with such frequency that they interfere with computer work. Schools and colleges have dedicated considerable resources to blocking them. Computer users sometimes respond unwittingly to **phishing** attempts, or emails that falsely claim to be a legitimate business in order to glean private information to be used for identity theft. For example, a teacher may get a message purporting to be from the school district information technology department, asking all users to update their records with passwords and other information. If the teacher supplies this information to the designated location, the "phisher" gets access to the teacher's account, which may contain a great deal of private information.

## Educational Issues

Trends in the educational system are intertwined with trends in technology and society. Several kinds of educational issues have special implications for the ways technology is used in teaching and learning:

### Lack of technology funding.

Recent economic downturns have meant decreased education funding, which also means fewer funds available for technology hardware, software, and training. This downturn comes at a time when technology expenses are on the rise. Although some educators are unwilling to advocate for technology funding over other priorities (e.g., music, arts), technology advocates point out strategies such as open-source options can make technology use more feasible by lowering costs.

### Teacher and student accountability for quality and progress.

Accountability emphases that began with the No Child Left Behind (NCLB) Act of 2001 remain strong and drive a trend toward using technology in ways that help teachers and students pass tests and meet required standards, rather than to support more innovative teaching strategies. Teachers hesitate to use technologies unless they address accountability goals.

### Digital literacy and digital citizenship.

The increasing role that technology plays in all areas of our society make it ever more essential that students become savvy consumers of technology resources and demonstrate **digital citizenship** or use of technology resources in safe, responsible, and legal ways. The responsibility for this instruction usually falls on schools.

### Debates on best practices with technologies.

Educators continue to debate the proper roles of traditional, teacher-directed methods versus student-led, inquiry-based methods. Long-used and well-validated teacher-directed uses of technology can address content standards, but many educators see them as passé. Inquiry-based, constructivist methods are considered more modern and innovative, but it is less clear how they address standards required to demonstrate teacher and student accountability.

### Reliance on online learning.

Increasing numbers of virtual K–12 courses are being offered, and virtual schools are becoming a mainstream part of U.S. education. Although this movement has increased access to high-quality courses and degrees, not all students have the skills needed to use them, even if they get access. Recognizing that learning at a distance is rapidly becoming commonplace in higher education, some states, including Michigan, Florida, Virginia, and Alabama, and some school districts, such as Putnam County, Tennessee, have made completing a distance course a high school graduation requirement.

## Cultural and Equity Issues

The power of technology is a double-edged sword, especially for education. While it presents obvious potential for changing education and empowering teachers and students, technology may also further divide members of our society along socioeconomic, ethnic, and cultural lines and widen the gender gap. Teachers will lead the struggle to make sure technology use promotes, rather than conflicts with, the goals of a democratic society.

### The Digital Divide.

Originally referred to as a discrepancy in access to technology resources among socioeconomic groups (although race and gender may also play a role), the **digital divide** has recently taken on a new and more subtle impact. While low-income and minority students have more access to technologies than ever before, dropout rates from distance courses are higher than rates for physical schools and usually affect underserved students more than

▲ Girls and boys need early opportunities to become involved in STEM activities such as robotics projects. (Photo by W. Wiencke)

others, which could further widen the digital divide. A study by Vigdor and Ladd (2010) found that simply providing access to home computers can actually be associated with decreased achievement, since unmonitored children tend to use them primarily in noneducational activities.

**Racial and gender equity.** When compared with males and whites, females, African Americans, and Hispanic minorities use computers less and enter careers in math, science, and technology areas at lower rates. Many educators believe that less frequent use of technology leads to lower entrance into technical careers. In addition, children in remedial programs may have access to computers, but they often use them mainly for remedial work rather than for email, multimedia production, and other personal empowerment activities.

**Students with special needs.** Devices and methods are available to help students compensate for their physical and mental deficits and allow them equal access to technology and learning opportunities. However, they remain difficult to purchase and implement, and often go unused. Parents clamor for the technology resources guaranteed their children by federal laws, but schools often claim insufficient funding to address these special needs. See ways that teachers can better meet the needs of these students in the Adapting for Special Needs feature.

## Legal and Ethical Issues

The legal and ethical issues educators face reflect those of the larger society. The major types of ethical and legal issues, discussed next, have a major impact on how technology activities are implemented.

**Hacking.** **Hackers** are those who use online systems to access the personal data of students in order to accomplish identity theft and commit other malicious acts. To combat these problems, schools are forced to install **firewalls**, software that blocks unauthorized access to classroom computers, and to spend larger portions of technology funds each year on preventing and cleaning up after illegal activities. They must also constantly educate teachers and students on strategies to prevent these attacks.

**Safety issues.** As students spend more time in online environments, attempts by online predators to contact students are more likely, and objectionable material is readily available and easy to access, sometimes referred to as **cyberporn** (Levy, 2010). To address these concerns, schools are requiring students/parents to sign an **Acceptable Use Policy (AUP)** that outlines

▲ Inform students about their school's Acceptable Use Policies (AUP) both to educate and protect them. (Photo by W. Wiencke)

appropriate use of school technologies for students and educators. This policy puts in place procedures to safeguard access to students' personal information.

### Academic dishonesty.
Greater online access to full-text documents on the Internet has resulted in increased incidents of student plagiarism, a practice often referred to as **cybercheating** or online cheating. Sites have emerged to help teachers catch plagiarizers, while teachers are also trying to structure assignments that make this kind of cheating more difficult. To make sure they comply with **copyright laws**, which give the creator of original works exclusive rights to use and profit from it, schools are making teachers and students aware of policies about copyright, AUP, and guidelines for **fair use** of published materials. Fair use gives limited rights to those who want to use brief excerpts of copyright material without the need for permission. Schools also are concerned that students signed up for an online course are actually the ones doing the work of the course. Some organizations have moved to proctoring systems with either cameras or biometric sensors to monitor students, while others have students come into a physical location to take required exams.

### Illegal downloads/software piracy.
An increasing number of sites offer ways to download copies of software, music, or media without paying for them, a practice known as **software piracy** or **music piracy**, and software and media companies are prosecuting even young offenders. Teachers are tasked with modeling and teaching ethical behaviors related to software and media. The most important of these issues in terms of their impact in shaping what we can and must do with technology in education are summarized in the **Top Ten** feature for this chapter.

**TECHNOLOGY LEARNING CHECK**
Complete **TLC 1.4** to review what you have learned from reading this section about various issues that shape technology uses in education.

## ⬤ TODAY'S EDUCATIONAL TECHNOLOGY SKILLS: STANDARDS, ASSESSMENTS, AND TEACHING COMPETENCIES

Clearly, 21st-century educators will have to deal with issues and situations that their predecessors could not even have imagined. New technology tools also mean new and different ways of accessing and processing information needed for teaching and learning. Both teachers and students must have the skills and knowledge that will prepare them to meet these new challenges and use these new and powerful strategies. Sets of skills and a framework for teacher education that have been created specifically to guide them are discussed below.

### The Common Core State Standards (CCSS)

The CCSS are statements of what students should learn and were developed by the National Governors Association Center for Best Practices (NGA Center) and the Council of Chief State School Officers (CCSSO). The standards cite the following under *College and Career Readiness Anchor Standards for Writing*:

CCSS.ELA-Literacy.CCRA.W.8 Gather relevant information from multiple print and digital sources, assess the credibility and accuracy of each source, and integrate the information while avoiding plagiarism.

## ISTE Standards for Teachers, Students, and Administrators

The International Society for Technology in Education (ISTE), a technology professional organization described earlier in this chapter, has developed standards for students, teachers, and school administrators. ISTE Standards for Teachers have become a benchmark for technology infusion in teacher education programs. Note that ISTE Standards for Students are considered to be the basic skills that students—and their teachers—should meet. ISTE Standards for Teachers, which assume that teachers have attained the student standards, focus on teaching skills that use technologies.

## The Partnerships for 21st Century Skills (P21) for Students and Teachers

P21 was formed in 2002 to create a successful model of learning based on incorporating "21st century skills into our system of education." Figure 1.4 is an image from the P21 website that shows three overarching categories of student outcomes and illustrates the support systems students and teachers will need to achieve these skills. In addition to a listing of specific "knowledge, skills, and expertise students should master to succeed in work and life in the 21st century," P21 has identified a set of essential core subjects (English, reading, or language arts, world languages, arts, mathematics, economics, science, geography, history and government/civics) as well as interdisciplinary themes that should be interwoven through these subjects. These themes, which also have skills listed under each one, include global awareness; financial, economic, business, and entrepreneurial literacy; civic literacy; health literacy; and environmental literacy. The P21 website also provides skills maps for each content area that list specific learning activities for each of the P21 competencies.

## The ICT Competency Framework for Teachers

UNESCO personnel collaborated with industry partners Cisco, Intel, ISTE, and Microsoft to create the **information and communication technology (ICT)** framework, which focuses on skills that teachers require to bring about three different levels of human capacity development: technology

### FIGURE 1.4  The P21 Skill Framework

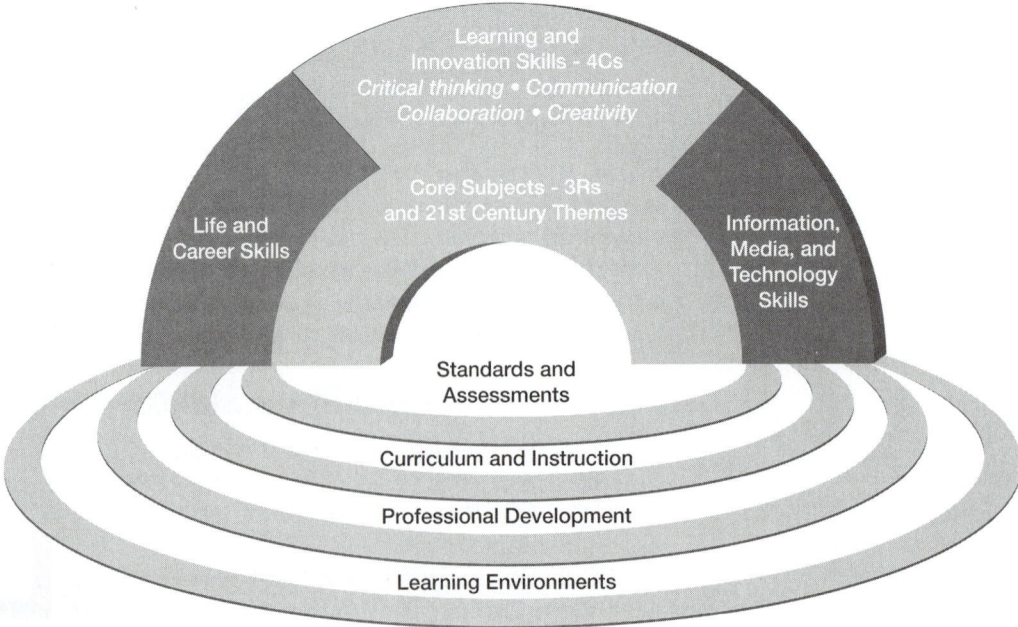

literacy, knowledge deepening, and knowledge creation. ICT is a term often used in place of the terms *instructional technology* and *educational technology,* especially outside the United States. UNESCO has Teacher Competency Standards Modules for each of these levels. Each module consists of curricular goals and teacher skills in six different areas: policy, curriculum and assessment, pedagogy, ICT, organization and administration, and teacher professional development.

## The Tech-PACK Framework

Teaching is a complex combination of what teachers know about the content they teach, how they decide to teach that content, and the tools they use to carry out their plans. Historically, teacher education has centered on content knowledge and pedagogy as separate concerns. But Shulman (1986) was first to stress the importance of how these "knowledge components" work together, rather than separately. Hughes (2000) extended Shulman's concept by adding technology as another component of knowledge needed by teachers. The result is a combination of technological, pedagogical, and content knowledge. See Figure 1.5 for an illustration of how these areas converge and overlap. Teachers who are in the "zone" at the center of the diagram when all three areas merge have the skills they need to integrate technologies into teaching (Mishra & Koehler, 2006).

Originally called **TPCK**, or the combination of technological pedagogical content knowledge required to integrate technology most effectively into instruction, this textbook refers to this combination as "Tech-PACK" to emphasize the critical contribution of technology to teaching. See Table 1.5 for a brief history of the development of this terminology. Teacher education programs have come to view the Tech-PACK framework as useful for several purposes. It gives students and their instructors a common vision and language for talking about their technology-related goals and illustrates to students the competencies they are aiming to develop. It also provides a common metric for gauging growth. Voogt, Fisser, Roblin, Tondeur, and van Braak (2012) reviewed the literature on how teacher education programs are using the Tech-PACK

**FIGURE 1.5** The Original TPACK Framework (from TPACK.org)

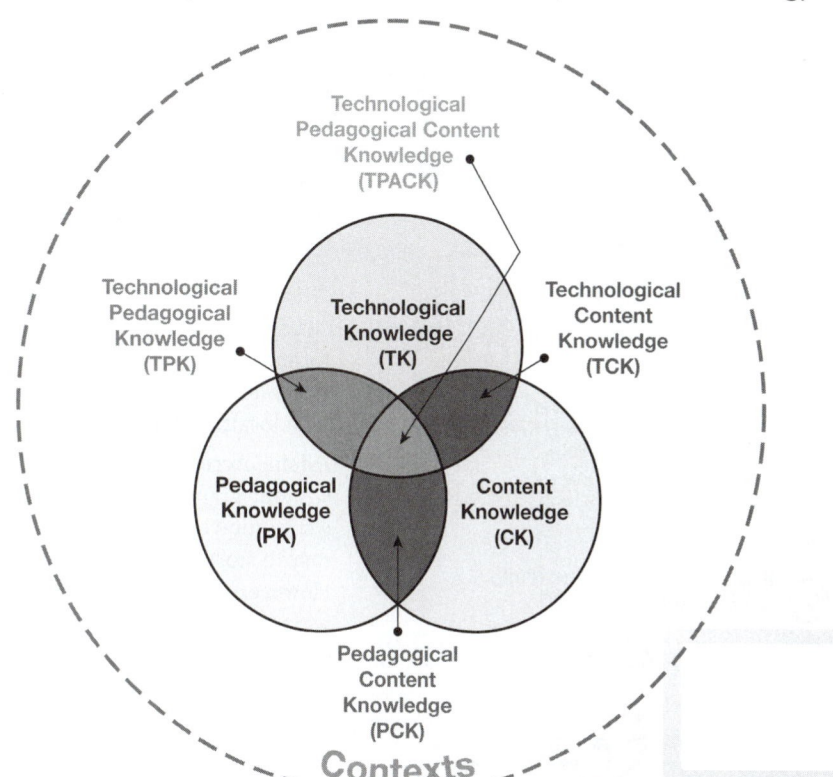

## TABLE 1.5 A Brief History of Tech-PACK Terminology

| | |
|---|---|
| 1986 | Shulman says pedagogy and content knowledge (PCK) must be considered together. |
| 2000 | Hughes adds technology to form TPCK (technological pedagogical content knowledge). |
| 2006 | Mishra and Koehler articulate the interdependence of content, pedagogy, and technology knowledge. |
| 2007 | TPCK becomes TPACK as Thompson and Mishra say it better represents the interdependence of the three knowledge domains and represents the "Total PACKage" of teacher knowledge required for technology integration. |
| 2012 | TPACK becomes Tech-PACK as Roblyer and Doering emphasize the critical contribution of technology to teaching. |

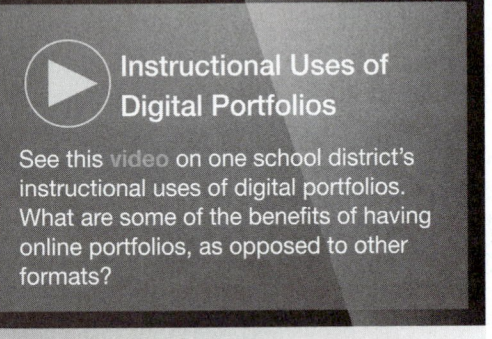

### Instructional Uses of Digital Portfolios

See this video on one school district's instructional uses of digital portfolios. What are some of the benefits of having online portfolios, as opposed to other formats?

**FIGURE 1.6** Electronic Portfolios: How to Develop Them

**DETERMINE PORTFOLIO REQUIREMENTS**

Find out products required, medium to use, and criteria to meet. See rubric for evaluating portfolio quality:
http://www.uwstout.edu/static/art/artedportfolios/evaluating/portevaluatiorubric.html

↓

**CREATE THE STRUCTURE**

Set up the portfolio structure on the medium (e.g., web, PowerPoint, Adobe Acrobat) you have chosen

↓

**ADD AND LINK COMPONENTS**

Create media and software products to demonstrate technology integration skills; add to portfolio by required deadlines

↕

**MONITOR THE COLLECTION; RECEIVE PERIODIC FEEDBACK**

Review products with instructors; determine if requirements are being met

↕

**REFLECT ON PRODUCTS; REVISE AS NEEDED**

Add or revise components based on reflection and feedback

framework and found that "Active involvement in (re)design and enactment of technology-enhanced lessons" (p. 109) was found to be a best practice in increasing competencies in teacher educators' technology integration skills. Harris, Grandgenett, and Hofer (2010) validated a rubric for assessing these skills. See this rubric and articles about it at the TPACK.org website.

## Demonstrating Technology Skills: Portfolio Options and Tech-PACK

Many teacher preparation programs require their candidates to develop a **teaching portfolio**, a collection of their work products from courses they take, to demonstrate their achievement of required skills and Tech-PACK growth as they go through the program. **Portfolios** can also serve as a collection of the student's work products over time, arranged so that they and others can see how their skills have developed and progressed. They also include criteria for selecting and judging content. Figure 1.6 shows a suggested sequence to follow in creating an electronic portfolio. Also see the feature Open Source Options for free materials to create portfolios.

In addition to showing their own technology development, teachers may want to have their students demonstrate their skills with a portfolio. Many teachers are turning to student **digital** or **electronic portfolios**, or a collection of work in a website or multimedia product, as the assessment strategy of choice. For free versions of portfolio materials, see **Open Source Options**.

Teachers usually provide the portfolio structure and tell students how to fill in the content. Resources available for creating portfolios are described here.

- **"Ready-made" portfolio software packages**. These packages provide a structure to which teachers can add content instead of creating their own format. Popular examples include Grady Profile by Auerbach and the online portfolio site Livetext. These systems usually are built on database software, with locations for attaching files of written and visual products.

- **Adobe Acrobat Professional**. To store and display documents (with or without graphics), teachers can use Adobe Acrobat Professional to create electronic versions of pages. PDFs are essentially pictures of pages and are easy to store and share with others by downloading the free Acrobat Reader. However, Adobe Acrobat Professional also has features that allows files that were created in different formats and applications (e.g., Word documents, email messages, spreadsheets, and PowerPoint presentations) to be combined in one portfolio file.

- **Multimedia authoring software**. Teachers can structure portfolios with presentation software such as Microsoft PowerPoint or Apple Keynote, or with multimedia development software such as Adobe Director, Travantis Lectora, or MediaWorks.

# OPEN SOURCE
## OPTIONS *for Electronic Portfolios*

| TYPES OF PORTFOLIO DEVELOPMENT MATERIALS | SOURCES |
|---|---|
| **Ready-made portfolio software packages** | *Mahara e-Portfolios*: mahara.org |
| | *Sakai's Open Source e-Portfolio System*: sakaiproject.org (Search on "eportfolios") |
| **Multimedia authoring software** | *Sophie*: sophieproject.org |
| **Relational databases** | *PostgreSQL*: postgresql.org |
| **Free websites with templates** | • *Firebird*: firebirdsql.org<br>• Google Sites – Steps for creating a Google Sites portfolio: learnnc.org<br>• Listing of other free sites at *Internet4Classrooms*: internet4classrooms.com |
| **Video editors** | *Open Movie Editor*: openmovieeditor.org |

- **Websites**. Portfolios can be posted on the Internet, where they can be more easily shared with others. Like multimedia packages, these portfolios can offer sophisticated video and audio presentations. Adobe's Creative Suite and Fireworks are popular Web-page development packages.
- **Video**. Today's digital video offers flexible, interactive formats for displaying portfolio elements. Video elements to document teacher or student accomplishments can also be inserted into multimedia products and websites described above.

**TECHNOLOGY LEARNING CHECK**

Complete TLC 1.5 to review what you have learned from reading this section about how teachers address technology standards and skills.

## TODAY'S EDUCATIONAL TECHNOLOGY USES: DEVELOPING A SOUND RATIONALE

The history of educational technology teaches us the importance of answering the "Why should I use technology?" question. Also, two current needs make it essential that teachers and schools are able to state a clear and compelling case for using technology in education. First, integrating technology into education requires substantial, ongoing investments in technology infrastructure and teacher training, so educators and policy makers need to offer a solid rationale for why these funds are well spent. Second, administrators want to see evidence that technology purchases help improve students' achievement, increase school attendance, or improve graduation rates. Developing a sound rationale for using technology in specific situations requires reviewing research findings and other evidence that technology is, indeed, helping to address some of education's most urgent needs and problems.

# What Does Research on Technology in Education Tell Us?

**Limitations of past research.** Even though electronic technologies have been in use in education since the 1950s, research results have not drawn a clear line between technology use and impact on educational quality indicators. Researchers such as Clark (1983, 1985, 1991, 1994) have openly criticized "computer-based effectiveness" research and **meta-analysis**, which is a statistical method designed by Glass (1976) to summarize results across studies and measure the size of the effect a "treatment" (e.g., a technology-based method) has over and above traditional methods. Clark concluded that most studies that have found a greater impact on achievement of one delivery method over the other did not control for factors such as different instructors, instructional methods, curriculum contents, or novelty. He famously said technologies make no more contribution to quality indicators than the truck that delivers the groceries does for nutrition. Though Kozma (1991, 1994) responded by asserting that research should look at technology not as an information delivery medium but as "the learner actively collaborating with the medium to construct knowledge" (1991, p. 179), policy makers still need evidence that this collaboration improves learning in measurable ways.

**Evidence from one-to-one initiatives.** Some of the most promising research results to date have come from the one-to-one computing initiatives, which provide a **laptop**, that is, a small portable personal computer, or other mobile computing device such as a tablet to every student in a given grade level or school and measure the impact on achievement, dropout rate, attendance, and other factors. Maine led this effort with a statewide program for middle school students in 2001 after a successful pilot project (Gulek & Demirtas, 2005). Bebell and O'Dwyer (2010) edited a group of articles reporting the results of four other one-to-one initiatives. These reports show that each initiative had an impact on quality indicators, but the amount of impact varied according to factors such as how projects were implemented, teacher acceptance, and students' use of the devices outside of school. Results of Project RED (Revolutionizing Education), an initiative completed with funding from computing industries, found similar results. Schools with one-to-one computing programs (Devaney, 2010) had fewer discipline problems, lower dropout rates, and higher rates of college attendance.

**Other recent reviews of research.** In February 2013, the educational magazine *Edutopia* published a summary of recent evidence of the impact of various technologies on quality indicators. Their review has links to all the recent reviews of research. The overall conclusions are that:

- Simply adding any technology to any learning environments does not necessarily improve learning. Teacher and student uses remain the most important factor.
- Successful technology integration requires accompanying changes in teacher training, curricula, and assessment practices.
- Blending technology with face-to-face teacher time generally produces better outcomes than face-to-face or online learning alone.
- Rigorous research on the specific features of technology integration that improve learning is limited.

## A Technology-Use Rationale Based on Problem Solving

As recent research shows, the case for using technology in teaching is one that must be made not just by isolating variables that make a difference, but by combining them. Educators have cited a number of reasons why we should integrate technology into teaching. These are described here in three different categories related to solving problems that limit learning, but it is when these contributions are combined that technology seems to make the greatest difference.

**Problem 1: How to motivate and engage students?** Technologies, when properly implemented, can use the following strategies to address the problem of unmotivated students:

- **Gaining their attention**. Teachers say technology's visual and interactive qualities can direct students' attention toward learning tasks.
- **Supporting manual operations during high-level learning**. Students are more motivated to learn complex skills (e.g., writing compositions and solving algebraic equations) when technology tools help them do the low-level skills involved (e.g., making corrections to written drafts or doing arithmetic).
- **Illustrating real-world relevance**. When students can see video and online examples of high-level math and science skills being used in real-life, it is no longer just "school work"; they are more willing to learn skills that have clear value to their future life and work.
- **Engaging students through production work**. Students who learn by creating their own products with technologies such as word processing, multimedia, and other technology products report higher engagement in learning and a greater sense of pride in their achievements.
- **Connecting students with audiences for their writing**. Educators say that students are much more motivated to write and do their best writing when they publish it online, since others outside the classroom will see their work.
- **Providing support for cooperative work**. Although students can do small-group work without technology, teachers report that students are often more motivated to work cooperatively on presentation software and website production projects.

**Problem 2: How to support students' learning needs?** The following are ways technologies can support students' learning by making their work more efficient and productive and by providing access to sources and ways of learning that they would not otherwise have:

- **Supporting effective skill practice**. When students need focused practice in order to comprehend and retain the skills they learn, drill-and-practice type software offers the privacy, self-pacing, and immediate feedback that makes practice most effective.
- **Visualizing underlying concepts in unfamiliar or abstract topics**. Simulations and other interactive software tools have unique abilities to illustrate science and mathematics concepts. Highly abstract mathematical and scientific principles become clearer and easier to understand.
- **Studying systems in unique ways**. Students use tools such as spreadsheets and simulations to answer "what if" questions that they would not be able to do easily by hand or that would not be feasible at all without the benefits of technology.
- **Giving access to unique information sources and populations**. The Internet connects students with information, research, data, and expertise not available locally.
- **Supplying self-paced learning for accelerated students**. Self-directed students can learn on their own with software tutorials and/or distance learning materials. They can surge ahead of the class or tackle topics that the school does not offer.
- **Turning disabilities into capabilities**. Students with disabilities depend on technology to compensate for vision, hearing, and/or manual dexterity they need to read, interact in class, and do projects to show what they have learned.
- **Saving time on production tasks**. Software tools such as word processing, desktop publishing, and spreadsheets allow quick and easy corrections to reports, presentations, budgets, and publications.
- **Grading and tracking student work**. Personalized learning systems and mobile, handheld technologies help teachers quickly assess and track student progress, giving them the rapid feedback they need to make adjustments to their learning paths.
- **Providing faster access to information sources**. Students use the Internet and email to do research and collect data that would take much longer to gather by other methods.
- **Saving money on consumables**. Software tools such as drill-and-practice and simulations optimize scarce funds by taking the place of materials (e.g., worksheets, handouts, animals for dissection) that are used and replaced each year.

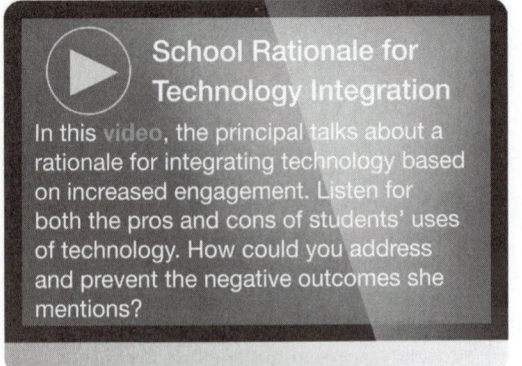

**School Rationale for Technology Integration**

In this video, the principal talks about a rationale for integrating technology based on increased engagement. Listen for both the pros and cons of students' uses of technology. How could you address and prevent the negative outcomes she mentions?

**Problem 3: How to prepare students for the future?** As the discussion of CCSS and 21st-Century Skills earlier in this chapter showed, skills that students will need in the future will focus more on skills such as thinking creatively and reasoning effectively, than on memorizing facts, definitions, and rules. To learn these skills, students will need the following:

- **Digital literacy**. As technologies are increasingly used to store and convey information, **digital literacy**, or skills in using both technologies and the information they carry, are viewed as essential (Pierce, 2013). For many library/media experts, digital literacy is becoming an umbrella term that encompasses **information literacy** (Beach & Swiss, 2011; Jewett, 2011; Stripling, 2010). Also, images and video are increasingly replacing text as communication media, requiring students to learn **visual literacy**, or skills in interpreting, creating, and using images. Because images are usually carried via digital media, visual literacy may be considered a subset of digital literacy.

- **Digital citizenship**. Schools are tasked with teaching students how to use technology resources in safe, responsible and legal ways.

All these reasons point out specific ways to integrate technology into teaching and learning and together form powerful rationale for why technology must become as commonplace in education as it is in other areas of society. See Figure 1.7 for a summary of elements underlying this rationale.

**FIGURE 1.7** Why Use Technology? A Summary Rationale Based on Problem Solving

| **Problem 1: How to motivate and engage students?** |
| --- |
| • Gains learner attention |
| • Supports manual operations during high-level learning |
| • Illustrates real-world relevance through highly visual presentations |
| • Engages students through production work |
| • Connects students with audiences for their writing |
| • Engages learners through real-world situations and collaborations |
| • Provides support for working cooperatively |
| **Problem 2: How to support students' learning needs?** |
| • Supports effective skill practice |
| • Helps students visualize underlying concepts in unfamiliar or abstract topics |
| • Lets students study systems in unique ways |
| • Gives access to unique information sources and populations |
| • Supplies self-paced learning for accelerated students |
| • Turns disabilities into capabilities |
| • Saves time on production tasks |
| • Grades and tracks student work |
| • Provides faster access to information sources |
| • Saves money on consumable materials |
| **Problem 3: How to prepare students for future learning?** |
| • Helps teach digital literacy |
| • Helps teach digital citizenship |

# ⦿ TOMORROW'S EDUCATIONAL TECHNOLOGY: EMERGING TRENDS IN TOOLS AND APPLICATIONS

Visions of the future are suffused with images of technologies that may seem magical and far-fetched now, just as cell phones and wearable technologies like Google Glass seemed only a few decades ago. We know that future education will mirror current technical trends and shape the goals and priorities we set today for tomorrow's education. As with so many "miraculous" technologies, the question is how we will take advantage of their capabilities to bring about the kind of future education systems our society wants and our economy needs.

## Trends in Hardware, Software, and System Development

For emerging developments with great potential for impact on education, we turn to the annual report of the New Media Consortium's (NMC) Horizon Project, established in 2002 to identify and describe emerging technologies that are likely to have great impact on our society. Though the focus of the education editions of this report are on postsecondary education, some of the trends listed here from recent reports also seem likely to impact K–12 education (Johnson, Adams Becker, Estrada, & Freeman, 2014; Johnson et al., 2013).

**Trend #1: Ubiquitous mobile computing.** The trend toward mobile devices in education is already widespread and having great impact on K–12 education, though concerns about curriculum, privacy, classroom management, and uniform access abound. Cloud-based storage and communications enables this trend.

**Trend #2: More sources of open content.** When combined with open-source materials, open content means that more courses and educational materials that were previously proprietary will now be free and available to everyone online. This trend also means more free content will be available to K–12 teachers and students.

**Trend #3: Massive open online courses (MOOCs).** One of the fastest growing of the new trends, MOOCs heralded a new way of looking at learning. One of the outcomes of the open-content movement, MOOCs hold the promise of a future where education is cheaper and available to anyone anywhere in the world.

**Trend #4: Increased e-book/e-text presence.** Though e-texts have been available for decades, their technical sophistication has recently increased dramatically. They are rapidly replacing paper books as the dominant medium for accessing information.

**Trend #5: Tablet computing.** The portability of these devices facilitate ubiquitous Internet access and rapid communications, as well as access to e-texts. A thriving software development movement for tablets is driving this trend and increasing the options they enable.

**Trend #6: Augmented reality systems.** Coined by a Boeing researcher in 1990, **augmented reality** refers to a computer-generated environment in which a real-life scene is overlaid with information that enhances our uses of it. Examples have been evident in industry,

▲ A growing hardware trend is use of e-texts. (Photo by W. Wiencke)

military, and entertainment (e.g., the movies *Avatar* and *Iron Man*) environments for years, but now simple versions of these systems are available to schools on mobile devices for uses such as GPS and maps of the sky. Devaney (2013) said that augmented reality is assuming a greater role in the classroom as learning tools based on it become available. For example, one teacher used an augmented reality app called Aurasma to lets students hover their tablets over images of famous paintings, thus calling up audio and text with features and notes about the artist's techniques. Other augmented reality apps include Layar, used to enhance print materials, and colAR which works with coloring-book pages.

### Trend #7: Wearable technologies.
In combination with augmented reality, a trend noted above, wearable technologies such as Google Glass are anticipated to impact education as new applications come on the market. Mineer (2014) cites predictions that BYOD will segue into "WYOD" or wear your own device. She describes one teacher's uses of Google Glass to record lectures as she gives them and let students record their progress on projects they are completing. Wearables such as AiQ's "smart textiles," which monitor the wearer's vital signs, and Recon Instruments' sports goggles, which monitor movements, have great potential for health-and sports-related areas. Other wearable products track location data, offering the potential for improving student safety in school settings.

### Trend #8: Gesture-based computing.
Devices that we can control through moving a hand or other body part are changing the way people interact with computers. With **gesture-recognition systems**, a camera or sensor reads body movements and communicates them to a computer, which processes the gestures as commands and uses them to control devices or displays. Gesture-based technology, especially in combination with wearable technologies, has the potential to enhance teaching simulations by making them more lifelike and intuitive to use.

### Trend #9: Games and gamification.
**Gamification**, or incorporating the most motivational aspects of games (e.g., badges awarded for success) into nongame activities, is attracting more attention from both software developers and educators. The hope is that driving interest and rewarding student achievement can increase the time spent on learning activities.

### Trend #10: Learning analytics.
Educators are also paying increased attention to **learning analytics**, or the ability to detect trends and patterns from sets of performance data (a.k.a. "big data") across large numbers of students. The goal is to find ways of applying findings across students to create a personalized approach to learning for each student.

### Trend #11: 3D printing.
Though currently seen in research and lab settings, **3D printers**, devices that can "print" models or actual products when a 2-D image is supplied, are predicted to play a greater role in science and other subjects that rely on models to illustrate and provide practice with new concepts.

## Trends in Educational Applications

Hardware/software trends are important because they support and drive current and emerging conditions for education. People expect to work, learn, and study whenever and wherever they want to, and they seek instruction that is responsive to their personal needs. These

▲ 3D printers offer students a new way to learn design strategies. (Photo by W. Wiencke)

technology trends and the conditions in which they are emerging augur a dramatically transformed education system:

### Trend #1: Flexible learning environments.

With wireless communications and portable devices, learning environments can be located beyond the walls of classrooms and schools. Students can take notes, gather data, or do research from wherever they are and have easy, fast access to resources such as writing labs and digital production labs. MOOC environments mean that students can supplement (or even circumvent) school learning with high-quality advanced courses offered at a distance. Though they are a "holdable technology," rather than a wearable technology, devices such as the LiveScribe Echo ("smart pens") offer instantaneous access to supportive information.

### Trend #2: Personalized learning.

Learning analytics has driven a fast-growing trend toward **personalized learning systems (PLS)**, or computer-based management programs that (1) assess individual student learning needs using complex algorithms and collections of data across students, and (2) provide a customized instructional experience matched to each student.

### Trend #3: New instructional models.

The ubiquity of computer power and Internet access has enabled both integration strategies, such as BYOD and new instructional models such as the MOOC and the **flipped classroom** models, in which students engage with concepts via lectures stored as downloadable videos or **vodcasts** before coming to class, then spend class time on other learning activities. Milman (2012) says that this model is also known as an inverted classroom, and the term's originators, Colorado chemistry teachers Jonathan Bergmann and Aaron Sams also called it "reverse instruction" (Makice, 2012). Milman says that this approach frees up class time "for more engaging (and often collaborative) activities typically facilitated by the instructor" (p. 85).

### Trend #4: Reliance on learning at a distance.

As high-speed connections become more readily available to schools and homes and handheld devices like tablets become capable of online access, more students are taking virtual courses and learning through virtual programs. The number of virtual schools operating across states is increasing (Watson, Murin, Vashaw, Gemin, & Rapp, 2013), and some schools now offer a completely online, virtual diploma. Though currently fraught with controversies such as funding and quality control, distance learning for K–12 students eventually will have the same degree of impact on reshaping schools as it has had on redefining higher education.

### Trend #5: Increased educational options for students with disabilities.

New technologies continue to make the most dramatic advances in opportunities for people with disabilities. On his website, innovator Ray Kurzweil describes physical immersion systems and intelligent programs that help people with sensory impairments and physical disabilities function effectively in learning situations. Bargerhuff, Cowan, Oliveira, Quek, and Fang (2010) describe **virtual reality (VR)** uses for those with visual impairments, but VR uses may now be expanding as a result of augmented reality, gesture-based computing, and other recent trends.

**TECHNOLOGY LEARNING CHECK**
Complete **TLC 1.7** to review what you have learned from reading this section about emerging trends in technologies and their uses in education.

# COLLABORATE, DISCUSS, REFLECT

Monkey Business/Fotolia

**The following questions may be used either for in-class, small-group discussions or may initiate discussions in blogs or online discussion boards:**

1. Visit the Common Sense Media website and review its Digital Citizenship Curriculum (under the Education menu button). How could a grasp of these skills and attitudes help young people in learning and in their social contacts with other students?

2. In his 2012 editorial "Will MOOCs Destroy Academia?" from the *Communications of the ACM*, Vardi opines that "due to the seductive possibilities of lower costs . . . the very value of college education is being seriously questioned" (p. 5). What evidence can you cite to support or refute the idea that MOOCs will threaten education as we know it? Will it have any impact on K–12 schools?

3. Gene Glass, originator of meta-analysis techniques, said, "Experienced education leaders worry that something is lost when teachers are replaced by avatars and real life is replaced by Facebook . . . only a fool believes everything that can be gained from face-to-face teaching and learning also can be acquired online" (2010, p. 34). Give examples from research and practice to support or refute Glass's analysis.

4. Go to *Edutopia*'s website and do the following two activities:

   a. In *Edutopia*'s "Technology Integration Research Review" from February 5, 2013, there is evidence summarizing the impact of educational technologies; learn what research can teach us about effective uses of technology for learning. Read especially the studies by subject area, such as science or writing. Summarize what you learned about the overall benefits of technology-based strategies and of using technology to teach your subject.

   b. Also at the *Edutopia* website, click on the Video tab to access the video collection. In the Search by Topic window, use the menu to browse videos by topic, and select Technology Integration. Watch one of the videos. (i) Which of the perspectives that shaped educational technology is evident in the video? (ii) Refer to Figure 1.7 in the text, and list elements that show which reasons the technology in the video is being used.

5. Educational technology historian Paul Saettler (1990) said, "Computer information systems are not just objective recording devices. They also reflect concepts, hopes, beliefs, attitudes" (p. 539). Contrast the concepts, hopes, beliefs, and attitudes that our past versus current uses of technology in education reflect.

6. Richard Clark's now-famous comment about the impact of computers on learning was that the best current evidence is that media are mere vehicles that deliver instruction but do not influence student achievement any more than the truck that delivers our groceries causes change in our nutrition (Clark, 1983, p. 445). Why has this statement had such a dramatic (and, in some cases, emotional) impact on educational technology practitioners? What evidence could you cite to respond to it?

7. In their study of students' reasons for online plagiarism, Comas-Forgas and Sureda-Negre (2010) found that some students say it "is easier, simpler and more comfortable than doing the work yourself" (p. 223). Can you suggest arguments that would help persuade students that online plagiarism, while easy and quick, is not in their best interests?

Chapter **1** Summary

**The following is a summary of the main points covered in this chapter.**

1. **Introduction: The "Big Picture" on Technology in Education**
   - This chapter's "big picture" review provides an important framework for viewing the field and consists of key terminology, reflections on the past, considerations about the present, and a look ahead to the future.
   - Four perspectives help define today's educational technology: educational technology as communications media (originally represented by AECT); educational technology as instructional systems and instructional design (originally represented by ISPI); educational technology as vocational training

(originally represented by ITEEA); and educational technology as computer systems (a.k.a., educational and instructional computing) (originally represented by ISTE).

- Important definitions in the field are:
  - Educational technology—A combination of the *processes* and *tools* involved in addressing educational needs and problems, with an emphasis on applying the most current digital and information tools.
  - Integrating educational technology—The process of *matching digital tools and methods* to given educational needs and problems.
  - Instructional technology—The *subset of educational technology* that deals directly with teaching and learning applications (rather than educational administrative ones).

2. **Yesterday's Educational Technology**
   - The history of educational computing/technology comprises four eras: the pre-microcomputer era (1950–late 1970s); the microcomputer era (late 1970s–1993); the Internet era (1990s); and mobile technologies, social media, and open access (2001–present).
   - We have learned the following from the history of technology in education: No technology is a panacea for education; teachers usually do not develop technology materials or curriculum; "technically possible" does not equal "desirable, feasible, or inevitable;" technologies change faster than teachers can keep up; older technologies can be useful, and teachers always will be more important than technology.

3. **Today's Educational Technology Resources: Systems and Applications**—These resources include:
   - An overview of digital technology tools includes these categories: hardware, software, and storage media (such as flash drives), as well as cloud computing storage.
   - Hardware tools include: microcomputers, handheld technologies, display technologies, imaging technologies, peripherals, and external storage.
   - Technology facilities that allow teachers and students to access these resources include laboratories of networked computers and classroom computer arrangements such as BYOD and one-to-one programs.
   - Software resources include programs for instruction, enhancing productivity, and administration.

4. **Today's Educational Technology Issues**—These include issues under the following categories:
   - Social issues such as privacy, health-related concerns, fears about technology misuses, and risks of online behaviors.
   - Educational issues such as lack of technology funding; teacher and student accountability for quality and progress; digital literacy and digital citizenship; debates on best practices with technologies; and reliance on online learning.
   - Cultural/equity issues such as the digital divide, racial and gender equity, and students with special needs.
   - Legal/ethical issues such as hacking, safety issues, academic dishonesty, and illegal downloads/software piracy.

5. **Today's Educational Technology Skills**
   - Skills include the following: at least one competency named in the Common Core State Standards; ISTE Standards for Students and Teachers; 21st Century Skills for Students and Teachers; ICT Competency Framework for Teachers; and the Tech-PACK framework.
   - Various portfolio options are available for teachers to document their skills in meeting these standards. These options include "ready-made" portfolio software packages, Adobe Acrobat Professional, multimedia authoring software, and websites.

6. **A Rationale for Using Educational Technology**
   - Items that can help build a rationale come from examining evidence from past research and from reviewing types of problems that the use of technologies has helped solve.
   - Technology can help to solve some educational problems, including how to motivate and engage students in learning, how to support learning needs, and how to prepare students for the future.

7. **Emerging Trends in Tools and Applications**
   - Trends in hardware, software, and system development include ubiquitous mobile computing, more sources of open content, massive open online courses (MOOCs), increased e-book/e-text presence, tablet computing, augmented reality systems, wearable technologies, gesture-based computing, games and gamification, learning analytics, and 3D printing.
   - Trends in educational applications resulting from these tools include flexible learning environments, personalized learning, new instructional models, reliance on learning at a distance, and increased educational options for students with disabilities.

# TECHNOLOGY INTEGRATION **WORKSHOP**

As you move through your teacher preparation program, you will see opportunities for adding products to a teaching portfolio that show what you know about and are able to do with technology. In this chapter, do the following to prepare for adding to your portfolio:

1. To apply the concepts and skills you've read about throughout this chapter, go to the Chapter 1 Technology Application Activity.

2. Review the section entitled "Demonstrating Technology Skills: Portfolio Options."

3. Determine portfolio requirements for your program and begin creating your own portfolio structure.

4. As you complete your own structure, include the following products:

- Products of your group's "Hot Topic Debates"
- Products of your group's "Collaborate, Discuss, Reflect" online or in-class activities.

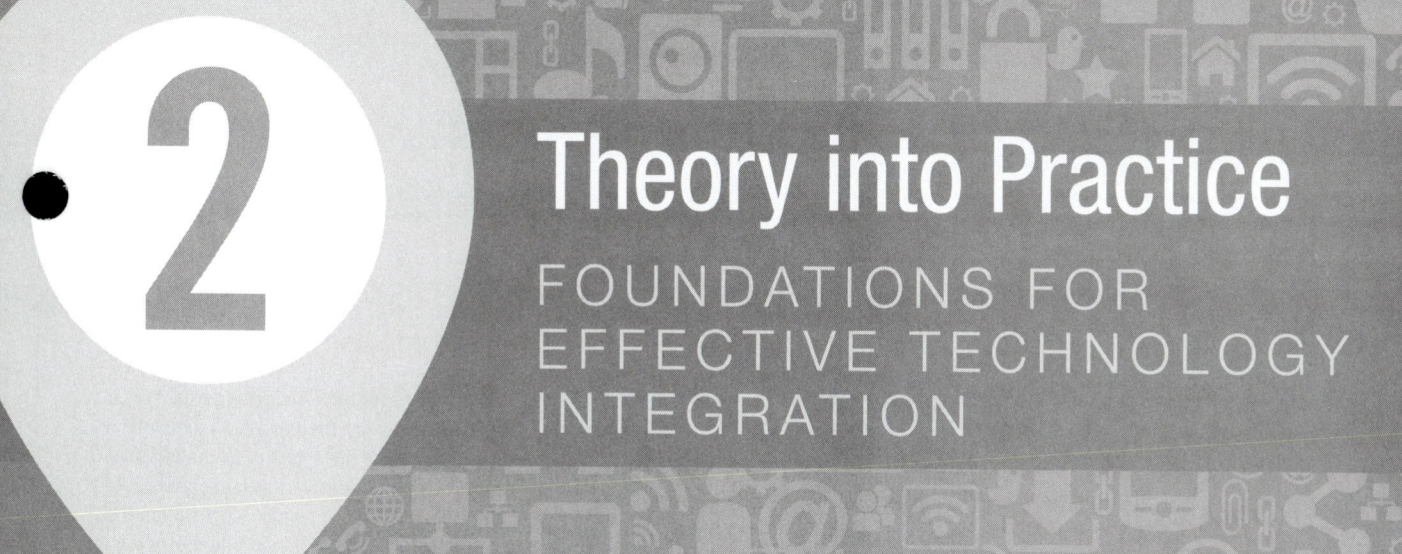

# 2 Theory into Practice

## FOUNDATIONS FOR EFFECTIVE TECHNOLOGY INTEGRATION

## Learning Outcomes

After reading this chapter and completing the learning activities, you should be able to:

1. Identify the contributions of each of three different factors to effective technology integration: learning theory foundations, the technology integration planning (TIP) model, and essential conditions for effective technology integration. (ISTE Standards•T 5)

2. Contrast objectivist and constructivist teaching strategies according to their language and epistemologies (i.e., beliefs about the nature of human knowledge and how to develop it). (ISTE Standards•T 5)

3. Analyze learning theories associated with directed instruction by identifying the theorists and beliefs associated with them and how they contributed to current directed technology integration strategies. (ISTE Standards•T 5)

4. Analyze learning theories associated with constructivist instruction by identifying the theorists and beliefs associated with them and how they contributed to current constructivist technology integration strategies. (ISTE Standards•T 5)

5. Analyze technology integration strategies in order to identify whether they reflect directed or constructivist approaches, or combinations of these. (ISTE Standards•T 5)

6. Determine planning needs for a sample classroom technology integration strategy by using steps in the Technology Integration Planning (TIP) Model. (ISTE Standards•T 2, 5)

7. Identify examples of each of the essential conditions to support effective classroom integration of technology. (ISTE Standards•T 2, 5)

# TECHNOLOGY INTEGRATION IN ACTION: THE ROLE OF CONTEXT

## STRATEGY A  PREPARING STUDENTS FOR STATE TESTS

Sophie Bluy/Pearson Education

One of Bill's responsibilities as mathematics department chair was helping all teachers make sure their students did well on the mathematics portion of the state's Test of Essential Skills for Success (TESS). Bill and the other math teachers were determined that every student in the school would pass the TESS-M, the math portion. They also decided that they would not just "teach to the test." They wanted the students to have a good grounding in math skills that would serve them well in their future education.

From practice test scores he had seen, Bill realized that there were too many students who needed help to provide individual coaches or tutors for each one, and he disliked the idea of making all students work on skills only some of them needed. At a school he had visited in another district, Bill had been impressed with how teachers relied on a computer-based system that included drills, tutorials, simulations, and problem-solving activities that they could access in their rooms or from the computer lab.

One of the benefits of the system was that students could take practice tests and teachers could get a list of skills with which they were having problems. Then the system would recommend specific activities, on and off the system, matched to each child's needs. The activities ranged from practice in very basic math skills to solving real-life problems that required algebra and other math skills. Bill persuaded his principal to purchase a year's subscription to this system, and he and the other math teachers agreed on ways they would use it to supplement their classroom instruction.

That year, every student at the school passed the TESS-M. The math teachers agreed that the computer-based activities had played a key role in students' preparation. They liked the way it helped them target students' specific needs more efficiently while not overemphasizing test taking. Bill asked the principal to make the system a permanent part of the school's budget.

## STRATEGY B  A SIMULATED FAMILY PROJECT

Wow/Shutterstock

Mayda's middle-school math students are usually fairly good at math skills; almost none of them has any trouble passing the state's criterion-referenced test. However, she likes to do at least one ongoing project each year to show students how their math skills apply to real-life situations. She also wants them to learn to work together to solve problems, just as they would be doing in college and in work situations when they graduate.

The first activity she does at the beginning of each year is to have her students work in small groups to simulate "families." They select a type of "job" their "wage earner" will have and create a monthly budget in a spreadsheet template she designed to show income earned from an imaginary job versus estimated monthly expenses for each of them and for the "family." To select jobs, the groups consult online newspaper Help Wanted sections to get an idea of what positions are available and how much they pay.

To estimate expenses, they look at online newspaper and real estate ads to see how much it costs to rent a house or an apartment in an area where they would like to live. Throughout the year, she gives each group unexpected expenses (e.g., the dog gets sick, the roof is leaking); the students must then adjust their spreadsheet budget to compensate for the extra expenses. If a group gets too far out of line with its budgeted expenses, she makes the students get a loan, which they do by researching available interest rates and adding a loan payment to their spreadsheet budgets that will pay off their debt.

Toward the end of the year, Mayda has students do estimated taxes on their earnings. Finally, they prepare a report using *PowerPoint* software that shows charts of their spending and what they learned about "making ends meet." The students always tell her this is the most meaningful math activity they have ever done.

# CHAPTER 2 BIG IDEAS OVERVIEW

Before you begin reading the rest of this chapter, listen to the Chapter 2 Big Ideas Overview. It will give you a two-minute audio overview of main concepts to look for and help prepare you to work through information and exercises to achieve this chapter's outcomes.

# OVERVIEW OF FACTORS IN SUCCESSFUL TECHNOLOGY INTEGRATION

As illustrated by the contrasting Technology Integration in Action examples that begin this chapter, the answer to the question, "Which kind of technology integration strategy works best?" is, "It depends on the situation." Effective technology integration calls for a well-planned match of learning needs with tools and strategies, as well as classroom conditions that support them. This chapter describes three complementary factors, as depicted in Figure 2.1, that work in combination to enable effective technology integration strategies.

## Learning Theory Foundations

To make use of all the insights we have gained from the study and research on how people acquire new knowledge, learning theories should inform teaching strategies. Thus, it is important to begin with a look at two very different, competing theories of how learning should take place and examine how various kinds of technology integration strategies were derived from them.

**FIGURE 2.1** Factors Required for an Enlightened Approach to Technology Integration

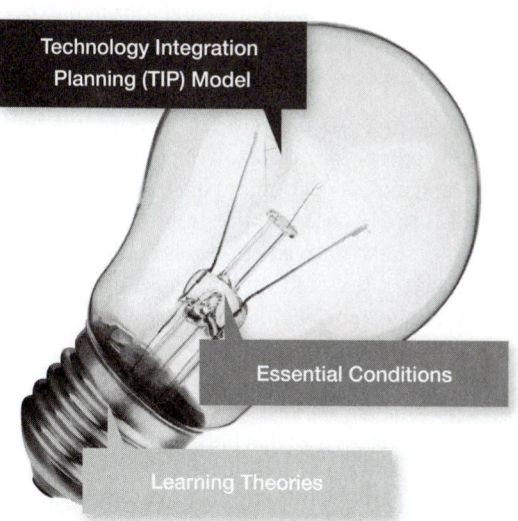

## Technology Integration Planning (TIP) Model

For the procedural and "people" issues involved in technology integration, we look to the steps of a three-phased TIP model and how teachers can assess the resources they require to plan and implement given technology-based lessons. This model specifies: analysis of teaching/learning needs/objectives, planning tasks, and post-instruction analysis and revisions.

## Essential Conditions for Effective Technology Integration

The International Society for Technology in Education (ISTE) emphasizes that technology-based strategies work best when **essential conditions**, or elements that form an optimal environment, are in place to support them.

Thus, a review of these conditions is the final piece in the foundation: a shared vision, skilled personnel, technical assistance, appropriate teaching and assessment strategies, supportive policies, access to hardware and software resources, and an engaged community.

**TECHNOLOGY LEARNING CHECK**
Complete TLC 2.1 to review what you have learned from reading this section about technology integration's three essential ingredients.

# OVERVIEW OF TWO PERSPECTIVES ON TECHNOLOGY INTEGRATION

Prior to about 1980, there seemed little question about the appropriate instructional role for technology, particularly computer technology. According to respected writers of the time (Taylor, 1980), there were three acceptable roles: computers as *tools* to support learning (e.g., word processing, calculations), as *tutors* to deliver instruction (e.g., drill and practice, tutorials), and as "*tutees*" (e.g., learning to program computers). However, as technology became more capable and complex, society changed in response, and with those changes came differing views of education and appropriate teaching strategies.

## Two Perspectives on Effective Instruction

In the past, educational goals reflected society's emphasis on the need for basic skills—such as reading, writing, and arithmetic—and an agreed-on body of information considered essential for everyone. Many educators now believe that the world is changing too quickly to define education in terms of specific information or skills; they believe it should focus instead on more general capabilities, such as "learning to learn" skills, that will help citizens cope with inevitable technological change. The emphasis on learning and innovation skills and critical thinking and problem solving in the 21st Century Student Outcomes created by the Partnership for 21st Century Skills (P21) reflect this belief.

While everyone seems to agree that changes in our educational methods are needed to respond to modern challenges, not everyone agrees on which strategies will serve today's educational goals. Statements of theorists and practitioners reflect two contrasting views of how learning should take place:

- **Directed instruction**. Teachers should transmit a predefined set of information to students through teacher-organized activities. This view is based on **objectivism**, a belief system grounded primarily in behaviorist learning theory and the information-processing branch of the cognitive learning theories.

- **Inquiry-based learning**. Learners should generate their own knowledge through experiences, while teachers serve only as facilitators. This view is based on **constructivism**, which evolved from other branches of thinking in cognitive learning theory.

A few technology applications, such as drill and practice and tutorial software functions, are associated only with directed instruction; most others (problem solving, multimedia production, Web-based learning) can inform either directed instruction or constructivist teaching and learning, depending on how they are used. This text is based on the premise that there are meaningful roles for both **directed instruction** and **constructivist** strategies and the technology applications associated with them. Both can help teachers and students meet the many and varied requirements of learning in today's information age society.

## Where Did the Perspectives Come From?

How did these differences come about? It is important to recognize that both people who espouse directed instruction methods and those who take constructivist approaches are attempting to identify what Gagné (1985) called the *conditions of learning*, or sets of circumstances that bring about learning. Both approaches are based on the work of respected learning theorists and psychologists who have studied both the behavior of human beings as learning organisms and the behavior of students in schools and classrooms.

Educators' views diverge, however, in the ways they define learning, how they identify the conditions required to make learning happen, and how they perceive the problems that interfere most with learning. They disagree because they subscribe to different life philosophies and learning theories and, consequently, they take different perspectives on improving current educational practice. The articles cited in the Hot Topic Debate reflects how these differing philosophies affect technology integration strategies.

The two perspectives have very different underlying **epistemologies** (beliefs about the nature of human knowledge and how to develop it). **Constructivists** (those who espouse inquiry-based methods) and **objectivists** (those who espouse directed methods) come from separate and different epistemological "planets," although both nurture many different tribes or cultures. The characteristics and theoretical origins of these philosophical differences can be briefly summarized in the following way:

- **Objectivists**—Knowledge has a separate, real existence of its own outside the human mind. Learning happens when this knowledge is transmitted to people and they store it in their minds in ways that can be retrieved later.

- **Constructivists**—Humans construct all knowledge in their minds by participating in certain experiences. Learning occurs when one constructs both mechanisms for learning and one's own unique version of the knowledge, colored by background, experiences, and aptitudes.

Sfard (1998) found that objectivists and constructivists view learning in such different ways that they actually use different metaphors for it: the *acquisition metaphor* and the *participation metaphor*. These differences in language signal fundamental differences in thinking about how learning takes place and how we can foster it. Figure 2.2 gives examples of these differing views and the language that signals them.

Sometimes differences of opinion among objectivists and constructivists have generated strident debate in the literature (Clark, Yates, Early, & Moulton, 2010; Baroody, Eiland, Purpura, & Reid, 2013). Objectivists say constructivist methods are unrealistic; constructivists

## Hot Topic Debate
## What are "Best Practices" in Technology Integration?

*Take a position for or against (based either on your own position or one assigned to you) on the following controversial statement. Discuss it in class or on an online discussion board, blog, or wiki, as assigned by your instructor. When the discussion is complete, write a summary of the main pros and cons that you and your classmates have stated, and put the summary document in your Teacher Portfolio.*

The dramatic differences in learning theories underlying traditional objectivist strategies and innovative constructivist strategies (a.k.a., discovery learning, inquiry-based learning, and experiential learning) have generated ongoing debate. Nowhere has this debate been more strident than in discussions about which best practices in using technologies can support learning. For example, Clark, Yates, Early, and Moulton (2010) summarize "a half-century of research evidence" that using "electronic media and discovery-based learning" has failed to produce results equal to "guided training methods" (p. 263). Adams, Mayer, MacNamara, Koenig, and Wainess (2012) say that this evidence of low or negative impact extends even to discovery

methods in today's computer-based games. Constructivists like Snape and Fox-Turnbull (2013) answer that today's "graveyard model of teaching" (everyone in rows and dead) needs to be replaced with students interacting, solving problems, applying skills, and making decisions about meaningful issues" (p. 52), and only "technological practice (that) uses authentic tools and processes" (p. 53) can meet this need. In addition, Baroody, Eiland, Purpura, and Reid (2013) found that computer-based discovery learning can even help young learners acquire basic mathematical concepts. It is also evident that many of today's T-PACK assessments are based on measuring teachers' growth in "authentic" (i.e., constructivist or inquiry-based) uses of technology in instruction. For example, Mouza, Karchmer-Klein, Nandakumar, Ozden, and Hu (2014) said that a "marker of effective teacher preparation" is the ability of teachers "to design inquiry-based activities around Web-based resources (p. 210).

What are the basic beliefs that underlie each of these opposing positions? Which one are you closer to and how would you respond to the opposing view?

# FIGURE 2.2 Perspectives from the Directed and Constructivist "Planets"

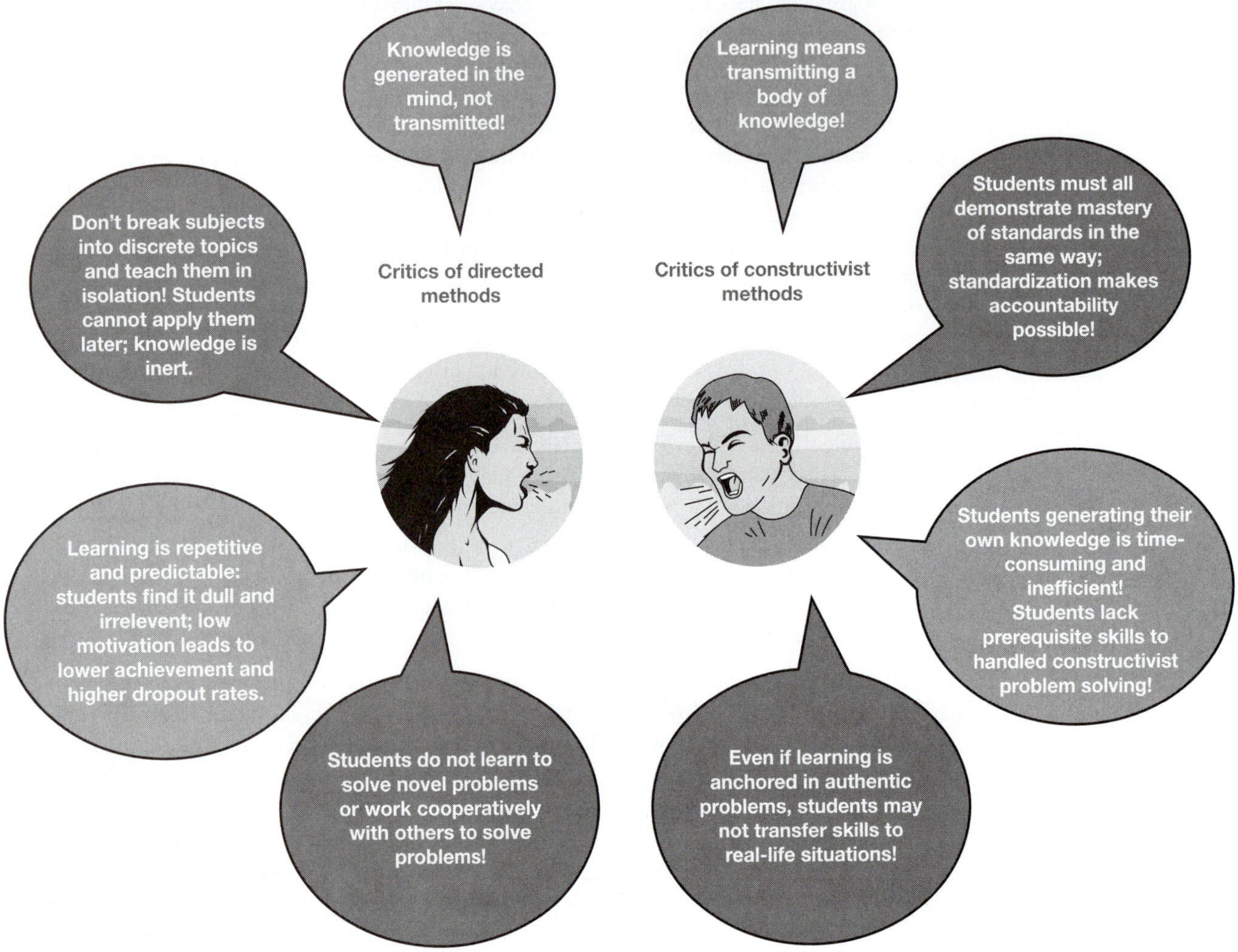

Critics of directed methods

- Knowledge is generated in the mind, not transmitted!
- Don't break subjects into discrete topics and teach them in isolation! Students cannot apply them later; knowledge is inert.
- Learning is repetitive and predictable: students find it dull and irrelevent; low motivation leads to lower achievement and higher dropout rates.
- Students do not learn to solve novel problems or work cooperatively with others to solve problems!

Critics of constructivist methods

- Learning means transmitting a body of knowledge!
- Students must all demonstrate mastery of standards in the same way; standardization makes accountability possible!
- Students generating their own knowledge is time-consuming and inefficient! Students lack prerequisite skills to handled constructivist problem solving!
- Even if learning is anchored in authentic problems, students may not transfer skills to real-life situations!

consider directed methods to be outmoded. The sections that follow will describe learning theories that underlie these belief systems. Subsequent sections will show how these theories give rise to different technology integration strategies.

**TECHNOLOGY LEARNING CHECK**
Complete TLC 2.2 to review what you have learned from reading this section about differing perspectives on teaching and learning.

# ⦿ LEARNING THEORY FOUNDATIONS OF DIRECTED INTEGRATION MODELS

Directed models of integrating technology were derived primarily from a combination of four theorists and theories, each of which contributed essential qualities and procedures: behaviorist, information-processing, and cognitive-behaviorist learning theories and the **systems approaches to instructional design** that were based on them. This section summarizes the basic concepts associated with these theories and their implications for education practices and for technology integration.

## Behaviorist Theories

These theories, among the earliest explanations for how people learn new things, are based primarily on the work of B. F. Skinner. Read background on Skinner and his theories in Figure 2.3. From Skinner's theories, we learned that instruction must provide the right stimuli and reinforcement to get students to make the desired behavioral responses, or learned skills. Computer-based instruction with teaching machines and programmed instruction quickly proved popular applications of this theory because they provided consistent, reliable stimuli and reinforcement on an individual basis.

## Information-Processing Theories

Educators found Skinner's stimulus-response view of learned behavior insufficient to guide all types of learning, so the first cognitive (as opposed to behavioral) learning theorists began to hypothesize *processes inside the brain* allow human beings to learn and remember. Much of the work of the information-processing theorists is based on a model of memory and storage proposed by Atkinson and Shiffrin (1968), and many teaching practices are based on this model.

**FIGURE 2.3** Skinner's Behaviorist Theories of Learning: Building on the S–R Connection

Corbis/Bettman

Before B. F. Skinner, theories of learning were dominated by **classical conditioning** concepts proposed by Russian physiologist Ivan Pavlov, who said that behavior is largely controlled by involuntary physical responses to outside stimuli (e.g., dogs salivating at the sight of a can of dog food). By contrast, Skinner's **operant conditioning theory** said that people can have voluntary mental control over their responses (e.g., a child reasons he will get praise if he behaves well in school). Eggen and Kauchak (2013) said Skinner believed that learning is "observable responses that change in frequency or duration as the result of consequences, (which are) events that occur following behaviors" (p. 296). Skinner's work showed that behaviors are controlled by the *consequences* of actions, rather than by events preceding the actions. A consequence is an outcome (stimulus) after the behavior, which can influence future behaviors. Skinner's work made him a highly influential figure during this time.

Skinner reasoned that the internal processes (those inside the mind) involved in learning could not be seen directly. (Scientific work had not advanced sufficiently at that time to observe brain activity.) Therefore, he concentrated on cause-and effect relationships that could be established by observation. He found that human behavior could be shaped by **contingencies of reinforcement** or situations in which reinforcement for a learner is made contingent on a desired response. He identified three kinds of situations that can shape behavior:

- **Positive reinforcement.** A situation is set up so that an increase in a desired behavior will result from a stimulus. For example, to earn praise or good grades (positive reinforcement), a learner studies hard for a test more often (desired behavior).

- **Negative reinforcement.** A situation is set up so that an increase in a desired behavior will result from avoiding or removing a stimulus. For example, a student dislikes going to detention (negative reinforcement), so to avoid detention again, the student is quiet in class more often (desired behavior).

- **Punishment.** A situation is set up so that a decrease in a desired behavior will result from undesirable consequences, such as when a student is given a failing grade (punishment) when she cheats on a test (undesirable behavior), so she is less likely to cheat in the future.

**Implications for education.** Skinner's influential book, *The Technology of Teaching* (1968), gave a detailed theory of how classroom instruction should reflect these behaviorist principles, and many of his classroom management and instructional techniques still are widely used today. To Skinner, teaching was a process of arranging contingencies of reinforcement effectively to bring about learning. He believed that even such high-level capabilities as critical thinking and creativity could be taught in this way; it was simply a matter of establishing chains of behavior through principles of reinforcement. Skinner felt that programmed instruction was the most efficient means available for learning skills. Educational psychologists such as Benjamin Bloom also used Skinner's principles to develop methods that became known as mastery learning. In summary:

- We know when people learn only by observing changes in their behavior.

- Behavior is shaped by stimulus-response connections.

- Reinforcement strengthens responses; if people do something and are reinforced for it, they learn to respond in predictable ways.

- Chains of behavior become skills.

**Implications for technology integration.** Most original drill-and-practice software was based on Skinner's reinforcement principles, for example, when students knew they would get praise or an entertaining graphic if they gave correct answers. Much tutorial software is based on the idea of programmed instruction. Because the idea behind drill-and-practice software is to increase the frequency of correct answering in response to stimuli, these packages often are used to help students memorize important basic information, while tutorial software gives students an efficient path through concepts they want to learn.

Computer programs provide ideal environments for the highly-structured cueing, attention-getting, visualization, and practice features that information-processing theorists found so essential to learning and remembering. See Figure 2.4 for information on on **information processing theories** of Atkinson and Shiffrin.

## Cognitive-Behaviorist Theory

Robert Gagné was a renowned educational psychologist who translated principles from behaviorist and information-processing theories into practical instructional strategies for educators. Read background on **cognitive-behaviorist theories** of Robert Gagné in Figure 2.5. Instruction based on this theory had to provide "conditions for learning" by offering activities matched to each type of skill. Students had to demonstrate they had learned prerequisite skills by demonstrating the type of behavior appropriate for the skill. Computer-based methods such as drills and tutorials were deemed useful since they could consistently provide the ideal events and conditions for learning.

## FIGURE 2.4 Information Processing Summary

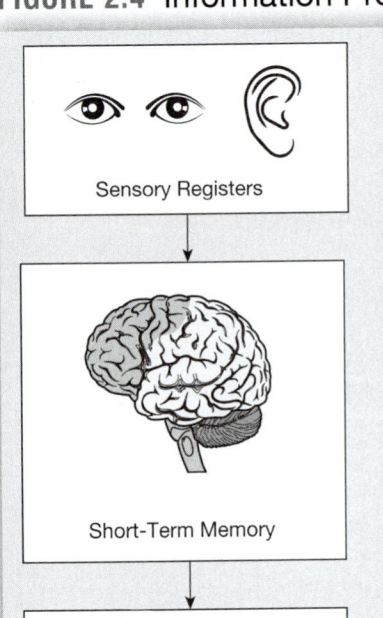

Sensory Registers

Short-Term Memory

Long-Term Memory

Behaviorists like Skinner focused only on external, directly observable indicators of human learning. Many people found this explanation insufficient to guide instruction. During the 1950s and 1960s, a group of researchers known as the cognitive-learning theorists began to hypothesize a model that would help people conceptualize processes they could not observe directly. Though some constructivists disassociate themselves with them, the information-processing theorists were among the first and most influential of the cognitive-learning theorists. They hypothesized processes inside the brain that allow human beings to learn and remember.

Although no single, cohesive information-processing theory of learning summarizes the field, the work of the information processing theorists is based on a model of memory and storage originally proposed by Atkinson and Shiffrin (1968). According to them, the brain contains certain structures that process information much like a computer. This model of the mind as computer hypothesizes that the human brain has three kinds of memory or "stores":

- **Sensory registers**. The part of memory that receives all the information a person senses
- **Short-term memory (STM)**. Also known as working memory, the part of memory where new information is held temporarily until it is either lost or placed into long-term memory
- **Long-term memory (LTM)**. The part of memory that has an unlimited capacity and can hold information indefinitely.

According to this model, learning begins when information is sensed through receptors: eyes, ears, nose, mouth, and/or hands. This information is held in the sensory registers for a very short time (perhaps a second), after which it either enters STM or is lost. Many Information-processing theorists believed that information can be sensed but lost before it gets to STM if the person is not paying attention to it. Anything people pay attention to goes into working memory, where it can stay for about 5 to 20 seconds. After this time, if information is not processed or practiced in a way that causes it to transfer to LTM, then it, too, is lost. Information-processing theorists believed that for new information to be transferred to LTM, it must be linked in some way to prior knowledge already in LTM. Once information does enter LTM, it is there essentially permanently, although some psychologists believed that even information stored in LTM can be lost if not used regularly.

**Implications for education.** Although subsequent studies have indicated that learning may be more complicated than the two-store model of memory would explain (Schunk, 2012), information-processing views have become the basis for many common classroom practices. Teaching practices based on these concepts include the use of: (1) interesting questions and eye-catching material to help students pay attention to a new topic; (2) mnemonic devices (e.g., saying that HOMES stands for the first letters in the five Great Lakes; (3) instructions that point out (or cue) important points in new material to help students remember them by linking them to information they already know; (4) visual explanations of abstract concepts; and (5) practice exercises to help transfer information from STM to LTM.

**Implications for technology integration.** Computer programs provide ideal environments for the highly structured cueing, attention-getting, visualization, and practice features that information-processing theorists found so essential to learning and remembering. Information-processing theories have also guided the development of artificial intelligence (AI) applications, an attempt to develop computer software that can simulate the thinking and learning behaviors of humans. Much of the drill and practice software available is designed to help students encode and store newly learned information into LTM.

## FIGURE 2.5 Gagné's Cognitive-Behaviorist Theory: Providing Conditions for Learning

Courtesy of Harriet Gagné

Gagné built on the work of behavioral and information-processing theorists by translating principles from their learning theories into practical instructional strategies that teachers could employ with directed instruction. He is best known for three of his contributions in this area: the Events of Instruction, the types of learning, and learning hierarchies. Gagné used the information-processing model of internal processes to derive a set of guidelines that teachers could follow to arrange optimal "conditions of learning." His set of nine **Events of Instruction** was perhaps the best known of these guidelines (Gagné, Briggs, & Wager, 1992):

1. Gaining attention
2. Informing the learner of the objective
3. Stimulating recall of prerequisite learning
4. Presenting new material
5. Providing learning guidance
6. Eliciting performance
7. Providing feedback about correctness
8. Assessing performance
9. Enhancing retention and recall

Gagné identified several types of learning as behaviors students demonstrate after acquiring knowledge. These differ according to the conditions necessary to foster them. He showed how the Events of Instruction would be carried out slightly differently from one type of learning to another (Gagné et al., 1992):

1. Intellectual skills:
   - Problem solving
   - Higher order rules
   - Defined concepts
   - Concrete concepts
   - Discriminations
2. Cognitive strategies
3. Verbal information
4. Motor skills
5. Attitudes

The development of "intellectual skills," Gagné believed, requires learning that amounts to a building process. Lower level skills provide a necessary foundation for higher level ones. For example, to learn to work long division problems, students first would have to learn all the prerequisite math skills, beginning with number recognition, number facts, simple addition and subtraction, multiplication, and simple division. Therefore, to teach a skill, a teacher must first identify its prerequisite skills and make sure the student possesses them. He called this list of building block skills a **learning hierarchy**.

**Implications for education.** Instruction based on this theory provides "conditions for learning" by offering activities matched to each type of skill. Students had to demonstrate they had learned prerequisite skills by demonstrating the type of behavior appropriate for the skill. For example, if the skill was using a grammar rule, students had to demonstrate they could correctly apply the rule in situations that required it. Gagné's Events of Instruction and learning hierarchies have been widely used to develop systematic instructional design principles. Although his work has had more impact on designing instruction for business, industry, and the military than for K–12 schools, many school curriculum development projects still use a learning hierarchy approach to sequencing skills.

**Implications for technology integration.** Computer-based methods such as drills and tutorials were deemed useful since they could consistently provide the ideal events and conditions for learning. Gagné, Wager, and Rojas (1981) showed how Gagné's Events of Instruction could be used to plan lessons using each kind of instructional software (drill, tutorial, simulation). They said that only a tutorial could "stand by itself" and accomplish all of the necessary events of instruction; the other kinds of software required teacher-led activities to accomplish events before and after software use.

## Systems Approaches: Instructional Design Models

The concept of instruction as a self-contained system with interdependent components is based on work of educational psychologists such as Robert Gagné and Leslie Briggs. They applied systems principles from military and industrial training to create models for designing school and college instruction. A system of instruction (based on behaviorist, information-processing, and cognitive-behaviorist theories) can be designed to achieve replicable results efficiently (i.e., good results over time and across student groups). See Figure 2.6 to read background on systems approaches to instructional design.

## Objectivist Theory Foundations for Directed Methods

Figure 2.7 shows how these four theories contribute to directed technology integration strategies based on **mastery learning** approaches, or sequences of objectives that, once met, define mastery of a subject. A considerable body of research indicates that directed methods work well to foster this kind of approach. For example, Clark, Yates, Early, and Moulton (2010) argue that directed instruction is more effective and efficient than minimally guided instruction when learners do not have enough prior knowledge to be self-guided. They say that minimally guided instruction ignores the fundamentals of human cognition and overloads working memory. Adams, Mayer, MacNamara, Koenig, and Wainess (2012) and other scholars have echoed Hirsch's (2002) early declaration that "one minute of explicit (directed) learning can be more effective than a month of implicit (exploratory) learning."

Objectivists focus primarily on technology integration strategies for systematically designed, structured learning products, such as drills, tutorials, and personalized learning systems (PLSs), discussed in Chapter 3. When they do use other materials such as simulations and some kinds of problem-solving software that have no innate structure, integration strategies are very structured, providing a step-by-step sequence of learning activities matched to specific performance objectives. When objectivists evaluate these products, they typically look for a match among

**FIGURE 2.6** Systems Approaches and the Design of Instruction: Managing the Complexity of Teaching

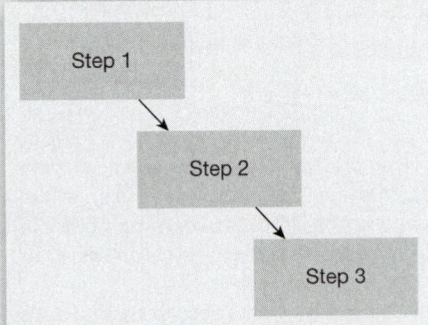

There are many versions of the systematic design process and many views on what constitutes instructional design (Roblyer, 2015). Saettler (1990) said that the development of "scientifically based instructional systems" (p. 343) precedes this century, but he also pointed out that modern instructional design models and methods have their roots in the collaborative work of Robert Gagné and Leslie Briggs. These notable educational psychologists developed a way to transfer "laboratory-based learning principles" gleaned from military and industrial training to create an efficient way of developing curriculum and instruction for schools.

Gagné specialized in the use of instructional task analysis to identify required subskills and conditions of learning for them. Briggs's expertise was in systematic methods of designing training programs to save companies time and money in training their personnel. When they combined their two areas of expertise, the result was a set of step-by-step processes known as a systems approach to instructional design, or **systematic instructional design**, which came into common use in the 1970s and 1980s. Designers created an instructional system by: stating goals and objectives, doing a task analysis to decide on learning conditions; aligning assessment and instructional strategies with goals and objectives; creating materials that deliver strategies; and testing and revising materials before finalizing them.

According to Saettler (1990), "the 1960s produced most of the major components of the instructional design process" (p. 345). Names associated with this era include Robert Mager (instructional objectives), Glaser (criterion-referenced testing), and Cronbach and Scriven (formative and summative evaluation). Other major contributors to modern instructional design models include David Merrill (component display theory) and Charles Reigeluth (elaboration theory).

**Implications for education.** Systems approaches to designing instruction have had great influence on training programs for business, industry, and the military, and somewhat less influence on K–12 education. However, performance objectives and sequences for instructional activities still are widely used. Most lesson planning models call for performance objectives (sometimes called behavioral objectives) to be stated in terms of measurable, observable learner behaviors.

**Implications for technology integration.** Most directed models for using technology resources are based on systems approaches; that is, teachers set objectives for a lesson, then develop a sequence of activities. A software package or an Internet activity is selected to carry out part of the instructional sequence. For example, the teacher may introduce a principle of genetics, then allow students to experiment with a simulation package to "breed" cats in order to see the principle in action. To those who espouse this approach, a system of instruction must be structured, sequential, and continually monitor student progress. Computer-based instruction is well-suited to delivering such an instructional system in a consistent and reliable way, while monitoring and giving fast feedback on student progress.

**FIGURE 2.7** How Objectivist Theories and Practices Lead to Directed Technology Integration Strategies

**Information processing theories (Atkinson & Shiffrin)** Attention-getting, repetitive, individual practice

**Behaviorist theories (Skinner)** Consistent presentation of stimuli & reinforcement

**Cognitive-behaviorist theories (Gagné)** Consistent presentation of sequences to fulfill events of instruction

**Systems approaches to instructional design** Consistent presentation of new information, practice, & assessment

*Implications for Technology Integration Strategies*

**Choose directed technology integration strategies when the goal is mastery learning:**
- Skills and content to be learned are clearly-defined, concrete, and unambiguous, and when a specific behavioral response (test performance) must be used to indicate learning has occurred.
- Students need individual tutoring and practice to learn and to demonstrate prerequisite skills.
- Students need to acquire specific skills as quickly and efficiently as possible.

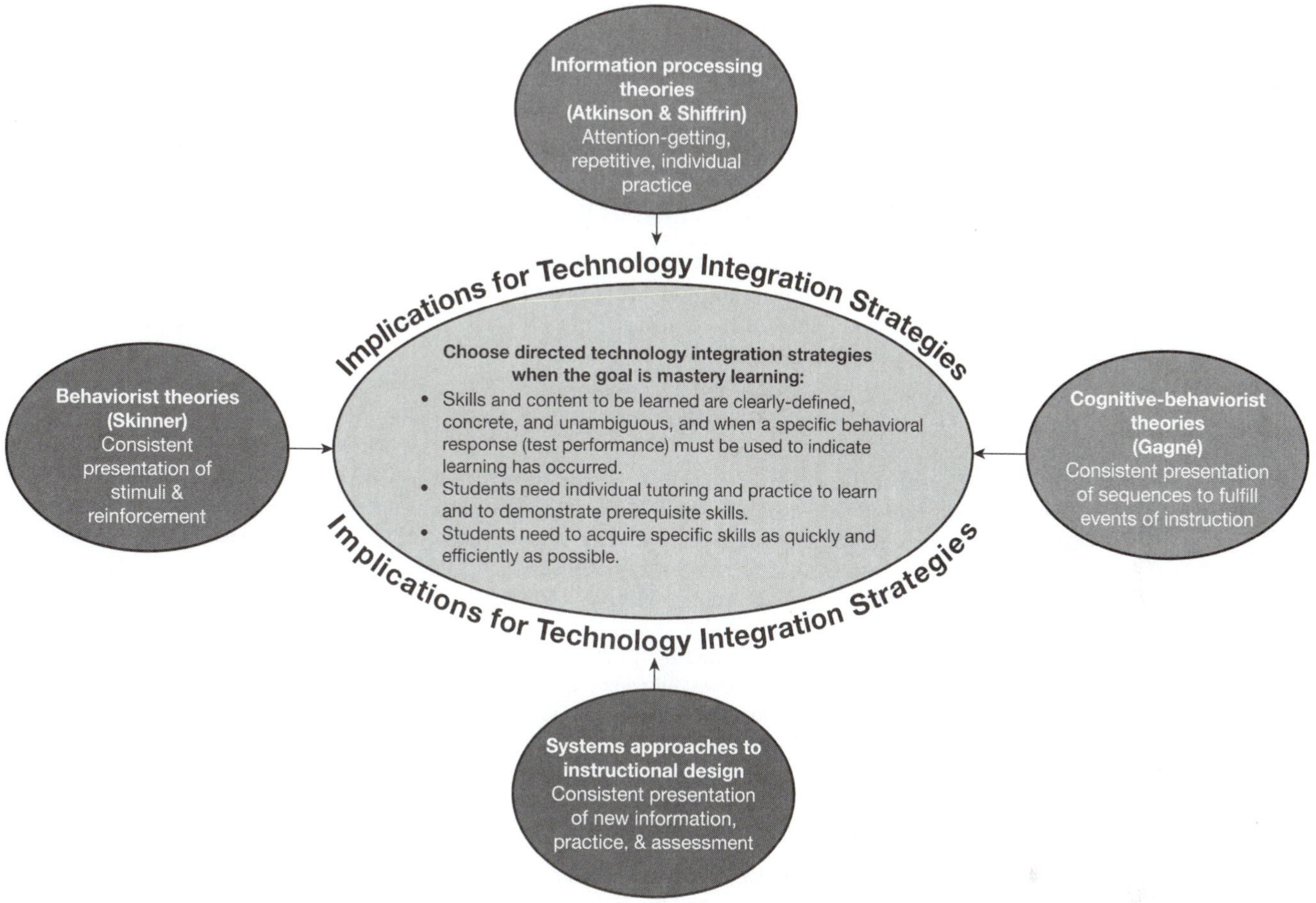

objectives, methods, and assessment strategies and how well they help teachers and students meet curriculum standards. To reflect objectivist principles, materials and integration strategies must have clearly defined objectives and a set sequence for their use.

**TECHNOLOGY LEARNING CHECK**

Complete TLC 2.3 to review what you have learned from reading this section about objectivist learning theories and technology integration strategies based on them.

# LEARNING THEORY: FOUNDATIONS OF CONSTRUCTIVIST INTEGRATION MODELS

Constructivist beliefs and methods were derived from a combination of six theorists and theories, each of which contributed essential qualities and procedures: social activism theory, social cognitive theory, scaffolding theory, child development theory, discovery learning and child development, and multiple intelligences theory. This section summarizes the basic concepts associated with each of these theories and their implications for education practices and for technology integration.

## Social Activism Theory

An early proponent of racial equality and women's suffrage, John Dewey's radical activism shaped his beliefs about education. Today's interdisciplinary curriculum and hands-on, experience-based learning are in tune with Dewey's lifelong message. His emphasis on the need for cooperative (social) learning would mesh well with uses of social media and technologies that enable group projects. Read background on John Dewey and **social activism theory** based on his beliefs in Figure 2.8.

## Social Cognitive Theory

The work of Albert Bandura was very much in keeping with Dewey's views of learning as a social process, but Bandura did pioneering research to show how this learning occurred. Bandura's focus on modeling and self-efficacy are reflected in many of today's instructional activities.

### FIGURE 2.8 John Dewey: Educational Reform as Social Activism

**Courtesy of the Library of Congress**

John Dewey is considered a philosopher rather than a learning theorist, an educational writer rather than an educational researcher. He was born in 1859 and most of his contributions to education predated those of the other famous individuals described here. Yet no one voice in education has had more pervasive and continuing influence on educational practice. In many ways, he can be thought of as the Grandfather of Constructivism, but he also advocated a merging of absolutism and experimentalism in much the same way as this chapter calls for using a combination of directed and constructivist methods.

Dewey's beliefs were very much shaped by his direct involvement in the social and cultural issues of the time; clearly he was a radical in his political views. An early proponent of racial equality and women's suffrage, he helped found a third American political party for liberals. His beliefs about education also reflected this radical activism. Though he did not himself originate the Progressive Education Movement, a reform initiative popular in the first half of the 1900s, he was identified closely with it; the movement survived his death in 1952 by only a few years. His philosophy of education, which he was able to see implemented at the turn of the century in a laboratory school established at the University of Chicago, focused on principles and concepts in direct opposition to those in education during that period. He believed the following:

- **Curriculum should arise from students' interests.** Dewey deplored standardization. He felt curriculum should be flexible and tailored to the needs of each student, a "pedocentric" strategy rather than the "scholiocentric" one of the time. He advocated letting each child's experiences determine individual learning activities.

- **Curriculum topics should be integrated, rather than isolated from each other.** He felt that isolating topics from one another prevented learners from grasping the whole of knowledge and caused skills and facts to be viewed as unrelated bits of information.

- **Education is growth, rather than an end in itself.** He did not share the common view of the time that education is preparation for work. He found that this view served to separate society into social classes and promote elitism. Rather, he looked on education as a way of helping individuals understand their culture and develop their relationship to society and their unique roles in it.

- **Education occurs through its connection with life, rather than through participation in curriculum.** He felt that social consciousness was the ultimate aim of all education. To be useful, all learning had to be in the context of social experience. However, he found that school skills such as reading and mathematics were becoming ends in themselves, disconnected from any meaningful social context.

- **Learning should be hands-on and experience based, rather than abstract.** He objected to commonly used teaching methods that used a "one-way channel of communication—from teacher to student through direct drill and memorization . . ." (Smith & Smith, 1994). He believed that meaningful learning resulted from students working cooperatively on tasks that were directly related to their interests. Dewey's writings (e.g., *The School and Society*, 1899; *The Child and the Curriculum*, 1902; *How We Think*, 1910; *Schools of Tomorrow*, 1915; *Democracy and Education*, 1916; *Experience and Education*, 1938) spanned an era of monumental change in America's cultural identity and helped reform the country's education system to reflect those changing times.

**Implications for education.** Although it is difficult to say whether or not Dewey's philosophies directly caused some of the trends in current educational practice, today's interdisciplinary curriculum and hands-on, experience-based learning are very much in tune with Dewey's lifelong message. However, it also is likely he would deplore the current standards movement and the use of testing programs to determine school promotion and readiness for graduation.

**Implications for technology integration.** As Bruce (2000) noted at the dawn of the Internet Age, Dewey would likely have approved of technologies like the Internet being used to help students communicate with each other and learn more about their society. Dewey's emphasis on the need for cooperative learning would mesh well with technologies used for developing group projects and presentations. However, as Dewey himself recognized, the central problem with all these resources is combining them into a curriculum that encourages intellectual challenge.

Technologies like video and social media provide models and either increase or decrease self-efficacy, depending on the messages these media carry. The teacher's job is to shape these messages and models so they have a positive impact on self-efficacy. Read background on Albert Bandura and social cognitive theory in Figure 2.9.

## Scaffolding Theories

Lev Semenovich Vygotsky's views were very much in tune with the social learning views of Dewey and Bandura. He felt that how children learn and think derives directly from the culture around them, but that a child perceives things much differently than an adult. Children learn by **scaffolding**, or building on what they know to what they need to know, with the help of adults. Today's educators espouse many of Vygotsky's beliefs that instruction should be tailored to each student's needs, scaffolding the student to higher levels of learning after ascertaining the student's current level of understanding. Many visual technology tools, from video-based scenarios to virtual reality, are designed to scaffold students' understanding through graphic examples and real-life experiences relevant to their individual needs. Read background on Lev Vygotsky and scaffolding theory in Figure 2.10.

## Child Development Theory

French biologist Jean Piaget added to what we know about learning by exploring early stages of development in children and the role of environment in these stages. Although Piaget was not interested in applying his ideas to school-based education, today's early childhood and elementary curriculum reflects many of Piaget's beliefs about children's developmental levels. Also, Piaget's pupil, MIT mathematician Seymour Papert (1980), used Piaget's theories as the basis of his work with Logo, a language designed to let young students solve design problems using an on-screen cursor they called a "turtle." This environment provided the vital link that Papert

**FIGURE 2.9** Albert Bandura's Social Cognitive Theory: Social Influences on Learning

Courtesy of Albert Bandura

Bandura's work challenged some of the major premises of conditioning theories that were most popular at that time. He said that, contrary to the behavioral theories of reinforcement, students learned a great deal through observation (which he called **vicarious learning**), rather than through their actions (which he called **enactive learning**) (Schunk, 2012). Bandura found, for example, that one of the most powerful ways students learned was through observing the behaviors modeled by those around them.

He also found there was a difference between learning and behaviors that showed learning. Learning was acquiring new information or concepts, but he found that students often learned information and concepts in social settings that they did not reflect in any immediate behavior. Though he acknowledged that enactive learning was learning from one's own actions, his ideas differed from Skinner's view that behavior changed automatically (i.e., without intention) as a result of reinforcement. Instead, Bandura found that it was students' beliefs and judgments as social beings that determined whether or not their actions changed; their internal cognitive processes shaped their actions, rather than solely as a result of external consequences resulting from reinforcement.

Motivation to learn also played a central role in Bandura's social cognitive theory. He found that students who were innately capable sometimes did not learn because they lacked **self-efficacy**, or belief in their abilities to accomplish the actions necessary to learn. Self-efficacy beliefs can be shaped by teachers and others and can affect whether or not students even try to learn, as well as how long they persist at learning tasks. Schunk (2012) reported a series of studies that showed students' self-efficacy and achievement increased from watching videos of their own or peers' performance. Self-efficacy differs from self-concept in that self-concept is a general self-perception of one's overall abilities; self-efficacy is belief specific to a certain area of learning.

**Implications for education.** Educators' practices acknowledge the importance of modeling. They frequently try to shape student behaviors and grow motivation to learn by showing other students of similar age and backgrounds exhibiting these behaviors. Teachers also provide models, though sometimes inadvertently. Students tend to imitate what teachers do, rather than attending to what teachers say.

**Implications for technology integration.** Video examples can provide many examples of models that teachers would not otherwise have at their disposal. In addition, studies have shown that self-modeling videos, in which students watch examples of their own successful performance, can increase their self-efficacy in the area.

**FIGURE 2.10** The Contributions of Lev Vygotsky: Building a Scaffold to Learning

Courtesy of the Library of Congress

For many years, the writings of Russian philosopher and educational psychologist Lev Semenovich Vygotsky had more influence on the development of educational theory and practice in America than in his own country. Vygotsky's landmark book, *Pedagogical Psychology*, though written in 1926, was not published in Russia until 1991. Davydov (1995) attributed this lack of attention to the nature of the Russian government up until the time of perestroika. ". . . Vygotsky's general ideas could not be used for such a long time in the education system of a totalitarian society—they simply contradict all of its principles" (p. 13). What were these educational concepts that were so threatening to a communistic state but found such a warm reception in a democracy?

Vygotsky felt that cognitive development was directly related to and based on social development (Eggen & Kauchak, 2013). What children learn and how they think are derived directly from the culture around them. An adult perceives things much differently than a child does, but this difference decreases as children gradually translate their social views into personal, psychological ones. Vygotsky's theories, with their emphasis on individual differences, personal creativity, and the influence of culture on learning, were discordant with the aims of the USSR, a government designed to "subjugate the education of young people to the interests of a militarized state that needed citizens only as devoted cogs" (Davydov, 1995, p. 12).

Vygotsky referred to the difference between these two levels of cognitive functioning (adult/expert and child/novice) as the **Zone of Proximal Development (ZPD)**. He felt that teachers could provide good instruction by finding out where each child was in his or her development and building on the child's experiences. He called this building process "scaffolding." Ormrod (2014) said that teachers promote students' cognitive development by presenting some classroom tasks that "they can complete only with assistance, that is, within each student's zone of proximal development" (p. 39). Problems occur when the teacher leaves too much for the child to do independently, thus slowing the child's intellectual growth.

**Implications for education.** Davydov (1995) found six basic implications for education in Vygotsky's ideas (p. 13):

1. Education is intended to develop children's personalities.

2. The human personality is linked to its creative potential, and education should be designed to discover and develop this potential to its fullest in each individual.

3. Teaching and learning assume that students master their inner values through some personal activity.

4. Teachers direct and guide the individual activities of the students, but they do not force their will on them or dictate to them.

5. The most valuable methods for student learning are those that correspond to their individual developmental stages and needs; therefore, these methods cannot be uniform across students.

6. These ideas had heavy influence on constructivist thought; Vygotsky's works were very much in tune with constructivist concepts of instruction based on each child's personal experiences and learning through collaborative, social activities.

**Implications for technology integration.** Many constructivist models of technology use the concepts of scaffolding and developing each individual's potential. Many of the more visual tools, from Logo to virtual reality, are used under the assumption that they can help bring the student up from their level of understanding to a higher level by showing graphic examples and by giving them real-life experiences relevant to their individual needs.

felt would allow children to move more easily from the concrete operations or earlier stages of development to more abstract (formal) operations. Papert's 1980 book, *Mindstorms*, challenged then-current instructional goals and methods for mathematics and became the first constructivist statement of educational practice with technology. Read background on Jean Piaget and developmental theory in Figure 2.11.

## Discovery Learning

Some of educational theorist Jerome Bruner's beliefs seem to coincide with those of Dewey, Vygotsky, and Piaget. Like Piaget, Bruner believed children go through various stages of intellectual development. But unlike Piaget, Bruner supported instructional intervention. Bruner's theories are associated with unstructured learning activities that he called **discovery learning**. This kind of learning can be supported with simulations, problem-solving environments, and exploring Internet sites for relevant information. Read background on Jerome Bruner's theories in Figure 2.12.

## Multiple Intelligences Theory

Gardner's **multiple intelligences theory** is the only learning theory that attempts to define the role of intelligence in learning. It posits there are at least eight different and relatively independent kinds of intelligence. Howard Gardner's work (Gardner & Hatch, 1989) is based on

# FIGURE 2.11  Jean Piaget's Theories: Cognitive Development in Children

Corbis/Bettman

Piaget's examination of how thinking and reasoning abilities develop in the human mind began with observations of his own children and developed into a career that spanned some 60 years. He referred to himself as a "genetic episte-mologist," or a scientist who studies how knowledge begins and develops in individuals. Both believers in and critics of Piagetian principles agree that his work was complex, profound, sometimes misunderstood, and usually oversimplified. However, at least two features of this work are widely recognized as underlying all of Piaget's theories: his stages of cognitive development and his processes of cognitive functioning.

Piaget believed that all children go through four stages of cognitive development. While the ages at which they experience these stages vary somewhat, he felt that each developed higher reasoning abilities in the same sequence:

- **Sensorimotor stage** (from birth to about 2 years). Characteristics of children: They explore the world around them through their senses and through motor activity. In the earliest stage, they cannot differentiate between themselves and their environments (if they cannot see something, it does not exist). Also, they begin to have some perception of cause and effect; develop the ability to follow something with their eyes.

- **Preoperational stage** (from about age 2 to about age 7). Characteristics of children: They develop greater abilities to communicate through speech and to engage in symbolic activities such as drawing objects and playing by pretending and imagining; develop numerical abilities such as the skill of assigning a number to each object in a group as it is counted; increase their level of self-control and are able to delay gratification, but are still fairly egocentric; and are unable to do what Piaget called conservation tasks (tasks that call for recognizing that a substance remains the same even though its appearance changes, e.g., shape is not related to quantity).

- **Concrete operational stage** (from about age 7 to about age 11). Characteristics of children: They increase in abstract reasoning ability and ability to generalize from concrete experiences; and can do conservation tasks.

- **Formal operations stage** (from about age 12 to about age 15). Characteristics of children: They can form and test hypotheses, organize information, and reason scientifically; they can show results of abstract thinking in the form of symbolic materials (e.g., writing, drama).

Piaget believed a child's development from one stage to another was a gradual process of interacting with the environment. Children develop as they confront new and unfamiliar features of their environment that do not fit with their current views of the world. When this happens, he said, a **"disequilibrium"** occurs that the child seeks to resolve through one of two processes of adaptation. The child either fits the new experi-ences into his or her existing view of the world (a process called **assimilation**) or changes that schema or view of the world to incorporate the new experiences, (a process called **accommodation**). Though recent research has raised questions about the ages at which children's abilities develop, and it is widely believed that age does not determine development alone, Ormrod (2014) summarizes Piaget's basic assumptions about children's cognitive development in the following way:

- Children are active and motivated learners.

- Children's knowledge of the world becomes more integrated and organized over time.

- Children learn through the processes of assimilation and accommodation.

- Cognitive development depends on interaction with one's physical and social environment.

- The processes of equilibration (resolving disequilibrium) help to develop increasingly complex levels of thought.

- Cognitive development can occur only after certain genetically controlled neurological changes occur.

- Cognitive development occurs in four qualitatively different stages.

**Implications for education.** Educators do not always agree on the implications of Piaget's theories for classroom instruction. One frequently expressed instructional principle based on Piaget's stages is the need for concrete examples and experiences when teaching abstract concepts to young children who may not yet have reached a formal operations stage. Piaget himself repeatedly expressed a lack of interest in how his work applied to school-based education, calling it "the American question." He pointed out that much learning occurs without any formal instruction, as a result of the child interacting with the environment. However, constructivist educators tend to claim Piaget as the philosophical mentor who guides their work.

**Implications for technology integration.** Many technology-using teachers feel that using visual resources such as Logo and simulations can help raise children's developmental levels more quickly than they would have occurred through maturation; thus children who use these resources can learn higher level concepts than they normally would not have been able to understand until they were older. Other educators feel that young children should experience things in the "real world" before seeing them represented in the more abstract ways they are shown in software, for example, in computer simulations.

Guilford's pioneering work on the structure of intellect and Sternberg's view of intelligence as influenced by culture. Though teachers have experimented with allowing students to demon-strate learning in various ways, this theory has had less impact on curriculum due to the need for students to pass high-stakes tests in only one format. This theory supports doing group work on multimedia products, assigning students group roles based on their type of intelligence (e.g.,

**FIGURE 2.12** The Contributions of Jerome Bruner: Learning as Discovery

Courtesy of Jerome Bruner

Like Piaget, Jerome Bruner was interested in children's stages of cognitive development. Bruner described development in three stages (Schunk, 2012):

- **Enactive stage (from birth to about age 3).** Children perceive the environment solely through actions that they initiate. They describe and explain objects strictly in terms of what they can do with them. The child cannot tell how a bicycle works but can show what to do with it. Showing and modeling have more learning value than telling for children at this stage.

- **Iconic stage (from about age 3 to about age 8).** Children can remember and use information through imagery (mental pictures or icons). Visual memory increases and children can imagine or think about actions without actually experiencing them. Decisions are still made on the basis of perceptions, rather than language.

- **Symbolic stage (from about age 8).** Children begin to use symbols (words or drawn pictures) to represent people, activities, and things. They have the ability to think and talk about things in abstract terms. They can also use and understand what Gagné would call "defined concepts." For example, they can discuss the concept of toys and identify various kinds of toys, rather than defining them only in terms of toys they have seen or handled. They can better understand mathematical principles and use symbolic idioms such as "Don't cry over spilt milk."

**Implications for education.** Unlike Piaget, Bruner was very concerned that school instruction build on the stages of cognitive development. The idea of discovery learning is largely attributed to him (Schunk, 2012). Discovery learning is "an approach to instruction in which students construct their own knowledge about a topic through firsthand interaction with an aspect of their environment" (Ormrod, 2014, p. G-4). They do this "by randomly exploring and manipulating objects or perhaps by performing systematic experiments" (Ormrod, 2014, p. 405). Bruner felt that students were more likely to understand and remember concepts they had discovered in the course of their own exploration. However, research findings have yielded mixed results for discovery learning, and the relatively unstructured methods recommended by Bruner have not found widespread support (Eggen & Kauchak, 2013; Ormrod, 2014). Teachers have found that discovery learning is most successful when students have prerequisite knowledge and undergo some structured experiences.

**Implications for technology integration.** Many of the more "radical constructivist" uses of technology employ a discovery learning approach suggested by Bruner. For example, rather than telling students how logic circuits work, a teacher might allow students to use a simulation that lets them discover the rules themselves. Most school uses of technology, however, use what Eggen and Kauchak (2013) call a guided discovery learning approach. For example, a teacher may introduce a video-based problem scenario, then help students develop their approaches to solving the problem.

those with high interpersonal intelligence are project coordinators, those with high logical–mathematical ability are technical experts, and those with spatial ability are designers). Read background on Gardner's theory in Figure 2.13.

## Constructivist Theory Foundations for Inquiry-Based Methods

Figure 2.14 shows how these six theories contribute to constructivist technology integration strategies based on an **inquiry-based approach** to learning. These qualities were designed to address a problem John Seely Brown called **inert knowledge**, a term introduced by Whitehead in 1929 to mean skills that students learned but did not know how to transfer later to problems that required them (Brown, Collins, & Duguid, 1989). Brown said that inert knowledge resulted from learning skills in isolation from each other and from real-life application; thus, he advocated cognitive apprenticeships, or activities that called for authentic problem solving, that is, solving problems in settings that are familiar and meaningful to students (CTGV, 1990). These ideas were based on the theories of Dewey, Bandura, Vygotsky, Piaget, and Bruner.

Today's technology-enabled environments were designed to provide learning environments that reflected **situated cognition**, or instruction anchored in experiences that learners considered authentic because they emulate the behavior of adults. These kinds of materials were intended to assist teachers in helping students build on or "scaffold" from experiences they already had to generate their own knowledge in an active, hands-on way, rather than receiving it passively. Today's constructivist integration strategies often focus on having students use data-gathering tools (e.g., mobile technologies) to study problems and issues in their locale, and on creating multimedia products to present their new knowledge and insights.

# FIGURE 2.13 Gardner's Theory of Multiple Intelligences

Courtesy of
Howard Gardner

Of all the learning and developmental theories embraced by constructivists, Howard Gardner's is the only one that attempts to define the role of intelligence in learning. His work is based on Guilford's pioneering work on the structure of intellect (Eggen & Kauchak, 2013) and Sternberg's view of intelligence as influenced by culture (Ormrod, 2014). Gardner's theory (1983) is that at least eight different and relatively independent types of intelligence exist, summarized in the following table:

| Types of Intelligences | Description | Reflected in Activities |
|---|---|---|
| Linguistic | • Uses language effectively<br>• Is sensitive to the uses of language<br>• Writes clearly and persuasively | Writer, journalist, poet |
| Musical | • Understands musical structure and composition<br>• Communicates by writing or playing music | Composer, pianist, conductor |
| Logical-mathematical | • Reasons logically in math terms<br>• Recognizes patterns in phenomena<br>• Formulates and tests hypotheses and solves<br>• problems in math and science | Scientist, mathematician, doctor |
| Spatial | • Perceives the world in visual terms<br>• Notices and remembers visual details<br>• Can recreate things after seeing them | Artist, sculptor, graphic artist |
| Bodily-kinesthetic | • Uses the body skillfully<br>• Manipulates things well with hands<br>• Uses tools skillfully | Dancer, athlete, watchmaker |
| Intrapersonal | • Is an introspective thinker<br>• Is aware of one's own motives<br>• Has heightened metacognitive abilities | Self-aware/self-motivated person |
| Interpersonal | • Notices moods and changes in others<br>• Can identify motives in others' behavior<br>• Relates well with others | Psychologist, therapist, salesperson |
| Naturalist | • Can discriminate among living things | Botanist, biologist |

**Implications for education.** If Gardner's theory is correct, then IQ tests (which tend to stress linguistic and logical-mathematical abilities) may not be the best way to judge a given student's ability to learn, and traditional academic tasks may not be the best reflection of ability. McDevitt and Ormrod (2010) point out that "to the extent that intelligence is culture-dependent, intelligent behavior is likely to take different forms in children from different ethnic backgrounds" (p. 301). Teachers, then, should try to determine which type or types of intelligence each student has and direct the student to learning activities that capitalize on these innate abilities. Gardner and Hatch (1989) gave suggestions for how best to do this. Also, teachers may consider learning activities based on distributed intelligence, where each student makes a different, but valued contribution to creating a product or solving a problem.

**Implications for technology integration.** Gardner's theory meshes well with the trend toward using technology to support group work. When educators assign students to groups to develop a multimedia product, they can assign students roles based on their type of intelligence. For example, those with high interpersonal intelligence may be the project coordinators, those with high logical–mathematical ability may be responsible for structure and links, and those with spatial ability may be responsible for graphics and aesthetics.

**FIGURE 2.14** How Constructivist Theories and Practices Lead to Inquiry-Based Technology Integration Strategies

**Social Cognitive theories (Bandura)**
Seeing others successfully modeling behaviors increases students' self-efficacy to learn behaviors

**Scaffolding theory (Vygotsky)**
Students learn from experts by building on what they already know; each learner's background shapes how he/she learns

*Implications for Technology Integration Strategies*

**Choose inquiry-based technology integration strategies when the goal is teaching inquiry/thinking skills**
- Concepts to be learned are abstract and complex; hands-on, visual activities are seen as essential so students can see how concepts apply to real world problem-solving.
- Teachers want to promote social collaboration and allow a variety of ways of learning and showing competence.
- Time permits students learning through unstructured exploration and discovering their own interest.
- Students need modeling to develop self-efficacy in order to increase their motivation to learn.

*Implications for Technology Integration Strategies*

**Social Activism (Dewey)**
Promote social interaction among students on problems and issues of direct interest to them

**Child Development Theory (Bruner)**
Learner abilities differ at each developmental level; children progress through stages through exploring their environment

**Discovery Learning (Bruner)**
Children learn and remember concepts better when they learn them through exploration

**Multiple Intelligences Theory (Gardner)**
Learning can occur and be demonstrated in different ways, depending on a learner's type of intelligence

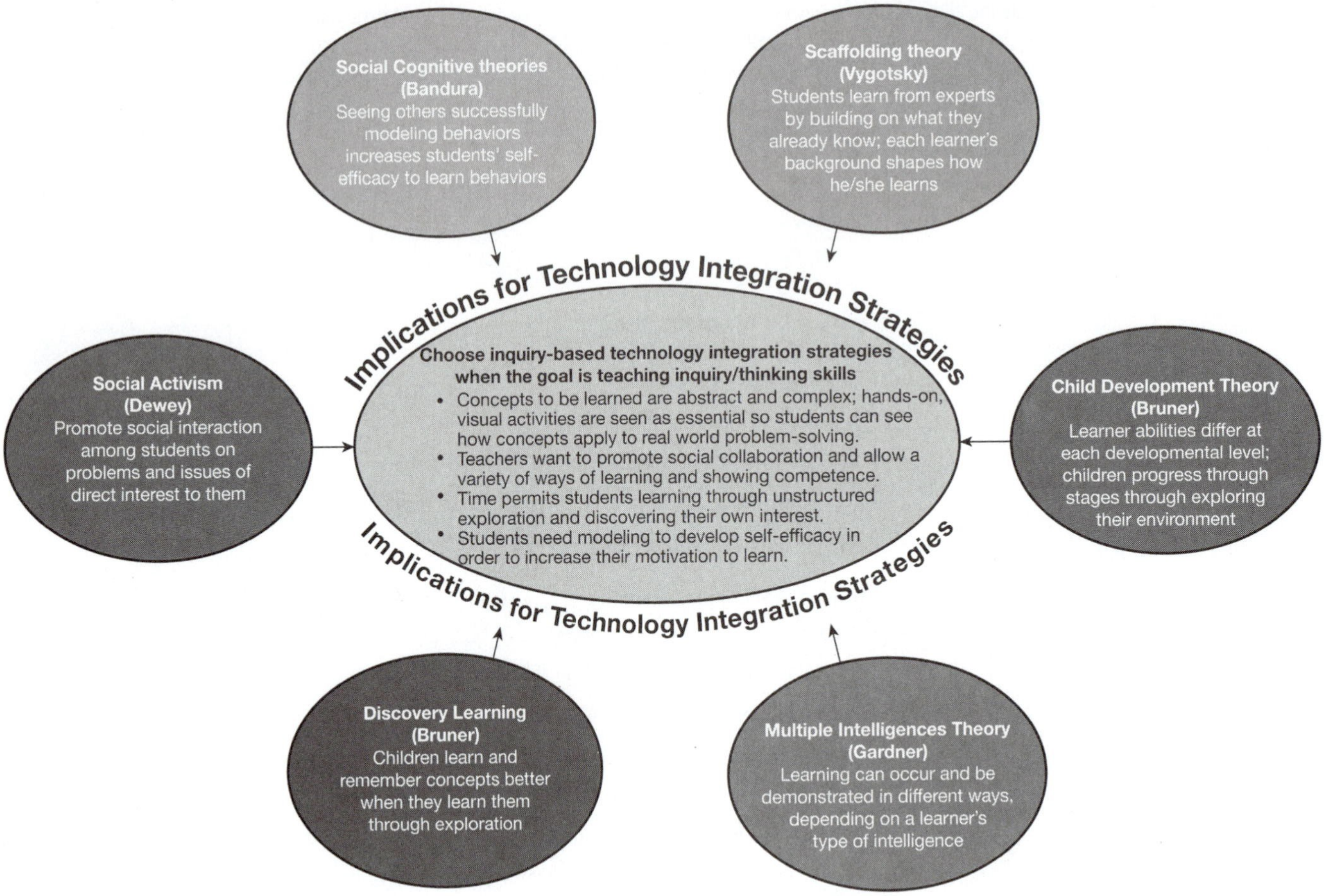

**TECHNOLOGY LEARNING CHECK**
Complete TLC 2.4 to review what you have learned from reading this section about constructivist learning theories and technology integration strategies based on them.

# TECHNOLOGY INTEGRATION STRATEGIES BASED ON DIRECTED AND CONSTRUCTIVIST THEORIES

The debate between objectivists and constructivists continues, in part because proponents of each view of learning focus on different kinds of problems (or different aspects of the same problems) confronting teachers and students in today's schools. Table 2.1a – 2c show how directed and constructivist models differ by needs and problems they address and instructional and assessment methods they use. The remainder of this section will focus on technology integration strategies that reflect each approach and possibilities for merging them.

## Future Directions for Merging Directed and Constructivist Approaches

Merging these two integration approaches in a way that benefits both learners and teachers requires an open-minded view of what constitutes "appropriate instruction." Of course, the most effective approach will depend on the topics and problems that define the learning activity and individual learning needs. Clearly, instructional problems identified by both objectivists and

## TABLE 2.1A A Comparison of Directed and Constructivist Models: Instructional Needs and Problems Targeted

| Directed Instructional Models | Constructivist Models |
| --- | --- |
| • *Accountability*: All students must meet required education standards to be considered educated.<br>• *Individualization*: Help meet individual needs of students working at many levels.<br>• *Quality assurance*: Quality of instruction must be consistently high across teachers and schools in various locations.<br>• *Convergent thinking*: All students must have the same skills. | • *Higher-level skills*: All students must be able to think critically and creatively and solve problems.<br>• *Cooperative group skills*: Help students learn to work with others to solve problems.<br>• *Increase relevancy*: Students must have active, visual, authentic learning experiences that relate to their own lives.<br>• *Divergent thinking*: Students must think on their own and solve novel problems as they occur. |

## TABLE 2.1B A Comparison of Directed and Constructivist Models: Methods

| Directed Instructional Models | Constructivist Models |
| --- | --- |
| • Stress individualized work.<br>• Have specific skill-based instructional goals and objectives; same for all students.<br>• Teachers transmit a set body of skills and/or knowledge to students.<br>• Students learn prerequisite skills required for each new skill.<br>• Sequences of carefully structured presentations and activities help students understand (process), remember (encode and store), and transfer (retrieve) information and skills.<br>• Traditional teacher-directed methods and materials are used: lectures, skill worksheets. | • Stress group-based, cooperative work.<br>• Have global goals such as problem solving and critical thinking that sometimes differ for each student.<br>• Have students generate their own knowledge through experiences anchored in real-life situations.<br>• Students learn lower-order skills in the context of higher-order problems that require them.<br>• Learning through problem-oriented activities (e.g., "what if" situations); visual formats and mental models; rich, complex, learning environments; and learning through exploration.<br>• Nontraditional materials are used to promote student-driven exploration and problem solving. |

## TABLE 2.1C A Comparison of Directed and Constructivist Models: Assessment Strategies

| Directed Instructional Models | Constructivist Models |
| --- | --- |
| • Traditional assessments (e.g., multiple choice, short answer) with specific expected responses; student products (e.g., essays) graded with checklists or rubrics. | • Nontraditional assessments (e.g., group products such as Web pages, multimedia projects) with varying contents or portfolios; student products graded with self-report instruments, rubrics. |

constructivists are common to most schools and classrooms, regardless of grade level, type of student, or content. Teachers will always use some directed instruction as the most efficient means of teaching required skills; teachers will always need motivating, cooperative learning activities to ensure that students want to learn and that they can transfer what they learn to problems they encounter. Proficient technology-oriented teachers must learn to combine directed instruction and constructivist approaches and to select technology resources and integration methods that are best suited to their specific needs.

These two ostensibly different views of reality will merge to form a new and powerful approach to solving some of the major problems of the educational system, each contributing an essential element of the new instructional formula. Each will address a different need:

- **Directed learning** may be best for providing a foundation of skills. Systematic approaches will ensure that specific prerequisite skills are learned.

- **Inquiry-based learning** may be best for developing global skills slowly over time.

Though constructivism could eventually dominate overall educational goals and objectives such as learning to apply scientific methods, directed approaches will ensure that students first have the prerequisite skills they need to do inquiry-based learning.

As Figure 2.15 shows, four technology integration strategies can be used to address either model, four strategies are based primarily on directed models, and four are based on constructivist models. These will be described in more detail in the following sections.

## Technology Integration Strategies Useful for Either Model

Currently, there are already four integration strategies that have a more general support role for instruction and can address the needs of either model. These "enabling" strategies seem to be appearing with increasing frequency in combination with other directed or constructivist strategies described in this chapter, supporting the other strategies and making them more feasible and practical. The four strategies are summarized in Table 2.2 and are described here.

**Integration to generate motivation to learn.** Teachers who work with at-risk students say that capturing students' interest and enthusiasm is key to success; frequently, they cite it as their greatest challenge. Some educators assert that today's entertainment-immersed students are increasingly likely to demand more motivational qualities in their instruction than students in previous generations did. Constructivists argue that instruction must address students' affective needs as well as their cognitive ones, saying that students will learn more if what they are learning is interesting and relevant to their needs. They recommend the highly visual and interactive qualities of Internet and multimedia resources as the basis of these strategies. Proponents of directed methods make similar claims about highly structured, self-instructional learning environments. They say that some students find it very motivating to learn at their own pace in a private environment because they receive immediate feedback on their progress. It seems evident that appropriate integration strategies to address motivation problems depend on the needs of the student; either constructivist or directed integration strategies can be used to increase motivation to learn.

**Integration to optimize scarce resources.** Current resources and numbers of personnel in schools are rarely optimal. Computer-based courseware materials can help make up for the lack of required resources in the school or classroom—from consumable supplies to qualified teachers. For example, drill-and-practice programs can replace worksheets, a good

## FIGURE 2.15 Technology Integration Strategies for Directed, Constructivist, or Both Models

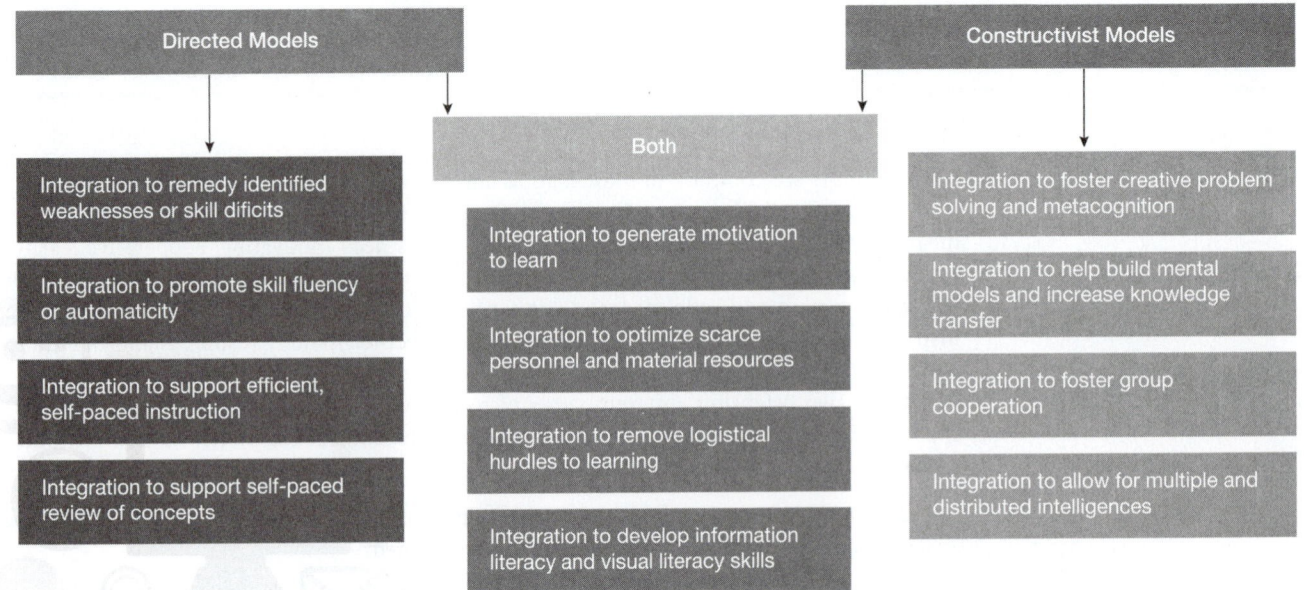

## TABLE 2.2 Technology Integration Strategies to Support Either Model

| Integration Strategies and Needs and Problems They Address | Example Activities |
|---|---|
| **To generate motivation to learn:**<br>• Due to past failures, at-risk students need more than usual motivation.<br>• Students need to see the relevance of new concepts and skills to their lives.<br>• Students need to be active, rather than passive, learners. | • Visual and interactive qualities of the Internet and multimedia resources draw and hold students' attention.<br>• Drill-and-practice/tutorial materials give students private environments for learning and practice.<br>• Video-based scenarios and simulations show relevance of science and math skills.<br>• Hands-on production work (e.g., multimedia, web pages) gives students an active role in learning. |
| **To optimize scarce personnel and material resources:**<br>• Schools have limited budgets; therefore, they must save money on consumables.<br>• Teachers are in short supply in some subject areas. | • Simulations allow repeated science experiments at no additional cost.<br>• Distance courses can offer subjects for which schools lack teachers. |
| **To remove logistical hurdles to learning:**<br>• Students find repetitive tasks (handwriting, calculations) boring and tedious.<br>• Students lack motor skills to show their designs.<br>• Students cannot travel to places to learn about them.<br>• Some social and physical phenomena occur too slowly, too quickly, or at too great a distance to allow observation. | Students can use:<br>• Word processing to make quick, easy revisions and corrections to written work.<br>• Calculators and spreadsheets to do low-level calculations involved in math/science problem solving.<br>• Computer-assisted design (CAD) and drawing software to try out and change designs.<br>• Virtual tours to see places the students could not go physically.<br>• Simulations to allow study of social systems (e.g., voting) and physical systems (chemical reactions). |
| **To develop information literacy/visual literacy skills:**<br>Students need to learn:<br>• Modern methods of communicating information.<br>• How to analyze the quality of visual presentations. | Students can:<br>• Do research reports as multimedia products or web pages.<br>• Become media savvy by using information on the Internet and video. |

distance program can offer instruction in topics for which local teachers are in short supply, and a simulation program (discussed in Chapter 3) can let students repeat experiments without depleting chemical supplies or other materials.

**Integration to remove logistical hurdles to learning.** Some technology tools offer no instructional sequence but help students complete learning tasks more efficiently. These tools support directed instruction by removing or reducing logistical hurdles to learning. For example, word processing programs do not teach students how to write, but they let students write and rewrite more quickly, without the labor of handwriting. CAD software does not teach students how to design a house, but it allows them to try out designs and features to see what they look like before building models or structures. A calculator lets students do lower-level calculations so they can focus on the high-level concepts of math problems. A website might contain only a set of pictures of sea life, but it lets a teacher illustrate concepts about sea creatures more quickly and easily than he or she could with books.

**Integration to develop information literacy and visual literacy skills.** A rationale underlying many of the most popular directed and constructivist integration strategies is the need to give students practice in using modern

▲ The highly visual and interactive qualities of Internet and multimedia resources make learning more interesting and relevant to students. (Photo courtesy W. Wiencke)

methods of communicating information. For example, when students use presentation software instead of paper charts to give a report, they gain experience for college classrooms and business offices, where computer-based presentations are the norm. Using technology to communicate visually represents information age skills that students will need both for higher education and in the workplace.

## Technology Integration Strategies Based on Directed Models

The four integration strategies based on directed methods are all designed to address individual instruction and practice (see Table 2.3).

**Integration to remedy identified weaknesses or skill deficits.** Constructivists say that students should learn prerequisite skills as they see the need for them in a group or individual project. However, experienced teachers know that even motivated students do not always learn skills as expected. These failures occur for a variety of reasons, many of which are related to learners' internal capabilities, and not all of which are thoroughly understood. When the absence of prerequisite skills presents a barrier to higher-level learning or to passing tests, directed instruction usually is the most efficient way of providing these skills. Materials such as drill-and-practice and tutorial software have proven to be valuable resources for providing this kind of individualized instruction. When students have failed to learn required skills, they frequently find technology-based materials more motivating and less threatening than teacher-delivered instruction.

**Integration to promote skill fluency or automaticity.** Some prerequisite skills must be applied quickly and without conscious effort in order to be most useful. Gagné (1982) and Bloom (1986) referred to this automatic recall as **automaticity**. Students need rapid recall and performance of a wide range of skills throughout the curriculum, including simple math facts, grammar and usage rules, and spelling. Some students acquire automaticity through repeated use of the skills in practical situations, while others acquire it more efficiently through isolated practice. Drill-and-practice, instructional games, and, sometimes, simulation courseware can provide practice tailored to individual skill needs and learning pace.

**TABLE 2.3** Technology Integration Strategies Based on Directed Teaching Models

| Integration Strategy | Needs and Problems Addressed | Example Activities |
|---|---|---|
| **To remedy identified weaknesses or skill deficits** | • At-risk students need individual instruction and practice.<br>• Students fail parts of high-stakes tests. | Tutorial or drill-and-practice software is targeted to identified skills. |
| **To promote skill fluency/automaticity** | • Students need to be able to recall and apply lower-level skills quickly, automatically.<br>• Students need to review for upcoming tests. | Drill-and-practice or instructional game software lets students practice math facts, vocabulary, or spelling words. |
| **To support efficient, self-paced learning** | • Students are motivated and able to learn on their own.<br>• No teacher is available for the content area. | Use tutorial software or distance learning courses for foreign languages, higher-level science or math, or other elective subjects. |
| **To support self-paced review of concepts** | • Students need help studying for test.<br>• Students need make-up instruction for missed work. | Use tutorial, drill-and-practice, or simulation software to cover specific concepts. |

Integration to support efficient, self-paced learning. When students are self-motivated and have the ability to structure their own learning, the most desirable method is often the one that offers the fastest and most efficient path. Sometimes these students are interested in topics not being covered in class or for which there is no instructor available. Directed instruction for these students can frequently be supported by well-designed, self-instructional tutorials and self-paced distance learning workshops and courses.

Integration to support self-paced review of concepts. When students cover a number of topics over time, they usually need a review prior to taking a test to help them remember and consolidate concepts. Sometimes students are absent when in-class instruction was given or need additional time going over the material to understand and remember it. In these situations, drill-and-practice and tutorial software materials are good ways to provide these kinds of self-paced reviews.

▲ Drill-and-practice and tutorial software materials can provide self-paced reviews on computers or handheld devices. (Photo courtesy W. Wiencke)

## Technology Integration Strategies Based on Constructivist Models

This section reviews the four integration strategies identified with constructivist methods. The strategies are summarized in Table 2.4.

Integration to foster creative problem solving and metacognition. Many people believe that our world is too complex and technical for students to learn ahead of time everything they may need for the future. Thus, our society is beginning to place a high value on the ability to solve novel problems in creative ways. If students are conscious of the procedures they use to solve problems, they often can more easily improve on their strategies and become more effective, creative problem solvers. Consequently, teachers often try to present students with novel problems to solve and to get them to analyze how they learn to solve them. Resources such as problem-solving courseware and multimedia applications are often considered ideal

## TABLE 2.4 Technology Integration Strategies Based on Constructivist Models

| Integration Strategy | Needs and Problems Addressed | Example Activities |
|---|---|---|
| **To foster creative problem solving and metacognition** | • Students need to be able to solve complex, novel problems as they occur.<br>• Teachers want to encourage students' self-awareness of their own learning strategies. | • Video-based scenarios pose problems and help support student problem solving.<br>• Graphic tools illustrate concepts and support student manipulation of variables.<br>• Simulations allow exploration of how systems work. |
| **To help build mental models and increase knowledge transfer** | • Students have trouble understanding complex and/or abstract concepts.<br>• Students have trouble seeing where skills apply to real-life problems. | • Video-based scenarios pose problems.<br>• Students create multimedia products to illustrate and report on their research.<br>• Simulations and problem-solving software illustrate and let students explore complex systems. |
| **To foster group cooperation skills** | Students need to be able to work with others to solve problems and create products. | Students collaborate to:<br>• Do Internet research.<br>• Create multimedia/web page products.<br>• Compete in instructional games. |
| **To allow for multiple and distributed intelligences** | Teachers want to allow students multiple ways to learn and to demonstrate achievement. | Students have varying roles in group work to create:<br>• Multimedia products.<br>• Web pages.<br>• Desktop-published newsletters, brochures. |

▲ Technology integration strategies support a variety of teaching and learning needs, including fostering group cooperation skills. (Photo courtesy of W. Wiencke)

environments for getting students to think about how they think and for offering opportunities to challenge their creativity and problem-solving abilities.

### Integration to help build mental models and increase knowledge transfer.
The problem of inert knowledge is believed to arise when students learn skills in isolation from problem applications. When students later encounter problems that require the skills, they do not realize how the skills could be relevant. Problem-solving materials in highly visual formats allow students to build rich mental models of problems to be solved. For example, visual information allows users to easily recognize patterns. Students need not depend on reading skills, which may be deficient, to build these mental models. Thus, supporters hypothesize that teaching skills in these highly visual, problem-solving environments helps ensure that knowledge will transfer to higher order skills. These technology-based methods are especially desirable for teachers who work with students in areas such as mathematics and science, where concepts are abstract and complex and where inert knowledge is frequently a problem.

### Integration to foster group cooperation skills.
One skill area currently identified as an important focus for schools' efforts to restructure curriculum is the ability to work cooperatively in a group to solve problems and develop products (Lynch, Lynch, & Bolyard, 2013; Schul, 2011; Wirth, 2013). Although schools certainly can teach cooperative work without technology resources, a growing body of evidence documents students' appreciation of cooperative work as both more motivating and easier to accomplish when it uses technology (Chin, 2013; Vargas, 2013).

### Integration to allow for multiple and distributed intelligences.
Integration strategies with group cooperative activities also give teachers a way to allow students of widely varying abilities to make valuable contributions on their own terms. Since each student is seen as an important member of the group in these activities, the activities themselves are viewed as problems for group—rather than individual—solution. This strategy has implications for enhancing students' self-esteem and for increasing their willingness to spend more time on learning tasks. It also allows students to see that they can help each other accomplish tasks and can learn from each other, as well as from the teacher or from media.

**TECHNOLOGY LEARNING CHECK**
Complete TLC 2.5 to review what you have learned from reading this section about technology integration strategies based on both models.

## A TECHNOLOGY INTEGRATION PLANNING (TIP) MODEL FOR TEACHERS

This section introduces a model to help teachers—especially those new to technology use—understand how to integrate technology into their teaching. Now that you know the general categories of technology integration strategies and the learning theories that gave rise to them, let's turn to how to make the strategies work in practice. Any well-designed lesson takes planning. The Technology Integration Planning (TIP) model, shown in Figure 2.16, is a problem-solving model that is useful when teachers are faced with selecting best strategies and materials, and they decide that they would like to try digital technologies to meet their needs.

Each step in the model's three broad phases helps ensure that technology use will be meaningful, efficient, and successful in meeting needs. Teachers experienced in using technology

## FIGURE 2.16  The Technology Integration Planning Model

| Phase 1: Analysis of Teaching/Learning Needs |
| --- |
| **Step 1:** Determine relative advantage |
| **Step 2:** Assess required resources & skills |
| **Phase 2: Designing an Integration Framework** |
| **Step 3:** Decide on objectives, assessments |
| **Step 4:** Design integration strategies |
| **Step 5:** Prepare instructional environment |
| **Phase 3: Post-instruction Analysis and Revisions** |
| **Step 6:** Analyze lesson results, impact |
| **Step 7:** Make revisions, based on results |

tend to do these steps intuitively. However, for new teachers or those just beginning to integrate technology, the TIP model provides a helpful guide on procedures and issues to address. The following sections will discuss each of its component steps, and give examples of tasks and products required in each step. As you read about the TIP model, also see a classroom example of how to implement the tasks: the Online Multicultural Project.

## Phase 1: Analysis of Learning and Teaching Needs

In this phase of technology integration, teachers analyze classroom problems and how technology-based strategies could address them. This section describes Phase 1 analysis steps and explains why each is necessary.

## TECHNOLOGY INTEGRATION

### Example 2.1 Phase 1: Analysis of Learning and Teaching Needs

Mia wanted to include more meaningful multicultural activities in the social studies curriculum since she and the other social studies teachers in her school focused primarily on studying various holidays and foods from other cultures. They sponsored an annual International Foods smorgasbord event that was very popular with the students, but she doubted it taught them much about the richness of other cultures or why they should respect and appreciate cultures different from their own. She sometimes overheard her students making disparaging comments about people in other ethnic groups and felt a better approach to multicultural education might help.

Mia concluded that she could follow a model she heard about while attending a workshop the previous summer. At the workshop, teachers in another school district described an online project with partner schools in countries around the world. One teacher told about her partners in Israel and Spain and said students exchanged information with designated partners and answered assigned questions to research each other's backgrounds and locales. Then they worked in groups on travel brochures or booklets to email to each other. They even took digital photos and videos of themselves to send. It sounded like a great way for kids to learn about other cultures in a meaningful way while also learning some geography and

civics. The teachers in the workshop remarked that it was difficult to demean people who look and talk differently from you when you've worked with and gotten to know them. Mia was so impressed with the online project they described that she decided to try it out in her own classroom. Even though she had not seen it modeled, she felt she could structure a good curriculum around these activities once she knew about what was needed.

### Phase 1 Analysis Questions

1. What is the problem Mia wants to address?
2. What evidence does she have that there is a problem?
3. What would be the relative advantage of the method she is proposing?
4. In what ways does she hope this method will be better than previous ones?
5. What special skills or resources would Mia need to carry out such a project?

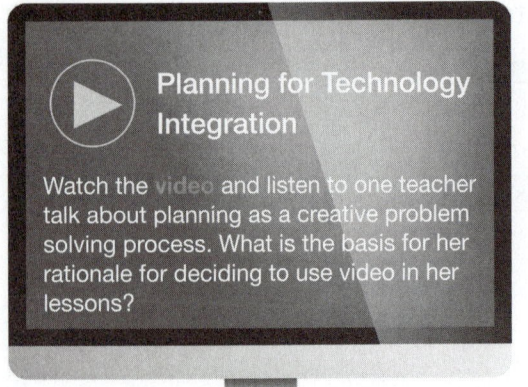

**Planning for Technology Integration**

Watch the video and listen to one teacher talk about planning as a creative problem solving process. What is the basis for her rationale for deciding to use video in her lessons?

**Step 1: Determining relative advantage.** Every teacher has topics—and sometimes whole subject areas—that have proven challenging to teach. Some concepts are so abstract or foreign to students that they struggle to understand them; some students find some topics so boring, tedious, or irrelevant that they have trouble attending to them. Some learning requires time-consuming tasks that students resist doing. Good teachers try to meet these challenges by making concepts more engaging or easier to grasp, making tasks more efficient to accomplish, or by completely rethinking curriculum goals. And, though technology-based strategies offer many benefits to teachers as they look for instructional solutions to these problems, time and effort (and often, expense) are required to plan and carry them out. Teachers have to consider the benefits of new methods compared to their current ones and decide if the benefits are worth the additional trouble.

Everett Rogers (2003), an expert on why and how people adopt innovative ideas and methods, called this seeing a **relative advantage**. Table 2.5 lists several kinds of learning problems and technology solutions with potential for high relative advantage to teachers. However, these lists are really just guidelines. Being able to recognize specific instances of these problems in a classroom context and knowing how to match them with an appropriate technology solution require knowledge of classroom problems, practice in addressing them, and an in-depth knowledge of the characteristics of each technology. Deciding whether to integrate technology requires answering the following two questions about technology's relative advantage in a given situation:

- **What is the problem?** To make sure a technology application is a good solution, begin with a clear statement of the teaching and learning problem. This is sometimes difficult to do. It is a natural human tendency to jump to a quick solution rather than to recognize the real problem. Also, everyone may not see a problem the same way. Use the following guidelines when answering the question, "What is the problem?"

  - *Nonuse of technologies may not be the problem.* When problems are stated in ways such as "Students do not know how to use spreadsheets," or "Teachers are not having their students use the Internet," the true nature of the problem is unclear and should be restated. For example, the problem may be lack of skills to use a specific technology (e.g., a spreadsheet or the Internet). In this case, the problem is, "Students lack digital literacy in key area." This kind of problem calls for *instruction in technology*, rather than *integrating technology into instruction*. On the other hand, if teachers are given a technology (e.g., "Here's your new iPad!") and told to implement it, they must decide if there is a real teaching or learning problem the new resource can help meet and state that. If teachers have a technology available, know how to use it, but choose not to use it, it may mean they can see no relative advantage to using it. Nonuse of a technology is not in itself a problem to address with the TIP model.

  - *Look for observable indications* that there really is a problem that technology integration can solve. Examples of evidence include: the curriculum is being revised and reconstituted around critical-thinking and problem-solving goals and requires resources to enable that move; students consistently achieve lower grades in a skill area; a formal or informal survey shows that teachers have trouble getting students to attend to learning tasks; or teachers observe that students are refusing to turn in required assignments in a certain area.

- **Do technology-based methods offer a solution with sufficient relative advantage?** Analyze the benefits of the technology-based method in light of the effort and cost to implement it, and then make a final decision. First, use the following guidelines to help determine whether your methods should be primarily directed or constructivist:

  - *Use directed strategies* when students need an efficient way to learn specific skills that must be assessed with traditional tests.

  - *Use constructivist strategies* when students need to develop global skills and insights over time (e.g., cooperative group skills, approaches to solving novel problems, mental models of highly complex topics) and when learning may be assessed with alternative measures, such as portfolios or group products.

## TABLE 2.5 Technology Solutions with Potential for High Relative Advantage

| Learning Problems | Technology Solutions | Relative Advantage |
|---|---|---|
| Concepts are new, foreign (e.g., mathematics, physics principles) | Graphic tools, simulations, video-based problem scenarios | Visual examples clarify concepts and applications. |
| Concepts are abstract, complex (e.g., physics principles, biology systems) | Math tools (Geometer's **SketchPad**), simulations, problem-solving software, spreadsheet exercises, graphing calculators | Graphics displays make abstract concepts more concrete; students can manipulate systems to see how they work. |
| Time-consuming manual skills (e.g., handwriting, calculations, data collection) interfere with learning high-level skills | Tool software (e.g., word processing, spreadsheets) and probeware | Takes low-level labor out of high-level tasks; students can focus on learning high-level concepts and skills. |
| Students find practice boring (e.g., basic math skills, spelling, vocabulary, test preparation) | Drill-and-practice software, instructional games | Attention-getting displays, immediate feedback, and interaction combine to create motivating practice. |
| Students cannot see relevance of concepts to their lives (e.g., history, social studies) | Simulations, Internet activities, video-based problem scenarios | Visual, interactive activities help teachers demonstrate relevance. |
| Skills are "inert," i.e., students can do them but do not see where they apply (e.g., mathematics, physics) | Simulations, problem-solving software, video-based problem scenarios, student development of Web pages, multimedia products | Project-based learning using these tools establishes clear links between skills and real-world problems. |
| Students dislike preparing research reports, presentations | Student development of desktop-published and web page/multimedia products | Students like products that look polished, professional. |
| Students need skills in working collaboratively, opportunities to demonstrate learning in alternative ways | Student development of desktop-published and Web page/multimedia products | Provides format in which group work makes sense; students can work together "virtually"; students make different contributions to one product based on their strengths. |
| Students need technological competence in preparation for the workplace | All software and productivity tools; all communications, presentation, and multimedia software | Illustrates and provides practice in skills and tools students will need in work situations. |
| Teachers have limited time for correcting students' individual practice items | Drill-and-practice software, handheld computers with assessment software | Feedback to students is immediate; frees teachers for work with students. |
| No teachers available for advanced courses | Self-instructional multimedia, distance courses | Provides structured, self-paced learning environments. |
| Students need individual reviews of missed work | Tutorial or multimedia software | Provides structured, self-paced environments for individual review of missed concepts. |
| Schools have insufficient consumable materials (e.g., science labs, workbooks) | Simulations, e-books | Materials are reusable; saves money on purchasing new copies. |
| Students need quick access to information and people not locally available | Internet and email projects; multimedia encyclopedias and atlases | Information is faster to access; people are easier, less expensive to contact. |

Then examine the needs and integration strategies described in Tables 2.3 through 2.5, and determine which one(s) apply for the situation. Select one that seems to be a good match to the problem and situation you have identified in your own classroom. Use the following guidelines to answer the question, "Is technology a good solution?"

- **Estimate the impact.** Consider the benefits others have gained from using the technology as a solution. Is it likely you will realize similar benefits?

- **Consider the required effort and expense.** How much time and work will it take to implement the technology solution? Is it likely to be worth it?

**Step 2: Assess required resources and skills.** A successful technology-enhanced lesson requires a combination of materials (i.e., hardware, software, other media) and teacher skills. First, teachers determine whether they have materials they need to carry out the strategy they have in mind. For example, if they want to do a lesson where their students work in groups on a research project and present a Prezi presentation, they might ask, "Do I have access to enough computers for enough time to let students complete it?" They must also decide if they have enough skills to carry out such a lesson. For example, do they know how to guide Internet searches, while keeping students safe and protected? Do they how to get students started with Prezi and help them troubleshoot if they run into technical problems? Then they must ask if they have experience in organizing this kind of technology-enhanced approach or have they seen it modeled.

If teachers could obtain all of the teaching resources they needed whenever they wanted them, they would make all the planning decisions described here *after* they had decided on the best instructional strategies in Step 1. In practice, however, teachers make many Step 1 and Step 2 decisions at the same time, since most usually decide how they will teach something in light of what is available for teaching it. Effective technology use means making sure that the instructional environment meets essential conditions required for successful technology integration. That means asking the following questions:

- **Question 1: What equipment, software, media, and materials will I need to carry out the instructional strategies?** As you create ways to stretch scarce resources, be sure that your strategies are ethical and in keeping with the reasons you chose a technology-based solution in the first place. Some guidelines:
  - *Computers*—If there are not enough computers available to support the individual format you wanted, consider organizing the integration plan around student pairs or small groups. Also consider having computer and noncomputer learning stations that individuals or groups cycle through, completing various activities at each one. However, if students must master skills on an individual basis, consider scheduling time in a computer lab when all students in the class can use resources at once.
  - *Copies of software and media*—Unless a software or media package specifically allows it, making copies of published software or media is illegal, even if copies are used on a temporary basis. Inquire about site licenses.
  - *Access to peripherals*—In addition to computers, remember to plan for adequate access to printers, printer paper, and any other needed peripherals (e.g., probes, handhelds).
- **Question 2: Do I have the technical skills I need to do this lesson?** Teachers must be familiar enough with the hardware and software to use it efficiently and do necessary troubleshooting. Insufficient skills can turn curriculum lessons into troubleshooting sessions.

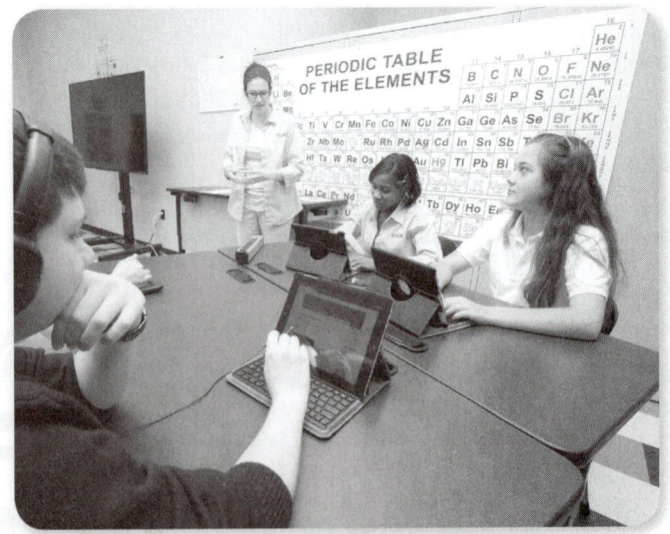

▲ Schools are increasingly providing handheld technologies such as tablets to give all students access to online resources and communications. (Photo courtesy W. Wiencke)

## Phase 2: Design of an Integration Framework

This phase requires making decisions about outcomes and how they will be assessed, and about how to arrange and carry out integration strategies.

**Step 3: Decide on objectives and assessments.** Writing objectives is a good way of setting clear expectations for what technology-based methods will accomplish and allowing a later measurement of how much these expectations have been met. Usually, teachers expect a new method will improve student behaviors—for example, that it will result in better achievement, more on-task behaviors, or improved attitudes. Sometimes, however, changes in teacher behaviors are important—for example, saving time on a task or helping to re-engineer curriculum. In either case, objectives should focus on outcomes that are observable (e.g., demonstrating, writing, completing, re-engineering),

## EXAMPLE 2.2 Phase 2: Design of an Integration Framework

Mia reflected on the problems she saw with her current multi-cultural goals and what she wanted her students to learn about other cultures that they didn't seem to be learning now. She decided on the following three outcomes: better attitudes toward people of other cultures, increased learning about similarities and differences among cultures, and knowledge of facts and concepts about the geography and government of the other country they would study. So that she could measure the success of her project later, she created objectives and instruments to measure the outcomes:

- **Attitudes toward cultures**—At least 75% of students will demonstrate an improved attitude toward the culture being studied with a higher score on the post-unit attitude measure than on the pre-unit measure. Instrument: She knew a good way to measure attitudes was with a semantic differential. Before and after the project, students would answer the question: "How do you feel about people from _____?" by marking a line between sets of adjectives to indicate how they feel.

- **Knowledge of cultures**—Each student group will score at least 90% on a rubric evaluating the brochure or booklet that reflects knowledge of the cultural characteristics (both unique and common to our own) about the people being studied. Instrument: After listing characteristics she wanted to see reflected in the products, she found a rubric to assess them. She decided they should get at least 15 of the 20 possible points on this rubric.

- Factual knowledge—Each student will score at least 80% on a short-answer test on the government and geography of the country being studied.

### Phase 2 Analysis Questions (Set 1)

1. How do you think Mia should use the product rubric to assign grades?
2. What kinds of questions could Mia include in a survey to measure how much students liked this way of learning?

Mia knew that her students would not achieve the insights and changed attitudes she had in mind through a strategy of telling them information and testing them on it. They would need to draw their own conclusions by working and communicating with people from other cultures. However, she felt she could use a directed approach to teach them the Internet and email skills they would need to carry out project activities. The project website had good suggestions on how to set up groups of four with designated tasks for each group member. It also suggested the following sequence of activities for introducing and carrying out the project:

> Step 1: Sign up on the project website; obtain partner school assignments.
>
> Step 2: Teachers in partner schools make contact and set a timeline.
>
> Step 3: Teachers organize classroom resources for work on project.

Step 4: Introduce the project to students: Display project information from the project website and discuss previous products done by other sites.

Step 5: Assign students to groups; discuss task assignments with all members.

Step 6: Determine students' email and Internet skills; begin teaching these skills.

Step 7: Students do initial email contacts/chats and introduce themselves to each other.

Step 8: Teacher works with groups to identify information for final product.

Step 9: Students do Internet searches to locate required information; take digital photos and scan required images; exchange information with partner sites.

Step 10: Students do production work; exchange final products with partners.

Step 11: Do debriefing and assessments of student work.

### Phase 2 Analysis Questions (Set 2)

1. Is Mia's approach primarily directed or constructivist?
2. Why did she decide to take this approach?
3. At which point should Mia do the pre-assessments to measure students' skills and attitudes prior
4. How should Mia determine students' levels of required Internet and email skills?

As soon as Mia knew that her students would be able to participate in the online project, she began to get organized. First, she examined the timeline of project activities so she would know when her students needed to use computers. She made sure to build in enough time to demonstrate the project site and to get students used to using the browser and search engine. Then she began the following planning and preparation activities:

- Handouts for students—To make sure groups knew the tasks each member should do, Mia created handouts specifying timelines and what should be accomplished at each stage of the project. She also made a checklist of information students were to collect and made copies so that students could check off what they had done as they went. She wanted to make sure everyone knew how she would grade their work, so she made copies of the assessments (the rubric and a description of the country information test), handed them out, and discussed them with the students.

- Computer schedule—Mia had a classroom workstation consisting of five networked computers, each with an Internet connection, so she set up a schedule for small groups to use the computers. She knew that some students would need to scan pictures, download image files from the digital camera, and process those files for sending to the partner schools, so she scheduled some additional time in the computer lab for this work. She thought that students could do other work in the library/media center after school if they needed still more time.

*(Continued)*

## EXAMPLE 2.2 Continued

### Phase 2 Analysis Questions (Set 3)

1  If Mia wanted to do a demonstration and display of the project website to the whole class at once, what resource(s) would she have to arrange to do this?

2  Mia was concerned about students revealing too much personal information about themselves to people in their partner schools. What guidelines should she give them about information exchanges to protect their privacy and security?

3  If the network or Internet access were interrupted for a day, what could Mia have the students do to make good use of their time during the delay?

---

rather than on internal results that cannot be seen or measured (e.g., being aware, knowing, understanding, or appreciating).

After stating objectives, teachers create ways to assess how well outcomes have been accomplished. Sometimes, they can use existing assessment instruments. In other cases, they have to create instruments or methods to measure the behaviors. (See the Open Source Options feature for some free tools to support assessment.) Here are a few example outcomes, objectives (which are used to state outcomes in a measurable form), and assessment methods matched to the outcomes:

- **Higher achievement outcome**—Overall average performance on an end-of-chapter test will improve by 20%. (Assess achievement with a test.)

- **Cooperative work outcome**—All students will score at least 15 out of 20 on the cooperative group skill rubric. (Use an existing rubric to grade skills.)

- **Attitude outcome**—Students will indicate satisfaction with the simulation lesson by an overall average score of 20 out of 25 points. (Create an attitude survey to assess satisfaction.)

# OPEN SOURCE
## OPTIONS *for Assessment Tools for Teachers*

### ASSESSMENT OPTIONS

**Online survey sites (most have a free, limited-feature option, as well as a fee-based option)**

**Rubric makers and free prepared rubrics**

**Test-makers and quiz-makers**

### FREE SOURCES

Advanced Survey: advancedsurvey.com
Survey Monkey: surveymonkey.com
Zoomerang: zoomerang.com
SurveyMethods: surveymethods.com

See links in Kathy Schrock's Guide to Everything (rubrics and other assessments): schrockguide.net/assessment-and-rubrics.html

Quiz Generator: quizgenerator.org
Content Generator: contentgenerator.net to practice creating documents that you will use in the classroom
Easton's list of quiz-maker sites and other free resources: eleaston.com/quizzes.html

- **Improved motivation**—Teachers will observe better on-task behavior in at least 75% of the students. (Create and use an observation sheet.)

This phase in integrating technology requires answering two questions about outcomes and assessment strategies:

- **Question 1: What outcomes do I expect from using the new methods?** Think about problems you are trying to solve and what would be acceptable indications that the technology solution has succeeded in resolving them. Use the following guidelines:

  - *Focus on results, not processes*—Think about the end results you want to achieve, rather than the processes to help you get there. Avoid statements that focus on a process students use to achieve an outcome; for example, "Students will learn cooperative group skills." Instead, state what you want students to be able to do as a result of having participated in the multimedia project—for example, "90% of students will score 4 out of 5 on a cooperative group skills rubric."

  - *Make statements observable and measurable*—Avoid vague statements that cannot be measured; for example, "Students will understand how to work cooperatively,"

- **Question 2: What are the best ways of assessing these outcomes?** The choice of assessment method depends on the nature of the outcome. Note the following guidelines:

  - *Use written tests to assess skill achievement outcomes*—Written cognitive tests (e.g., short answer, multiple choice, true/false, matching) and essay exams remain the most common classroom assessment strategy for many formal knowledge skills.

  - *Use evaluation criteria checklists to assess complex tasks or products*—When students must create complex products, such as multimedia presentations, reports, or web pages, teachers may give students a checklist like the one shown here: a set of criteria that specify the requirements each product must meet. Points are awarded for meeting each criterion.

  - *Use rubrics to assess complex tasks or products*—Rubrics like the one shown here fulfill the same role as evaluation criteria checklists and are sometimes used in addition to them. **Rubrics** are instruments consisting of a set of elements that define important aspects of a given performance or product and provide ratings that describe levels of quality for each element. Their added value is giving students descriptions of various levels of quality. Teachers usually associate a letter grade with each level of quality (Level 5 = A, Level 4 = B, etc.).

  - *Use Likert scale–type surveys or semantic differentials to assess attitude outcomes*—When the desired outcome is improved attitudes, teachers design a survey in **Likert scale** format or with a **semantic differential**. In a semantic differential like the one shown here, students respond to a question by checking a line between each of several sets of bipolar adjectives to indicate their level of feeling about the topic of the question. The teacher sums the item scores to obtain a measure of student perceptions. A Likert Scale like the example shown here is a series of statements that students use to indicate their degree of agreement or disagreement. Teachers sum responses across items to get an estimate of the change.

Use observation instruments like this one to measure frequency of behaviors—For example, if teachers wanted to see an increase in students' use of scientific language, they could create a chart to keep track of this use on a daily basis so they could track baseline performance and improvement over time.

## Step 4: Design integration strategies.
What usually drives integration design decisions is whether the learning environment will be primarily directed (a teacher or expert source presents information for students to absorb) or primarily inquiry based or constructivist (students do activities to generate their own learning). In light of this decision, which you made in Step 1, consider each of the following implementation decisions:

- **Question 1: What kind of content approach is needed?** Should the approach be single subject or interdisciplinary? Sometimes school or district requirements dictate this decision, and sometimes teachers combine subjects into a single unit of instruction as a way to cover concepts and topics they may not otherwise have time to teach. Most often, however, interdisciplinary approaches are used to model how real-life activities require the use of a combination of skills from several content areas.

- **Question 2: What grouping approach should I use?** Should the students work as individuals, in pairs, in small groups, or as a whole class? This decision is made in light of how many computers or software copies are available, as well as the following guidelines:
  - *Whole class:* For demonstrations or to guide whole-class discussion prior to student work
  - *Individual:* When students have to demonstrate individual mastery of skills at the end of the lesson or project
  - *Pairs:* For peer tutoring; higher-ability students work with those of lesser ability
  - *Small group:* To model real-world work skills by giving students experience in cooperative group work.

- **Question 3: How can I prepare students adequately to use technologies?** When designing a sequence of activities that incorporates technology tools, be sure to leave enough time for demonstrating the tools to students and allowing them to become comfortable using them before they do a graded product.

Step 5: Prepare the instructional environment. This step requires answering two questions about preparing an instructional environment that will support technology integration:

- **Question 1: How should resources be arranged to support instruction and learning?** Guidelines here include:
  - *Access by students with disabilities*—For students with visual or hearing deficits, consider software or adaptive devices created especially to address these disabilities. An important concern here is Universal Design for Learning or UDL. For more on this, see the Adapting for Special Needs feature.
  - *Privacy and safety issues*—School students should never use the Internet (including social networking sites) without adult supervision and should never participate in unplanned chat sessions. If possible, firewall software should be used to prevent accidental access to inappropriate sites.
  - *Handouts and other materials*—Prepare and copy (or post) necessary support materials. Unless learning to use the software without guidance is a goal of the project, consider creating summary sheets to remind students how to do basic operations.

- **Question 2: What steps are required to make sure technology resources work well?** Guidelines here include:
  - *Troubleshooting*—Computers, like all machines, occasionally break down. Learn simple diagnostic procedures so you can correct some problems without assistance.
  - *Test runs and backup plans*—Leave sufficient time to learn and practice using resources before students use them, but also try out the resources again just before class begins. Have a backup plan in case something goes wrong at the last minute.

## Phase 3: Post-Instruction Analysis and Revisions

This section gives a detailed description of Phase 3 steps and an explanation of why each is necessary. As teachers complete a technology-based project with students, they begin reviewing evidence on how successful the strategies and plans were in solving the problems they identified. They use this evidence to decide what should be changed with respect to objectives, strategies, and implementation tasks to ensure even more success next time.

Step 6. Analyze results. To do a post-instruction analysis, teachers look at the following issues:

- **Were the objectives achieved?** This is the primary criterion of success for the activity. Teachers review achievement, attitude, and observation data they have collected and decide if the technology-based method solved the problem(s) they had in mind. These data help them determine what should be changed to make the activity work better.

# Adapting for Special Needs

## Universal Design for Learning

Universal Design for Learning (UDL) is a framework that has important implications for technology use in the classroom. UDL proactively values academic diversity through strategies that offer students multiple ways to access, engage, and demonstrate their mastery of the learning outcomes. One of the mantras of UDL is that instructional design that is deliberately created for individuals with disabilities often provides significant benefits to all students. The essence of UDL involves three components:

- Providing multiple means of **representation** to give learners various ways of acquiring information and knowledge

- **Providing** multiple means of **expression** to provide learners with alternatives for demonstrating what they know

- **Providing** multiple means of **engagement** to tap into learners' interests, to challenge them appropriately, and to motivate them to learn

Traditionally, when educators fail to recognize that 25 to 50 percent of the students in their classroom may not read at grade level, they distribute textbooks that have a readability level *above* grade level. However, using the principle of multiple means of representation, an educator plans instruction to provide access to digital text so that students can manipulate the physical nature of the text (e.g., change the font size, color contrasts), as well as alter the cognitive difficulty by using tools such as text-to-speech (e.g., Natural Reader) or text-summarization (e.g., the free program Text Compactor).

Learn more about universal design for learning in order to understand its applications for your own classroom by visiting the Teaching Every Student in the Digital Age (at the Center for Applied Special Technology or CAST website).

—*Contributed by Dave Edyburn*

- **What do students say?** Some of the best suggestions on needed improvements come from students. Informal discussions with them yield a unique "consumer" focus on the activity.

- **Could improving instructional strategies improve results?** Technologies in themselves do not usually improve results significantly; it is the way teachers use them that is critical. Look at the design of both the technology use and the learning activities surrounding it.

# TECHNOLOGY INTEGRATION

## EXAMPLE 2.3   Phase 3: Post-Instruction Analysis and Revisions

Mia was generally pleased with the results of the multicultural project. According to the semantic differential, most students showed a major improvement in how they perceived people from the country they were studying. Students she had spoken with were very enthusiastic about their chats and email exchanges. Some group brochures and booklets were more polished than others, but they all showed good insights into the similarities and differences between cultures, and every group had met the rubric criteria on content. The web searches they had done seemed to have helped a lot. One thing that became clear was that production work on their published products was very time consuming; in the future, either they would have to do a simpler product or the schedule would have to be changed to allow more time. Mia also realized she had to stress that the deadlines are firm. Students would search for and take digital photos forever if she let them, and that put them behind on doing their products and left little time to discuss their findings on comparisons of cultures. Results varied on the short-answer test on the government and geography of the country being studied. Only about half the students met the 80% criterion. Mia realized she would have to schedule a review of this information before the test. She decided to make this a final group task after the production work was done.

### Phase 3 Analysis Questions

1  Although all of Mia's groups did well on context overall, rubric scores revealed that most groups scored lower in one area: spelling, grammar, and punctuation in the products. What steps could Mia add to the production work checklist that might improve this outcome next time?

2  If Mia found that only five of the seven groups in the class were doing well on their final products, what might she do to find out more about why this was happening?

3  One teacher who observed the project told Mia that it might be good to have the school district media/materials production office do the final work on the products for the students. Does this seem like a good idea? Why or why not?

- **Could improving the environment improve results?** Sometimes a small change, such as better scheduling or access to a printer, can make a big difference in a project's success.
- **Have I integrated technology well? How well has the technology integration strategy worked?** Use the Assessment Tools: Technology Impact Checklist to determine if the activity has been "worth it." Also check the available data:
  - *Achievement data*—If the problem was low student achievement, do data show students are achieving better than they were before? If the goal was improved motivation or attitudes, are students achieving at least as well as they did before? Is higher achievement consistent across the class, or did some students seem to profit more than others?
  - *Attitude data*—If the original problem was low motivation or students refusing to do required work, are there indications this behavior has improved? Has it improved for everyone or just for certain students?
  - *Students' comments*—Be sure to ask both lower-achieving and higher-achieving students for their opinions. Even if achievement and motivation seem to have improved, what do students say about the activity? Do they want to do similar activities again?
- **What could be improved to make the technology integration strategy work better?** The first time you do a technology-based activity, you can expect it will take longer and you will encounter more errors than in subsequent uses. The following areas are most often cited as needing improvement:
  - *Scheduling*—If students request any change, it is usually for more time. This may or may not be feasible, but you can review the schedule to determine if additional time can be built in for learning software and/or for production work.
  - *Technical skills*—It usually takes longer than expected for students to learn the technology tools. How can this learning be expedited or supported better?
  - *Efficiency*—From the teacher's point of view, the complaint is usually that the activity took longer than expected to plan and carry out. Review the schedule to see if there is any way the activity can be expedited.

**Step 7. Make revisions.** Based on the results from Step 6, teachers make adjustments to materials, logistics, and/or strategies. Revision activities are on a continuum ranging from small changes in how materials are used all the way to going back to Step 1 and re-analyzing the problem–solution match. Evidence in the form of student outcomes must drive these decisions.

As a planning tool, the TIP model makes the questions concrete that teachers need to think through when designing instruction that uses technology. The combination of theory foundation and thoughtful planning make technology integration purposeful, effective, and meaningful for teachers and students alike.

**TECHNOLOGY LEARNING CHECK**
Complete TLC 2.6 to review what you have learned from reading this section about the TIP model for technology integration.

# WHEN TECHNOLOGY WORKS BEST: ESSENTIAL CONDITIONS FOR TECHNOLOGY INTEGRATION

The ISTE website summarizes conditions necessary for teachers to exploit the potential power of technology. Teachers' ability to use technology to good advantage is determined in large part by whether their workplace has the conditions described here. A summary of the essential conditions for effective technology integration is shown in Figure 2.17.

**FIGURE 2.17** Essential Conditions for Effective Technology Integration

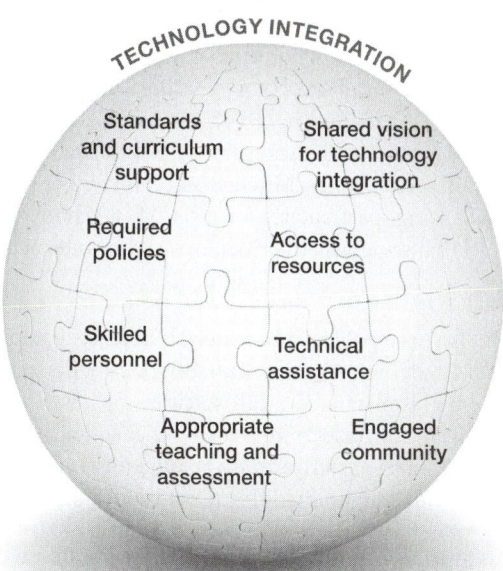

TECHNOLOGY INTEGRATION

- Standards and curriculum support
- Shared vision for technology integration
- Required policies
- Access to resources
- Skilled personnel
- Technical assistance
- Appropriate teaching and assessment
- Engaged community

## Essential Condition: A Shared Vision for Technology Integration

Teachers need system-wide support to implement technology. This means that the school, district, local community, and state share with teachers a commitment to using technology to support teaching and learning. Usually, this commitment is reflected in a statewide and/or district-wide plan created as a cooperative effort of teachers, administrators, and community business partners. The National Center for Technology Planning offers guidelines for planning strategies and examples of school and district plans. To ensure that teachers and administrators have a shared vision for how technology should be supported, all technology plans should reflect the following qualities.

**Coordinate school and district planning, and involve teachers and other personnel at all levels.** Plans at the school and district levels should be coordinated with each other and involve all stakeholders. Also helpful are technology liaison/coordinators who act as each school's representative on a district-wide planning committee.

**Budget yearly amounts for technology purchases, and plan for sustainability.** Technology changes too rapidly for schools to expect that one-time purchases of equipment or software will suffice. Thus, a technology plan should identify a specific amount to spend each year and a prioritized list of activities to fund over the life of the plan. Schools find that the computers that were new just four years ago cannot run the latest software packages. Funding must address both initial purchases and upgrades needed to sustain schools' technical capacities over time.

**Emphasize continuing teacher training.** Knowledgeable people are as important to a technology plan as up-to-date technology resources. Successful technology programs hinge on well-trained, motivated teachers who update their skills over time.

**Match technology to curriculum needs.** Rather than asking, "How can we use this equipment and software?" an effective vision focuses on questions such as these:

- What are current, unmet educational needs, and can technology address them?
- What are we teaching now that we can teach better with technology?
- What can we teach with technology that we could not teach before, but that should be taught?

## Essential Condition: Standards and Curriculum Support

The Common Core Standards, ISTE Standards for Students, 21st Century Student Outcomes, and the ICT Framework identify higher-order thinking skills and digital citizenship as critical for life-long learning and productivity in our emerging global society. Students learn these technology standards in the context of their content-area course work, rather than as a separate subject area. Therefore, it is critical to situate technology skills in content-area curriculum in ways that support both the subject-area content and the technology skills. This essential condition is met best when technology and content-area standards are designed to support each other.

## Essential Condition: Required Policies

As discussed early in this chapter, legal, ethical, and equity conditions in our society profoundly affect how technology is used in schools. The following policies are required to ensure appropriate behavior, safety, equitable treatment of all students, financial assistance, incentives, and accountability at all levels of integration:

Online use policies. The increasing use of online resources for communications and research also means risks for students. In 2000, the U.S. Congress passed the Children's Internet Protection Act to encourage schools to take measures that keep children away from Internet materials that could be harmful to them. Partly as a result of awareness-raising programs by schools and other organizations, recent studies have found that various harms experienced by underage online users have decreased in recent years and are not increasing with the rise in access to mobile and online technologies (Livingston & Smith, 2014). Although Livingstone and Smith found that cyberbullying, unwanted contact with strangers, sexual messaging and pornography affect only about 20 percent of adolescents, Jones, Mitchell, and Finkelhore (2013) found that that online harassment may be increasing, particularly for girls. Most schools have students sign an **Acceptable Use Policy (AUP)** that stipulates the risks involved in Internet use and outlines appropriate, safe online behavior.

Legal/ethical use polices. Schools also have policies and materials in place to address issues such as illegal access to school servers (hacking), viruses, and software/media piracy. Districts usually address illegal access problems by placing firewall software on district and school networks to prevent access to specific website addresses or to websites that contain certain keywords or phrases. (Unfortunately, firewalls and filtering software also create a new set of problems for schools by preventing their users from connecting to many legitimate educational sites.)

Policies to ensure equity. Schools are also responsible for ensuring equitable access to and use of technology resources by all students, especially those who are traditionally underserved or underrepresented in mathematics, science, and technology occupations.

Financial assistance, incentives, and accountability policies. Schools need to support teachers in their efforts to integrate technology effectively. Important aspects of this support include financial assistance for purchasing software for use in their classrooms and attending professional development opportunities; offering incentives to teachers for trying to integrate technology, ranging from monetary incentives to release time; and accountability for teachers who do and do not support district technology initiatives.

## Essential Condition: Access to Hardware, Software, and Other Resources

Finding funding. Experts agree that adequate funding can determine the success or failure of even the best technology plans. The summary of guidelines on funding shown in Figure 2.18 is a good way to get started. Schools will never have the budgets for technology that they want or need. Strategies for optimizing available funds include requiring competitive bids, scheduling hardware and software upgrades, using donated equipment, and using broken computers for spare parts.

Purchasing hardware and software. Although teachers depend on their schools and district offices to provide necessary resources, teacher input in this process is critically important. When schools and districts make hardware and software purchases, they are making curricular decisions. Therefore, it is important for purchases to begin with those that fulfill the curriculum needs for which teachers most need technology support.

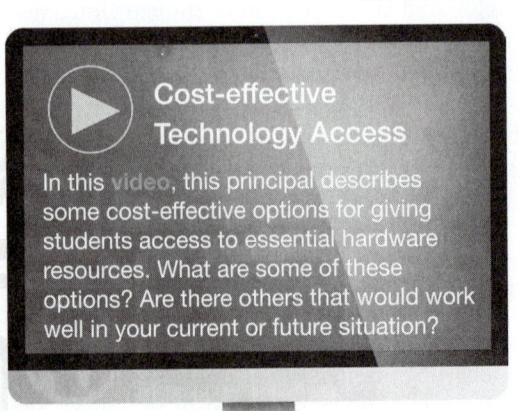

**Cost-effective Technology Access**

In this video, this principal describes some cost-effective options for giving students access to essential hardware resources. What are some of these options? Are there others that would work well in your current or future situation?

Setting up and maintaining physical facilities. Schools have developed several arrangements to help ensure that computer equipment supports teachers' various curriculum needs. They minimize technology repair problems by insisting that their users follow safety rules and conduct preventive maintenance procedures. In addition, they usually a maintenance options that best meets their needs. Securing equipment is an equally important maintenance issue, since vandalism and theft are recurring problems in schools. Again, schools can choose from among several options, including monitoring and alarm systems, security cabinets, and lockdown systems.

**FIGURE 2.18** Funding Information

**Funding Sources**

Hundreds of sources can be found under the following five categories. The first four usually have budgets for funding larger projects, but schools and teachers usually have smaller projects that can be funded from community sources (e.g., companies, individuals, and groups):

1. **Federal funding sources:** grants.gov

2. **Sources specific to your state:** Look for links from your state's Department of Education website

3. **Foundations of large companies:** Go to company websites; look for "Funding" links. Examples include:
   - **The Honda Foundation**
   - **Verizon Foundation**

4. **Private foundations:** Examples include:
   - **The Annenberg Foundation**
   - **The NEA Foundation**
   - **The Bill and Melinda Gates Foundation**
   - **The William & Flora Hewlett Foundation**
   - **Pearson's funding resources** Go to the Pearson school web site.

5. **Professional education publications:** Examples include:
   - **Edutopia** Go to the Edutopia web site and search on Grant Information: Resources to Get You Started.
   - **eSchoolNews** Go to the eSchoolNews website and search the site for Grant Information.

**Guidelines for Writing Successful Proposals**

- **Read and follow the guidelines.** This is the most important (and most-often neglected) guideline of all. Your idea MUST address directly the primary goals of the agency (e.g., some agencies cannot fund equipment; some accept only proposals from K–12 schools, and some only from higher education).

- **Organize the proposal.** Have: a concise overview (one-to-two pages maximum), a statement of needs the proposal addresses, specific goals and objectives, a narrative summary (as brief as possible), a budget spreadsheet that identifies costs in categories, and a budget narrative that explains the costs.

- **Write in clear and compelling language.** Ask as many people as possible to read the proposal and suggest changes to sharpen its language before you submit it.

**Characteristics of Successful Applicants**

Schools and projects that obtain funding have several characteristics in common:

- Have ideas for how to make things better.
- Constantly stay in constant touch with funding opportunities.
- Foster ongoing relationships with community groups and individuals.
- Maintain boilerplate material so they are able to respond quickly when opportunities arise and have one or more good writers handy.
- Express passion about their work and know how to describe what they do.

**Building on Success**

To continue receiving outside funding, educators who have a funded project must do three things on a continuing basis:

1. **Carry out what you proposed.** Show you did good things with what you already received.

2. **Publicize your success.** Publicize through school and district public relations personnel. Create publications and websites to document accomplishments. Ask the local newspaper or TV and radio stations to come for a show-and-tell session. Give talks and presentations to local groups, and get your project on the agendas of school meetings.

3. **Generate new funding opportunities.** View funded projects as seeds for new opportunities rather than one-time activities.

# Essential Condition: Skilled Personnel

Most preservice teacher training programs include at least some preparation in how to integrate technology effectively into teaching. However, because technology resources and applications change so quickly, continuing professional staff development in technology resources and applications remains an essential condition for effective technology integration.

**Hands-on integration emphasis.** Technology integration skills cannot be learned by sitting passively in a classroom, listening to an instructor, or watching demonstrations. Participants must have hands-on opportunities with technologies, and the focus must be on how to use technologies in classrooms rather than just on technical skills.

**Training over time.** The "one-shot" in service approach is ineffective for helping teachers develop methods to use computers as instructional tools. In service training in technology uses must be ongoing.

**Modeling, mentoring, and coaching.** The most effective teacher educators are those who model the use of technology in their own teaching. One-to-one mentoring and coaching programs and linking teachers to each other and to staff developers have also been shown to be effective. Most teachers seem to learn computer skills through colleague interaction and information sharing.

**Just-in-time training.** To be most effective, teachers must learn technologies just prior to applying them. This means they must have access to required resources immediately following training.

## Essential Condition: Technical Assistance

Each teacher needs training in simple troubleshooting procedures, such as what to do if a URL doesn't work or a computer doesn't come on. But teachers should not be expected to address more complicated diagnostic and maintenance problems. Nothing is more frustrating than depending on computer access for an important student project only to discover that equipment is malfunctioning or Internet access is down. Schools must support teachers by providing and maintaining resources vital to classroom use, as well as by offering continuing professional development in using resources effectively.

## Essential Condition: Appropriate Teaching and Assessment Models

Models of technology integration range from add-ons to substitutes. Brown (2013) describes four different levels of integration referred to as the SAMR (for substitute, augmentation, modification, redefinition) model:

- Substitution, with no functional change.
- Augmentation: Technology acts as a direct tool substitute, with functional improvement.
- Modification: Technology allows for significant task redesign.
- Redefinition: Technology allows for new tasks that were previously not possible.

Puentedura (2009), the model's creator, conceived of these integration types as "levels," going from lowest (substitution) to highest (redefinition). However, each technology integration strategy is appropriate depending on the instructional need, and teachers should be encouraged to use all of them.

Assessment practices will vary with the technology integration model. (See assessment strategies in Phase

▲ Effective technology integration depends in large part on the "essential condition" of well-trained teachers. **Thomas Barrat/Shutterstock**

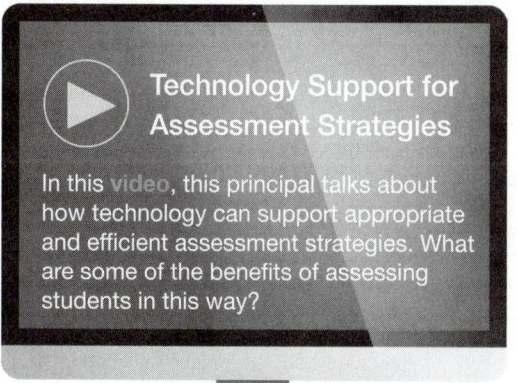

**Technology Support for Assessment Strategies**

In this video, this principal talks about how technology can support appropriate and efficient assessment strategies. What are some of the benefits of assessing students in this way?

2 of the TIP model.) The critical factor is matching the teaching strategy with an appropriate assessment strategy. For example, if students are creating Web pages, a grading rubric would measure their achievement better than a traditional written test would. Depending on the integration model, teachers may want to use a combination of assessment strategies (e.g., written tests as well as products evaluated with a rubric or checklist).

## Essential Condition: Engaged Community

Technology has the most impact on achieving educational goals when schools involve the entire local community. This means holding public forums about technology initiatives, bringing community members into the classroom, educating those who can play key roles, and fostering partnerships among schools, businesses, corporations, individual entrepreneurs, and educators. Businesses often partner with school programs to make a dream a reality. This is not only a way to extend school technology budgets, it brings many talents together to work toward a common purpose: school improvement.

**FIGURE 2.19** The SAMR Model (based on concepts from Puentedura, 2009)

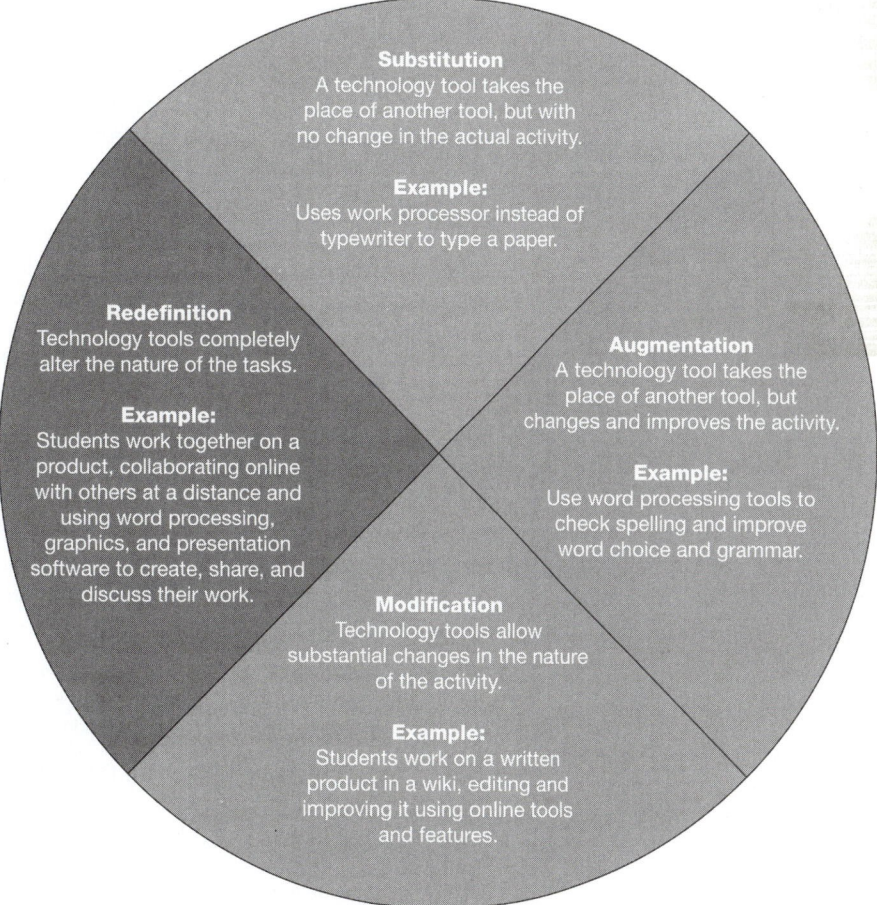

**Substitution**
A technology tool takes the place of another tool, but with no change in the actual activity.

**Example:**
Uses work processor instead of typewriter to type a paper.

**Augmentation**
A technology tool takes the place of another tool, but changes and improves the activity.

**Example:**
Use word processing tools to check spelling and improve word choice and grammar.

**Modification**
Technology tools allow substantial changes in the nature of the activity.

**Example:**
Students work on a written product in a wiki, editing and improving it using online tools and features.

**Redefinition**
Technology tools completely alter the nature of the tasks.

**Example:**
Students work together on a product, collaborating online with others at a distance and using word processing, graphics, and presentation software to create, share, and discuss their work.

**TECHNOLOGY LEARNING CHECK**
Complete TLC 2.7 to review what you have learned from reading this section about essential conditions for technology integration.

**The following questions may be used either for in-class, small-group discussions or may initiate discussions in blogs or online discussion boards:**

1. An analysis of studies on discovery learning research by Alfieri, Brooks, Aldrich, and Tenenbaum (2011) illustrated that not all discovery-learning approaches are created equal. They found that unassisted discovery strategies nearly always resulted in lower achievement when compared with explicit instruction. However, strategies they referred to as "enhanced discovery" methods often compared favorably with explicit instruction. What can you find out about each of these types of discovery learning methods? How are they carried out? What characteristics of enhanced discovery methods would be likely to make them more successful than unassisted strategies?

2. Search online or in your college's database for the article "The Poor Scholar's Soliloquy," (S. M. Corey, 1944, *Childhood Education*, Volume 33, 219–220.). This piece was written about 70 years ago. Is the situation the boy describes still typical of American education? Can you cite ways in which more constructivist approaches could benefit this child?

**Chapter** **2** ## Summary

1. **Overview of factors in successful technology integration**—Three interrelated factors help ensure effective technology integration: learning theory foundations; an integration planning model; and essential conditions for integration.

2. **Overview of learning theory foundations**—Two lines of learning theories have given rise to two types of integration models: directed and constructivist.
   - Directed integration models were shaped by objectivist theories: behaviorist (Skinner), information-processing (Atkinson and Shiffrin), cognitive-behavioral (Gagné), and systems theories.
   - Constructivist models were shaped by constructivist theories: social activism (Dewey), social learning (Bandura), scaffolding (Vygotsky), child development (Piaget), discovery learning (Bruner), and multiple intelligences (Gardner) theories.

3. **Technology integration strategies based on directed models include**—Integration to remedy identified weaknesses or skill deficits; integration to promote skill fluency or automaticity; integration to support efficient, self-paced learning; and integration to support self-paced review of concepts.

4. **Technology integration strategies based on constructivist strategies include**—Integration to foster creative problem-solving and metacognition; integration to help build mental models and increase knowledge transfer; integration to foster group cooperation skills; and integration to allow for multiple and distributed intelligences.

5. **Technology integration strategies based on either model**—Integration to generate motivation to learn; integration to optimize scarce resources; integration to remove logistical hurdles to learning; and integration to develop information literacy and visual literacy skills.

6. **The Technology Integration Planning (TIP) Model**—This model is designed to help teachers (especially those new to technology) plan for effective classroom uses of technology. The model consists of seven steps within three phases:
   - Phase 1: Analysis of Learning and Teaching Needs
   - Phase 2: Design of an Integration Framework
   - Phase 3: Post-Instruction Analysis and Revisions

7. **Essential conditions for technology integration**—For technology to have the desired impact on improved teaching and learning, the following conditions must be in place: a shared vision for technology integration; standards and curriculum support; required policies; access to hardware, software, and other resources; skilled personnel; technical assistance; appropriate teaching and assessment approaches; and an engaged community.

# TECHNOLOGY INTEGRATION **WORKSHOP**

## 1. APPLY WHAT YOU LEARNED

To apply the concepts and skills you've read about throughout this chapter, go to the Chapter 2 Technology Application Activity.

## 2. TECHNOLOGY INTEGRATION LESSON PLANNING: PART 1—EVALUATING AND CREATING LESSON PLANS

Complete the following exercise using the sample lesson plans found on any lesson planning site that you find on the Internet.

a. Locate lesson ideas—Identify three lesson plans that focus on any of the tools or strategies you learned about in this chapter. For example, select those that reflect:
- Directed integration strategies
- Constructivist integration strategies
- Integration strategies useful to support with directed or constructivist approaches

b. Evaluate the lessons—Use the Technology Lesson Plan Evaluation Checklist to evaluate each of the lessons you found.

c. Create your own lesson—After you have reviewed and evaluated some sample lessons, create one of your own using a lesson plan format of your choice (or one your instructor gives you). Be sure the lesson focuses on one of the strategies discussed in this chapter.

## 3. TECHNOLOGY INTEGRATION LESSON PLANNING: PART 2—IMPLEMENTING THE TIP MODEL

Review how to implement the TIP Model in your classroom by doing the following activities with the lesson you created in the Technology Integration Lesson Planning exercise above.

a. Describe the Phase 1—Planning activities you would do to use this lesson in your classroom:
- What is the relative advantage of using the technology(ies) in this lesson?
- Do you have resources and skills you need to carry it out?

b. Describe the Phase 2—Implementation activities you would do to use this lesson in your classroom:
- What are the objectives of the lesson plan?
- How will you assess your students' accomplishment of the objectives?
- What integration strategies are used in this lesson plan?
- How would you prepare the learning environment?

c. Describe the Phase 3—Evaluation/Revision activities you would do to use this lesson in your classroom: What strategies and/or instruments would you use to evaluate the success of this lesson in your classroom, in order to determine revision needs?

d. Add lesson descriptors—Create descriptors for your new lesson (e.g., grade level, content and topic areas, technologies used, ISTE standards, 21st Century Learning standards).

e. Save your new lesson—Save your lesson plan with all its descriptors and TIP Model notes.

## 4. FOR YOUR TEACHING PORTFOLIO

- Lesson plan evaluations, lesson plans and products you created above
- Products of your group's Hot Topic Debates
- Products of your group's Collaborate, Discuss, Reflect online or in-class activities.

# 3 Instructional Software for 21st Century Teaching

## Learning Outcomes

After reading this chapter and completing the learning activities, you should be able to:

1. Identify characteristics, sources, and roles of instructional software products. (ISTE Standards•T 2, 3)

2. Analyze an instructional situation that is using drill and practice functions, and describe the integration strategy, selection criteria, benefits, and limitations of drill-and-practice software for the situation. (ISTE Standards•T 2, 3)

3. Analyze an instructional situation that is using tutorial functions, and describe the integration strategy, selection criteria, benefits, and limitations of tutorial software for the situation. (ISTE Standards•T 2, 3)

4. Analyze an instructional situation that is using simulation functions, and describe the integration strategy, selection criteria, benefits, and limitations of simulation software for the situation. (ISTE Standards•T 2, 3)

5. Analyze an instructional situation that is using instructional game functions, and describe the integration strategy, selection criteria, benefits, and limitations of instructional game software for the situation. (ISTE Standards•T 2, 3)

6. Analyze an instructional situation that is using problem-solving functions, and describe the integration strategy, selection criteria, benefits, and limitations of problem-solving software for the situation. (ISTE Standards•T 2, 3)

7. Analyze an instructional situation that is using a personalized learning system (PLS), and identify the benefits and limitations of a PLS for the situation. (ISTE Standards•T 2, 3)

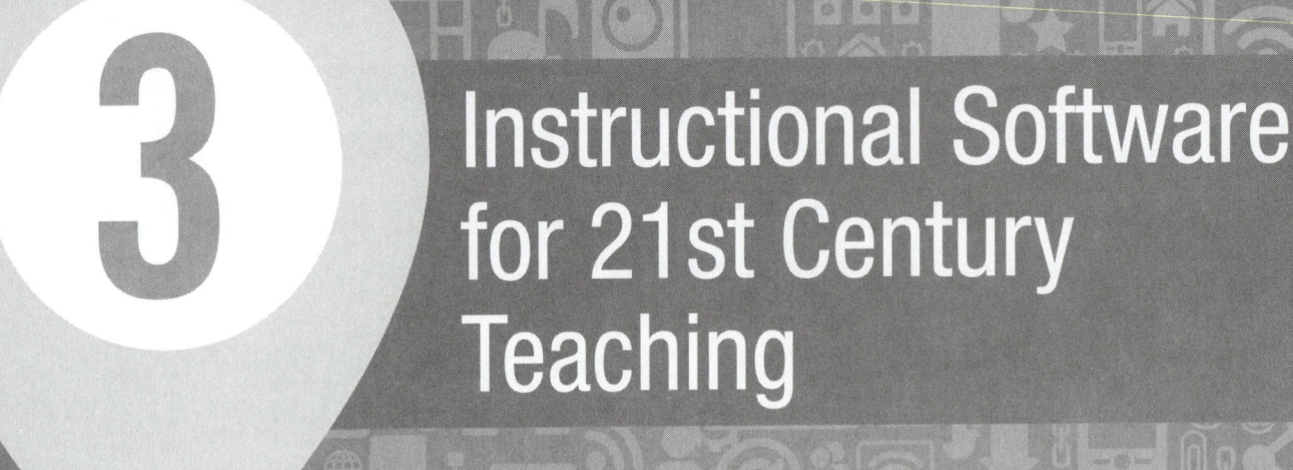

# TECHNOLOGY INTEGRATION IN ACTION
# MATH BY DESIGN

GRADE LEVEL: Middle school • CONTENT AREA/TOPIC: Geometry and measurement • LENGTH OF TIME: Two weeks

## PHASE 1 ANALYSIS OF LEARNING AND TEACHING NEEDS

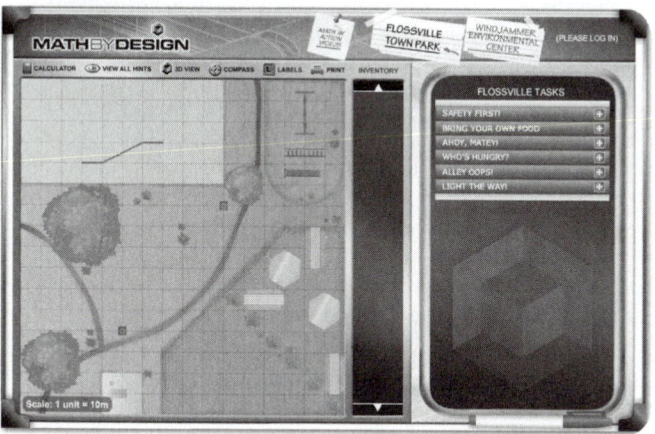

*Source:* Reprinted by permission of Maryland Public Television, © 2009, from http://mathbydesign.thinkport.org

### Step 1: Determine relative advantage.

Ms. Paige was a veteran middle school mathematics teacher who was always able to get a high percentage of her students to pass required state tests, yet she continued to struggle with engaging them in geometry skills. She was always looking for examples to show her students practical applications of geometry concepts in everyday life, but each year she taught she found students were increasingly disinterested. Though they were learning geometry skills and passing tests, she doubted they would remember the concepts or be able to connect these skills to practical problems and situations in the world around them. While perusing the state's websites to support teaching science, technology, engineering, and mathematics (STEM) subjects, she learned of Math by Design, in which students solved geometry and measurement problems by becoming "junior architects" and redesigning a park in an imaginary town called Flossville. She thought that these hands-on activities that required applying geometry skills in a fun environment might have relative advantage for her geometry instruction, since they could stir students' interest more than just seeing examples.

### Step 2: Assess Required Resources and Skills.

She spent several hours reviewing the website's materials and working through each of the unit's design problems. Though she was a competent geometry teacher, she realized she would have to teach each of the geometry skills in a way that would help students connect them with Flossville design tasks. It made her think about how to sequence and assess concepts in a much different way than she had been used to doing, but the website's teaching hints and sample lessons were most helpful. She had never worked with a website project before, but she found the site easy to use and intuitive. After her review and reflection, she felt ready to begin planning.

## PHASE 2 PLANNING FOR INTEGRATION

### Step 3: Decide on objectives and assessments.

Ms. Paige also realized that she wanted her students to achieve more with these materials than just passing tests. She wanted the experience to be interesting and challenging in ways that would change their attitudes about geometry. She developed the following outcomes, objectives, and assessments that would help her determine later if she had accomplished her aims:

Outcome: Select and use appropriate geometry concepts to solve graphic design problems.
Objective: All students, working in groups, will create correct solutions for assigned Flossville design problems.
Assessment: Score at least 20 out of 25 on a teacher-designed rubric assessing group work and design solutions.

Outcome: Transfer geometry skills from Flossville to teacher-designed situations.
Objective: All students, working individually, will achieve a score of at least 80% on a post-unit test requiring transfer of geometry concepts covered in Flossville to novel design scenarios.
Assessment: Teacher-designed, multiple-choice test of 12 scenario items (two scenario items per geometry concept).

Outcome: Demonstrate achievement of state geometry standards.
Objective: All students will achieve at least a passing score (80%) on the state-required post-course geometry test.
Assessment: State multiple-choice, post-course geometry exam.

Outcome: Enjoy learning geometry skills and appreciate their value.

Objective: At least 90% of students will demonstrate improved attitudes toward learning geometry skills.

Assessment: A teacher-designed, ten-item survey that students complete anonymously.

## Step 4: Design integration strategies.

Ms. Paige felt that students would find the Math by Design materials most motivating if they did the design tasks themselves using the hints and tutorial explanations, so she would provide very little direct instruction. Even though the site was really a problem-solving environment, it had a game-like feel to it, so she resolved to introduce it as a game that students could play as a reward for learning geometry skills. She also felt they would do well with this project after she had taught several of the prerequisite geometry skills, so she would introduce the Flossville activity later in the course. With these aspects in mind, she created the following activity sequence:

Day 1: Introduce to the whole class the environment and its design tasks and illustrate on the whiteboard how to access the hints, calculator, and other features. Tell them that, using the two computers in the classroom, they will work in pairs or groups of three to solve an assigned design task. Each of the groups would become "expert" in one of the design tasks and the skills and procedures required to solve them. Then, when the class was able to go to the computer lab, students would work individually on all design tasks, one at a time, with the "experts" on each task assisting them. Each "expert" would be expected to know the design task well enough to answer any questions other students might have. Students would also complete a pre-assessment of geometry attitudes using the survey she had created.

Days 2–6: The groups begin their work in the classroom. While they work on the Math by Design site, the other students work on assigned review activities and complete makeup work from the previous unit.

Days 7–9: The whole class goes to the computer lab to work on the other design tasks they have not yet completed. The students act as experts and assist other students with the design tasks.

Day 10: The class completes the post-project assessment and geometry attitudes survey.

## Step 5: Prepare instructional environment.

Ms. Paige knew that working with technology materials required some additional planning, so she did the following to make sure everything needed for the project was in place:

Materials: She made a chart showing which students were assigned to be experts on each of the six design tasks. She also made notes on which geometry skills were required for each task so she could be sure she covered these in her instruction and reviews before students began working with Math by Design. She set up a schedule designating which groups would work on her classroom computers each day.

Computer scheduling: The computer lab was much in demand for students' general production work (e.g., word processing) and work for other classes, so she met with the computer lab director and explained the project to her before requesting use of the lab for a three-day period.

Parent letter: The Math by Design website provided a letter to send home to parents about the project. She thought it was a good idea to let parents know what students were doing, so she printed out the letters for students to take home. She also posted a copy of the letter on her page on the school's website.

Backup plans: Since the computer lab sometimes closed unexpectedly due to technical issues, she made some "just-in-case" plans. Her backup plan would be to show the whole class one or more of the short Math in Action videos on the Math by Design website, hold a discussion using the questions the site provided, and follow up by having students work the practice problems the site offered to support each video.

# PHASE 3 POST-INSTRUCTION ANALYSIS AND REVISIONS

## Step 6: Analyze results.

Ms. Paige was delighted with the students' obvious enthusiasm for the Math by Design activities. They especially liked being named experts on a design task and helping "teach" other students how to do it. Some of the students began to bring in and share their own examples of geometry principles and examples they had identified outside the classroom, and the geometry attitudes survey reflected a definite pre-to-post improvement. A couple students asked if she had materials on careers in architecture. The only real problem she noticed was that one of the design tasks was more difficult than others and the "student experts" assigned to it required more teacher assistance. Also, on the post-assessment to measure transfer of skills to design situations similar to Flossville, she found that some geometry skills transferred more than others. There was no difference in the number of students passing the end-of-course geometry test, but that did not surprise her, since most usually passed it.

## Step 7: Make revisions.

Ms. Paige made a note to remember to make the following changes:

- Assign the more difficult Flossville design task to the best students.
- Review and discuss more (aided by Math in Action videos) before post-assessment.
- Expand the Flossville project to include other Math by Design environments.
- Use the bulletin board in the computer lab to display printouts from the Flossville environment and describe the geometry standards students had achieved.

# CHAPTER 3 BIG IDEAS OVERVIEW

Before you begin reading the rest of this chapter, listen to the Chapter 3 Big Ideas Overview. It will give you a two-minute audio overview of main concepts to look for and help prepare you to work through information and exercises to achieve this chapter's outcomes.

# AN INTRODUCTION TO INSTRUCTIONAL SOFTWARE

In the 1960s and 1970s, educators and software developers alike began to pursue the idea that computers could be programmed to teach. Some believed that education would be more efficient if computers took over the traditional role of teachers. Some 35 years later, we talk less about computers replacing teachers and more about helping teachers transform the teaching process. This chapter shows how software empowers teachers, rather than replaces them. We begin with some basic definitions and terms for instructional software and the roles these products can play in teaching and learning.

## Basic Information about Instructional Software

**Instructional software** is a general term for computer programs used specifically to deliver instruction or assist with the delivery of instruction on a topic. Although tool software, such as word processing and spreadsheets, can also enhance or support instructional activities, this text differentiates between tool software and instructional software. Software tools serve many purposes other than teaching; instructional software packages are used solely to support instruction and/or learning.

Programming languages as instructional software. **Logo** was a programming language designed especially for educational purposes, which makes it a hybrid type of instructional software, since it merges the capabilities of instructional and tool software. Initially, Logo was used to introduce young children to problem solving through programming, allowing them to explore concepts in content areas such as mathematics, science, and language arts. The work of Seymour Papert (1980) and his colleagues at the Massachusetts Institute of Technology popularized Logo in the 1980s. Although not as popular now, Logo and some of its derivative materials are still used for instructional purposes (Feurzeig, 2010; Ratcliff & Anderson, 2011).

A more recent trend along the same lines is having students program their own games to learn science, technology, engineering, and mathematics (STEM) skills like the following, based on Shapiro's analysis (2013):

- **Systems-thinking** – Basics about how dynamic systems work, a foundation of many STEM topics
- **Interdisciplinary thinking** – Problem solving and how to locate and synthesize relevant information from many sources.

- **User-centered design** – How to design systems that reflect what they know about how humans want to interact with software and each other
- **Specialist language** – How to use technical language and symbols from many different areas
- **Meta-level reflection** – How to explain and defend their ideas, describe issues, create and test hypotheses, and analyze the impact of their software solutions on others

Instructional software terms. In the early days—when the purpose of instructional software was primarily tutoring—it was called **computer-assisted instruction (CAI)** or **courseware.** The term is still in common use, but some kinds of instructional software such as simulations, instructional games, and problem-solving software are designed with more constructivist purposes in mind; they support, rather than deliver, instruction. Therefore, teachers also may hear instructional software referred to as computer-based instruction (CBI), computer-based

# OPEN SOURCE
## OPTIONS for Instructional Software Sites

## TYPES OF INSTRUCTIONAL SOFTWARE

**Drill and practice**
Drills in SAT, vocabulary, and math
Drills in chemistry
Drills in music concepts
Drills in language arts skills
Drills in history and geography concepts
Drills in math concepts
Self-test drills for English language learners
Flash card creation site

**Tutorial**
Technology how-to tutorials
Physics tutorials
Economics tutorials
Chemistry tutorials
Math tutorials
U.S. government tutorials

**Simulations**
Stock market simulation
Chemistry simulations
Genetics simulations (GenScope)

**Instructional games**
Social studies games
Civics games
Science games
Brain Games
Jeopardy game-maker and library

**Problem solving**
Memory Challenge
Thinkport-STEM Collaborative
Triana Open-Source Problem Solving Environment

Additional sites and information found at educational-freeware.com

learning (CBL), or computer-assisted learning (CAL), or in more generic terms, such as software learning tools.

**Software sources.** The number of commercial instructional software products has grown so much that new sites have emerged to help teachers, parents, and schools select ones that meet criteria for quality and alignment to Common Core State Standards (CCSS), a reemergence of a trend from the 1980s when availability of instructional software products for microcomputers exploded. Molnar (2013) says that these sites include edshelf, Graphite, PowerMyLearning, and emerging sites like EduStar (based on PowerMyLearning) and Learning List. All of these sites are free except for Learning List, which Molnar says provides additional analysis of both digital and print resources.

Teachers can also tap many sources of free software. See the Open Source Options feature. Also, programs can now be used from virtually any Internet-enabled device (e.g., a microcomputer, handheld device, or cell phone). Allowing access to software for all students remains an issue. See Adapting for Special Needs for how to address this concern.

## Teaching Roles for Instructional Software

It used to be easy to classify a software package by the type of teaching function it served—drill-and-practice, tutorial, simulation, instructional game, or problem-solving program. (See descriptions in Table 3.1) But many of today's software packages or systems fulfill several different functions. For example, a language-learning system may have a number of straight drill activities, along with activities that fulfill problem-solving and game functions. Though software teaching functions are distinct, developers tend to use the terms for these functions interchangeably. Some developers refer to a drill program that gives extensive feedback as a tutorial. Others refer to simulations or problem-solving functions as games.

Software still reflects the same five functions, but in light of current trends toward multiple-function software systems, teachers must analyze a package carefully to determine which instructional function(s) it serves to ensure it supports their specific teaching needs. They may not be able to refer to an entire package as a drill or a simulation, but it is possible and desirable to identify whether it provides, for example, science vocabulary skill practice (drill-and-practice

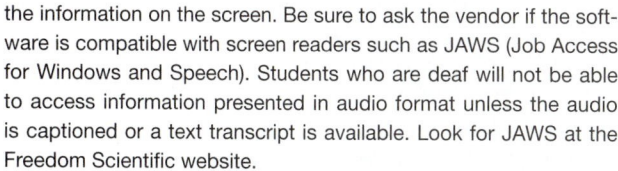

## Adapting for Special Needs

### Instructional Apps, Software, and Web Resources

When selecting apps, software, and web resources for the classroom, teachers, technology specialists, and administrators should be mindful of special needs that may impact student access and engagement. For example, some students may not be able to use the standard mouse and keyboard due to physical disabilities that impair gross and fine motor movement. In these situations, schools will need to provide items such as the following that allow an individual with a special need to operate the computer with adaptive equipment:

- Expanded keyboards, such as Key Technologies' Intellikeys
- Keyboards with guards, such as the Beyond Adaptive website
- Adaptive switch interfaces, such as those listed in the Enablemart catalog

Students with sensory impairments may be unable to access software that has not been properly designed to be accessible. Students who are blind use screen-reading software to read them the information on the screen. Be sure to ask the vendor if the software is compatible with screen readers such as JAWS (Job Access for Windows and Speech). Students who are deaf will not be able to access information presented in audio format unless the audio is captioned or a text transcript is available. Look for JAWS at the Freedom Scientific website.

Finally, students with cognitive disabilities may encounter difficulty using apps, software, and Web resources that have extensive commands and complex interfaces. In these situations, look for software such as the following that offers simplified user interfaces:

- Scholastic Keys at Tom Snyder, Inc.
- Inspire Data at Inspiration, Inc.

For more about accessible software, see the Microsoft's Developer Networks Designing Accessible Applications website.

—*Contributed by Dave Edyburn*

# TABLE 3.1 Five Instructional Software Functions

| Software Function and Example | Description of Teaching Uses |
|---|---|
| **Drill and Practice: Brainpop**  | Users can work problems or answer questions and get feedback on correctness—directed teaching strategy |
| **Tutorial: ETCAI** 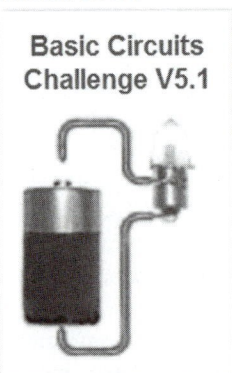 | Acts like a human tutor by providing all the information and instructional activities a learner needs to master a topic (i.e., information summaries, explanation, practice routines, feedback and assessment)—directed teaching strategy |
| **Simulation: Digital Frog** 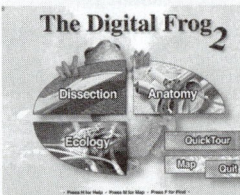 | Models real or imaginary systems to show how those systems (or similar ones) work to demonstrate underlying concepts—directed or constructivist teaching strategy |
| **Instructional Game: iCivics** 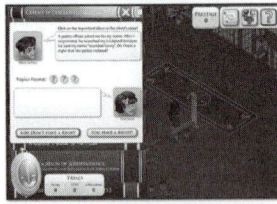 | Adds game rule to drills or simulations—directed or constructivist teaching strategy |
| **Problem Solving: Memory Challenge** 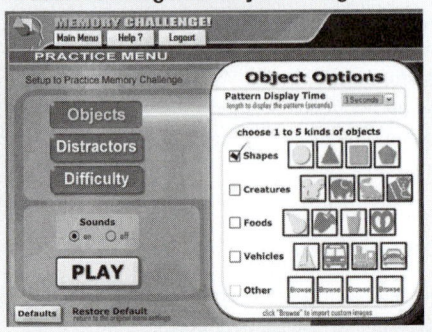 | A. Teaches directly (through explanation and/or practice) the steps involved in solving problems—directed teaching strategy<br>B. Gives learners opportunities to learn problem solving strategies—constructivist teaching strategy |

function) and/or opportunities for studying plant growth in action (simulation function). Each software function serves a different purpose during learning and, consequently, has its own appropriate integration strategies.

The first instructional software products reflected the behavioral and cognitive learning theories that were popular at the time. Some software functions (e.g., drill and practice, tutorial) remain focused on directed strategies that grew out of these theories, delivering information to help students acquire and retain information and skills. Later, instructional software was designed to support more constructivist aims of helping students explore topics and generate their own knowledge. Therefore, some software functions (e.g., simulation, games) can be used in either directed or constructivist ways, depending on how they are designed. See Table 3.1 for a summary of the five software functions described in this chapter.

Gagné, Wager, and Rojas (1981) suggested a way to look at software that can help educators analyze a given product with respect to its instructional function(s) and design appropriate integration strategies that make use of these functions. Gagné et al. said that drills, tutorials, and simulations each accomplish a different combination of the **Nine Events of Instruction**. The nine events are guidelines identified by Gagné that can help teachers arrange optimal "conditions for learning" for various types of knowledge and skills. By determining which of the events a software package fulfills, he said, educators can determine the teaching role it serves and where it might fit in the instructional process. This chapter describes both directed and constructivist strategies for instructional software. Look at the Top Ten feature for good ideas on how to integrate instructional software products of various kinds.

**TECHNOLOGY LEARNING CHECK**

Complete TLC 3.1 to review what you have learned from reading this section about basic instructional software concepts.

## DRILL-AND-PRACTICE TEACHING FUNCTIONS

**Drill-and-practice** software functions are exercises in which students work example items, usually one at a time, and receive feedback on their correctness. Programs vary considerably in the kind of feedback they provide in response to student input. Feedback can range from a simple "OK" or "No, try again" to elaborate animated displays or verbal explanations. Some programs simply present the next item if the student answers correctly. Types of drill and practice are sometimes distinguished by how the program tailors the practice session to student needs. Types of drill functions are described below:

- **Flash card activity**—This is the most basic drill-and-practice function, arising from the popularity of real-world flash cards. A student sees a set number of questions or problems, presented one at a time. The student chooses or types an answer, and the program responds with positive or negative feedback depending on whether the student answered correctly.

  - **Chart fill-in activities**—In this kind of practice, students are asked to complete a whole set of answers (e.g., multiplication facts) by filling in a chart, usually on a timed basis to test for fluency. Then they receive feedback on all the answers at once.

  - **Branching drill**—In branching drills, a more sophisticated form of drill and practice, the software moves students on to advanced questions after they get a number of questions correct at some predetermined mastery level; it may also send them back to lower levels if they answer a certain number wrong. Some programs automatically review questions that students get wrong before going on to other levels. Students may not realize that branching is happening,

▲ A popular use of drill-and- practice software is helping students prepare for high-stakes tests. (Photo courtesy of W. Wiencke)

since the program may do it automatically without alerting them to this fact. Sometimes, however, the program may congratulate students on good progress before proceeding to the next level, or it may allow them to choose their next activities.

- **Extensive feedback activities**—In these drills, students get more than just correct/incorrect feedback. Some programs give detailed feedback on why the student got a problem wrong. This feedback is sometimes so thorough that the software function is often mistaken for a tutorial. (See the next section for a description of tutorial functions.) However, the function of a drill is not instruction, but rather practice *after* instruction. Consequently, drill and tutorial functions have different integration strategies.

## Selecting Good Drill-and-Practice Software

In addition to meeting general criteria for good instructional software, well-designed drill-and-practice programs should also meet specific criteria:

- **Control over the presentation rate**—Unless questions are part of a timed review, students should have as much time as they wish to answer and examine the feedback before proceeding to later questions. A student usually signals readiness to go to the next question by simply pressing a key.

- **Answer judging**—If programs allow students to enter a short answer rather than simply choosing one, a good drill program must be able to discriminate between correct and incorrect answers.

- **Appropriate feedback for correct and incorrect answers**—If students' responses are timed, or if their session time is limited, they may find it more motivating simply to move quickly to the next question, rather than receiving recognition for correctness. When drills do give feedback, they must avoid two common errors. First, feedback must be simple and display quickly. Students rapidly tire of elaborate displays, and the feedback ceases to motivate them. Second, some programs inadvertently motivate students to get *wrong* answers by giving more exciting or interesting feedback for wrong answers than for correct ones. The most famous example of this design error occurred in an early version of a popular microcomputer-based math drill series. Each correct answer got a smiling face, but two or more wrong answers produced a full-screen, animated crying face that students found amusing. Consequently, many students tried to answer incorrectly so they could see it. The company corrected this flaw, but this classic error continues today in other forms.

- **Characteristics tailored to young learners**—Luik (2011) also offers advice specific to programs for young learners. Recommendations from her study focus primarily on keeping instructions and procedures simple and avoid screen elements that could distract them.

## Benefits of Drill and Practice

Though often disparaged by constructivists as "drill and kill," the benefits of drill-and-practice software functions have been well established by research. Indeed, its effects were so well documented in the early days of computer-based learning that little current research focuses on it. It long ago became clear that drill activities can allow the effective rehearsal students need to transfer newly learned information into long-term memory (Merrill & Salisbury, 1984; Salisbury, 1990). To help them master higher-order skills more quickly and easily, students must have what Gagné (1982) and Bloom (1986) call **automaticity**, or automatic recall of lower order prerequisite skills. The usefulness of drill programs seems especially popular among teachers of students with learning disabilities (Graham, Bellert, Thomas, & Pegg, 2007).

Schoppek and Tulis (2010) found that fluency in basic math skills is essential for mathematical problem solving. However, they noted that contemporary mathematics instruction does not emphasize the importance of these skills (p. 239). Their results with third graders showed that even a moderate amount of individualized practice with drill software greatly improved both arithmetic skills and problem solving, an impact that continued in follow-up testing three months later. The researchers felt that individualized practice with drill software was a more efficient use of time than other kinds of practice. Drill software has been found to yield equivalent or better benefits when compared to paper-pencil practice, and drill software is both more efficient and often more appealing to students.

Recent focuses on educational accountability and meeting standards that began with the No Child Left Behind (NCLB) Act has breathed new life into strategies that were once considered passé. Even in research circles, some authors have claimed that directed teaching strategies are more effective than minimally guided teaching techniques (Kirshner, Sweller, & Clark, 2006). As constructivist methods became more popular in the 1980s and 1990s, the demand for drill-and-practice and tutorial instructional software waned, and use of simulation and problem-solving software increased. Now, directed strategies that drills and tutorials support—strategies that are ideal for preparing students for tests—are once again on the rise.

Although curriculum increasingly emphasizes problem-solving and higher-order skills, teachers still give students on-paper practice (e.g., worksheets or exercises) for many skills to help them learn and remember correct procedures. The following are acknowledged benefits of drill software as compared to paper exercises:

- **Immediate feedback**—When students practice skills on paper, they often do not know until much later whether or not they did their work correctly. To quote a common saying, "Practice does not make perfect; practice makes permanent." If they practice incorrect answers, students may be memorizing the wrong skills. Drill-and-practice software informs them immediately whether their responses are accurate so they can make quick corrections. This helps both "debugging" (identifying errors in their procedures) and retention (placing the skills in long-term memory for future access).

- **Increased motivation**—Many students refuse to do the practice they need on paper, either because they have failed so much that the whole idea is abhorrent, they have poor handwriting skills, or they simply dislike writing. In these cases, computer-based practice may motivate students to do the practice they need. Computers don't get impatient or give disgusted looks when a student gives a wrong answer.

- **Saving teacher time**—Since teachers do not have to present or grade drill and practice, students can practice on their own while the teacher addresses other student needs. The curriculum has dozens of areas in which the benefits of drill and practice apply. Some of these are:

  - Math facts
  - Typing skills
  - English and foreign-language vocabulary
  - Countries and capitals
  - Preparation for SAT, ACT, TOEFL, and other high-stakes tests
  - Musical keys and notations

## Limitations and Problems Related to Drill and Practice

Although drill and practice can be extremely useful to both students and teachers, it is also frequently maligned by its critics as "drill and kill." This criticism comes from the following two sources:

- **Instructional overuse or misuses**—Some authors have criticized teachers for presenting drills for overly long periods or for teaching functions that drills are ill-suited to accomplish. For example, teachers may give students drill-and-practice software as a way of introducing new concepts rather than just for practicing and reinforcing familiar ones.

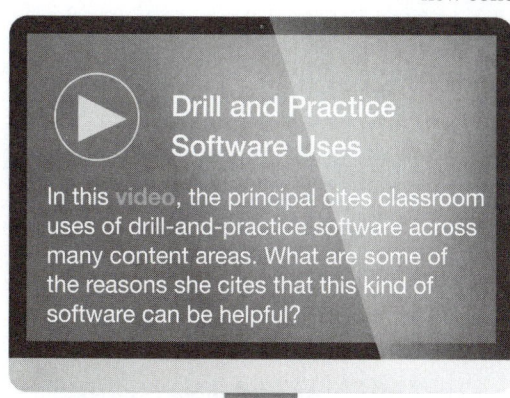

**Drill and Practice Software Uses**

In this video, the principal cites classroom uses of drill-and-practice software across many content areas. What are some of the reasons she cites that this kind of software can be helpful?

- **Criticism by constructivists**—Since it is identified so closely with traditional instructional methods, drill-and-practice software has become an icon for what many people consider an outmoded approach to teaching. Critics claim that introducing isolated skills and directing students to practice them contradicts the trend toward restructured curriculum in which students learn and use skills in an integrated way within the context of their own projects that specifically require the skills.

Despite these criticisms, it is likely that some form of drill-and-practice software will be useful in many classrooms for some time to come. Rather than ignoring drill-and-practice software or criticizing it as outmoded, teachers should seek to identify needs that drills can meet and use the software in ways that take advantage of its capabilities. See Figure 3.1 for examples of drill software and a summary of drill features.

# FIGURE 3.1 Drill-and-Practice Software Functions in Brief

| Description of Drill and Practice | | |
|---|---|---|
| **Characteristics** | **Criteria for Effective Drill Software** | **Benefits** |
| • Presents items for students to answer<br>• Gives feedback on correctness<br>• Sometimes gives explanation of why answers are incorrect | • User control over presentation rate<br>• Good answer judging<br>• Appropriate feedback for correct, incorrect answers | • Gives immediate, private feedback<br>• Motivates students to practice<br>• Saves teacher time correcting student work |
| *Vocabulary Practice*<br>by BrainPop | *Chemistry Formulas*<br>by Chemistry Drills.com | *Name the Note*<br>by Music Drills.com |
| Practice in word identification: drag each word into the correct category | Practice in creating correct chemical formulas | Downloadable app for practicing keyboard note identification |

## TABLE 3.2 Integration Strategies and Guidelines for Using Drill and Practice Programs

| Strategy | Explanation |
|---|---|
| **Supplement and/or replace worksheets and homework exercises** | Use whenever students lack specific skills that are prerequisite to higher-order ones. The motivation, immediate feedback, and self-pacing can make it more productive for students to practice skills on the computer than on paper. |
| **Prepare for tests** | Use when students need to prepare to demonstrate mastery of specific skills in important examinations (e.g., for end-of-year grades or for college entrance). |

| Guideline | Explanation |
|---|---|
| **Set time limits** | Limit the time for drill assignments to 10 to 15 minutes per day to ensure that students will not become bored and that the drill-and-practice strategy will retain its effectiveness. Also, teachers should be sure students have been introduced previously to concepts underlying the drills. Use drills only to debug students' strategies and helps them retain their grasp of concepts. |
| **Use only after teaching the concepts** | Never use drill to introduce new topics. Use only to debug students' understanding and help them retain their grasp of familiar concepts. |
| **Assign individually** | Take advantage of self-pacing and personalized feedback by allowing individual, rather than group, use. If technology resources are limited and all students in a class will benefit from practice in a skill, divide them into small groups to compete with each other for the best group scores, or divide into two groups for a "relay race" competition to see which group can complete the assignment the fastest with the most correct answers. |
| **Use learning stations** | If not all students need the kind of practice that a drill provides, make software one of several learning stations to serve students with identified weaknesses in one or more key skills. |

# TECHNOLOGY INTEGRATION

## Example 3.1

**TITLE:** Using Ratios

**CONTENT AREA/TOPIC:** Mathematics—Ratios and Proportions

**GRADE LEVELS:** 4-5

**ISTE STANDARDS•S:** Standard 2–Communication and Collaboration; Standard 6–Technology Operations and Concepts

**CCSS:** MATH.CONTENT.4.NF.A.1, MATH.CONTENT.5.NF.A.1, **MATH.**CONTENT.6.RP.A.1

**DESCRIPTION:** One of the activities at Cynthia Lanius's Mathematics Lessons website provides practice in recognizing

pictured examples of ratios and proportions. After students learn about ratio concepts in the classroom, the teacher may either print out the on-screen exercises or have students access the site on classroom computers. Students also get a sheet to mark down how many they get correct. Students get a 10-minure period to practice the concepts by completing the items, and they check their own correctness by clicking an on-screen tab to reveal each correct answer.

*SOURCE:* Based on online resources at Cynthia Lanius's Mathematics Lessons website

## Using Drill and Practice in Teaching

Teachers may take advantage of the benefits of drill-and-practice software to give students practice using isolated skills. Follow the integration strategies and guidelines shown in Table 3.2 to make best use of drill-and practice-programs. Also, an example integration strategy for drill functions is shown in Technology Integration Example 3.1.

**TECHNOLOGY LEARNING CHECK**

Complete TLC 3.2 to review what you have learned from reading this section about drill and practice software concepts.

## TUTORIAL TEACHING FUNCTIONS

**Tutorial** software is an entire instructional sequence on a topic, similar to a teacher's classroom instruction. This instruction usually is expected to be a self-contained instructional unit rather than a supplement to other instruction. Students should be able to learn the topic without any other help or materials. Unlike other types of instructional software, tutorials are true teaching materials. Gagné et al. (1981) said that good tutorial software should address all nine instructional events. Today's technologies (e.g., Camtasia, Youtube) make video demonstrations possible, and these are often referred to as "tutorials." However, demonstrations alone do not fulfill software tutorial functions; instructional software tutorials require practice and feedback capabilities.

Also, people may confuse tutorial and drill activities for two reasons. First, drill software may provide elaborate feedback that reviewers may mistake for tutorial explanations. Even software developers may claim that a package is a tutorial when it is, in fact, a drill activity with detailed feedback. Second, a good tutorial should include one or more practice sequences to check students' comprehension. Since this kind of checking is a drill-and-practice function, teachers reviewing tutorial software can become confused about the primary purpose of the activity.

Tutorials often are categorized as linear or branching tutorials (Alessi & Trollip, 2001):

- **Linear tutorial**—A simple, linear tutorial gives the same instructional sequence of explanation, practice, and feedback to all learners regardless of differences in their performance.

- **Branching tutorial**—A more sophisticated, branching tutorial directs learners along alternate paths depending on how they respond to questions and whether they show mastery of certain parts of the material. Branching tutorials can range in complexity by the number of paths they allow and how fully they diagnose the kinds of instruction a student needs. More complex tutorials may also have computer-management capabilities; teachers can place each student at an appropriate level and get progress reports as each one goes through the instruction.

Tutorials are usually geared toward learners who can read fairly well and who are older students or adults. Since tutorial instruction is expected to stand alone, it is difficult to explain or give appropriate guidance on-screen to a nonreader. However, some tutorials aimed at younger learners have found clever ways to explain and demonstrate concepts with graphics, succinct phrases or sentences, or audio/video directions and illustrations.

## Selecting Good Tutorial Software

Being a good teacher is a difficult assignment for any human, let alone a computer. However, to fulfill tutorial functions, teaching is exactly what tutorials are supposed to do. In addition to meeting general criteria for good instructional software, well-designed tutorial programs should also meet the following standards:

- **Extensive interactivity**—Give frequent and thoughtful responses to questions and supply appropriate practice and feedback to guide students' learning. The most frequent criticism of tutorials is that they are "page-turners"—that is, they ask students to do very little other than read.

- **Thorough user control**—First, students should always be able to control the rate at which text appears on the screen. The program should not go on to the next information or activity screen until the user has signaled readiness (e.g., by pressing a key). Next, the program should offer students the flexibility to review explanations, examples, or sequences of instruction or to move ahead to other instruction and should also provide frequent opportunities to exit the program.

- **Appropriate pedagogy**—The program's structure should provide a suggested or required sequence of instruction that builds on concepts and covers the content adequately. It should provide sufficient explanation and examples in both original and remedial sequences. In sum, it should compare favorably to an expert teacher's presentation sequence for the topic.

- **Adequate answer-judging and feedback capabilities**—Whenever possible, programs should allow students to answer in natural language and should accept all correct answers and possible variations of correct answers. They should also give appropriate corrective feedback when needed, supplying this feedback after only one or two tries rather than frustrating students by making them keep trying indefinitely to answer something they may not know.

- **Appropriate graphics and/or video**—Most experts say that graphics should be used sparingly and not interfere with the purpose of the instruction. Where graphics are used, they should fulfill an instructional, aesthetic, or otherwise supportive function. Video-based tutorials should provide clear, uncluttered demonstrations of procedures.

- **Adequate recordkeeping**—Depending on the purpose of the tutorial, teachers may need to keep track of student progress. If the program keeps records on student work, teachers should be able to get progress summaries quickly and easily.

## Benefits of Tutorials

Since a tutorial includes drill-and-practice activities, helpful features include the same ones as for drills (immediate feedback to learners, motivation, and time savings) plus the additional benefit of offering a self-paced instructional experience. Many successful uses of tutorials have been documented over the years. For examples, see Ellington and Hardin (2008), Offner and Pohlman (2010), Criswell, (2011), and Wilson and Wilson (2013).

Another, more sophisticated kind of tutorial software is **intelligent tutoring systems**, a kind of branching tutorial software that adapts the sequence of instruction to the needs of each learner. Steenbergen-Hu and Cooper (2013) report encouraging results using such systems designed to teach mathematics.

## Limitations and Problems Related to Tutorials

Tutorials can fulfill many much-needed instructional functions, but like drill and practice, they also attract their share of criticism, including:

- **Criticism by constructivists**—Constructivists criticize tutorials because they deliver directed instruction rather than allowing students to generate their own knowledge through hands-on projects. Thus, they feel tutorials are trivial uses of the computer.

- **Lack of well-designed products**—The difficulty and expense of designing and developing true tutorial functions make such programs scarcer than other kinds of software. A well-designed tutorial sequence emerges from extensive research into how to teach the topic well. Designers must know what learning tasks the topic requires, the best sequence

### FIGURE 3.2 Tutorial Software Functions in Brief

| Description of Tutorials | | |
| --- | --- | --- |
| **Characteristics** | **Criteria for Effective Tutorial Software** | **Benefits** |
| • Presents an entire instructional sequence<br>• Is complete, rather than supplemental, instruction<br>• Includes drill-and-practice functions<br>• Can be either linear or branching | • Extensive interactivity<br>• Thorough user control<br>• Appropriate pedagogy<br>• Adequate answer judging and feedback<br>• Appropriate graphics<br>• Adequate record keeping | • Same as drill and practice (immediate, private feedback, time savings)<br>• Offers instruction that can stand on its own |
| ***Trigonometry Challenge***<br>**by ETCAI** | ***Laws of Motion***<br>**by The Physics Classroom** | ***The Constitution***<br>**by Congress for Kids** |
| Instruction in trigonometry concepts: Sequence of screens gives information on concepts such as the Pythagorean Theorem, followed by practice items with feedback | Instruction in physics concepts: Sequence of screens gives information and animated demonstrations to teach concepts such as Newton's Laws of Motion, followed by practice items | Instruction in aspects of U.S. government: Sequence of screens gives explanation of how the government works, with assessment items to review concepts and check comprehension |
| | | |

*Source:* A special thanks to the Dirksen Congressional Center for permission to use information and screenshots from Congress for Kids (http:www.congressforkids .net). Images reprinted by permission of ETCAI Products (http://www.etcai.com), The Physics Classroom (http://www.physicsclassroom.com/), and the Dirksen Congressional Center.

for students to follow, how best to explain and demonstrate essential concepts, common errors students are likely to make, and how to provide instruction and feedback to correct those errors. Though programs identified as "video tutorials" have emerged in recent years, most are demonstrations and explanations that may or may not be well-researched, and most do not contain the practice and feedback elements.

- **Reflect only one instructional approach**—True tutorial programs that have adequate feedback are difficult to design because teachers frequently disagree about what should be taught for a given topic, how to teach it most effectively, and in what order to present the learning tasks. For instance, a teacher may choose not to purchase a tutorial with a sound instructional sequence because it does not cover the topic the way he or she presents it. Not surprisingly, software companies tend to avoid programs that are difficult to develop and market. However, use of website-based tutorials is increasing.

Although tutorials have considerable value and are popular in military and industrial training, schools and colleges have never fully tapped their potential as teaching resources. However, recent trends toward combining a tutorial approach with new technologies (online and streaming video) are bringing tutorial functions into more common use. See Figure 3.2 for examples of tutorial software and a summary of tutorial features.

## Using Tutorials in Teaching

Tutorial software can serve several classroom needs. This section describes integration strategies to meet each of these needs and offers guidelines and practical tips on how to integrate these strategies in the classroom.

Self-instructional tutorials are becoming more useful in light of new strategies such as the **flipped classroom** model and easier to develop due to new technologies such as **screencasting,** or video captures of actions on a computer screen, usually accompanied by narration (Stagg, Kimmins, & Pavlovski, 2013). The tutorial's unique capability of presenting an entire interactive instructional sequence can assist in several classroom situations. Follow the integration strategies and guidelines shown in Table 3.3 to make best use of tutorial programs.

### TABLE 3.3 Integration Strategies and Guidelines for Using Tutorial Programs

| Strategies | Explanation |
| --- | --- |
| **Self-paced reviews of instruction** | Use when students are slower to understand concepts and need to spend additional time on them, learn better in a self-paced mode without the pressure to move at the same pace as the rest of the class, and need a review before a test. |
| **Alternative learning strategies** | Use when students at advanced levels prefer to structure their own learning activities and proceed at their own pace or when they are able use tutorials prior to meeting with a teacher for assessment and/or further work assignments |
| **Instruction when teachers are unavailable** | Use when students surge ahead of their class and the teacher cannot leave the rest of the class to provide advanced instruction, or when no teacher is available for the comparatively few students who need a course (e.g., physics, German, trigonometry, or other lower-demand courses). |
| Guidelines | Explanation |
| **Assign individually** | Like drill-and-practice functions, tutorial functions are designed for use by individuals rather than by groups of students. |
| **Use learning stations or individual checkout** | Depending on which strategy it promotes, a tutorial may be used in a classroom learning station or may be available for checkout at any time in a library/media center. Sometimes teachers send students to learning stations with tutorials in order to review previously presented material while the teacher works with other students. (See Technology Integration Example 3.2.) |

## Example 3.2

**TITLE:** Minds on Physics

**CONTENT AREA/TOPIC:** Physics—Newton's Laws of Motion

**GRADE LEVELS:** 9–12

**ISTE STANDARDS•S:** Standard 1–Creativity and Innovation; Standard 6–Technology Operations and Concepts

**CCSS:** ELA/Literacy RST.11-12.7, WHST.9-12.7, Mathematics MP.2, Math.Content.HSN.Q.A.1, Math.Content.HSA-CED.A.4

**NSTA:** HS-PS2-1, HS-PS2-4

**DESCRIPTION:** After presenting the topic in the classroom using usual instructional strategies, the teacher assigns the Minds on Physics (MOP) module at the Physics Classroom website as a mastery learning activity. Students complete the assigned online materials as homework or classwork and submit their encrypted "success codes" to their teacher. The teacher then checks that students have completed them successfully by using a decryption page provided on the site. The teacher then assigns one or more of the online labs to illustrate application of Newton's Laws, and uses the scoring rubric provided to assess students' write-up(s) of their results.

*SOURCE:* Based on The Physics Classroom materials developed by Tom Henderson at http://www.physicsclassroom.com/mop/join.cfm

**TECHNOLOGY LEARNING CHECK**

Complete TLC 3.3 to review what you have learned from reading this section about tutorial software concepts.

# SIMULATION TEACHING FUNCTIONS

A **simulation** is a computerized model of a real or imagined system that is designed to teach how the system works. Unlike tutorial and drill-and-practice activities, in which the teaching structure is built into the package, learners using simulations usually must choose tasks to do and the order in which to do them. Alessi and Trollip (2001) identified two main types of simulations: those that teach about something and those that teach how to do something; they also divide the "how to" simulations into procedural and situational types.

## Simulations That Teach About Something

Alessi and Trollip (2001) further divide "simulations that teach about something" into two other categories: physical simulations and iterative simulations. These sub-categories are based on how users interact with them.

- **Physical simulations.** These simulations allow users to manipulate things or processes represented on the screen. For example, students might see selections of chemicals with instructions on how to combine them to see the result, or they might see how various electrical circuits operate. More recent investigations of simulation software include the use of three-dimensional models (Kim, 2006).

- **Iterative simulations.** These simulations speed up or slow down processes that usually happen either so slowly or so quickly that students cannot see the events unfold. For example, software may show the effects of changes in demographic variables on population growth, or the effects of environmental factors on ecosystems. Alessi and Trollip (2001) refer to this type as "iterative" because students can run it over and over again with different values, observing the results each time. Biological simulations, such as those on genetics, are popular since they help students experiment with natural processes. Genetics simulations let students pair animals with given characteristics and see the resulting offspring.

## Simulations That Teach How to Do Something

Alessi and Trollip (2001) divide the "how to" simulations into procedural and situational types. Again, these categories are based on how users are able to interact with them.

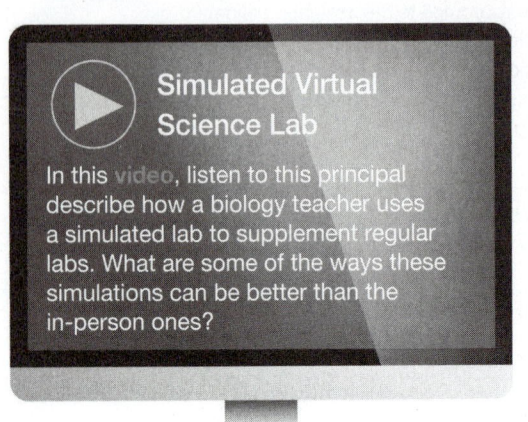

**Simulated Virtual Science Lab**

In this video, listen to this principal describe how a biology teacher uses a simulated lab to supplement regular labs. What are some of the ways these simulations can be better than the in-person ones?

- **Procedural simulations.** These activities teach the appropriate sequences of steps to perform certain procedures. They include diagnostic programs, in which students try to identify the sources of medical or mechanical problems, and flight simulators, in which students simulate piloting an airplane or other vehicle.

- **Situational simulations.** These programs give students hypothetical problem situations and ask them to react. Some simulations allow for various successful strategies, such as letting students play the stock market or operate businesses. Others have most desirable and least desirable options, such as choices when encountering a potentially volatile classroom situation.

The descriptions above clarify the various forms a simulation might take, but teachers need not feel they should be able to classify a given simulation into one of these categories. Simulations usually emphasize learning about the *system itself* rather than learning general problem-solving strategies. For example, a program called The Factory has students build products by selecting machines and placing them in the correct sequence. Since the program emphasizes solving problems in correct sequence rather than manufacturing in factories, it should probably be called a problem-solving activity rather than a simulation. Programs such as City Creator, which let students design their own cities, provide more accurate examples of building-type simulations.

## Selecting Good Simulation Software

Simulations vary so much in type and purpose that a uniform set of criteria is not possible. For some simulations, a realistic and accurate representation of a system is essential, but for others, it is important only to know what screen elements represent. Since the screen often presents no set sequence of steps, simulations need good accompanying documentation—more than most software. These help the teacher more quickly learn how to use the program and show the students how to use it. See Figure 3.3 for examples of simulation software and a summary of simulation features.

## Benefits of Simulations

Simulations are more prevalent in science than any other area (Brunsell, & Horejsi, 2012; Eskrootchi & Oskrochi, 2010; Evagoroua, Nicolaoub, & Constantinoub, 2010; Jaakkola & Nurmi, 2008; Lalley, Piotrowski, Battaglia, Brophy, & Chugh, 2010; Urban-Woldron, 2009), but they are also popular in teaching social science topics (Bartels, McCown, & Wilkie, 2013; Iannou, Brown, Hannafin, & Boyer, 2009). Simulations are currently available in other content areas; nearly all are now able to be accessed online. Some updated products combine the control, safety, and interactive features of computer simulations with the visual impact of pictures of real-life devices and processes.

Research comparing simulations to "real" activities often qualify the benefits they report by saying that the impact of simulations depends on how and with whom they are used. For example, in a study of a simulation of environmental concepts, Eskrootchi and Oskrochi (2010) report that, "Simulations do not work on their own; there needs to be some structuring of the students' interactions with the simulation to increase effectiveness" (p. 236). Gelbart, Brill, and Yarden (2009) found that some students learn more than others from simulations designed to teach genetics concepts. Research on teaching "systems thinking" skills to elementary school students by using environmental simulations (Evagoroua, Nicolaoub, & Constantinoub, 2010) reported good impact on some skills but not others. One common finding is that simulations work best when combined with nonsimulation activities. Urban-Woldron (2009) found that physics simulations were most useful as a follow-up to hands-on activities, and Jaakkola and Nurmi (2008) reported that simulations in electrical concepts had more positive benefits with elementary school children when accompanied by hands-on learning.

However, other studies report unqualified positive results from simulations. Lalley et al. (2010) compared the effectiveness of simulated and physical frog dissections on learning,

# FIGURE 3.3  Simulation Software Functions in Brief

| Description of Simulations | | |
| --- | --- | --- |
| **Characteristics** | **Criteria for Effective Simulation Software** | **Benefits** |
| • Models a real or imaginary system<br>• Can model physical phenomena (e.g., growth), procedures (e.g., dissections), and hypothetical situations (e.g., stock market)<br>• Users can see the impact of their actions | • System fidelity and accuracy (for some simulations)<br>• Good documentation to explain system characteristics and uses | • Compresses time or slows down processes<br>• Gets students involved<br>• Makes experimentation safe<br>• Makes the impossible possible<br>• Saves money and other resources<br>• Allows repetition with variations<br>• Allows observation of complex processes |
| ***BioLab Fly***<br>**by BioLab** | ***Stock Market Simulation***<br>**by National SMS** | ***Digital Frog***<br>**by Digital Frog International** |
| Simulated breeding of fruit flies: Students learn genetics concepts through repeatable experiments | Simulated stock market: Student teams learn how the stock market works by "investing" money and seeing resulting profits and losses | Simulated dissection: Students can "dissect" a virtual frog using digital tools and images |

retention, and student satisfaction and found no significant differences on any measure. They concluded that the simulated dissection "provides a viable alternative to physical dissection . . . and may be appealing to teachers and students for a number of practical and/or ethical reasons" (p. 189). Iannou et al. (2009) reported that a problem-based simulation designed to teach world issues made students more motivated to learn social studies than did text-based materials.

Wieman and Perkins (2005) reported research that indicates interactive simulations in physics are frequently much more effective than seeing actual demonstrations. They believe that real-life demonstrations and labs include peripheral information that is not central to the concept being learned. While an expert can easily filter out the "extra" information to focus on the phenomenon of interest, a novice does not even know what to filter out. Thus, the extra information produces confusion and much higher cognitive loads for novice learners.

Depending on the topic and the way it is used, a simulation has potential to provide one or more of the following instructional benefits.

▲ Simulation software can be used instead of or as a supplement to science lab activities such as dissections. (Photo courtesy of W. Wiencke)

**Compress time.**  This feature is important whenever students study the growth or development of living things (e.g., pairing animals to observe their offspring's characteristics) or other processes that take a long time (e.g., the movement of the sun across the sky). A simulation can make something happen in seconds that normally takes days, months, or longer, so that students can cover more variations of the activity in a shorter time.

**Slow down processes.** Conversely, a simulation can also model processes normally invisible to the human eye because they happen so quickly. For example, physical education students can study the slowed-down movement of muscles and limbs as a simulated athlete throws a ball or swings a golf club.

**Get students involved.** Simulations can capture students' attention by placing them in charge of things and asking, "What would you do?" The results of their choices can be immediate and graphic. Users can also interact with the program instead of just seeing its output.

**Make experimentation safe.** Whenever learning involves physical danger, simulations are the strategy of choice. This is true when students are learning to drive vehicles, handle volatile substances, or react to potentially dangerous situations. They can experiment with strategies in simulated environments that might result in personal injury to themselves or others in real life. For example, the First Responders Simulation and Training Environment (FiRSTE) allows for the training of civilian first responders to respond to attacks employing weapons of mass destruction (Tichon, Hall, Hilgers, Leu, & Agarwal, 2003).

**Make the impossible possible.** Very often, teachers simply cannot give students access to the resources or situations that simulations can. Simulations can show students, for example, what it would be like to walk on the moon or how to react to emergencies in a nuclear power plant. They can see cells mutating or hold countrywide elections. They can even design new societies or planets and see the results of their choices. For example, one researcher at the University of California–Davis (Virtual Schizophrenia in Second Life, 2007) recreated a mental health treatment ward in a virtual world and gave each of his students a taste of what it means to experience schizophrenia in the real world. As students' virtual characters walked the hallways, they were overcome by hallucinations, including "the floor disappearing from underfoot, writing on posters that morphs into derogatory words, a pulsating gun that suddenly appears on a table, and menacing voices that laugh."

**Save money and other resources.** Many school systems are finding dissections of animals on a computer screen to be much less expensive and just as instructional as using real frogs or cats. (It is also easier on the animals!) Depending on the subject, a simulated experiment may be just as effective a learning experience as an actual experiment is, but at a fraction of the cost.

**Allow repetition with variations.** Unlike in real life, simulations let students repeat events as many times as they wish and with unlimited variations. They can pair any number of cats or make endless spaceship landings in a variety of conditions to compare the results of each set of choices.

**Allow observation of complex processes.** Real-life events often are so complex that they are confusing—especially to those seeing them for the first time. When many things happen at once, students find it difficult to focus on the operation of individual components. Who could understand the operation of a stock market by looking at the real thing without some introduction? Simulations can isolate parts of activities and control background noise. This makes it easier for students to see what is happening when, later, all the parts come together in the actual activity.

## Limitations and Problems Related to Simulations

Most educators acknowledge the instructional usefulness of simulations. There are some concerns, however, including the following:

- **Criticism of virtual lab software.** Though modern simulation software makes it possible to do simulated labs for topics in biology and chemistry, both the American Chemical Society

▲ Though modern simulation software makes it possible to do many chemistry and biology lab activities on the computer, both the American Chemical Society and the National Science Teachers Association say that simulations should be used only to supplement, not replace, traditional labs. (Photo courtesy of W. Wiencke)

(2008) and the National Science Teachers Association (Davis, 2009; NSTA, 2007) have come out strongly against replacing hands-on, in-class labs with virtual ones, saying that simulations should be used only as supplements to regular labs. The College Board has also indicated that students may not get Advanced Placement (AP) course credit for any courses that substitute virtual labs for hands-on labs.

- **Accuracy of models.** When students see simplified versions of systems in a controlled situation, they may get inaccurate or imprecise perspectives on the systems' complexity. For example, students may feel they know all about how to react to driving situations because they have experienced simulated versions of them. Many educators feel strongly that situational simulations must be followed at some point by real experiences, a position with which organizations such as the NSTA and the American Chemical Society concur. In addition, many teachers of very young children feel that learners at early stages of their cognitive development should experience things first with their five senses rather than on computer screens.

- **Instructional misuses.** Sometimes, simulations are used to teach concepts that could just as easily be demonstrated on paper, with manipulatives, or with real objects. If students can master the activities of a simulation without actually developing effective problem-solving skills, such applications can actually encourage counterproductive behaviors.

## TABLE 3.4 Integration Strategies and Guidelines for Using Simulation Programs

| Strategies | Explanation |
| --- | --- |
| In place of or as supplements to lab experiments | Use as replacements for labs when adequate lab materials are not available or for experiments that would be unmanageable or too dangerous in person. Use as supplements to prepare students for actual labs, or as follow-ups with variations of the original experiments without using consumable materials. |
| In place of or as supplements to role-playing | Use when students either refuse to role-play in front of a class or get too enthusiastic and disrupt the classroom. |
| In place of or as supplements to field trips | Use when desired locations are not within reach of the school, and a simulated experience of all or part of the process is the next best thing. Simulations also provide good introductions or follow-ups to field trips. |
| To introduce and/or clarify a topic | Use to provide a nonthreatening (ungraded), get-acquainted look at a new topic and build students' initial interest in it. Some software helps students see how earlier learning relates to the topic. (Simulations such as Tulane University's Crisis at Fort Sumter helps students see the impact of events leading up to the U.S. Civil War.) |
| To foster exploration and process learning | Use to emulate in-class science labs and to illustrate and provide practice in using scientific methods |
| To encourage cooperation and group work | Use to interest students in working together on a product. For example, a simulation on immigration or colonization might launch a group project in a social studies unit. |
| **Guidelines** | **Explanation** |
| Provide usage instruction and guidelines | Since simulations are unstructured, students need to know how to make them work and what they are to do with them. |
| Use either with groups or individuals | Because they instigate discussion and collaborative work so well, simulations usually are considered more appropriate for pairs and small groups than for individuals. However, individual use certainly is not precluded. |

# TECHNOLOGY INTEGRATION

## Example 3.3

**TITLE:** Crisis at Fort Sumter

**CONTENT AREA/TOPIC:** U.S. History—Civil War period

**GRADE LEVELS:** 10–12

**ISTE STANDARDS•S:** Standard 1–Creativity and Innovation; Standard 2–Communication and Collaboration; Standard 4–Critical Thinking, Problem Solving, and Decision Making

**CCSS:** ELA-LITERACY.RH.9-10.5 ELA-LITERACY.RH.11-12.2

**SSCS:** Theme 2-Time, Continuity, and Change

**DESCRIPTION:** Introduce students to the historical simulation website Crisis at Fort Sumter. The simulation outlines the decisions that President Abraham Lincoln had to make concerning Fort Sumter. Tell them to choose one decision on which they disagree with the President, outline what they would have done differently, and write a description defending their alternative solution. They post the description on the discussion board, and the class discusses the merits of the various proposals and the impact each might have made on the situation.

*SOURCE:* Based on an exercise idea submitted at the MERLOT website for use with the Crisis at Fort Sumter simulation website.

## How to Use Simulations in Teaching: Integration Strategies and Guidelines

Simulations are considered among the most potentially powerful computer software resources; as with most software, however, their usefulness depends largely on the program's purpose and how well it fits in with the purpose of the lesson and student needs. Teachers are responsible for recognizing the unique instructional value of each simulation and using it to its best advantage. Lee and Guo (2008) offer teacher guidelines for using simulations in physics instruction to achieve the most impact. Real systems are often preferable to simulations, but a simulation is useful when the real situation is too time consuming, dangerous, expensive, or unrealistic for a classroom presentation. Follow the integration strategies and guidelines shown in Table 3.4 to make best use of simulations.

**TECHNOLOGY LEARNING CHECK**

Complete TLC 3.4 to review what you have learned from reading this section about simulation software concepts.

## INSTRUCTIONAL GAME TEACHING FUNCTIONS

Technology-based games bridge the worlds of gaming, entertainment, and education in an attempt to deliver fun and effective learning. Young et al. (2012) define digital-learning games as those that focus on the acquisition of knowledge and foster "habits of mind" that are academically useful (p. 63). But more simply defined, **instructional games** are software products that add game-like rules and/or competition to learning activities. Tobias and Fletcher (2012) note that other names for instructional games include computer games, video games, serious games, and educational software.

Even though teachers often use them in the same way as they do drill-and-practice or simulation software, games are considered a separate software function because they have a different instructional connotation to students. When students know they will be playing a game, they expect a fun and entertaining activity because of the challenge of the competition and the potential for winning. Though many writers and researchers tend to conflate

▲ Instructional game software uses students' natural love of games to lure them into learning. **Alice McBroom/Pearson Education**

games and simulations, Young et al. (2012) emphasizes that "Simulations are designed to model real systems . . . whereas the object of games is to score points and win" (p. 64). Teachers frequently intersperse games with other activities to hold students' attention or as a reward for accomplishing other activities, even though games, by themselves, can be powerful teaching tools.

It is important to recognize the common characteristics that set instructional games apart from other types of software: game rules, elements of competition or challenge, and amusing or entertaining formats. These elements generate a set of mental and emotional expectations in students that make game-based instructional activities different from nongame ones.

Devaney (2013) notes that while interest in video games seems to be growing, adoption in schools has been slow. One reason is that because effective educational video games take so much time to develop, there are few good models for teachers to see and try out. However, video games of various kinds are emerging from elementary school to high school levels, all designed to immerse young people in alternate worlds for the purpose of learning various content and skills. She cites examples such as Minecraft, SimCity, Surge EpiGame, and Satisfraction. Other available products include those from a company called Dig-It! Games, which let students learn about ancient civilizations. Finally, she notes that Educade is a free site that links standards-aligned lesson plans with various interactive activities, including video games.

## Selecting Good Instructional Games

Since instructional games often amount to drills or simulations overlaid with game rules, these three types of software often share many of the same criteria (e.g., better reinforcement for correct answers than for incorrect ones). Hong, Cheng, Hwang, Lee, and Chang (2009) surveyed educators to create a checklist of criteria that determine the educational value of a game. The seven categories they identified included: mentality challenge, emotional fulfillment, knowledge enhancement, thinking-skill development, interpersonal skills, spatial ability development, and bodily coordination. Teachers can use the following criteria to choose effective instructional games:

**Appealing and appropriate formats and activities.** The most popular games include elements of adventure and uncertainty as well as levels of complexity matched to learners' abilities.

**Instructional value.** Teachers should examine instructional games carefully for their value as both educational and motivational tools. Do they meet a need that other formats cannot? While a number of researchers argue for the benefits of educational games, others question their value.

**Physical dexterity is reasonable.** Teachers should ensure that students will be motivated rather than frustrated by the activities. Unless the object of the game is to learn physical dexterity (e.g., for students with physical challenges), the focus of the game should be learning content-area skills, rather than physical dexterity. For content-area games, the level of physical dexterity should be manageable by all students.

**Social, societal, and cultural considerations are addressed.** Games may be inappropriate for children if they are not designed with a respectful outlook. For instance, games that call for violence or combat require careful screening, not only to avoid students' modeling this behavior, but also because girls often perceive the attraction of these activities differently than boys do. In addition, games may present females and various ethnic and cultural groups in stereotypical roles. Ideally, teachers should choose games that do not perpetuate stereotypes, while at the same time highlighting positive messages (e.g., peace and friendship) rather than unnecessary violence (e.g., aggression).

## Benefits of Instructional Games

A classroom without elements of games and fun would be a dry, barren landscape for students to traverse. Successful uses of games have been reported in many content areas (Bai, Pan, Hirumi, & Kebritchi, 2012; Young et al, 2012). Their appeal seems to center around students' desire to compete and play. Though they may provide the same actual function as a drill or simulation, games provide teachers with opportunities for taking advantage of the innate desire to play in order to get students to spend more time on a curriculum topic. Some educators and observers feel strongly that video games hold special promises for improving classroom teaching strategies and making learning more engaging and motivational (Ash, 2011; Corbett, 2010). Recent research focuses on games' ability to foster what Herold (2013) calls "noncognitive skills" or abilities such as empathy, attention, and tenacity. See Figure 3.4 for examples of instructional game software and a summary of game features.

## Limitations and Problems Related to Instructional Games

Some teachers believe that any time they can sneak in learning under the guise of a game, it is altogether a good thing. However, games are also criticized from several standpoints:

- **Learning versus having fun.** Some schools forbid any use of games because they believe games convince students that they are escaping from learning, thus drawing attention away

**FIGURE 3.4** Instructional Game Software Functions in Brief

| Description of Instructional Games | | |
| --- | --- | --- |
| **Characteristics** | **Criteria for Effective Instructional Game Software** | **Benefits** |
| **Crystals of Kaydor** **by the University of Wisconsin-Madison** Game to foster empathy and ability to pay attention: Students must successfully interact with aliens | **Lure of the Labyrinth** **by Thinkport** Game to apply pre-algebra skills: Students use math skills to locate a missing pet in the labyrinth | **Jeopardy Review Generator** **by Super Teacher Tools** Game to practice any content area skills: Teachers generate content review items for a Jeopardy game |

*Source:* Crystals of Kaydor image © Learning Games Network- LGN (http://www.gameslearningsociety.org); Lure of the Labyrinth (http://www.labyrinth.thinkport .org) reprinted by permission from Maryland Public Television. Copyright © Maryland Public Television; Jeopardy Review Generator reprinted by permission of SuperTeacher Tools (www.superteachertools.com), courtesy of Jason Kries. Copyright © Jason Kries.

from the intrinsic value and motivation of learning. Critics also feel that winning the game becomes a student's primary focus and that the instructional purpose is lost in the pursuit of this goal. Observers disagree about whether "getting lost in the game" is a benefit or a problem. See the Hot Topic Debate, which addresses this issue.

- **Confusion of game rules and real-life rules.** Some teachers have observed that students can become confused about which part of the activity is the game and which part is the skill; they may then have difficulty transferring their skill to later nongame situations. For example, the teacher's manual for Sunburst's *How the West Was One + Three × Four* game reminded teachers that some students can confuse the math operations rules with the game rules and that teachers must help them recognize the need to focus on math rules and use them outside the game.

- **Inefficient learning.** Although students obviously find many computer games exciting and stimulating, it is sometimes difficult to pinpoint their educational value. Teachers must try to balance the motivation that instructional games bring to learning against the classroom time they take away from nongame strategies. For example, students may become immersed in the challenge of the *Spore* game series, but more efficient ways to teach evolution concepts may be just as motivating.

- **Classroom barriers.** In a review of research on video games for instruction, Rice (2007) found six barriers to widespread classroom implementation. These included negative teacher perceptions toward video games, as well as a lack of several characteristics required to make best use of these materials: state of the art graphics, adequate computing hardware required to run advanced video games, short class periods that hindered long-term engagement in complex games, real-world affordances, and alignment to state standards. More recent research found that, though most teachers would like to use games for learning, substantial barriers include cost, access to technology resources, and schools' emphasis on standardized test results (Millstone, 2012).

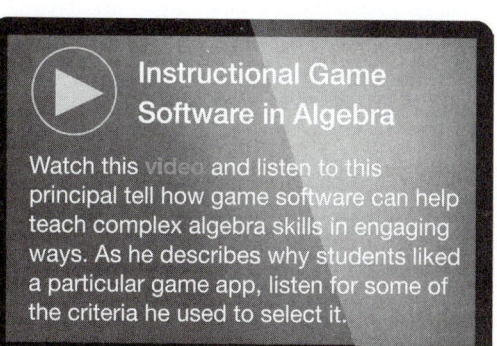

**Instructional Game Software in Algebra**

Watch this video and listen to this principal tell how game software can help teach complex algebra skills in engaging ways. As he describes why students liked a particular game app, listen for some of the criteria he used to select it.

## Using Instructional Games in Teaching

Instructional games can serve several classroom needs. Follow the integration strategies and guidelines shown in Table 3.5 to make best use of instructional games.

## TABLE 3.5 Integration Strategies and Guidelines for Using Instructional Games

| Strategies | Explanation |
|---|---|
| In place of worksheets and exercises | As with drill-and-practice software, teachers can use games to help students acquire automatic recall of prerequisite skills. |
| As a reward | The single most common use of games is to reward good work. However, using games as rewards disregards the power of games to be teaching software and limits them to use as a behaviorist tool. Some schools actually bar games from classrooms for fear that they overemphasize the need for students to be entertained. |
| To teach "noncognitive skills" | Some newer games are designed especially to teach skills such as attention and perseverance, which are useful across content areas. |
| To teach cooperative group working skills | Like simulations, many instructional games serve as the basis for or introduction to group work. In addition, some games can be played collaboratively over the Internet (e.g., via an Internet-enabled game console). A game's competitive qualities can present opportunities for competition among groups. |

| Guidelines | Explanation |
|---|---|
| Use sparingly | Use games sparingly so that students learn effectively from them and continue to stay motivated by the game play. |
| Involve all students | Make sure that girls and boys alike are participating and that all students have a meaningful role. |
| Emphasize the content-area skills first | Before students begin playing, make sure they know the relationship between game rules and content-area (e.g., math) rules. Students should recognize which rules they will be using in their later work and which are merely part of the game environment. (See Technology Integration Example 3.4.) |

# TECHNOLOGY INTEGRATION

## Example 3.4

**TITLE:** Do I Have a Right?

**CONTENT AREA/TOPIC:** Civics—The Bill of Rights

**GRADE LEVELS:** 8–10

**ISTE STANDARDS•S:** Standard 4—Critical Thinking, Problem Solving, and Decision Making

**CCSS:** ELA-LITERACY.RH.6-8.3 ELA-LITERACY.RH.9-10.6, ELA-LITERACY.RH.11-12.5

**NCSS:** Theme 6-Power, Authority, and Governance

**DESCRIPTION:** Using a packet of materials on the Bill of Rights, the teacher reads a scenario in which the world has been destroyed and a "Pamphlet of Protections" must be created to define the rights people will have. Students identify their "top ten" rights from a checklist and the teacher polls the class to see which were selected. The teacher compares this task to the challenge that framers of the Constitution faced and reviews each of the Bill of Rights they created. After review and discussion, students apply what they learned with "Do I Have a Right?" online game software. They become lawyers who must decide whether potential clients "have a right." The more clients they serve, the more cases they win, and the faster the law firm grows.

*SOURCE:* Based on ideas from lesson plan at the iCivics free lesson plans website.

 **TECHNOLOGY LEARNING CHECK**
Complete **TLC 3.5** to review what you have learned from reading this section about instructional game software concepts.

# PROBLEM-SOLVING TEACHING FUNCTIONS

Although simulations and instructional games are often used to help teach problem-solving skills, **problem-solving software** is designed especially for this purpose. Problem-solving software functions may focus on fostering component skills in or approaches to general problem-solving ability, or provide opportunities to practice solving various kinds of content-area problems. According to Mayes (1992), problem solving is cognitive processing directed at achieving a goal when the solution is not obvious. One way to think about problem solving is through three of its most important components: recognition of a goal (an opportunity for solving a problem), a process (a sequence of physical activities or operations), and mental activity (cognitive operations to pursue a solution).

Though most problem-solving literature focuses on skills in solving mathematical problems, research on problem solving covers a wide variety of desired component behaviors. The literature mentions such varied subskills for problem solving as metacognition, observing, recalling information, sequencing, analyzing, finding and organizing information, inferring, predicting outcomes, making analogies, and formulating ideas. Although there are many opinions about the proper role of instructional software in fostering these abilities, there seem to be two main approaches:

- **Content-area problem-solving skills**—Some problem-solving software focuses on teaching content-area skills, primarily in mathematics and science. For example, Seo and Bryant (2012) report using a program called Math Explorer to help students learn a systematic approach to solving mathematics word problems. Others are what might be called problem-solving "environments." These complex, multifaceted packages offer a variety of tools that allow students to create solutions to science-related problems presented by a scenario. One of these is like Alien Rescue developed by the University of Texas (edb.utexas.edu/alien-rescue), which helps students solve problems in science environments. Still others provide opportunities to practice solving specific kinds of math or science problems.

- **Content-free problem-solving skills**—Some educators feel that general problem-solving ability can be taught directly by specific instruction and practice in its component strategies and subskills (e.g., recalling facts, breaking a problem into a sequence of steps, or predicting outcomes). Others suggest placing students in problem-solving environments and, with some coaching and guidance, letting them develop their own heuristics for attacking and solving problems.

The purposes of the two views overlap somewhat, but the first is directed more toward motivating students to attack problems and to recognize problem solving as an integral part of everyday life, while the second aims to help students practice component skills in specific kinds of problem solving.

## Selecting Good Problem-Solving Software

Qualities to look for in good problem-solving software depend on the purpose of the software. In general, problem formats should be interesting and challenging, and software should have a clear link to developing a specific problem-solving ability. Software documentation should state clearly which specific problem-solving skills students will learn and how the software fosters them. See Figure 3.5 for examples of problem-solving software and a summary of problem-solving features.

## Benefits of Problem-Solving Software

Research and practice indicates that problem-solving software can help students in at least three different ways:

- **Promotes visualization in mathematics problem solving.** Research results in mathematical problem-solving skills tend to support the hypothesis that software, such as Geometer's

## FIGURE 3.5 Problem Solving Software Functions in Brief

| Description of Problem Solving Software | | |
|---|---|---|
| **Characteristics** | **Criteria for Effective Problem Solving Software** | **Benefits** |
| Four different types:<br>1. Tools to help students solve problems<br>2. Environments that challenge students to create solutions to complex problems<br>3. Problems to help develop component problem-solving skills (e.g., recalling facts, following a sequence)<br>4. Opportunities for practice in solving content-area problems | • Challenging, interesting formats<br>• Clear links to developing specific problem-solving skills or abilities | • Challenging activities motivate students to spend more time on the topic<br>• Prevents inert knowledge by illustrating situations in which skills apply |
| *Memory Challenge*<br>**by The Critical Thinking Co.** | *Sequences*<br>**by The Tool Factory, Inc.** | *Crazy Machines*<br>**by Viva Media LLC** |
| Practice exercises to improve visual memory skills required for reading and math activities 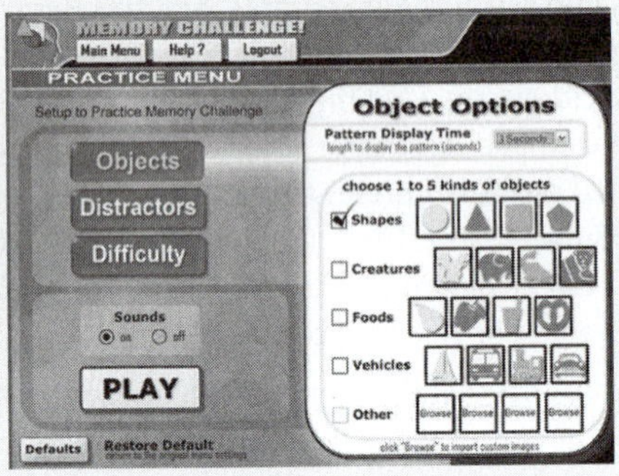 | Text-free practice in teaching sequencing by ordering events in a correct sequence  | Teaches how to recognize math situations in word problems and use graphic organizers to understand and plan solutions 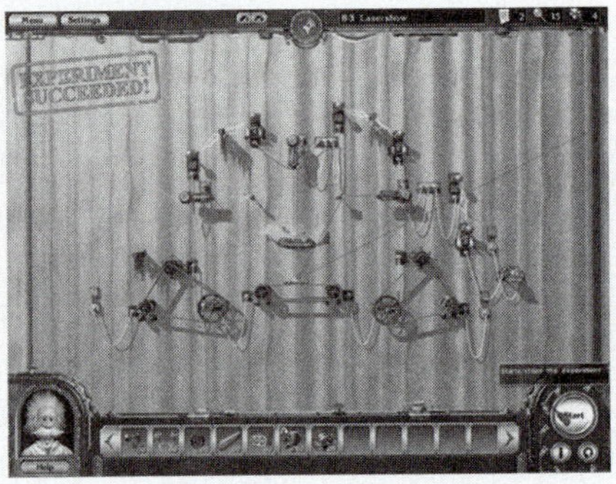 |

*Source:* Memory Challenge reprinted by permission of the Critical Thinking Co. (http://www.criticalthinking.com); Sequences is a Sherston Software product (http://www.sherstonamerica.com), reprinted by permission; Crazy Machines 2: The Wacky Contraptions Game © FAKT (http:// www.viva-media.com) published by Viva Media, reprinted by permission.

Sketchpad and other software that rely on graphical displays, helps students visualize abstract concepts and, thus, better understand how to solve problems that call for those concepts. For example, Salden, Koedinger, Renkl, Alevne, and McLaren (2010) used a program called Cognitive Tutors that "supports problem solving while . . . providing prompts for problem sub-goals, step-based immediate feedback, and context-sensitive hints" (p. 379).

• **Improves interest and motivation.** Students are more likely to practice solving problems in activities they find interesting and motivating. Some educators also feel that students will become more active, spontaneous problem solvers if they experience success in their initial problem-solving efforts. For example, in reporting research results with problem-based environments such as the Alien Rescue software, Pedersen (2003) found that these environments can be highly motivational, although Samsonov, Pedersen, and Hill (2006) also found that this kind of software was more motivational to higher-achieving students.

• **Prevents inert knowledge.** Content-area problem-solving environments, such as Thinkport's Flossville Town Park and Windjammer Environmental Center, can make knowledge and skills more meaningful to students because they illustrate how and where information applies to actual problems. Students learn both the knowledge and its application at the same time. Also, students gain opportunities to discover concepts themselves, which they frequently find more motivating than simply being told concepts.

## Limitations and Problems Related to Problem-Solving Software

Problem-solving software packages are among the most popular of all software functions; however, the following issues are still of concern to educators:

- **Names versus skills.** Software packages use many terms to describe problem solving, and their exact meanings are not always clear. Terms that appear in software catalogs as synonyms for problem solving include *thinking skills, critical thinking, higher level thinking, higher-order cognitive outcomes, reasoning, use of logic,* and *decision making.* In light

**TABLE 3.6** Integration Strategies and Guidelines for Using Problem Solving

| Strategies | Explanation |
|---|---|
| **To teach component skills in problem-solving strategies** | Many problem-solving packages provide good, hands-on experience with one or more of the skills required to use a problem-solving approach. These include identifying and following a logical sequence, identifying relevant information to solve problems, not jumping to conclusions too quickly, and remembering relevant information. |
| **To provide support in solving problems** | Some software packages are specifically designed to scaffold students as they practice solving complex problems. For example, Geometer's Sketchpad helps students draw objects and investigate their mathematical properties. |
| **To encourage group problem solving** | Some software provides environments that lend themselves to solving problems in small groups. For example, software at the Thinkport site provides opportunities for collaborative problem solving. |
| **To provide practice in solving problems** | Some packages provide opportunities to practice applying problem solving in ways that make it more likely the skills will transfer to real-life situations. |
| **Strategies** | **Explanation** |
| **Guidelines for directed teaching** | The following six steps can help you integrate problem-solving software for directed teaching: <br><br>1. Identify problem-solving skills or general capabilities to build or foster skills in:<br> • solving one or more kinds of content-area problems (e.g., building algebra equations);<br> • using a scientific approach to problem solving (i.e., identifying the problem, posing hypotheses, planning a systematic approach); and<br> • identifying the components of problem solving, such as following a sequence of steps or recalling facts.<br>2. Decide on an activity or a series of activities that will help teach the desired skills.<br>3. Examine software to locate materials that closely match the desired abilities, remembering not to judge capabilities on the basis of vendor claims alone.<br>4. Determine where the software fits into the teaching sequence (for example, to introduce the skill and gain attention, as a practice activity after demonstrating problem solving, or both).<br>5. Demonstrate the software and the steps to follow in solving problems.<br>6. Build in transfer activities and make students aware of the skills they are using in the software. |
| **Guidelines for constructivist teaching** | The following seven steps can help you integrate problem-solving software according to constructivist models:<br><br>1. Allow students sufficient time to explore and interact with the software, but provide some structure in the form of directions, goals, a work schedule, and organized times for sharing and discussing results.<br>2. Vary the amount of direction and assistance provided, depending on each student's needs.<br>3. Promote a reflective learning environment; let students talk about the methods they use.<br>4. Stress thinking processes rather than correct answers.<br>5. Point out the relationship between software activities and other kinds of problem solving.<br>6. Let students work together in pairs or small groups.<br>7. For assessments, use alternatives to traditional paper-and-pencil tests. |

of this diversity of language, teachers must identify the skills that a software package addresses by looking at its activities. For example, for a software package that claims to teach inference skills, one would have to see how it defines *inference* by examining the tasks it presents, which may range from determining the next number in a sequence to using visual clues to predict a pattern.

- **Software claims versus effectiveness.** It would be difficult to find a software catalog that did not claim that its products foster problem solving, yet few publishers of software packages that purport to teach specific problem-solving skills have data to support their claims. When students play a game that requires skills related to problem solving, they do not necessarily learn these skills. They may enjoy the game thoroughly—and even be successful at it—without learning any of the intended skills. Teachers may have to use problem-solving software themselves to confirm that it achieves the results they want.

- **Lack of skill transfer.** Although some educators feel that general problem-solving skills, such as inference and pattern recognition, will transfer to content-area skills, scant evidence supports this view. In the 1970s and 1980s, for example, many schools taught programming in mathematics classes under the hypothesis that the planning and sequencing skills required for programming would transfer to problem-solving skills in math. Research results never supported this hypothesis. In general, research tends to show that skill in one kind of problem solving will transfer primarily to similar kinds of problems that use the same solution strategies. Researchers have identified nothing like "general thinking skills," except in relation to intelligence (IQ) variables.

## Using Problem-Solving Software in Teaching

Problem-solving software can serve several classroom needs. This section describes integration strategies to meet each of these needs and offers guidelines and practical tips on how to integrate these strategies in the classroom. For an example of a problem-solving software that supports both directed and constructivist applications, see Technology Integration Example 3.5.

# TECHNOLOGY INTEGRATION

## Example 3.5

**TITLE:** Wait for a Date: Calculating Probability with Geometer's Sketchpad

**CONTENT AREA/TOPIC:** Mathematics—Precaluclus

**GRADE LEVELS:** 8–10

**ISTE STANDARDS•S:** Standard 4—Critical Thinking, Problem Solving, and Decision Making; Standard 6—Technology Operations and Concepts

**CCSS:** MATH.CONTENT.HSS.CP.A.1, CCSS.MATH.PRACTICE.MP5

**DESCRIPTION:** The teacher presents students with a scenario: "You and a friend arrange for a lunch date next week between 12:00 and 1:00 p.m. However, neither of you remembers the exact meeting time. Each of you arrives at a random time between 12:00 and 1:00 p.m. and waits exactly 10 minutes, then leaves if the other person has not come. Under these circumstances, what is the probability that you two will meet?" Students use a premade Sketchpad model (available at the Geometer's Sketchpad site) to gather sample data and, by viewing data as points in a plane, they uncover a geometric pattern that allows them to compute a precise probability. Sketchpad also supports activities called "black box tasks" for students with more sophisticated knowledge of the software. In these activities, students use the software to re-create a given figure or deduce underlying properties that two or more objects have in common.

*SOURCE:* Based on lesson plan idea at the Geometer's Sketchpad website.

**TECHNOLOGY LEARNING CHECK**
Complete TLC 3.6 to review what you have learned from reading this section about problem solving software concepts.

**Personalized learning systems (PLSs)** are computer-based management programs that (1) assess individual student learning needs using complex algorithms and collections of data across students, and (2) provide a customized instructional experience matched to each student. PLSs are an evolved form of an **Integrated Learning System (ILS)**, a product introduced in the early 1970s that provided assessment, instruction, and reports on student progress. Recent software developments have combined adaptive testing and databases of instructional strategies to enable systems that can personalize a given student's path through a topic based on his or her performance. The accountability emphasis that began with the No Child Left Behind Act of 2001 created a demand for products such as PLSs that can helps teachers assess needs and assign instructional solutions quickly and efficiently. PLSs vary widely in how they work, but three qualities are currently characteristic of all PLSs. Screenshots from two well-known PLS companies, Amplify and Knewton, are used as illustrations:

## FIGURE 3.6 Amplify Learning Map Showing Progress on CCSs in a Topic Area

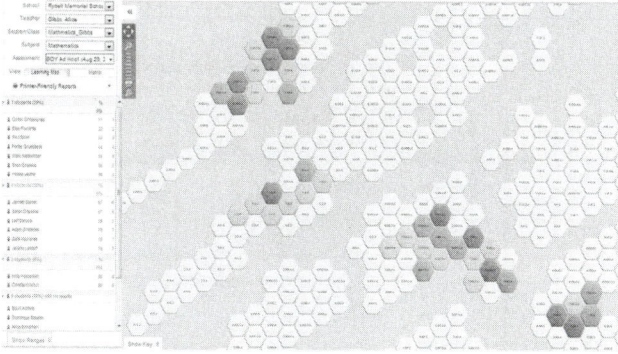

© 2014 Amplify Education

## FIGURE 3.7 Amplify Learning Map Detail by Common Core Standard

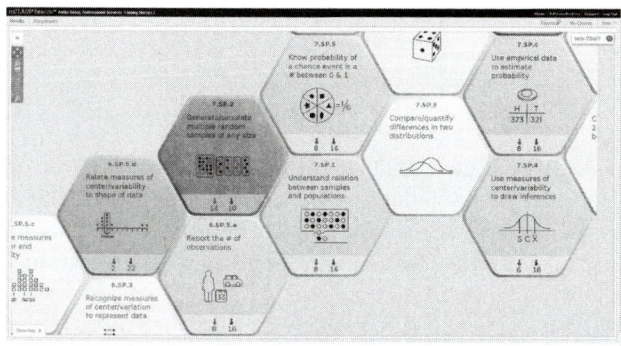

© 2014 Amplify Education

## FIGURE 3.8 Amplify Report on Progress by Student and Class

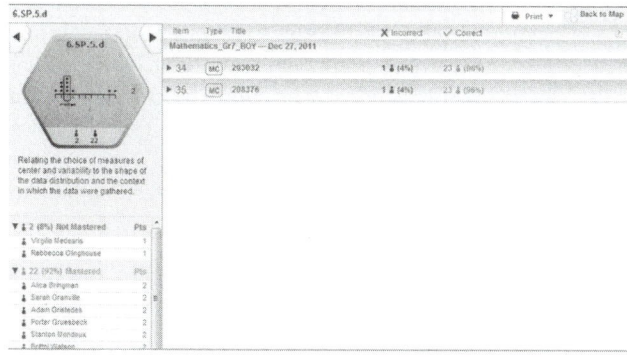

© 2014 Amplify Education

- **Adaptive assessment** – Adaptive assessment strategies are the heart of the PLS approach. Students use electronic devices (e.g., computers, tablet) to take tests in a given topic, and teachers get results that enable decisions on what to do next to support learning. For example, Figure 3.6 shows Amplify's report on progress in sixth and seventh grade probability and statistics standards. It displays results on a progression of skills by difficulty from lower left to upper right. Every skill is mapped by subject to the CCSs. The colors represent levels of mastery.

- **Curriculum matched to Common Core State Standards** – Each report the PLS generates ties to performance on the CCSS that most states have now adopted as their own. Figure 3.7 shows clusters of statistics and probability skills labeled by CCSS and color coded to show a class of strength in each standard. Green indicates that most students have mastered the standard; red indicates that it probably needs more instruction.

- **Reports on individual and group progress** – PLSs are able to give summary reports on progress by CCSS for any designated students. For example, Figure 3.8 illustrates individual and class progress on a specific CCSS, which helps teachers know which students have and have not mastered standards and make decisions on next instructional steps for the topic.

- **Multiple learning media** – Unlike ILSs, which provided all instruction in the same computer-based system, each PLS prescription sends students to a variety of materials, many online or electronic. However, the trend seems to be to place more students on digital curriculum to more easily track progress and integrate assessment and instructional solutions. Today's PLSs are often accessible on handheld devices such as tablets.

## Selecting PLSs

One way to ensure the appropriate use of PLSs is to have a careful, well-planned initial review and selection process that involves both teachers and school administrators. Since PLSs are a new way of thinking about assessment and curriculum, criteria for the selection process are usually based on the ease of implementation and the amount of company support and professional development offered, as well as how the PLS approach supports district and state priorities. See Figure 3.9 for examples of PLS products and a summary of PLS features.

# FIGURE 3.9 Personalized Learning System Functions in Brief

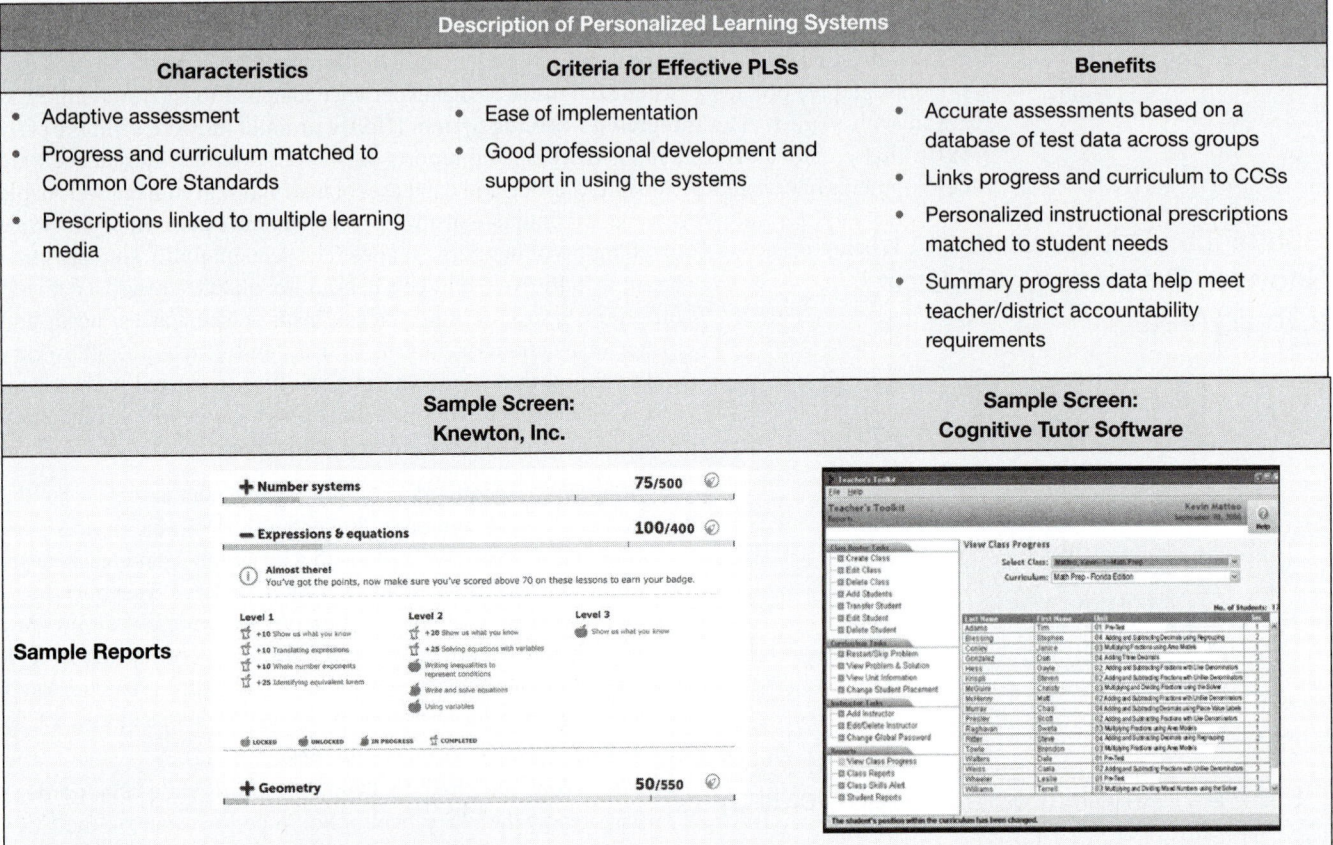

| Description of Personalized Learning Systems | | |
|---|---|---|
| **Characteristics** | **Criteria for Effective PLSs** | **Benefits** |
| • Adaptive assessment<br>• Progress and curriculum matched to Common Core Standards<br>• Prescriptions linked to multiple learning media | • Ease of implementation<br>• Good professional development and support in using the systems | • Accurate assessments based on a database of test data across groups<br>• Links progress and curriculum to CCSs<br>• Personalized instructional prescriptions matched to student needs<br>• Summary progress data help meet teacher/district accountability requirements |
| | **Sample Screen:**<br>**Knewton, Inc.** | **Sample Screen:**<br>**Cognitive Tutor Software** |

## Benefits of PLSs

PLSs are becoming popular in school districts for their ability to use a wealth of available data on student performance to produce personal learning solutions by CCSSs, as well as their ability to provide achievement information by student, teacher, class, or school. This approach to diagnosing and selecting materials targeted to learning needs frees teacher time for guiding student learning.

## Limitations and Problems Related to PLSs

Though we know a great deal about ILS impact, PLSs have a shorter track record. Studies of ILS impact have been carried out since they emerged in the 1970s. Initial research seemed promising, but large-scale studies using controlled experimental methods show no significant differences in achievement between classrooms using these systems and those using traditional materials and methods (U.S. Department of Education, 2010; Wijekumar, Hitchcock, Turner, Lei, & Peck, 2009).

Since large-scale research on PLS is lacking, Fletcher (2013) says that both proponents and critics of PLS are stating their cases. He says that learning proponents say that technology has enabled individualized instruction to be delivered to every student at an affordable cost, "to discard the factory model that has dominated Western education for the past two centuries" (p. 65). Critics, however, say that teachers already do the task of matching a student's strengths and weaknesses to appropriate strategies and materials. "Instead of delegating these tasks to computers, opponents say, we should be spending more on training, hiring and retaining good teachers" (p. 65).

**TECHNOLOGY LEARNING CHECK**

Complete TLC 3.7 to review what you have learned from reading this section about PLS concepts.

Monkey Business/Fotolia

The following questions may be used either for in-class, small-group discussions or may initiate discussions in blogs or online discussion boards:

1. The College Board has joined the American Chemical Society and the National Science Teachers Association in objecting to simulated lab software (e.g., online frog dissections, mixing chemicals) when used to replace in-class, hands-on labs. Read the ACS and NSTA statements and analyze the objections they voice. What evidence can you cite to support or refute their positions?

2. The perception that drill-and-practice software is a "drill and kill" activity is based on misuses of the practice activity. What are occasions in which drill and practice does and does not lead to better performance? Search for articles like the following and read for background: Jay Greene's (2010) article "False Claim on Drill and Kill" on the *Education Next* website; Mary Brabeck's article "Practice for Knowledge Acquisition (Not Drill and Kill)" on the American Psychological Association (APA) website; and the theories of E. D. Hirsch on various websites.

Chapter  **3**

# Summary

The following is a summary of the main points covered in this chapter.

1. **Introduction to instructional software**
   - Instructional software (a.k.a., computer-assisted instruction or courseware) are computer programs that were designed specifically to deliver instruction or assist with the delivery of instruction on a topic.
   - Functions fulfilled by instructional software include: drill-and-practice, tutorial, simulation, instructional game, or problem-solving programs.
   - Programming languages such as Logo that were designed specifically to teach problem-solving concepts are also considered a kind of hybrid instructional software. Today, programming languages in addition to Logo are used to teach STEM skills that include: systems-thinking, interdisciplinary thinking, user-centered design, specialist language, and meta-level reflection.
   - Websites have emerged to help educators select well-designed instructional software products aligned to CCSS. These include: edshelf, Graphite, PowerMyLearning, EduStar, and Learning List.

2. **Drill-and-practice software functions**—These are programs that provide exercises in which students work example items, usually one at a time, and receive feedback on their correctness.
   - Types of drill and practice include flash card activities, chart fill-in activities, branching drills, and extensive feedback activities.
   - Effective drill and practice includes: answer judging, appropriate feedback for correct and incorrect answers, and characteristics tailored to young learners.
   - Benefits include immediate feedback, increased motivations, and saving teacher time.
   - Limitations and/or problems include instructional misuses and criticism by constructivists.
   - Integration strategies for drill-and-practice software are to supplement or replace worksheets and homework exercises and to prepare for tests.

3. **Tutorial software functions**—These are programs that provide an entire instructional sequence on a topic, similar to a teacher's classroom instruction.
   - Types of tutorials include linear and branching activities.
   - Effective tutorials include extensive interactivity, thorough user control, appropriate pedagogy, adequate answer-judging and feedback capabilities, appropriate graphics and/or video, and adequate recordkeeping.
   - Benefits include all the same benefits of drill and practice, as well as self-paced instruction.
   - Limitations and/or problems include criticism by constructivists, lack of well-designed products, and the fact that they reflect only one instructional approach.

- Integration strategies for tutorial software are to provide alternative learning strategies and to give instruction when teachers are unavailable.

4. **Simulation software functions**—These are programs that provide computerized models of a real or imagined system that is designed to teach how the system works.
   - Types of simulations include: products that teach about something, which include physical and iterative simulations; and products that teach how to do something, which include procedural and situational simulations.
   - Simulations are most effective when they are used in conjunction with hands-on activities.
   - Benefits include their abilities to compress time, slow down processes, get students involved, make experimentation safe, make the impossible possible, save money and other resources, allow repetition with variations, and allow observation of complex processes.
   - Limitations and/or problems include: Criticism of virtual lab software, accuracy of models, and misuses of simulations.
   - Integration strategies for simulation software are: to use in place of or as supplements to lab experiments, role-playing, or field trips; to introduce and/or clarify a new topic; to foster exploration and process learning; and to encourage cooperation and group work.

5. **Instructional game functions**—These are programs that add game-like rules and/or competition to learning activities.
   - Types of instructional games are the same as for drills and simulations, dependent on the game format.
   - Effective instructional games include appealing formats and activities; instructional value; reasonable physical dexterity; and social, societal, and cultural considerations.
   - Benefits are the same as for drill or simulation function, as well as offering highly motivating formats.
   - Limitations and/or problems include learning versus having fun, confusion of game rules and real-life rules, inefficient learning, and classroom barriers.
   - Integration strategies for simulation software are to use in place of worksheets and exercises, to teach cooperative group working skills, and to use as a reward.

6. **Problem-solving functions**—Software designed especially for the purpose of teaching component skills in problem solving.
   - Types of problem-solving programs include programs to teach content areas as well as programs to teach content-free problem-solving skills.
   - Effective problem-solving programs are interesting and challenging, and have a clear link to developing a specific problem-solving ability
   - Benefits include abilities to promote visualization in mathematics problem solving, improve interest and motivation, and prevent inert knowledge
   - Limitations and/or problems revolve around names versus skills, software claims versus effectiveness, and lack of skill transfer.
   - Integration strategies for simulation software are to teach component skills in problem-solving strategies, to provide support in solving problems, and to encourage group problem solving.

7. **Personalized learning systems (PLSs)**—These are systems that test students, summarize progress data, and help teachers build provide personal learning strategies for groups of students.
   - Components of PLSs include adaptive assessment, curriculum matched to Common Core Standards, and multiple learning media.
   - Selecting PLSs requires a careful, well-planned initial review and selection process that involves both teachers and school administrators.
   - Benefits include their ability to use data to produce personal learning solutions; provide achievement information by student, teacher, class, or school; and free teacher time for guiding student learning.
   - Limitations and problems for PLSs include the fact that research on their effects is lacking.

# TECHNOLOGY INTEGRATION **WORKSHOP**

## 1. APPLY WHAT YOU LEARNED

To apply the concepts and skills you've read about throughout this chapter, go to the Chapter 3 Technology Application Activity.

## 2. TECHNOLOGY INTEGRATION LESSON PLANNING: PART 1—EVALUATING AND CREATING LESSON PLANS

Complete the following exercise using the sample lesson plans found on any lesson planning site that you find on the Internet.

**a.** Locate lesson ideas—Identify three lesson plans that focus on any of the tools or strategies you learned about in this chapter. For example:

- Drill and practice software
- Tutorial software
- Simulation software
- Instructional game software
- Problem solving software
- Personalized Learning Systems

**b.** Evaluate the lessons—Use the Technology Lesson Plan Evaluation Checklist to evaluate each of the lessons you found.

**c.** Create your own lesson—After you have reviewed and evaluated some sample lessons, create one of your own using a lesson plan format of your choice (or one your instructor gives you). Be sure the lesson focuses on one of the technologies or strategies discussed in this chapter.

## 3. TECHNOLOGY INTEGRATION LESSON PLANNING: PART 2—IMPLEMENTING THE TIP MODEL

Review how to implement the TIP model in your classroom by doing the following activities with the lesson you created in the Technology Integration Lesson Planning exercise above.

**a.** Describe the Phase 1—Planning activities you would do to use this lesson in your classroom:

- What is the relative advantage of using the technology(ies) in this lesson?
- Do you have resources and skills you need to carry it out?

**b.** Describe the Phase 2—Implementation activities you would do to use this lesson in your classroom:

- What are the objectives of the lesson plan?
- How will you assess your students' accomplishment of the objectives?
- What integration strategies are used in this lesson plan?
- How would you prepare the learning environment?

**c.** Describe the Phase 3—Evaluation/Revision activities you would do to use this lesson in your classroom: What strategies and/or instruments would you use to evaluate the success of this lesson in your classroom, in order to determine revision needs?

**d.** Add lesson descriptors—Create descriptors for your new lesson (e.g., grade level, content and topic areas, technologies used, ISTE standards, 21st Century Learning standards).

**e.** Save your new lesson—Save your lesson plan with all its descriptors and TIP model notes.

## 4. FOR YOUR TEACHING PORTFOLIO—add the following to your teaching portfolio:

- Lesson plan evaluations, lesson plans, and products you created above.
- Products of your group's Hot Topic Debates.
- Products of your group's Collaborate, Discuss, Reflect online or in-class activities.

# 4 Technology Tools for 21st Century Teaching
## THE BASIC SUITE

## Learning Outcomes

After reading this chapter and completing the learning activities, you should be able to:

1. Analyze given instructional or productivity needs to identify which of the "basic three" software tools would be most appropriate to meet the need. (ISTE Standards•T 2, 3)

2. Select word processing uses and integration strategies that take advantage of the software's unique features and characteristics and reflect what we have learned from research and practice about how it can meet instructional and productivity needs. (ISTE Standards•T 2, 3)

3. Select spreadsheet uses and integration strategies that take advantage of the software's unique features and characteristics and reflect what we have learned from research and practice about how it can meet instructional and productivity needs. (ISTE Standards•T 2, 3)

4. Select presentation software uses and integration strategies that take advantage of the software's unique features and characteristics and reflect what we have learned from research and practice about how it can meet instructional and productivity needs. (ISTE Standards•T 2, 3)

Vladgrin/Shutterstock

# TECHNOLOGY INTEGRATION IN ACTION: CAN YOU AFFORD YOUR DREAM CAR?

**GRADE LEVEL: Middle to high school • CONTENT AREA/TOPIC: Applied math skills • LENGTH OF TIME: One week**

## PHASE 1   ANALYSIS OF LEARNING AND TEACHING NEEDS

Lisa Turay/Shutterstock

### Step 1: Determine relative advantage.

Whenever Ms. Kiley teaches her applied mathematics class for grades 9 through 12, she has teenagers of many ages and ability levels. She wants all of them to have experience applying math skills to real problems they will encounter in their daily lives. She tries to include projects that are interesting and relevant to all of them and that require a combination of research, mathematical problem solving, and production skills. One activity she found that meets all her criteria is called, "Can You Afford Your Dream Car?" She selected this project from a list she found on the Internet and felt it would be a much better way to teach these concepts than she had used before. Almost all of her students are beginning drivers and are interested in car purchases, and, so that they can do calculations quickly and focus on the underlying concepts (e.g., the relationship among down payment, interest rate, and loan period), she would create a template with spreadsheet software for students to use. Each student does Internet research to locate the best price on a car he or she would like to buy. Then they enter the information into the spreadsheet template and present their findings to the class, answering various questions about loan amounts and car payments.

### Step 2: Assess Required Resources and Skills.

Ms. Kiley had learned about spreadsheets in a workshop held by her local professional organization, and she learned how to create the template and transfer it to the students' computers. Then she worked with the spreadsheet in order to get proficient enough with the software to help her students. Each of the lab computers had the basic suite of tool software on them.

## PHASE 2   PLANNING FOR INTEGRATION

### Step 3: Decide on outcomes, objectives, and assessments.

To keep her students on track and to make sure they learn what she has in mind for this project, Ms. Kiley created outcomes, objectives, and assessments to measure their research, problem-solving, and production outcomes. The outcomes, objectives, and assessments are:

Outcome:  Select a car to purchase and complete background research on it.
Objective:  Each student completes all required steps to select a car to "buy"; completes a list of the activities required to research and locate comparison information about its price, loan, and features; and enters the information into a spreadsheet template.
Assessment:  A checklist with points for each required activity.

Outcome:  Do mathematical problem solving.
Objective:  Each student uses the spreadsheet to answer a series of questions about the amount of the car loan and the payments at various interest rates and time periods.
Assessment:  Worksheet questions with points for each one; 80% is passing.

Outcome:  Do a final report.
Objective:  Each student achieves a rubric score of at least 90% on a word-processed report that describes and illustrates the car, tells why it is a cost-effective purchase, and includes a spreadsheet (based on the template provided) showing how he or she will pay for it.
Assessment:  Rubric on report quality and accuracy.

### Step 4: Design integration strategies.

Ms. Kiley wanted to make sure each student had hands-on experience with the research and production activities and was able to master each of the skills she outlined, so she decided to make this an individual activity. She designed the following activity sequence to carry out the project:

Day 1: Introduce the project. Encourage students to talk about cars they have already purchased or are considering purchasing, and ask them to describe how they went about selecting one and, if they actually bought it, how they decided on a loan amount, term, and payment size. Demonstrate the spreadsheet template, and show students how the payments and total amount paid change automatically depending on the loan amount, interest, and period entered into the spreadsheet. Review the project checklists and rubrics as well as the timeframe for completing the work. Introduce the problems students are to work using their completed spreadsheets.

Day 2: Take students to the computer lab, and demonstrate some of the sites they may want to use to check out makes and models of cars. Also, demonstrate once again how to use the spreadsheet template. Have students do some calculations with the spreadsheet, and answer any questions they have. Let them begin researching cars they want to buy.

Day 3: In the computer lab, allow students to continue their research. Some students may have completed research on their home computers. These students can begin work on their final reports or complete the problem-solving exercise.

Day 4: In the computer lab, allow students to continue work on their reports and the exercises with the spreadsheet template.

Day 5: Back in the classroom, let selected students present their "dream car purchase." Use the classroom computer workstation to show an online example of the car model and the dealer from which they would buy it. Students who need more time can go to the computer lab.

Day 6: Students turn in their projects and exercises.

### Step 5: Prepare instructional environment.

The first time Ms. Kiley taught this project, she had to create the spreadsheet template and handouts of the checklists and rubric for students to use. For subsequent times, she had to do the following:

Handouts: Ms. Kiley made copies of the project requirements and grading criteria sheets (i.e., checklists and rubrics) to hand out to students. She also made sure these handouts were online at her classroom website as PDF files, so students could download additional copies if needed.

Software skills: Although Ms. Kiley demonstrated how to use the spreadsheet template, she checked with students individually as they worked in the lab to make sure they knew how to enter the required information in the cells and could copy and paste their completed worksheet into their report.

Computer scheduling: Ms. Kiley made sure she could have her whole class in the computer lab for the three days she would need it; she also made sure individual students could come to the lab for the two subsequent days to complete their research and reports.

Template copies: Ms. Kiley made sure that a copy of the template was on the classroom website so that students could download it to their own computers at school or even at home, if they liked.

## PHASE 3 POST-INSTRUCTION ANALYSIS AND REVISIONS

### Step 6: Analyze results.

Each time she taught the project, Ms. Kiley reviewed students' work and asked for their comments on how she could make the project even more meaningful. She quickly realized that students who did not have a home computer were at a disadvantage in completing the work in a timely way. She found that, although students usually completed their spreadsheets correctly and could answer questions about them, their reports varied considerably in quality.

### Step 7: Make revisions.

In light of the fact that not all students had a home computer with the required software, Ms. Kiley made a special effort to help these students during their time in the lab and made sure they knew they could have additional lab time outside class or before or after school to use the classroom workstation. Also, since students' written reports did not always meet required criteria, she decided to consider other ways of having students present their work.

# CHAPTER 4 **BIG IDEAS OVERVIEW**

Before you begin reading the rest of this chapter, listen to the Chapter 4 Big Ideas Overview. It will give you a two-minute audio overview of main concepts to look for and help prepare you to work through information and exercises to achieve this chapter's outcomes.

# INTRODUCTION TO THE BASIC SOFTWARE TOOL SUITE

In education and, indeed, in most other areas of modern society, three of the most widely used software support tools are word processing, spreadsheet, and presentation programs. **Word processing** software allows production and revision of text-based information but also allows adding many kinds of graphic elements to text products. **Spreadsheets** are programs designed to allow storage of numerical data by row–column positions and enable calculations and other manipulations of the data. **Presentation software** is a program that enables both text and graphical information to be organized and displayed as a set of slides. For many professionals in education and other fields, these tools have become an indispensable part of their daily work. They are frequently sold as **software suites**, separate tool programs placed in the same package and designed to work well together. Teachers choose them not only because they have qualities that aid classroom instruction and help make classroom time more productive, but also because they give students experience with 21st-century tools that they will see again and again in their workplaces.

## Why Use Software Tools?

Depending on the capabilities of the tool and the needs of the situation, these programs can offer several benefits:

- **Improved productivity**—Getting organized, producing instructional materials, and accomplishing paperwork tasks all go much faster when software tools are used. Using a technology tool to do these tasks can free up valuable time that can be rechanneled toward working with students or designing learning activities.

- **Improved appearance**—Software tools help teachers and students produce polished-looking materials that resemble the work of professional designers. The quality of classroom products is limited only by the talents and skills of the teachers and students using the tools. Students appreciate receiving attractive-looking materials and find it rewarding and challenging to produce handsome products of their own.

- **Improved accuracy**—Software tools make it easier to keep precise, accurate records of events and student accomplishments. More accurate information can support better instructional decisions about curriculum and student activities.

- **More support for interaction and collaboration**—Software tools have capabilities that promote interaction and collaboration among students, allowing input from several people at once. These qualities can encourage creative, cooperative group-learning activities. (For hints on making sure these powerful tools are available to all students, see the Adapting for Special Needs feature.)

## Overview of Uses for the "Basic Three" Software Tools

Since the early days of microcomputers, word processing and spreadsheet programs have served as two of the most basic components in the teacher's "technology toolkit." **Database software**, a program that allows information to be collected and organized to allow easy retrieval through keyword searching, used to be one of the basic programs. Though still used in education and elsewhere, it is not typically used as part of the basic suite anymore. Instead,

# Adapting for Special Needs

## Word Processing and Other Basic Software Tools

**W**ord processing skills are expected of all students across all subjects and grades. However, some students with disabilities have difficulty with this task because of physical, sensory, or cognitive impairments that interfere with written expression. In order to support struggling writers, educators may use tools like the following that encourage written expression for diverse learners:

• Clicker Writer (available at the Crick Software website)—A word processor that lets students click on letters, words, or short phrases to send into the word processor, so they can write sentences without using the keyboard. Ideal for students with autism, intellectual disabilities, or learning disabilities because of the visual supports.

• Co: Writer (at the Don Johnston website)—A word prediction program that helps students who have illegible handwriting, poor phonetic spelling, a physical disability that makes typing difficult, or difficulty translating thoughts into writing. Ideal for students with learning disabilities or physical disabilities.

• Picture It (at the SunCastle Technology website)—Allows teachers to create picture-assisted reading materials to help struggling readers and writers. Ideal for young children, second language learners, and students with intellectual disabilities.

• Scholastic Keys (formerly called Max's Toolbox) (Available at the Tom Snyder, Inc. website)—Gives elementary students an early introduction to using Microsoft Office by providing a kid-friendly interface for Word, Excel, and PowerPoint. Ideal for young children, second language learners, and students with intellectual disabilities.

*—Contributed by Dave Edyburn*

presentation programs have emerged in its place. As Table 4.1 shows, each of these programs performs specific functions and each helps support specific productivity and teaching/learning activities. However, the three programs are usually designed to work together. For example, in the Technology Integration in Action Example at the beginning of this chapter, a student completes a spreadsheet that demonstrates a mathematical concept (loan terms), and then he or she inserts this spreadsheet into a word-processed report or presentation.

**Overview of productivity uses.** These three software products are often referred to as the "basic productivity tools," because they were among the first such tools to be designed to save time on clerical types of tasks and because they are now the ones that software companies such as Microsoft most often include in their software suites. In schools, word processing is the most frequently used of the three for productivity purposes, since teachers and students employ it across all subject areas whenever they need to do typed work, such as taking notes or completing a composition or report. Spreadsheet software also enhances teacher and student productivity by allowing more efficient work with numbers, and presentation software helps them organize and communicate complex information more quickly as slides or frames.

**Overview of instructional uses.** Word processing is used instructionally primarily to support English and foreign language exercises, such as learning vocabulary and punctuation.

## TABLE 4.1 An Overview of the "Basic Three" Software Tools

| Software Tool | Software Functions | Sample Products |
|---|---|---|
| **Word processing**<br>Example: Microsoft Word | Creates documents consisting of pages with text and graphics | Student compositions, poetry, and reports; flyers; simple newsletters; letters |
| **Spreadsheet**<br>Example: Microsoft Excel | Puts numerical information in row–column format; allows quick calculations and recalculations | Budgets, checkbooks, gradebooks, illustrations of mathematics concepts |
| **Presentation**<br>Example: Microsoft PowerPoint | Displays text and graphics (with or without audio and/or) in a slide show | Teacher demonstrations and support for lectures, student projects, book reports, tutorials, and practice items |

Spreadsheets are used most often for demonstrations in mathematics, science, and business education areas. They also support instructional activities such as science experiments or social studies surveys. Presentation software has become especially popular in business and journalism to show students how to design graphics and other media that communicate concepts clearly and persuasively. Look at the Top Ten feature for good ideas on how to integrate these basic tools into classroom instruction.

## Recent Developments in Software Tools

Although software tools have been in existence for many years, they are constantly being updated with new features and capabilities. The following developments have made these tools even more useful in the classroom:

- **Web-based collaboration tools**—There has been a surge of software tools that are now available via the Internet, and many are free of charge. **Google Docs**, for instance, is a tool that provides users access to online programs for word processing, spreadsheets, and presentations. The site offers easy storage and sorting of documents in a "cloud computing" environment that allows for sharing of documents among multiple users.

- **Open-source software**—Open-source software, computer software whose source code is made available in the public domain and that permits users to use, change, and improve the software and to redistribute it in modified or unmodified form, is also becoming more popular. Open-source alternatives to many of the most popular programs are now available. See the Open Source Options feature for free productivity software sites.

- **Mobile apps**—All of the basic software tools are now available on tablets and handheld devices. This portable format makes them easily accessible and flexible to use for both

# OPEN SOURCE
## OPTIONS for Software Tools from the Basic Suite

| TYPES | FREE SOURCES |
|---|---|
| **Suites** (all tool software in one site) | Feng Office (formerly OpenGoo): fengoffice.com<br>GNOME Office: live.gnome.org/GnomeOffice<br>Google Docs: docs.google.com<br>NeoOffice: neooffice.org<br>Open Office: openoffice.org<br>Simple Groupware: simple-groupware.de |
| **Word processing only** | AbiWord: abisource.com<br>Writer: why.openoffice.org/images/writer-big.png<br>Zoho Writer: writer.zoho.com |
| **Spreadsheet only** | Calc: why.openoffice.org/images/calc-big.png<br>Gnumeric: projects.gnome.org/gnumeric |
| **Presentation** | Ease: live.gnome.org/Ease/0.1<br>Prezi: prezi.com/ |

teachers and students. Since these basic software tools have been transferred to hand-held format, the devices themselves have become even more functional for school and classroom use.

- **Web-enabled features**—All of the basic software tools now allow insertion of "live" Web page links in documents, and most allow documents to be saved in **Hypertext Markup Language (HTML)**, the programming language that creates Web pages, or in other web page formats or as **portable document files (PDFs)**. This makes it even easier to connect documents to web page resources that embellish or add to the document's content. For example, students may include links in a project report to some of the resources they consulted during their research.

- **Better file-exchange compatibility**—In the early days of software tools, programs were often incompatible. That is, **files**, or products created in one program, could not be opened in another program. Incompatibility was especially problematic between programs on Macintosh and Windows (PC) computers. This problem limited file sharing and hindered collaborative work, since people often had different **computer platforms** or types of computer operating systems (e.g., Macintosh vs. Windows) and tool programs. Today's software tools, both online and on a local computer, are designed to be much more compatible across programs and platforms, making it much easier for teachers and students to transfer documents and to work together on projects.

- **Software suites**—Because it is usually cheaper to buy several tools as a package rather than separately, tool functions are increasingly used as parts of **software suites**, which combine several functions such as word processing, spreadsheet, database, and graphics in the same package. There are software suites for all platforms. Apple developed the iWork suite for use on all Apple hardware; it includes Pages for word processing, Keynote for presentations, and Numbers for a spreadsheet. Similarly, Microsoft Office is a software suite for both Macintosh and Windows-based systems and includes Microsoft Word, Microsoft Excel, and Microsoft PowerPoint.

**TECHNOLOGY LEARNING CHECK**
Complete **TLC 4.1** to review what you have learned from reading this section about the basic software tool suite.

## USING WORD PROCESSING SOFTWARE IN TEACHING AND LEARNING

Word processing programs allow people to produce typed documents on a computer screen. Although the lines between word processing and desktop publishing have become increasingly blurred, the programs still differ in the way they produce documents. Word processing programs essentially produce documents as a stream of text, whereas desktop publishing software produces them as individual pages. Despite this difference, most word processing programs allow at least some desktop publishing capabilities, such as inserting text boxes and graphics at any location on a page. Table 4.2 summarizes word processing features.

### The Impact of Word Processing in Education

Perhaps no other technology resource has had as great an impact on education as word processing. This section reviews the reasons teachers use this software tool and the research that has been done to confirm its impact. Also see Figure 4.1 for an illustration of a word processing template that students could use to do a sample Civil War "daily newspaper," labeled with word processing capabilities teachers and students find most useful.

**Why teachers use word processing.** Not only does word processing offer high versatility and flexibility, it also is "model-free" instructional software—that is, it reflects no

# TABLE 4.2 A Summary of Word Processing Features

| Feature Categories/General Benefits | Description of Features and Specific Benefits |
|---|---|
| **Basic features** save time writing text and make changing text easier and more flexible. | **Save documents for later use.** Documents saved to disc can be changed without reentering text.<br>• Rich Text Format (RTF) removes all or most formatting commands so other word processors can read the file.<br>• PDF format allows files to be read as formatted documents with Adobe Acrobat Reader.<br>• HTML format allows documents to be placed on the Internet.<br><br>**Erase and insert.** Allows easy insertion of additional letters, spaces, lines, paragraphs, or pages.<br><br>**Search and replace.** One command allows all occurrences of a word or phrase to be changed as specified.<br><br>**Move or copy text.** Allows cutting and pasting (deleting text and inserting it elsewhere) or copying and pasting (repeating text in several places).<br><br>**Automatic word wraparound.** Goes to next line at end of a line without pressing Enter or Return. (Also hyphenates words, as needed.) |
| **Desktop publishing features** make flyers, reports, newsletters, brochures, and student handouts more attractive and professional looking. | **Text alignment.** Centers or justifies (right, left, or full).<br><br>**Change styles, appearance.** Allows a variety of fonts, type styles, font colors, margins, line spacing, tabs, and indentations in the same document.<br><br>**Automatic headers, footers, and pagination.** Automatically places text at the top (header) or bottom (footer) of each page in a document with or without page numbering (pagination).<br><br>**Graphics.** Inserts clip art or image files into documents and formats them: some programs allow image editing.<br><br>**Insert colors, shading, borders, watermarks.** Text lines/boxes or graphics can be filled with color or degrees of shading. Pages can be bordered or stamped with graphics that appear on every page underneath text.<br><br>**Tables.** Organizes information into rows and columns without using tabs or indentations.<br><br>**Text boxes.** Allows text blocks to be inserted in any location in or around a document.<br><br>**Shapes and callouts.** Allows inserting shapes, callouts, and other figures to enhance documents. |
| **Language features** help teachers and students correct their work and do various language, spelling, and usage exercises. | **Spell-checker.** Compares words in a document to those stored in the program's dictionary files.<br><br>**Thesaurus.** Suggests synonyms for any word.<br><br>**Grammar checkers.** Review documents for items such as sentence length, frequency of word use, and subject-verb agreement. Also marks phrases or sentences to be corrected. |
| **Web features** allow teachers and students to connect documents with Internet resources and create Web page announcements, reports, and projects. | **Live URLs.** Allows person reading the document to click on text and go automatically to a website. (*Note:* Web browser must be active.)<br><br>**Simple Web page development.** Allows creation of HTML pages. |
| **Support features** make using the program easier and more flexible. | **Templates.** Users can easily adapt preformatted models of resumes, newsletters, and brochures to their own needs.<br><br>**Voice recognition and speech synthesis:**<br>• Receives and enters text via dictated words rather than as typed entries.<br>• Reads words as they are typed.<br><br>**Merges text with data fields:**<br>• Automatically inserts words (e.g., names and addresses) into documents such as letters (i.e., mail-merges)<br>• Lists of data can be stored within the word processing program or merged from a database. |

**FIGURE 4.1** Sample Template with Highlighted Word Processing Features

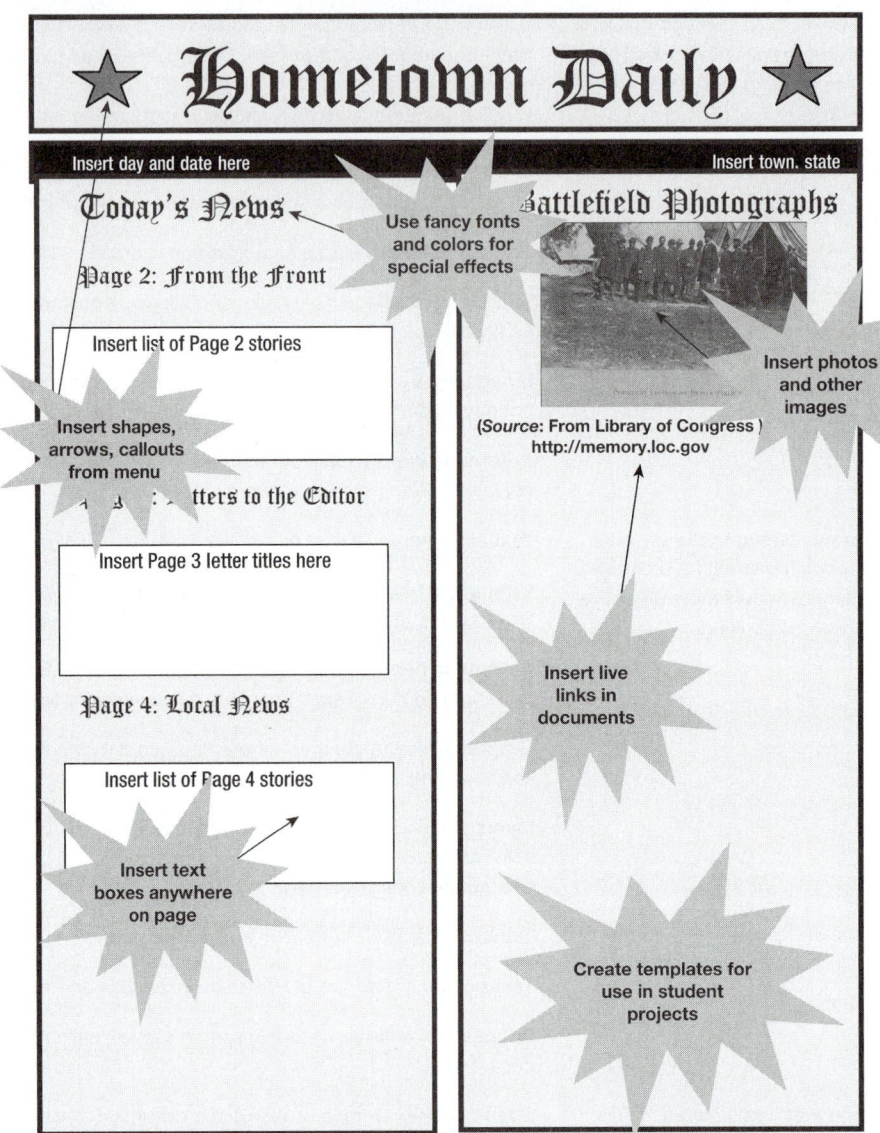

This sample of a word-processed template was created for a history lesson to engage students in events of the Civil War. Using material they learn in class and obtain online, they create a newspaper as it might have appeared during the Civil War, filled with descriptions of battles, as well as local events. Some of the most useful word processing features used to create this template are pointed out in the figure.

particular instructional approach. A teacher can use it to support any directed instruction or constructivist activity. Since its value as an aid to teaching and learning is universally acknowledged, word processing has become the most commonly used software in education. It offers many general **relative advantages** (unique benefits over and above other methods) to teachers and students:

- **Saves time**—Word processing helps teachers use preparation time more efficiently by letting them modify materials instead of creating new ones. Writers can also make corrections to word processing documents more quickly than they could on a typewriter or by hand.

- **Enhances document appearance**—Materials created with word processing software look more polished and professional than handwritten or typed materials. It is not surprising that students seem to like the improved appearance that word processing gives to their

▲ Perhaps no other technology resource has had as great an impact on education as word processing. Even young students can use it to write and revise their work more quickly. **Digital Media Pro/Shutterstock**

work. This is especially possible with the many templates that are part of the software suites today.

- **Allows sharing of documents.** Word processing allows materials to be shared easily among writers. Teachers can exchange lesson plans, worksheets, or other materials on disc and modify them to fit their needs. Students can also share ideas and products among themselves.

- **Allows collaboration on documents.** Especially since the release of products such as Google Docs and Wikispaces, teachers and students can now create, edit, and share documents synchronously. Ullman (2013) described several strategies schools are using to connect students around the globe and engage them in collaborative document projects in ways that accomplish Common Core State Standards in writing and language.

- **Supports student writing and language learning.** Adaptive keyboard and voice recognition capabilities make writing more accessible for students with physical challenges. Word processors also have optional features that support writing in many languages, complete with appropriate spell-checking and diacritical marks.

**Research on the impact of word processing.** Research on the benefits of word processing in education has yielded more positive results over time. Results of early studies of the effects of word processing on quality and quantity of writing were mixed (Bangert-Drowns, 1993). Three reviews of research (Bangert-Drowns, 1993; Hawisher, 1989; Snyder, 1993) found that these differences in findings may reflect differences in researchers' choices of types of word processing systems, prior experience and writing ability of students, and types of writing instruction evaluated. Generally, word processing seemed to improve writing and attitudes toward writing only if it was used in the context of good writing instruction and if students had enough time to learn word processing procedures before the study began. In a 2003 review of research, Goldberg, Russell, and Cook found that students who use computers during writing instruction produce written work that is about 0.4 of a standard deviation (SD) better than students who develop writing skills on paper. SD is a statistical unit of deviation or difference from the mean or average score.

When Graham and Perin (2007) compared research results on word processing as an intervention to improve writing with other such interventions, they found that with a .55 SD effect, word processing had a greater impact than sentence combining (0.50), inquiry (0.32), prewriting activities (0.32), a process writing approach (0.32), or study of models (0.25), but had less effect than strategy instruction (0.82), summarization (0.82), peer assistance (0.75), or setting product goals (0.70). A subsequent analysis of word processing effects on weaker writers (Morphy & Graham, 2012) yielded greater effects than had been previously found, indicating that weaker writers profit more from word processing use (.52 SD). Table 4.3 summarizes some of the findings of all the major research reviews.

Dave and Russell (2010) observe that, though word processing does not always lead to better quality writing, it definitely has had a dramatic impact on the practice of writing. Noting that "drafting and revision were developed out of process theory and research done in the early 1980s . . . when word processing was not as pervasive or standardized as it is now" (p. 406), they find that this technology has altered our very definition of "draft" and made continuous revision a reality. However, they also note that most revisions remain concerned primarily with surface-level corrections, such as spelling and grammatical errors, and word processors seem to have had limited effect on promoting global revision, or overall improvements in depth and quality of written communication. "Despite the ease with which global revisions can be made with current word processors, students' perception of the task of revision may not have changed much in this regard over the last 20 years" (p. 418).

## TABLE 4.3  Findings from Reviews of Word Processing in Education

| | Hawisher (26 studies) (1989) | Snyder (57 studies) (1993) | Bangert-Drowns (32 studies) (1993) | Goldberg, Russell, & Cook (14 studies) (2003) | Morphy & Graham (27 studies) (2012) |
|---|---|---|---|---|---|
| Better quality of writing | No conclusion | No conclusion | Positive results | Positive results | Positive results |
| Greater quantity of writing | Positive results | Positive results | Positive results | Positive results | Positive results |
| More surface (mechanical) revisions | No conclusion | Positive results | No conclusion | Not reviewed | Not reviewed |
| More substantive (meaning) revisions | No conclusion | No improvement | No conclusion | Not reviewed | Not reviewed |
| Fewer mechanical errors | Positive results | Positive results | Not reviewed | Not reviewed | Not reviewed |
| Better attitude toward writing | Positive results | Positive results | No improvement | Not reviewed | Positive results |
| Better attitude toward word processing | No conclusion | Positive results | Not reviewed | Not reviewed | Positive results |

Dave and Russell also found that students tend not to print out work from word processors to help them revise their drafts as much as they used to, preferring to revise on-screen instead.

Issues in using word processing.  Educators seem to agree that although word processing is a valuable application, its use in education can be controversial:

- **Questions about what age students should start word processing**—Word processing software designed for young children is available, and schools can introduce it to students as young as four or five years old. Some educators feel that word processing will free students from the physical constraints of handwriting, allowing them to develop written expression skills. Others worry that it will make students unwilling to spend time developing handwriting abilities and other activities requiring fine-motor skills.

- **The need to teach keyboarding skills**—Discussion is ongoing about whether students need to learn keyboarding ("10-finger typing" on the computer) either prior to or in conjunction with word processing activities. Some educators feel that students will never become really productive on the computer until they learn 10-finger keyboarding. Others feel that the extensive time spent on keyboarding instruction and practice could be better spent on more important skills, and that students will pick up typing skills on their own.

- **The effects of word processing on handwriting**—While no researchers have conducted formal studies of the impact of frequent word processing use on handwriting legibility, computer users commonly complain that their handwriting isn't what it used to be, ostensibly because of infrequent opportunities to use their handwriting skills. In addition, cursive writing, long a staple in elementary school curriculum, is on the wane, due in no small part to the influence of word processing and other technologies (Supon, 2009). Debate still swirls, however, around the question of whether word processing should replace cursive writing (Vacek & Fuhrhop, 2013).

- **Impact of word processing on assessment**—Some organizations either have students choose between word processing and handwritten formats for answering essay-type test questions, but there is an increasing tendency toward requiring students to take all tests on a computer. This practice introduces several issues. First, some researchers have found that essay graders tend to discriminate against word-processed papers, consistently giving them lower scores than handwritten ones (Mogey, Paterson, Burk, & Purcell, 2010).

Educational organizations that allow students to choose either handwriting or word processing must be careful to establish guidelines and special training to ensure that raters do not inadvertently discriminate against students who choose word processing. Second, schools that require word-processed writing for tests must assure that students are experienced enough with the software so their lack of word processing skill does not affect the quality of their written expression.

- **Problems with inadvertent errors**—Link (2009) warned that the auto correction feature built into most word processors can replace typed words with ones the software selects as more correct, leading to typos that interfere with intended meaning. For example, Link noted that an important German article appeared in print with every instance of the correct phrase "DNA-Polymerase" changed to "DANN-Polymerase." "Dann" means "then" in German, so the software replaced what it perceived as a misspelling with a known word. Teachers and students must be aware of this built-in feature and either turn it off or proofread even more carefully.

Teachers and administrators are still deciding how best to deal with these issues. Despite these obstacles, education's dependence on word processing continues to grow.

## Word Processing in the Classroom: Productivity and Teaching Strategies

Word processing has a variety of benefits for both productivity and teaching practices. An overview of both these strategies is given here.

### Productivity strategies.
Word processing can save teachers preparation time for classroom materials such as handouts or other instructional materials, lesson plans and notes, reports, forms, letters to parents or students, flyers, and newsletters, especially if a teacher uses the same documents every year. For example, a teacher may send the same letter to parents each year simply by changing the dates and adding new information. Teachers may want to keep electronic templates or model documents they can easily update and reuse. The following are suggested list of reusable word-processed documents teachers may want to have on hand.

- Beginning of the year welcome letter
- Name tags
- Permission letters for field trips and other events
- Flyers and other announcements
- Request for fee payments letter
- Fund-raising letter
- Posted flyer of class rules
- Letterhead stationery
- Periodic student progress letters to parents
- Lesson plans and notes
- Students information sheets and handouts
- Newsletters
- Annual reports required by the school
- Frequently used worksheets and exercises

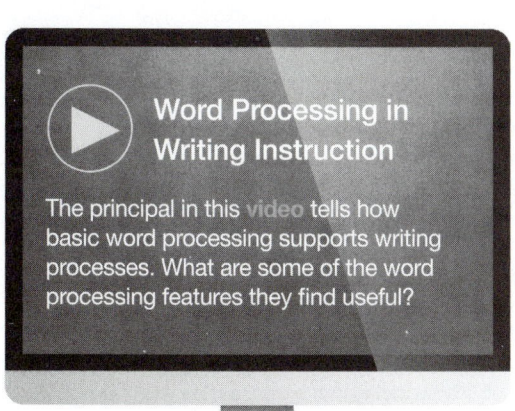

**Word Processing in Writing Instruction**

The principal in this video tells how basic word processing supports writing processes. What are some of the word processing features they find useful?

### Instructional integration strategies for word processing.
Research shows that word processing alone cannot improve the quality of student writing but can help students make corrections more efficiently; this can motivate them to write more and take more interest in

improving their written work. Some current word processing integration strategies include the following:

- **Supporting the learning of writing processes**—Students can use word processing to write, edit, and illustrate stories; to produce reports in content areas; to keep notes and logs on classroom activities; and for any written assignments. Using word processing in the classroom can make it easier for students to get started writing as well as to revise and improve their writing. (See Technology Integration Example 4.1.) Teachers can make good use of the **track changes** feature, which allows one to put typed "red marks" on students' written works to guide them in how to revise and improve their writing. Teachers can also use **comment boxes**, a word processing feature that allows them to insert written notes in margins. AbuSeileek (2013) found that students who received corrective feedback using such features were more likely to eliminate targeted writing errors (e.g., sentence fragments and run-ons) than those who did not.

- **Using a dynamic group product approach**—Teachers can assign group poems or letters to various students, allowing students to add and change lines or produce elements of the whole document in a word processing program. Using word processing software, students find it easier to share, exchange, and add onto drafts, as well as to work together on written projects at a distance.

- **Assigning individual language, writing, and reading exercises**—Special word processing exercises allow for meaningful, hands-on practice in language use as individual students work on-screen combining sentences, adding or correcting punctuation, or writing sentences for spelling words. Word processing may also make possible a variety of reading/language-related activities ranging from decoding to writing poetry and enjoying literature. Identifying and correcting errors becomes a more visual process.

- **Encouraging writing-through-the-curriculum**—A trend in education is to encourage writing skills in courses and activities other than those designed to teach English and language arts. This practice of writing-through-the-curriculum is in keeping with the emphasis on integrated, interdisciplinary, and thematic curricula. Word processing can encourage these integrated activities. (See Technology Integration Example 4.2.) Its font and graphics features allow students to represent concepts in mathematics, science, and other content areas. Word processors are also available in other languages to support foreign language learning.

## Teaching Word Processing Skills: Recommended Skills and Activities

Students new to word processing must have adequate time to develop skills in using the software before teachers can begin to grade their word-processed products. Many online tutorials are available for teaching various software packages, but these may not always be accessible to

# TECHNOLOGY INTEGRATION

## Example 4.1

**TITLE:** Mystery Writers!

**CONTENT AREA/TOPIC:** Language arts, creative writing

**GRADE LEVELS:** 3–5

**ISTE STANDARDS•S:** Standard 1—Creativity and Innovation; Standard 2—Communication and Collaboration; Standard 6—Technology Operations and Concepts

**CCSS:** CCSS.ELA-LITERACY.RL.3.3, CCSS.ELA-LITERACY.W.3.3, CCSS.ELA-LITERACY.W.3.6, CCSS.ELA-LITERACY.W.4.3.D, CCSS.ELA-LITERACY.W.4.10, CCSS.ELA-LITERACY.RL.5.9, CCSS.ELA-LITERACY.W.5.3.A

**DESCRIPTION:** Students assume the identity of private investigators as they read, solve, and write mysteries in order to learn about the genre and encourage creative writing. The teacher helps students outline the critical elements of a mystery story and allows them to map a sample mystery to illustrate these elements and a story line. Then the teacher introduces nursery rhymes as mystery story-starters (e.g., Why did Humpty Dumpty fall off that wall? How did Mother Hubbard's cupboard become empty?). Students organize their stories with a sticky-note story map, then word process their stories, doing drafts with teacher assistance.

*SOURCE:* Based on a concept in an EducationWorld.com lesson at http://www.educationworld.com/

# TECHNOLOGY INTEGRATION

## Example 4.2

**TITLE:** The Language of Jazz—An Integral Part of American History and Culture

**CONTENT AREA/TOPIC:** Music/history

**GRADE LEVELS:** Elementary to middle school

**ISTE STANDARDS•S:** Standard 1—Creativity and Innovation; Standard 2—Communication and Collaboration; Standard 3—Research and Information Fluency; Standard 6—Technology Operations and Concepts

**CCSS:** CCSS.ELA-LITERACY.RH.6-8.1, CSS.ELA-LITERACY. RH.6-8.4, CCSS.ELA-LITERACY.RH.6-8.8

**DESCRIPTION:** Students use the Internet to research the history of jazz and the life of one jazz musician and his or her effect on American culture. Then they use word processing software (Microsoft Word) to create a brochure about their musician and share it with the class. The Microsoft Education website provides step-by-step directions to carry out the lesson and two handouts for students (prepared with Microsoft Word).

*SOURCE:* Based on a concept in a Lesson Plan from Microsoft Education collection.

---

students. Also, younger or less independent learners may not have the ability to use these self-instructional methods and may need teacher-led instruction.

For all of these reasons, teachers who would like to use word processing in classroom lessons may have to introduce their students to word processing and show them the features and uses of the software. Table 4.4 shows a recommended sequence for introducing word processing to students. Note that some features and steps are labeled "optional." Teachers may choose to introduce these on an as-needed basis or only with older, more experienced students. Also see Figure 4.2 for some tips you can give students just learning word processing. Finally, be sure to see the end-of-chapter pop up activity on how you can use track changes, comment boxes, **tables**, a **thesaurus**, and **symbols**.

## FIGURE 4.2  Tips for Teaching Students New to Word Processing

The following are useful to tell students or place on a poster where students can see it.

1. **Highlight first, then format.** If you want to change margins, font, color, or size for some text, highlight it (darken by dragging the mouse over it) FIRST. The software formats only what you highlight.

2. **Don't hit Enter or Return at ends of lines.** The software automatically wraps around text at the ends of lines. Hitting Enter/Return at the ends of lines will put unwanted spaces in the text.

3. **Delete blank lines before you print.** Blank lines will not always be evident on the screen but the computer knows they're there and leaves space for them on a printed page. If you see unexpected blank spaces at ends of pages or anywhere in a printed document, highlight them on the screen and delete them before printing again.

4. **Be careful with search and replace.** Before changing all instances of a word or phrase to something else, be sure you can predict the result. For example, if you change all instances of the word "TO" to "BY," remember that some words also contain "TO." (The word "together" would become "bygether!")

5. **Spell-checking isn't proofreading.** Spell-checking is no substitute for reviewing your paper carefully before you finalize it. For example, "cite" is spelled correctly, but "site" may be what you want.

## TABLE 4.4 Tips on Teaching Students How to Do Word Processing
### (Also go to the internet4classrooms website and look for Word tutorials)

| Suggested Steps | Tasks Under Each Step |
|---|---|
| **Step 1**—Prepare for teaching. | **Arrange for:**<br>• A big screen and projection system, or interactive whiteboard (IWB).<br>• A disc or flash drive for each student, or a cloud-based storage location.<br>• Copying sample file(s) onto network or student media.<br>• One computing device per student.<br>• Alternative keyboards or other adaptive devices for students with disabilities.<br><br>**Create or obtain:**<br>• Handouts or wall posters on **word processing** features and common errors. |
| **Step 2**—Demonstrate the basics. | **Using a big screen and projection system or IWB, show how to:**<br>• Transfer a file to a computing device (if needed).<br>• Open a file.<br>• Move around in a document using the cursor and scroll bars.<br>• Add and delete text; undo changes.<br>• Name, save, and close document.<br><br>**Point out common errors:**<br>• Forgetting to move cursor before typing.<br>• Forgetting about automatic wraparound (pressing Enter or Return at end of lines).<br>• Forgetting to save all changes before closing a file. |
| **Step 3**—Assign individual practice. | **Give students a sample word processing file and have them:**<br>• Open the file.<br>• Do a list of changes to the file (e.g., inserting spaces, deleting lines, undoing changes).<br>• Name, save, and close document. |
| **Step 4**—Demonstrate formatting features. | **Using a big screen and projection system or IWB, show how to:**<br>• Change fonts, styles, and alignment.<br>• Add clip art.<br>• Spell-check the document.<br>• Print the document.<br>• **Optional:** Search and replace procedures.<br>• **Optional:** Add bullets and numbering.<br><br>**Point out common errors:**<br>• Inserting too many spaces at top or bottom of document (by pressing Enter or Return).<br>• Unexpected errors from Search and Replace feature (failing to predict results). |
| **Step 5**—Assign more individual practice. | **Have students open their sample word processing file from Step 3 and do the following:**<br>• Change fonts, styles, and alignment.<br>• Add clip art.<br>• Spell-check the document.<br>• Print the document.<br>• **Optional:** Search and replace text.<br>• **Optional:** Add bullets and page numbering. |
| **Step 6**—Demonstrate procedures with new files. | **Show students how to:**<br>• Open a new file.<br>• Name and save under different names (Save vs. Save As).<br>• **Optional:** Set up a new document (e.g., set margins and line spacing).<br>• **Optional:** Do headers, footers, and pagination. |
| **Step 7**—Assign more individual practice. | **Do the following:**<br>• Assign a product for them to copy (for younger students) or create (for older students).<br>• Monitor students as they work and give individual help as needed. |

# USING SPREADSHEET SOFTWARE IN TEACHING AND LEARNING

Spreadsheets are programs designed to organize and manipulate numerical data. The term spreadsheet comes from the precomputer word for an accountant's ledger: a book for keeping records of numerical information such as budgets and cash flow. Unlike the term word processing, which refers only to the computer software or program, the term spreadsheet can refer either to the program itself or to the product it produces. Spreadsheet products are sometimes also called **worksheets**. The information in a spreadsheet is stored in rows and columns. Each row–column position is called a **cell** and may contain numerical values, words or character data, and **formulas** or calculation commands.

A spreadsheet helps users manage numbers in the same way that word processing helps them manage words. Spreadsheet software was the earliest application software available for microcomputers. Some people credit spreadsheets with starting the microcomputer revolution, since the availability of the first spreadsheet software, Visicalc, motivated many people to buy a microcomputer for their homes. Spreadsheet features are listed in Table 4.5. Also see Figure 4.3, which shows spreadsheet features used to create a Magic Squares exercise to engage students in number patterns.

## The Impact of Spreadsheets in Education

Like word processing, spreadsheets have seen widespread adoption throughout education. This section gives the reasons for this tool's popularity and summarizes both the research on using this software and an issue that may affect its integration.

### Why teachers use spreadsheets.
Spreadsheet programs are in widespread use in classrooms at all levels of education. Teachers use them primarily to keep budgets and gradebooks and to help teach mathematical topics. Spreadsheets offer teachers and students several unique benefits:

- **Save time**—Spreadsheets save valuable time by allowing teachers and students to complete essential calculations quickly. They save time not only by making initial calculations faster and more accurate, but their automatic recalculation features also make it easy to update products such as grades and budgets. Entries also can be changed, added, or deleted easily, with formulas that automatically recalculate final grades.

- **Organize displays of information**—Although spreadsheet programs are intended for numerical data, their capability to store information in columns makes them ideal tools for designing informational charts, such as schedules and attendance lists, that may contain few numbers and no calculations at all.

- **Support asking "what if" questions**—Spreadsheets help people visualize the impact of changes in numbers. Since values are automatically recalculated when changes are made in a worksheet, a user can play with numbers and immediately see the result. This capability makes it feasible to pose "what if" questions and to answer them quickly and easily.

- **Increase motivation to work with mathematics**—Many teachers feel that spreadsheets make working with numbers more fun. Students sometimes perceive mathematical concepts as dry and boring; spreadsheets can make these concepts so graphic that students express real delight with seeing how they work.

- **Research on the impact of spreadsheet use**—Although spreadsheets are widely believed to help students visualize numerical concepts better than other, less dynamic tools, few studies have attempted to capture their comparative impact on achievement. Ray (2013) used pre–post achievement data to indicate the impact of "spreadsheet simulations," or exercises that ask students to collect data in two or more different ways, insert the sets of data on a spreadsheet, and compare the results of the data-collection strategies. He found these exercises improve comprehension of highly abstract concepts in biology. There is

# TABLE 4.5 A Summary of Spreadsheet Features

| Feature Categories/General Benefits | Description of Features and Specific Benefits |
|---|---|
| **Basic features** make it easier to display and manipulate budget, grade, or survey data; and do mathematics problem solving. | **Line up information in rows and columns.** Row–column format makes numerical and other information easier to read and digest at a glance.<br><br>**Do basic calculations.** Use formulas in cells to do:<br>• Basic arithmetic functions: adding, subtracting, multiplying, dividing.<br>• Weighted averages by combining these functions.<br><br>**Do complex calculations.** Enter formulas in cells to do:<br>• Mathematical functions such as logarithms and roots.<br>• Statistical functions such as sums and averages.<br>• Trigonometric functions such as sines and tangents.<br>• Logical functions such as Boolean comparisons.<br>• Financial functions such as periodic payments and rates.<br>• Special-purpose functions such as looking up and comparing data entries with other information (e.g., counting the number of grades above a certain number).<br><br>**Do automatic recalculation.** When a number in one cell changes (e.g., a grade), a **spreadsheet** formula automatically updates all calculations related to that number (e.g., an average grade).<br><br>**Copy cells.** Numbers, formulas, or other information in cells can be copied and pasted to any other cells.<br><br>**Sort data.** Data can be organized alphabetically or numerically.<br><br>**Search and replace.** One command allows all occurrences of a specified word, phrase, number, or formula to be changed. |
| **Formatting features** | **Alignment.** Centers or right- or left-justifies cell entries.<br><br>**Changes styles/appearance.** Allows:<br>• A variety of fonts, sizes, font colors, and type styles in the same document.<br>• Cells and graphics to be filled with color or degrees of shading.<br><br>**Insert automatic headers, footers, and pagination.** Allows text to be automatically placed at the top (header) or bottom (footer) of each page in a worksheet with or without page numbering (pagination). |
| **Graphics/interactive features** allow **spreadsheet** data to be shown in more visual formats. | **Charting.** Creates charts and graphs automatically from **spreadsheet** data.<br><br>**Insert graphics or movies.** Clip art or other still or moving images can be pasted into cells to illustrate concepts or to change document appearance.<br><br>**Insert drawn figures.** Allows inserting shapes, callouts, and other figures to enhance worksheet appearance. |
| **Web features** allow teachers and students to connect documents with Internet resources and create Web page announcements, reports, and projects. | **Insert "live" URLs.** Allows person using the **spreadsheet** to click on text and go automatically to a website. (*Note:* Web browser must be active.)<br><br>**Save as Web pages.** Allows worksheets to be displayed online. |
| **Support features** make using the program easier and more flexible. | **Read and save to other formats. Spreadsheets** can:<br>• Read and use other data files such as those produced by Statistical Packages for the Social Sciences (SPSS) software.<br>• Save documents in formats (e.g., tab-delimited) for use in SPSS or other programs.<br><br>**Use templates.** Users can easily adapt preformatted models of worksheets (e.g., budgets, checkbooks, and gradekeepers) to their own needs. |

also considerable evidence that spreadsheets have proven useful for teaching concepts in many areas, including probability (Beigie, 2010), meteorology (Krall, 2010), business topics (McDermott, 2010), physics (Benacka, 2010), and even sports (Bennett, O'Shaughnessy, & Bedford, 2011). Baker (2013) found that of all the technology skills that those in accounting professions could learn (accounting software, databases, e-mail or Internet, programming, spreadsheets, and word processing), accounting interns felt that spreadsheets are by far the most important. The literature contains numerous testimonials by teachers who have used

**FIGURE 4.3** Sample Spreadsheet from a Lesson on Magic Squares

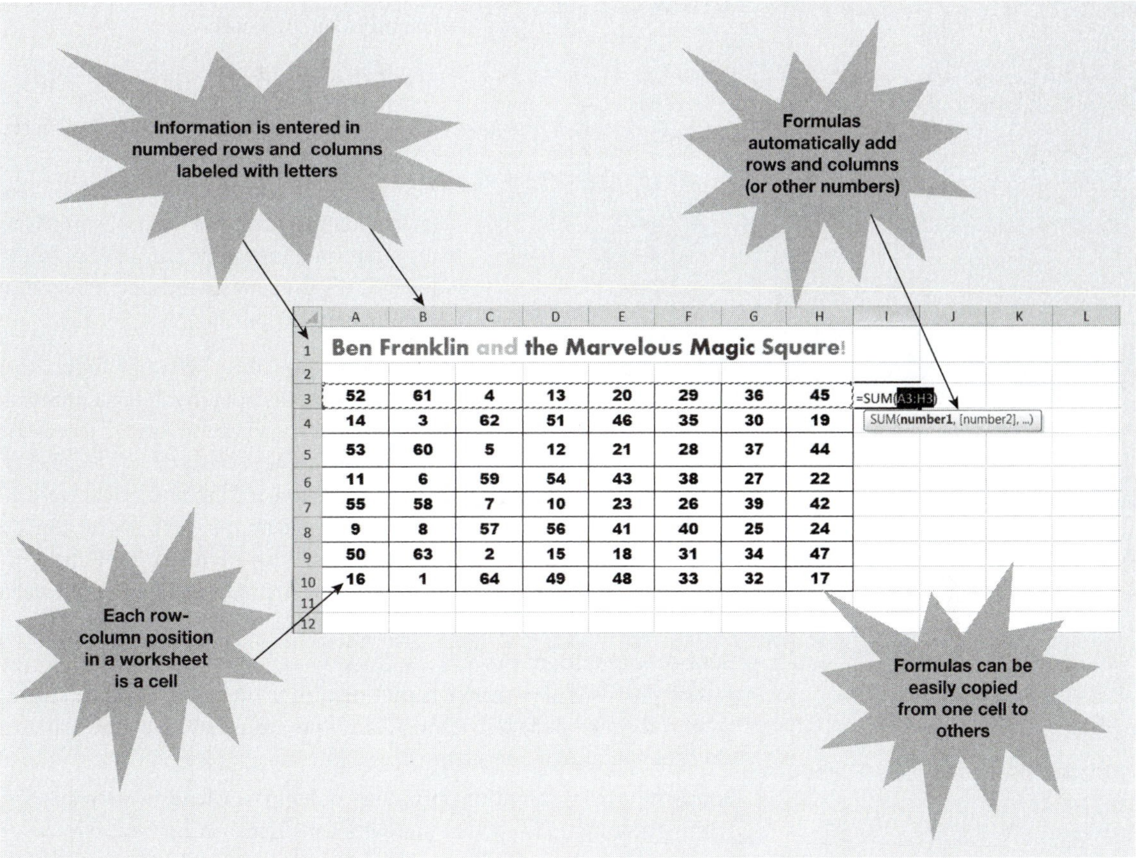

A Magic Square is a square grid of numbers in which numbers in each row, each column, and each forward and backward diagonal add up to the same number. In this example, we inserted a Magic Square created by Ben Franklin into a spreadsheet. The numbers each add to 260. Students insert formulas to discover this principle, then create their own, smaller Magic Square version assigned by the teacher (e.g., a 3 x 3 grid in which numbers add to 15.) Some of the spreadsheet features used to carry out this lesson are shown here.

spreadsheets successfully in teaching topics ranging from mathematics to social studies. Wu (2007) found that spreadsheet templates helped students better understand the concepts underlying statistical graphs.

Issues in using spreadsheets. Though spreadsheets have a reputation in education for utility and versatility in teaching, they still present more of a problem for many students than do tools such as word processing. Teachers who would employ this versatile software must first address students' tendency to fear mathematics. They are not afraid to process words, but processing numbers is quite another matter. Teachers usually have to allow time for students to become comfortable with the software and discover that it is an aid to them, rather than a further challenge to their math ability.

## Spreadsheets in the Classroom: Productivity and Teaching Strategies

**Spreadsheets** offer benefits for both productivity and teaching practices. An overview of both these strategies is given here.

Productivity strategies. Teachers can use spreadsheets to help them prepare classroom materials and complete calculations that they would otherwise have to do by hand or with a calculator. The most common uses of spreadsheets are for keeping school club and classroom budgets, preparing performance checklists for assessment purposes, and keeping gradebooks.

▲ Spreadsheets can let students visualize math concepts, solve numerical problems, and experiment with mathematics principles.
Sean Nel/Shutterstock

The latter use is becoming less common as schools and districts obtain gradebook software for use by all personnel who have to keep and calculate grades.

### Instructional integration strategies for spreadsheets.

Teachers can use spreadsheets in many ways to enhance learning. The literature, in fact, reflects an increasing variety of applications. Although their teaching role focuses primarily on mathematics lessons, spreadsheets have also effectively supported instruction in science, social studies, and even language arts. Current spreadsheet integration strategies include the following:

- **Making possible visual teaching demonstrations.** Whenever concepts involving numbers can be clarified by concrete representation, spreadsheets contribute to effective teaching demonstrations. Spreadsheets offer an efficient way of demonstrating numerical concepts such as multiplication and percentages and numerical applications, such as the concept of electoral votes versus popular votes. A worksheet can make a picture out of abstract concepts and provide a graphic illustration of what the teacher is trying to communicate. (See Technology Integration Example 4.3.)

- **Supporting student products**—Students can use spreadsheets to create timelines, charts, and graphs, as well as products that require them to store and calculate numbers. Creating graphic displays of data in a spreadsheet program can save time, particularly when changes or corrections are made to the data.

- **Supporting mathematical problem solving**—Spreadsheets take over the task of doing arithmetic functions so that students can focus on higher level concepts. By answering "what if" questions in a highly graphic format, spreadsheets help teachers encourage logical thinking, develop organizational skills, and promote problem solving.

- **Storing and allowing analysis of data**—Whenever students must keep track of data from classroom experiments or online surveys, spreadsheets help organize these data and allow students to perform required descriptive statistical analyses on them. (See Technology Integration Example 4.4.)

# TECHNOLOGY INTEGRATION

## Example 4.3

**TITLE:** How the Electoral College Works—A Visual Demonstration

**CONTENT AREA/TOPIC:** Civics, elections

**GRADE LEVEL:** 9

**ISTE STANDARDS•S:** Standard 2—Communication and Collaboration; Standard 3—Research and Information Fluency; Standard 4—Critical Thinking, Problem Solving, and Decision Making

**CCSS:** MATH.CONTENT.HSS.ID.A.2, CCSS.MATH.CONTENT. HSS.ID.A.3

**NCSS THEMES:** Thematic Standards: 6 – Power, Authority, and Governance; Disciplinary Standards: Civics and Government;

**DESCRIPTION:** After the class holds a mock election and assigns electoral votes to each class in the school based on enrollment numbers, the teacher creates a spreadsheet to match the list of classes and their popular and electoral votes. Students enter data on election results, and the teacher displays the spreadsheet on a large monitor so the whole class can see the results as they are entered. Through this activity, students are able to see that if a very few of the popular votes in key areas are changed, the results of the election would be reversed. The class discusses these results as well as the possibility that a candidate could win the popular vote and lose the electoral vote.

*SOURCE:* Based on a concept from the Getting into the Electoral College lesson at the NCTM Illuminations site: http://illuminations.nctm.org.

# TECHNOLOGY INTEGRATION

## Example 4.4

**TITLE:** Comparing the Weather in Two Locations

**CONTENT AREA/TOPIC:** Science, weather

**GRADE LEVEL:** 8

**ISTE STANDARDS•S:** Standard 1—Creativity and Innovation; Standard 2—Communication and Collaboration; Standard 4—Critical Thinking, Problem Solving, and Decision Making

**CCSS:** CCSS.MATH.CONTENT.8.SP.A.1, CCSS.MATH.CONTENT.8.F.B.5, CCSS.MATH.PRACTICE.MP5

**NSTA:** MS-ESS2-1, MS-ESS2-5, MS-ESS3-5

**DESCRIPTION:** Students work in small groups to gather weather data from NOAA's National Weather Service website on two cities the teacher assigns them. They enter the data on a spreadsheet and do calculations to determine temperature and rainfall averages for given periods of time. They compare the two cities' weather patterns and analyze them to determine reasons for the differences they find. Finally, they report on their findings to the class.

*SOURCE:* Based on a concept in a lesson plan at the Hotchalk website: http://www.lessonplanspage.com

---

- **Projecting grades**—Students can be taught to use spreadsheets to keep track of their own grades. They can do their own "what if" questions to see what scores they need to make on their assignments to achieve desired class grades. This simple activity can play an important role in encouraging students to take responsibility for setting goals and achieving them.

## Teaching Spreadsheet Skills: Recommended Skills and Activities

Just as with word processing, students new to spreadsheets must have time to develop skills in using the software before teachers can begin to grade their work. Some lessons require students to know only the most basic operations, as shown in Step 2 of Table 4.6. Other activities require students to create their own spreadsheets and formulas, as shown in Step 4. In the latter case, if students are not able to use the online tutorials that are available for teaching spreadsheet software, teachers can use the strategies outlined in Table 4.6. Even when teaching these advanced concepts, teachers may choose to introduce more complex functions and features on an as-needed basis, depending on the requirements of the lesson.

**TECHNOLOGY LEARNING CHECK**

Complete TLC 4.3 to review what you have learned from reading this section about spreadsheet features and uses.

## USING PRESENTATION SOFTWARE IN TEACHING AND LEARNING

**Presentation software** is designed to display information, including text, images, audio, and video, in a slideshow format. It took the place of photo slides presented in a slide projector and, like the technology it replaced, was originally designed to accompany and support marketing presentations and business training and reports. But like word processing and spreadsheet software, it quickly made the transition from business to education and home use. Though Microsoft PowerPoint was not the first such software, and though there are many other packages available for sale and as open-source options, the name PowerPoint is often used interchangeably with presentation software, much as the brand name Kleenex is often used instead of facial issue.

## TABLE 4.6 Tips on Teaching Spreadsheets
### (Also see Spreadsheet tutorials)

| Suggested Steps | Tasks Under Each Step |
|---|---|
| **Step 1**—Prepare for teaching. | **Arrange for:**<br>• A big screen and projection system, or interactive whiteboard (IWB)<br>• A disc or flash drive for each student, or a cloud-based storage location<br>• Copying sample file(s) onto network or student media<br>• One computing device per student<br>• Alternative keyboards or other adaptive devices for students with disabilities<br><br>**Create or obtain:**<br>• Handouts or wall posters on spreadsheet features and common errors |
| **Step 2**—Demonstrate the basics. | **Using a big screen and projection system or IWB, show how to:**<br>• Transfer a file to a computing device (if needed).<br>• Open a spreadsheet file from a storage location or medium<br>• Select a worksheet to work on in the file by clicking a tab at the bottom.<br>• Select any given cell location by row–column position.<br><br>**Then demonstrate:**<br>• Spreadsheet "magic": Show how it recalculates automatically when a number is changed.<br><br>**Finally, show how to:**<br>• Enter new information into a cell.<br>• Format given cells for appearance and as various kinds of numbers.<br>• Change column width.<br>• Copy information in a cell down the column or across a row.<br><br>**Point out a common error:**<br>• Forgetting to highlight cells to be formatted before selecting a format option. |
| **Step 3**—Assign individual practice. | **Give students a sample spreadsheet file on disc and have them:**<br>• Open the file.<br>• Make changes to the file (e.g., insert new data, copy down a column or across a row, format cells).<br>• Name, save, and close the document. |
| **Step 4**—Demonstrate formatting features. | **Using a big screen and projection system or IWB, show how to:**<br>• Create a formula to add numbers in a column.<br>• Copy a formula across the row to add numbers in other columns.<br>• **Optional:** Functions such as SUM and AVERAGE.<br>• **Optional:** Charting functions.<br>• **Optional:** Adding graphics and URLs.<br><br>**Point out common errors with formulas:**<br>• Forgetting to place the cursor in the cell where you want the formula<br>• Pressing the Right Arrow key (instead of the Return or Enter Key) to leave the cell while creating a formula (Show that this action adds something to the formula, rather than exiting the cell.)<br>• Including the formula cell itself in the formula's calculation (i.e., circular reference error) |
| **Step 5**—Assign more individual practice. | **Have students open their sample spreadsheet file from Step 3 and do the following:**<br>• Enter and format various new formulas.<br>• **Optional:** Create a chart based on the data.<br>• **Optional:** Add a graphic and/or a URL.<br><br>Monitor students as they work, and give individual help as needed. |

Slides or frames created in this software are usually presented in the order in which they appear in the slideshow product. However, presentation software also has features allow hypermedia capabilities, permitting the display of frames in any order by clicking on links or "buttons." Presentation software features are summarized in Table 4.7.

## The Impact of Presentation Software in Education

**Why teachers use presentation software.** Though presentation software is generally used in the same way in education as it is in business, to support speakers (teachers and students) as they present information to listeners, it has evolved additional uses in education that make it a more complex, multipurpose classroom tool. Current uses are described later in this chapter. Presentation software offers educators the following benefits:

▲ Presentations offer a way to engage students with sound and images. (Photo by W. Wiencke)

- **Helps organize thinking about a topic**—When teachers or students create a presentation with this software, it helps them think through what they will say and in what order they should present information. Though using presentation software does not ensure an organized, coherent talk, its emphasis on sequencing and breaking information into component parts can promote a more organized approach. Use of presentation software can allow a teacher to illustrate and provide students with practice in information organization skills.

- **Enhances the impact of spoken information**—When a presentation product is well designed, it supports and supplements what the speaker says, using graphics and multimedia to give illustrations and drive home points with images and sound.

- **Allows collaboration on presentations**—Working together on presentations of project work or research results gives students important practice in collaborative skills. It also allows students to contribute in a variety of ways to the product, rather than just in writing; for example, some may focus on text message design and some on selecting and creating appropriate graphics.

**Research on the instructional uses of presentation software.** This software is a much-studied technology, and researchers have looked at its impact on both educational processes and outcomes. Jordan and Papp (2013) reviewed and summarized the body of research on the impact of PowerPoint. They found that while overall findings show no impact on desired outcomes, they were also able to demonstrate that impact depends almost exclusively on how it is used. They cite several limitations and problems of less-then-effective uses, including the following:

- Overuse or improper use of bullets and lists can cause problems for learners as they process information they are hearing.

- Sometimes students focus so much on the slides they neglect other important information or sources.

- They can be a loss of "connection" between the person presenting the slides and the listeners when the focus is on the slides and not on the concepts behind them.

- Slideshows tend to be used the same way across all audiences, leading to a single teaching style that may not be appropriate for everyone.

- Many people who create slideshows do not have a good grasp of visual design principles that would help them achieve better results.

These findings indicate that creating and using presentation software effectively requires substantial background in specific pedagogical and visual design principles. Like the other basic tools, presentation software is easy to use but difficult to use well as a teaching tool.

**Issues in using presentation software.** Use of presentation software has produced strong reactions by several observers. Issues related to presentation software use include:

# TABLE 4.7 A Summary of Presentation Software Features

| Feature Categories/ General Benefits | Description of Features and Specific Benefits |
|---|---|
| **Basic features** allow display of frames or slides of information in a set sequence. | **Create a slideshow made of separate frames.** Frame-by-frame organization breaks up information into logical units that can be presented one at a time. |
| | **Add frames with various formats.** Frame styles can be different on each page; styles can range from a blank frame to one with locations marked for where text and graphics should be inserted. |
| | **Copy and paste slides.** Slides can be added by duplicating other slides. |
| | **Add speaker notes to slides.** Helps users plan what to say as each frame is presented. |
| | **Search and replace.** One command allows all occurrences of a specified word or phrase to be changed as specified. |
| **Display features** allow various ways to view slideshows. | **Display in various ways as single frame.** Displays a slide that either: allows changes to be made on it before presentation, or a full-screen display during a presentation. |
| | **Display as storyboards.** Shows all frames at once for review and/or changing frame sequence. |
| **Formatting features** allow variation in text spacing and frame appearance. | **Format font size and type.** Allows text variety to enhance frame appearance. |
| | **Format background color.** Allows each frame to have different background color to better highlight information and focus viewers' attention. |
| **Graphics and interactive features** make frames have more impact and utility. | **Insert images.** Clip art from a library that comes with the software and includes photos and animations; or images from other sources. |
| | **Insert drawn figures.** Allows inserting shapes, callouts, lines, or other figures to enhance frame appearance or to help illustrate concepts. |
| | **Insert videos and animations.** Allows inserting short videos to supplement slide information from text and images or GIF animations, primarily for gaining attention. |
| | **Insert charts and graphs.** Allows creation of charts or graphs to insert on frames to illustrate concepts. |
| | **Insert products created in other software.** Allows word-processed text or spreadsheet products, including charts and graphs, to be added to frames. |
| | **Interactive buttons or "hotspots."** Links can be inserted to allow users to "jump" to other parts of the presentation out of the order in which slides are stored in presentation. |
| **Web features** allow teachers and students to connect frames to Internet resources | **Insert "live" URLS.** Allows person displaying the presentation to click on text or images and go automatically to a website. (*Note:* Web browser must be active.) |
| | **Save presentations as web pages.** Allows presentations to be accessed and displayed online. |
| **Support features** make using the program easier and more flexible. | **Use templates.** Users can add information to already formatted files that come with themed graphics already on each slide. |
| | **Save to other formats.** Presentations can be saved as PDFs to allow use as documents or as read-only presentations for sharing with others. |
| | **Print presentations.** Presentations can be printed with varying numbers of slides per page and given to listeners for following and note-taking. |
| | **Use timed slideshows.** Presentations can be set up to display frames automatically using timing settings or to play narration or music during the show. |

## Hot Topic Debate
## Is Powerpoint Really Evil?

Take a position for or against (based either on your own position or one assigned to you) on the following controversial statement. Discuss it in class or on an online discussion board, blog, or wiki, as assigned by your instructor. When the discussion is complete, write a summary of the main pros and cons that you and your classmates have stated, and put the summary document in your Teacher Portfolio.

In a 2003 article entitled "PowerPoint is Evil," Edward Tufte said that "the PowerPoint style routinely disrupts, dominates, and trivializes content. Thus PowerPoint presentations too often resemble a school play—very loud, very slow, and very simple." The *New York Times* published an article entitled "We Have Met the Enemy and He Is PowerPoint." What characteristics serve to make presentations with PowerPoint or other software less than helpful? What guidelines can you cite to make sure such presentations are helpful?

- **Impact of presentation software on information presented**—Tufte (2003) famously said that "Power corrupts; PowerPoint corrupts absolutely." He is among those who feel that presentation software makes people focus on the slides, rather than the message, saying that "rather than supplementing a presentation, [PowerPoint] has become a substitute for it" (p. 3). See the Hot Topic Debate feature for more on this issue.

- **Impact of presentation software on teaching style**—There are also complaints about the effects that using slide-based software has on teaching style and impact. Adams (2006) said that using PowerPoint makes educators reshape what they present in a way that is inconsistent with developing higher-level skills. On the other hand, Elliott and Gordon (2006) said that proper use of presentation software can support constructivist activities and promote higher-level thinking and "deep understanding" (p. 34).

Criticisms of this tool seem best addressed by teachers becoming more aware of the most effective uses of presentation software. Klemm (2007) offers several tips for avoiding uses of presentation software that make them a "trap for bad teaching" (p. 121). These include showing only a few slides at a time before having students apply the information, having some slides with no text (images or diagrams only), moving around the room while showing slides, taking the last slide off the screen when moving on to student work, and not giving out hard copies of slides.

## Presentation Software in the Classroom: Productivity and Teaching Strategies

The benefits that presentation software offers are primarily to teaching practices. This section offers an overview of these strategies, as well as how to make time spent with presentations more productive.

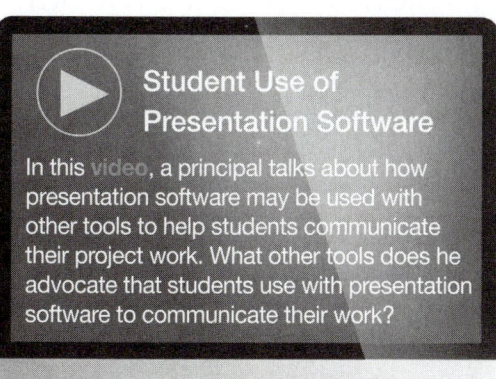

**Student Use of Presentation Software**

In this video, a principal talks about how presentation software may be used with other tools to help students communicate their project work. What other tools does he advocate that students use with presentation software to communicate their work?

Productivity strategies. Since presentation software is designed specifically for presenting information, it has no real productivity applications. However, PowerPoint presentations can be made more productive by following the design and usage rules listed in Figure 4.4, as well as Klemm's (2007) guidelines, given previously.

Instructional integration strategies for presentation software. Since presentation software can support instruction in any content area, the literature reflects many examples of effective uses. Presentation strategies began when software allowed only **electronic slide shows**, sequences of frames with clip art and text, displayed in a linear way. When it became possible to add complex graphics and video sequences to frames, they evolved into popular multimedia authoring tools. Then, when presentation software began to offer branching and links to external information such as Internet sites, this tool became a

**FIGURE 4.4** Guidelines for Designing Presentations with Presentation Software

All of the following are qualities that can greatly enhance readability, audience engagement, and/or communication of content during a PowerPoint or Keynote presentation.

1. **Use large type**—Use at least a 32-point font; use a larger type size if the audience is large and a long distance away from the presenter. Smaller type (no less than a 20-point font) may be used to provide citations, references, and sources, which are typically positioned in the lower-left or -right corner of the appropriate slide.

2. **Contrast the text and background colors**—The audience cannot see text that is too similar in hue to the background on which it appears. Use text with high contrast to the background (e.g., dark text on light-colored backgrounds, white text on dark-colored backgrounds).

3. **Minimize the amount of text on each frame**—Use text to focus attention on main points, not to present large amounts of information. Summarize ideas in brief phrases and make sure that you, not the projection screen, are the focus of the presentation. In other words, use the presentation to enhance, strengthen, and expand upon points that are outlined briefly on each frame.

4. **Keep frames simple**—Frame designs should be simple, clear, and free of distractions. Too many items on one frame can interfere with reading, especially if some items are in motion. In addition, try to employ photographs and images in place of lengthy text when describing a context or event. Finally, try to minimize the number of bullet points (not to exceed three to five points) on each individual slide.

5. **Avoid using too many "fancy" fonts**—Many fonts are unreadable when projected on a screen. Use a plain sans serif (straight lines with no "hands" and "feet") font for titles and a plain serif font for other text. Avoid using more than three different fonts throughout the presentation to maintain consistency of headings, body text, and pull-out text.

6. **Avoid using gratuitous graphics and clip art**—Graphics interfere with communication when used solely for decoration. Use graphics to help communicate and expand upon the content, not for the sake of using graphics alone.

7. **Avoid using gratuitous sounds**—Sounds interfere with communication when used solely for effect. They should always help communicate the content and not be used as a transition effect.

8. **Use graphics, not just text**—Well-chosen graphics can help communicate messages. Text alone does not make the best use of the capabilities of presentation software. However, with the ever-increasing ease of finding and downloading images and media from online sources, it is important to introduce concepts of copyright and fair use, require students to document where materials come from, and teach them how to cite the proper sources in their presentations.

9. **Present in a dark room**—Frames can fade away if the room is too bright. Make sure to cover windows and turn off lights during a presentation.

10. **Avoid reading text aloud**—Do not read what the audience can read for themselves. Use text to guide the main points of discussion. This will help you focus on presenting to the audience as opposed to speaking at the screen. Remember, you—not the PowerPoint—are doing the presenting.

hypermedia environment. Today's presentation software also allows authors to add clickable buttons or **hot spots** to jump to any location in the presentation, giving users control of what they want to see and when they can see it. This expanded the number and type of integration possibilities for students and teachers.

For large classes and other groups, presentation software products typically are used in conjunction with computer projection systems, which may include large, high-definition monitor panels, digital projectors and wall-mounted screens, or systems that operate as

**TABLE 4.8** Comparison of Design Criteria for Projected and Individual Presentations

| Criteria for Presentations Projected to *Groups* | Criteria for Presentations Used by *Individuals* |
| --- | --- |
| **Use large type**—So it can be seen from the back of the room (usually 32-point or more) | **Type may be smaller**—For viewing on an individual's computer |
| **Minimize text on each frame**—Use text mainly to focus attention on main points | **More text on each frame is okay**—If product is for tutoring, more text may be needed |
| **Avoid using fancy fonts**—These may be unreadable | Same criterion |
| **Avoid using gratuitous graphics, clip art, and sounds**—These interfere with understanding when used only for decoration | Same criterion |
| **Use graphics, not just text**—These help convey messages | Same criterion |

stand-alone devices. All of these devices enlarge the image produced by the software by projecting it from a computer screen onto a wall screen. However, some integration strategies with interactive presentation hypermedia call for products to be used by individuals working at their own computers. Many of the criteria that are appropriate for projected presentations are not required for individual ones. See Table 4.8 for a comparison of group and individual design guidelines.

Current integration strategies for presentation software include the following:

- **Presentation of information summaries**—By far the most popular use of these tools is for supporting and strengthening classroom presentations. Teachers use them to focus student attention and guide note-taking.

- **Demonstrations of materials for discussion**—In this strategy, the teacher displays a complex diagram such as an electrical circuit or light spectrum, or a series of examples such as works of art, types of animals, or instruments in an orchestra. This is an ideal way to focus student attention while explaining important concepts or pointing out essential features.

- **Presentation of illustrative problems and solutions**—Projection with presentation software is useful when the whole class needs to see example problems and how to solve them (e.g., in mathematics or chemistry) prior to doing their own problems.

- **Automatically-forwarding practice screens**—Many teachers set up automatic presentations of spelling or vocabulary words or objects to identify (e.g., lab equipment, famous names or places) to run automatically in the classroom, knowing that students' eyes are drawn to the moving slides.

- **Assessment screens**—When teachers need students to identify pictures of items (e.g., lab equipment, famous people), presentation screens can enable visual assessment strategies.

- **Brief or full tutorials**—Teachers can create brief tutorials with presentation software. These can be used for reviews of simple concepts (e.g., grammar rules) or "how-to" procedures (e.g., steps to carry out a lab, computer software demonstrations) that allow students to work independently, either for in-class work or make up work. They may also be used to prepare for tests. See an example in Figure 4.5. Full tutorials are complete instructional sequences that usually have practice items following an explanation, which makes interactive buttons especially useful. The program can then branch to different feedback depending on the answer the user selects.

**FIGURE 4.5 Example Frame from Biology Tutorial Created with Presentation Software**

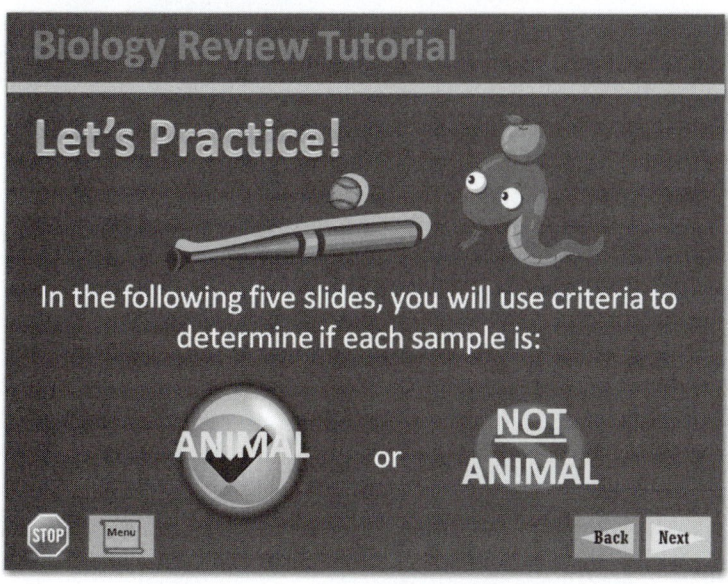

- **Book reports**—Instead of presenting book reports verbally or as written summaries, it is becoming increasingly common for students to report on their reading using presentation slideshows. Teachers often design a standard format or template, and students fill in the required information and add their own illustrations.

- **Game-based reviews**—Interactive presentations based on popular games like Jeopardy have become increasingly popular ways to review skills or content. (See Figure 4.6 for an example game.) The buttons inserted on the screens send users to various items and can also send them to frames with answers and feedback. The Super Teacher Tools site has a large and useful collection of games in a Jeopardy format that review content for a variety of content topics ranging from mathematics to history.

- **Interactive storybooks**—With this strategy, students document existing stories or write their own so they can be read interactively by others. Those reading these hypermedia stories can click on various places on the screen to hear or view parts of a

## FIGURE 4.6 Example Jeopardy Game Created with Presentation Software

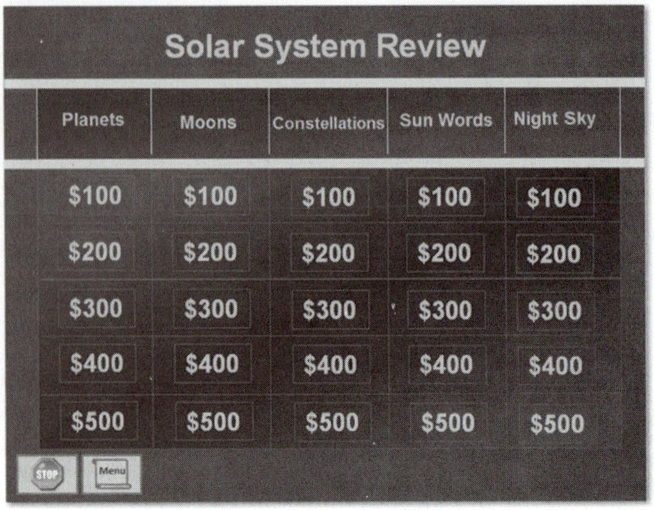

story. This format also lets students go beyond one basic sequence and create their own branches and endings to stories. Candreva (2010) described this strategy as a way to reinforce and enhance children's literacy skills. Thesen and Kira-Soteriou (2011) used a free software called Photo Story 3 (listed in the Open-Source Options feature) to allow students to create their own digital stories. They, too, felt it was a powerful way to enrich all young students' literacy skills. Technology Integration Example 4.5 illustrates the use of these "talking storybooks."

- **Student presentations of project work**—The most powerful strategy for integrating presentation software is for students to create individual or small-group presentations to document and display results of research they have done and/or to practice making persuasive presentations. Having learners become the designers and experts of content, in the end presenting their work to the class, can serve as a powerful technology integration lesson for any domain of learning. Franklin (2008) described a lesson that has each student choose a chemical element to

learn about and create a PowerPoint presentation to teach others. Henson (2008) used a similar strategy to have students research animal behavior and present their findings. McVee, Bailey, and Shanahan (2008) told of students using PowerPoint to help display their interpretation of poems. Schwebach (2008) describes how students used PowerPoint to present their capstone research projects. O'Hara and Pritchard (2008) found that students who created interactive PowerPoint products to illustrate new vocabulary words were more active and engaged than other students and demonstrated greater understanding of words and concepts they studied. PowerPoint-type presentations have become so popular for classroom projects that many assessment rubrics for them are now available online (see especially Kathy Schrock's listing of PowerPoint rubrics (Also, see Technology Integration Examples 4.6 and 4.7.)

# TECHNOLOGY INTEGRATION

## Example 4.5

**TITLE:** Talking Books Enhance Literacy for Kids with Special Needs

**CONTENT AREA/TOPIC:** Language arts, literacy

**GRADE LEVELS:** Elementary students with physical disabilities

**ISTE STANDARDS•S:** Standard 1—Creativity and Innovation

**CCSS:** CCSS.ELA-LITERACY.RF.K.1.A, CCSS.ELA-LITERACY.RF.2.3, CCSS.ELA-LITERACY.RF.3.4, CCSS.ELA-LITERACY.RL.3.1, CCSS.ELA-LITERACY.SL.4.2, CCSS.ELA-LITERACY.SL.5.5

**DESCRIPTION:** When students cannot read independently because of their physical difficulties, their reading development is often delayed. They may not be able to turn pages of a book or turn back to reread a page they enjoy, so they always have to ask someone else to do these things for them. The result is less reading and poorer overall literacy. By making popular children's books into electronic format with PowerPoint, students can access these books using a variety of computer access aids. They turn "pages" by activating a switch with whatever part of their body has the best voluntary control.

*SOURCE:* Based on a concept from "Creating Talking Books in PowerPoint" at http://atto.buffalo.edu/registered/Tutorials/talking Books/powerpoint.php.

# TECHNOLOGY INTEGRATION

## Example 4.6

TITLE: Cave Drawings

CONTENT AREA/TOPIC: Social studies (history), art

GRADE LEVEL: 6–8

ISTE STANDARDS•S: Standard 1—Creativity and Innovation; Standard 2—Communication and Collaboration

CCSS: CCSS.ELA-LITERACY.RH.6-8.3, CCSS.ELA-LITERACY. RH.6-8.7

NCSS THEMES: Thematic Standards: 1 - Culture and Diversity; 2 - Time, Continuity, and Change; 3 - People, Places, and Environments; Disciplinary Standards: 1- History

DESCRIPTION: Students learn about prehistoric man and the messages left in caves from that time. The teacher displays a presentation with example drawings. Students discuss the messages being communicated in pictures. Then, they try their hand at "drawing messages." The lesson wraps up with a discussion on similarities between cave drawings and television, magazines, or newspapers. Students can also create a newspaper advertisement using only pictures and/ or symbols, then see if others can guess the topic of the advertisement.

SOURCE: Based on a concept in Cave Drawing lesson plan at Teachnology website: http://www.teach-nology.com/.

## TECHNOLOGY INTEGRATION

## Example 4.7

TITLE: Here's My Hero

CONTENT AREA/TOPIC: Language arts and technology

GRADE LEVELS: 4–5

ISTE STANDARDS•S: Standard 1—Creativity and Innovation; Standard 2—Communication and Collaboration; Standard 3— Research and Information Fluency; Standard 6—Technology Operations and Concepts

CCSS: CCSS.ELA-LITERACY.RI.4.3, CCSS.ELA-LITERACY.RI.4.9, CCSS.ELA-LITERACY.RI.5.7, CCSS.ELA-LITERACY.W.4.2.B, CCSS.ELA-LITERACY.W.4.4, CCSS.ELA-LITERACY.W.5.7

DESCRIPTION: Students identify a historical figure they regard as a hero and make a presentation about him/her to share with the class. They gather images and data from the Internet to add to their slides. They use PowerPoint features to format their slides, create a timeline of significant events in their hero's life (organizational chart), and insert a table comparing themselves to their hero. Before making their presentations, they learn how to organize speaker notes for their slides and rearrange slides for maximum impact during the presentation.

SOURCE: Based on a concept in a lesson plan at the TechnoKids website: http://www.technokids.com/computer-curriculum/junior/powerpoint-lesson-plans-technohero.aspx.

## Teaching Presentation Software Skills: Recommended Skills and Activities

If students are to develop their own presentations, as is required in some of the integration strategies described in this chapter, they must have time to learn the software before their products are graded. Ideally, they will have time to play with the software and explore its capabilities. However, direct instruction may be a more efficient use of classroom time. If students are not able to use the online tutorials that provide direct instruction in how to use presentation software (see link in Table 4.9), teachers can use the strategies outlined in Table 4.9 to teach this software. Teachers may decide to teach other functions and features of presentation software gradually over time, depending on the needs of the lessons.

# TABLE 4.9 Tips on Teaching Students How to Create Presentations
## (Also see PowerPoint tutorials)

| Suggested Steps | Tasks Under Each Step |
| --- | --- |
| **Step 1**—Prepare for teaching. | **Arrange for:**<br>• A big screen and projection system or interactive whiteboard (IWB).<br>• A disc or flash drive for each student, or a cloud-based storage location.<br>• Copying sample file(s) onto network or student media.<br>• One computing device per student.<br>• Alternative keyboards or other adaptive devices for students with disabilities.<br><br>**Create or obtain:**<br>Handouts or wall posters on **presentation software** features and common errors. |
| **Step 2**—Demonstrate the basics using a sample prepared presentation. | **Using a big screen and projection system or IWB, show how to:**<br>• Open a sample slideshow.<br>• Page through the frames using the slide-bar and thumbnail views.<br>• See all frames at once in slide sorter format.<br>• Get from one view to another using menus or icons at bottom of screen.<br><br>**Then demonstrate:**<br>• How to display the slideshow as a presentation.<br><br>**Finally, show how to:**<br>• Create an additional slide at any location in the presentation.<br>• Select a slide format from those available.<br>• Add text to the slide and format it.<br>• Add clip art from a library.<br>• Add an image from a hard drive or a flash drive. |
| **Step 3**—Assign individual or small-group practice. | **Give students a sample presentation file and have them:**<br>• Open the file.<br>• Do a list of changes to the file (e.g., add new slides, insert text and images).<br>• Name, save, and close the document. |
| **Step 4**—Demonstrate advanced features. | **Using a big screen or projection system, show how to:**<br>• Add transitions to slides.<br>• **Optional:** Insert shapes and lines.<br>• **Optional:** Add WordArt or charts.<br>• **Optional:** Do notes.<br>• **Optional:** Do headers and footers for handouts.<br>• **Optional:** Print handouts. |
| **Step 5**—Assign more practice. | **Do the following:**<br>• Assign a product for them to copy or experiment with (for young students) or create (for older students).<br>• Monitor students as they work and give individual help where needed. |
| **Step 6**—Demonstrate interactive features using a sample interactive presentation. | **Demonstrate:**<br>• How buttons work to "jump" from various locations.<br>• How to insert a button.<br>• How to storyboard using slide sorter option. |
| **Step 7**—Assign more practice. | **Do the following:**<br>• Assign a product for them to copy or experiment with (for young students) or create (for older students).<br>• Monitor students as they work and give individual help as needed. |

The effectiveness of interactive presentations depends largely on the designer's authoring skills. The most common error in presentation hypermedia is when links fail to work as intended. Using and teaching two design steps can prevent this.

1. Lay out frames using sticky notes or the **slide sorter** option, and make notes on each interactive button to show where users go to when they click it.
2. Try out the finished product and/or have others try it out, and go through it, taking various paths through the slides. Make sure all buttons work and send users to the locations the buttons indicate, no matter which frame students come from in the presentation.

▲ The most powerful strategy for integrating presentation software is for students to create individual or small-group presentations to document and display results of their research and/or to practice making persuasive presentations. (Photo courtesy of W. Wiencke)

### TECHNOLOGY LEARNING CHECK

Complete **TLC 4.4** to review what you have learned from reading this section about presentation software features and uses.

# COLLABORATE, DISCUSS, REFLECT

Monkey Business/Fotolia

**The following questions may be used either for in-class, small-group discussions or may initiate discussions in blogs or online discussion boards:**

1. In his *New York Times* blog post, "Ending the Curse of Cursive," John Tierney quoted Vanderbilt professor Steve Graham: "If every young child had a computer to write on, and the keyboards were built for young children, and we provided instruction to help them type fluently, then the need for handwriting would be questionable." Do you agree with Dr. Graham that we should eschew teaching cursive writing in favor of focusing on word processing instruction? What arguments could be made for and against this substitution?

2. In an article, "Spreadsheets Across the Curriculum," for the ICT in Education website, Freedman responded to critics who say that spreadsheets are, by their very nature, boring. Freedman maintains that spreadsheets can be interesting and exciting, depending on how you use them. For example, she assigned students to do a party plan and decide how many bottles of "fizzy drink" and other supplies were needed and how much they could purchase within a given budget. She also gives examples of how spreadsheets can add interest to studies that are not usually thought of as "numerical" For example, counting, plotting, and comparing the instances of jokes or murders in various Shakespearean plays. Can you create other ways to use spreadsheets in various content areas to create learning activities that are both important and engaging to students?

# Summary

**The following is a summary of the main points covered in this chapter.**

1. **Overview of the "Basic Three"**—Three software tools that are usually part of the basic suite of programs most people buy are: word processing, spreadsheet, and presentation software.
   - Benefits of these programs include improved productivity, appearance, and accuracy, and more support for interaction and collaboration.
   - Developments since these products were first made available include Web-based collaboration tools, open-source software, mobile tools, Web-enabled features, better file-exchange compatibility, and software suites.

2. **Word processing is a software tool that allows people to produce typed documents on a computer screen.**
   - Word processing benefits include saving time, improving document appearance, allowing easy exchange of work, allowing collaboration, and support for student writing and language learning.
   - Word processing issues include questions about the age students should start word processing, necessity to teach keyboarding skills, effects of word processing on handwriting, impact of word processing on assessment, and problems with inadvertent errors.
   - Word processing productivity applications include creating handouts or other instructional materials, lesson plans and notes, reports, forms, letters to parents or students, flyers, and newsletters.
   - Word processing instructional integration strategies include supporting the learning of writing processes; using a dynamic group process approach; assigning individual language, writing, and reading exercises; and encouraging writing through the curriculum.

3. **Spreadsheets are software tools designed to organize and manipulate numerical data.**
   - Spreadsheet benefits include saving time, organizing displays of information, and increasing motivation to work with mathematics.
   - Spreadsheet productivity applications include keeping club and classroom budgets, preparing performance checklists, and keeping gradebooks.
   - Spreadsheet instructional integration strategies include making possible visual teaching demonstrations, supporting student products, supporting mathematical and "what if" problem solving, storing and allowing analysis of data, and projecting grades.

4. **Presentation programs are software tools that are designed to display information, including text, images, audio, and video, in a slideshow format.**
   - Presentation software benefits include helping organize thinking about a topic, enhancing the impact of spoken information, and allowing collaboration on presentations.
   - Presentation software issues include the impact of presentation software on information presented and teaching style.
   - Presentation software integration strategies include presentation of information summaries, demonstrations of materials for discussion, presentation of illustrative problems and solutions, automatically forwarding practice screens, assessment screens, brief or full tutorials, book reports, game-based reviews, interactive storybooks, and student presentations of project work.

# TECHNOLOGY INTEGRATION WORKSHOP

## 1. APPLY WHAT YOU LEARNED

To apply the concepts and skills you've read about throughout this chapter, go to the Chapter 4 Technology Application Activity.

## 2. TECHNOLOGY INTEGRATION LESSON PLANNING: PART 1—EVALUATING AND CREATING LESSON PLANS

Complete the following exercise using the sample lesson plans found on any lesson planning site that you find on the Internet.

a. Locate lesson ideas—Identify three lesson plans that focus on any of the tools or strategies you learned about in this chapter. For example:
   - Word processing software tools
   - Spreadsheet software tools
   - Presentation software tools

b. Evaluate the lessons—Use the Technology Lesson Plan Evaluation Checklist to evaluate each of the lessons you found.

c. Create your own lesson—After you have reviewed and evaluated some sample lessons, create one of your own using a lesson plan format of your choice (or one your instructor gives you). Be sure the lesson focuses on one of the technologies or strategies discussed in this chapter.

## 3. TECHNOLOGY INTEGRATION LESSON PLANNING: PART 2—IMPLEMENTING THE TIP MODEL

Review how to implement the TIP model in your classroom by doing the following activities with the lesson you created in the Technology Integration Lesson Planning exercise above.

a. Describe the Phase 1—Planning activities you would do to use this lesson in your classroom:
   - What is the relative advantage of using the technology(ies) in this lesson?
   - Do you have resources and skills you need to carry it out?

b. Describe the Phase 2—Implementation activities you would do to use this lesson in your classroom:
   - What are the objectives of the lesson plan?
   - How will you assess your students' accomplishment of the objectives?
   - What integration strategies are used in this lesson plan?
   - How would you prepare the learning environment?

c. Describe the Phase 3—Evaluation/Revision activities you would do to use this lesson in your classroom: What strategies and/or instruments would you use to evaluate the success of this lesson in your classroom, in order to determine revision needs?

d. Add lesson descriptors—Create descriptors for your new lesson (e.g., grade level, content and topic areas, technologies used, ISTE standards, 21st Century Learning standards).

e. Save your new lesson—Save your lesson plan with all its descriptors and TIP Model notes.

## 4. FOR YOUR TEACHING PORTFOLIO

Add the following to your Teaching Portfolio:
   - Lesson plan evaluations, lesson plans, and products you created above.
   - Products of your group's Hot Topic Debates.
   - Products of your group's Collaborate, Discuss, Reflect online or in-class activities.

# Technology Tools for 21st Century Teaching

## BEYOND THE BASICS

## Learning Outcomes

After reading this chapter and completing the learning activities, you should be able to:

1. Identify the uses and contributions to teaching and learning of each of the seven categories of software tools. (ISTE Standards•T 1, 2, 3, 5)

2. Select a materials generator software tool that would most effectively support a given teaching and/or learning task. (ISTE Standards•T 1, 2, 3, 5)

3. Select data collection and analysis software tools that would most effectively support a given teaching and/or learning task. (ISTE Standards•T 1, 2, 3, 5)

4. Select a testing software tool that would most effectively support a given teaching and/or learning task. (ISTE Standards•T 1, 2, 3, 5)

5. Select a graphics software tool that would most effectively support a given teaching and/or learning task. (ISTE Standards•T 1, 2, 3, 5)

6. Select a planning and organizing software tool that would most effectively support a given teaching and/or learning task. (ISTE Standards•T 1, 2, 3, 5)

7. Select a research and reference tool that would most effectively support a given teaching and/or learning task. (ISTE Standards•T 1, 2, 3, 5)

8. Select a content-area software tool that would most effectively support a given teaching and/or learning task. (ISTE Standards•T 1, 2, 3, 5)

# TECHNOLOGY INTEGRATION IN ACTION
# SHARING A PASSION FOR POETRY

GRADE LEVEL: Grades 4–5 • CONTENT AREA/TOPIC: Language arts, poetry • LENGTH OF TIME: An hour each day for 6 days

## PHASE 1 ANALYSIS OF LEARNING AND TEACHING NEEDS

ZouZou/Shutterstock

### Step 1: Determine relative advantage.

Mr. Lipe is a fifth grade teacher who has great difficulty getting his young students to share his passion for poetry. He tried various teaching approaches, but many students remained indifferent, and few are interested enough to read or write poems after the unit is over. When he taught mathematics activities, he had found that using his interactive whiteboard made it easier to engage students, especially if they played a part in illustrating and practicing concepts. He felt that with the right kinds of activities, he might also engage them in learning about and writing poetry. From a blog for teachers, he learned about some online materials to help teach poetry, some of which could be used with interactive whiteboards and allowed students to publish their work online. After reviewing the materials, he decided to restructure his poetry unit around these activities. He would display the online "poetry engine" on the whiteboard to illustrate several types of poems that kids can write, and it would also allow students some initial practice in writing poems. After more practice in pairs and small groups, each would have to write one poem of each kind, with or without the poetry engine, and each would be allowed to publish one poem on the website.

### Step 2: Assess required resources and skills.

Mr. Lipe felt he knew a great deal about writing poetry, since he had had good instructors in his undergraduate program and was a poet himself. But after three years of unsuccessful efforts to engage his students in poetry writing, he felt less confident in his ability to motivate young people on this topic. To improve his instructional approaches, he read through a variety of blogs and online materials looking for ideas on how to teach poetry better. After reading these materials and blogging with colleagues who gave him good leads, he felt more confident that the new approach would be much more motivating to students.

## PHASE 2 PLANNING FOR INTEGRATION

### Step 3: Decide on objectives and assessments.

To help him see if students were achieving what he hoped in the poetry unit, Mr. Lipe created objectives and assessments to measure students' progress in poetry skills, as well as their attitudes toward poetry. The outcomes, objectives, and assessments were:

Outcome: Write three different poems reflecting three different poetry genres.
Objective: After participating in the practice activities, each student writes three poems in correct format, using either a poetry engine or writing on the word processor, and provides an illustration for at least one.
Assessment: A rubric of criteria and points.

Outcome: Feel more positively about poetry.
Objective: At least 80% of students express interest in reading or writing additional poems, as reflected in comments to the teacher or poems they offer.
Assessment: Teacher observation.

### Step 4: Design integration strategies.

Mr. Lipe knew that the initial activities would be group based, followed up by individual ones. He designed the following sequence of activities to be done in one hour each day for one week:

Day 1: **Introduce the unit.** Begin by reading two short poems from a book of popular poems for young people (e.g., Shel Silverstein's *Where the Sidewalk Ends*), while displaying on the whiteboard an image for each poem from the book. Ask students to close their eyes while a poem is read; ask if the poem brought an image to mind for any of them. Tell students that they can write, illustrate, and publish poems of their own. Demonstrate the poetry engine on the whiteboard and let students come to the whiteboard and practice generating poems of each genre in front of the class. Tell students they may bring a favorite poem to share with the class the next day, if they like.

Day 2: **Allow student practice and sharing.** Ask one or two students to share the poem they found or wrote. Show students the part of the site on which students can publish their work. Tell them that by the end of the week, they will write three poems and select one to publish. Display and discuss the rubrics on the whiteboard. Allow students to work in small groups with the three classroom computers using the poetry engine. Other students work on illustrations that can accompany poems, writing other poems, and on reviewing books of popular poetry for young people. Facilitate their work and answer questions, as needed. Ask them to begin thinking about which poem they would like to upload to the site in order to become a published poet. Tell students that some of them may share one of their own poems with the class each day of this week.

Day 3: **Continue practice and sharing.** Ask a few students to share the poems they wrote the day before, and remind students they may bring a poem to share with the class the next day. Continue work with the poetry engines and seatwork on illustrations and reading and writing additional poems.

Day 4: **Continue practice and sharing.** Ask more students to share their poems by displaying them on the whiteboard and talk about their poetry ideas. Ask students to change or move around words in ways that improve the poems. Encourage them to express their thoughts about poetry and what they like and don't like about it. Remind them that they must select only one poem to publish.

Day 5: **Select and publish poems.** Ask more students to share their poems. Allow students to begin publishing their selected poems on the classroom computers, while other students complete work on their poems and illustrations.

Day 6: **Complete work.** Ask more students to share their poems. Finish publishing all poems to the site. Give students a handout to give to parents with the website where they may find their child's published poem.

Post-unit activity. Arrange for a poetry reading event where children get to read aloud their published poems.

### Step 5: Prepare instructional environment.

The first time Mr. Lipe taught this project, he created the rubric and student and parent handouts, and he created a whiteboard file to allow touch-screen use of the poetry engine display. For subsequent times, he had to do the following:

Prepare for whiteboard displays: He selected the images to display from the computer and checked to make sure the whiteboard was working with the software file he would use with the poetry engine.

Prepare classroom computers: He checked each of the classroom computers and made sure the poetry website was in the Bookmarks/Favorites list.

Make handout copies: He made copies of the students' rubric and parent handouts.

## PHASE 3   POST-INSTRUCTION ANALYSIS AND REVISIONS

### Step 6: Analyze results.

Mr. Lipe was delighted with the response from his students. Nearly all of them completed all three required poems, and most were in good shape. In the weeks following the unit, about 50% of them asked how they could write or read more poems. Though he didn't meet his own criterion of 80% of the students, he felt he was on the right track with this approach. Several parents had contacted either him or his principal expressing their delight with their child's published poems.

### Step 7: Make revisions.

Though the unit generally went smoothly, there was not enough time in the six days for all students to publish their poems, and some students needed more time to complete their work. Also, not all students had the opportunity to read a poem in front of the class. Since these were the most motivational of the activities, Mr. Lipe decided to schedule a computer lab day to do uploading of poems and allow students to continue reading a poem each day until everyone had a chance.

*Source:* Based on a concept presented in Scholastic's *Writing with Writers: Poetry* activities and resources.

# CHAPTER 5 **BIG IDEAS OVERVIEW**

Before you begin reading the rest of this chapter, listen to the **Chapter 5 Big Ideas Overview**. It will give you a two-minute audio overview of main concepts to look for and help prepare you to work through information and exercises to achieve this chapter's outcomes.

# INTRODUCTION TO OTHER SOFTWARE SUPPORT TOOLS

An ever-increasing number of software tools are available that go beyond what many people think of as the "basic" capabilities of word processing, spreadsheets, and presentation software. These additional materials serve teachers and students in a variety of ways, making possible many kinds of freedom in the classroom. These tools vary greatly in their purposes and the benefits they offer. Since teachers should choose them for the qualities and benefits they bring to the classroom, rather than simply because they are available, this chapter will focus on unique features and classroom needs each of them can meet. The tools described in this chapter range in importance from nearly essential to "nice to have," and in function from presenting instruction to supporting background tasks that make a classroom run smoothly. Depending on the tool and the needs of the situation, a software support tool can offer the following benefits:

- Improved efficiency and productivity
- Improved appearance of product
- Better accuracy and timeliness of information
- More support for interaction and sharing

## Types of Software Support Tools

This chapter describes seven general categories of software support tools. Table 5.1 provides examples of software products under each of the following categories:

- **Materials generators**—Help teachers and students produce instructional materials on paper and online.
- **Data collection and analysis tools**—Help teachers collect and organize information to provide feedback and support decision making.
- **Testing and grading tools**—Help teachers collect and track assessment information to measure student progress.
- **Graphics tools**—Allow manipulation of images to illustrate documents and Web pages.
- **Planning and organizing tools**—Help teachers and students conceptualize, organize, and communicate their ideas.
- **Research and reference tools**—Let students look up information in electronic versions of encyclopedias, atlases, and dictionaries.
- **Content-area tools**—Support teaching and learning activities in various subject matter areas.

## Recent Developments in Software Support Tools

Although some of these tools have been in existence for many years, they are constantly being updated with new features and capabilities. The following developments have made these tools even more useful in the classroom.

- **Mobile devices**—Handheld devices such as tablets and cell phones have made software tools even more portable and accessible to teachers and students, and this more portable format has made software tools even more popular.

- **Web and cloud availability**—Though a few software tools continue to be packaged and sold on discs, most are now available only as downloads from the Internet. Others aim for maximum access with **cloud computing**, which is storage outside one's own computer on servers that are accessed through the Internet.

- **Software suites**—Just as word processing, spreadsheets, and presentation software are packaged together as "software suites" in order to combine their capabilities and make them easier to use together, other software tools are also available in packages matched to various needs. For example, if a teacher wanted to do complex print publications, Adobe's Creative Suite Design Standard combines high-end desktop publishing software (Adobe InDesign) with Adobe Photoshop (image editor), Adobe Illustrator (drawing software), and Adobe Acrobat (portable document software). If the goal was designing full-featured Web pages, Adobe's Creative Suite Web Premium package would include Adobe Dreamweaver and Adobe Fireworks. While these highly capable suites are fairly expensive for educators, other software suites (as well as separate software tools) are available as free downloads (see Open-Source Options).

## TABLE 5.1 Overview of Software Tool Categories

| Tool Category and Uses | Example Software Tools |
| --- | --- |
| **Materials generators** allow creation and use of documents, Web pages, and various lessons and exercises | • Desktop publishing software<br>• Web design software<br>• Interactive whiteboard software<br>• Worksheet and puzzle generators<br>• IEP Generators<br>• Graphic document makers<br>• PDF and forms makers |
| **Data collection and analysis** tools make it easier to collect and process data to provide feedback and support decision making | • Database software<br>• Online survey software<br>• Statistical packages<br>• Student information systems<br>• Student response systems |
| **Testing and grading tools** allow collection and tracking of assessment information to measure student progress | • Electronic gradebooks<br>• Test generators and rubric generators<br>• Computer-based testing systems |
| **Graphics tools** allow creation of illustrations for use in documents and Web pagess and create visual data summaries | • Draw/paint programs<br>• Image editing software<br>• Charting and graphing tools<br>• Media collections<br>• Word cloud generators |
| **Planning and organizing tools** help organize ideas for writing and discussion; help organize, plan, and schedule activities | • Outlining and concept-mapping software<br>• Lesson planning software<br>• Calendars; scheduling and time-management tools |
| **Research and reference tools** help students research on assigned topics; assist with using correct spelling and word use | • Online encyclopedias<br>• Digital atlases and mapping tools<br>• Digital dictionaries and thesauruses |
| **Content-area tools** support tasks specific to content areas such as technology education, music, reading, science, math, social studies, and foreign languages | • MIDI tools: music editors and synthesizers<br>• CAD systems<br>• Reading tools<br>• MBLs/CBLs<br>• GPS/GIS systems<br>• Online language translators |

**TECHNOLOGY LEARNING CHECK**

Complete TLC 5.1 to review what you have learned from reading this section about the categories of software tools.

## USING MATERIALS GENERATORS

Materials generators include desktop publishing software, Web page editors, whiteboard activity software, worksheet and puzzle generators, IEP generators, graphic document makers, and PDF and forms makers. A summary of these, with sample products and classroom uses, is shown in Table 5.2. Also see here a summary of free software tools in Open Source Options.

# OPEN SOURCE
## OPTIONS
### for Software Tools Beyond the Basics

| TYPES | FREE SOURCES |
|---|---|
| Materials generators | Scribus: scribus.net<br>NVu Web design software: nvu.com<br>Puzzle maker: discoveryeducation.com/free-puzzlemaker/<br>Certificate maker: certificatemaker.com<br>PDFforge PDF maker: pdfforge.org<br>PageBreeze forms maker: formbreeze.com |
| Data collection and analysis tools | Listing of free statistical software: freestatistics.info/en |
| Testing and grading tools | Gradebook (*Engrade*): engrade.com<br>Test generator: mytest.vocabtest.com<br>Rubric maker—*RubiStar* (use program to create a rubric or use pre-made rubrics): rubistar.4teachers.org |
| Graphics tools | Inkscape graphics editor: inkscape.org<br>Tux Paint drawing software for kids: tuxpaint.org<br>Gimp image editing software: gimp.org<br>Charting/graphing tools: educational-freeware.com<br>Free WAV sound files: thefreesite.com/Free_Sounds/<br>Sourceforge font collections: sourceforge.net/projects/worldfonts<br>Open font library: launchpad.net/openfontlibrary<br>Free animations: free-animations.co.uk |
| Planning and organizing tools | OpenSIS student information system: opensis.com<br>SchoolForge SIS: schoolforge.net<br>Parent–teacher conference scheduler: ptcfast.com |
| Research and reference tools | GoldenDict: goldendict.org/<br>Lingoes: lingoes.net/<br>Wikipedia: en.wikipedia.org |
| Content-area tools | Archimedes *CAD* system: archimedes.codeplex.com<br>Audacity sound editor software: audacity.sourceforge.net<br>Music Editor Free: music-editor.net<br>Free online readability calculators: readabilityformulas.com/free-readability-calculators.php<br>Online graphing calculator: coolmath.com/graphit<br>GPS education resources: gpseducationresource.com<br>U.S. Census Bureau TIGERLine GIS files: census.gov/geo/maps-data/data/tiger.html<br>Language translators: babelfish.com/ or translate.google.com/ |

## TABLE 5.2 Overview of Materials Generators Tools

| Tool Category | Example Software Tools |
|---|---|
| **Desktop publishing software:** Students create their own letterhead, brochures, flyers/posters, newsletters, newspapers, and books | • Microsoft Publisher<br>• Adobe InDesign and Pagemaker<br>• Quark Express |
| **Web page design software:** Teachers design Web pages or websites to give information or house often-used links or lessons such as webquests; students design Web pages to learn the skill or to display results of project work or research | • Adobe Dreamweaver<br>• Microsoft WebMatrix |
| **Whiteboard activity software:** Teachers create lessons for use with interactive whiteboards | • Notebook (for use with Smart Boards)<br>• ActivStudio or ActivInspire (for use with Prometheus Boards) |
| **Worksheet and puzzle generators:** Teachers create puzzles and worksheets to allow skill practice | • Crossword Puzzle Maker<br>• Worksheet Works<br>• Quia Web |
| **IEP Generators:** Teachers create individual education plans (IEP) for special education students | • IEP Online and EasyIEP<br>• IEP Planet<br>• IEP4U |
| **Graphic document makers:** Teachers and students create awards, recognitions, flyers, cards, and other decorated documents | • Print Shop Deluxe<br>• Smart Draw |
| **PDF and forms makers:** Teachers and students create documents in Portable Document Format (PDF) and create forms that can be completed online | • Adobe Acrobat Pro<br>• PDF Maker Pilot<br>• Cute PDF<br>• FormArtist Professional |

## Desktop Publishing Software

It is perhaps ironic that one of the most useful and widely used of the technology tools is one that communicates information in a traditional medium: the printed page. By allowing teachers and students to design elaborate printed products, however, desktop publishing tools give them the important advantage of complete control over a potentially powerful form of communication. This control over the form and appearance of the printed page is the defining quality of **desktop publishing**, a term coined in 1984 by Paul Brainerd, founder of the Aldus Corporation, to mean using a combination of software, microcomputers, and printers to allow individuals to be their own publishers.

Desktop publishing versus word processing software. Though desktop publishing software and word processing software are different tools, it is possible to do some kinds of desktop publishing with word processing software. Just as with desktop publishing software, word processing programs allow users to mix text and graphics on each page. The primary difference between word processing software and desktop publishing software is that the latter is designed to create documents as separate pages that are then linked together; the user clicks on an icon representing each page, and only one page or facing pages display. On the other hand, word processing "flows" pages in a continuous stream through a document; the user scrolls down to view pages in the document. Because desktop publishing software allows pages to be viewed as separate units, it provides more flexibility with the placement and format of both text and graphics on individual pages.

You can use any available word processing software package to create most of the desktop publishing products you want to produce in a school environment (e.g., classroom brochures and newsletters). The more advanced layout features offered by desktop publishing software (e.g., elaborate layering of text and graphics elements) are needed only if you are teaching students how to design and lay out large, complex documents such as newspapers and books.

Example classroom applications. Desktop publishing software can be used for many of the same classroom activities and products as word processing software. Desktop publishing is the strategy of choice, however, to produce elaborate, graphic-oriented documents (e.g., flyers and posters, brochures, newsletters and magazines, and books and booklets), and teachers can structure some highly motivating classroom projects around these products. Instructional benefits for desktop publishing include increases in children's self-esteem when they publish their own work, heightened interest in writing and in motivation to write for audiences outside the classroom, and improved learning through small group collaboration. Here is a list of common classroom applications and ideas for implementing them:

- **Practice in grammar, spelling, and communication**—The activity of creating a flyer or brochure can become an opportunity to learn about designing attractive and interesting communications and to apply language usage skills.
- **Methods of reporting research findings**—Popular examples of using desktop publishing projects to report on students' research include creating travel brochures that report on student exploration during field trips, descriptions of the local region, and creative descriptions of organizations or activities. Sometimes this type of activity represents the culmination of a large project, such as a series of science experiments or a social studies research unit; sometimes it is a way for every student to contribute writing for a class project. All of these projects are highly motivational to students, and they attract "good press" for the teacher and the school.
- **Opportunities for creative works**—Even very young students are thrilled to produce and display their own personal books, which sometimes represent work produced over the course of a school year. Sometimes the books show creative works resulting from a competition; frequently, examples of students' best work are collected for a particular topic or time period. Students can sell their publications as a fund-raising activity, but this kind of project also reaps other benefits for students of all abilities. Teachers report that getting published increases students' pride in their work and makes them want to spend more time on it.

### Criteria for effective desktop publishing.
Desktop-published products have greater impact and communicate the author's intent more clearly if they reflect some fairly simple design criteria. These include:

- **Using a limited number of typefaces (fonts)**—Unusual typefaces or **fonts** can help direct the eye toward text, but too many different fonts on a page can be distracting, and some fancy fonts are difficult to read.
- **Using different fonts for title and text**—To aid the reader, use a **serif typeface** (a font with small curves or "hands and feet" that extend from the ends of the letters) for text in the main body of the document. Use a **sans serif typeface**, a font without extensions, for titles and headlines.
- **Using appropriate sizes for type**—Make the type large enough to assist the reader (e.g., younger readers usually need large point sizes), but not too large to dominate the page.
- **Avoiding overuse of type styles**—Breaking up text with too many style changes interferes with reading. Avoid excessive underlining, boldfacing, and italics.
- **Matching text and background colors**—Use white or yellow type on a black block to add drama. Avoid color combinations that can be difficult to read (e.g., orange on green or red on blue).
- **Using visual cues**—Attract reader attention to important information on the page by using frames or boxes around text; bullets or arrows to designate important points; shading of the part of the page behind the important text; different text styles (e.g., boldface or italic type); and captions for pictures and diagrams.
- **Using white space well**—There is a saying in advertising that "white space sells." Don't be afraid to leave areas in a document with nothing in them at all to help focus attention on areas that do contain information.
- **Creating and using graphics carefully**—Use pictures and designs to focus attention and convey information, but remember that too many elaborate pictures or graphic design elements can be distracting.

- **Avoiding common text format errors**—Common desktop design pitfalls include using irregularly shaped text blocks and angled type, both of which are difficult to read.
- **Avoiding common text break errors**—Use desktop publishing software features to control for widows and orphans (leftover single words and phrases at the tops or bottoms of pages) and excessive hyphenation.

## Web Design Software

Although educators and others can create Web pages and websites using a high-level programming language called **HTML** (which stands for hypertext markup language), it is easier and faster to use a tool called **Web design software**. Also known as **Web page editors**, these tools are authoring programs that allow people to create Web pages in the same way they would use word processing to create documents. They insert text, graphics, and hypermedia links to create the pages, and the editor software automatically creates the HTML that allows the pages to be linked together and placed on the Internet.

Teachers and students can use Web design software to create Web pages for both instructional and productivity applications. Some common uses include:

- **Classroom news, activities, and resources**—Many teachers use HTML editors to create their own classroom websites. These are multipurpose sites with items ranging from announcements and information about current curriculum to locations from which students and/or parents may download handouts or homework. They can also have links to Internet sites that teachers know they will be using often to support instruction. For example, if they use certain puzzles and games to provide student practice, they can have part of the site that has links to these activities.

- **Web-based lessons**—Teachers can use HTML editors to create their own instructional activities students can do on the Web. More details and examples of these lessons will be presented in Chapter 7.

- **Student-produced work**—Teachers may choose to have students create Web pages instead of documents to show off their creative work or research results. Students find it very motivating when they realize that their work will be available online and can be seen by others.

## Interactive Whiteboard Activity Software

**An interactive whiteboard** is a display screen connected to a computer and digital projector and allows information projected on the screen to be manipulated with special pens or one's hands. Some systems also allow drawings or notes from a given session to be saved and brought back later. The most popular interactive whiteboards are Prometheus' Promethean ActivBoard and SMART Technology's SMART Board. A related device also developed by Prometheus is the **SMART Table Interactive Learning Center**, which is an electronic table with a touch-screen surface that several students can give input to at the same time. Each brand of interactive whiteboards comes with its own programs, called **interactive whiteboard activity software**, that allows teachers to author and display lessons for use with the systems. For example, the interactive whiteboard activity software used with a SMART Board is called Notebook (see Figure 5.1), and the programs used with the Promethean ActivBoard interactive whiteboard are called ActivStudio and ActivInspire. The programs come with a resource bank of images, graphics tools, and text tools that teachers can use to author programs in much the same way as they would use PowerPoint's program and resources to create slides. Whiteboard activity software is required to give whiteboard lessons their interactive qualities. For example, teachers may use it to develop a lesson that

▲ Teachers may use interactive whiteboard activity software to develop lessons in which students move objects around on the whiteboard or touch the screen to select or enter answers. (Photo courtesy of W. Wiencke)

## FIGURE 5.1 Sample Screen from SmartBoard Notebook Software

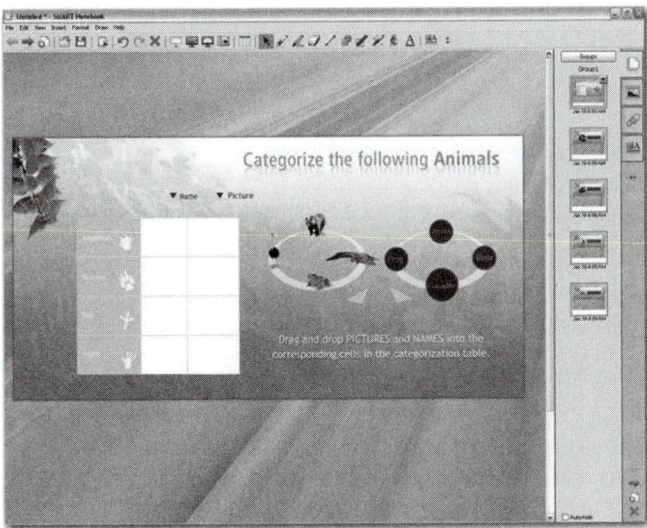

Categorize the following Animals

Drag and drop PICTURES and NAMES into the corresponding cells in the categorization table.

allows students to move objects around on the whiteboard or touch the screen to select or enter an answer to a mathematics problem.

Companies that market interactive whiteboards provide the software as a free download to those who purchase their whiteboards. Whiteboards have become very popular in schools, so this chapter includes a list of **Top Ten** ways teachers can use them as well as a Hot Topic for Debate that focuses on their use. For a sample lesson designed with this kind of software tool, see Technology Integration Example 5.1.

## Worksheet and Puzzle Generators

Teachers also use software to produce worksheets, in much the same way as they do to generate tests. **Worksheet generators** help teachers produce exercises for practice rather than test items. Like test generator software, worksheet generator software prompts the teacher to enter questions of various kinds, but it usually offers no options for completing exercises on-screen or for grading them. In many cases, test generator software and worksheet generator software are similar enough to be used interchangeably, and some packages are intended for both purposes. **Puzzle generators** automatically format and create crosswords, word search puzzles, and similar game-like activities. The teacher enters the content, and the software formats the puzzle. Refer to Table 5.2 for popular worksheet and puzzle generation sites. Common uses of worksheet and puzzle generators include:

- Practice for lower level skills, such as math facts
- Cloze exercises (comprehension exercises with certain words removed and students fill in the blanks)
- Exercises to review words and definitions

## Individualized Education Program (IEP) Generators

The increased emphasis on school and teacher accountability means more paperwork on student progress, and teachers of students with special needs seem to have the most paperwork requirements of all. Federal legislation, such as the Individuals with Disabilities Education Act (IDEA) and the Americans with Disabilities Act (ADA), requires that schools prepare an **individualized educational program,** or IEP, for each special needs student. These IEPs

## Hot Topic Debate
### Do Classrooms Need Interactive Whiteboards?

*Take a position for or against (based either on your own position or one assigned to you) on the following controversial statement. Discuss it in class or on an online discussion board, blog, or wiki, as assigned by your instructor. When the discussion is complete, write a summary of the main pros and cons that you and your classmates have stated, and put the summary document in your Teacher Portfolio.*

In her February 2011 (vol. 8, no. 2) article in the *Teacher.Net Gazette,* "Top 10 Ways to Use Interactive Whiteboards in Elementary Classrooms," Yenner says that interactive whiteboards are a breakthrough technology, making possible a variety of new ways to engage students and make teachers' work more efficient. However, other authors are more critical. One post in the Innovative Educator blog gave "10 Reasons to Ditch the Board," saying whiteboards have few additional capabilities to make them worth the money. Do interactive whiteboards have unique and powerful characteristics that energize teaching and learning, or are they being oversold? What evidence can you cite that they have (or have the potential to have) substantial impact on teacher practice and student outcomes?

# TECHNOLOGY INTEGRATION

## Example 5.1

serve as blueprints for each special student's instructional activities, and teachers must provide documentation that such a plan is on file and that it governs classroom activities. **IEP generator** software assists teachers in preparing IEPs (Wilson, Michaels, & Margolis, 2005). Like test and worksheet generators, IEP generators provide on-screen prompts that remind users of the required components in the plan. When a teacher finishes entering all the necessary information, the program prints out the IEP in a standard format. Some IEP generation programs also accept data updates on each student's progress. See also the Adapting for Special Needs feature.

## Graphic Document Makers

**Graphic document makers** are software tools that simplify the activity of making highly graphic materials, such as awards certificates and greeting cards. They offer sets of clip art and predesigned templates to which teachers and students can add their own content. For example, teachers have found certificates to be a useful kind of recognition. Certificates congratulate students for accomplishments, and the students can take them home and share them with parents and friends. Most certificate makers include numerous templates for various kinds of achievements, a feature that makes teachers prefer them over word processing software for these kinds of tasks. You can select the template that is appropriate for the kind of recognition intended (e.g., completing an activity, being a first-place winner) and enter the personal information for each recipient. Also, students frequently find it motivating to use these packages to design their own certificates, cards, and flyers. The most popular of these document makers is Printshop (Broderbund). This and similar software tools are listed in Table 5.2. Though graphic document makers are still being used, word processing and drawing software packages now offer many of the same advantages, including a variety of templates for various awards.

## PDF and Forms Makers

**Portable Document Format (PDF)** file software, created by Adobe, permits the viewing and sending of documents as images. Since they are viewed as images, the PDF document displays all of the formatting and design elements (e.g., margins, graphics) of the original document without requiring access to the software used to create it. Adobe Acrobat Pro or a similar program is used to create these files, but Adobe also provides free software to read documents saved in PDF format (Adobe Reader). PDF software is often used in conjunction with **forms makers** such as PDF Maker Pilot, a software tool that creates documents and Web pages with forms that can be filled in on-screen. Teachers find forms makers useful because they make it easier to create forms to

# Adapting for Special Needs

## Software Tools

As students enter middle school, the demands of changing class-rooms and teachers each hour challenge the organizational abilities of even the best students. Suddenly, they have to do assignments in many different subjects and must have books and folders to keep track of each subject. Fortunately, most middle schools have a school-wide system (e.g., assignment notebooks, folders, homework-help Web pages) to help students get organized and keep track of all that they are supposed to know and do. However, by October each year some students are "organizationally failing," which makes it difficult for them to do well in their classes.

While staying organized and keeping track of important details is a lifelong challenge for everyone, difficulties with memory storage and retrieval is a fundamental characteristic of many individuals with learning disabilities. As a result, it is important to help these students find an information management system that is highly effective for them. Many of the following organizational tools have features that offer benefits to these students. However, please note that tools alone will not help students overcome deficits in organization and planning. Teachers and parents must commit to monitor the use of the tools and teaching new strategies to that the student can maximize the power of the tool.

- Evernote (at the Evernote website)—Encourages users to make artifacts (a note, image, or URL) of things they have to do, which are then indexed and made searchable.
- PocketMod (at the Pocketmod website)—Provides a way of creating a pocket guide of things to do and remember.
- Remember the Milk (at the Remember the Milk website)—Helps users create a system of reminders of tasks to do.
- Things 2 (at the Cultured Code website)—Lets users create an agenda and daily/weekly/monthly to-do lists.
- Toodledo (at the Toodledo website)—Helps users organize tasks they have to do into folders and subtasks.
- Todoist (at the To Do List website)—An online task manager to help users keep organized.
- Vitalist (at the Vitalist website)—A personal organization and productivity system.
- Voo2Do (at the Voo2do website)—An online system that helps users track priority, due dates, and time estimates for a number of different tasks.

—*Contributed by Dave Edyburn*

collect information from students, parents, or faculty or to implement surveys as part of research projects. Formatting even the simplest form can be time consuming on a word processor. These software tools structure the process and make the design simple to accomplish. As teachers create these forms, they can store them as templates for later use, perhaps with revisions.

**TECHNOLOGY LEARNING CHECK**
Complete TLC 5.2 to review what you have learned from reading this section about materials generator features and uses.

# USING DATA COLLECTION AND ANALYSIS TOOLS

Data collection and analysis tools include database software, statistical software packages, online survey sites, student information systems, online and computer-based testing systems, and student response systems, or clickers. A summary of these tools, with sample products and classroom uses, is shown in Table 5.3.

## Database Software

**Databases** are computer programs that allow users to store, organize, and manipulate information, including both text and numerical data. Database software can perform some calculations, but its real power lies in allowing people to locate information through keyword searches. A database program is most often compared to a file cabinet or a Rolodex card file. Like these precomputer devices, the purpose of a database is to store important information in a way that makes it easy to locate later. This capability has become increasingly important as society's store of essential information grows in volume and complexity.

## TABLE 5.3 | Overview of Data Collection and Analysis Tools

| Tool Category | Example Software Tools |
|---|---|
| **Database software:** Teachers teach how to build and use database software in business and technology classes | • FileMaker<br>• Quickbase<br>• Microsoft Access |
| **Statistical packages:** Teachers use statistical procedures to analyze data from experiments and action research studies | • SPSS<br>• SAS<br>• Analyse-it<br>• XLStat<br>• NCSS<br>• Stata |
| **Online survey tools:** Teachers design and implement online surveys to collect data for instructional purposes | • SurveyMonkey<br>• Zoomerang |
| **Student information systems:** Teachers, administrators, and parents keep track of student and class progress on required curriculum objectives | • PowerSchool<br>• Pinnacle SIS<br>• Tyler SIS<br>• QuickSchools |
| **Student response systems or clickers:** Teacher displays a question or problem (sometimes on interactive whiteboard), all students answer it at the same time, and the system summarizes and displays results immediately; teachers use the systems to engage students and check comprehension | • Student Response Solutions<br>• Smart Response<br>• ActiVote, ActivExpression, ActivEngage<br>• iRespond |

People often use the term *database* to refer both to the computer program and to the product it creates; however, database products are also called files. Whereas a spreadsheet stores an item of data in a cell, a database stores one item of data in a location usually called a **field**. Although each field represents one item of information in a database, perhaps the more important unit of information is a **record**, which stores all items of information related to a particular database entry.

For example, in a database of student records, each record corresponds to a student, and a record consists of several fields of information about the student, such as name, address, age, and parents' names. In a database of information about a school's inventory of instructional resources, each record represents one resource and consists of several fields describing aspects such as title, publisher, date published, and location.

### A shift in database uses and instruction.

After microcomputers became popular in the 1980s, database programs became nearly as widely used as word processing and spreadsheet programs. Teachers used them for recordkeeping tasks and taught students how to build and use database files. But nowadays, most teachers don't create their own management systems to keep inventories of classroom materials or records on student performance; they rely instead on systems in the main office for such vital information. Teachers use prepared databases much more widely than ever before, but they do not usually create them. Instructional uses, too, have become more focused on using existing databases, rather than building them. Though database construction is still taught in some classrooms (e.g., business and technology classes), more often database use focuses on using existing database files in science or social studies. For example, Southworth, Mokros, Dorsey, and Smith (2010) report using a program called GENIQUEST, a database of fictional information about dragons that helps teach genetic concepts in biology. Southworth et al. stressed the importance of such tools in helping students become "computational thinkers" in a modern world that is "increasingly defined by data" (p. 29). Wilson, Trautmann, MaKinster, and Barker (2010) describe using Science Pipes, a product designed by the Cornell Lab of Ornithology, to help students "conduct guided inquiries or hypothesis-driven research to investigate patterns and trends—such as the distribution of plant and animal species across biomes or the migration routes of various bird species" (p. 35).

Though most database instruction is in science and social studies, integration strategies have been designed for a variety of topics across the curriculum. These strategies include the following.

- **Teaching research and study skills**—Skills in locating and organizing information to answer questions and learn new concepts have always been as fundamental as reading and writing skills. Much of the world's information is stored in databases that are becoming more available to students and other nontechnical people for everyday use. As the volume of information in our society increases, students' need to learn how to locate important information quickly. Many database activities are designed to instruct students in these kinds of searches and provide them with practice in looking for information in various sources.

- **Understanding the power of information "pictures"**—Students need to be able to do their own **data mining**, or looking for hidden patterns in a group of data. To do that, they need to understand the persuasive power of information organized into databases. Sometimes a database can generate information "pictures" or relationships among bits of information that may not be visible in any other way. For example, social media or online shopping destinations use their vast databases of user information to generate profiles of users and display advertisements tailored to their perceived interests. Students can learn to use database information to generate these types of information pictures.

- **Posing and testing hypotheses**—Many problem-solving activities involve asking questions and locating information to answer them. Using databases is an ideal way to teach and provide practice with this kind of problem solving. Students can either research prepared databases full of information related to a content area, or they can create their own databases, which is not as common. Either way, these activities encourage them to look for information that will support or refute a position.

## Statistical Software Packages

As researcher and author L. R. Gay (1992) once joked, many teachers believe that the field of statistics should be renamed "sadistics." Yet teachers may find several uses for statistical analyses. Teachers who do action research in the classrooms must collect and analyze data on student performance. Depending on the type of research, several typical analyses yield helpful information, including descriptive statistics (e.g., means and standard deviations) and inferential statistics (e.g., $t$ tests and analyses of variance). **Statistical software packages** allow users to enter data and perform calculations needed to accomplish these analysis procedures. Teachers may also find statistical software useful when they have to teach statistical procedures to their students in, for example, a business education course or an AP statistics course. Though a teacher must have considerable knowledge of the proper applications of various statistical procedures, the software can save considerable time on the arithmetic and calculations. Popular statistical software tools are listed in Table 5.3.

## Online Survey Tools

A number of online sites, such as SurveyMonkey and Zoomerang, are available to allow teachers and students to design and implement their own surveys and questionnaires. This way of collecting data has become increasingly popular, since it eliminates the need for postal mailings or for respondents being in any particular location to complete a survey. An example of an online survey site is shown in Figure 5.2.

**Features of online survey tools.** Though online survey tools vary in format and capabilities, they have certain basic features in common. These include:

- **Variety of item formats**—Items can be in formats that include multiple choice, true/false, short answer, essay, and Likert scale (e.g., strongly disagree to strongly agree). Various item formats can appear in the same survey.

## FIGURE 5.2 Sample Screen from Survey Monkey Site

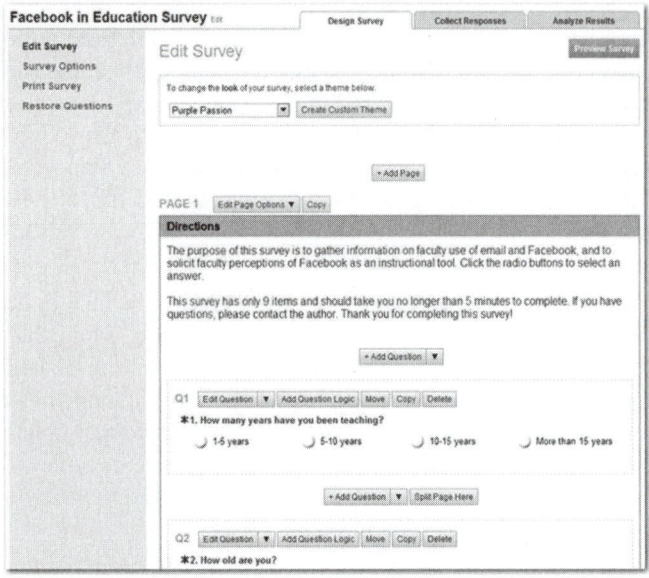

Reprinted by permission from SurveyMonkey, LLC (http://www.SurveyMonkey.com)

- **Instant tracking and visual summaries of results**—After the survey is implemented and people begin completing it, one can get immediate updates on how many people have participated and what the data look like in bar or graph form.
- **Data downloads**—Systems also permit users to get a file of data resulting from surveys in spreadsheet-ready formats.

Most online survey tools have a free version with fewer capabilities than the fee-based version.

### Integration strategies for online survey tools.
Both productivity and instructional uses have been reported for online survey tools. For example, Looney (2008) says that online surveys are an ideal way to allow students to give their feedback on any given topic, such as how they liked a classroom activity or how they feel about candidates up for election. For a sample lesson designed with this kind of software tool, see Technology Integration Example 5.2. Instructional integration strategies for online surveys include the following:

- **Student polling**—Either the teacher or students design items that poll students on their opinions. Then the teacher summarizes data produced by the poll to show students the class opinions on a given topic. The purpose for doing this activity can range from simply illustrating how a poll works to providing data that are meaningful to students in order to teach analysis skills.
- **Generating data for graphic illustrations**—Either the teacher or students design a survey and place it online for the purpose of gathering data to create a graphic such as a pie chart or bar graph. Students get practice in reading and interpreting the graphic displays.
- **Teaching survey design**—Students create and implement online surveys in order to learn how to create well-designed items and develop a survey instrument that communicates well and obtains the desired data.

# TECHNOLOGY INTEGRATION

## Example 5.2

**TITLE:** Polling the Class Prior to a Statewide Vote

**CONTENT AREA/TOPIC:** Civics, electio\ns

**GRADE LEVELS:** 9–12

**ISTE STANDARDS•S:** Standard 3—Research and Information Fluency; Standard 4—Critical Thinking, Problem Solving, and Decision Making; Standard 6—Technology Operations and Concepts

**CCSS:** CCSS.ELA-LITERACY.RH.9-10.7, CCSS.ELA-LITERACY. RH.9-10.8, CCSS.ELA-LITERACY.RH.11-12.9, CCSS.MATH. CONTENT.HSS.ID.A.1, CCSS.MATH.CONTENT.HSS.ID.B.6

**NCSS THEMES:** Thematic Standards: 6 - Power, Authority, Governance; Disciplinary Standards: 3 - Civics and Government

**DESCRIPTION:** Prior to a statewide vote on proposed amendments to the statewide constitution, students create a class or school survey to poll students on how and why they think the state's citizens should vote. After the survey is implemented and data are available, they use data to make charts and graphs of results on each item. After the election, they analyze and discuss reasons for similarities and differences between a poll's results and those of the actual election.

*SOURCE:* Based on a concept from the "Constitutional Amendments Survey" lesson plan submitted to the Teachnology website (http://www .teachnology.com).

- **Teaching data analysis**—Either the teacher or students design a survey to gather data for the purpose of illustrating and allowing practice in how to do analyses such as means (averages), medians, modes, and percentages.
- **Teaching math concepts**—The teacher implements an online survey that will provide data to illustrate math concepts such as probability.

## Student Information Systems

**Student information systems (SISs)** are software tools that help educators keep track of student, class, and school data (e.g., attendance, test scores) to maintain records and support decision making. Schools purchase various operations they want the system to keep track of. Depending on what they choose, the system may do any or all of the following:

- Track and report on attendance
- Maintain records on student demographic data (e.g., birth date, address)
- Develop class scheduling
- Track and report on test scores and achievement by objective
- Allow parents to have online access to student grades and attendance information
- Notify parents about problems with grades or attendance

**FIGURE 5.3** Sample Screen from PowerSchool

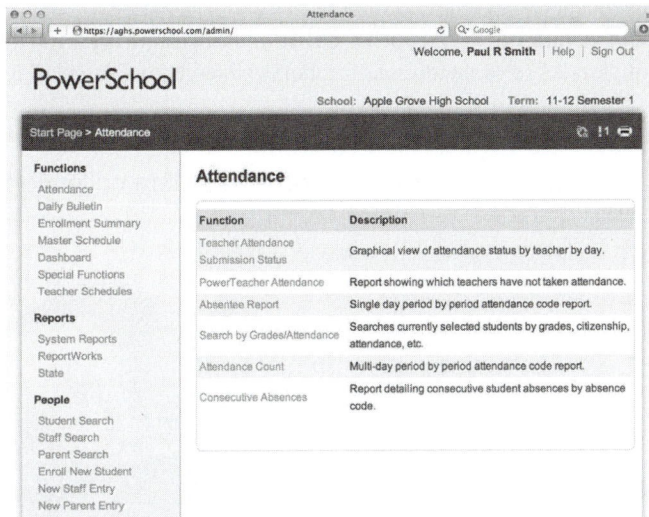

**Clickers Used With Whiteboards**

In this video, as this principal explains how teachers combine student response systems or clickers with interactive whiteboard activity software tools, listen for some of the reasons teachers use these resources. What other uses can you think of that may work well in your current or future situation?

In the 1970s, these systems were known by the general term **computer-managed instruction (CMI) systems**. At that time, there was a burgeoning interest in mastery learning in which teachers specified a sequence of objectives for students to learn and prescribed instruction to help the students master each objective. The teacher had to keep track of each student's performance on each objective—a mammoth record-keeping task. CMI systems, such as the Teaching Information Processing System (TIPS) and the Program for Learning in Accordance with Needs (PLAN), ran on large, mainframe computers and were designed to support teachers in these efforts.

Today's educators must also be concerned about monitoring student progress, but the concern now is in complying with accountability requirements such as those specified by the No Child Left Behind Act. Also, these systems can make it easier for teachers to keep parents notified about student progress. Systems such as Pearson's PowerSchool and GlobalScholar's Pinnacle SIS allow parents and educators online access to students' grade reports. See Figure 5.3 for an example screen from one such system.

Some SISs are components of personalized learning systems (PLS). Integration with PLSs allows instruction to be tailored to each student's needs and collects data as students go through the instruction. Reports show the teacher what students have accomplished and point out areas where they may still need assistance and off-computer work.

## Student Response Systems (Clickers)

Unique among data collection resources, **student response systems (SRS)** (also called audience response systems, personal response systems, **clickers**, or classroom response systems) are a combination of handheld hardware and software that permits each student in a classroom to answer a question simultaneously and permits the teacher to see and display a summary of results immediately. The software ranges from that sold with a textbook to new technologies where cellular phones can be used to respond to questions

Student Response Systems or "clickers" provide immediate feedback to support several kinds of whole-group teaching strategies. (Photo courtesy of W. Wiencke)

posed by the instructor. Tomei (2013) cites them as one of the top 10 technologies to support 21st-century learning. Caldwell (2007) offered categories of activities teachers can do with these devices, as well as guidelines for writing good questions and a list of best-practice tips.

### Research on student response systems.
Though studies of these tools tend to be in large-section courses in higher education, they usually report improved student engagement, more active learning, and greater achievement (Blood & Neel, 2008; Gauci, Dantas, Williams, & Kemm, 2009; Shaffer & Collura, 2009). DeSorbo, Noble, Shaffer, Gerin, and Williams (2012) found that both paper-pencil groups and SRS groups of elementary school students achieved about the same in a health education program, but that both students and teachers preferred the clickers over the traditional way of gauging progress. Stowell, Oldham, and Bennett (2010) also found that students were less likely to conform to the group's opinion and felt more comfortable responding with this tool than raising their hands when questions being discussed were controversial.

### Integration strategies for student response systems.
Uses for this kind of system range from vocabulary games to comprehension checks during a classroom presentation and offer an easy way to engage all students at once. Successful uses have been reported in science (Moss & Crowley, 2011; Walgren, 2011), mathematics (Popelka, 2010), and English (Miller, 2009). For a sample lesson designed with this kind of software tool, see Technology Integration Example 5.3.

**TECHNOLOGY LEARNING CHECK**

Complete TLC 5.3 to review what you have learned from reading this section about data collection and analysis tool features and uses.

# TECHNOLOGY INTEGRATION

## Example 5.3

**TITLE:** Fraction to Decimal Jeopardy

**CONTENT AREA/TOPIC:** Mathematics, fractions/decimals

**GRADE LEVEL:** 4

**ISTE STANDARDS•S:** Standard 1—Creativity and Innovation; Standard 2—Communication and Collaboration; Standard 4—Critical Thinking, Problem Solving, and Decision Making

**CCSS:** CCSS.MATH.CONTENT.4.NF.C.5, CCSS.MATH.CONTENT.4.NF.C.6, CCSS.MATH.CONTENT.4.NF.C.7, CCSS.MATH.PRACTICE.MP5

**DESCRIPTION:** The teacher uses an interactive whiteboard and creates or downloads a Jeopardy game file to let students practice various skills in changing decimals to fractions, fractions to decimals, and expressing results in words. The class divides into two teams to play the game and divides up the response keys so that each team is using A–D or E–H keys to respond. For each question, the team with the highest percentage of correct responses earns the points and picks the next category and question to answer. The team with the most points at the end of the game wins.

*SOURCE:* Based on a concept from the lesson plan "Fraction to Decimal Jeopardy" at the SMART Exchange website http://exchange.smarttech.com.

## ⦿ USING TESTING AND GRADING TOOLS

These tools include electronic gradebooks, test and rubric generators, and computer-based testing systems. A summary of these tools, with sample products and classroom uses, is shown in Table 5.4

# TABLE 5.4 Overview of Testing and Grading Tools

| Tool Category and Uses/Purposes | Example Software Tools |
|---|---|
| **Electronic gradebooks:** Teachers keep track of and calculate student grades | • PinnacleGrade Gradebook<br>• Teacher Planet's listing of gradebook packages |
| **Test and rubric generators:** Teachers create tests and test item banks, administer tests online; teachers create or adopt rubrics for grading complex products or performances | • Exam View Learning Series<br>• Test Creator<br>• Wondershare QuizCreator<br>• EasyTestMaker<br>• RubiStar (a creation program or pre-made rubrics)<br>• Rubric Maker |
| **Computer-based testing systems:** Students take tests on the computer or online, and the software grades tests and compiles data for grading and decision making | • ExamBuilder<br>• Easy Test<br>• ComputerTest 2.0 |

## Electronic Gradebooks

Although some teachers prefer to keep their grades on flexible spreadsheet software, many prefer to use software designed exclusively for this purpose. An **electronic gradebook** (electronic gradekeeping) program allows a teacher to enter student names, test/assignment names, data from tests, and weighting information for specific test scores. The program then analyzes the data and prints reports based on this information. Some gradebooks even offer limited-purpose word-processing capabilities to enter notes about tests. The software automatically generates averages and weighted averages for each student and averages across all students on a given test. Gradebooks require less teacher setup time than spreadsheets do, but they also allow less flexibility on format options. Many schools today use district-wide gradebooks, often as part of student information systems (described later in this chapter), for uniformity across all grading programs. A sample gradebook screen is shown in Figure 5.4.

## Test Generators and Rubric Generators

Software tools are available to help teachers with what many consider to be one of their most onerous and time-consuming instructional tasks: producing tests and other kinds of assessments. Test generators and rubric generators are shown in Table 5.4, which also lists where to locate several of these tools.

**Test generators.** Teachers use **test generators** to create and enter questions, and then the program prepares the test. The teacher may print the required number of copies on the printer or print only one copy and make the required number of copies on a copy machine. The features of test generators vary, but the following capabilities are common and offer several advantages, even over word processing programs:

- **Test creation and revision procedures—**The software produces tests in a standard layout; the teacher need not worry about arranging the spacing and format of the page. The software prompts teachers to create tests item by item in formats such as multiple choice, fill in the blank, true/false, matching, and—less often—short answer and essay. Changes, deletions, and updates to questions are also easy to accomplish, again without concern for page format.

- **Random generation of questions—**Test items are selected randomly from an item pool to create different versions of

### FIGURE 5.4 Sample Screen from the Track My Gradebook Software

Reprinted by permission from TrackMyGrades.com, LLC. (www.TrackMyGrades.com)

a test. This is especially helpful when a teacher wants to prevent "wandering eye syndrome" as students take a test.

- **Selection of questions based on criteria**—Programs usually allow teachers to specify criteria for generating a test. For example, items can be requested in a specific content area, matched to certain objectives, or set up in a certain format, such as short-answer items only.

- **Answer keys**—Most programs automatically provide an answer key at the time the test is generated. This is helpful with grading, especially if different versions of the test are used.

- **Test item banks**—Many test generators allow use of existing question pools, or **test item banks**, and some offer these banks for purchase in various content areas. Some programs also import question banks prepared on word processors.

Most test generators offer only on-paper versions of tests, but some allow students to take tests on-screen after they are prepared. The latter type is also discussed in the next section under Computer-Based Testing Systems.

**Rubric generators.** The popularity of rubrics has grown to such an extent that several Internet sites offer free rubric generators. The teacher follows a set of prompts, and the system creates a rubric that can be printed out or referred to online. These generator sites usually also have a bank of prepared rubrics teachers can select and use. See a list of rubric generation sites in Table 5.4 and in the Open-Source Options feature.

## Computer-Based Testing Systems

Also known as **computer-assisted testing,** computer-based testing systems allow students to take tests on-screen or to put test answers on optically scanned "bubble sheets," and provide reports on performance data afterward. Some current testing systems overlap with the function of true test generators, which are designed to produce tests from data banks. Some of the major standardized tests, such as the SAT and GRE, are now given on computerized testing systems, which offers benefits such as immediate knowledge of results. The capabilities of computerized testing systems let educators go beyond the limits of multiple-choice tests and make possible alternative assessments. These systems also simplify test scheduling, because everyone need not take tests at the same time.

With testing systems, tests can be shorter, since the software assesses each person's ability level with fewer questions. The software continuously analyzes performance and presents more or less difficult questions based on the student's performance, a capability known as **computer adaptive testing (CAT)** (Barla et al., 2010). CAT is being used more and more frequently for testing in professional courses like those in nursing education. Computer-based testing of all kinds remains controversial, however. Some people feel that computer-based testing is not equivalent to other kinds of testing and may cause increased test anxiety in some students (Fritts & Marszalek, 2010). Herold (2013) notes that there are "disagreements over how computer-adaptive assessment should function . . . have reignited long-standing concerns held by advocates for students with disabilities" (p. 18).

**TECHNOLOGY LEARNING CHECK**
Complete TLC 5.4 to review what you have learned from reading this section about testing and grading tool features and uses.

## ◯ USING GRAPHICS TOOLS

Graphics tools include draw/paint programs; image editing tools; charting/graphing tools; clip art, photo, animation, sound, video, and font collections; and word cloud generators. A summary of these, with sample products and classroom uses, is shown in Table 5.5.

## TABLE 5.5 Overview of Graphics Tools

| Tool Category | Example Software Tools |
|---|---|
| **Draw/paint programs:** Teachers and students create their own drawings and illustrations to display on-screen or print. | • Adobe Illustrator<br>• CorelDraw<br>• KidPix |
| **Image editing software:** Teachers and students create, modify, and combine images (e.g., clip art, photos, drawings) to illustrate documents and Web pages. | • Adobe Photoshop<br>• ACDSee Pro Photo Manager |
| **Charting/graphing software:** Students create charts and graphs to illustrate and study data summaries. | • SmartDraw<br>• The Graph Club 2.0 |
| **Media collections:** Teachers and students insert these media items into documents and media they create. | • Graphics for Teachers<br>• Microsoft Media Collections<br>• Istock Photos<br>• Digital Sound Factory (musical instruments)<br>• Flaming Text<br>• Adobe Fonts Collection<br>• Animation Factory |
| **Word cloud generators:** These tools allow creation of a unique graphic display called a "word cloud," which shows most frequent words from a text passage as larger. | • Abcya<br>• Tagxedo<br>• Tagul<br>• Worditout<br>• Wordle<br>• Wordsift |

## Draw/Paint Programs

Drawing and painting software tools help teachers and students create their own graphics to insert into documents or Web pages. In simpler draw/paint programs, such as Kid Pix, users select graphics components (e.g., colors, shapes, lines) from menus and toolbars, making the programs so easy to use that anyone can sit down and create an image in a matter of minutes. Students may use these programs to illustrate their work or to help convey information in reports. Cause and Chen (2010) say that for young children, drawing is a representational form of communication that is a precursor to writing, and recommend drawing software on a tablet computer for its versatility. Walker-Dalhouse and Risko (2008) agree, finding that "children can use drawing software to illustrate text content and represent their interpretations of concepts learned" (p. 423). Lach, Little, and Nazzaro (2003) say the tools make possible a multiple-intelligences approach to science and art instruction. Higher-end programs, such as Adobe Illustrator, make possible more complex drawings and require more knowledge of art and graphic techniques. These are usually used in high school level communications and technology education courses. See Figure 5.5 for an example of a product at the secondary level.

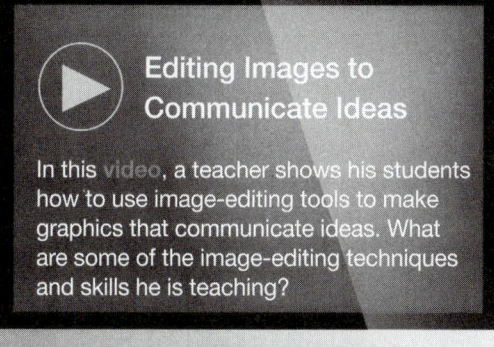

### Editing Images to Communicate Ideas

In this video, a teacher shows his students how to use image-editing tools to make graphics that communicate ideas. What are some of the image-editing techniques and skills he is teaching?

## Image Editing Tools

To modify photographic images, **image editing programs** are the technology software tool of choice. These tools usually are used to enhance and format photos that are then imported into desktop publishing systems or Web page products. Image editing programs are known for their sophistication and wide-ranging capabilities. Many of these packages, such as Adobe Photoshop, require considerable time to learn if one wants to become familiar with all facets of the technology, but new tools such as Instagram, Hipstamatic, and Snapseed, which work on mobile devices, make image editing more accessible in the K–12 classroom. Gran (2013) talks about these tools primarily from the standpoint of teaching photography and the arts, but image editing can also be used in many other subject areas. For example, Technology Integration Example 5.4 shows how image editing tools could be used in a math/astronomy lesson.

## FIGURE 5.5 Sample Draw/Paint Software at Secondary Level

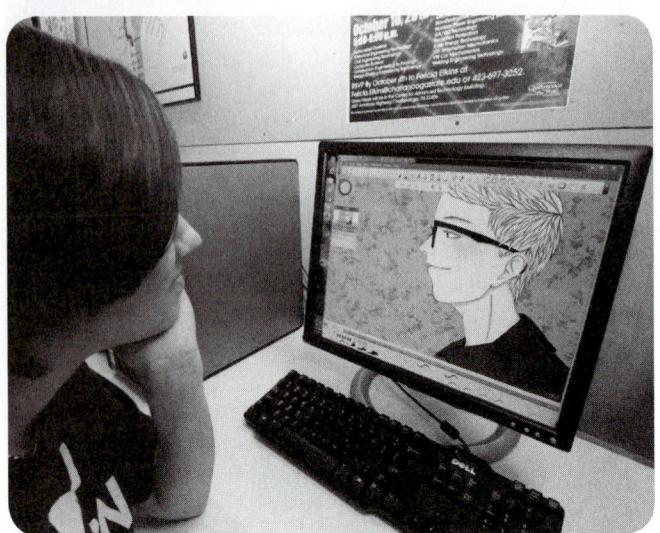

(Photo courtesy of W. Wiencke)

## Charting and Graphing Tools

**Charting/graphing tools** automatically draw and print desired charts or graphs from data entered by users. The skills involved in reading, interpreting, and producing graphs and charts are useful both to students in school and adults in the workplace. Because people with limited artistic ability usually find it difficult to draw charts and graphics freehand, charting and graphing software takes the mechanical drudgery out of producing these useful "data pictures." Since students now need not labor over rulers and pencils as they try to plot coordinates and set points, they can concentrate on the more important aspects of the graphics: the meaning of the data and what they represent. This kind of activity supports students in their efforts at visualizing mathematical concepts and engaging in inquiry tasks.

Graphing activities in science, social studies, and geography also profit from applications of these kinds of software tools. Ruthven, Deaney, and Hennessy (2009) are among those who view graphing as an essential tool to enhance algebra and other mathematics instruction. Though software on graphing calculators is often used for charting and graphing tasks and charting/graphing software packages are still available, features of spreadsheet software (discussed in Chapter 4) are being cited more frequently. See Technology Integration Example 5.5 for an example lesson with graphing software.

## Clip Art, Photo, Animation, Sound, Video, and Font Collections

**Clip art** packages were originally collections of still pictures drawn by artists and graphics designers and placed in a book or on a disc for use by others. Nowadays, the idea of clip art has expanded to include drawings, cartoons, photos, and animations—all of which are found easily on the Internet.

# TECHNOLOGY INTEGRATION

## Example 5.4

**TITLE:** Bringing the Planets Closer to Home

**CONTENT AREA/TOPIC:** Mathematics (measurement), astronomy

**GRADE LEVEL:** 8–12

**ISTE STANDARDS•S:** Standard 3—Research and Information Fluency; Standard 4—Critical Thinking, Problem Solving, and Decision Making; Standard 6—Technology Operations and Concepts

**CCSS:** CCSS.MATH.CONTENT.7.RP.A.2, CCSS.MATH.CONTENT. HSA.CED.A.1, CCSS.MATH.CONTENT.HSA.REI.B.3, CCSS. MATH.CONTENT.HSG.SRT.A.2, CCSS.MATH.CONTENT.HSG. SRT.B.5, CCSS.MATH.CONTENT.HSG.C.A.1

**DESCRIPTION:** Students begin by downloading NASA photos from the Internet (e.g., look for images at the Solarviews website

or the Solarsystem portion of the NASA website). Then convert them to an uncompressed TIF format using an image editing program such as Adobe Photoshop. Their task is to learn how to measure the images. First, they use the software to calibrate the images (determine the scale) by comparing the size of each image to a known measurement, such as the diameter of Mars. Then they multiply the measured distance by the scale to determine the size of other features they have downloaded. In this way, the students can measure and compare features that change, such as the Martian and Earth polar ice caps. These measurements can be the basis of many projects to study space phenomena.

*SOURCE:* Based on a concept from Slater, T., & Beaudrie, B. (2000). Far out measurements: Bringing the planets closer to home using image-processing techniques. *Learning and Leading with Technology, 27*(5), 36–41.

## Example 5.5

**TITLE:** Engaging Special Education Students in Math Concepts

**CONTENT AREA/TOPIC:** Mathematics, special education

**GRADE LEVEL:** 2

**ISTE STANDARDS•S:** Standard 1—Creativity and Innovation; Standard 4—Critical Thinking, Problem Solving, and Decision Making; Standard 3—Research and Information Fluency; Standard 6—Technology Operations and Concepts

**CCSS:** CCSS.MATH.CONTENT.2.MD.D.10, CCSS.MATH.PRACTICE.MP5

**DESCRIPTION:** In a two-week project that emphasizes authentic problem solving, students collect data about the success of their school's food drive and use graphing software to graph the information. They enter data into a table, generate a bar graph, and hang the graph in the room as a focal point of discussion. The activity especially benefits students with challenges such as autism by preventing frustration with graphing tasks and keeping them focused on the concepts that data illustrate.

*SOURCE:* Based on a concept from Ward, R. (2006). Engage students with graphing software. *Learning and Leading with Technology, 34*(1), 35.

---

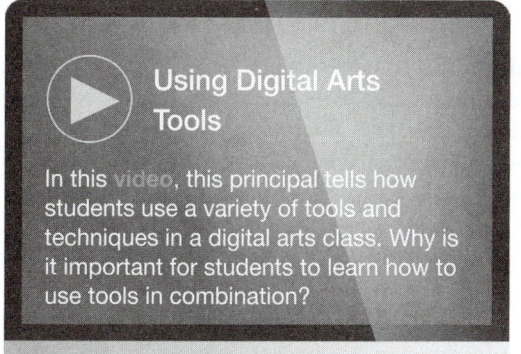

**Using Digital Arts Tools**

In this video, this principal tells how students use a variety of tools and techniques in a digital arts class. Why is it important for students to learn how to use tools in combination?

For example, high-quality photos, illustrations, and videos can be found online at sites such as the ones shown in Table 5.5. When preparing presentations, you can use available art instead of drawing your own original images or taking your own photos. Most word processing, desktop publishing, image editing, and draw/paint programs can import these items from a disc or a website. Font collections are also available to expand the font options that come with a computer or software.

These collections offer valuable resources that help illustrate and decorate written products. Teachers find that such pictures help make flyers, books, and even letters and notices look more polished and professional. Some teachers feel that students are more motivated to write their own stories and reports when they can also illustrate them.

For teachers and students who want to develop their own websites or multimedia presentations, collections of sound effects and video clips (e.g., MPEG files) are also becoming common on the Internet, and many are free of charge. However, a system may need special software plug-ins, such as Quicktime or Adobe Flash, to incorporate these elements.

## Word Cloud Generators

These tools create a graphic arrangement of words from a text passage that shows the most-frequent words as bigger than the others. (See example in Figure 5.6.) Wordle was the first such tools, but was quickly followed by many others, as shown in Table 5.6, because instructors recognized they could exploit word clouds for any topic where word frequency was a concern. For example, Perry (2012), a speech teacher, described how she used word clouds to help students understand the importance of repetition, style, and focus in their speeches. But these tools can be used for learning activities in any subject area, as Gorman illustrates in his online list of "108 Ways to Use Word Clouds in the Classroom." Search for this title online to see the latest list. Examples include:

- **Any subject** — See patterns in students' views by surveying them on a topic and creating a word cloud from results.
- **Science** — Create a word cloud to illustrate occurrences of weather or geographic events (e.g., compare earthquake magnitudes or locations).
- **Language arts** — Compare and contrast persuasive writing samples (from editorials or students' own work) using word clouds to illustrate how they use words.
- **Social studies** — Compare and analyze word clouds created from two presidential speeches.

**FIGURE 5.6** Sample Word Cloud Created with Wordle

- **Mathematics** — Create word clouds of objects that have a given geometric shapes and use Tagul or Tagxedo to fit the words into the shape. (Also see Nickel (2012) for more math ideas.)
- **Music** — Study and compare song lyrics by or across artists by doing word clouds of each song.

**TECHNOLOGY LEARNING CHECK**

Complete **TLC 5.5** to review what you have learned from reading this section about graphics tool features and uses.

# USING PLANNING AND ORGANIZING TOOLS

Planning and organizing tools include outlining and concept mapping software, lesson planning software, and scheduling/time management tools. A summary of these, with sample products and classroom uses, is shown in Table 5.6.

## Outlining Tools and Concept Mapping Software

Several kinds of technology tools are available to help students learn writing skills or to assist accomplished writers in setting their thoughts in order prior to writing. **Outlining tools,** sometimes called electronic outliners, are programs designed to prompt writers as they develop outlines. For example, the software may automatically indent and/or supply the appropriate number or letter for each line in the outline. Outlining tools are offered either within word processing packages or as separate software packages for use before word processing.

Other writing aids include software designed to get students started on writing reports or stories: a story starter. This kind of program provides a first line and invites students to supply subsequent lines. Other tools give students topic ideas and supply information about each topic that they can use in a writing assignment. Sometimes a software package combines outlining tools and other writing aids.

**Concept mapping software** tools are designed to help people think through and explore ideas or topics by developing concept maps. Concept maps are visual outlines of ideas that can offer useful alternatives to the strictly verbal representations provided by content outlines. The number of concept mapping software programs has grown over the past few years, with many of the programs being web-based or even free of charge. Inspiration is one of the most popular of these tools (see Figure 5.7).

**FIGURE 5.7** Sample Concept Map in Inspiration

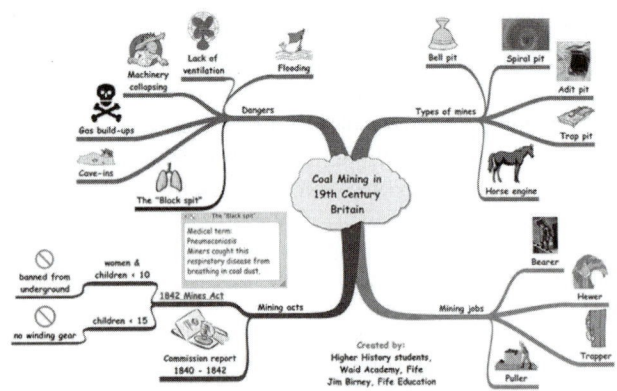

World History Analysis Mind Map: Coal Mining in 19th Century Britain

*Source:* Mindmap created using Inspiration®, by Inspiration Software, Inc.

## TABLE 5.6 Overview of Planning and Organizing Tools

| Tool Category | Example Software Tools |
|---|---|
| **Outlining and concept mapping software:** Help students organize their ideas in outline or concept map to prepare for writing or to examine story structures | • Inspiration<br>• Kidspiration<br>• SmartDraw |
| **Lesson planners:** Help teachers prepare and document lesson plans | • PlanbookEdu<br>• ILessonPlan<br>• MyLessonPlanner |
| **Scheduling, calendar, and time management tools:** Help teachers organize their time and plan activities | • FileBuzz Teacher Calendar Software<br>• Reel Logix Calendar Software<br>• Easy Schedule Maker |

## FIGURE 5.8 Sample Tools in Kidspiration

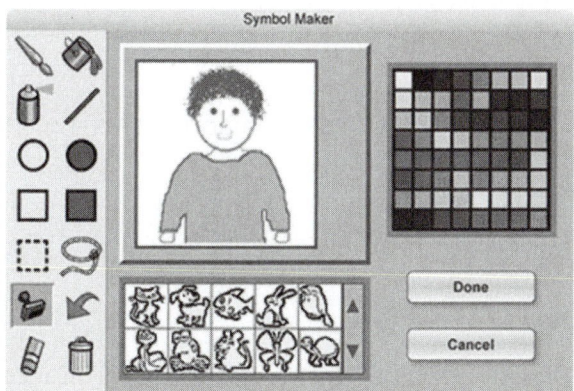

*Source:* Symbol Maker in Kidspiration®3, created by Inspiration Software, Inc.

## FIGURE 5.9 Lesson Planner from Pearson's SuccessNet Online Lesson Planner

Pearson SuccessNet

**Lesson Planner**

Teachers use the Lesson Planner to access lesson plans, schedule them to the calendar, and generate lesson plan reports. Lesson plan content can be modified to create customized lesson plans.

**Related Topics**

- Planner Setup
- Planner View
- Change Dates
- Customize Lesson Plans
- View Lesson Plan
- Edit Lesson Plan
- Add Standards
- Lesson Builder
- Add to Planner
- Shift Schedule
- Auto-scheduling
- Lesson Plan by Date Report Setup and Lesson Plan by Standard Report Setup
- View Lesson Plan by Date Report and View Lesson Plans by Standard Report

PEARSON

Kidspiration (Figure 5.8) is a version of this software designed for younger users. MacArthur (2009) discusses the research conducted on these powerful instructional tools and gives good examples of how they may be used to help struggling writers. (See Technology Integration Example 5.6.)

## Lesson Planning Software

Not all teachers rely heavily on written lesson plans to guide their teaching activities. However, many occasions demand some form of documentation to show what teachers are teaching and how they are teaching it. Tools that help teachers develop and document their descriptions of lessons are sometimes called lesson makers or lesson planners. Most of these programs are online and provide on-screen prompts for specific lesson components, such as objectives, materials, and activity descriptions. They also print out lessons in standard formats, similar to the way test generators format printouts of tests. See Figure 5.9 for an example.

## Scheduling, Calendar, and Time Management Tools

Several kinds of tools have been designed to help teachers organize their time and plan their activities. Schedule makers help formulate plans for daily, weekly, or monthly sequences of appointments and events. Calendar makers are similar planning tools that actually print graphic calendars of chosen months or years with the planned events printed under each day. Other time management tools are available to help remind users of events and responsibilities. The teacher enters activities and the dates on which they are to occur. Then, when he or she turns on the computer each day, the software displays on the screen a list of things to do. Some integrated packages combine all of

# TECHNOLOGY INTEGRATION

## Example 5.6

TITLE: Writing Our Own Fairy Tales

CONTENT AREA/TOPIC: Language arts, writing

GRADE LEVELS: Grades 3–4

ISTE STANDARDS•S: Standard 1—Creativity and Innovation; Standard 4—Critical Thinking, Problem Solving, and Decision Making; Standard 3—Research and Information Fluency; Standard 6—Technology Operations and Concepts

CCSS: RL.3.3, RF.3.4(a), W.3.5, RL.4.6, W.4.3(e), SL.4.6, CCSS. ELA-LITERACY.SL.5.5

DESCRIPTION: The teacher first reads two different fairy tales aloud to the class and helps the students brainstorm what

the stories have in common. As they talk about the stories, the teacher uses Inspiration software to illustrate the common aspects and themes that make fairy tales so interesting (e.g., central character(s), colorful setting, conflict or challenge, resolution, moral or lesson). The concept map shows how these aspects appear in both fairy tales. She asks students to tell one of their other favorite fairy tales and fills in the concept map template with them. She asks students to work in pairs or threes to create their own fairy tale, first sketching out the elements in an Inspiration template, then writing and illustrating them. Finally, the groups share their fairy tales, showing the concept map that illustrates their "essential elements" for their fairy tale.

*SOURCE:* Based on a concept from the Fairy Tale Picture Books lesson plan at the ReadWriteThink website: http://www.readwritethink.org/.

these tools. Time management tools are especially popular applications on handheld computers, as the user can update the calendar at any time and place.

**TECHNOLOGY LEARNING CHECK**
Complete **TLC 5.6** to review what you have learned from reading this section about planning and organizing tool features and uses.

# USING RESEARCH AND REFERENCE TOOLS

Research and reference tools include digital versions of encyclopedias, atlases and mapping tools, and dictionaries and thesauruses. Today's reference tools are online and usually available as apps. A summary of these, with sample products and classroom uses, is shown in Table 5.7.

## Online Encyclopedias

Encyclopedias have come a long way from the sets of books that American families kept to support their children's education. Young people used these books for research on school projects, and parents used them to take advantage of teachable moments when their children required more than quick answers. Now most major encyclopedias are online with a searchable database structure. Digital encyclopedias allow users to locate either one specific item or all references on a given topic, and they usually offer multimedia formats that include sound and/or film clips as well as hypertext links to related information on any topic.

## Digital Atlases and Mapping Tools

Like encyclopedias, atlases are popular educational reference tools for families as well as schools. They summarize geographic and demographic information ranging from population statistics to national products. Online versions of these atlases are especially helpful because they are so interactive. Students can either see information on a specific country or city or gather information on all countries or cities that meet certain criteria. Some atlases even play national songs on request! Mapping sites such as MapQuest also help teach geographic concepts by showing distances between points.

## TABLE 5.7 Overview of Research and Reference Tools

| Tool Category | Example Software Tools |
|---|---|
| **Online encyclopedias:** Help students research any topic | • Encyclopedia Brittanica Online<br>• Encyclopedia.com<br>• Wikipedia |
| **Online atlases and mapping tools:** Help students learn about and use local, national, world, and extraterrestrial geography | • Worldatlas<br>• Rand McNally<br>• Mapquest<br>• The National Map (geological)<br>• U.S. Atlas<br>• Atlas of the Universe<br>• Google Maps |
| **Online dictionaries and thesauruses:** Give definitions and synonyms | • Technology words: *Webopedia*<br>• Any words/thesaurus<br>• Merriam-Webster<br>• Any words/thesaurus<br>• Dictionary.com |

## Digital Dictionaries (Word Atlases)

Sometimes called **word atlases**, digital dictionaries and thesauruses give pronunciations, definitions, and example uses for each word entry. They also offer many search and multimedia features similar to those of encyclopedias and atlases. Many digital dictionaries can play an audio clip of the pronunciation of any desired word, which helps young users and others who cannot read diacritical marks.

**TECHNOLOGY LEARNING CHECK**

Complete **TLC 5.7** to review what you have learned from reading this section about research and reference tool features and uses.

# USING TOOLS TO SUPPORT SPECIFIC CONTENT AREAS

Numerous content-specific technologies support teaching within a content area. Some of these tools are described within this chapter; you will find additional content-specific tools within each subject-matter chapter (Chapters 9 through 15). Examples of content-area tools are CAD systems; music tools such as music editors, sequencers, and MIDI tools; reading tools; microcomputer-based labs; graphing calculators and calculator-based labs; and Geographic Information Systems and Global Positioning Systems. A summary of these, with sample products and classroom uses, is shown in Table 5.8.

## CAD and 3-D Modeling/Animation Systems

A **computer-assisted (or computer-aided) design (CAD)** system is a special kind of graphics production tool that allows users to prepare sophisticated, precise drawings of objects such as houses and cars. Like presentation tools, CAD systems began to appear in classrooms after they had been introduced in business and industry. This kind of software is usually employed in vocational-technical classrooms to teach architecture and

### TABLE 5.8 Overview of Content-Area Specific Tools

| Tool Category | Example Software Tools |
|---|---|
| **CAD systems:** Students create visual models of houses and other structures as they study design concepts | • AutoCAD<br>• Alibre |
| **Music editors, sequencers, and MIDI tools:** Students create their own musical pieces or revise those of others | • iLike and Garageband |
| **Reading tools:** Support reading instruction in various ways | • Readability calculation software<br>• Accelerated Reader (AR)<br>• Digital storybooks |
| **Microcomputer-based labs (MBL), calculator-based labs (CBL), and graphing calculators:** Students collect and analyze data from problems or experiments | • Texas Instruments graphing<br>• Vernier LabQuest |
| **Geographic information systems (GIS) and global positioning systems (GPS):** Students study geographic and social studies information and concepts | • ARCView GIS<br>• GPS curriculum<br>• Magellan GPS<br>• Garmin GPS |
| **Online foreign language dictionaries and language translators:** Students use these as references in the study of languages other than their native ones | • Look for a listing of foreign language dictionaries at the Foreignword website<br>• WorldLingo<br>• Babylon 9 |

## FIGURE 5.10 Sample Screen from CAD Software

*Source:* From CAD Software, Autodesk. Copyright © 2014 by Autodesk.

engineering skills. However, some teachers use CAD software to teach drawing concepts in art and related topics. (See Figure 5.10 for an example of CAD software.) More advanced graphics students may use 3-D modeling and animation software systems to do fancy visual effects such as **morphing** (short for metamorphosing, an animation technique in which one image gradually turns into another).

## Music Editors, Sequencers, and MIDI Tools

**Music editor** software provides blank musical staffs on which the user enters the musical key, time, and notes that constitute a piece of sheet music. This software is designed to help people develop musical compositions on-screen, usually in conjunction with hardware such as a **Musical Instrument Digital Interface (MIDI)** device, a standard adopted by the electronic music industry for controlling devices that play music (for example, **music synthesizers**). Music editors allow a user either to hear the music after it is written or to create music on the keyboard and automatically produce a written score.

**Music sequencers** are software packages that support the creation of music scores with several parts. Music editors offer powerful assistance in the processes of precomposing, composing, revising, and even performing. These tools play a prominent part in the music classroom, but Mishra and Koehler (2009) remind us that they can also be used to teach concepts in other areas, such as using a music editor to analyze music clips and relate math concepts such as ratios and percentages to rhythm, music, and tempo.

## Reading Tools

Both reading teachers and teachers of other topics occasionally need to determine the approximate reading level of specific documents. A teacher may want to select a story or book for use in a lesson or to confirm that works are correctly labeled as appropriate for certain grade levels. Several methods are available for calculating the reading level of a written work; all of them are time consuming and tedious to do by hand. Readability analysis software automates calculations of word count, average word length, number of sentences, or other measures of reading difficulty.

**Cloze software.** Another software tool related to reading instruction, Cloze software, provides passages with words missing in a given pattern; for example, every fifth word or every tenth word. Students read the sentences and try to fill in the words. Cloze passages have been found to be good measures of reading comprehension. Some teachers also like to use them as exercises to improve reading comprehension.

**Digital storybooks.** Many books for children as well as adults are available in interactive versions called **interactive storybooks** or **electronic storybooks**, which can be read from a computer screen, on mobile devices, or as print books with interactive buttons. Some of these allow children to hear narrations in English or other languages such as Spanish. Others let children explore the screen, activating animations and sounds when they click in various locations. These books are designed to provide an interesting, interactive way to read and to increase reading fluency. However, Pearman and Chang (2010) say that though the features of electronic storybooks can support reading acquisition, they can also distract children's productive reading and should be carefully supervised.

**Accelerated Reader.** A product called Accelerated Reader or AR designed to track students' reading skills, has seen popular use. Its purpose is to motivate students to increase the amount of reading they do for enjoyment. It keeps track of the number of books they read and tests them on comprehension. Teachers can get individual or aggregate data on books read at each readability level. This gives them a better idea of how students are progressing in their reading abilities and whether they are spending enough time reading at desired levels. Early studies found that schools using AR for longer periods of time show higher rates of reading, which may correlate with higher tested reading levels. However, subsequent reviews of research performed by the U.S. Government's What Works Clearinghouse found "no discernible effects in reading fluency and comprehension for adolescent learners" (U.S. Department of Education, 2010, p. 5) and "no discernible effects for reading fluency, mixed effects for comprehension, and potentially positive effects for general reading achievement" for K–3 students (U.S. Department of Education, 2008, p. 4). The What Works Clearinghouse also reviewed research for English Language Learners (ELL), but found that too few studies met criteria to allow it to draw conclusions (U.S. Department of Education, 2009).

## Microcomputer-Based Labs (Probeware)

A technology tool that has proven particularly useful in math and science classrooms is the **microcomputer-based lab (MBL)**, sometimes referred to as **probeware**. MBL packages consist of software accompanied by special hardware sensors designed to measure light, temperature, voltage, and/or speed. The probes are connected to the microcomputer, and the software processes the collected data. Computer-based probeware actually can replace several traditional items of lab equipment, such as oscilloscopes and voltmeters. Brunsell and Horejsi (2010) say that probeware devices are standard equipment for the modern science classroom and have software interfaces with other cutting-edge equipment like digital microscopes, GPSs, and robots. Blanchard, Sharp, and Grable (2009) point out that probeware can also be useful to integrate science and mathematics in authentic and motivating projects. For one such project, see Technology Integration Example 5.7.

## Calculators, Graphing Calculators and Calculator-Based Labs

For many years, calculators have played a widespread—and often controversial—role in mathematics education. **Graphing calculators**, which are software-programmed devices that have small screens and can illustrate equations in graphs, have emerged and have become indispensable tools in both mathematics and higher-level science curricula. Jaqua (2010) describes a variety of

# TECHNOLOGY INTEGRATION

## Example 5.7

TITLE: Car Lab Project

CONTENT AREA/TOPIC: Physical science, mathematics

GRADE LEVELS: 9–12

ISTE STANDARDS•S: Standard 4—Critical Thinking, Problem Solving, and Decision Making; Standard 6—Technology Operations and Concepts

CCSS: CCSS.MATH.PRACTICE.MP5, CCSS.MATH.CONTENT. HSF.LE.A.1, CCSS.MATH.CONTENT.HSF.LE.A.1.A, CCSS.MATH. CONTENT.HSF.LE.A.2NSTA: HS-PS2-1

DESCRIPTION: This project, which connects physical science and mathematics skills, builds on teenagers' natural excitement about cars and getting a driver's license. Students are asked to design a rubber-band car that will go the fastest and/or farthest in a drag race. In an initial race, they collect data by placing their car directly in front of a motion detector attached to a graphing calculator. As they race their cars, the graphing calculator displays the velocity graph and slope. The class discusses what a straight versus a curved line means for observations of velocity and acceleration. Students then go to each of four different stations, each of which uses probes and graphing calculators to collect data and create graphic representations for discussion and analysis: (1) Going the Distance (additional speed trials to generate and analyze graphs of velocity and acceleration), (2) Piston Pressure (to experiment with and observe physical principles about pressure in closed systems), (3) The Color of Headlights (experiments with light intensity), and (4) Soda Can Radiator (experiments with energy and temperature).

SOURCE: Based on a concept from Blanchard, M., Sharp, J., & Grable, L. (2009). Rev your engines! The Science Teacher, 76(2), 35–40.

▲ For many years, calculators have played a widespread—and often controversial—role in mathematics education. (Photo by W. Wiencke.)

classroom activities, appropriate for students from sixth grade up to the college level, that use these devices to teach graphing skills. Browning and Garza-Kling (2010) review four ways graphing calculators can be used to investigate mathematical ideas at the middle school level. Other articles in the special issue of *Mathematics Teaching in the Middle School* (vol. 16, nos. 5–6) offer a wealth of ideas and activities on how to use graphing calculators in teaching algebra and geometry for middle school students. When probes or sensors are connected to a graphing calculator rather than to a computer (as described in the previous section on MBLs), they are called **calculator-based labs (CBLs)**.

## Geographic Information Systems and Global Positioning Systems

A **Geographic Information System (GIS)** is a computer system that is able to store in a database a variety of information about geographic locations. After it has stored all the data that describe a given location, the GIS can then display the data in map form. GISs allow uses of large amounts of geographic information to produce, analyze, and compare maps. Kerski, Demirci, and Milson (2013) reviewed uses of GIS in secondary education around the world. They found teachers in over 30 countries using it in subjects "ranging from geography, environmental studies, and social sciences to science, biology, and mathematics" (p. 232) making it one of the world's most popular and versatile software tools.

A **Global Positioning System (GPS)** is a worldwide radio-navigation system made possible by a bank of 24 satellites and their ground stations. Using satellites as reference points, a GPS unit can calculate positions of anything on earth accurate to a matter of feet or inches. A GPS receiver connected to mapping software is what most people think of as a GPS; however, the use of these systems is growing, from finding your way in an unfamiliar community to guiding farmers as they plant and harvest their crops. These small devices can be useful in a car, agricultural equipment, the home, or even a portable laptop. Though GIS and GPS tools are used primarily in teaching science and social studies, uses for a variety of other content areas have been reported. Figure 5.11 shows children using a GPS in an outside-school learning activity.

## FIGURE 5.11 GPS Activity in the Field

▲ Global Positioning Systems (GPS) are so portable, they can be used to support field activities like this one in which children are looking for locations to collect data for a science project. © Thinkstock

## Online Foreign Language Dictionaries and Language Translators (Machine Translation)

Two online tools that can support students as they learn additional languages are foreign language dictionaries and language translators, with the latter usually referred to in foreign language education as **machine translation**. Online **foreign language dictionaries** function like other dictionaries in that they allow people to look up definitions for words and phrases in common usage. However, foreign language dictionaries allow users to look up a word or phrase in one language (e.g., French or German) and get the definition and synonyms for it in another language (e.g., English). These online tools are used like any quick reference to help students learn and use a language new to them.

**Language translators** work as the name implies: they allow users to input sentences and paragraphs of text in one language and get a translation into another language. In foreign language education, the practice of using these machine translation tools is viewed as highly problematic. Translators often provide literal translations that are not accurate representations of meaning, and students who are new to the language are not able to make judgments about grammar and usage that allow them to judge correctness of translations. Steding (2009) offers strategies for using these tools in the classroom in ways that best support students' burgeoning skills.

### TECHNOLOGY LEARNING CHECK

Complete **TLC 5.8** to review what you have learned from reading this section about content-area tool features and uses.

## COLLABORATE, DISCUSS, REFLECT

Monkey Business/Fotolia

**The following questions may be used either for in-class, small-group discussions or may initiate discussions in blogs or online discussion boards:**

1. Some educators object to the use of tools such as test generators and worksheet generators, saying that they encourage teachers to use technology to maintain current methods, rather than using technology in more innovative ways. What case can you make for keeping software tools like these in classrooms?

2. The use of online and on-computer testing systems is becoming a popular, albeit controversial, practice. What are the main points raised by critics of these systems? How would you address them?

3. Online language translators are proliferating, despite the fact they rarely provide completely accurate translations from one language to another. An essay called "Do online translators really work, or are they more trouble than they're worth?" (see a copy by searching on this title) gives examples of these inaccuracies. Since these literal translations can cause problems for students of foreign languages, what is a proper role for these tools in foreign language learning?

**Chapter 5** Summary

**The following is a summary of the main points covered in this chapter.**

1. **Benefits of software tools—These tools provide** improved efficiency and productivity, improved appearance, better accuracy and timeliness of information, and more support for interaction and sharing.

2. **Materials generators**—These are tools that help teachers and students produce instructional materials. They include desktop publishing software, Web design software, whiteboard lesson software, test generators and rubric generators, worksheet and puzzle generators, IEP generators, graphic document makers, and PDF and forms makers.

3. **Data collection and analysis tools**—These are tools that help teachers collect and organize information that indicates student progress. They include electronic gradebooks, statistical packages, online survey systems, student information systems, and student response systems (clickers).

4. **Testing and grading tools**—These tools help teachers assess student progress. They include electronic gradebooks, test and rubric generators, and online and computer-based testing systems.

5. **Graphics tools**—These are tools that allow the manipulation of images to illustrate documents and Web pages. They include draw/paint programs; image editing tools; charting/graphing tools; clip art, photo, animation, sound, video, and font collections; and word cloud generators.

6. **Planning and organizing tools**—These are tools that help teachers and students organize for more productive use of their time and help students conceptualize and communicate their ideas. They include lesson planning software; scheduling, calendar, and time management tools; and outlining and concept mapping software.

7. **Research and reference tools**—These are tools that let students look up information in electronic versions of encyclopedias, atlases, and dictionaries for research projects and other learning activities. They include electronic versions of the following tools: encyclopedias, atlases and mapping tools, and dictionaries and thesauruses.

8. **Content-area tools**—These are tools that support teaching and learning activities in various content areas. They include CAD systems, music tools such as music editors and sequencers, reading tools, microcomputer-based labs, graphing calculators and calculator-based labs, Geographic Information Systems and Global Positioning Systems, and online foreign language dictionaries and language translators (machine translation).

# TECHNOLOGY INTEGRATION **WORKSHOP**

## 1. APPLY WHAT YOU LEARNED

To apply the concepts and skills you've read about throughout this chapter, go to the Chapter 5 Technology Application Activity.

## 2. TECHNOLOGY INTEGRATION LESSON PLANNING: PART 1—EVALUATING AND CREATING LESSON PLANS

Complete the following exercise using the sample lesson plans found on any lesson planning site that you find on the Internet.

a. Locate lesson ideas—Identify three lesson plans that focus on any of the tools or strategies you learned about in this chapter. For example:

- Materials generator software tools
- Data collection and analysis software tools
- Testing and grading tools
- Graphics software tools
- Planning and organizing software tools
- Research and reference software tools
- Content-area software tools

b. Evaluate the lessons—Use the Technology Lesson Plan Evaluation Checklist to evaluate each of the lessons you found.

c. Create your own lesson—After you have reviewed and evaluated some sample lessons, create one of your own using a lesson plan format of your choice (or one your instructor gives you). Be sure the lesson focuses on one of the technologies or strategies discussed in this chapter.

# 3. TECHNOLOGY INTEGRATION LESSON PLANNING: PART 2—IMPLEMENTING THE TIP MODEL

Review how to implement the TIP model in your classroom by doing the following activities with the lesson you created in the Technology Integration Lesson Planning exercise above.

**a.** Describe the Phase 1 Planning activities you would do to use this lesson in your classroom:
   - What is the relative advantage of using the technology(ies) in this lesson?
   - Do you have resources and skills you need to carry it out?

**b.** Describe the Phase 2 Implementation activities you would do to use this lesson in your classroom:
   - What are the objectives of the lesson plan?
   - How will you assess your students' accomplishment of the objectives?
   - What integration strategies are used in this lesson plan?
   - How would you prepare the learning environment?

**c.** Describe the Phase 3 Evaluation/Revision activities you would do to use this lesson in your classroom—What strategies and/or instruments would you use to evaluate the success of this lesson in your classroom, in order to determine revision needs?

**d.** Add lesson descriptors—Create descriptors for your new lesson (e.g., grade level, content and topic areas, technologies used, ISTE standards, 21st Century Learning standards).

**e.** Save your new lesson—Save your lesson plan with all its descriptors and TIP model notes.

# 4. FOR YOUR TEACHING PORTFOLIO

Add the following to your Teaching Portfolio:
   - Lesson plan evaluations, lesson plans, and products you created above.
   - Products of your group's Hot Topic Debates
   - Products of your group's Collaborate, Discuss, Reflect online or in-class activities

# 6

# Online Tools, Uses, and Web-Based Development

## Learning Outcomes

After reading this chapter and completing the learning activities, you should be able to:

1. Select a rule or guideline for online behavior that could help teachers and students address each of the problems and issues they are likely to encounter in the online environment. (ISTE Standards•T 4, 5)

2. Identify a procedure or problem-solving strategy that would allow teachers and students to navigate the Internet efficiently in a given situation. (ISTE Standards•T 3, 5)

3. Identify a strategy and/or resource to address given needs to locate or store information online. (ISTE Standards•T 3, 5)

4. Identify the features and uses of various online communications options. (ISTE Standards•T 3, 5)

5. Select online social networking tools that would be most effective for a given educational use. (ISTE Standards•T 1, 3, 5)

6. Locate apps to meet various educational needs. (ISTE Standards•T 2, 3)

7. Identify authoring skills and resources required for online Web page or website creation. (ISTE Standards•T 3, 5)

8. Explain how each recommended development step and website criteria contribute to efficient development of high quality Web content. (ISTE Standards•T 3, 5)

# TECHNOLOGY INTEGRATION IN ACTION
# A RESEARCH PAPER

GRADE LEVEL: High school • CONTENT AREA/TOPIC: Research, study skills • LENGTH OF TIME: Nine weeks

## PHASE 1   ANALYSIS OF LEARNING AND TEACHING NEEDS

Konstantin Chagin/Shutterstock

### Step 1: Determine relative advantage.

Ms. Almon was the library media specialist at Werebest High School. One of her tasks was to help all teachers and students use the library's resources effectively for students' research paper assignments. Over the years, she had compiled a substantial collection of handouts, lists of sources, and assessment materials, which she copied, placed in notebooks, and updated periodically. However, she and the teachers agreed it was difficult to get students to use these notebooks. The students' study skills and organizational strategies left a lot to be desired, and each teacher seemed to have a different approach to teaching these important skills. Also, students wanted a more digital approach, in tune with their burgeoning social media preferences. As she and the teachers talked about this situation, they agreed that it would be better to have these materials available on a website, so that students could access them wherever they were, the materials could be easily updated, and the approach for doing research would be consistent across all classes. They decided to work together to create a research paper resource website. They also decided they would use this site and a set of video tutorials to structure a series of teaching activities to help students complete research paper assignments.

### Step 2: Assess required skills and resources.

Ms. Almon had never designed a website, but she had attended a district workshop on free website development resources, and she had consulted the district technology resource person about the best option for their needs. They decided that in light of the number of different items she wanted to create and upload, the district website linked to her school would be the best place to host it. The resource person agreed to help her design the site and show her how to upload items to it.

## PHASE 2   PLANNING FOR INTEGRATION

### Step 3: Decide on objectives and assessments.

Ms. Almon and the teachers decided they would structure their assessments around the "Big6" information literacy skills (search to locate this website) as well as around the quality of content in the students' research papers. To make sure that all teachers structured students' learning in the same way, they agreed on objectives for each of these skill areas and created assessment methods to measure each of them. They also decided to measure student attitudes toward research and writing. The outcomes, objectives, and assessments they decided on were as follows:

Big6 information skills 1–3.
Outcome: Defining, searching for, and acquiring information.
Objective: Students will identify a topic for a research paper, use the project website to identify published sources of information related to the topic, and locate the items of information.
Assessment: Checklist of required tasks and products from information searches.

Big6 information skills 4–6.
Outcome: Analyze, synthesize, and evaluate information.
Objective: Students will write summary analyses of the information in each item they locate, write a synthesis across all information, and prepare an outline of the points they will emphasize in their research papers.
Assessment: Checklist of required tasks and products from information analyses.

Final paper.
Outcome: Write a research paper.
Objective: Students will achieve a rubric score of at least 15 of 20 possible points on an assigned research paper.
Assessment: Rubric on research paper content, structure, mechanics, and creativity.

Attitudes toward writing and research. Outcome: Positive attitude toward research and writing. Objective: The students will demonstrate a good attitude toward the writing approach and research used in the project by reporting a rating of at least 45 of 50 possible points on an attitude survey.
Assessment: Likert scale attitude survey.

## Step 4: Design integration strategies.

Ms. Almon and the teachers worked together to determine what they would place on the resource website and how students would use it. They decided the site would be most useful if it provided links to other helpful sites and a structure to help students work through the process of doing their searches and writing their papers. They also decided they should create short video tutorials on key points in the process, such as how to select a research paper topic and how to use a graphic organizer to create a visual outline. The website and the tutorials should also help make the teaching process more consistent across classes. They decided to recommend the following time frame for the research paper project:

Week 1: **Introducing the project and identifying a topic.** All teachers introduce the research paper project by displaying the website to the whole class, using the interactive whiteboard. They review the steps, discuss the process (displaying some of the links at each step), show the first video tutorial, and help students select their research paper topics.

Weeks 2–3: **Helping students obtain information.** The teachers show students how to use website links to search for information related to their topic. One of the activities is deciding which type of resource to use. For resources that can best be found in the library, Ms. Almon arranges to show students how to access these resources in the library media center, using a video tutorial as an overview. Students use the website resources at the classroom workstation or in the computer center, depending on what else the teacher is doing in the classroom during this time.

Weeks 4–6: **Helping students analyze and synthesize information.** The teachers help students review their information and make decisions on how to structure their paper and what to include in it. They show videos on graphic organizers and let students practice using these techniques.

Weeks 7–8: **Writing the papers.** During this time, students complete most of the writing on their papers at home or in the library media center after school. Some teachers allocate class time for students to work in class and to review and give feedback on students' word-processed drafts.

Week 9: **Presentations.** Students present their papers using the strategy selected by their teacher. Some prepare PowerPoint presentations to accompany their oral presentations; others create a video or a Web page with links to other resources.

## Step 5: Prepare instructional environment.

The main preparation task for the project was creating the website and video tutorials and deciding what to include in each. However, Ms. Almon also had to coordinate the students' trips to the library media center. Preparation tasks included:

Creation of website content. Ms. Almon and the teachers decided on the sections of content to include. Then each of them searched for the best links to include, made a Bookmarks/Favorites file of the sites they found, and wrote the content for that section of the site. Ms. Almon compiled the materials into a website and, with the district resource person's help, uploaded the site to the school server.

Video development. The teachers also decided on four topics that would support the teaching of research paper strategies and could be presented well via video. Ms. Almon worked with the district media department to create the four brief video tutorials—how to select a research paper topic, how to create a graphic organizer, how to use the library media center resources, and strategies for presenting a research paper. These were placed on the school server for easy online access.

Handout. To make sure students understood the assignment and had access to all resources, Ms. Almon created a handout that all teachers could give their students. She also posted this handout on the website so that students could **download** it (transfer it from the Internet to their computer) whenever they wished.

Library media center and computer lab scheduling. Before students began work on the projects, the teachers scheduled time for their students in the lab and in the library media center.

### Step 6: Analyze results.

After all students had completed their research papers, the teachers met to review the data they had collected. Students did very well on the first set of information skills but less well on the second set. Student attitudes toward the writing process were generally high: About 75% of students rated it 20 points or more. Comments volunteered by students on their surveys indicated they would like more in-class time to revise their products and more individual assistance with the revision process. Rubric scores on research papers were also generally good, with noticeable improvement in the areas of structure and content. Scores were lowest on mechanics.

### Step 7: Make revisions.

The teachers decided to create a set of writing exercises to give students more concentrated practice on analysis and synthesis skills before doing their own written summaries. They also decided to target one or two mechanics skills for special practice with word-processed exercises. All the teachers agreed that the website and video tutorials had been critical focal points in making instruction across classes more consistent and easier to follow.

Based on concepts from "So You Have to Do a Research Project?" from East Greenwich Public Schools.

## CHAPTER 6 **BIG IDEAS OVERVIEW**

Before you begin reading the rest of this chapter, listen to the Chapter 6 Big Ideas Overview. It will give you a two-minute audio overview of main concepts to look for and help prepare you to work through information and exercises to achieve this chapter's outcomes.

## DIGITAL CITIZENSHIP ISSUES AND NEEDS FOR THE ONLINE ENVIRONMENT

Most of us cannot remember a time when cell phones and social media were not the norm, when we couldn't "Google" something we did not know or had forgotten, or a time when communicating with mobile devices was not a daily activity. Even in the rapid environment of technological evolution, remarkable changes in communications have come about with incredible speed. Some resources have gone from possible to pervasive in only a few years. These changes are not slowing down.

The primary reason for this breathtaking revolution in communications is society's recognition of the importance of ready access to people and resources. If "knowledge is power," as Francis Bacon said, then communication is freedom—freedom for people to reach information they need in order to acquire knowledge that can empower them. This heady freedom permeates the atmosphere of a 21st-century information society. The development that made this revolution possible is the emergence of an online, Web-based environment. This chapter, the first of three that focus on online education, will review how this environment came about and the online tools that are currently available for teachers and students to take full advantage of it.

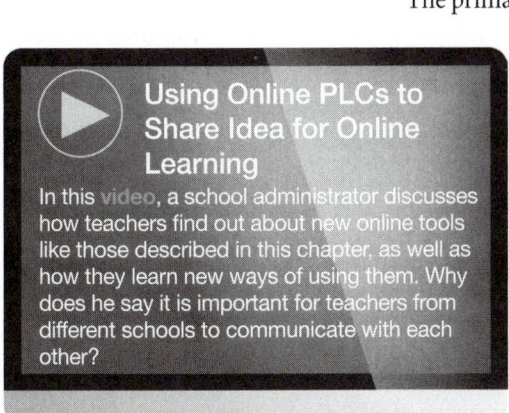

Using Online PLCs to Share Idea for Online Learning

In this video, a school administrator discusses how teachers find out about new online tools like those described in this chapter, as well as how they learn new ways of using them. Why does he say it is important for teachers from different schools to communicate with each other?

### How "Online" Emerged: A Brief History

We inherited our online world from a U.S. Department of Defense (DOD) project that developed the first version of the Internet during the 1970s. Its purpose was to allow quick communication among researchers working on

DOD projects in about 30 locations. The DOD also saw it as a way to continue communications among these important defense sites in the event of a worldwide catastrophe such as a nuclear attack. Because these projects were funded by the DOD's Advanced Research Projects Agency (ARPA), the network was originally called **ARPAnet**.

In the 1980s, just as desktop computers were becoming common, the National Science Foundation funded a high-speed connection among university centers based on the ARPAnet structure. By connecting their individual networks, universities could communicate and exchange information in the same way the DOD's projects had. However, these new connections had an additional, unexpected benefit. A person accessing a university network from home or school could also get access to any site connected to that network. This connection began to be called a gateway to all networks, and what we now call the Internet was born. Though most people think of the Internet as synonymous with the **World Wide Web (WWW)**, the latter really is a subset of the Internet system that came about around 1993 with the development of browser software. The WWW is an Internet service that links sites around the world through **hypertext**, texts that contain links to other texts. Everyday many people use a **Web browser** or software that allows users to load websites that are connected to each other via the WWW, and in this way, they "navigate" around the Internet from site to site.

Mobile devices have further accelerated this trend toward storing and accessing information and communicating online. Anyone with a device such as a smartphone, tablet, or a wearable technology such as Google Glass can communicate with individuals in other locations and can access course spaces from wherever they are.

## Online Safety and Security Issues

In addition to its benefits, the online world also has its share of society-wide debates, problems, and controversies. In many ways, it is a reflection of the best and worst qualities of our society. Five potential problems related to safety and security are discussed here, along with strategies that educators can use to make the online environment a safer, more worry-free place for teaching and learning.

### Accessing sites with inappropriate materials.
Like a big-city bookstore, the Internet has materials that parents and teachers may not want students to see, either because they are inappropriate for an age level or because they contain information or images that some consider objectionable. Because online information is easily obtainable, such materials can be accessed all too easily by accident. For example, until only a few years ago, a suffix such as .gov, .com, .edu, and .info differentiated the website for our nation's executive branch of government from a pornography site. Because it is so easy to access these sites, preventing students from accidentally visiting these pages is difficult.

The Children's Internet Protection Act, signed into law on December 21, 2000, is designed to ensure that libraries receiving federal e-rate funds take measures to keep children away from Internet materials that could be harmful to them. Most schools have found that the best way to prevent access to sites with inappropriate materials is to install firewall hardware and/or filtering software on individual computers or on the school or district network that connects them to the Internet. **Firewall software** (e.g., Norton) protects a computer from attempts by others to gain unauthorized access to it and also prevents access to certain sites. **Filtering software** (e.g., Cyber Patrol and Net Nanny) limits access to sites on the basis of keywords, a list of off-limit sites, or a combination of these. Although there is software and hardware to prevent students from accessing inappropriate material, nothing is foolproof and/or without issues. For example, students and/or teachers wanting to use YouTube within the classroom many times find that the districts filtering software has blocked it. Whether a piece of software or an individual is in charge of filtering content, content that is important for learning may be blocked or controlled.

### Safety and privacy issues for students.
Social networking sites (SNS) are online locations that allow users to upload their own content, meet and connect with friends from around the world, and share media and interests. Although most public SNSs are blocked in schools today, the dominance of them outside of school and the lack of experience most students have may put young people at special risk. Though Facebook "boots" underage users when it can find them, many preteens in the United States are using social network sites, despite not meeting the minimum age requirement of 13 years old. Students can be impacted negatively in online social environments in many ways, including the ones described here.

- **Online predators**—Many times young people tend to believe everything they hear and read. Therefore, in a variety of online discussion rooms or chat rooms (online locations where people can drop in and exchange messages in real time), they may not consider the possibility that a 12-year-old named "Mary" may actually be a 50-year-old man. Students should be instructed never to provide their complete names, addresses, or telephone numbers to any stranger they "meet" on the Internet, and they should report to teachers any people who try to get them to do so.

- **Sales pitches aimed at children**—This is a problem similar to that posed by television commercials. Many Internet sites have colorful, compelling images that encourage people to buy. Young people may make purchase commitments they cannot fulfill. Schools and teachers must also be sensitive to these sites and make students aware of the sales messages implicit in them.

- **Privacy issues**—In their Web products, teachers should be careful not to identify students with last names, addresses, and other personal information. Another privacy issue surrounds the use of **cookies**, or small text files placed on a hard drive by a Web server contacted on the Internet. The purpose of cookies is to provide the server with information that can help personalize Web activity to your needs, but cookies also may track behavior on the Internet in ways that violate privacy. Students and teachers can learn how to manage cookies in ways that prevent unwanted tracking.

- **Cyberbullying**—The practice of using technology to harass, threaten, embarrass, or target another person has become an acknowledged problem and the subject of this chapter's Hot Topic Debate. Cyberbullying is the online version of regular school bullying and can produce the same harmful consequences to young people. Several sites have been set up to document and combat this problem, but the first line of defense remains school-based programs to raise awareness among students of what constitutes cyberbullying and to teach how to respond if they observe or are a victim of this online mistreatment.

**Computer viruses and hacking.** Viruses are programs written for malicious purposes. Two of the most common ways to get viruses on your computer from the Internet are through email attachments and downloaded files.

- **Email attachments with viruses**—Email attachments can contain viruses, and when files are exchanged, many senders are not even aware that emails are being sent under their names. If a computer contains a virus programmed to attach itself to files, the virus can inadvertently be sent along with the file. When the person receiving the attachment opens it, the virus transfers to his or her computer.

## Hot Topic Debate
## Does Social Networking Promote Cyberbullying?

*Take a position for or against (based either on your own position or one assigned to you) the following controversial statement. Discuss it in class or on an online discussion board, blog, or wiki, as assigned by your instructor. When the discussion is complete, write a summary of the main pros and cons that you and your classmates have stated, and put the summary document in your Teacher Portfolio.*

"A person is bullied when he or she is exposed, repeatedly and over time to negative actions on the part of one or more other persons, and he or she had difficulty defending him or herself" (see the Olweus Bullying Prevention program website). The number of teens who are bullied online is increasing as social networking sites become ubiquitous. Today 73% of U.S. teens use one or more online social network sites, and 37% of these teens use them on a daily basis. In 2010, between 21% and 30% of U.S. youth had harassed others online (see the Prevent Cyberbullying and Internet Harassment website). An important distinction between teens bullied on social networks and those bullied elsewhere is that the former are more likely to report it. Some argue that the very nature of social networking promotes cyberbullying. Others point to the meager attention given to the problem by parents, educators, schools, and policy makers. Some people have pointed to the lack of online etiquette (netiquette), and few safe-browsing skills exhibited by teens. Do you see evidence that bullying behavior is worse in social networks than in school? What is the school's role in reducing cyberbullying?

## FIGURE 6.1 Strategies to Prevent Computer Viruses

Use and update frequently a virus protection software that protects your computer!

Avoid shareware! Download programs only from reputable sites!

Do not open attachments from unknown senders! If you weren't expected an attachment from someone, confirm it was they who sent it!

Gualtiero Boffi/Shutterstock

- **Downloaded files and programs with viruses**—As with email attachments, viruses can attach themselves to files and programs and be received along with the item being downloaded. Figure 6.1 identifies strategies to address these virus problems.

Fraud and phishing.     Although the Internet is becoming more secure for credit card use, online consumers, teachers, and even students must be sure to purchase products only from well-known, reputable sites that offer a secure server. Though secure servers have special programs to prevent outside monitoring of transactions, even large, well-known stores have seen data breaches that put customer data at risk. The **uniform resource locator (URL),** or Web address, for a secure server usually begins with "https" instead of the usual "http," and has a symbol of a lock in the Web browser. Teachers and students must be vigilant to avoid offers and alerts that are **phishing** attempts, or emails that claim to be from a legitimate organization or business and ask for personal information but is actually used for identify theft. For example, someone gains access to your password by sending an email claiming to be from your online service provider, saying your account has been compromised; they send you to a site to enter and change your password. No reputable organization would ask its member to do this, so all such requests should be viewed as phishing attempts.

Online identity and reputation issues.     The same online features that make information and media so easy to store and share also mean that they are not private, and, once shared, they have a permanent online presence. As many students, teachers, public officials, and others have learned to their distress, shared messages and media establish an online identity that, though it may be misleading, is difficult to change. For example, someone may post a **selfie**, or a self-taken photo, that reflects an undesirable image. A **digital footprint** is the trail that people leave behind as a result of their social media interactions (Careless, 2012). Because colleges and employers often review an individual's digital footprint before making decisions on applications, students' "digital decisions" can have "unanticipated negative consequences . . . from lost job opportunities and denied college admission to national scandals" (Cooper, 2013, p. 51). In light of this, teachers have to instruct students to evaluate carefully the potential impact of their actions on their online reputation.

## Online Ethical and Legal Issues

Some online behaviors are risky not because they endanger students' safety or reputation, but because they violate ethical and legal rules that could result in punishment. Two of these are plagiarism (a.k.a. cybercheating) and piracy.

**Online plagiarism.** **Online plagiarism** or **cybercheating** is academic dishonesty in which someone uses another's work obtained from the Internet as his/her own. In an environment in which information is so readily available, students often do not realize that they cannot use text or images without attribution. Teaching students when and how to attribute their sources has become an essential skill for teachers to include in their instruction on how to do online research.

**Online piracy.** The free-flowing nature of online information and the ease with which students can locate it leads many students to the erroneous conclusion that everything they find online should be free. To make sure they comply with copyright laws, schools are making teachers and students aware of policies about copyright, **Acceptable Usage Policy (AUP),** and guidelines for fair use of published materials. However, illegal downloading of music, video, and documents remains a widespread problem. These practices are all considered **online piracy**.

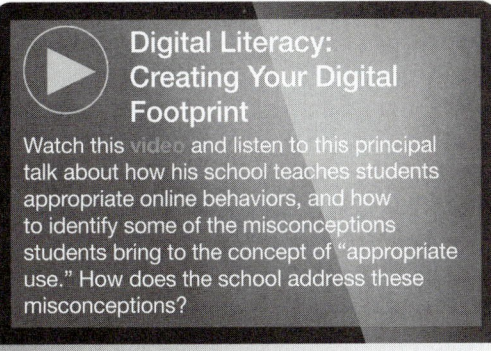

**Digital Literacy: Creating Your Digital Footprint**

Watch this video and listen to this principal talk about how his school teaches students appropriate online behaviors, and how to identify some of the misconceptions students bring to the concept of "appropriate use." How does the school address these misconceptions?

## Rules and Guidelines for Online Behavior: Digital Citizenship, Netiquette, and More

In light of the issues, challenges and risks presented by online use, several kinds of standards have emerged for guiding online behavior for various situations. All these fall under the general heading of fostering **digital citizenship,** or the responsible, civil, safe, and productive use of modern technologies. Becoming a good digital citizen requires an array of skills, including netiquette concepts and rules of behavior in online learning environments. Because schools are increasingly asking students to use technology tools and go online, schools are also tasked with teaching students all the digital citizenship concepts and skills described in this section.

**Teaching digital citizenship concepts.** They key to promoting online safety and appropriate online behavior is instruction in digital citizenship. The organization Common Sense Media has created a free, online curriculum that teachers may use in their own classrooms. It contains sets of standards and objectives, lesson plans, and assessments matched to each of the following topics in its scope and sequence:

- **Internet safety**—Optimizing Internet use by using safe strategies such as distinguishing between inappropriate contact and positive connections.
- **Privacy and security**—Managing online information and keeping it secure by creating good passwords, avoiding scams and schemes, and analyzing privacy policies.
- **Relationships and communications**—Using intrapersonal and interpersonal skills to build and strengthen positive online communication and communities.
- **Cyberbullying**—Handling cyberbullying situations and building positive, supportive online communities.
- **Digital footprint and reputation**—Protecting privacy, respecting others' privacy, and becoming aware of one's digital footprint.
- **Self-image and identity**—Comparing online versus offline identity and becoming aware of how representation through different online personas affects one's sense of self, reputation, and relationships.
- **Information literacy**—Identifying, locating, evaluating, and using information effectively, as well as evaluating the quality, credibility, and validity of websites, and giving proper credit.
- **Creative credit and copyright**—Addressing plagiarism, piracy, copyright, and fair use.

Technology Integration Example 6.1 illustrates a lesson plan to use at the beginning of a school year to get students thinking about their **digital footprint**, or the kind of online presence they establish when they use social media.

## Example 6.1

**TITLE:** Online Safety: What Would You Do?

**CONTENT AREA/TOPIC:** Digital literacy

**GRADE LEVELS:** Middle school

**ISTE STANDARDS•S:** Standard 5a

**CCSS:** CSS.ELA-LITERACY.SL.6.2, CCSS.ELA-LITERACY.SL.6.3, CCSS.ELA-LITERACY.SL.7.4, CCSS.ELA-LITERACY.SL.8.1.D

**DESCRIPTION:** Students begin learning how to behave safely online by discussing how they know that someone on the phone is who they say they are. Then they talk about how this is different online and focus on why someone might pretend to be someone they aren't. They go over the basic rules for staying safe online. Next, divide the class into small groups and give each a scenario about someone they "meet" online. They are to discuss and decide how they would react and why. As groups share their scenarios and responses, the class discusses them and why their response is or is not a good one. End up with the whole class generating their own list of "Online Dos and Don'ts."

*SOURCE:* Based on an idea from the lesson plan *Be Street Smart* at the Google Digital Literacy and Citizenship Curriculum website.

## FIGURE 6.2 Netiquette: Rules for Good Manners in Digital Communications

Studio 8/Pearson Education

**Be courteous when using technologies to communicate:**
- Silence device sounds when requested.
- Talk on phones in public only when permitted.
- When communicating with devices in public, be respectful of others by talking and texting quietly.

**Identify yourself:**
- Begin messages with a salutation and end them with your name.
- Use a signature (a footer with your identifying information) at the end of a message.

**Include a subject line.** Give a descriptive phrase in the subject line of the message header that tells the topic of the message (not just "Hi, there!").

**Avoid sarcasm.** People who don't know you may misinterpret its meaning.

**Respect others' privacy.** Do not quote or forward personal email without the original author's permission.

**Acknowledge and return messages promptly.**

**Copy with caution.** Don't copy everyone you know on each message.

**No spam (a.k.a. junk mail).** Don't contribute to worthless information on the Internet by sending or responding to mass postings of chain letters, rumors, etc.

**Be concise.** Keep messages as concise as possible—about one screen, as a rule of thumb.

**Use appropriate language:**
- Avoid coarse, rough, or rude language.
- Observe good grammar and spelling.

**Use appropriate emotions (emotion icons) to help convey meaning.** Use emoticons to convey emotions only if you are sure that your readers know their meaning.

**Use appropriate intensifiers to help convey meaning.**
- Avoid "flaming" (online "screaming") or sentences typed in all caps.
- Use asterisks surrounding words to indicate italics used for emphasis (*at last*).
- Use words in brackets, such as (grin), to show a state of mind.
- Use common acronyms (e.g., LOL for "laugh out loud").

Teaching netiquette concepts. The guidelines that govern civil, courteous behavior in online communications have become known as **netiquette**, a combination of net and etiquette. Netiquette is considered a subset of digital citizenship skills and covers rules of behavior for email, messaging, and discussions. A summary of netiquette rules in Figure 6.2 is based on published sources (Shea, 2004; Senning & Post, 2013).

Rules of online learning etiquette: The ROLE Model. Additional guidelines are available to govern civil and constructive behavior in online courses. Roblyer (2013) refers to the following list as the Rules for Online Learning Etiquette, or the ROLE Model, as part of a rubric to guide and assess online discussions.

1. **Make postings and responses friendly and helpful.** This guideline helps students realize that they have a "voice" or manner of speaking online that is perceptible to others. Working with others online is more constructive if this voice is congenial and supportive, rather than negative or argumentative.

2. **Allow for differences of opinion; disagree in a professional way.** This is the most difficult of the rules for students to learn. In a learning environment, where new ideas and diverse opinions are the norm, students must be prepared for disagreement and not be surprised, intimidated, or angered by it. Instead, they must learn how to make a case and defend a position without becoming negative or abusive.

3. **Always assume benign intent; request clarification when necessary.** Because there are usually no facial cues or body language in online "conversations," the meaning behind words in text may be unclear. Students must be taught to keep an open mind and not assume the worst, as some are inclined to do.

4. **Avoid sarcasm, which can often be misinterpreted.** Because jokes and sarcastic remarks can be misinterpreted as serious statements, they should be avoided. Even when accompanied by helpful intensifiers or emoticons, sarcasm and humor can have unintended impact.

5. **Never use profanity or "flaming" language, regardless of the situation.** Though good advice in any situation, students must be reminded that angry or profane words have no place in a classroom – online or otherwise.

**TECHNOLOGY LEARNING CHECK**
Complete **TLC 6.1** to review what you have learned from reading this section about digital citizenship in the online environment.

#  NAVIGATION OPTIONS

There are several different ways to "travel" around the Internet. Background on each of these methods is discussed here, along with tips on how to troubleshoot navigation problems and issues.

## Using Uniform Resource Locators (URLs)

Our use of the Internet depends on the use of common procedures or Internet protocols that allow computers to communicate with each other despite differences in programs or operating systems. One important protocol is the manner of listing website addresses. Just about every home in the world has an address so that people can find it and make deliveries of mail and other items. Each place you "visit" on the Internet also has an address, for many of the same reasons. However, the Internet is less tolerant of mistakes in an address than is the U.S. Post Office! Each address must be entered exactly, with every punctuation mark in place, or it will not work.

Parts of Web addresses. Internet addresses are called **uniform resource locators**, or **URLs**. Look at the example URL shown in a browser window in Figure 6.3. The line where

## FIGURE 6.3 Parts of a URL

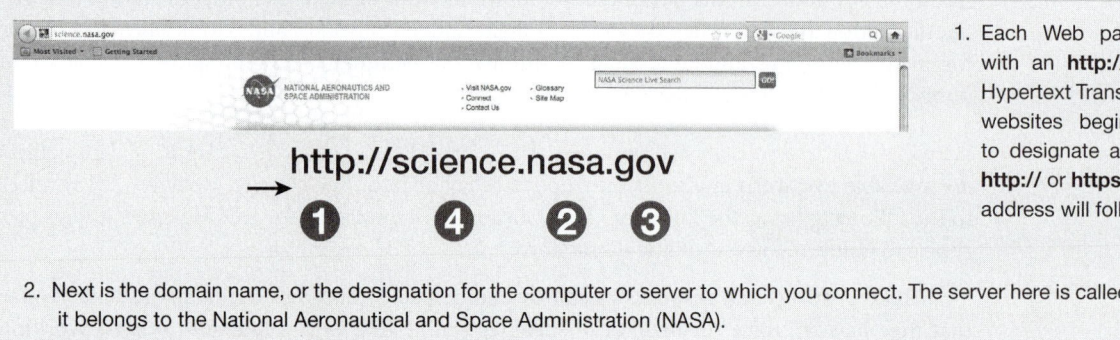

**http://science.nasa.gov**
❶ ❹ ❷ ❸

1. Each Web page address begins with an **http://**, which stands for Hypertext Transfer Protocol. (Secure websites begin with an **https://** to designate a secure server.) The **http://** or **https://** shows an Internet address will follow.

2. Next is the domain name, or the designation for the computer or server to which you connect. The server here is called **nasa**, which shows it belongs to the National Aeronautical and Space Administration (NASA).

3. The last required part of the URL is the domain designator, a suffix that tells what kind of group owns the server. This group is **.gov** a website of the U.S. government.

4. **OPTIONAL:** Large organizations often have more than one server, or may split up a large server into subdomains. When this is done, the domain name will have more parts. The above example has a separate domain for the Science topics of NASA.

the URL is entered is called the address line. The last three letters in the address line constitute what is called a **domain designator**, a suffix that typically indicates the type of content one would find at the website. The most common designators are shown in the figure. The U.S. nonprofit organization that sets up domain names is the Internet Corporation for Assigned Names and Numbers (ICANN). In 2011, it announced that it would allow expanding the number of domain names. For example, a company such as IBM could have its own domain name of .ibm.

### Two important aspects of URL use.
Two things to learn about URLs are how to locate them and how to read them.

- **Locating URLs**—If you want to visit a site, but you don't know its URL, one way to find it is to make an educated guess. For example, let's say you want to find the website for the National Council of Social Studies. Since you know it probably will have a ".org" designator, and organizations usually use their initials in URLs, a good guess would be **http://www.ncss.org**.

- **Reading URLs**—If someone gives you a URL, very often you can tell what and where it is by reading its parts. Look at an example: **http://www.noaa.gov**. If you knew that the URL someone gave you was one on the subject of weather, you might guess this is for the National Oceanic and Atmospheric Administration (NOAA), a government agency that offers students and teachers a wealth of up-to-date information on the weather.

## Four Methods for Navigating the Net

You can move around from website to website on the Internet by using any of four different options described below.

### Method #1: Navigating with links.
You can "travel" on the Internet by clicking or tapping **links** (also known as **hot links** or hot spots), text or images that have been programmed into the website to send your browser to another location on the Internet, either within the site or to another site, when you click on them. How do users know when images are links? On a computer, there is a visible change when a user passes a cursor over an image (without clicking); the words or image change color or the pointer turns into a "browser hand." On a smartphone or tablet, links may be designated with a different color text.

### Method #2: Navigating with buttons.
Forward and Back buttons are available on browser menu bars. This has been the most common way to navigate back and forward to a previously viewed page.

**FIGURE 6.4** Sample QR Code: The Pearson CourseSmart Website

**Method #3: Navigating with the "History."** Although not as common for navigation, every browser keeps a list of sites the user has visited. The user can click and hold down the Back button to see this list, and scroll down to select a site name on the list and navigate to it without having to retype a URL address into the address bar.

**Method #4: Navigating with Quick Response (QR) codes.** The newest method of getting to Internet sites and Web-based resources quickly is by scanning **QR codes**. These are small, two-dimensional barcode-like images (see Figure 6.4) that can be scanned with a mobile device such as a smartphone in order to send the user to an Internet site. QR codes are becoming ubiquitous in all areas of society, including education. Teachers use them to help students go quickly to online educational materials such as videos, worksheets, supplements to textbooks, or school-related information. To create QR codes, users can go to a free code-generator site such as Kaywa. QR code readers are needed to scan QR codes, and free code-reader apps may be downloaded from the Internet.

## Bookmarks, Favorites, and Online Organizers

You can visit so many sites on the Internet that you quickly lose track of where you found a valuable site on a certain topic. You could write all of them down, but a quicker way to go to such sites is to let a feature in your browser help you create a list or use an online organization tool. This browser-based list is called a **Bookmarks file** (in Firefox and Safari) or **Favorites file** (in Internet Explorer).

**Adding a Bookmark or Favorite.** To make a Bookmark or Favorite, first navigate to the site you would like to visit. Once it is on the screen, go to the Bookmarks or Favorites menu at the top of the browser frame and select Bookmark or Favorite (the names of these options may vary, depending on the version of the browser).

**Organizing a Bookmarks or Favorites file.** For a Bookmarks/Favorites collection to be most useful to its creator and others, it should be organized into sections, much like a library or any collection of materials. After Bookmarks/Favorites are created, they can be organized into categories of related items.

**Using an online organizer.** Websites such as Delicious, Evernote, and Diigo allow users to access their favorite sites at any location by saving the website URLs online in one place. At these sites, they can also bookmark pages for their friends and see what other people are bookmarking.

## Basic Internet Troubleshooting

Like most technologies, the Internet presents its share of "head scratchers." The majority of these errors and problems can be corrected easily; others require more complicated fixes or adjustments. Two of the most common difficulties for Internet users are discussed here.

**Problem type #1: Site connection failures.** After entering the URL, the site won't come up on the screen; you may get an error such as "Page not found." This is the most common problem people encounter; it may occur because of URL syntax errors, problems with the local or domain server, bad links, or firewall issues. The error message for each problem indicates the cause.

- **URL syntax errors**—As mentioned earlier, each dot, punctuation mark, and letter in a URL has to be correct, or the site will not load. If the "Page not found" message appears, or if the Browser instead presents a list of possible sites, check the URL syntax and make sure you have not done any of the following:
  - Confused the letter "l" with the number "1"
  - Confused the letter "O" with the number "0"
  - Confused the hyphen "-" with the underscore "_"

- Confused the forward slash "/" with the backward slash "\" in "http://" or in suffixes
- Omitted a required punctuation mark
- Misspelled a part of the URL
- Used the wrong domain designator (e.g., .edu instead of .org)

Many URL errors occur in suffixes that follow the domain designator. Try omitting all suffixes beyond the slash and going directly to the main part of the URL. The main page may show the links you want, or the site may have a built-in search engine you can use.

- **Local or domain server down**—If you have checked the URL syntax and are positive it is correct, it may be that the server that hosts the website is not working temporarily. It may have a technical problem, or it simply may be down for regular maintenance. In this case, you may get an error message like the one shown previously. Wait an hour or two, and try it again.

- **Server traffic**—A more rare cause of connection failures is that the server handling Internet traffic for the network or for users in the geographic region is not working properly. Error messages say: "Failure to resolve domain error. Try this site again later."; or "Page has no content."

- **Bad or dead links**—If a URL repeatedly fails to connect and you are sure the syntax is correct, the site may have been taken off the Internet. This is known as a bad or dead link. If this is the case, you may get the same error message given previously, or the site may provide a message that says: "Bad link."

- **Firewalls**—Sometimes a site will not connect because a network's firewall blocks it. If you think your network's firewall is blocking your access to a site in error, contact your network administrator and request that this be adjusted.

**Problem type #2: Feature on the site will not work.** If an Internet site indicates that it has a special feature, such as a video or PDF, but it will not work, there are three possible causes:

- **Plug-in or reader required**—It may be that the computer does not have the special player program or plug-in required to play the video or see the document. Usually, if a special program is needed, the site will have a link to a location where you can download and install it on your computer.

- **Compatibility errors**—The Internet works because there are agreements in place about how to make various machines and programs "talk" to each other. However, sometimes differences exist between operating systems or versions of software that make them incompatible. One of the most recent problems is that Adobe Flash will not usually work on Apple devices such as the iPhone or iPad. This issue is a result of two companies not agreeing on common standards, but it is still an issue that users should be aware of.

**TECHNOLOGY LEARNING CHECK**
Complete **TLC 6.2** to review what you have learned from reading this section about online navigation options.

## ◉ SEARCHING AND STORING OPTIONS

Before the Internet, it was difficult to locate specific resources or items of information. Now there is so much information that companies have developed special searching programs to help us locate items. These searching programs are called **search engines**. Some popular search engines and how to use them are described here.

**FIGURE 6.5** Subject Index in DMOZ Search Engine

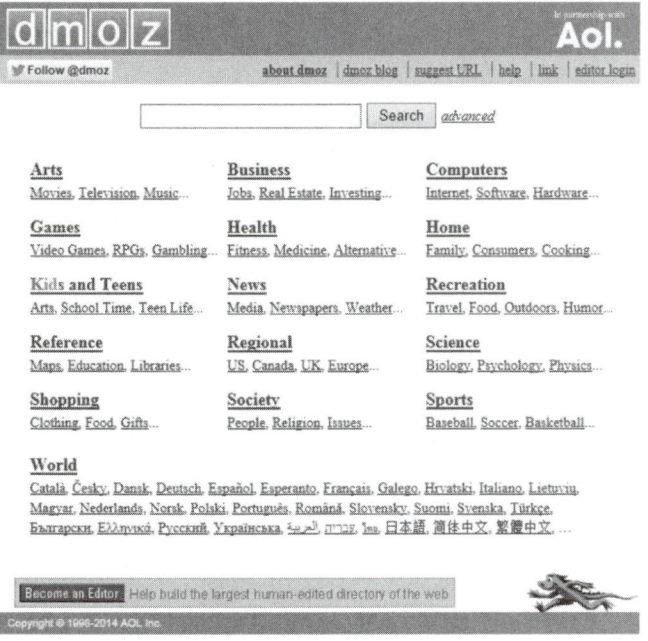

## Types of Search Engines

According to Search Engine Watch, a site with information on all available search engines, there are many kinds of search engines. Check out the Search Engine Watch site to learn about most popular searches, recent search-related news, and various types of sites (e.g., filtered ones for kids, social networking search engines). Two commonly cited types of search engines are:

- **Major search engines**—According to the Search Engine Watch site, in the United States the "Big 5" search engines are: Google, Bing, Yahoo, Ask.com, and AOL. Other search engines are more popular in other countries. For example, the Search Engine Watch site says Baidu is most popular in China, and Tandex is the most popular of the Russian language search engines. Terra is a popular Spanish-language search engine and portal.

- **Metacrawlers**—These programs use more than one search engine at the same time to locate things. The top five metacrawlers cited by Search Engine Watch are: Dogpile, Vivisimo, Kartoo, Mamma, and Surfwax.

## Search Tools and Strategies

Search engines can be used in several ways, depending on how you want to narrow the search. These include using subject index searches, keyword searches, and advanced searches:

- **For subject index searches**—The search engine site provides a list of topics you can click on. For example, see a subject index at DMOZ, a search engine site of the Open Directory project. See Figure 6.5.

- **For keyword searches**—Type in a combination of words that could be found in the URLs of the sites or documents you want. When using Google, you are doing a keyword search. Just type in the search word or phrase, and the search engine displays a list of websites whose URLs contain the word or phrase. The pages listed as results of the search are sometimes called **hits**.

- **For advanced searches**— Keyword searches in search engines allow several kinds of "advanced search" options to narrow the search for you so you won't get so many irrelevant hits (see Figure 6.6). You can put quotations marks around the phrase, or use an advanced search, which most search engines have available. For example, in Google, let's say you want to know about literary criticism on the novel *Showboat* by Edna Ferber. A keyword search with the phrase Edna Ferber's "Showboat" yields hundreds of hits on the music and the movie. However, you want to know ONLY about the book. An advanced search would be the following:

  - At the Google search engine site, click on Settings and select the Advanced Search button.
  - Fill in the terms *Showboat* and *Edna Ferber*, separated by commas, in the "all these words" box.

**FIGURE 6.6** Keyword Search in DMOZ Search Engine

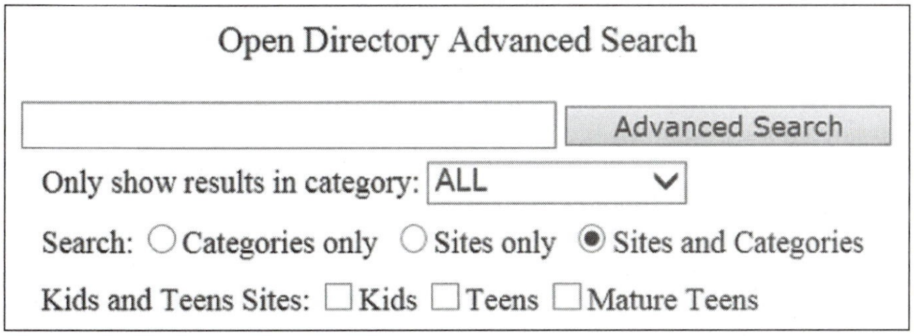

Open Directory Advanced Search

[ _____ ] [ Advanced Search ]

Only show results in category: [ ALL ▾ ]

Search: ○ Categories only  ○ Sites only  ● Sites and Categories

Kids and Teens Sites: ☐ Kids  ☐ Teens  ☐ Mature Teens

- Fill in the terms *musical*, *theater*, and *movie*, separated by commas, in the "none of these words" box. The results should give you primarily hits on the book *Showboat*.

Byrne (2012) give teachers three guidelines for teaching students good searching skills.

1. Do not give research assignments that can be done with a quick Google search. Make assignments that require a thoughtful search.
2. Teach students to search with keywords, rather than with questions.
3. Show them how they can use advanced search tools to narrow their searches.

**TECHNOLOGY LEARNING CHECK**
Complete TLC 6.3 to review what you have learned from reading this section about online searching and storing options.

##  COMMUNICATIONS OPTIONS

Online communications are increasingly replacing traditional channels such as sending letters and making telephone calls. The tools described in this section are considered primarily for one-to-one communications, rather than social collaboration and networking among groups. However, the line between the two is becoming increasingly blurry. Communications options are available in both **synchronous** (intended to be seen immediately) and **asynchronous** (left for people to read later) formats. E-mails and listservs are considered asynchronous, while text and instant messaging and videoconferencing are usually considered synchronous.

### Email and Listservs

**Electronic mail** (email) is a common way to exchange personal, written messages between individuals or small groups. Email may be sent via a program (e.g., Microsoft Outlook) or through capability built into an Internet browser. This versatile medium supports a variety of classroom activities. Teachers have used email to improve communications among students, teachers, and parents (Legg & Wilson, 2009; Sheer & Fung, 2009). E-mail use among young people is rapidly being replaced by other forms of communication such as the messaging systems discussed in the next section.

    **Listservs** are programs that store and maintain mailing lists and make possible ongoing email "conversations" among groups who belong to an organization or share common interests. When an e-mail message is addressed to a listserv mailing list, it is automatically duplicated and sent to everyone who is a member of the list. Replies to a listserv also go to list members, but only those on the list can send a message to a listserv.

### Instant Messaging and Text Messaging

**Instant messaging (IM)** and **text messaging** are two electronic services that allow users to see messages immediately. In technical terms, they differ in the kind of program that makes them possible. IM is done with an online program to which users must subscribe, while text messaging is a device feature. However, some broadband providers tend to conflate the two, calling messages sent to users within the company's system instant messages, and referring to messages sent to others as text messages.

    In online communications, IM uses a private chatroom format in which members use system features to alert each other when they wish to chat. Members then may send messages that are received immediately—like a telephone conversation but with text messages instead of voice. IMs are usually exchanged instantaneously, but they also may be left as messages to be read later, and the person notified can then initiate a chat session. Common IM programs are Apple iChat and Yahoo Messenger.

Texting has become increasingly popular among young people, but texting while driving has caused such problems that many states have already banned the practice. **Andresr/Shutterstock**

Like instant messaging, text messaging, a.k.a **texting** allows for instant communications between people but is done as a cell or smartphone feature, rather than with an online program, and allows for sending images and short videos, as well as text. Text messaging has become such a primary means of communications that it has overtaken voice communications on cell phones in frequency of use. It has become so frequent, in fact, that people even do it while driving, causing such problems that some states have already banned the practice.

The two kinds of communications share some common features and uses. For example, users make frequent use of abbreviations, such as RUOK for "Are you okay?" and CUL for "See you later." Although some research has found a link between "techspeak" in texting and poor grammar skills (Cingel & Rundar, 2012), text messaging is becoming a common practice for synchronous communications. Faure and Orthober (2011) found that text messaging helped increase course-related interaction. Byrne (2011), a social studies teacher, reported on activities with texting to get parents involved in civics lessons. The primary barrier to classroom use of text messaging is that many school districts prohibit cell phone use in schools.

## Videoconferencing in Online and Blended Environments

This form of two-way interactive communication allows those involved to see and hear each other. Each person must have a camera, an audio input device such as a microphone, and an output device such as speakers. In addition, each participant must use a program such as Skype or a Web browser feature that enables video communications. It is also helpful to have a high-speed connection so the video will move smoothly.

Videoconferencing is used more in higher education than in K–12 schools, but it is becoming more common as high-speed connections in schools become more available. It is especially used in the context of language-learning programs, where hearing the spoken language is an essential component of instruction. Lawrence and Chang (2011) remind potential users that successful use of videoconferencing for language learning requires familiarity with the technology, clear teaching and learning objectives, and pedagogical strategies appropriate for the medium. Richardson, Fox, and Lehman (2012) also say that videoconferencing can play a vital role in teacher education programs. They describe integration strategies that include student teaching, clinical experiences, courses, virtual field experiences, and guest speakers.

**TECHNOLOGY LEARNING CHECK**

Complete TLC 6.4 to review what you have learned from reading this section about online communications options.

## SOCIAL NETWORKING AND COLLABORATING OPTIONS

Online spaces that allow people in any geographic location to come together for the purpose of sharing and creating content are broadly referred to as **social networking tools**. They are also referred to as **Web 2.0 tools** because they changed online interaction from users merely

## FIGURE 6.7 Social Networking Tools

▲ Social networking tools bring together communities from around the world. **Thomas Bethge/Shutterstock**

viewing other's content (i.e., Web 1.0 tools) to allowing them to contribute their own content. These tools, which include blogs, microblogs, chatrooms, wikis and crowdsourcing sites, video- and photo-sharing communities, and social networking sites (SNS) (see Figure 6.7), have not only seen faster widespread adoption than most previous technologies, they have had unprecedented impact on society and civilization. Social networking tools bring together communities from around the world whose members may be diverse in nearly every way except for a shared interest in a topic or activity, and they have enabled endeavors ranging from funding research to supporting revolutions. Education, too, has experienced revolutionary impact from social networking. This section will focus on the most powerful educational uses and integration strategies for each of these tools.

## Blogs and Microblogs

**Blogs.** Short for Web log, a **blog** is a Web page that serves as a publicly accessible location for discussing a topic or issue. Blogs began as personal journals, but their use rapidly expanded to become public discussion forums in which anyone could give opinions on any given topic. Blogs are interactive websites for discussion, potentially among many people, but are created, designed, managed, and updated by an individual, with regular entries of event descriptions, opinions, narratives, and commentaries added over time. Blog authors can upload images, video, links, and other documents to support their content. Users do not have to understand HTML or other authoring languages to create and update blogs; rather, most blogging sites provide a system that consists of easy-to-use forms in which users enter their text, images, and content, with the page immediately published online for anyone to see. Some of these are shown in the Open Source Options feature.

**Blog integration strategies.** Blogs have supported a variety of productivity, instructional, and administrative purposes. Some of these are:

- **Support for engaged writing.** The most high-profile use of blogs has been to encourage more frequent, engaged writing among students in English and foreign language settings. These activities emerged soon after blogs became widely available and have been ongoing for over a decade. Vurdien (2013) reported on one of these strategies in advanced-level English language learning courses, in which students kept personal blogs to read and comment on each other's work. They were encouraged to use their peers' comments to edit and improve their writing. Nichols (2012) described a yearlong project intended to improve low test language scores of students in Grades 3–5. Teachers posted prompts as blog entries, and students responded in math, science, and technology labs. Though Nichols reported that students tended to ignore language mechanics (e.g., punctuation and spelling) in their blog posts, they had high levels of engagement in the writing activity. At the end of the year, state-mandated test scores improved by 50% for Grade 5 students, partly as a result of increased language use from blogging.

- **Collaboration in content area topics.** Blog activities have been reported in a wide range of content areas to improve collaboration skills in ways that enhance content learning. For example, Manfra (2012) found that a "whole-class educational blog could facilitate culturally relevant instruction and authentic intellectual work in U.S. history" (p. 118). Hossain and Wiest (2013) used blogs in a middle school geometry classroom to increase students' collaboration on mathematics problems. Still other teachers have their students follow blogs of professionals in various areas, analyzing their content and even posting comments, thus becoming a part of a professional community while still in school.

# OPEN SOURCE
## OPTIONS *for Web Development Tools*

| | |
|---|---|
| **Blogs** | WordPress: wordpress.com<br>Blogger: blogger.com/features |
| **Web page editor software** | openWYSIWYG: openwebware.com<br>NVU (pronounced "N-view,"): nvu.com/<br>TinyMCE: tinymce.moxiecode.com<br>eIRTE: elrte.org |
| **Wiki development and hosting sites** | MediaWiki: mediawiki.org<br>FreewareWiki: freewarewiki.com/<br>Wikispaces: wikispaces.com |
| **FTP software** | SmartFTP: smartftp.com/<br>Cyberduck: cyberduck.io/ |

- **Communication among teacher communities of practice.** Teachers also get involved in blogs as a professional development strategy, from getting ideas on lesson plans to gaining new skills in their content area. By "talking" with others who teach their grade level, topic, or population, teachers become part of a thriving community of practice that helps them reflect on and develop skills and solve problems with the help of knowledgeable peers.

- **Increasing interaction with parents and community members.** Some schools keep blogs for certain programs (e.g., the school library/media center), the better to communicate with stakeholders. They post notices of events and hold discussions about how to get funding, solve problems, and make best use of school resources. These uses keep open lines of communications and forge working partnerships between school and community.

- **Updates and insights on education topics.** Educators of all kinds, including school administrators, follow blogs for the same reasons that they read education newsletters, columns, and professional journals. They get insights and timely updates on topics ranging from education issues to free resources for technology integration. In her listing of "education blogs worth following," Stansbury (2012) suggest blogs such as Edudemic (on social media issues and uses in education), The Innovative Educator (with fresh ideas for teaching), and ZDNet (technology product reviews and comments).

Microblogs. These are services that permit a series of brief postings that others can follow and reply to. With over 500 million followers, **Twitter** is the most well-known of these systems. It allows posts (called **tweets**) up to 140 characters posted under a person's profile page. Tweets can include images and brief videos and may be public or restricted, depending on how a user sets a profile. Each tweet consists of a **hash tag**, or a prefix consisting of a pound sign (#) and a topic name, followed by a message. Hash tags allow others to identify topics and create their own messages on the same topic. For example, when Apple founder Steve Jobs died, people on Twitter could express condolences by sending messages with the hash tag #ripstevejobs. An increasing number of young people are using microblogs. Madden et al. (2013) found that a quarter of teens who go online use Twitter.

In his blog, Basu (2013) describes some of the ways to use Twitter in education. These include:

- **Support for classroom topics.** Set up hashtags around whatever teachers are teaching at the time. Students can follow these postings to track what was taught in class and engage in discussions around the topics.

- **Reviews and quizzes.** Set Twitter to give periodic quizzes on lesson topics.

- **Bulletin boards.** Take the place of traditional means of making quick, important announcements by setting up hashtags that students and parents can check for late-breaking news.

- **Twitter walls.** This use requires users to download an app that makes a visual display of Tweets on a given topic. This "wall display of tweets" supports analysis of comments on a given topic and promotes discussion.

- **Support for role playing.** Some educators create "live-tweet" projects in which they talk as famous historical figures would have, and anyone can follow their "events." For example, the Massachusetts Historical Society live-tweet the life of John Quincy Adams. This makes history come alive for students and encourages discussion.

- **Classroom newspaper from Twitter streams.** Tweets on topics of interest to a school or classrooms can be turned into a news stream.

- **Mentor searches.** Finally, students can connect with professionals in an area of study, follow their postings, and interact with them to get inspiration and tips on careers.

## Chatrooms

**Chatrooms** are Internet locations that allow "live" communications between two or more users. As users in a chatroom type in their comments, everyone in the "room" sees what they type. Users of chatrooms sometimes use **avatars**, moving 3-D figures that represent people in virtual environments. Avatars may or may not actually look like the person they represent. This use remains more common in higher education than in K–12 environments. Common areas where chatrooms are used are within educational **content management systems (CMS)** such as **Blackboard** or **Moodle**, which are online structures set up especially to house courses, and in education-based social networking environments such as Edmodo.

## Wikis and Crowdsourcing Sites

**Wikis for classroom use.** **Wikis** are a collection of Web pages that encourage collaboration and communication of ideas by having users contribute or modify content. Many instructors use wikis in their classes for their students to use as they develop products, or teachers develop wikis to communicate their own content. Reich, Murnane, and Willett (2012) studied wiki use in K–12 settings and found four types of applications: "(a) trial wikis and teacher resource-sharing sites (40%), (b) teacher content-delivery sites (34%), (c) individual student assignments and portfolios (25%), and (d) collaborative student presentations and workspaces (1%)" (p. 7). They also found that wiki uses are developing 21st-century skills such as complex communications and new media literacy. Their analysis of patterns of wiki uses found many learning activities that included "publishing homework assignments, portfolios, peer review writing, post artwork, download music for rehearsals, and review drills for physical education" (p. 10). Figure 6.8 shows a wiki collection sponsored by the Clark County School District, which any teacher may join to get lesson ideas and resources for using wiki resources. Also see the Open Source Options feature for free wiki sites. Finally, Technology Integration Example 6.2 illustrates a collaborative use of wikis.

**FIGURE 6.8** Clark County School District Wiki Collection

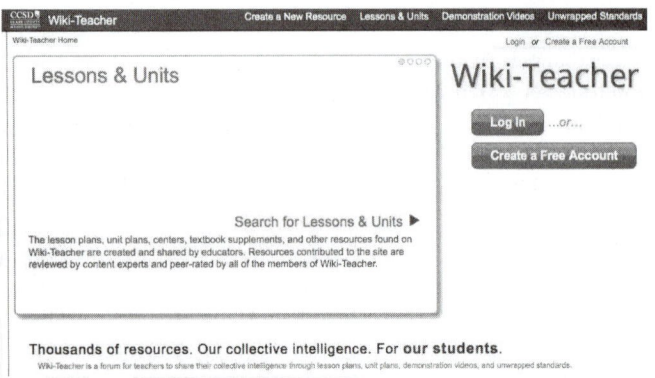

From Clark SD Wiki Collection copyright © by Clark County School District (CCSD), Las Vegas, NV 89146, USA. Reprinted by permission.

**Crowdsourced wikis.** Some wiki sites are built around a specific purpose and use the contributions of a

## Example 6.2

**TITLE:** Wiki Tales

**CONTENT AREA/TOPIC:** Language arts, literacy

**GRADE LEVELS:** 6–8

**ISTE STANDARDS•S:** Standard 1—Creativity and Innovation, Standard 2—Communication and Collaboration, Standard 4—Critical Thinking, Problem Solving, and Decision Making

**CCSS:** RL.6.2, SL.6.1, SL.7.1(c), W.8.3.

**DESCRIPTION:** Divide students into groups of two or three. Using wikis (your school may have a wiki engine it uses, or there are free wiki sites available, such as Wikispaces), have each group begin by creating a page and collaboratively writing an introduction to a story. The introduction must include enough unique characters that each group member can focus on at least one. Students should discuss what will happen to these characters and how their stories will diverge and then weave together at the end. Each group member will create individual pages about their chosen character(s) linked to the collaborative group introduction. Encourage students to brainstorm, with their group members, ways they can link back to common pages where their characters interact with each other. Groups can also include images and outside links within their stories that help convey their tale and the personalities of their characters. The project can be extended by having groups try to link their stories to other group's stories within the class and/or by having groups edit each other's work.

*SOURCE:* Based on the lesson Collaborating, Writing, Linking: Using Wikis to Tell Stories Online at the readwritethink website: http://www.readwritethink.org.

diverse group of individuals who form a community, even though they may not even know each other and never meet in person. These are commonly referred to as **crowdsourced sites**. Wikipedia is probably the most high-profile of these sites. Its mission is to produce a "free encyclopedia" that is created, constantly updated, and self-policed by its users, and it has generated many similar sites such as Scholarpedia and Wikimedia. Though many educators do not permit students to use Wikipedia or other crowdsourced sites for their research projects, some educators encourage it as a way for students to get leads or glean basic understanding that will enable more informed searches of academic sources.

Crowdfunding sites. Another high-profile type of crowdsourced site is to obtain funding for new projects and is referred to as **crowdfunding sites**. Kickstarter is one of the most well-known of these, but others include Indiegogo, Crowdfunder, Rockethub, Crowdrise, Somolend, appbackr, Angelist, Invested.in, and Quirky (Barnett, 2013). Education projects are among those funded at these sites, and students also use them to obtain underwriting for their college expenses. In all these sites, applicants ask for funding in return for future profits or other payments.

## Video- and Photo-Sharing Communities

Video- and photo-sharing communities (e.g., YouTube, TeacherTube, Tumblr, Vimeo, Instgram, Flickr.com, Vine) are websites that provide users with easy-to-use tools to upload video and photo files to a server for online sharing with either selected or all viewers. Teachers and students can comment on the videos and photos, tag (i.e., attach keywords to) the content for increased ease of searching, and rate the quality of content. A 2013 study from the Pew Internet and American Life Project (Duggan, 2013) found that "54% of Internet users have posted original photos or videos to websites and 47% share photos or videos they found elsewhere online" (p. 1). Byrne (2012) describes tools that allow users to make best use of these communities. For example, SynchTube and Watch2gether allow users to chat about videos as they watch them. Vialogues allows discussions of videos that may not be online, and TedEd offers a space for teachers to post videos and share lessons around them, including those in a flipped classroom format. As discussed in Chapter 1, a **flipped classroom model** is one in which students engage with concepts via video lecture or vodcast before coming to class, then spend class time on other learning activities.

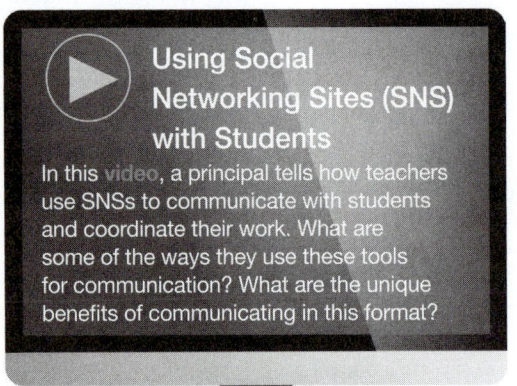

**Using Social Networking Sites (SNS) with Students**

In this video, a principal tells how teachers use SNSs to communicate with students and coordinate their work. What are some of the ways they use these tools for communication? What are the unique benefits of communicating in this format?

# Social Networking Sites

Social networking sites are websites that give members a space in which they can create a personal profile, contribute content, and connect and interact with others. These sites also make it possible for members to contribute to blogs and share media such as images and videos. **Social networking sites (SNSs)** include Facebook, LinkedIn, Google Plus, and the education-oriented Edmodo, created especially for use by teachers, schools, and districts. The most common SNS is still Facebook, which began in 2004 and has over a billion and a half users worldwide.

### Research on SNSs.
Much of what we know about use of social media by young people is from a continuing series of survey studies by the Pew Internet and American Life Project. One of these reports (Madden et al., 2013) focused on teens' use of social media and how they handle privacy issues. They found that teens "have waning enthusiasm for Facebook, disliking the increasing adult presence, people sharing excessively, and stressful 'drama,' but they keep using it because participation is an important part of overall teenage socializing" (p. 1). The report also revealed that while teens are concerned about privacy issues such as others getting access to their personal information, they often engage in practices that compromise privacy. For example, over 90% posted a photo of themselves online and attached their real name to their profile, and 82% post their birth date.

In a study of preteen use of social media, Weeden, Cooke, and McVey (2013) found that many young people begin to use social media at age 9, and almost all were on Facebook by age 12. The children also acknowledged that they misrepresented their age in order to join Facebook, since the published age requirement was 13. All these findings have important implications for those teaching young people appropriate uses of social media as part of digital citizenship skills.

Manca and Ranierit (2013) reported results of a critical review of research on use of Facebook in education. They concluded that, while hopes remained high among researchers that social networking would overcome "the boundaries of formal education" (p. 496) and make possible highly engaging new learning environments, few cases were found where Facebook's affordances were exploited. There was evidence that, despite widespread popularity for social uses, many cultural and pedagogical obstacles remain to "prevent a full adoption of Facebook as a learning environment" (p. 487).

### Integration strategies for SNSs.
The highly social nature of SNSs make them ideal for keeping in touch with parents and carrying out collaborative and constructivist strategies. Two of the more common of these strategies include:

- **Collaborating and commenting on student work.** SNSs are frequently used as collaborative spaces for teachers and students to work together. For example, Hammett (2013) describes a project in which ninth graders studied Shakespeare's *Romeo and Juliet* and created collaborative digital projects that included e-zines, presentations, digital videos and photo-stories. They used an SNS called Ning to share their products and to communicate about them throughout the unit.

- **Communicating with parents and community members.** As with blogs and other social media, schools can invite parents and other community members to "friend" their SNSs and keep apprised of school events and achievements. SNSs also provide stakeholders with an additional way to keep communication lines open with educators about issues of mutual concern. Chairatchatakul, Jantaburom, and Kanarkard (2012) found that social networking had the impact of creating a "home-school partnership" and increased parental involvement through "idea generation, parent service, public relations, reputation management and parent-school communications" (p. 378).

**TECHNOLOGY LEARNING CHECK**

Complete TLC 6.5 to review what you have learned from reading this section about social networking options.

# APPLYING APPS IN EDUCATION

**App** is an abbreviation for application software and refers to any program specifically designed to run on mobile devices such as smartphones or tablets. Apps are often designed exclusively for a given platform (e.g., Apple or Anroid). **Universal apps** are programs that work on all platforms. "There's an app for that" has quickly become a catchphrase as people have become dependent on their handheld devices to go online.

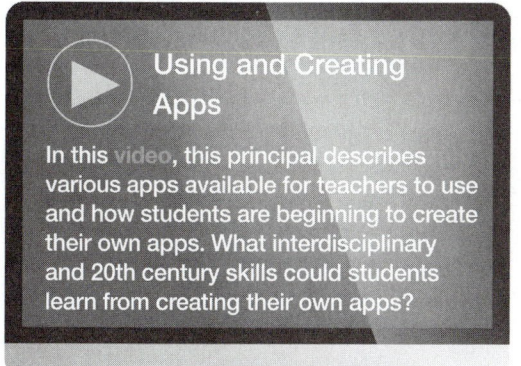

In this video, this principal describes various apps available for teachers to use and how students are beginning to create their own apps. What interdisciplinary and 20th century skills could students learn from creating their own apps?

## Locating Apps

Most people use keyword or app name searches to locate apps in an app-finding program on their smartphone or tablet. They can also locate apps by going to various online app outlets such as Apple iTunes or the Mac App Store. Schools and districts that want their teachers to have access to apps identified as especially useful may use volume discount options such as Apple's Volume Purchase Program (for Apple apps) and Google Play (for Android). These programs provide a way to purchase large numbers of app copies and distribute them efficiently to multiple devices.

## Using Apps in Education

Since apps are just programs that run primarily on handheld devices, they can fulfill the same roles as any of the instructional software types discussed in Chapter 3 or tool software types described in Chapters 4 and 5. Hundreds of worthwhile apps are available and still more being developed each year. Teachers are encouraged to do their own searches, based on their needs. The Top Ten Sites for Locating Apps in Education can serve as a starting point.

**TECHNOLOGY LEARNING CHECK**

Complete **TLC 6.6** to review what you have learned from reading this section about applying apps in education.

# WEB PAGE AND WEBSITE AUTHORING SKILLS AND RESOURCES

In addition to the many ready-to-use online sites, teachers and students can also develop their own websites. An array of authoring tools is available for the design Web pages and websites, but would-be Web authors must also have the skills and resources to make use of them. This section describes Web development skills, tools, and media that teachers and students need for Web authoring, as well as a recommended development sequence and criteria for judging the quality of finished products.

## Web Development Skills

To create Web-based media, teachers and students must learn how to use software such as HTML editors (e.g., Adobe Dreamweaver), photo editing (Adobe PhotoShop), and video editing (TubeChop, Apple iMovie). They can get started with these skills by using video and print tutorials at sites such as the Internet4Classrooms or Khan Academy sites, or search YouTube for links to many video tutorials. In addition to these skills, the following are some categories of capabilities Web authors must develop over time in order to create high-quality products.

Digital literacy. Nowadays anyone can adapt and alter existing media, thus creating visual displays that may be misleading or incorrect. Therefore, a critically important prerequisite for effective Web authoring is media literacy, now often called **digital literacy**, which includes the ability to be critical and ethical producers and consumers of media.

**Using music and art.** Visual arts and music play major roles in the effectiveness of Web-based products. As teachers and students gain more knowledge in the theory and aesthetics of music and art, they will use these resources more productively in the authoring process, ultimately enhancing the quality of their media development.

**Print and graphic design principles.** Many principles of desktop publishing also apply to Web-based media designs. When students first see the array of graphics and sound options available, they typically use so many colors, graphics, and sounds that it overshadows the message. Design principles to guide judicious use of these options are described later in the Evaluating Quality of Web-based Hypermedia Products section.

**Video design principles.** For video products, skills are needed in effective ways to illustrate concepts by using motion and camera effects. Authors also learn how to edit video sequences and apply print and animated effects in their video projects.

**Creativity and novel thinking.** One of the strands in the framework of 21st Century Skills is "Creativity and Innovation," and Web-based hypermedia projects are a great place to encourage these skills. Website design assignments for students must go beyond replicating existing materials and models to take advantage of the true power and affordances (i.e., opportunities for action and interactivity) of the medium.

**Considering the audience.** Whenever possible, novice Web authors should display their projects both locally and to broader audiences made possible by Web publishing. Research on writing has shown that students invest more effort in the writing process when they know others will read their writing. Hayes and Desler (2009) and others have observed that this sense of audience carries over to hypermedia authoring. Younger students in particular should be reminded constantly to think of their projects from the user's point of view. Projects should be tested on other students, family members, or friends, focusing on the usability of the project in addition to the embedded content.

## Hypermedia Resources for Web Page and Website Development

Over time, hypermedia programs have become increasingly more powerful and user-friendly, and features and capabilities are being added with every new version. Authors now can draw on a variety of resources to put sound and motion in their Web-based hypermedia products. However, with the ready online availability of samples, it is important to keep in mind principles of copyright, fair use, and plagiarism discussed in Chapter 1. Table 6.1 summarizes sources of development resources materials under audio, video, photos, images, and text categories.

## Web Authoring Tools

Only a short time ago, Web pages could not be developed without program authoring languages and scripting tools. Now, thanks to Web page development software, it is possible to develop whole sites without writing a line of code or script. However, even if one uses a Web development tool, such as Adobe Dreamweaver, that generates code automatically, it is good to know enough about each of the major program authoring languages to make minor adjustments to developed pages or to troubleshoot problems as they occur. Program authoring languages include Hypertext Markup Language (HTML and HTML 5), Java, **Virtual Reality Modeling Language (VRML),** ActionScript in Adobe Flash, and others. Programming languages for coding apps are Objective-C and Javascript. Also described here are Web page and website software tools that allow teachers and students to create Web products without programming.

**HTML and HTML 5.** **HTML** is the Internet standard for formatting and displaying Web pages. **HTML 5** is the latest revision of the HTML standard and has become mainstream since

**TABLE 6.1  Summary of Web-Based Hypermedia Design and Development Resources**

| Types of Resources | Items of Each Type | Roles in Websites |
| --- | --- | --- |
| **Audio** | • CD audio—Digitized music, speech, or sound effects captured from audio CD or video DVD<br>• Recorded sounds—Authors' or others' own voice recordings<br>• Prerecorded sounds—From collections of sound effects offered in multimedia software or from CD-ROM collections | • Background music for presentations<br>• Illustrations of musical types<br>• Portions of famous speeches<br>• Readings of poetry<br>• Directions to students<br>• Sound effects to add interest or humor or to signal transitions<br>• Teacher and student generated podcast audio files |
| **Video** | • Digitized videos—Imported from DVD or other digital sources using video digitizer, or from camcorder and edited with movie software (e.g., Apple iMovie, Windows Movie Maker)<br>• Recorded from live **webcam**, a video camera connected to a computer in order to gather video for viewing at other locations<br>• Collections of prerecorded video clips—Available on CD-ROM or DVD | • Demonstrations of procedures (e.g., labs, sport movements)<br>• Recorded lectures<br>• Illustrative examples of topics being discussed<br>• Video decision-making simulations<br>• Video problem-solving situations<br>• Screen capture video for software demonstration |
| **Photos** | • Scanned photos—Digitized from print photographs using scanners<br>• Captured from video sources—Freeze-frames from DVD or VCR<br>• Digital camera images—Downloaded from camera to computer<br>• Commercial collections—From CD-ROM and stock photography collections | • Historical events, documents, or famous people<br>• Geographical locations or objects in outer space<br>• Illustrative tools (e.g., machines or art implements) |
| **Graphic images** | • Created or imported—Using draw/paint software, from clip art collections, or images scanned from drawings or hard copy images<br>• Animations—From CD-ROM collections or created using animation tools | • Illustrative cartoons (e.g., political)<br>• Attention-getting cues<br>• Introductory animations for websites and software<br>• Charts and visualizations |
| **Text** | • Entered by author—Typed into product or added as a graphic item (e.g., Apple iWork, Microsoft Office)<br>• Imported—From word processing files and graphic design software | • Signs or titles<br>• Summaries of written procedures or explanations<br>• Definitions |

Adobe **Flash** is not supported on products such as the Apple iPad. For developing Apple web pages, HTML5 can be used instead of Flash.

Java and Javascript.   Originally called OAK, **Java** is a high-level programming language developed by Sun Microsystems. A language similar to C++, it was originally developed for more general use but has become popular because of its ability to allow users to create interactive graphic and animation activities on Web pages. Many developed Java applications, called **Java applets,** are available for online downloading and can be run on any computer that has a Java-compatible Web browser. Java used to be extremely popular as it made Web page features such as animations and special effects, graphics and buttons, interactive displays, and Web data collection forms possible. Now, many of these features are accomplished through other means that are described later. **Javascript** is an object-oriented scripting language that is client-side, meaning it is implemented as part of a Web browser. Javascript and other programming languages, such as Java, and C++, are used to create dynamic websites.

## FIGURE 6.9 App Example

▲ The code projected on the screen was written by this young app designer to create a game app. (Photo courtesy of W. Wiencke)

**VRML.** Although not in common use by most developers, **VRML** develops and displays 3-D objects on Web pages. These objects give the illusion of being "real," much more than videos or animations do, and they can be used to create multiuser virtual worlds, which are sometimes referred to as MUDs (multiuser dimensions or domains). These virtual areas allow several people to interact at once using graphic representations of themselves.

**ActionScript in Adobe Flash.** **ActionScript** within Adobe Flash software provides an advanced authoring environment for creating content for the web, a mobile device, or virtually any digital platform. In applications ranging from instructional media and games to interactive websites, Flash can take a typical HTML-designed website and make it into an interactive experience.

**App programming languages.** Depending on the device on which the app will run, it may be programmed in Java, Javascript, C++, CSS, Objective–C, or combinations of these. A sample of programming code to develop an app that creates a game called Python 2.7 is shown in Figure 6.9, along with its young programmer.

**Web development software.** Web development tools called **Web editors** are also available to generate HTML, Javascript, and other code so that users can develop Web page and website products without having to know programming languages. These tools range from the WYSIWYG editors (shown in the Open Source Options feature) to complex, full-featured software packages (e.g., Adobe Dreamweaver) that allow development of multiple-page websites with sophisticated multimedia components. View the Adapting for Special Needs feature for this chapter to learn about Web accessibility for learners with special needs.

**Web development hosting sites.** For teachers who do not want to learn programming languages, **Web hosting sites** are available that let users choose from various formats and templates and insert their own content. Free sites designed especially for teacher use are shown in the Open Source Options feature.

**Web management tools.** Some Web development software automatically uploads your Web pages to the server provided by the software company, while others require manual transfer or upload to a server to be viewed publicly. To do the latter manual transfer, one needs **File Transfer Protocol** or **FTP** capability. If the website will be housed on a school or district server, technical personnel there may provide an FTP capability or they may want to upload the pages themselves. If the site will be on another server, contact that server's Web administrator to determine the required procedures. Google Sites stores websites on Google's server, and thus, FTP as described is not needed. If an FTP program is needed, popular ones are SmartFTP and Cyberduck.

Finally, if one is going to use Web development software, such as Adobe Dreamweaver, one will need to have a "home," that is, a computer or server on which it resides. Most teachers choose to have their website on their school or district server. In this case, they may want to learn about the procedures that have been established in their school or district for obtaining required permissions and for uploading pages to the server.

▲ Thanks to Web page development software, it is possible for teachers and students to create whole websites without writing a line of code or script.
Ian Wedgewood/Pearson Education

## Downloading Images, Programs, and Plug-Ins

Several of the resources that are useful in both developing and using Web pages can be **downloaded**—that is, transferred from a website to your computer—for free from company sites. Some of these downloadable resources are images, programs (e.g., updated versions of browsers), extensions, and **plug-ins** or "player" programs that allow you to play audio and video clips in Web pages. Most of today's browsers come with the plug-ins already installed when you download the browser.

Downloading images. Downloading an image from the Internet is easy, but remember that many images you find on Web pages are copyrighted. Their legal use is determined by copyright law and by the owner of the website. If you are not sure if you can use an image legally, contact the website owner to request permission. If you have determined you have rights to use an image, use your browser to "capture" or download it and store it on your computer. Once you download an image, you can use it in your own Web pages.

After you save an image on your computer, normally accomplished by right-clicking on an image and selecting "Save Image As," you can insert it in documents or other Web pages. However, you may need to change the image format from the original file format. Several **image formats,** or ways of storing images, have been developed over the years to serve various purposes: either a certain computer or operating system required it, or certain formats were found to deal better with differences among image types (e.g., photos rather than drawn images). You can tell the format of an image by the suffix in its filename. The most common formats are:

- **GIF**—Stands for "Graphics Interchange Format." Used for drawn images, illustrations, clip art, or animations.
- **JPEG**—Stands for "Joint Photographic Experts Group," and the filename extension is .jpg. Used for photographs.

Images downloaded from Web pages will most commonly be in JPEG format. If you want to use images in your own Web pages, they must be in either JPEG or GIF formats. If you want to change an image to one of these formats, you need to bring it into an image manipulation program (e.g., Adobe Photoshop) and save it in either GIF or JPEG format.

Downloading programs and plug-ins. Web browsers made the Internet visual, but subsequent developments gave it sound and motion. Special programs called **plug-ins** have been created to allow people to see and hear the multimedia features that make the Internet increasingly lifelike. Although plug-ins tend to change and update frequently, the online environment has a built-in way of allowing people to take full advantage of its multimedia features and to keep up with advancements required for their use. Users can download many of the plug-ins directly from the company sites. Five of the most commonly downloaded programs and plug-ins are described here.

▲ Movie players are one of several free plug-in programs teachers and students can download in order to view media online. Dusit/Shutterstock

1. **Updated browser versions**—Most new computers come with a browser program already installed. However, browsers update frequently, constantly adding new features and capabilities. It is necessary to use an up-to-date version in order to see newer Internet features. You can download newer versions of browsers from the Apple, Firefox, and Microsoft websites.

2. **PDF reader**—This program lets you see **Portable Document Format** files. These are pages stored as images so they may be printed out with a page appearance identical to the original document. A PDF format is particularly important when the original text contains both print and images or when one wants to see the appearance of the original document. For example, one might photograph and store the pages of the Declaration of Independence so that history students could see them. Numerous companies have developed software for creating PDF files from any type of file. For example, if one owns a Macintosh computer that uses a recent operating system version, one can create a PDF file from the Print menu. A program to create PDF files from Adobe is also available for purchase, but the Adobe Reader viewer plug-in required to see already-stored PDF files. Reader is available free from Adobe; Apple has its own program called Preview.

3. **Streaming video and audio player plug-ins**—An online capability is being able to see action or hear sounds live on the Internet. **Streamed video and audio** sends or "streams" images and sounds a little at a time so one need not download the files completely before using the contents. This is especially useful for large videos that take a long time to download. Video quality is dependent on the quality and speed of the line connecting the computer to the Internet.

4. **Movie player plug-ins**—Videos that have been digitized and stored as movie files may be viewed through a plug-in. Programs such as Apple's QuickTime or Windows MovieMaker are used to create these movies, which usually are shot with a digital camera and stored in a .mov format. To see them, one needs player software. Although originally designed as a movie player, more recent versions of QuickTime can also be used with streaming video and audio.

5. **Animation plug-ins**—Special programs that create animated content (e.g., sliding menus, games, movies) for the Web also come with their own players, such as Adobe Flash.

 **TECHNOLOGY LEARNING CHECK**
Complete **TLC 6.7** to review what you have learned from reading this section about website authoring skills and resources.

 # WEB PAGE AND WEBSITE AUTHORING STEPS AND CRITERIA

Recommendations for efficient authoring of Web products are given in this section. Also, since teachers and students should use the same criteria for their own pages that they wish to see in other sites, website criteria for effective communication and navigation are described here.

## Recommended Sequence for Authoring Web Pages and Sites

The following seven steps are recommended as a sequence for Web page development. As noted earlier, many website development sites now have templates that eliminate some steps or make them much easier. For a summary of these steps, see Figure 6.10.

**Step 1: Review existing products.** An effective way of developing new hypermedia products such as Web pages and websites is to look at what others have done. Review other teachers' sites and look for ideas that would work for your own site. For students doing their own websites to present results of research or a product they have developed (e.g., a newsletter), this is an important

# FIGURE 6.10 Recommended Website Authoring Sequence

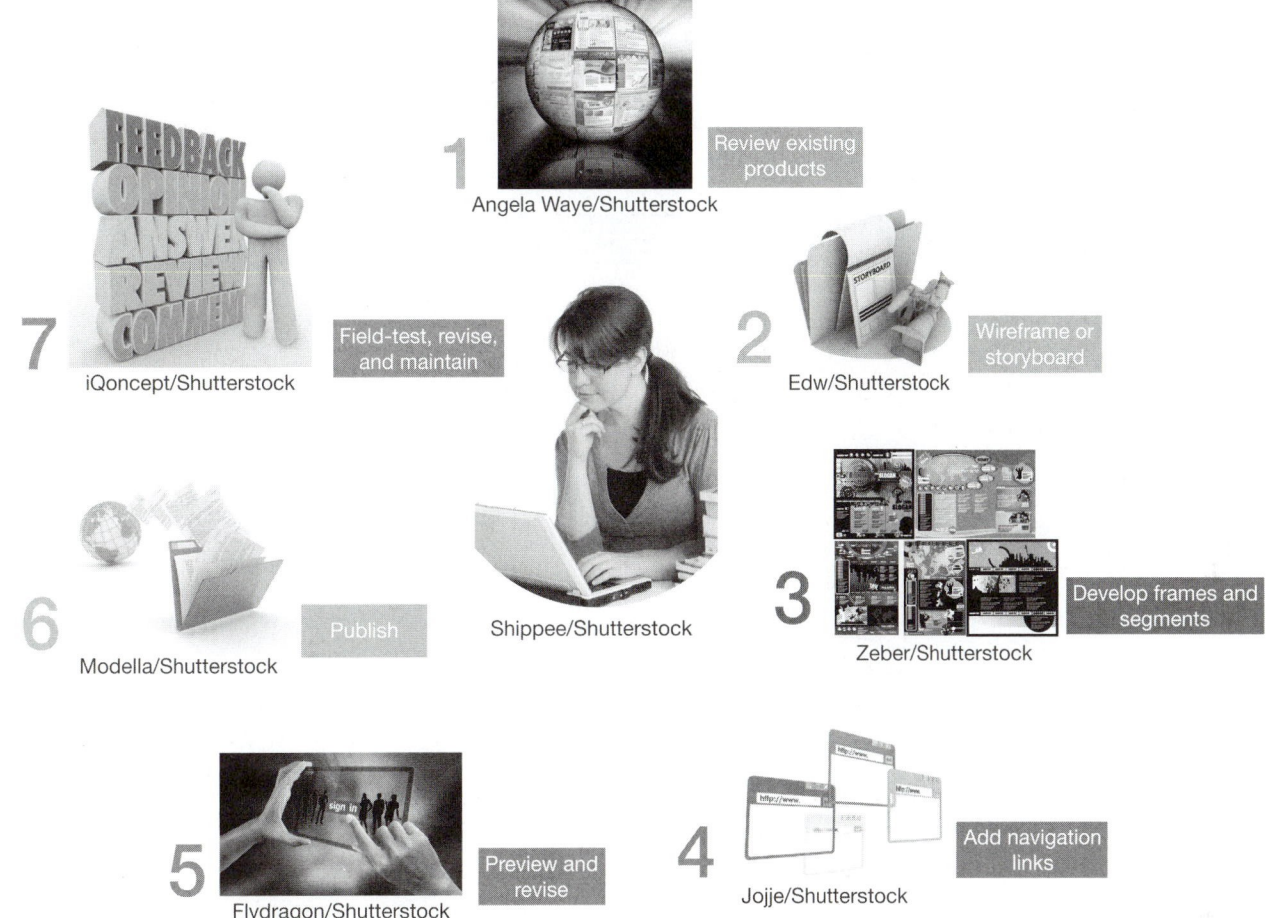

1 Review existing products — Angela Waye/Shutterstock

7 Field-test, revise, and maintain — iQoncept/Shutterstock

2 Wireframe or storyboard — Edw/Shutterstock

— Shippee/Shutterstock

3 Develop frames and segments — Zeber/Shutterstock

6 Publish — Modella/Shutterstock

5 Preview and revise — Flydragon/Shutterstock

4 Add navigation links — Jojje/Shutterstock

part of the learning process of communicating in digital products. Even experienced designers spend a great deal of time viewing websites to learn and understand how to display information effectively.

**Step 2: Wireframing or storyboarding.** Planning and designing, the first steps in developing a website, are the most difficult and important—and most frequently neglected—of all the steps. Most people want to get right to the fun of development, but professional media creators have learned that this kind of planning saves time in the long run. Even famous movie directors, such as Alfred Hitchcock and Steven Spielberg, were known to have storyboarded entire movies before doing a single camera shot. They found that being able to visualize how the product should look and how segments would work together prevented needless reworking and, thus, prevented wasting time and materials. This planning step calls for **wireframing** or **storyboarding**, or mocking up a blueprint for what should appear on each frame and how the pages will work together. To do this step, map out the pages in terms of functions, giving a general idea of content on each page and showing how users navigate from one page to another. A useful resource to accomplish this step is cognitive mapping software such as Inspiration, or even sticky notes placed on large pieces of poster board to represent the Web pages. Storyboards should include sketches of tables, navigation elements, photos, and details on other graphic elements on each page.

**Step 3: Developing frames and segments.** Now comes the fun of actually developing your individual pages using the website development tool of choice. This phase is based on storyboards and includes creating the tables, inserting the images and other media, inserting the interactive elements and links, and any other features you may want on your site.

**Step 4: Add navigation links.** After developing individual pages, add navigations links that will connect pages together into a functional site. The use of storyboards is also helpful at this stage.

# FIGURE 6.11  Website Evaluation Criteria Checklist

**Site Name:** _____  **Topic:** _____

**Site Purpose (check one):**

_____ Business _____ Entertainment _____ Instructional _____ News _____ Personal _____ Political _____ Other

**URL:** _____

| Criteria | Yes | No |
|---|---|---|
| **Site Authors and Sponsors** | | |
| Site author(s) and/or sponsorship are clearly identified. | | |
| Author(s) is/are clearly qualified to present reliable information on the topic. | | |
| Contact is provided so site users can ask questions and get further information. | | |
| **Site author/sponsor comments:** | | |
| **Content** | | |
| All information is the most current and up-to-date available. | | |
| All information is factually accurate. | | |
| The site is complete (i.e., no "under construction" signs). | | |
| The site has a creation and/or revision date. | | |
| Sufficient information on the topic is provided; it is not missing key elements. | | |
| Appropriate helpful links to other, related sites are provided. | | |
| Content is free from typos and misspellings and from punctuation and grammatical errors. | | |
| Content is free from ethnic, slang, or rude names or words; information is presented in a professional manner. | | |
| Content sources (including sources of graphics) are properly referenced. | | |
| In informational sites, content is free from bias. | | |
| In persuasive sites, author bias is clearly stated. | | |
| **Content comments:** | | |
| **Organization and Navigation** | | |
| Pages load quickly. | | |
| Every page shows clearly how to navigate to parts of the site. | | |
| Content is organized and presented in a logical way. | | |
| Menus, site maps, and other navigation tools are used effectively to aid navigation. | | |
| The product has a consistent look and feel throughout. | | |
| Buttons and links all work as indicated. | | |
| Users can get to any content within three clicks. | | |
| **Organization and navigation comments:** | | |
| **Visual Design** | | |
| Use of fonts and type sizes is controlled so as not to interfere with readability. | | |
| Screen design is optimized for use on smaller-screen devices. | | |
| Color contrasts with background for easy reading. | | |
| To add interest and motivation for users, information is presented in an innovative and creative way. | | |
| **Visual design comments:** | | |
| **Media** | | |
| Graphics, videos, and sound are included to help communicate information on the topic; their purpose is not just decorative. | | |
| Audio is audible and understandable. | | |
| Video content is clear and visible. | | |
| No obscene or rude graphics or visuals are included. | | |
| Use of graphics (e.g., images, animations) on a page does not distract from reading. | | |
| Pictures and sounds associated with buttons and links are appropriate to the purpose and content of the frames. | | |
| **Media comments:** | | |

**Step 5: Preview and revise.** Developers should always be testing how the website actually looks in a Web browser as they develop it. Many development programs have a built-in preview system, but it is essential to preview the site with an actual browser to observe how it will work when it is published on the Web.

**Step 6: Publish.** For others to see the newly created website, place the pages on a server. This is called "publishing" the site. If you use a website hosting service, this step may be done for you. If not, use an FTP procedure to upload your website to a server so that it is live for the public. Much like the testing and development phases, you will be uploading the website through numerous iterations to make sure it views correctly and works well on different types of Web browsers. Everyone remembers website URL addresses that are simple, such as Ed.gov, the Department of Education's website, and many URL addresses reflect the content of the website. Website developers can purchase a **domain name** that is simple and easily remembered while also reflecting the content of the website. Website domain names can be purchased at numerous places, such as Network Solutions, GoDaddy, or Register.com.

**Step 7: Field-test, revise, and maintain the site.** The best websites are those that are updated regularly based on user comments and the continuing insights of the developers. Obtaining user feedback may be done through interactive forms built into the page or through inviting emailed comments.

## Criteria for Evaluating Website Information and Design

As students learn how to make use of online sources for school purposes and create their own websites, an essential skill they must acquire is being able to evaluate information critically and to look for indications that content is accurate and reliable. The Internet's vast information storehouse, unfortunately, contains some information that is incomplete, misleading, inaccurate, and/or out of date. It even has some sites that are works of complete fiction presented as fact. However, students frequently accept as authoritative any information they find on the Internet. They must learn that blind acceptance of any information (on the Internet or elsewhere) is a risky practice and that they have a responsibility to make any information they add worthwhile and useful.

There are numerous rubrics and checklists available for evaluating website content and design. These can be used to teach students these important information evaluation strategies.

Users evaluate a Web page by the usefulness and reliability of its content and the quality of its design, so Web developers must be aware of these criteria. The Web Quality Criteria Checklist shown in Figure 6.11 is a compilation of many checklists and formatted for use in website reviews. Website criteria are listed in five categories:

1. **Authorship.** A site must provide enough background about its authors for users to determine if the site is reliable and useful.

2. **Content.** Site information must not only be complete, accurate, and up-to-date, it must also free from the sources of problems often inherent in written communications: mechanical errors, inappropriate language, lack of appropriate source referencing, and bias.

3. **Organization and navigation.** The site must reflect characteristics and features that make it easy to use.

4. **Visual design.** Information must be presented in an attractive, creative, yet readable way.

5. **Media.** Items such as video, audio, images, and animations must meet the same criteria as all the content: appropriate language and usable presentation.

As students begin to create their own websites, it is helpful to give them criteria in the form of rubrics that describe the quality they are aiming for in each of several aspects. Many such Web page rubrics are available; one of the most popular sites for rubrics is in Kathy Schrock's Guide to Everything.

**TECHNOLOGY LEARNING CHECK**
Complete **TLC 6.8** to review what you have learned from reading this section about Web-page and website authoring steps and criteria for developing a Web presence.

Monkey Business/Fotolia

The following questions may be used either for in-class, small-group discussions or may be used to initiate discussions in blogs or online discussion boards:

**1.** Despite decades of research evidence to the contrary, a popular belief persists among teachers and students that students learn better when they are allowed to use their preferred learning styles. (Search for and locate the 2008 article "Learning Styles Concepts and Evidence" by Pashler, McDaniel, Rohrer, and Bjork, available free online.) Online environments are felt to be one way of allowing students to have their choice of learning formats. Why do you think this belief in the usefulness of learning styles–based instruction persists in the face of compiled evidence?

**2.** Cingel and Sundar (2012) reported results of a study that showed texting was linked with poor grammar skills in middle school students. What could teachers do to curb the possible negative consequences of texting on grammar and writing, while acknowledging students' love of this medium and their likely continued use of "techspeak" in social situations?

**Chapter 6**

# Summary

### 1. Introducing the Online Environment
- The Internet began as a U.S. Department of Defense (DOD) project called ARPAnet. Today's online environment came about in 1993 with the development of Internet browser software.
- Online safety and security issues for teachers and students include accessing sites with inappropriate materials, safety and privacy issues for students, computer viruses and hacking, fraud and phishing, and online identity and reputation issues.
- Online ethical and legal issues for teachers and students include online plagiarism and online piracy.
- Three kinds of rules and guidelines for online behavior have been developed and include digital citizenship concepts (Internet safety, privacy and security, relationships and communications, cyberbullying, digital footprint and reputation, self-image and identity, information literacy, and creative credit and copyright), netiquette concepts that govern courtesy in online communications, and rules governing behavior in online learning environments.

### 2. Navigation Options
- Internet addresses are called uniform resource locators, or URLs. There are optional parts of a URL that determine its address. Uses of URLs include locating them and reading them.
- Four ways to navigate the net include links, buttons, browser history, and QR codes.
- Bookmarks, Favorites, and Online Organizers are ways to keep track of most-used online sites. Users can add a Bookmark or Favorite, create files of them on a browser, or use an online organizer.
- Basic Internet troubleshooting includes solving two kinds of problems: site connection failures and feature on the site that will not work.

### 3. Searching and Storing Options
- Search engines are online programs that allow keyword searches to locate websites. Types include regular search engines and metacrawlers.
- Search strategies include subject index searches and keyword searches.
- Strategies for storing and interacting with files online.

### 4. Communications Options
- Tools described in this section are considered primarily for one-to-one communications, rather than social collaboration and networking among groups
- Electronic mail (email) is a common way to exchange personal, written messages between individuals or small groups, while listservs are programs that store and maintain mailing lists and make possible ongoing email "conversations" among groups who belong to an organization or share common interests.
- Instant messaging (IM) and text messaging are two electronic services that allow users to see messages immediately. In technical terms, they differ in the kind of program that makes them possible.
- Videoconferencing is two-way interactive communication allows those involved to see and hear each other. Each person must have a camera, an audio input device such as a microphone, and an output device such as speakers.

5. **Social Networking and Collaborating Options**
   - Blogs are Web pages that serve as a publicly accessible location for discussing a topic or issue. Integration strategies include support for engaged writing, collaboration in content area topics, communication among teacher communities of practice, increasing interaction with parents and community members, and updates and insights on education topics.
   - Microblogs (e.g., Twitter) are services that permit a series of brief postings that others can follow and reply to. Integration strategies include support for classroom topics, reviews and quizzes, bulletin boards, Twitter walls, support for role playing, classroom newspaper from Twitter streams, and mentor searches.
   - Chatrooms are Internet locations that allow "live" communications between two or more users.
   - Wikis are a collection of Web pages that encourage collaboration and communication of ideas by having users contribute or modify content. Other crowdsourced sites include Wikipedia and crowd-funding sites.
   - Video- and photo-sharing communities (Tumblr, Instagram, Vine, etc.) are websites that provide users with easy-to-use tools to upload video and photo files to a server for online sharing with either selected or all viewers.
   - Social networking sites (SNSs) are websites that give members a space in which they can create a personal profile, contribute content, and connect and interact with others. Research shows that while young people are concerned about privacy, they often do not take steps that would assure privacy. Integration strategies include collaborating and commenting on student work and communicating with parents and community members.

6. **Applying Apps in Education**
   - App is an abbreviation for application software and refers to any program specifically designed to run on mobile devices such as smartphones or tablets. They are located through keyword or name searches on mobile devices.
   - Since apps are just programs that run primarily on handheld devices, they can fulfill the same roles as any of the instructional software types discussed in Chapter 3 or tool software types described in Chapters 4 and 5.

7. **Web Page and Website Authoring Skills and Resources**
   - Web development skills that developers must acquire over time include digital literacy, using music and art, print and graphic design principles, video design principles, creativity and novel thinking, and considering the audience.
   - Hypermedia resources for Web page and website development include items in audio, video, photos, images, and text categories.
   - Web authoring tools include HTML and HTML 5, Java, Javascript, VRML, PHP, Microsoft ASP.NET, ActionScript in Adobe Flash, and other languages such as C++, CSS, and Objective-C, or a combination of these options. Developers may also use Web development software and Web development hosting sites.
   - Developers may also download images, programs, and plug-ins to help their work.

8. **Web Page and Website Authoring Steps and Criteria**
   - Sequence for authoring Web pages and sites is: Step 1: Review existing products; Step 2: Wireframe or storyboard; Step 3: Develop frames and segments; Step 4: Add navigation links; Step 5: Test and revise; Step 6: Publish (upload); and Step 7: Gather evaluation comments, revise, and maintain the site.
   - Criteria for evaluating website information and design include items under five areas: authorship, content, organization and navigation, visual design, media. Teachers also may want to give students rubrics to guide their website design.

# TECHNOLOGY INTEGRATION **WORKSHOP**

## 1. APPLY WHAT YOU LEARNED

To apply the concepts and skills you've read about throughout this chapter, go to the Chapter 6 Technology Application Activity.

## 2. TECHNOLOGY INTEGRATION LESSON PLANNING: PART 1—EVALUATING AND CREATING LESSON PLANS

Complete the following exercise using the sample lesson plans found on any lesson planning site that you find on the Internet.

**a.** Locate lesson ideas—Identify three lesson plans that focus on any of the tools or strategies you learned about in this chapter. For example:

- Online organizers and organizing sites
- Social networking tools such as blogs, microblogs, chatrooms, wikis, video- and photo-sharing communities, and SNSs
- Apps

**b.** Evaluate the lessons—Use the Technology Lesson Plan Evaluation Checklist to evaluate each of the lessons you found.

**c.** Create your own lesson—After you have reviewed and evaluated some sample lessons, create one of your own using a lesson plan format of your choice (or one your instructor gives you). Be sure the lesson focuses on one of the technologies or strategies discussed in this chapter.

## 3. TECHNOLOGY INTEGRATION LESSON PLANNING: PART 2—IMPLEMENTING THE TIP MODEL

Review how to implement the TIP model in your classroom by doing the following activities with the lesson you created in the Technology Integration Lesson Planning exercise above.

**a.** Describe the Phase 1 Planning activities you would do to use this lesson in your classroom:

- What is the relative advantage of using the technology(ies) in this lesson?
- Do you have resources and skills you need to carry it out?

**b.** Describe the Phase 2 Implementation activities you would do to use this lesson in your classroom:

- What are the objectives of the lesson plan?
- How will you assess your students' accomplishment of the objectives?
- What integration strategies are used in this lesson plan?
- How would you prepare the learning environment?

**c.** Describe the Phase 3 Evaluation/Revision activities you would do to use this lesson in your classroom: What strategies and/or instruments would you use to evaluate the success of this lesson in your classroom, in order to determine revision needs?

**d.** Add lesson descriptors—Create descriptors for your new lesson (e.g., grade level, content and topic areas, technologies used, ISTE standards, 21st Century Learning standards).

**e.** Save your new lesson—Save your lesson plan with all its descriptors and TIP model notes.

## 4. FOR YOUR TEACHING PORTFOLIO

Add the following to your Teaching Portfolio:

- Lesson plan evaluations, lesson plans, and products you created above
- Products of your group's Hot Topic Debates
- Products of your group's Collaborate, Discuss, Reflect online or in-class activities

# 7

# Introduction to Distance Education

## ONLINE AND BLENDED ENVIRONMENTS

## Learning Outcomes

After reading this chapter and completing the learning activities, you should be able to:

1. Identify examples of current distance education models, and describe distance education issues and research-based practices. (ISTE Standards•T 2, 5)

2. Describe types of blended learning models, including the flipped classroom model. (ISTE Standards•T 2, 5)

3. Select online audio- and video-based integration strategies for use in blended-learning environments. (ISTE Standards•T 2, 5)

4. Identify and describe types of Web-based activities used in blended-learning environments. (ISTE Standards•T 2, 5)

5. Select Web-based activities for use in blended-learning environments. (ISTE Standards•T 2, 5)

# TECHNOLOGY INTEGRATION IN ACTION: FLIPPING FOR PRE-ALGEBRA MASTERY

**GRADE LEVEL:** Middle school • **CONTENT AREA/TOPIC:** Pre-algebra • **LENGTH OF TIME:** Two weeks (plus pre-project introduction)

## PHASE 1 ANALYSIS OF LEARNING AND TEACHING NEEDS

Apops/Fotolia

### Step 1: Determine relative advantage.

Mr. Patel knew that he and the other pre-algebra teachers at his middle school needed a better approach to presenting the course content. Passing rates for the end-of-course tests were lower than they had ever been, and an analysis of students' test performance showed that their skills began to drop sharply as linear equations were introduced. Mr. Patel first heard about flipped classroom methods at a state technology conference, and he had learned a lot more since becoming a member of the Flipped Learning Network (FLN) online community. He could see how this approach might be more motivating to students and allow him to spend more time with students who were struggling. Though he read teacher postings about innovative applications like the "Explore-Flip-Apply" flipped model, he didn't think an exploration approach would work well with pre-algebra, which had a limited timeframe in which to prepare students for exams. Several math teachers on the FLN encouraged him to try a "flipping for mastery" model, in which students watch videos at home and answer questions about them, then come into class to apply and "debug" or correct errors and fine-tune skills they had learned. Everyone advised him to start small and build, so he decided to begin with a two-week unit on linear equations.

### Step 2: Assess required skills and resources.

From what Mr. Patel had read on the FLN, one of the main obstacles in a flipped model was students' access to a broadband Internet connection that would allow them to watch videos online. He informally polled students to identify which ones might have problems with this kind of access and was surprised that only three out of all his students lacked the needed access. When he told his principal about his flipped classroom idea and the three students, she arranged for him to check out school district tablets that would permit the needed connection. Mr. Patel was also a little apprehensive about creating videos, which he had never done before, but his school technology resource person offered his help with video recording procedures. Mr. Patel knew there would be a learning curve for him to get up to speed on these technologies, but based on the success stories and encouragement of FLN math teachers, he decided it was worth the investment.

## PHASE 2 PLANNING FOR INTEGRATION

### Step 3: Decide on objectives and assessments.

Mr. Patel had some specific outcomes in mind to measure the success of this new venture and to decide if it was worth expanding to other units. He wanted to make sure students were actually watching the videos at home before class, if their performance on his weekly quizzes was improving, and if they liked the new strategy better than the old way. The outcomes, objectives, and assessments he decided on were as follows:

**Video-viewing exercises.**
**Outcome:** Watching required videos and completing questions on them prior to class.
**Objective:** At least 90% of all students will indicate they have watched videos by successfully completing (i.e., getting at least 2 of 3 items correct) on at least 90% of required question sets.
**Assessment:** Graded items on question sets; matrix set up to allow across-student calculation.

**Weekly quizzes.**
**Outcome:** Achieving passing grades on weekly quizzes.
**Objective:** At least 90% of all students will achieve a passing score (85% or more) on each weekly quiz.
**Assessment:** Graded quizzes.

Attitudes toward flipped classroom method.
Outcome: Positive attitude toward flipped classroom tasks and outcomes.
Objective: The students will demonstrate a good attitude toward the flipped approach by an overall, across-students rating of at least 18 of 20 possible points (90%) on an attitude survey.
Assessment: Likert scale attitude survey.

## Step 4: Design integration strategies.

After reviewing recommendations from FLN teachers and reviewing how he currently taught his linear equations, Mr. Patel decided to break up curriculum into six different steps, each with a video and exercises matched to it. For each of the two weeks, students would watch one video and complete preclass exercises on it each night before Monday, Tuesday, and Wednesday classes. Monday–Wednesday classes would revolve around application of the principles introduced in the videos. Thursday would be dedicated to prequiz review and individual help for students who had specific problems. Friday would be designated quiz day, and review of answers. The project would have the following timeframe:

Week 1: Introduce flipped classroom methods. The week before the project was to begin, Mr. Patel told his students about the method he was going to use and emphasized it was experimental. If students didn't like it or outcomes were no better than with the previous method, he told them he would not continue it. He gave them a preproject video to watch at home and set aside some class time for them to watch it in the school computer lab, as well. He contacted parents and encouraged them to watch it to be informed on what their children would be doing.

Week 2, Days 1–3: Watch videos. On Monday through Friday evenings, students were to watch assigned videos and complete exercises to answer questions about them. Mr. Patel inserted the videos into Google forms, and students were to watch the video, complete the form as an exercise, and submit it to him online before class the next day. When students came to class, Mr. Patel had small-group projects for students to apply what they had learned about linear equations. He had made up learning activity packets for them to work through as he went from group to group assisting and facilitating work.

Week 2, Day 4: Tutoring sessions. On Thursday, Mr. Patel set aside most of the period for individual and small-group help for those who needed extra assistance.

Week 2, Day 5: In-class quizzes. At the end of the week, a quiz covered all the material from that week. Then Mr. Patel went over all the answers and posted a discussion online about problem areas. He allowed students to retake different versions of the quiz after school if they had failed to demonstrate mastery on the initial quiz.

Week 3, Days 1–4: Repeat activities. This was a repeat of the first week's Days 1–3 activities.

Week 3, Day 5: In-class quizzes, project debriefing, and final attitude questions. After students took their final quizzes and Mr. Patel reviewed them, he gave students a link to his SurveyMonkey attitude questionnaire and asked them to complete this after class.

## Step 5: Prepare instructional environment.

There was much to do before beginning the actual flipping period. Preparation tasks included:

Quizzes, exercises, and survey development: Mr. Patel did these instruments first so he would be sure to gear his instruction toward students' being able to demonstrate mastery on them. For the survey, he wanted to clarify in his own mind what aspects of the program he wanted students to feel positively about.

Video development: Mr. Patel considered carefully the skills he wanted students to master on the quizzes and what demonstrations and discussions would be best captured on video. He knew videos had to be no longer than 10 minutes, so he had to write scripts for what he would cover before beginning actual videotaping. Then, with the help of the school's technology resource teacher, he created the six videos.

Activity packages for small-group work: He created these for the in-class work.

# PHASE 3 POST-INSTRUCTION ANALYSIS AND REVISIONS

## Step 6: Analyze results.

After all students completed all quizzes and the attitude questionnaires, Mr. Patel reviewed the results for each. He was happy to find that all students but two had watched the videos and successfully completed the exercises in Week 1, and all students were successful in Week 2. Weekly quiz performances were another story. He came close to meeting his own objectives on Weekly Quiz 1; 85% of students passed it, and 100% passed it if the "second-chance" quizzes were considered. However, on Weekly Quiz 2, only about 50% of students passed; 80% when second-chance quizzes were considered. Still he was encouraged by the attitude questionnaires. The most common finding is that students wanted more of this flipping experience. He even had a few parents email him to say they had learned a lot by watching the videos.

### Step 7: Make revisions.

Mr. Patel knew that some of his videos needed improvement. He went over them with his colleagues, and they pointed out places where examples could be improved or expanded. Two students offered to review places on videos where they had difficulty understanding. Also, he knew that directions in some of his activity packets needed to be much clearer so that students could follow them and complete required work more quickly. After making these revisions, he was ready to move on to "flipping" another unit for mastery.

Based on concepts from "Ms. Garcia's Flipped Pre-algebra Class" on FLN and George Phillip's blog "Reversing Instruction in Social Studies"

## CHAPTER 7 BIG IDEAS OVERVIEW

Before you begin reading the rest of this chapter, listen to the Chapter 7 Big Ideas Overview. It will give you a two-minute audio overview of main concepts to look for and help prepare you to work through information and exercises to achieve this chapter's outcomes.

## OVERVIEW OF DISTANCE EDUCATION

The United States Distance Learning Association (USDLA) defined **distance education** as "structured learning that takes place without the physical presence of the instructor" (Holden & Westfall, 2010, p. 3). Thanks to technologies such the Internet that enable distance education, learning has escaped the physical boundaries of the classroom and the school, and students and teachers have become part of a worldwide virtual classroom. This chapter, the second of three about online education, begins with some foundation concepts about distance learning: current distance learning models and issues and research that tell us how the models work and how well issues are being addressed. Also see Chapters 6 and 8 for more on distance learning.

### Distance Learning Models

Although the Internet was the catalyst for an explosion of interest in distance learning, it is by no means the only distance delivery system. Indeed, distance learning can be done without any electronic assistance at all; at one time it was done by correspondence study via postal mail (a.k.a., **snail mail**). Changes in our technological capabilities have brought about gradual changes to our methods of delivering instruction at a distance. The first major change to mailed correspondence courses came when presentations were placed on videotape and mailed along with print materials. Later improvements in the quality and availability of broadcast technologies made it possible to send audio and video information, either live or taped.

Distance models can be classified in any of several ways. Two of those are described here. First, Simonson, Smaldino, Albright, and Zvacek (2012, pp. 92–93) suggested a classification scheme based on Edgar Dale's **Cone of Experience**, a system designed to categorize media according to their degree of realism. Dale said media range from concrete (e.g., hands-on or multisensory experience) to abstract (verbal symbols such as text descriptions), and that younger or less experienced students require more concrete experiences before they can understand abstract ones. Thus, distance delivery systems can be classified according to the degree to which they approximate reality (see Figure 7.1). However, this classification system also may be overlaid with the methods and technologies used to deliver them. For

# FIGURE 7.1 Classification System for Distance Learning by Types of Interaction

| | Types of Interaction | Delivery Methods |
|---|---|---|
| **Most abstract, least realistic**<br><br>Pearson Education | • One-way, print-based<br>• Recorded or broadcast audio<br>• One-way, synchronous audio from instructor to students<br>• Two-way, synchronous audio between students and instructor<br>• Recorded or broadcast video (no synchronous interaction with instructor) | • Correspondence courses via postal mail and/or fax<br>• Prerecorded audio (e.g., online podcasts)<br>• Broadcast radio<br>• Audio-conferencing telephone systems<br>• Broadcast television: microwave or satellite link |
| **Most realistic, least abstract**<br><br>John Foxx Collection/Imagestate | • Text and multimedia interactions<br>• Live video from instructor to students (with synchronous audio interaction)<br>• Two-way synchronous video between instructor and students | • Web-based course management systems<br>• Teleconferencing<br>• Videoconferencing |

example, a more abstract system such as recorded or broadcast audio could be delivered via an online podcast, while interactive text or multimedia could be accessed through a content management system.

Since today's distance education is nearly always web-based, a second way of classifying types of distance learning is either as one of the **online models**, in which all course activities are done via the Internet, or one of the **blended models**, that is, a combination of in-person and online activities. This chapter focuses primarily on blended models. However, there are also many other courses (and some programs) in which students never meet in person with their instructor, and all interaction is done in online course spaces, e-mail, and other forms of electronic communication. These online models are described in Chapter 8.

## Current Issues in Distance Learning

As communications became more global and accessible, hopes were high that it would mean better access to quality education for all students, regardless of location and economic status. These hopes have not been universally realized, and unexpected problems have included the widening of the digital divide, student developmental issues, and varying kinds of impact on education reform.

**Digital divide issues.** Greater dependence on the Internet has served to widen still further the digital divide. Recent studies show that while more students are using the Internet and other distance resources, children from underserved populations (i.e., low-income and some minority students) still have far less access at home and school than other students (Ritzhaupt, Liu, Dawson, & Barron, 2013; Wei, Teo, Chan, & Tan, 2011; Xu & Jaggers, 2013). Leu et al. (2014) found that gaps in online reading skills were linked to family income. If these gaps persist, it augurs future problems in providing equitable access to the resources distance learning offers. Xu and Jaggers (2013) found that some groups of students who have exhibited performance deficits in traditional classrooms have even greater deficits in online courses. Their study results showed that "males, black students, and students with lower levels of academic preparation experienced significantly stronger negative coefficients for online learning compared with their counterparts, in terms of both course persistence and course grade . . . This is troubling from an equity perspective: If this pattern holds true across other states and educational sectors, it would imply that the continued expansion of online learning could strengthen, rather than ameliorate, educational inequity" (p. 23).

Developmental issues for students. Spending too much time on computers has been cited as harmful to children's development of relationships and social skills. The American Academy of Pediatricians (AAP), recognizing these potentially harmful effects of overexposure to mass media (including the Internet), calls for limiting children's use of media (AAP, 2013) to no more than two hours per day. The AAP does, however, make exceptions for children enrolled in virtual courses when medical conditions prevent them from attending regular schools.

Variable impact on education reform. Some educators continue to predict that distance learning will spearhead educational reform by altering traditional, teacher-centered methods and bringing about richer, more constructivist methods. However, reports to date have disputed this belief (Savin-Baden et al., 2010; Tao, Ramsey, & Watson, 2011), finding that distance resources are usually used to support traditional approaches. Virtual K–12 schools are a growing phenomenon, but their impact on educational reform is often hampered by issues such as high dropout rates, disputes over funding, and policies for maintaining quality. Virtual schooling has also become a political issue, since some educators and parents fear that virtual schools could become the primary vehicle that would allow federal and state funding for private and home-schooled students (Glass, 2009, 2010). Further, critics question whether current funding is being directed at virtual school programs that are consistently being monitored for quality (Chingos, 2013; Miron & Urshel, 2012). There are continued calls for regulations and policies to evaluate and ensure continued quality of virtual schooling even as they struggle to keep up with the rapid pace of technological advancement and their own rapid expansion (Glass & Welner, 2011).

## Distance Learning Research

The continued growth of support for distance learning has already proven wrong those who said that it was just a passing fad (Allen & Seaman, 2013). Years of research have confirmed the effectiveness of some forms of distance learning, and studies of other strategies are on the increase. This section captures the current status of distance learning and some current research that indicates how distance learning is helping shape the future of teaching and learning. In the past, the most popular kind of research compared a distance learning method with a traditional method. However, other kinds of questions have proven more useful in shaping the impact of distance learning. Findings on these topics are described here and summarized in Table 7.1.

Effectiveness of distance learning compared with face-to-face (FTF) learning. A meta-analysis and review of online learning conducted by the U.S. Department of Education (2010) comparing **face-to-face (FTF)**, blended, and online courses confirmed that students in online courses performed modestly better than those learning face-to-face. Though the greatest difference was between blended and face-to-face courses, with blended courses performing best of all formats, report authors do not conclude the blended model itself was responsible. Instead they pointed out that "blended conditions often included additional learning time and instructional elements not received by students in control conditions (thus) . . . the positive effects associated with blended learning should not be attributed to the media, per se" (p. ix).

Research reviews and meta-analyses tend to show that synchronous courses, or those in which information and messages are left for the receiver to read later, tended to show greater gains than synchronous ones, in which communications are sent and received immediately (Bernard et al., 2009; Queen, Lewis, & Coopersmith, 2011). Finally, there is also no doubt that distance students tend to drop out at higher rates than students in face-to-face courses (Breslow et al, 2013; Lee & Choi, 2011; Miron & Urschel, 2012; Park & Choi, 2009). Research results about the contributions and uses of distance education have raised debates, one of which is shown in the Hot Topic Debate feature for this chapter.

## TABLE 7.1 Summary of Research Findings on Distance Learning

| Research Topic | Findings |
|---|---|
| **Effectiveness and impact:** Are distance courses as effective as FTF courses? | <ul><li>No significant overall differences in achievement between distance and FTF courses.</li><li>Asynchronous courses tend to reflect higher achievement than synchronous ones.</li><li>Dropout rate usually higher in distance courses.</li></ul> |
| **Course quality:** What are the characteristics of effective distance courses? | The most successful courses have:<ul><li>High interaction.</li><li>Instructor and other support throughout the course.</li><li>Fewer technical problems and good technical support when problems occur.</li></ul> |
| **Effective distance learners:** What are the characteristics of students who are effective distance learners? | <ul><li>Students likely drop out due to a combination of variables.</li><li>Characteristics of successful distance learners include self-motivation and ability to structure one's own learning, previous experience with technology, good attitude toward course subject matter, and internal locus of control.</li><li>Other contributors to success include spending more time online and increased computer self-efficacy.</li></ul> |
| **Effective distance instructors:** What are the characteristics of effective distance instructors? | Effective distance instructors have good:<ul><li>Course planning and organization that capitalize on distance learning strengths and minimize constraints.</li><li>Verbal and nonverbal presentation skills specific to distance learning situations.</li><li>Collaborative work with others to produce effective courses.</li><li>Ability to use questioning strategies.</li><li>Ability to involve and coordinate student activities among several sites.</li></ul> |
| **Cost-effectiveness:** What can make online instruction more efficient and productive? | <ul><li>Broadening access to reduce overall costs.</li><li>Use of research-based principles and best practices from the learning sciences.</li><li>Individualizing and differentiating instruction based on diagnostic assessments and preferred pace of learning.</li><li>Building on student interests, which can result in increased student motivation, time on task and better learning outcomes.</li><li>Making better use of teacher and student time by automating routine tasks.</li><li>Increasing the rate of student learning.</li><li>Reducing school-based facilities costs.</li><li>Reducing salary costs by transferring some educational activities to computers.</li><li>Economies of scale through reuse and large-scale distribution.</li></ul> |

**Course characteristics that affect success.** The majority of studies in this area focus on attitudes of students who complete distance learning courses. Researchers agree that the handful of factors described here are the major contributors to course satisfaction (Beauchamp & Kennewell, 2010; Robinson & Sebba, 2010).

- **High interaction.** Though some studies find that the convenience of distance learning means more to students than teacher interaction does, the single greatest determinant of satisfaction across studies is the amount of interaction between teacher and students (Beauchamp & Kennewell, 2010; Clayton, Blumberg, & Auld, 2010; Ravenna, Foster, & Bishop, 2012).

- **Preparation for the course.** The practice of required course orientations is becoming more common to increase retention in online courses (Blumenstyk, 2011). Also, Colucci

# Hot Topic Debate
## Can Students Learn as Well Online as Face-to-Face?

*Take a position for or against (based either on your own position or one assigned to you) on the following controversial statement. Discuss it in class or on an online discussion board, blog, or wiki, as assigned by your instructor. When the discussion is complete, write a summary of the main pros and cons that you and your classmates have stated, and put the summary document in your Teacher Portfolio.*

One of the biggest debates and discussions in distance education is whether learning online is as effective as face-to-face (FTF). There have been decades of media comparison studies in which student outcomes were compared in classrooms using and not using various technologies. Similar studies have been done comparing distance learning and traditional learning (Bernard et al., 2009), yielding the same results: no significant differences. However, we also know that the dropout rate is higher in distance learning. Many recent studies report the quality and experiences of online student learning are impacted by issues ranging from the amount of interaction with the instructor to the type of media used. If researchers are correct that the learning medium or distance format makes no difference in learning outcomes, why is the dropout rate so high? Can you cite evidence to support or refute the position that all students are able to learn well online?

and Koppel (2010) suggest that meeting students face-to-face for the first class meeting helps establish a rapport that can lead to better interaction throughout the course.

- **Support during the course.** Many studies show that students value and profit from teacher and other support, both technical and logistical, during their course experiences, from registration through course activities and evaluation. DiPietro (2010) observed that supportive interactions help establish a sense of community among learners, resulting in both increased engagement and motivation. McBrien, Cheng, and Jones (2009) find that feelings of isolation or disconnectedness from the teacher and classmates, as well as frustration with technology problems, can also negatively affect course satisfaction.

- **Minimal technical problems.** Consistent evidence exists that technical problems can doom the best-planned course (Ko & Rosen, 2010; McBrien et al., 2009). Successful courses are those that minimize technical problems so that the student can focus on the learning rather than on computer and technical issues. Not having to mediate technology problems also frees the teacher to spend more time on instruction and accommodating student needs.

Characteristics of successful distance learners. Some researchers have tried to identify student capabilities or other factors that could predict whether a student might drop out, be less satisfied, or not perform as well in an online activity. A study conducted by Patterson and McFadden (2009) concluded that there is no single theory that can fully explain student attrition in distance learning; students likely drop out due to a combination of variables. Hypothesized characteristics of successful distance learners include self-motivation and ability to structure one's own learning (Robinson & Sebba, 2010), previous experience with technology (Johnson, Gueutal, & Falbe, 2009), good attitude toward course subject matter (Hung, Chou, Chen, & Own, 2010), and internal locus of control, or a personality characteristic of believing that one can control events that affect them (Vandewaetere & Clarebout, 2011). A study conducted by Damianov et al. (2009) suggested that spending more time online can predict whether students will be successful in online learning environments. Some studies that support a correlation between increased computer self-efficacy and improved outcomes in online courses. For example, Alshare, Freeze, Lane, and Wen (2011) found that students level of comfort with online learning and their "Web self-efficacy" (p. 437), or belief that they were good at using the Internet, could predict their satisfaction in online courses.

Characteristics of successful distance instructors. Fish and Wickersham (2009) found that distance learning instructors need different skills than instructors for traditional courses do. Their review of the research reveals several areas of unique competence, all of which require experience with distance learning environments:

- Course planning and organization that capitalize on distance learning strengths and minimize constraints
- Verbal and nonverbal presentation skills specific to distance learning situations
- Collaborative work with others to produce effective courses
- Ability to use questioning strategies
- Ability to involve and coordinate student activities among several sites

**Cost-effectiveness of online and blended programs.** A U. S. Department of Education study by Bakia, Shear, Toyama, and Lasseter (2012) focused on the potential impact of online learning on educational productivity. While they found few studies that could address this satisfactorily, the ones they did find suggested that nine applications of online and blended learning could be pathways to improved productivity. These include (p. vii):

1. Broadening access in ways that dramatically reduce the cost of providing access to quality educational resources and experiences, particularly for students in remote locations or other situations where challenges such as low student enrollments make the traditional school model impractical;

2. Engaging students in active learning with instructional materials and access to a wealth of resources that can facilitate the adoption of research-based principles and best practices from the learning sciences, an application that might improve student outcomes without substantially increasing costs;

3. Individualizing and differentiating instruction based on student performance on diagnostic assessments and preferred pace of learning, thereby improving the efficiency with which students move through a learning progression;

4. Personalizing learning by building on student interests, which can result in increased student motivation, time on task and ultimately better learning outcomes;

5. Making better use of teacher and student time by automating routine tasks and enabling teacher time to focus on high-value activities;

6. Increasing the rate of student learning by increasing motivation and helping students grasp concepts and demonstrate competency more efficiently;

7. Reducing school-based facilities costs by leveraging home and community spaces in addition to traditional school buildings;

8. Reducing salary costs by transferring some educational activities to computers, by increasing teacher-student ratios or by otherwise redesigning processes that allow for more effective use of teacher time; and

9. Realizing opportunities for economies of scale through reuse of materials and their large-scale distribution.

**TECHNOLOGY LEARNING CHECK**
Complete **TLC 7.1** to review what you have learned from reading this section about distance education models, issues, and research.

# BLENDED LEARNING ENVIRONMENTS

Some organizations such as universities or large school districts adopt policies that designate a course as online if a certain percentage of its activities (e.g., over 50% or over 80%) are online. But in practice, any instructional units that include combinations of online and in-person activities are actually **blended environments**, so there are really an infinite number of blended course

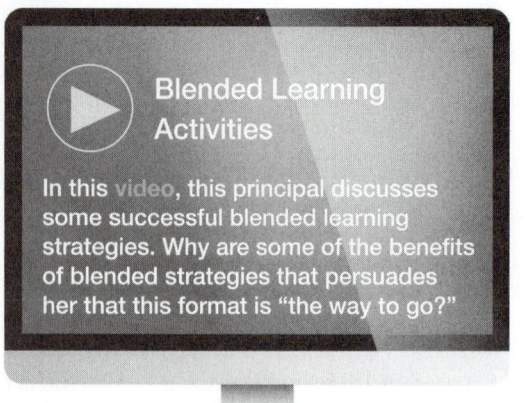

**Blended Learning Activities**

In this video, this principal discusses some successful blended learning strategies. Why are some of the benefits of blended strategies that persuades her that this format is "the way to go?"

models in operation. This section describes characteristics of three types of blended learning models and reviews implementation requirements of one model that has attracted substantial attention in recent years: the flipped classroom model. Subsequent sections will review the online elements that enable blended models: video components and Web-based lessons.

## Blended Learning Models

Staker and Horn (2012) described four different blended-learning models for K–12 classes and programs: rotation, flex, self-blended, and enriched virtual. The rotation and flex models call for blending traditional and online modes within a given course, while self-blended and enriched virtual models are combinations of online and in-person courses within programs. Roblyer (2015) said that the following are the three most common blended models used in education and training courses.

**Traditional classroom with online activities.** Many of today's courses are offered in an in-person classroom but include one or more online activities. For traditional, in-person classrooms, these online activities are usually enrichment activities such as webquests or virtual field trips or to locate sources on topics students have been assigned to research.

**Online classroom with in-person events.** Because of the concern about reports of student fraud and cheating, some organizations require even courses labeled as "all online" to have students come in person to a testing center to complete exams. Other organizations are responding to research reports that blended experiences result in better learning outcomes than either traditional or fully online ones (Means, et al., 2010). For this reason even programs such the Florida Virtual School, which had been completely online since it began in 1997, have begun using blended methods with some courses. For example, a course may offer a field trip to enhance its online activities, or an online teacher might visit the school building to meet with students individually and teach minilessons (Davis, 2012). Davis noted that these events inject a personal connection that helps keep students engaged.

**Flipped classroom model.** Currently, in one of the most popular blended models, students engage with concepts via a technology such as a **vodcast,** or a video uploaded to an online site, before coming to class, then spend class time on learning activities in which they apply and expand on their pre-class activities. Sometimes this flipped classroom model is referred to as an *inverted classroom* (Milman, 2012). Colorado chemistry teachers Jonathan Bergmann and Aaron Sams, who originated the term flipped classroom, also called it "reverse instruction" (Bergmann & Sams, 2014; Makice, 2012). Milman said that this approach frees up class time for the instructor to help with hands-on activities that engage students.

In one of their later articles about the flipped classroom model, Bergmann and Sams (2014) said they placed too much emphasis on the pre-class activity being a video. Indeed, they said the preclass activity can center around any of a number of **learning objects**, or self-contained, single-purpose instructional components that can be reused a number of times in different learning contexts. These learning objects can include using online simulations or even reading books or articles.

## Implementing a Flipped Classroom Model

**Flipped classroom models** are instructional approaches in which students do activities such as listen to or watch recorded lectures and/or demonstrations, then come to class and use hands-on methods to apply what they learned from their preclass activities. The "flipped" element is that activities students traditionally did in class (listening to lectures or watching a teacher demonstrate procedures) is now done outside of class; activities in which students apply what they learned, traditionally done as homework, is

**Flipping for Engagement**

In this video, this principal discusses how flipping strategies are one way to insure students are engaged in learning. What are some of the characteristics of the "active school" he describes?

In flipped-learning models, students do outside-class activities such as watching videos before coming to class to do hands-on work.
Apops/Fotolia

now done in class. Flipped classrooms have taken education by storm, generating great enthusiasm and many followers in both K12 and higher education. This section gives background on the model, as well as practical tips for implementing it effectively.

The Flipped Learning Network (FLN) is a free online resource that teachers may join to get access to a wealth of classroom materials and lesson ideas, as well as a growing community of "flippers." The FLN emphasizes that flipping the classroom does not necessarily result in "flipped learning." They said that to achieve the real benefits of flipping, the strategy must be a truly remodeled learning environment where the focus is on students' active involvement.

### Background and research on flipped models.
In a report from the FLN Research Committee, Hamdan, McKnight, McKnight, and Arfstrom (2013) said that for this model to achieve the goal of revitalizing and improving instructional methods, flipped-learning activities must have four features they refer to as the "four pillars of F-L-I-P" (pp. 5–6) which are listed and briefly summarized here:

1. **Flexible learning environments.** Students choose when and where they learn, and teachers (and though not named, probably also administrators) acknowledge that the learning environment will be "chaotic and noisy," rather than orderly and quiet. Teachers allow for flexibility in learning and assessment timelines, and that they measure progress in ways that are most meaningful for them and their students.

2. **Learning culture shift.** There must be a transition from objectivist principles to more constructivist ones: from students as passive receivers of knowledge and the teacher as "sage on the stage," to students' active involvement in choosing their own learning and assessment paths, scaffolding from what they already know to higher skills levels.

3. **Intentional content.** Teachers must continually analyze content for what should be in videos as opposed to classroom activities. Depending on the grade level and topic, they select instructional methods such as problem-based learning (PBL), mastery learning, or Socratic methods.

4. **Professional educators.** Finally, this pillar calls for an acknowledgement of the indispensable role of teachers and asserts that professional educators are reflective and collaborative and know how to accept criticism that can improve their practice.

Hamdan et al. also confirmed that a flipped-learning approach that reflects these four features uses several popular theory-based strategies, included active learning, peer instruction, **priming** or exposing students to topics that will be revisited later, and **pretraining** or "receiving some instruction before in-class instruction" (p. 8). Cognitive load theory, which holds that working memory is limited and can be overloaded if too many new concepts are presented at one time, offers a theoretical foundation for flipped learning, because instructional methods that introduce and then cycle back through concepts later (e.g., priming or pretraining) is thought to reduce that load and make it more manageable.

LaFee (2013) tempers the enthusiasm for flipped classroom methods with some commonly cited caveats. For example, some educators question whether the strategy can work when students or schools lack access to technologies they need and whether or not it is scalable or able to be implemented more broadly across various types of teachers and classrooms. Finally, they question whether or not flipped-learning strategies improve outcomes when compared to traditional methods.

### Flipped classroom research.
Goodwin and Miller (2013) said that evidence is still coming in as to whether a flipped strategy improves educational outcomes, but studies to date seem split between equal or better outcomes. Berrett (2012) reports on a study conducted by

## Example 7.1

**TITLE:** Student-Generated Flipped Review Exercises

**CONTENT AREA/TOPIC:** Social studies

**GRADE LEVELS:** 5th grade

**ISTE STANDARDS•S:** Standard 2—Communication and Collaboration; Standard 3—Research and Information Fluency

**CCSS:** CCSS.ELA-LITERACY, RH.6-8.1, CCSS.ELA-LITERACY, RH.6-8.4 CCSS, ELA-LITERACY, RH.6-8.7

**DESCRIPTION:** To help students prepare for social studies end-of-semester or end-of-course final exams, arrange small groups and assign each group a part of the content that it is responsible to review. Each group uses available movie equipment and software to make a movie (or series of brief clips) about the assigned content. The class watches each video at home the night before the review, and other students post questions of the other groups. In class, they discuss what they learned from the video and questions that were posted about it. Make sure directions are clear that the video lessons should cover main ideas instead of incidental ones. Based on ideas In George Phillip's Flipped Classroom Blog "Reversing Instruction In Social Studies"

Nobel laureate Carl Wieman, who compared a flipped method with the traditional one for a physics course and found the "flipped group" achieved nearly twice as much. McLaughlin et al. (2014) report improved attitudes toward a flipping strategy, but do not cite achievement outcomes. Fell (2013) cites preliminary results from a college economics course that showed equal achievement outcomes for traditional and flipped classrooms.

**Flipped classroom implementation tips.** The FLN is a good source of up-to-date information and ideas for more effective uses of flipped classroom activities. In addition, Raths (2013) offers "tips for a better flipped classroom," which include recommendations such as starting small and getting student and parent buy-in before beginning the project. It is also important to teach students how to watch videos for instructional purposes, which is far different than viewing for entertainment. Bergmann and Sams (2014) said that the key to a successful implementation of this model is effective use of "face time." For example, science teachers may focus on in-class assistance to individual students as they solve challenging problems and do hands-on activities. Physical education teachers might have students actually do the movements they reviewed before class.

There is a consensus among teachers who have tried flipping that videos used for this purpose should be short, about five to eight minutes, though they may be shorter or slightly longer, depending on the grade level. The maximum recommended length even in high school and college is 15 minutes. See Technology Integration Example 7.1 for an example of a flipped classroom lesson.

**TECHNOLOGY LEARNING CHECK**

Complete **TLC 7.2** to review what you have learned from reading this section about blended learning environments.

## ONLINE AUDIO AND VIDEO STRATEGIES IN BLENDED ENVIRONMENTS

Many blended models, including the flipped classroom model, depend on ready access to online audio and video content. Once the exclusive domain of media professionals, such content can now be produced by anyone, including teachers and students, and shared with others on free websites like YouTube, TeacherTube, and Tumblr. These same sites also provide a wealth of video that others have produced and made available for public use. Teachers are taking advantage of students' desire to produce and use online audio and video content by both including it in their own lessons and by allowing students to create their own videos that show what they have learned. This section gives background on audio and video production and describes integration strategies for incorporating these online media to create blended learning environments.

## Background on Podcasts and Vodcasts

**Podcast**, a term that combines "iPod" and "broadcast," coined by British journalist Ben Hammersley in 2004, originally meant posting audio on a website. Now podcasts can also mean posting video on an online site such as YouTube, a practice also sometimes referred to as a **vodcast**, or **video sharing**. Young people were among the first to make audio and video sharing popular, but it has evolved into a new form of multimedia publishing used around the world by people of all ages.

## Audio and Video Development

Video and audio editing software is to media what word processing is to text. With the emergence of audio/video capability on mobile phones and easy uploading to online sites, there has been an explosion in media production to rival the rapid increase in word processing of documents.

**Creating digital media from imported files.** Audio-video files can be imported onto a computer from a source, such as a phone, digital camera, or **webcam**, in one of several formats (e.g., **Audio Video Interleave (AVI) format, Moving Picture Experts Group (MPEG) format, QuickTime movie (MOV) format**). Once stored on a computer, the resulting digitized clips can be inserted into a multimedia package or uploaded to the Internet. Media clips stored in this way are often viewed with free player software, such as Apple's QuickTime or Windows Media Player. **Video editing software** allows digital videos to be edited and combined with special effects, such as titles, screen fades, transitions, and voice-over audio/sound effects. If teachers need only audio to post a musical selection or a lecture, software such as Audacity is available to allow audio recording and editing.

An example screen from an open-source video editing software is shown in Figure 7.2. The top of the screen offers video editing options, and the bottom part allows users to manipulate the audio track. By sliding markers on these tracks and dragging the video clips to their intended destinations in the file, students can cut, copy, and/or paste sections of a video and/or combine them with special effects such as fades or background music. The end result can then be uploaded to a website.

**Creating media with screen-capture software.** Another way to produce videos for instructional use is through a **screen-capture software** such as Camtasia. This software allows recording one's on-screen activity (e.g., typing and cursor motions), along with accompanying audio descriptions, storing the sequence as a digital file, and adding special effects, such as circling or highlighting certain words or actions. Bull (2013) described how teachers may use this kind of software to create their own interactive media to serve instructional purposes ranging from demonstration to assessment.

## Audio and Video Lesson Integration Strategies

As Rudd and Rudd (2014) observed, video is becoming much more prevalent in online and blended courses. Students and teachers are using audio and video they have created and placed

**FIGURE 7.2** Sample Video Editor: *Open Movie Editor*

*Source: Open Movie Editor*, from http://www.openmovieeditor.org. Reprinted by permission.

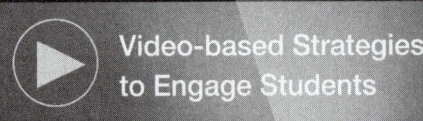

**Video-based Strategies to Engage Students**

In this video, a principal talks about video lessons across the curriculum that help students stay engaged in learning. Can you identify video-based strategies that might be useful in your current or future situation?

online for a variety of purposes, ranging from presenting the daily school news to creating video lessons that enable a flipped classroom model. Some of these media-based strategies are described here.

## Demonstrations of frequently performed procedures.

For activities that are frequently repeated (for example, procedures for science experiments), teachers can film themselves or others completing the steps. These short clips, which provide demonstrations that can be viewed and repeated as many times as desired by students, are useful across curriculum areas. Ehrmann (2011) advises teachers to share video demonstrations among themselves to save both money and time. Some examples of video-demonstration strategies are:

- In physical education, use videos to demonstrate fitness and sports skills and methods (Shumack & Reilly, 2011).
- For students with cognitive disabilities who need reminders of frequently used steps, use video demonstrations that can be repeated on demand (Brown, 2010).
- **Video modeling** is a technique that has been used successfully with individuals with special needs, especially students with autism spectrum disorders (ASD). In this technique, students either watch themselves or their peers doing desired behaviors. According to The Autism Teacher website, video modeling works well because children tend to pay more attention to them than to people they actually encounter. Also, students can watch videos as many times as they want to, which frees up teacher time for other activities. Video modeling has been used successfully to build social and communication skills in students with ASD (Buggey & Ogle, 2013; Wilson, 2013).

## Student-created presentations.

Although students can produce a video as a way of documenting research findings (as they do with PowerPoint and Keynote presentations), they often create videos that illustrate real-life examples of concepts they have learned (e.g., showing how algebra applies to everyday situations) or make documentaries of events and conditions around them. Bedrossian (2010) described a project that made important scientific and technological discoveries come alive for students as they interviewed, recorded, and made podcasts of oral histories of people who lived during the time these innovations happened. The ready availability of YouTube makes sharing student-created presentations easy and fun. Criswell (2013) described making video recordings of students' musical performances as a way to help them self-assess their work.

## Adapting for Special Needs

### Online Teaching and Learning: Blended Environments

As teachers and administrators work to implement new blended learning environments, it is increasingly important to ensure that the digital learning resources are accessible. The following websites are maintained by online learning and accessibility experts and feature a wealth of resources.

- Center for Online Learning and Students with Disabilities
- Knowbility website
- Usability.gov
- Web Accessibility in Mind (WebAIM) website

*—Contributed by Dave Edyburn*

▲ Students can create videos that illustrate real-life examples of concepts they have learned or make documentaries of events and conditions around them. (Photo courtesy W. Wiencke)

### Audio or video classroom discussion starters.

Teachers can use either audio or video examples as a way to spark discussion or to help students analyze their own behaviors. For example, Pannell and Hutchison (2010) recorded students explaining how they solved math problems involving fractions. The teacher played each recording as she illustrated the problem solution on the whiteboard. Students then discussed which methods were better and compared them to the ones they had been using. Webcams that provide images of local or distant phenomena can also be helpful resources. Technology Integration Example 7.2 illustrates one of these uses.

### Expert lectures and speakers.

Prerecorded lectures and speakers have become especially popular in flipped classroom models. Some of these uses include the following:

- Interviews with local community experts can be prerecorded to make their "visits" even more useful for later discussion. Note that permission to use recorded video of speakers is always needed. Make sure they are aware you will be recording them, and obtain their written permission to reuse the video for future classes.

- Videos of classroom lectures, demonstrations, and/or or discussions come in handy if students miss the original presentation or want to review material later.

- Ware and Stein (2013) found that video vignettes and profiles of people in STEM careers can provide valuable mentors and role models for school students to encourage their interest in pursuing such careers.

### Video portfolios.

Student portfolios of their work products over time have become more common for assessment purposes, and video systems have assumed a central role in portfolio development. Additionally, many teachers develop portfolios to document their teaching methods in preparation for a promotion or additional certification (Delacruz & Bales, 2010).

### Video decision-making/problem-solving simulations.

This strategy was made popular with the *Adventures of Jasper Woodbury* videodiscs in the mid-1990s and has been widely used since then. Videos are used to depict problem scenarios that require math,

## TECHNOLOGY INTEGRATION

### Example 7.2

**TITLE:** Webcams Bring Weather to Life

**CONTENT AREA/TOPIC:** Science, physical sciences

**GRADE LEVELS:** High school

**ISTE STANDARDS•S:** Standard 3—Research and Information Fluency; Standard 6—Technology Operations and Concepts

**NSTA:** HS-ESS2-4, HS-ESS2-5

**DESCRIPTION:** Teachers who want a vivid and engaging way to teach physical science and weather concepts can create classroom activities around webcam images of various locations.

For example, a flood cam is designed to provide readings of a river's height, along with safety advice and weather predictions. Teachers can use weather webcams in distant locations to illustrate weather concepts. As local weather events occur, they can take advantage of "teachable moments" to show how physical science concepts apply to real-world events.

*SOURCE:* Based on a concept from *A Study in Natural Disasters* at the Education World site.

science, or geography skills, and students can review information in the videos as they create solutions to the problems.

### Documentation of school activities.

Many middle and secondary schools use video cameras and video editing software to produce a daily news show or morning announcements. These productions "star" the students themselves, and students control the camera and perform the necessary editing work. News shows offer valuable opportunities to help students develop their research and interviewing skills, on-camera presentation skills, and technical production skills. When schools create video yearbooks, students capture video clips of events and merge them into a collage of the year's events.

### Visual literacy instruction.

Now that online video has established itself as playing a significant social role in our society, visual literacy is a requirement for academic success, as well as success in many careers. Through creating and/or analyzing information in video format, students learn how people can use visual images to communicate biases and make persuasive arguments in advertisements and news stories. This enables students to become more thoughtful (and sometimes more cautious) consumers of digital information and marketing.

### Video production instruction.

Technology education labs typically feature video production as one of the required learning stations. Students in these labs usually create the school's news shows and morning announcements. Pinkstone (2010) said that, "Filmmaking crosses several curriculum areas (English, visual arts, drama, and media studies) and is an excellent way to engage students in their learning and develop their practical skills" (p. 12). She also tells of filmmaking competitions that invite student-produced works, thus providing even greater motivation to acquire skills in these important areas. Online sites such as SchoolTube and TeacherTube, which are especially designed for hosting student video projects, provide a rich, yet safe environment for using and posting these kinds of projects. Lorenzi's (2012) article on "creating future filmmakers" is a must-read for teachers seeking to work meaningful and motivating video projects into their curriculum. For each of the following six ideas for video assignments, she first tells how to prepare students before sending them out as amateur filmmakers. Also see Technology Integration Example 7.3 based on one of her ideas:

1. **The interview.** Students research a talk-show guest they would like to interview. For example, they might choose a fictional character or a famous person from history.

# TECHNOLOGY INTEGRATION

## Example 7.3

**TITLE:** Students as Feature Filmmakers

**CONTENT AREA/TOPIC:** Language arts

**GRADE LEVELS:** Elementary to middle school

**ISTE STANDARDS•S:** Standard 1—Creativity and innovation; Standard 2—Communication and Collaboration; Standard 6—Technology Operations and Concepts

**CCSS:** RL.6.2., W.6.6, SL.6.1, SL.7.1(c), W.8.3, CCSS. ELA-LITERACY, SL.8.5

**DESCRIPTION:** Students choose a favorite book and brainstorm what might happen to the characters after the end of the story.

Then they work in small groups to write their own sequels and film them. Each group creates storyboards to map out the setting, action, and dialog. Finally, they role-play and film the sequels. An alternative is to use photos or scanned illustrations for a narrated slide show. With either format, students can insert a musical sound track or dub in their own narration over the pictured events, depending on their skill levels.

*SOURCE:* Based on a concept from *Creating Future Filmmakers* by Natalie Lorenzi (2011) in Instructor, *121*(6), 57–58. Retrieved at http://www.scholastic.com/teachers/instructor.

2. **Field (trip) correspondents.** The teacher brings along a video camera on a field trip, capturing students' thoughts and allowing them to shoot footage themselves.
3. **The sequel.** Students make a video or a narrated slide show on what happened after the end of one of their favorite books.
4. **The commercial.** Students make up a product to sell and create commercials for it.
5. **Destinations.** Students create films as though they are reporting from the site of a historical period they are studying.
6. **Tour guides.** Students film a tour of their school and interview "VIPs" such as the principal or school nurse.

**TECHNOLOGY LEARNING CHECK**
Complete TLC 7.3 to review what you have learned from reading this section about online audio and video components and how to integrate them.

## TYPES OF WEB-BASED LESSONS IN BLENDED MODELS

One way to create a blended environment is integrating one or more Web-based lessons. This section describes types of lessons that meet various instructional purposes, how to implement them, and how to evaluate their success.

### Types of Web-Based Lessons and Projects

On her website Virtual Architecture, Harris describes three general categories of online learning activities:

- **Interpersonal exchanges**—Students communicating via technology with other students or with teachers or other experts
- **Information collection and analysis**—Using information collections that provide data and information on request
- **Problem solving**—Student-oriented and cooperative problem-solving projects

Harris lists strategies she calls activity structures that fall under these three categories. Lessons based on a given activity structure all follow the same basic design, even though their content and objectives may vary. Detailed descriptions of these activity structures may be found at the Virtual Architecture website. Some forms these models can take are described here, and examples of each are given in Table 7.2.

**Electronic pen pals or "key pals."** Teachers link up each student with a partner or pen pal in a distant location to whom the student writes letters or diary-type entries. Recently, teachers have attempted to do this with social networking sites such as Facebook. However, as with any online environment, there can be risks to using such an approach. One risk is cyberbullying, which was discussed in Chapter 6.

**Electronic Mentoring.** Students can link with mentors in the form of other students, individual experts in a given field, or expert resources such as learning communities. Links may take the form of chats, discussion groups, or collaboration zones. For example, teachers put students in touch with scientists who volunteer to ask questions about their areas of research and recent findings.

**Virtual field trips.** Kirchen said, "A **virtual field trip** (VFT) is a technology-based experience that allows children to take an educational journey without leaving the classroom" (p. 27). Real field trips present a variety of logistical problems, including expense. Electronic field trips are a way

## TABLE 7.2 Types and Examples of Web-Based Lessons and Projects

| Type of Web-Based Activity | Sample Sites (search on these titles) |
|---|---|
| **Electronic pen pals (keypals):** Links students at a distance to exchange information | • ePals<br>• OneWorld Classrooms |
| **Electronic mentoring:** Links students with experts to answer questions and support learning | • International Telementor Program<br>• Mad Scientist Network<br>• Writing with Writers |
| **Virtual field trips:** Visit sites to view people, places, and resources not locally available | • National Health Museum<br>• Internet for Classrooms |
| **Electronic publishing:** Share written and artistic products on websites | • Midlink Magazine<br>• VoiceThread: Conversations in the Cloud |
| **Group product development:** Work on written or artistic products with students at different sites | • The Center for Innovation in Engineering and Science Education (CIESE) online classroom projects (Click on Programs and Curriculum)<br>• Thinkquest |
| **Problem-based learning:** Explore topics, obtain and analyze data, or participate in simulated problem solving with other students | • The GLOBE Program<br>• The PathFinder Science Network for Student and Citizen Science<br>• International Schools CyberFair<br>• WISE (Web-based Inquiry Science Environment) at Berkeley |
| **Social action projects:** Discuss and create solutions for social or environmental problems with other students | • IEARN Network<br>• Earth Day Groceries Project |

to circumvent these problems and bring real-world situations into the classroom. These activities explore unique locations around the world, and by involving learners at those sites, students share the experience with other learners at remote locations. For example, suppose a teacher wanted students to take a tour of the White House in Washington, DC, but the distance and cost was prohibitive. Instead, they might take a virtual tour like the one at the Whitehouse.gov website. Stoddard (2009) provided a conceptual model for successful virtual field trips and noted that virtual field trips allow student learning to be more authentic and that there is a need for teachers to receive professional development in this area. Stansberry (2013) recommended "10 of the best virtual field trips" that range from a tour of the Louvre Museum in Paris to the Hershey factory in Hershey, Pennsylvania. Also see the Global Schoolnet site's list of field trips classes can join.

### Electronic publishing.

When students submit their written or artistic products to a website, it is called **electronic publishing.** This allows their work to be shared with other students and visitors to the site. They may use free tools such as wikis and blogs or websites such as the Student Newspapers Online site, which charges an annual fee to host a school newspaper and offers free templates modeled on actual newspapers that schools can use for their own designs.

### Group product development.

Teachers have developed many variations of online group development of products. One approach is to have students work independently toward an agreed-on goal, with each student or group adding a portion of the final product. This is sometimes called chain writing.

### Problem-based learning.

**Problem-based learning (PBL)** has long been recognized as a strategy to help students develop higher-order thinking skills (Ak, 2011). Casia and Zubiaga (2010) noted that PBL is an authentic way of learning that provides students with real-life experiences in ways that help students build on their prior knowledge in contexts they find most meaningful. Tsai and Cheng (2013) reviewed research on PBL environments from 2004–2012 and found that PBL was on the rise in the United States and that it has proven to be an especially effective method in online learning environments. This kind of problem solving can take many forms, four of which are described here:

▲ In collaborative problem-solving models, several students or student groups working together to solve a problem. **Monkey Business Images/Shutterstock**

- **Collaborative problem solving.** This model involves several students or student groups working together to solve a problem. These kinds of lessons were dubbed **webquests** by Bernie Dodge in 1995 at San Diego State University and became a model for teachers across the country in creating their own lessons. According to the Webquest.org website, a webquest is a lesson format in which students search for information on the Web to answer questions and/or solve problems. All of these lessons give students a scenario and a task to do in response to that scenario; usually they have a problem to solve or a project to complete. An example webquest is shown in Technology Integration Example 7.4.

- **Parallel problem solving.** In this strategy, students in a number of different locations work on similar problems. They solve their problem independently and then compare their methods and results, or they may build a database or other product with information gathered from all participants during the activity.

- **Data analysis.** These activities give students access to data from real phenomena, such as weather or solar activity. Using these data, students are able to answer questions and solve problems posed by their teachers, their peers, and themselves.

- **Simulated activities.** These are the Web equivalent of simulation software. In these activities, students participate in real-life activities such as managing a city or investing in the stock market. Spinello and Fischbach (2008) found that students who participated in online public health simulations produced higher exam scores than those who participated in the traditional face-to-face environment.

## Social Action Projects

In these projects, the focus is on learning about and addressing important global social, economic, political, or environmental conditions. For example, students collaborating on a peace project might write congressional representatives to voice concerns and present their viewpoints. Or as in Kidlink's "I Have a Dream" project, they might collaborate to articulate a dream for making the world a better place, then as the website says, they "organize their dream projects and create a plan of action to make them a reality." The emphasis in this kind of project is group collaboration to offer solutions to an issue of practical community (global or local) concern.

# TECHNOLOGY INTEGRATION

## Example 7.4

TITLE: Webquest—Introducing the English Language!

CONTENT AREA/TOPIC: English as a Second Language

GRADE LEVELS: 9–10

ISTE STANDARDS•S: Standard 2—Communication and Collaboration; Standard 3—Research and Information Fluency; Standard 6—Technology Operations and Concepts

CCSS: CCSS.ELA-LITERACY.L.9-10.4, CCSS.ELA-LITERACY.L.9-10.6

DESCRIPTION: ESL students use webquest directions and links to build a factbook on an English-speaking country of their choice. Doing the activities in small groups, they build their collaborative skills, knowledge of the history of the English language, and their English listening, reading, vocabulary, and writing skills.

*SOURCE:* Based on a concept from "A Guide to the World of the English Language" in the webquest collection at http://questgarden.com.

The **Top Ten Feature** for this chapter identifies good sources of award-winning, Web-based lesson plans, activities, and collaborative projects based on these models.

## Integration Strategies for Web-Based Activities

The following strategies address a variety of classroom needs; it is this match of activity types with needs that defines and shapes integration strategies. The Web-based activities and lessons described previously can be used with more than one of the integration strategies discussed next.

**Support for student research.** Students frequently use websites and Web-based video resources and videoconferencing to gain insights into topics they are studying and to locate information for research papers and presentations. This work may be in the form of individual or group-based research projects or electronic mentoring. (See Technology Integration Example 7.5.)

Strategies in which students write for distance audiences help motivate them to write more and to do their best writing. Lesson activities that make use of this strategy include keypals and electronic publishing. (See Technology Integration Example 7.6.)

# TECHNOLOGY INTEGRATION

## Example 7.5

**TITLE:** Connecting Science Students with NASA Resources

**CONTENT AREA/TOPIC:** Earth science

**GRADE LEVELS:** All grades

**ISTE STANDARDS•S:** Standard 1—Creativity and Innovation; Standard 2—Communication and Collaboration; Standard 3—Research and Information Fluency; Standard 4—Critical Thinking, Problem Solving, and Decision Making

**NSTA:** 2-ESS1-1, 2-ESS2-3, 4-ESS2-2, 5-ESS2-2, 5-ESS3-1, MS-ESS1-1, HS-ESS2-2, HS-ESS2-3, HS-ESS2-5, HS-ESS2-6, HS-ESS2-7

**DESCRIPTION:** The project begins by having students learn how to analyze photographic detail. They then obtain images taken from the International Space Station's Window Observational Research Facility (WORF) from four Earth locations, analyze them, and document their findings. Each student develops five questions he or she would like to ask in a videoconference or online session with NASA experts. Each class involved in the project forwards its best 10 questions, which the experts address in a live online session.

*SOURCE:* Based on an idea from Peterson, R., Starr, B., & Anderson, S. (2003). Real NASA inspiration in virtual space. *Learning and Leading with Technology, 31*(1), 14–19.

# TECHNOLOGY INTEGRATION

## Example 7.6

**TITLE:** Fractured Fairy Tales

**CONTENT AREA/TOPIC:** Language arts, literacy

**GRADE LEVELS:** 3–6

**ISTE STANDARDS•S:** Standard 1—Creativity and Innovation; Standard 2—Communication and Collaboration; Standard 4—Critical Thinking, Problem Solving, and Decision Making

**CCSS:** RL.3.9, W.3.6, RL.4.2, W.4.9, L.5.1

**DESCRIPTION:** Students use traditional and fractured fairy tales to study story structure. After reading and examining several traditional and fractured fairy tales, students work in groups to plan their own original fractured fairy tale, using the online Fractured Fairy Tales tool as an idea generator. Each group then publishes its story using either presentation software (e.g., PowerPoint) or a collaborative website (e.g., in wikis or Google Docs), adding images and other linked media to enhance the tale. Groups share their stories with the entire class and can vote on the best retelling of a fairy tale.

*SOURCE:* Based on ideas from the lesson Once Upon a Link: A PowerPoint Adventure with Fractured Fairy Tales at the ReadWriteThink website.

# TECHNOLOGY INTEGRATION

## Example 7.7

**TITLE:** Westward Expansion

**CONTENT AREA/TOPIC:** Social studies, history

**GRADE LEVELS:** 7–12

**ISTE STANDARDS•S:** Standard 2—Communication and Collaboration; Standard 3—Research and Information Fluency; Standard 4—Critical Thinking, Problem Solving, and Decision Making

**CCSS:** CCSS.ELA-LITERACY.RH.6-8.1, CCSS.ELA-LITERACY.RH.6-8.5, CCSS.ELA-LITERACY, RH.9-10.2, CCSS.ELA-LITERACY.RH.9-10.8, CCSS.ELA-LITERACY.RH.9-10.9, CCSS.ELA-LITERACY.RH.11-12.6

**NCSS THEMES:** 2 – Time, Continuity, and Change; 3 – People, Places, and Environments 4 – Individual, Groups, Institutions; Disciplinary Standards: 1 – History, 2 – Geography, 4 – Economics

**DESCRIPTION:** Begin by asking the class to hypothesize why Americans may have wanted to move west in the middle of the 19th century.

- Discuss general reasons why humans leave one place to move to another, as well as the cultural and political climate of the United States during this era.

- Have students work in pairs researching, examining, and discussing primary documents and images from this time period available online through the National Archives.

- Using tools available at the National Archives Docs Teach website, or a collaborative online tool such as Google Docs or Google Sites, students then choose 5–10 documents to share with the class and place their documents in chronological sequence, compiling a list of possible reasons why Americans moved westward during this era.

- Have groups share their findings with the class.

*SOURCE:* Based on ideas from the lesson Reasons for Westward Expansion at the National Archives Experience Docs Teach website.

---

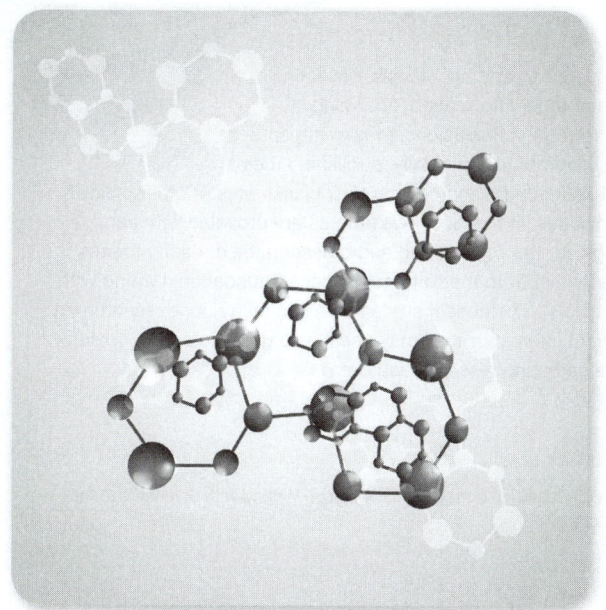

▲ Real-world data, images, animations, and videos available online can help students better understand complex problems and visualize possible solutions. **YasnaTen/Shutterstock**

**Practice for information literacy skills.** Locating and using information from online sources has become a key part of classroom learning. Growth in students' digital literacy skills requires that they have opportunities to learn how to use Web resources to locate information they need efficiently. Possible activities include individual and cooperative research projects. (See Technology Integration Example 7.7.)

**Visual learning problems and solutions.** The real-world data, images, animations, and videos available online can help students better understand complex problems and visualize possible solutions. Activities that work for this strategy include individual and cooperative research projects, as well as problem-based learning projects. (See Technology Integration Example 7.8.)

**Development of collaboration skills.** Web-based projects provide rich opportunities for students to learn how to work together, just as they will be required to do in real-life workplaces. Many Web-based projects call for students to work together to produce a product (e.g., a brochure, Web page, or multimedia presentation), either to display results of their joint research or just to gain skill in working with others on common problems. Projects that promote collaboration skills include individual and cooperative research projects, electronic publishing, group development of products, problem-based learning, and social action projects. (See Technology Integration Example 7.9.)

# TECHNOLOGY INTEGRATION

## Example 7.8

**TITLE:** OF2—Our Footprints, Our Future

**CONTENT AREA/TOPIC:** Environmental science

**GRADE LEVELS:** All grades

**ISTE STANDARDS•S:** Standard 2—Communication and Collaboration; Standard 4—Critical Thinking, Problem Solving, and Decision Making

**NSTA:** MS-PS1-4, MS-ESS3-5, HS-LS1-6 –LS2-5 HS-ESS2-6

**DESCRIPTION:** OF2—Our Footprints, Our Future is an international initiative that encourages individuals younger than 19 from around the world to use online tools and resources to measure their carbon footprint and develop ways to reduce their carbon usage. The goal of OF2 is to engage students, their families, schools, and communities to reduce the total global carbon footprint. Students input data based on their lifestyles into an online carbon footprint calculator to estimate their annual contribution (e.g., see the Zerofootprint Youth calculator for younger students or the What's Your Carbon Footprint? calculator at the Nature Conservancy website for older students). Because the tool has been adapted to recognize different cultural and socio-economic settings, housing, modes of transportation, and food consumption, students will be able to find a close estimate. Once students receive their results, they can blog or discuss in groups how their lifestyle affects climate changes around the world.

*SOURCE:* Based on an idea from the Our Footprints, Our Future lesson at the iEARN website.

---

# TECHNOLOGY INTEGRATION

## Example 7.9

**TITLE:** Writing with Scientists

**CONTENT AREA/TOPIC:** Science, writing

**GRADE LEVELS:** High school

**ISTE STANDARDS•S:** Standard 3—Research and Information Fluency; Standard 4—Critical Thinking, Problem Solving, and Decision Making

**CCSS:** CCSS.ELA-LITERACY.W.9-10.2, CCSS.ELA-LITERACY.W.9-10.8, CCSS.ELA-LITERACY.W.11-12.1, CCSS.ELA-LITERACY.WHST.11-12.4, CCSS.ELA-LITERACY.RST.11-12.9

**DESCRIPTION:** Writing with Scientists helps students write a research paper, and takes them through the process of describing their questions and hypothesis, collecting data and other information, analyzing results, writing conclusions, presenting sources in a bibliography, and, finally, publishing their report online to be shared with their classmates or other online communities. In this activity, students are provided with sample writings as well as recorded audio description of each process by a scientist from the National Science Foundation. Writing with Scientists can be used if students have already done research on a topic of interest or they may use it as a guide to set up goals before gathering research and data.

*SOURCE:* Based on concepts in the lesson Writing with Scientists at the Scholastic site.

---

**Multicultural immersion.** Many Web-based projects focus on broadening students' perspectives on their own and other cultures, and providing insights into how their culture relates to others in the world. Appropriate Web-based activities include electronic (virtual) field trips and social action projects. (See Technology Integration Example 7.10.)

## Example 7.10

**TITLE:** Comparing Local Histories

**CONTENT AREA/TOPIC:** Social studies, history

**GRADE LEVELS:** Middle school

**ISTE STANDARDS•S:** Standard 2—Communication and Collaboration; Standard 3—Research and Information Fluency

**NCSS THEMES:** 1 – Culture and Cultural Diversity, 3 – People, Places, and Environments, 4 – Individual Development and Identity, 5 – Individuals, Groups, and Institutions, 9 – Global Connections; Disciplinary Standards: 1 – History, 2 – Geography, 3 – Civics and Government, 4 - Economics

**DESCRIPTION:** After researching the geography and history of their own town or community, students use Web 2.0 tools to share their findings with their peers in other countries. Students practice numerous research skills, such as interviewing and document analysis, while acquiring an understanding of how the history of the region they studied is connected to their lives. They work in small groups to produce a Web page and use social networking tools (e.g., a blog) to compare and discuss their communities.

*SOURCE:* Based on ideas from the Local History Project lesson at iEARN website.

---

**TECHNOLOGY LEARNING CHECK**

Complete **TLC 7.4** to review what you have learned from reading this section about types of Web-based lessons and how to integrate them in ways that assure their quality.

## IMPLEMENTING WEB-BASED LESSONS IN BLENDED ENVIRONMENTS

The Web-based lessons and integration strategies described in previous sections share two common features: all require a website of some kind to support them and enable communication of important information to participants, and all need good assessment strategies to gauge their impact and the quality of their products. This section discusses both of these features.

# OPEN SOURCE
## OPTIONS *for Web-Hosting Sites*

### FREE SOURCES

Google Sites: sites.google.com

Weebly Websites: weebly.com

iTeach: iteach.org/

SchoolRack: schoolrack.com

# Support Sites for Web-Based Activities

Some online lessons take place in a **content management system or CMS** (a.k.a **Learning Management System or LMS**) such as Blackboard or Moodle. However, the majority of K12 lessons take place on public websites that have been designed to serve functions ranging from announcing and describing the lesson to displaying student projects from past lessons. The type(s) of functions the website must serve depends on the nature of the lesson. A website to be used only by one classroom will look far different from one supporting classrooms in multiple sites. The following review of website support functions is based on Harris's description of website functions in her Virtual Architecture website. Note that a single website can serve one or more of these support functions.

## FIGURE 7.3 Example of Lesson Support Type 2—Tutorial Instruction: Mind Lab

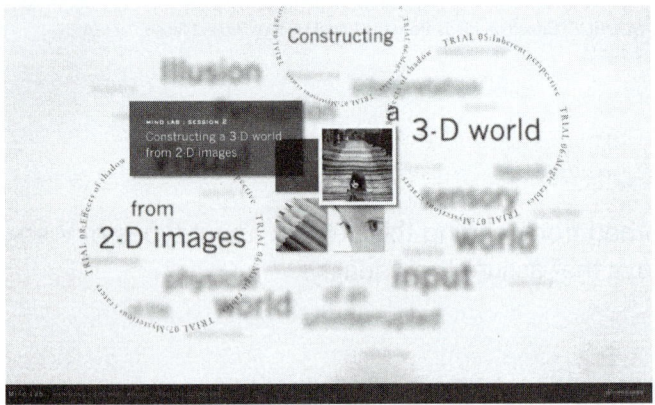

## FIGURE 7.4 Example of Lesson Support Type 4—Communication and Support

**Support Function 1: Project host site.** Sites can host a learning activity, introducing the project's goals and purposes and inviting people to participate in it. For example, see Global SchoolNet's Geogame website, which hosts a project that develops students' understanding of geographic terms, increases their ability to use maps, and raises their awareness of cultural diversity. Educators to want to host their own projects can use one of the free web-hosting sites shown in the Open Source Options feature.

**Support Function 2: Tutorial instruction.** A website can be structured to deliver actual instruction and information on a topic. For example, Mind Lab, shown in Figure 7.3, provides four descriptions of how the mind works to receive and process visual phenomena around us. For example, there are lessons titled "Illusion of an uninterrupted world," and "Constructing a 3D world from 2D images." These lessons are followed by sessions to let users experience these processes themselves.

**Support Function 3: Information exchanges.** Students can use websites to add information to a collection that will be shared with others. For example, the goal of the Kidlink website is to make possible a "global dialogue among youth of the world," both in terms of messages and media. Many of these projects have been supplanted by blogs on various topics that anyone can join.

**Support Function 4: Communication and support.** A website can serve as a virtual meeting place to support students as they learn in distant locations. For example, the Math Forum @ Drexel (shown in Figure 7.4), which has been in operation since 1992, has a popular service called "Ask Dr. Math," which provides homework help from "volunteer math doctors" as well as from an archive of math problems and answers.

**Support Function 5: Displays of student work.** Websites can be used as Web publication centers in which students show examples of their poems, stories, pictures, and multimedia products. Some sites also show ongoing descriptions of past, current, and planned project activities. For example, the KidPub website (Figure 7.5) hosts student work samples from around the world.

## FIGURE 7.5 Example of Lesson Support Type 5—Displays of student work: KidPub

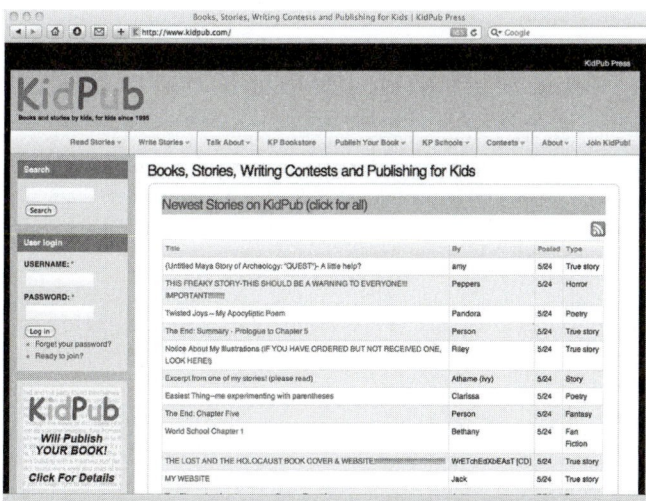

*Source:* KidPub website at http://www.kidpub.com. Copyright 1995, 2013 KidPub Press LLC. Reprinted by permission.

## FIGURE 7.6 Example of Lesson Support Type 6—Project Development: Global SchoolNet

*Source:* Copyright GlobalSchoolNet.org – Linking Kids Around the World. Reprinted by permission.

**Support Function 6: Project development centers.** Websites are sometimes set up for the specific purpose of inviting new distance learning projects. The Global SchoolNet Foundation (see Figure 7.6) has hundreds of existing projects and invites teachers around the world to register new ones.

# Evaluating Quality of Web-Based Lessons and Student Products from Lessons

Assessment is a critically important aspect all online activities. First, it is used to select high-quality lessons and confirm they work well for their intended audience. Second, student success must be assessed in terms of what they learned and the quality of the products they created during the lessons.

**Assessing lesson quality.** Hundreds of Web-based activities are available for teachers to use in their classrooms or join online; many have been tried out by teachers, and some work better than others. How can teachers assess quality of given activities and select those that will work best for their students? One useful assessment instrument is the Rubric for Evaluating WebQuests. Although webquests represent just one of many possible types of Web-based lessons, the elements of this rubric apply to most Web-based lessons. Another good instrument is the **Technology Lesson Plan Evaluation Checklist**, which is based on the Technology Integration Planning (TIP) model described earlier in chapter 2. Finally, to assess how well the lesson met your own objectives, use the **Technology Impact Checklist for Assessment of Technology-Integrated Lessons**.

**Assessing student contributions.** Rubrics are helpful not only to assess student work, but also to give them criteria and clearly articulated descriptions of what constitutes a high-quality product. Many rubrics for assessing quality of presentations, podcasts, and vodcasts that students create may be found at Kathy Schrock's Guide to Everything website under Assessments and Rubrics.

## TECHNOLOGY LEARNING CHECK

Complete **TLC 7.5** to review what you have learned from reading this section about how to support Web-based lessons with websites and appropriate assessment strategies.

Monkey Business/Fotolia

The following questions may be used either for in-class, small-group discussions or may be used to initiate discussions in blogs or online discussion boards:

1. Glass and Welner (2011) are highly critical of those who equate learning online with learning face-to-face. They said it is not reasonable to believe that people can learn as much from a computer as they learn from teachers in a traditional classroom. Based on what you have read and experienced about online learning, what evidence could you cite to support or refute their position? Are there skills or knowledge that cannot be learned online? If so, what are they?

2. LaFee (2013) poses several questions about the scalability of flipped classroom models. For example, he asks whether the technique can be applied to all subjects and whether it can be expanded to whole schools or districts. From what you have read about this model and what you know about educational practices in general, what evidence can you cite to answer his questions?

Chapter **7**

# Summary

The following is a summary of the main points covered in this chapter.

1. **Overview of Distance Education**
   - **Distance learning models.** These can be classified using (1) Edgar Dale's cone of experience, a system designed to categorize media according to their degree of realism, as to the degree to which their delivery systems permit them to approximate reality, and (2) as one of the online or blended models.
   - **Current issues in distance learning.** These include digital divide issues, developmental and socialization issues for students, and variable impact on education reform.
   - **Distance learning research.** Results are summarized on the effectiveness of distance learning compared with face-to-face (FTF) learning, course characteristics that affect success, characteristics of successful distance learners, characteristics of successful distance instructors; and cost-effectiveness of online programs.

2. **Blended Learning Environments**
   - **Blended learning models.** Any instructional units that include combinations of online and in-person activities are actually blended courses. While there are really an infinite number of blended course models in operation, models may be categorized as traditional classroom with online activities, online classroom with in-person events, and the flipped classroom model.
   - **Implementing a flipped classroom model.** Research results on flipped classroom outcomes are split between equal or better outcomes. Tips on implementing flipped classrooms include starting small, getting student and parent buy-in, teaching students how to watch videos for instructional purposes, and keeping videos short (usually between five and eight minutes).

3. **Online Audio and Video Strategies**
   - **Background on podcasts and vodcasts.** *Podcast* is a term that combines "iPod" and "broadcast" and originally meant posting audio on a website; now it can also mean posting video on a site such as YouTube, a practice also sometimes referred to as a vodcast, or video sharing.
   - **Audio and video development.** Audio and video files can be imported onto a computer from a source, such as a phone, digital camera, or webcam, in one of several formats or can be created using screen-capture software such as Camtasia.
   - **Audio and video lesson integration strategies.** These include demonstrations of frequently performed procedures; student-created presentations; audio or video of classroom discussion starters, expert lectures, and speakers.; video portfolios; video decision-making/problem-solving simulations; documentation of school activities; visual literacy instruction; and teaching video production.

4. **Types of Web-Based Lessons in Blended Environments**
   - **Types of Web-based lessons and projects.** Types of activity structures are interpersonal exchanges, information collection and analysis, **and** problem solving. Lesson and project types that reflect these

structures include electronic pen pals or "key pals," electronic mentoring, virtual field trips, electronic publishing, group product development, and problem-based learning.

- **Integration strategies for Web-based activities** – These include support for student research, practice for information literacy skills, visual learning problems and solutions, development of collaboration skills, and multicultural immersion.

5. **Implementing Web-Based Lessons in Blended Environments**
   - **Support for Web-based activities.** All Web-based projects or lessons require a website. Website support functions include project host site, tutorial instruction, information exchanges, communication and support, displays of student work, and project development centers.
   - **Assessing quality of Web-based lessons.** Two kinds of assessment are required in relation to Web-based lessons and projects. First, teachers must assure they are high quality and confirm they work well for their intended audience. Second, student success must be assessed in terms of what they learned and the quality of the products they created during the lessons.

# TECHNOLOGY INTEGRATION **WORKSHOP**

## 1. APPLY WHAT YOU LEARNED

To apply the concepts and skills you've read about throughout this chapter, go to the Chapter 7 Technology Application Activity.

## 2. TECHNOLOGY INTEGRATION LESSON PLANNING: PART 1—EVALUATING AND CREATING LESSON PLANS

Complete the following exercise using the sample lesson plans found on any lesson planning site that you find on the Internet.

**a.** Locate lesson ideas—Identify three lesson plans that focus on any of the tools or strategies you learned about in this chapter. For example:

- Web-based lessons and projects
- Podcasts and vodcasts
- Flipped classroom and other blended models

**b.** Evaluate the lessons—Use the Technology Lesson Plan Evaluation Checklist to evaluate each of the lessons you found.

**c.** Create your own lesson—After you have reviewed and evaluated some sample lessons, create one of your own using a lesson plan format of your choice (or one your instructor gives you). Be sure the lesson focuses on one of the technologies or strategies discussed in this chapter.

## 3. TECHNOLOGY INTEGRATION LESSON PLANNING: PART 2—IMPLEMENTING THE TIP MODEL

Review how to implement the TIP model in your classroom by doing the following activities with the lesson you created in the Technology Integration Lesson Planning exercise above.

**a.** Describe the Phase 1—Planning activities you would do to use this lesson in your classroom:

- What is the relative advantage of using the technology(ies) in this lesson?
- Do you have resources and skills you need to carry it out?

**b.** Describe the Phase 2—Implementation activities you would do to use this lesson in your classroom:

- What are the objectives of the lesson plan?
- How will you assess your students' accomplishment of the objectives?
- What integration strategies are used in this lesson plan?
- How would you prepare the learning environment?

**c.** Describe the Phase 3—Evaluation/Revision activities you would do to use this lesson in your classroom: What strategies and/or instruments would you use to evaluate the success of this lesson in your classroom, in order to determine revision needs?

**d.** Add lesson descriptors—Create descriptors for your new lesson (e.g., grade level, content and topic areas, technologies used, ISTE standards, 21st Century Learning standards).

**e.** Save your new lesson—Save your lesson plan with all its descriptors and TIP model notes.

## 4. FOR YOUR TEACHING PORTFOLIO

Add the following to your Teaching Portfolio:

- Lesson plan evaluations, lesson plans, and products you created above
- Products of your group's Hot Topic Debates
- Products of your group's Collaborate, Discuss, Reflect online or in-class activities

# 8

# Online Models, Courses, and Programs

## Learning Outcomes

After reading this chapter and completing the learning activities, you should be able to:

1. Identify the characteristics of four online course models in current use. (ISTE Standards•T 4, 5)

2. Select tools and strategies to build into an online course's infrastructure, and identify the contributions they make to student success. (ISTE Standards•T 4, 5)

3. Describe procedures for developing effective online courses. (ISTE Standards•T 4, 5)

4. Describe five best practices for online programs, and identify the contribution each makes to course success. (ISTE Standards•T 3, 5)

5. Identify features of today's virtual schools and diploma programs, and describe issues, trends, and research findings on their impact and effectiveness. (ISTE Standards•T 3, 5)

6. Identify integration strategies for each of the three kinds of virtual environments used in K–12 education. (ISTE Standards•T 3, 5)

# TECHNOLOGY INTEGRATION IN ACTION
# VIRTUAL HEALTH

**GRADE LEVEL:** High school • **CONTENT AREA/TOPIC:** Health Education • **LENGTH OF TIME:** One or two semesters

## PHASE 1 ANALYSIS OF LEARNING AND TEACHING NEEDS

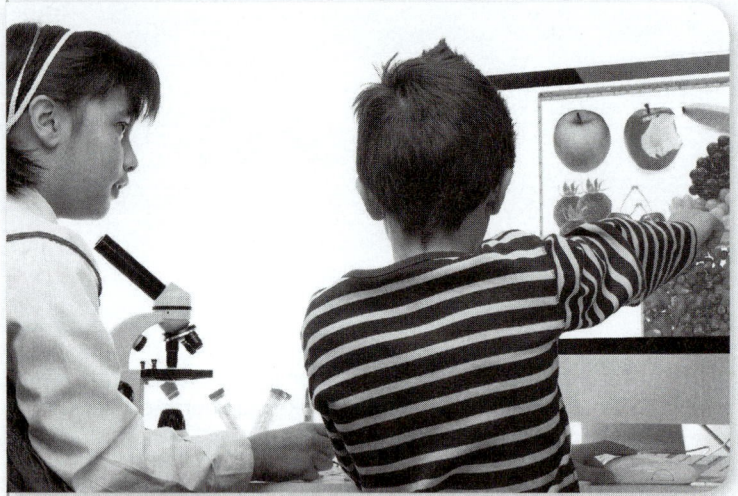

Lucky Dragon/Fotolia

### Step 1: Determine relative advantage.

One state's department of education had recently mandated that all eighth graders take a health education course. It had provided a scope and sequence for the curriculum, as well as standards and objectives, and a written exam each student had to pass to receive credit. However, it left the format of the course up to individual school districts. After discussions with school administrators, the Wunderkind School District decided to make the course online, so that each student could access it either at home or school and could have maximum flexibility on when they finished it; they could take it either as a one-semester or two-semester course. District administrators also knew they didn't have enough teachers in each school certified to teach health education, especially in the rural schools, and the online format would allow instruction to be offered from any location. Finally, they felt that if students were given extra scaffolding to learn this new format, they might be able to take other online courses in topics for which certified teachers were lacking. They asked Ms. Haas, the district's health and physical education supervisor, to oversee the task of locating or creating the online course.

### Step 2: Assess required skills and resources.

Ms. Haas had never developed an online course, but she had taken two online courses in her master's degree program and knew teachers who had taken other online courses. After she was given the assignment to create an online health education course, she reviewed three such courses available from various virtual school vendors. She especially liked one that had been created by a well-known virtual school with franchises across the United States, but it did not exactly match the state's required curriculum. The district gave her a small budget to have teachers work with her on revising the course, so she selected two science teachers who had taught courses for the virtual school in their spare time and who were familiar with the health education curriculum. She knew she would be learning a lot in this project, but she felt confident her team could develop a good course.

## PHASE 2 PLANNING FOR INTEGRATION

### Step 3: Decide on objectives and assessments

The state had already provided standards, objectives, and an end-of-course assessment. Ms. Haas and her team decided that in addition to ascertaining numbers of students dropping the course or failing the final exam, they also wanted to gauge progress in various parts of the course so they could determine which topics presented the most difficulties. They also wanted to measure student and teacher attitudes toward the class and its online format. Outcomes and measures they decided on were as follows:

**End-of-course exam.**
**Outcome:** Achieving passing grades on final exam.
**Objective:** At least 90% of all students taking the course will achieve a passing score (80% or better) on the final exam.
**Assessment:** Graded exams.

**Unit tests.**
**Outcome:** Achieving passing grades on unit tests.
**Objective:** At least 90% of all students taking the course will achieve a passing score (80% or better) on each unit test.
**Assessment:** Graded tests.

Teacher attitudes toward the course.
Outcome: Positive course evaluations.
Objective: Teachers will evaluate the course positively as demonstrated by an overall, across-teacher rating of at least 25 of 30 possible points (83%) on an attitude survey.
Assessment: Likert scale attitude survey.

Student attitudes toward the course.
Outcome: Positive course evaluations.
Objective: The students will evaluate the course positively as demonstrated by an overall, across-student rating of at least 25 of 30 possible points (83%) on an attitude survey.
Assessment: Likert scale attitude survey.

### Step 4: Design integration strategies.

Ms. Haas and her team compared the current course with the state-mandated health education course curriculum and found that two of the five units would have to be modified to match the state's requirements. They liked the interactive activities in all units, which included:

- Small-group discussions on health-related issues
- Exercises to do after viewing brief videos of health experts, doctors, and the First Lady
- Webquests with online sites to gather and analyze various kinds of information for children and young people
- Apps to download and use to support healthy lifestyles
- A final small-group project to develop healthy living plans

Their revisions would require developing some additional activities and posting them in the course, as well as changing course grading criteria to meet the new assessment strategies.

### Step 5: Prepare instructional environment.

Ms. Haas knew that preparing parents and students, as well as schools, for the requirements of the course would be key to the success of the program. The team's preparation tasks included:

Development of new activities. New learning activities were created, field-tested with students, and added to the course space.

Preparation for parents. Ms. Haas wrote a letter to the superintendent to sign and send out to principals for distribution to parents of eighth grade students who would be taking the health course. It described the reason for the course, the new online format, and how the district would prepare and support the students to be successful in the course.

Preparation for students. The teachers created an orientation to online learning that all eighth grade students would take prior to being allowed to register for the course. They based their orientation on others they have located, and tailored it to review the online course space they would be using.

Course handbooks. To make sure everyone had a summary of course content, procedures, and FAQs in a format they were used to (i.e., print), the team developed a handbook and emailed copies to each teacher and principal. They also posted it in the online course space and sent printed copies to each of the computer labs.

Computer lab scheduling. The team decided that schools should provide a class period in their computer labs dedicated to students taking the course. Facilitators would staff each lab to help students with any problems they might encounter. Students would also be required to tale the end-of-course exam in the school's computer lab.

Personnel training. Teachers and lab facilitators were brought in for hands-on training on how to support students and troubleshoot common problems they would encounter.

## PHASE 3  POST-INSTRUCTION ANALYSIS AND REVISIONS

### Step 6: Analyze results.

At mid-semester the first time the course was offered, students were asked to complete a required mid-course feedback instrument to gather comments on what was and was not working well. From these comments, it became apparent that some students were not prepared for the amount of time they would have to spend completing some assignments and had not allocated their time very well. Also, some links were not working consistently, and some students experienced problems that facilitators seemed ill-prepared to handle. Links were corrected immediately. At the end of the semester, the team gathered and reviewed the mid-semester comments, as well as unit test results, and end-of-course evaluations.

## Step 7: Make revisions.

From the mid-course comments and course evaluations, it was apparent that facilitator training has been inadequate, so adjustments were made to this workshop's design to allow additional hands-on training. Unit test grades met the specified criteria in all but the final unit, where it was clear that additional time was needed. Course evaluations of teachers and course completers met criteria for everything except facilitator support and time required for assignments. The single greatest problem was that approximately 25% of all students had either not appeared in the course space or had stopped posting and completing assignments after the first unit; these students either dropped or failed the course. The design team felt that more emphasis and preparation on time management requirements had to be added to the orientation to prepare students for taking an online course. They also decided to have a follow-up procedure in place for students who did not "appear" by the end of the first week or failed to post any required assignment. Teachers were to email students, call them at home if they received no reply within a week, and report all follow-up procedures and results to Ms. Haas. The design team decided to implement these measures for the second semester and review data again at that time.

## CHAPTER 8 BIG IDEAS OVERVIEW

Before you begin reading the rest of this chapter, listen to the Chapter 8 Big Ideas Overview. It will give you a two-minute audio overview of main concepts to look for and help prepare you to work through information and exercises to achieve this chapter's outcomes.

## DEVELOPING ONLINE COURSES: MODELS

Though "all-online" courses are often thought of as those with no in-person components and, therefore, different from blended ones, some organizations such as large school districts often adopt policies that designate a course as "all online" if a certain percentage of its activities (e.g., over 50% or over 80%) are online. However, to differentiate online courses from blended ones, this chapter defines online courses as those that have no required in-person class meetings at all. The four models for structuring online courses described here are based on Roblyer's (2015) classification system.

### The Noninteractive Online Model

The **noninteractive online model** is the most basic online model, which consists of content presentations with built-in assessments. Students read and study the information in the form of text, links to online sites, videos, simulations, and/or self-led exercises, then take online tests to demonstrate mastery of the material. Though students in noninteractive courses do interact with content designed by content experts (who may be instructors), they have no interaction with instructors or other students during the course. Noninteractive courses are not as common as other online courses but serve important purposes. For example, organizations such as school districts may offer them to their employees to update their skills or to provide a required certification.

### The Interactive, Asynchronous Online Model

In an **interactive asynchronous online model**, the most common online model used at all levels of education, students "meet" and interact with their instructor (and often with other students) in a course space enabled by a Content Management System (CMS), also known as a Learning Management System or (LMS), such a Blackboard or Moodle. Courses are usually designed using the features of a proprietary or open-source CMS, though some organizations may choose to design and use their own CMSs or course structure. Interactive online models vary in the nature of their activities, but many include whole class and/or small-group discussions, individual and/or small-group assignments, materials to read and study, practice exercises to complete, and assessments of various kinds.

## The Interactive Online Model with Synchronous Events

Less common than asynchronous online courses are those that have synchronous, real-time class meetings. Roblyer (2015) notes that "in this model, students are at a distance from the instructor and each other but 'meet' and communicate in the course space with the aid of cameras and online tools such as Adobe Connect, GotoMeeting, or Blackboard's collaborative tools Elluminate or Wimba" (p. 177). In this model, students and the instructor may either see each other using cameras connected to the computer or may only hear each other through the computer's built-in microphone. Usually these courses combine these meetings with online activities described in the previous section.

## The MOOC Model

One of the newest online-only models is the **Massive Open Online Course (MOOC) model**, so named because it originally aimed at large-scale participation and allowed anyone anywhere in the world to register for the course for free. Later MOOC models varied this approach, and either allowed open enrollment or enrollment only by members of the organization and charged participants who completed the course and wished a formal credit or certificate. As with the interactive online model, the pedagogical approach used in a MOOC model varies considerably but usually involves viewing videos of professor lectures and demonstrations, interspersed with practice and interactive activities such as simulations or problem solving, and whole-class or small-group online discussions, ending up with assessments. Though anyone can sign up for these courses for free, students must complete all required course activities and pass assessments in order to obtain a completion certificate or "badge" of completion. MOOC assignments are often corrected by automatic grading programs (Marovich, 2012). MOOCs are offered primarily by large universities and school districts that have the resources to support the high costs of development and implementation. The first CMSs to support MOOCs were Coursera designed by Stanford professors, EdX designed by Harvard and MIT personnel, and Udacity, designed by a Stanford professor (Azvedo, 2012). However, others have been added by other organizations that see a potentially large international market for MOOCs.

The initial research reports on MOOC performance in higher education have yielded a common finding: course completion rates range from 2–10% and average closer to the lower end (Youngman, 2013). For example, Breslow et al. (2013) reported on a MOOC offered in 2012 by a consortium of institutions headed by MIT and Harvard. While it initially registered over 155,000 students, only about 10% of these completed the course (still a high number for a single course). Breslow et al. discovered that the single greatest predictor of success in a MOOC is whether or not a student was working outside the course space with someone who taught a course or had expertise in that topic. Thus, as Means, Toyama, Murphy, Bakia, and Jones (2010) found about distance learning in general, MOOC models appear to be more successful when implemented as a blended-learning experience, rather than an exclusively online one.

The MOOC trend that began in universities is moving to some K–12 environments. This format may serve several roles for schools, including advanced and special-topics courses not offered by local schools due to limited resources, individual enrichment to build on courses and topics students are required to take, and professional development for teachers. Cavanagh (2013) reported that Coursera has already begun offering free professional development to K–12 teachers in the

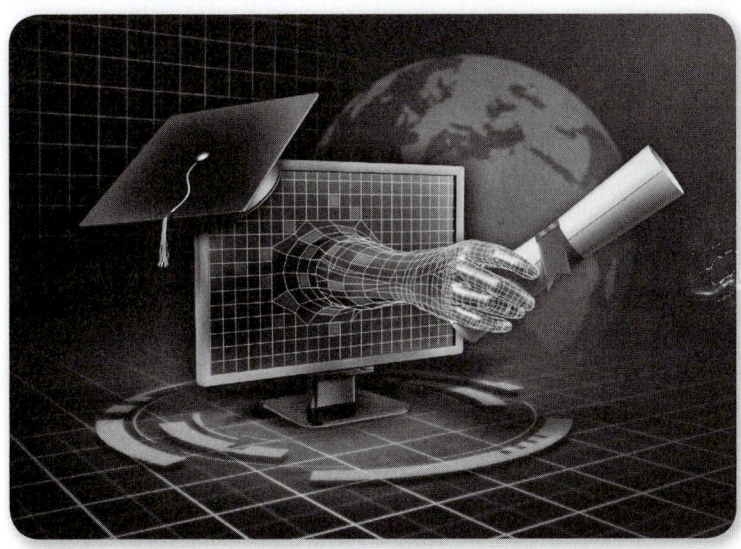

▲ Models of online courses include the noninteractive online model, the interactive, asynchronous online model, the interactive online model with synchronous events, and the MOOC model. **Andrea Danti/Shutterstock**

United States and abroad. Test preparation courses have become a primary use of MOOCs at the high school level. For example, the University of Houston system offered two MOOCs to help high school students prepare for the College Board's Advanced Placement (AP) Calculus and AP Statistics exams (Barmer, 2014), and the University of Miami's Global Academy, a virtual high school, developed a MOOC to help juniors prepare for the SAT test in biology (Jackson, 2013).

**TECHNOLOGY LEARNING CHECK**

Complete TLC 8.1 to review what you have learned from reading this section about models of online courses.

## DEVELOPING ONLINE COURSES: CONTENT MANAGEMENT SYSTEMS (CMS) AND OTHER REQUIRED INFRASTRUCTURE

Several elements of infrastructure are required to deliver any of the models of courses described previously. Some of these resources deliver content and allow an online location in which students and teachers may interact. But others are designed especially to ensure that learners have as trouble-free an online learning experience as possible.

### Content Management Systems (CMS)

CMSs provide an online environment that contains tools for teaching an online course. CMSs have become the most common means of designing and delivering Web-based courses. A school or district usually buys a license for a system, such as Blackboard or Desire2Learn, and its personnel use the system's features (e.g., graphics, conferences, discussion forums, email, links to PDFs and Web pages) to design and deliver courses hosted by its servers. The content management system also includes grade-keeping and student-tracking features, such as an electronic portfolio for each student. More recently, open-source CMSs have become available and are shown in the Open Source Options feature. Some distance education instructors eschew CMSs in favor of creating their own websites with free website tools (Rees, 2014). However, most use CMSs because they lack the time and/or expertise to build their own.

## OPEN SOURCE
### OPTIONS *for Online Content*

| | FREE SOURCES |
|---|---|
| **CMSs** | Drupal: drupal.org/<br>Joomla: joomla.org/<br>Moodle: moodle.org/<br>Sakai: longsight.com/technologies/sakai |
| **Virtual environments (MUVEs)** | Quest Atlantis: atlantisremixed.org<br>Sloodle: sloodle.org/ |

## Course Support Tools

Other tools are available to supplement CMS features, though some CMSs include their own versions of such tools. These include video environments, such as GoToMeeting and Elluminate Live, which allow groups of individuals to hear and see each other and exchange information such as PowerPoint presentations. Some online courses also use blogs, wikis, and other social media tools that are outside the CMS.

## Technical Support

Research on what makes online courses successful has indicated that providing continuous technical support and troubleshooting are as important as knowledgeable, trained instructors and students who are ready to learn in the less-structured environment of online courses. Nothing is more frustrating to students and instructors as encountering features or links that will not work as advertised or problems with accessing the course or its features. Some organizations provide a helpdesk that students and instructors may contact in the event of problems with a CMS.

## Support for Students with Special Needs

Online courses must be usable by students with special needs such as vision or hearing impairments. Enhancement to address these needs include ability to enlarge text; alternatives to mouse controls, such as special switches and joy sticks, for students with mobility issues; alternative keyboards; alternatives to videos (e.g., podcast descriptions) for students with visual deficits; and alternatives to text presentation (e.g., podcasts or text readers) in all areas for students with visual deficits. See the Adapting for Special Needs feature for more on this kind of support. All online courses must include these capabilities in order to meet **Universal Design for Learning (UDL)** requirements.

## Resources to Monitor Course Outcomes

One feature available in most CMSs is a **data dashboard,** or a location that summarizes course data in ways that allow instructors to track student participation and progress. For example, it summarizes statistics for each student and across assignments on the number of times students sign on

## Adapting for Special Needs

### Online Teaching and Learning: Online-Only Environments

Web accessibility is a critical aspect of effective website development and Web page design. Federal law requires all agencies receiving federal funds to demonstrate compliance with Web accessibility standards. When website designers fail to consider the needs of individuals with disabilities, they may use inappropriate design techniques, such as the following:

- Text may be inside an image, which makes it impossible to enlarge.
- Colors cannot be adjusted to improve text-to-background contrast.
- Alternatives to mouse controls are not provided for navigation.
- Text descriptions do not accompany visual images.

In these situations, equitable access is denied to individuals with disabilities since they are prevented from accessing the information that is available to their peers who do not have special needs. The following sites give useful information on how to design Web pages and websites for maximum accessibility:

- CSS Zen Garden (at the CSS Zen Garden website)—To experience how Cascading Style Sheets (CSS) can be used to alter how a Web page looks while maintaining the same content. This is an important advance as it means that users are able to apply their own style sheet to a web page to alter the readability in ways that are personally beneficial.
- Readability (at the Readability.com website)—To explore free tools for Web and mobile devices. Users will discover that they can enhance the reading experience by customizing the CSS they use to view Web-based information.
- Ten Quick Tests for Website Accessibility (at the UK's Webcredible website, search on "accessibility testing")—Describes 10 easy ways to assess the accessibility of a specific website.
- WAVE (at the Web AIM website)—A free, Web-based tool to help Web developers make their Web content more accessible.

*—Contributed by Dave Edyburn*

and how often they posted responses or products. Macfadyen and Dawson (2010) found that data dashboards are valuable not only to track progress and task completion but also to predict learning problems and help instructors identify which students might need extra help. For example, a data dashboard can identify **lurkers,** or students who sign on to and spend time in a course space but never post anything. There are various reasons for this behavior, but because it is nonproductive, it signals to the instructor that a personal communication with that student is in order.

## Resources and Strategies to Ensure Academic Integrity

Academic fraud is one of the main concerns with online courses. Instructors and administrators want tools in place that can help ensure that the students who are signed up for a course are actually the ones submitting work and taking tests. Four common strategies courses use to ensure this integrity are given here. Some programs use a combination of all these methods:

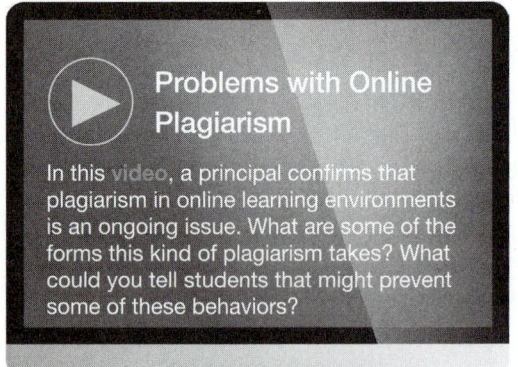

**Problems with Online Plagiarism**

In this video, a principal confirms that plagiarism in online learning environments is an ongoing issue. What are some of the forms this kind of plagiarism takes? What could you tell students that might prevent some of these behaviors?

1. **Online honor codes.** Some courses include an honor code in the syllabus that students must agree to before beginning the course. The instructor asks students to sign and submit a signed honor code via email or in an online posting.

2. **Information about plagiarism.** It is also helpful to include in the syllabus information and examples on what constitutes plagiarism violations and the repercussions for students who commit them. Students do not always know what is and is not permitted, so this kind of information often proves instructive.

3. **Student discussions about academic integrity.** Some courses have an initial online discussion about the importance of academic integrity. The discussion may be as a whole class or small-group-based, and usually poses a question such as "Who does cheating cheat?" or "A person of integrity: What does that mean?"

4. **Physical monitoring systems.** Finally, some technologies make it possible to ascertain the identity of individuals completing assessments for online courses. Video monitoring systems may be used to proctor student work at a distance (Shaffer, 2012). Other tools fall under the general heading of **biometric monitoring systems,** or tools to take physical readings from a student's body to ascertain identify. Rodchua, Yiadom-Boakye, and Woolsey (2011) say that these systems include fingerprint, retina, and facial identification.

**TECHNOLOGY LEARNING CHECK**

Complete TLC 8.2 to review what you have learned from reading this section about required resources for online courses.

# DEVELOPING ONLINE COURSES: PROCEDURES

Designing online environments takes considerable expertise in applying a variety of different strategies for presenting instruction and assessing learned skills. As with the Technology Integration in Action example that opened this chapter, sometimes those who teach the course have little to no control over the course design. When they are able to design "from scratch," designers can use the following recommended 10-step sequence, based on Roblyer's (2015) recommendations.

## Step 1: Select the Online Model

A course with a noninteractive model will have a far different design than one based on one of the interactive ones, and each model has a unique presentation. Thus, the decision on which model to use has far-reaching impact on other choices related to course structure and design.

## Step 2: Design and Document Learning Activities

This step also calls for a critical set of decisions on the instructional design of the course: what students will need to do to achieve course objectives. There is no cookbook-type strategy for completing this set of activities. If a course is being transferred from in-person to online format, it will likely retain some of the structural aspects (e.g., objectives, how many content units there are, and in which order students will go through them), but most actual learning activities will change substantially to support learning in the online format. See Roblyer (2015) for key concepts and advice on making informed instructional design decisions for online environments.

After activities are designed, they are documented in a detailed course syllabus, which provides an overview of course structure, requirements, and expectations. A comprehensive syllabus usually includes:

- Details such as instructor name
- Contact information (e.g., office address, email, phone number)
- Office hours and meeting dates and times (if any)
- Catalog description and course topics and objectives
- Required and recommended course materials
- Graded activities
- Grading criteria and grading scale
- Weekly course schedule
- Policies governing academic integrity, confidentiality, and appropriate behavior in the course space
- Other information such as access guidelines for students with disabilities and how to drop a course

Ko and Rossen (2012) say that the syllabus should also make clear how often students are required to visit or interact in the course space.

## Step 3: Create Course Space Structure

In this step, the decisions made in Step 2 take shape in the course space. Studies show that the single most important quality of an effective course space is how it encourages and manages interaction (Roblyer & Wiencke, 2004). Moore (1986) was first to identify three kinds of interaction: learner–content, learner–instructor, and learner–learner. In noninteractive models, interaction is exclusively learner–content. Moore (1993) also said that activities must be structured to address what he called **transactional distance**, or the potential gap in communications between instructors and learners that must be bridged for most students to learn successfully. Online courses bridge this distance through the following types of communication and information posted in the course space.

### Learner–content interaction.
The course space must be designed to require and support students to engage with materials that carry the course content. This usually means that students cannot merely read text or view videos; they must do activities that show they have understood them. The course space must communicate clearly what the activities are, where they are located in the course space, and what students are required to do with them. This is the only type of interaction that is required for all course models. One popular way to begin student engagement with the content is through a scavenger hunt that requires them to locate items such as words or images in various parts of the course space. As they locate items, they also learn the course space structure and where various kinds of resources are located. Their first assignment in this activity would be to create a document that shows the scavenger hunt answers and submit it in the required area.

### Learner–instructor interaction.
In most online or blended courses, learners will also interact with instructors. The course space must provide locations for this to occur (e.g., chatrooms or instant-messaging areas) and make sure students know where they are and how to use them. Some courses also announce **virtual office hours**, in which the instructor is available (usually via course space options such as chatrooms) to answer questions immediately.

To keep from having to answer the same question multiple times for different students via email, it is a good idea to have an asynchronous area of the course where students and instructors can interact with posted messages. In this space, when a student asks a question, everyone sees both the question and the instructor's answer. If a student emails a question instead of posting it in the course space, the instructor thanks the student for the question and asks him or her to post it in the designated course space so that everyone will see the question and answer. After one or two such emails, students learn to communicate in the "Ask the Instructor" space.

### Learner–learner interaction.

The final kind of interaction is not required in every course but has become more popular as studies have confirmed the power of students learning with and from each other. Opportunities for social interaction in course spaces are also important, because non-online students often learn from each other in outside-class situations such as libraries and coffee shops. Online courses are often designed to emulate and promote this social interaction. The following are some ways to accomplish learner–learner interaction:

- **An "introduce yourself" forum.** Just as in-person courses sometimes open with an activity to help students get to know each other, effective course spaces provide an engaging opening activity that gets students talking to each other on a social level. Some example introduction strategies are shown in Figure 8.1. These strategies serve to get students talking with each other and give them nonthreatening, hands-on experience with how an online discussion works.

- **A "learner lounge" forum.** This is a location for social talk on anything of interest to the students, such as movie reviews, recipes, links to topics of interest, or comments about what they are learning. Students can post items of interest there throughout the course.

- **Discussion groups.** With the exception of social forums such as the learner lounge, it is difficult to engage in a whole-class discussion because threads can get very long and hard to follow. Instead, effective courses break up students into small groups of three to six students and post discussion topics there. Recommendations for managing small groups are given later in this chapter under Teaching Online Courses.

## FIGURE 8.1 Example Opening Activities to Promote Social Interaction in Online Courses

IdeaStepConceptStock/Shutterstock

**Ask students to post the following and reply to each other as they see common links:**

- Make an acrostic with the letters of their first name. Each word should be something that could describe them.
- Tell why they want to become a teacher (or whatever they are studying to be).
- Provide a link to where they work, go to church, or another location that is important to them and give a little background on it.
- Post a photo of themselves (or an image or cartoon character they want to represent them) and give a paragraph of personal background.
- Post a photo of their pet(s) and tell a little about them.
- Post two things they feel are most important to know about them.
- Describe their proudest (or scariest, most inspiring, etc.) moment.
- Tell their three most important life goals.
- Name their favorite book and why they liked it.
- Tell which sports teams they cheer for and why.

## Step 4: Create Assignment Materials

This tells students the course structure and how they will use it. It should be a step-by-step sequence, but it is frequently set it up by content units. See Figure 8.2 for an example assignments area.

## Step 5: Create Assessment Materials

All products and activities for which students are graded must have an instrument that lets students know the expectations; this includes discussion assignments. Figure 8.3 shows an example rubric for assessing student performance in online discussion forums. All instruments must be placed in course space locations that are clearly labeled so students will know where to locate them. Note that the "ROLE Model" shown at the bottom of Figure 8.3 provides helpful netiquette, or guidelines for posting messages to online services (e.g., email or discussion boards) to demonstrate courtesy and regard for other users.

## Step 6: Create Content Presentation Materials

In this step, create methods for presenting materials and information. In models that are completely online, new information must be delivered via one of the following options or a combination of them: posted documents, Web pages, videos or vodcasts of lectures, audios or podcasts, slide presentations (e.g., PowerPoints), and textbook reading assignments.

## Step 7: Create Small-Group Activities

Discussion activities have already been mentioned as a way to promote learner–learner interaction. Other small-group activities (e.g., webquests, research and/or presentation projects) can be placed in the same area of the course space. These may be designed so only group members can see their own area and cannot see each other's work, or they may be set up so that all groups are free to see each other's work. Each group's area must be clearly labeled with tasks and responsibilities for each group and group member. (See more on this work in the next section of this chapter.)

**FIGURE 8.2** Example Assignments Area in a Course Space

- **Unit 1: Weeks 1–3—*Learning Theories & Teaching Practice***
  - **Go to Teacher Lounge (on main Discussion Board) and do activities:** Introduce yourself, learn about your fellow students, learn how to evaluate and select websites for usefulness and information accuracy and integrity.
  - **Listen to Unit 1 overview audio and review Unit 1 Learning Module (click Documents button).**
  - **Readings and Exercises:** Read Ch. 1; answer questions.
  - **Discussion/Sharing #1 in Group Forum (click My Group Forum button):** Post required information in Group Forum.

- **Unit 2: Weeks 4–7—*Learning as Shaping Behavior and Memory***
  - **Listen to Unit 2 overview audio and review Unit 2 Learning Module (click Documents button).**
  - **Readings and Exercises:** Read Chs. 2 and 4; answer questions.
  - **Discussion/Sharing #2 in Group Forum (click My Group Forum button):** Post required information on chapter concepts, contribute to group summary product, post product in main Discussion Board.
  - **Take Midterm Exam (available end of Week 7).**

- **Unit 3: Weeks 8–11—*Social Environment and Human Development***
  - **Listen to Unit 3 overview audio and review Unit 3 Learning Module (click Documents button).**
  - **Readings and Exercises:** Read Chs. 3 and 8; answer questions.
  - **Discussion/Sharing #3 in Group Forum (click My Group Forum button):** Post required information on chapter concepts, contribute to the group summary product, and post product in main Discussion Board.

- **Unit 4: Weeks 12–16—*Constructivism & Knowledge Construction***
  - **Listen to Unit 4 overview audio and Review Unit 4 Learning Module (click Documents button).**
  - **Readings and Exercises:** Read Ch. 6 and Baines/Stanley article; answer questions.
  - **Discussion/Sharing #4 in Group Forum (click My Group Forum button):** Post required information on chapter concepts, contribute to the group discussion/debate.
  - **Final Project:** Complete projects and post in main Discussion Board (Final Product topic) for sharing with class.
  - **Take Final Exam (available end of Week 16).**

# FIGURE 8.3 Conference Participation Rubric

| Rubric for Guiding and Assessing Online Discussion Participation | | | | | |
|---|---|---|---|---|---|
| | Dimension #1: Timeliness of Interaction | Dimension #2: Frequency of Interaction | Dimension #3: Direction of Interaction | Dimension #4: Language Quality and Voice | Dimension #5: Quality of Contribution |
| **Level 1: Basic** (1 point for each dimension) | Joins discussion later than deadline. | Posts only one comment. | Posts only own comment(s); does not respond to anyone else's comments. | Comment(s) are poorly written and difficult to understand, too wordy, too terse, and/or at least one does not observe the ROLE Model.* | Comments are general and/or unrelated to discussion topic (e.g. "I agree!" or "I hear what you're saying."). |
| **Level 2: Low** (2 points for each dimension) | Joins by the deadline, but late enough that it does not leave time for good participation in the discussion. | Posts two comments but only at the beginning or end of the discussion period. | Posts own comments and responds once to another person's comment. | Comments are sometimes poorly written and difficult to understand, or are too wordy and rambling or terse. | Offers comments related to the topic but do not clearly reflect knowledge of topic or required content. |
| **Level 3: Medium** (3 points for each dimension) | Joins by the deadline, but is late in responding to other's postings. | Posts more than two comments but only at beginning or end of discussion period. | Posts own comments and responds more than once to other's comments or questions. | Comments are usually understandable but at least one is either wordy and rambling or terse. | Offers comments related to the topic and required content, but comments are not always very logical or helpful ones. |
| **Level 4: High** (4 points each dimension) | Posts well before the deadline to leave time for good participation in the discussion; responds fairly promptly to others' postings (within a day). | Posts more than two comments interspersed throughout the discussion period. | Posts own comments and responds more than once to other's postings and to any other questions directed at her or him. | Comments are always well formulated and articulate. | Offers comments that are directly related to the topic and content and are helpful, logical comments. |
| **Total =** ____/20 possible points | **Total on Timeliness of Interaction =** ____ of 4 points | **Total on Frequency of Interaction =** ____ of 4 points | **Total on Direction of Interaction =** ____ of 4 points | **Total on Language Quality and Voice =** ____ of 4 points | **Total on Quality of Contribution =** ____ of 4 points |

| **\* The ROLE Model** | **Grading Scale:** |
|---|---|
| 1. Make postings and responses friendly and helpful. | 18–20 points = Very good, A work |
| 2. Allow for differences of opinion; disagree in a professional way. | 16–17 points = Good, B work |
| 3. Always assume benign intent; request clarification when necessary. | 14–15 points = Average or C work |
| 4. Avoid sarcasm, which can often be misinterpreted. | Under 14 = Work below standards |
| 5. Never use profanity or "flaming" language, regardless of the situation. | |
| * Rules of Online Learning Etiquette | |

## Step 8: Create Resource Links and Other Materials

Online courses usually have incidental materials for enrichment and information, as well as other areas to support course assignments that have been posted previously under Step 4. These include links to websites outside the course space, locations for turning in completed exercises or assignments (e.g., dropbox), how to contact help in case of technical problems, and a gradebook area where students may keep track of grades.

## Step 9: Decide On and Signal the Course Path

To a student who enters a course space for the first time, nothing is self-evident; every course space is like entering a new town for the first time. Students who have used previous course spaces can usually figure out what to do, but there is no such thing as a course space that is too clear. To help students navigate, the instructor must signal a clear path: tell the student where to go first and how to learn where materials and activities are located in the space. This is usually done with an introductory email and announcements page. An introductory email is sent to students a week or two before the course opens and welcomes them and explains where to get a username and password, how to sign on and where to go first, and how to get technical assistance for sign-on issues. An announcements page appears automatically when the student signs on and gives detailed instructions on what to do.

## Step 10: Determine and Document Course Logistics and Requirements

Finally, decisions must be made and documented about how the course will be delivered. These include:

- **A timetable for displaying course components.** Decisions made at this point include:
  - Should the course be shown all at once or parts at a time?
  - After one part (e.g., a unit or discussion) is complete, should it be locked or removed from student view to prevent further comments or work?
- **Mid-course feedback.** Anonymous feedback from students gathered using CMS tools and solicited during the course helps spot problems or issues that may have an impact on coursework.
- **Requirements to visit course space.** Students must know how often and when they are expected to visit the course space. Decisions on this requirement depend on the content and the assignments that require interaction with other students.

**TECHNOLOGY LEARNING CHECK**
Complete TLC 8.3 to review what you have learned from reading this section about procedures for designing online courses.

# 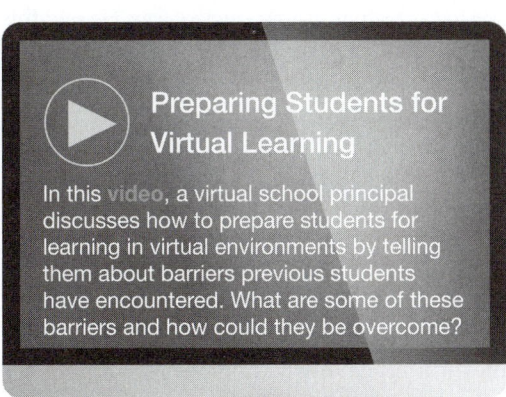 BEST PRACTICES FOR EFFECTIVE ONLINE COURSES

Decisions made about the design of a course space are intertwined with decisions on how the course will be taught. For example, setting up communications, assignments, assessment strategies, and a path students should take through the course determine in large part how instruction will take place. The instructor's role becomes one of managing the interactive activities set up in the course space. This management takes three forms: best practices for facilitating online programs, working with small groups, and assessing the quality of online courses. Each is discussed in this section.

## Best Practices for Teaching Online Programs

Stansbury (2014) reported on results of a survey to determine best practices and lessons learned from implementing online learning programs in K–12 schools. Respondents included school district administrators, curriculum directors, principals, and exemplary virtual teachers. They agreed that particular characteristics and methods need to be in place to ensure

Preparing Students for Virtual Learning

In this video, a virtual school principal discusses how to prepare students for learning in virtual environments by telling them about barriers previous students have encountered. What are some of these barriers and how could they be overcome?

that programs not only don't fail but are not mediocre. These critical characteristics include those discussed here.

Use tools to monitor progress. Because teachers cannot rely on a student's verbal responses or body language to indicate difficulties, monitoring tools must be in place to indicate when students are having problems with assignments. This is crucial because studies have shown that students who fall behind are more likely to drop the course.

Have personnel available to assist struggling students. Though monitoring tools can provide feedback, teachers and mentors are the ones who must interact with students to address their needs. One administrator reported that "the most successful teachers are those who build relationships with students," which is why districts often have on-site mentors who can help students with everything from how to log in to how to use the technology required to take the class. Another administrator said her district provides three tiers of support: an online teacher, a content teacher or a learning mentor, and an online tutor available round the clock every day.

Employ well-trained online instructors. Effective online teachers not only need to know how to teach an online course, they also need to have personality traits and communication skills that lend themselves to online work. For example, teachers must know techniques for communicating well with students they may never see and knowing which students need special assistance. Stansbury (2014) notes that hiring online teachers is different from hiring traditional ones. In addition to the usual characteristics of good teachers, online teachers must be even more self-directed and possess extremely strong technology and people skills. Teachers must also have frequent professional development to build their online skills.

Offer rigorous and engaging curriculum. Engaging curriculum is one that keeps students interested and provides a variety of methods of delivering content. Lacking face-to-face contact with engaging teachers, students need hands-on activities that require frequent interaction.

Provide students with preparation and clear expectations. Past studies have indicated that students who fail in online courses frequently have inaccurate expectations of what an online course entails. The survey respondents acknowledged that training students in how to use the course technology and making sure they know what they have to do to pass the course can make the difference between success and failure.

## Best Practices for Managing Online Small-group Work

Small-group work is a frequently used strategy in interactive online courses, but it is not easy to do effectively. Students tend to dislike it because it requires depending on others whose schedules may be different than their own and who may not complete the work for which the group is responsible. There are several best practices for supporting group work in ways that make it more efficient and productive.

Tuckman (1965) said that before small groups can work well together, group members usually go through a process of learning how to relate to each other in a productive way. He said this process has four stages: forming (testing), storming (intragroup conflict), norming (developing group cohesion), and performing (productive work). His observations were based primarily on adult therapy groups, but these stages may also occur in younger collaborative groups as early as middle-school age. Online instructors can take several measures to make sure groups go through formation stages and more quickly to effective collaboration. The following recommendations for how to do this are based on Roblyer (2015):

1. Assign the group a clearly stated problem, and show them how they will be graded.
2. Assign roles and specific responsibilities for each group member.
3. Have groups begin by agreeing on some "norms" (e.g., how they will resolve issues such as someone not doing their "job" and when they will ask an instructor for help).
4. Encourage group cohesion by asking the group members to agree on a group name.
5. Monitor all group activities, but intercede in group work only when necessary.

If one of the course objectives is for students to learn how to work collaboratively to solve a problem or produce a product, several instruments are available to assess this ability. Visit Collaboration Rubrics at the website Kathy Schrock's Guide to Everything: Assessments and Rubrics.

## Best Practices for Assessing Quality of Online Courses

Several rubrics and checklists are available to assess the quality of distance courses. Roblyer and Wiencke (2004) developed a postcourse evaluation instrument that focuses on five characteristics to promote interaction: social/rapport-building designs, instructional designs for interaction, interactivity of instructional resources, and evidence of learner and instructor engagement. See this rubric in Figure 8.4.

In addition, the Quality Matters program is a faculty-centered, peer review process designed to certify the quality of distance learning courses. Quality Matters has developed a set of 40 elements that are distributed across the following eight broad standards. It is these elements that are used to evaluate the design of online and hybrid courses:

1. Course Overview and Introduction
2. Learning Objectives
3. Assessment and Measurement
4. Resources and Materials
5. Learner Engagement
6. Course Technology
7. Learner Support
8. Accessibility

Finally, the Rubric for Online Instruction, designed and hosted online by California State University–Chico, focuses on the following characteristics:

- Learner Support and Resource
- Instructional Design and Delivery
- Innovative Teaching with Technology
- Online Organization and Design
- Assessment and Evaluation of Student Learning
- Faculty Use of Student Feedback

**TECHNOLOGY LEARNING CHECK**
Complete TLC 8.4 to review what you have learned from reading this section about best practices for online courses and programs.

#  VIRTUAL SCHOOLS

**Virtual schools** is the term usually used to refer to the K–12 version of distance learning, though the literature on this area also uses the term **cyberschools** (Watson, Murin, Vashaw, Gemin, & Rapp, 2013) or simply **online schools**. This section reviews background on these schools, as well as implementation trends, issues, and research findings.

## Background on Virtual Schools

Prior to 1996, online learning was limited primarily to postsecondary institutions, but schools established in 1994 by Utah and in 1996 by Florida began a movement that accelerated quickly. By 2014, virtual schools were considered a permanent and accepted part of

# FIGURE 8.4 Rubric for Assessing Interactive Quality of Distance Courses

**RUBRIC DIRECTIONS:** The rubric shown below has five (5) separate elements that contribute to a course's level of interaction and interactivity. For each of these five elements, circle a description below it that applies best to your course. After reviewing all elements and circling the appropriate level, add up the points to determine the course's level of interactive qualities (e.g., low, moderate, or high)

| | |
|---|---|
| Low interactive qualities | **1–9 points** |
| Moderate interactive qualities | **10–17 points** |
| High interactive qualities | **18–25 points** |

| Scale (see points below) | Element #1: Social/Rapport-Building Designs for Interaction | Element #2: Instructional Designs for Interaction | Element #3: Interactivity of Technology Resources | Element #4: Evidence of Learner Engagement | Element #5: Evidence of Instructor Engagement |
|---|---|---|---|---|---|
| **Low Interactive Qualities (1 point each)** | The instructor does not encourage students to get to know one another on a personal basis. No activities require social interaction, or are limited to brief introductions at the beginning of the course. | Instructional activities do not require two-way interaction between the instructor and students; they call for one-way delivery of information (e.g., instructor lectures, text delivery) and student products based on the information. | Fax, Web pages, or other technology resource allows one-way delivery of information (text and/or graphics). | By the end of course, most students (50–75%) *reply to* messages from the instructor, but only when required; messages are sometimes unresponsive to topics and tend to be either brief or wordy and rambling. | Instructor responds only randomly to student queries; responses usually take more than 48 hours; feedback is brief and provides little analysis of student work or suggestions for improvement. |
| **Minimum Interactive Qualities (2 points each)** | In addition to brief introductions, the instructor requires one other exchange of personal information among students, (e.g., written bio of personal background and experiences). | Instructional activities require students to communicate with the instructor on an individual basis only (e.g., asking/responding to instructor questions). | Email, listserv, conference/bulletin board or other technology resource allows two-way, asynchronous exchanges of information (text and graphics). | By the end of course, most students (50–75%) *reply to* messages from the instructor and other students, both when required and on a voluntary basis; replies are usually responsive to topics but often are either brief or wordy and rambling. | Instructor responds to most student queries; responses usually are within 48 hours; feedback sometimes offers some analysis of student work and suggestions for improvement. |
| **Moderate Interactive Qualities (3 points each)** | In addition to providing for exchanges of personal information among students, the instructor provides at least one other in-class activity designed to increase communication and social rapport among students. | In addition to requiring students to communicate with the instructor, instructional activities require students to communicate with one another (e. g., discussions in pairs or small groups). | In addition to technologies used for two-way asynchronous exchanges of information, chatroom, or other technology allows synchronous exchanges of primarily written information. | By the end of course, all or nearly all students (90–100%) are *replying to* messages from the instructor and other students, both when required and voluntarily; replies are always responsive to topics but sometimes are either brief or wordy and rambling. | Instructor responds to all student queries; responses usually are within 48 hours; feedback usually offers some analysis of student work and suggestions for improvement. |
| **Above Average Interactive Qualities (4 points each)** | In addition to providing for exchanges of personal information among students and encouraging | In addition to requiring students to communicate with the instructor, instructional activities require students to | In addition to technologies used for two-way synchronous and asynchronous exchanges of written information, additional | By the end of course, most students (50–75%) *both reply to and initiate* messages when required and | Instructor responds to all student queries; responses usually are prompt (i.e., within 24 hours); feedback always offers detailed |

| Scale (see points below) (*cont.*) | Element #1: Social/Rapport-Building Designs for Interaction (*cont.*) | Element #2: Instructional Designs for Interaction (*cont.*) | Element #3: Interactivity of Technology Resources (*cont.*) | Element #4: Evidence of Learner Engagement (*cont.*) | Element #5: Evidence of Instructor Engagement (*cont.*) |
|---|---|---|---|---|---|
| | communication and social interaction, the instructor also interacts with students on a social/personal basis. | develop products by working together cooperatively (e.g., in pairs or small groups) and sharing feedback. | technologies (e.g., teleconferencing) allow one-way visual and two-way voice communications between the instructor and students. | voluntarily; messages are detailed and responsive to topics, and usually reflect an effort to communicate well. | analysis of student work and suggestions for improvement. |
| **High Level of Interactive Qualities (5 points each)** | In addition to providing for exchanges of information and encouraging student–student and instructor–student interaction, the instructor provides ongoing course structures designed to promote social rapport among students and the instructor. | In addition to requiring students to communicate with the instructor, instructional activities require students to develop products by working together cooperatively (e.g., in pairs or small groups) and share results and feedback with other groups in the class. | In addition to technologies to allow two-way exchanges of text information, visual technologies such as two-way video or videoconferencing technologies allow synchronous voice and visual communications between the instructor and students and among students. | By the end of course, all or nearly all students (90–100%) both *reply to and initiate messages*, both when required and voluntarily; messages are detailed, responsive to topics, and are well-developed communications. | Instructor responds to all student queries; responses are always prompt (i.e. within 24 hours); feedback always offers detailed analysis of student work and suggestions for improvement, along with additional hints and information to supplement learning. |
| **Total Each:** | _____ pts. | _____ pts. | _____ pts. | _____ pts. | _____ pts. |
| **TOTAL :** | _____ pts. | | | | |

mainstream U. S. education. In the 2013 version of the annual *Keeping Pace with K12 Online and Blended Learning* report, Watson, et al. classified virtual schools by the following six types:

1. **Single-district programs.** These are created by a district and serve only that district's students.

2. **Blended schools.** In these schools, attendance is required at a physical site during the school year but the curriculum is delivered in a blended form (partially in-person and partially online). Many of these are charter schools.

3. **Multidistrict fully online schools.** These schools are the primary providers for their students, who may (but need not) attend a physical school for part of their education. Schools that serve more than half of all fully online students are operated by **education management organizations (EMOs)**. These include Advanced Academics, Connections Academy, Insight Schools, K12 Inc., Mosaica, and Provost Academy (Watson, 2013).

4. **Consortium programs.** These are developed by districts or other organizations that combine resources in order to serve their students more efficiently. Districts join the consortium in order to serve their students without needing to create their own virtual school.

5. **State-supported supplemental options.** These include two different subcategories of online options: state-run virtual schools (e.g., the Florida Virtual School) that serve students both inside the state and elsewhere, and course-choice options that allow students in the state to take courses from any of a number of different providers.

6. **Private/independent schools.** As the name implies, these are nonpublic, nonprofit schools developed with private funds or endowments.

▲ Some virtual school students access courses from home and some from a school computer lab where they meet for a regularly scheduled school session. **Left: Annie Pickert Fuller/Pearson Education; Right: Sophie Bluy/Pearson Education**

Students participate in virtual school courses from various locations. For example, some students take them from home or a library, while others attend a school computer lab for a regularly scheduled session each day and access their courses in that way. Annual reviews by the Southern Regional Education Board (SREB, 2013) and Watson et al. (2013) revealed several trends discussed here.

### Single-district and multidistrict online schools growing.

Watson et al. (2013) say that the number of new district-level virtual school initiatives has grown every year. The SREB report confirms this trend, noting that "some states require districts to provide online courses to their students, while others require that districts allow students to take online courses from the state-run virtual schools" (p. 2). Other reports (Miron, Horvitz, & Gulosino, 2013) show that the number of students served by multidistrict schools that are supported by EMOS such as K12 Inc. are growing rapidly.

### Quality-control measures are growing.

After reports of underperforming virtual schools in some states (Hubbard & Mitchell, 2011; Miron et al., 2013), more states seem to be instituting accountability measures to ensure virtual school quality (SREB, 2013).

### Online-learning graduation requirement trend growing slowly.

The innovation begun by Michigan to require that students have an online course experience for high school graduation also continues to grow, but much more slowly. Four states now require an online learning experience to earn a high school diploma. Michigan was the first to adopt the measure, followed by Alabama, Florida, and Virginia. Idaho also passed a law requiring an online course for graduation but repealed it in 2012. Watson et al. (2013) say that North Carolina and Arkansas are also exploring such a requirement. Several individual school districts have this requirement; this district-level trend may be growing faster than the statewide requirement.

## Virtual School Issues

Although an increasingly popular strategy, K–12 virtual courses and programs have ongoing challenges. The National Education Policy Center (NEPC) at the University of Colorado, Boulder developed a series of reports that analyze the performance of full-time, publicly funded K–12 virtual schools in terms of policy issues and research evidence. Huerta, Rice, and Shafer

(2013) discuss policy issues in one of the NEPC reports. The following issues are based on their report and on those of Miron et al. (2013) and Watson et al. (2013). Because virtual schools are having an increasing impact on the operations of all schools, teachers and administrators should be prepared to take a position on each of these virtual school issues

**Program quality and accountability.** Huerta et al. (2013) say that "Quality of content, quality and quantity of instruction, and quality of student achievement are all important aspects of program quality" (p. 7). They find that structures to ensure quality monitoring of these aspects vary considerable and are often insufficient to give policy makers information they need to make future decisions. Outcome measures that are available are sometimes less than positive. For example, Miron et al. (2013) report that "the on-time graduation rate for the full-time virtual schools was less than half the national average: 37.6% and 79.4%, respectively" (p. 12).

**Curriculum alignment.** To be awarded credit, virtual school curriculum standards have to be aligned to state and local standards where the students reside. This is especially difficult when students from a given virtual school come from more than one state.

**Teacher certification.** To ensure they are qualified, online teachers must receive certification from a state agency. Schools must either identify one agency or accept teachers from several different certifying agencies.

**Program accreditation.** Course credit can be granted either by the virtual school or the school district, and accrediting agencies have emerged to certify online schools. However, it is sometimes difficult to tell if the agency itself is reliable.

**Funding formulas.** Virtual schools typically receive an amount for each successful virtual school students, and Huerta et al. find that funding formulas vary considerably from state to state. Two funding issues they cite are the need to tie funding to actual virtual school costs and the need to prevent "profiteering" by for-profit EMOs, which serve about two-thirds of full-time virtual school students. Lawsuits that have arisen over virtual schools' use of public funds sometimes point to the fact that home-schooled students who use virtual school courses do so at public expense. Huerta et al. find that "as students move across district and county lines, their resident districts struggle to monitor which virtual schools are providing substantive education services to which students" (p. 5). Thus, they recommend a greater state-level role in auditing virtual course use and allocating funds accordingly. Ash (2014) also discussed similar funding issues for virtual charter schools.

**Consequences for virtual school students.** Possible negative effects of virtual schooling on students' socialization have been cited (Davis, 2011). Also, the dropout rate is usually higher for online courses, and it has become clear that not all students can succeed online without prior help. Successful online students seem to need more than the usual degree of organizational skills and self-motivation, as well as better-than-average computer skills. Online students must also be afforded ready and reliable access to technology resources, which may place children in lower socio-economic classes at a disadvantage. While it may expand educational access for many, there have been questions about whether distance learning is a realistic option for underserved students, and if this contributes to widening the opportunity gap in education (Miron et al., 2013).

## Virtual School Research

Several studies have yielded valuable insights on the growth of the virtual school movement and how virtual school outcomes compare with those of traditional schools. These are important trends for educators to follow, not only because they describe a changing job

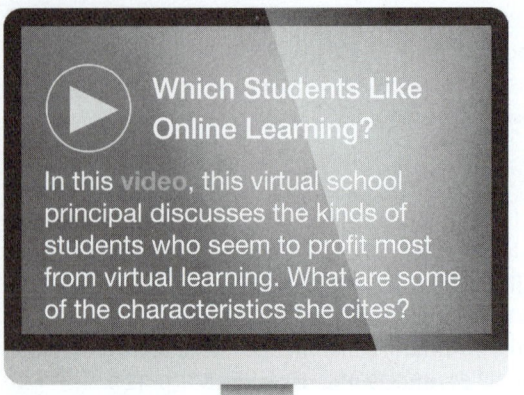

**Which Students Like Online Learning?**

In this video, this virtual school principal discusses the kinds of students who seem to profit most from virtual learning. What are some of the characteristics she cites?

market for K–12 teachers, but also because they may determine skills teachers may be expected to have in the near future. Studies also provide good information on best practices in online courses and programs. Though best practices for postsecondary distance education generally apply for virtual schools, studies specific to virtual schools have also provided K12-specific information on what works best at this level. All information on best practices can guide educators who design online courses and teach in virtual schools.

### Descriptive reviews of virtual schools.

The last report from the U.S. Department of Education's National Center for Education Statistics that focused exclusively on virtual schools described the characteristics of schools, district's monitoring policies, and enrollment figures during the 2009–2010 school year (Queen, Lewis, & Coopersmith, 2011). It found that 55% of U.S. school districts had students enrolled in distance courses, and 95% of those were at the high school level. It also found there were 1,816,400 enrollments in distance education courses, and 79% of districts reported enrolling 100 or fewer students.

### Comparing performance of virtual school and traditional schools.

Another national study commissioned by the U.S. Department of Education (Means et al., 2010) did a meta-analysis of experimental studies that compared outcomes of traditional, in-person courses with those of distance courses. They focused only on studies that could meet their rigorous research design requirements and that provided adequate information on learning outcomes to calculate the required meta-analysis information. However, only five such studies at the K–12 level could be located that met their criteria and, thus, recommended caution in generalizing results to the K–12 population.

Studies by Miron and Urschel (2012) and Miron, Horvitz, and Gulosino (2013) have provided more concrete, albeit controversial, insights about virtual school performance. Miron and Urschel focused exclusively on outcomes of schools operated by K12, Inc. the single largest for-profit provider of virtual courses. They found that when compared with the general student population in the states where they operated, students in K12 Inc. courses were more likely to be white (75% versus 55%), less likely to be from poor families (i.e., to qualify for free or reduced lunch: 40% versus 47%), and much less likely to be English language learners (.3% versus 13.8%). They also found the K12 Inc. courses had weak performance outcomes on several measures. For example, only 27.7% of K12 schools reported meeting Adequate Yearly Progress (AYP) in 2010–2011, as compared to 52% nationwide; and as mentioned previously, the on-time graduation rate was 49.1%, compared with a national rate of 79.4%. (See Hot Topic Debate.)

Miron, Horvitz, and Gulosino also used publicly available federal and state data to focus on all public virtual schools, this time seeking to determine the number of full-time virtual schools operating in the United States, the number of students they enroll and their demographic characteristics, and how full-time virtual schools perform in terms of student achievement as compared with other public schools. They found approximately the same demographic proportion as in their other study: 75% versus 54% nonwhite. The number of virtual school students qualifying for free or reduced lunch was 35% in virtual schools and 45% in other schools. The number of full-time virtual schools meeting AYP was about 24% versus 52% in virtual schools. Finally, the on-time graduation rate for the full-time virtual schools was 37.6% versus the national average of 79.4%. The study authors point out that the nature of virtual schools is evolving rapidly, and that performance outcomes could vary from the 2011–12 data that was available to them. Thus, their studies could point the way toward future studies that both seek to explain findings and control for other relevant factors.

K–12 online courses and programs have been found to meet a need for students who wish to study advanced levels of content (e.g., Advanced Placement or AP courses) and special topic courses (e.g., Russian or Chinese languages) that are not available to many schools because they cannot afford teachers for the relatively few who want to take these courses. At the same time, studies have found that students in at least one large virtual school were more likely to be white and from wealthier families and much less likely to be speakers of English as a second language (Miron et al., 2013). Other studies have found that black and Hispanic students registered for virtual courses in lower numbers when compared with the state's population, yet tended to drop out of such courses in proportionately higher numbers (Miron, & Urschel, 2012). In light of these findings, what arguments can you bring to the debate that virtual schools are widening, rather than addressing, the digital divide. What can be done to alleviate such a problem?

**Best practices for virtual schools.** Studies confirm that high interaction is an essential ingredient for virtual school success. A study examining a statewide virtual high school conducted by Oliver, Osborne, Patel, and Kleiman (2009) indicated that online students value high levels of interaction and feedback from teachers, content delivered in multiple modalities, and a mix of opportunities to communicate both synchronously and asynchronously with others. An in-depth study of K–12 virtual school teachers' beliefs and practices conducted by DiPietro (2010) indicated that increased interaction with the teacher and others leads to increased perceptions of students' engagement with the content, and ultimately, a more positive learning experience. Clearly, to maintain and support the motivation necessary for success in distance learning courses, teachers must build in and maintain high levels of interaction with students.

Finally, virtual schools have begun to recognize the potential for social isolation due to online learning. Consequently, they have begun adding face-to-face experiences to address the need for socialization in young people (Davis, 2011).

**TECHNOLOGY LEARNING CHECK**

Complete **TLC 8.5** to review what you have learned from reading this section about virtual schools and virtual diploma programs.

# VIRTUAL REALITY ENVIRONMENTS

The potential of virtual reality (VR) systems to make cyberspace seem real has been talked about since William Gibson's 1984 novel, *Neuromancer*, in which people used **avatars**, or graphic icons, to represent themselves in virtual environments. Until recently, however, that potential has been tapped more for video games than for education. That is changing as better, more useful educational tools become available. Three types of environments are described here, along with integration strategies for them. Also, a sample of these virtual tools is shown in the Top Ten Virtual Education Environments.

## Types of Virtual Reality Environments

Three types of **virtual reality (VR)** environments are described here: full immersion environments, multi-user virtual environments (MUVE), screen-based VR, and 3-D models. Only the latter three have seen much use in schools.

**FIGURE 8.5** Example of a Virtual Reality Immersion Activity

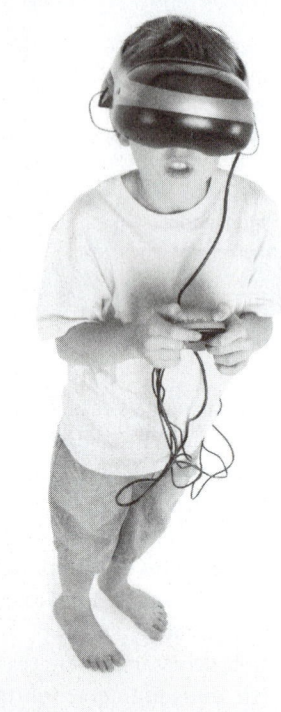

Leah-Anne Thompson/Shutterstock

**FIGURE 8.6** Opening Page from the Quest Atlantis MUVE

**Full immersion systems.** These are not often used in education, though they are typically what people envision when they think of VR. In **full immersion systems**, the user places a headset (e.g., goggles or a helmet) over the eyes. Known as a **head-mounted display (HMD)**, this headset is the channel through which the wearer "sees" the computer-generated environment. Other configurations use a large curved projection screen to immerse the user in the environment. In both VR systems, views of the "real" world are replaced with views of the virtual one, and the senses create an illusion of actually being in the environment the system displays. Other devices for full immersion systems include sound and tactile or **haptic interfaces** such as a data glove. See an example of a boy engaged in a VR activity in Figure 8.5. Though there were many articles and high hopes for immersive VR in the 1990s, these systems have made few inroads into K–12 education, and are still mainly a topic for military and industry research and experimentation.

**Multi-user virtual environments (MUVE).** Although not as realistic as full immersion VR, **MUVEs** are Web-based VR in which users have their avatars meet in 3-D environments on a computer screen; it costs much less to implement than immersive VR and has the added advantage of allowing several people to use it at the same time. The technical requirements for creating MUVEs limited their use in education until 2003, when Linden Labs released the online VR environment Second Life, an online virtual world created entirely by its users. In such "worlds," users create an avatar to represent their digital presence; then they explore the digital world to connect and collaborate with others, build houses and communities, and even sell items in the environment in exchange for real money.

K–12 educators had high hopes that Second Life would become a teaching platform for schools, but it is considered primarily an adult learning environment, and its use in education has been limited and is usually in postsecondary courses. Similar virtual environments have been designed especially for children and teenagers, and these are seeing more use in schools. For example, students in various physical locations can use their avatars in Quest Atlantis to solve various problems posed in scenarios (see Figure 8.6). See other free virtual environments listed in the Open Source Options feature.

**Web-based VR.** Like MUVEs, **Web-based VR**s are 3-D environments viewed on a computer screen, but they are designed for use by one person at a time. These environments are usually found in applications for students with physical or cognitive disabilities. These are also sometimes referred to as immersive environments, but they offer a different immersive experience than full immersion systems with HMDs. However, the technology is changing quickly in this area, and Sony's decision to add an HMD to its PlayStation (Martin, 2014) may signal a trend toward merging the capabilities of full immersion and web-based VR.

**3-D models.** These are made possible with sophisticated software that creates three-dimensional replicas of objects or locations. The products are then viewed on a flat screen computer (as opposed to an immersive environment). Some 3-D models are transferred to be viewed via Web browsers, as described above. **Virtual manipulatives**, or replicas of real manipulatives that are accessed via the Internet (Li & Ma, 2010), are one of the most popular types of 3-D models. The National Center for Virtual Manipulatives at Utah State University has a large collection of these tools to support math and science topics, along with instructions for teachers on how to use them. Wang, Kenzie, McGuire, and Pan (2010) find that virtual manipulatives support inquiry learning by allowing children to "manipulate representations by flipping, turning, or rotating objects (e.g., geometric shapes), helpful for reinforcing critical mathematics skills, such as numbers and operations, algebra, geometry, and measurement" (p. 385).

## Example 8.1

TITLE: IMMERSE YOURSELF IN THE SMITHSONIAN

CONTENT AREA/TOPIC: History and geology

GRADE LEVELS: All grades

ISTE STANDARDS•S: Standard 2—Communication and Collaboration; Standard 3—Research and Information Fluency; Standard 6—Technology Operations and Concepts

CCSS: CCSS.ELA-LITERACY.RI.3.3, CCSS.ELA-LITERACY. SL.8.5, CCSS.ELA-LITERACY.RI.11-12.4, CCSS.ELA-LITERACY. RI.11-12.7

DESCRIPTION: Students take a tour through the museum in a 3-D environment made up of panoramic pictures of actual

Smithsonian exhibits. They use their computer mouse to "walk" through the museum room by room, while camera icons throughout the museum show them hot spots where they can get close to an exhibit panel. Exhibits include the ocean hall, ancient seas, dinosaurs, early life, fossils, plants, mammals, African cultures, the Ice Age, Western cultures, reptiles, insects, butterflies, bones, geology, gems, and minerals. The teacher forms small groups of two or three students, each of which is assigned an exhibit to explore. Then they become the expert on their exhibit, acting as a tour guide for the class as their exhibit is projected on an interactive whiteboard or screen.

SOURCE: Based on a concept from the Teaching Community virtual field trip lesson plans website: http://teaching.monster.com/education/articles/8847-5-best-virtual-field-trips.

## Integration Strategies for Virtual Environments

VR is generating interest as a tool that can meet many kinds of instructional needs. Some of the more common classroom applications of VR resources are described here.

Virtual field trips.    Teachers use "3-D tours" of famous locations to take virtual field trips as substitutes for actual field trips when the latter are not accessible to students. Popular sites include museums, and famous landmarks and buildings, and national parks. The Digital Human Library provides a listing of many 3-D tours that teachers may use. An example virtual field trip using the Smithsonian Museum's 3-D resources is shown in Technology Integration Example 8.1.

3-D models to illustrate how systems work.    Although still limited to more technical topics in the areas of mathematics, science, architecture, and engineering, 3-D modeling is experiencing increased use in education as a way to help students visualize mathematics and science concepts. Example models are described to study characteristics of the solar system and processes of photosynthesis. Bradley and Farland-Smith (2010) say that 3-D models are an important resource for science, helping teach common high school concepts like "Punnett square, cell membranes, photosynthesis, and microscope usage" (p. 34). Sun, Lin, and Wang (2010) report good results with using a 3-D model to help children learn abstract concepts related to movements of the earth, sun, and moon.

Immersive practice and exploration.    In education, Web-based VR systems are seen primarily in university settings, but there has been considerable interest in the research community for testing these environments in special education to allow students to practice skills in a realistic but safe setting. For example, Subrahmaniyan et al., (2012) describe studies with a Web-based environment to improve visual-motor integration in children with learning disabilities. Using a haptic robotic device that permits them to simulate objects and environments virtually, they allowed children to participate in game-based activities and concluded that they had promise for occupational therapy. Ke and Im (2013) described research with a virtual-reality–based program to teach social interaction and communication strategies to children with high functioning autism. Inman, Loge, Cram, and Peterson (2011) report successful use of a virtual reality program to help children with physical disabilities learn to use a wheelchair.

### Virtual collaboration and problem solving.

MUVEs can be used to carry out constructivist lessons to allow students to work together to explore content and solve problems. For example, the Quest Atlantis MUVE shown in Figure 8.6 focuses on science topics. One activity has students working together to "analyze a water quality problem through using data collected in a virtual park."

**TECHNOLOGY LEARNING CHECK**

Complete **TLC 8.6** to review what you have learned from reading this section about virtual learning environments and how to integrate them.

# COLLABORATE, DISCUSS, REFLECT

Monkey Business/Fotolia

**The following questions may be used either for in-class, small-group discussions or may be used to initiate discussions in blogs or online discussion boards:**

1. In Aoun's (2011) article, "Learning today: The lasting value of place," he cites predictions that "place-based" learning (i.e., brick-and-mortar sites) will be less important due to the increasing popularity of online learning. However, he feels that this view is oversimplified and that despite the increase in online learning, place-based education is central to receiving a good education. Make a table of the pros and cons of learning at a distance versus learning in a physical location. Analyze your table in order to address the question, "What will be the place of place-based learning in future education?" Is the answer different for K–12 students than it is for college students?

2. Socialization is an important goal of K–12 schools, and some critics of virtual schools have argued that socialization is not possible in virtual environments. Some virtual schools say they have addressed this need with online clubs and other virtual social activities. Other schools add face-to-face meetings to their virtual courses or encourage their students to join brick-and-mortar school field trips, clubs, study groups, and extracurricular activities. Do you believe that the socialization of virtual school students will suffer due to isolation from experiences with people in the physical world? What theoretical, anecdotal, and/or research evidence can you cite to bolster your arguments?

Chapter **8** ## Summary

**The following is a summary of the main points covered in this chapter.**

1. **Developing Online Courses: Models and Required Resources.** Online course models in popular use include:
   - **The noninteractive online model.** Students have no interaction with an instructor or other students. They read documents or view videos and take assessments

- **The interactive, asynchronous online model.** Students interact with an instructor and, usually, other students. Activities vary but usually include whole class and/or small-group discussions, individual and/or small-group assignments, materials to read and study, practice exercises to complete, and assessments.
- The interactive online classroom with synchronous events. Students are at a distance from the instructor and each other but "meet" and communicate in the course space with the aid of cameras and online tools and combine these meetings with online activities.
- The MOOC model. A course that aims at large-scale participation and allows anyone anywhere in the world to register for the course for free. Teaching approach usually involves viewing videos of professor lectures and demonstrations, interspersed with practice and interactive activities such as simulations or problem-solving, whole-class or small-group online discussions, and assessments.

2. **Developing Online Courses: Content Management Systems (CMS) and Other Required Infrastructure**
   - **Content management systems (CMS).** This software provides an online environment containing tools for teaching an online course.
   - **Course support tools.** These include software that allows students and instructors to meet synchronously and see each other as they communicate.
   - **Technical support.** These are resources and strategies students and instructors may use when they experience technical challenges in the course space.
   - **Support for students with special needs.** These include the ability to enlarge given text, alternatives to mouse controls for students with mobility issues, alternatives to videos for students with visual deficits, and alternatives to text presentation in all areas for students with visual deficits.
   - **Tools to monitor course outcomes.** This is usually done with a **data dashboard,** or a location that summarizes course data in ways that allow instructors to track student participation and progress.
   - **Tools and strategies to ensure academic integrity.** These include online honor codes, providing students with information about plagiarism, student discussions about academic integrity, and physical monitoring systems.

3. **Developing Online Courses: Procedures.** Steps in the development of an online course include:
   - **Step 1: Select the Online Model**
   - **Step 2: Design and Document Learning Activities**
   - **Step 3: Create Course Space Structure**
   - **Step 4: Create Assignment Materials**
   - **Step 5: Create Assessment Materials**
   - **Step 6: Create Content Presentation Materials**
   - **Step 7: Create Small-Group Activities**
   - **Step 8: Create Resource Links Other Materials**
   - **Step 9: Decide On and Signal the Course Path**
   - **Step 10: Determine and Document Course Logistics and Requirements**

4. **Teaching Online Courses**
   - **Best practices for online programs.** These include using tools to monitor progress, having personnel available to assist struggling students, employing well-trained online instructors, offering rigorous and engaging curriculum, and providing students with preparation and clear expectations.
   - **Managing small-group work in online courses.** While small-group work is an effective strategy in online courses, making it work well requires the following: assigning the group a clearly stated problem, and showing them how they will be graded; assigning roles and specific responsibilities for each group member; having groups begin by agreeing on some "norms" (e.g., how they will resolve issues such as someone not doing their "job" and when they will ask an instructor for help); encouraging group cohesion by asking the group members to agree on a group name; and instructor monitoring all group activities, intervening in group work only when necessary.
   - **Assessing quality of online courses: Criteria and rubrics.** To monitor quality of online courses, use available rubrics such as: Rubric for Assessing Interactive Quality of Distance Courses, the Quality Matters Rubric, and the Rubric for Online Instruction.

5. **Virtual Schools**
   - **Background on virtual schools.** According to the annual Watson et al. report of K–12 virtual programs, categories of virtual schools include single-district programs, blended schools, multidistrict fully online schools, consortium programs, state-supported supplemental options, and

private/independent schools. Major trends include the following: single-district and multidistrict online schools are growing; quality-control measures are growing; but the online-learning graduation requirement trend is growing slowly.

- **Virtual school issues.** These include problems and concerns with program quality and accountability, curriculum alignment, teacher certification, program accreditation, funding formulas, and consequences for virtual school students.
- **Virtual school research.** There are comparatively few studies on K–12 online learning. One recent federally funded study shows about 1.8 million students enrolled in online courses. Another study of one major virtual school provider showed that compared with the general student population in the states where they operated, students in virtual school were more likely to be white, less likely to be from poor families, and much less likely to be English language learners. Weaker performance outcomes were observed in virtual schools compared with national figures.

6. **Virtual Environments**

- **Types of virtual environments.** Four types include full immersion systems, in which the user places a headset (e.g., goggles or a helmet) over the eyes and the wearer "sees" only the computer-generated environment; multi-user virtual environments (MUVEs), in which 3-D environments are represented on a computer screen; Web-based VR, in which the user experienced a 3-D setting in an on-screen environment; and 3-D models, which are 3-D replicas of objects or locations.
- **Integration strategies for virtual environments.** These include virtual field trips, 3-D models to illustrate systems work;, immersive practice and exploration, and virtual collaboration and problem solving.

# TECHNOLOGY INTEGRATION **WORKSHOP**

## 1. APPLY WHAT YOU LEARNED

To apply the concepts and skills you've read about throughout this chapter, go to the Chapter 8 Technology Application Activity.

## 2. TECHNOLOGY INTEGRATION LESSON PLANNING: PART 1—EVALUATING AND CREATING LESSON PLANS

Complete the following exercise using the sample lesson plans found on any lesson planning site that you find on the Internet.

**a.** Locate lesson ideas—Identify three lesson plans that focus on any of the tools or strategies you learned about in this chapter. For example:
- Small-group work in online courses
- Virtual environments (e.g., 3-D environments and immersive systems)

**b.** Evaluate the lessons—Use the Technology Lesson Plan Evaluation Checklist to evaluate each of the lessons you found.

**c.** Create your own lesson—After you have reviewed and evaluated some sample lessons, create one of your own using a lesson plan format of your choice (or one your instructor gives you). Be sure the lesson focuses on one of the technologies or strategies discussed in this chapter.

## 3. TECHNOLOGY INTEGRATION LESSON PLANNING: PART 2—IMPLEMENTING THE TIP MODEL

Review how to implement the TIP model in your classroom by doing the following activities with the lesson you created in the Technology Integration Lesson Planning exercise above.

**a.** Describe the Phase 1—Planning activities you would do to use this lesson in your classroom:
- What is the relative advantage of using the technology(ies) in this lesson?
- Do you have resources and skills you need to carry it out?

**b.** Describe the Phase 2—Implementation activities you would do to use this lesson in your classroom:
- What are the objectives of the lesson plan?
- How will you assess your students' accomplishment of the objectives?
- What integration strategies are used in this lesson plan?
- How would you prepare the learning environment?

**c.** Describe the Phase 3—Evaluation/Revision activities you would do to use this lesson in your classroom: What strategies and/or instruments would you use to evaluate the success of this lesson in your classroom, in order to determine revision needs?

**d.** Add lesson descriptors—Create descriptors for your new lesson (e.g., grade level, content and topic areas, technologies used, ISTE standards, 21st Century Learning standards).

**e.** Save your new lesson—Save your lesson plan with all its descriptors and TIP model notes.

## 4. FOR YOUR TEACHING PORTFOLIO

Add the following to your Teaching Portfolio:
- Lesson plan evaluations, lesson plans, and products you created above
- Products of your group's Hot Topic Debates
- Products of your group's Collaborate, Discuss, Reflect online or in-class activities

Joan E. Hughes and M. D. Roblyer

# 9

# Teaching and Learning with Technology in English and Language Arts

## Learning Outcomes

After reading this chapter and completing the learning activities, you should be able to:

1. Identify implications for technology integration of each current issue faced by English/language arts teachers. (ISTE Standards•T 4, 5)

2. Select technology integration strategies that can meet various needs for instruction in English/language arts curricula. (ISTE Standards•T 2, 5)

3. Design a strategy for how to build teacher knowledge and skills in technology integration for English and language arts. (ISTE Standards•T 5)

# TECHNOLOGY INTEGRATION IN ACTION
# MY SIDE OF THE STORY: TEACHING DIGITAL LITERACIES WITH A MULTIMEDIA STORYTELLING PROJECT

GRADE LEVELS: 6–8 • CONTENT AREA/TOPIC: English/language arts, literature, creative writing • LENGTH OF TIME: Three weeks

## PHASE 1  ANALYSIS OF LEARNING AND TEACHING NEEDS

Suslik1983/Shutterstock

### Step 1: Determine relative advantage.

Mr. Caruso is a seventh grade teacher who teaches literature and composition. He had been reading about the new "digital literacies" that required skills in using many different media to communicate information in a variety of ways, in addition to print. He also thought this might be a good way to confront a perennial problem he has with teaching literature: getting students to connect more with characters in stories by analyzing their traits, motivations, conflicts, points of view, and relationships with others. He felt character analysis was one of the most powerful and instructive aspects of literature, since it teaches students about why they and others act as they do in various situations and how different people can view the same situation in very different ways. The project he had in mind would ask students to choose a character in a popular story and create a different telling of the story from the point of view of that character. This approach would require his students to analyze the characters more closely and use narration and images they select to illustrate the "new and improved" version they create. He had also been using blogs to encourage students' journaling, and he liked the idea of posting all the stories online and using blogs to allow students to critique each other's work. This would give them an audience for their stories other than himself, which he felt would be very motivating.

### Step 2: Review required resources and skills.

Mr. Caruso knew his strategy would hinge on having continuing and frequent online access and use of software tools. He arranged for a set of tablets to be on hand for the duration of the project. He felt that if the project were successful, he would secure funding for a permanent set of tablets.

## PHASE 2  PLANNING FOR INTEGRATION

### Step 3: Decide on objectives and assessments.

Mr. Caruso identified state and national language arts standards he wanted to help achieve with this project. Since he wanted to make sure students really achieved what he had in mind, he identified the following project outcomes, objectives, and assessments:

Outcome:  Create a multimedia presentation that takes a different perspective on a popular story.
Objective:  At least 90% of students will achieve an 80% or better rubric score on a multimedia project designed to tell a popular story from the perspective of one of the characters.
Assessment:  Rubric to assess the quality of character analysis, narration, and images in the project.

Outcome:  Make blog posts that reflect good character analysis.
Objective:  At least 90% of students will post at least five comments, including at least one that reflects insights on a character in the original or revised versions of the story.
Assessment:  Checklist of requirements for blog posts.

### Step 4: Design integration strategies.

Mr. Caruso designed the following sequence of daily activities for the three-week project:

Days 1–2: **Introduce the unit.** The teacher introduces the project by having students read and discuss *The True Story of the Three Little Pigs* by Jon Scieszka, which tells the traditional fairy tale through the wolf's eyes. The teacher leads a discussion on character traits and motivations reflected in the story and how this influences the narrative and plot. Then the teacher asks students to analyze another story that is currently popular with young people of their age. Again, they discuss how one of the characters might tell the same story from a different perspective. Finally, the teacher introduces the project and hands out and discusses the assessment rubric.

Days 3–4: **Library work and individual meetings.** The teacher takes students to the library/media center to review books and stories he has selected. He asks them to select a story for their project focus from a set he has identified; or they may identify one of their own choosing. As the students are ready to identify selections, he meets with them and confirms that their idea will work for the project.

Day 5: **Demonstration of a presentation software template and copyright discussion.** Using a template designed for the project, the teacher shows students the interactive and narration features they will use and shows how to "grab" images from the Internet and insert them into their presentation. He discussed copyright and Creative Commons and how to credit shareable works they use in their projects.

Days 6–10: **Individual student work on projects.** Students work on classroom computers to create their projects. The teacher circulates around to each student, answering questions and offering assistance and suggestions.

Days 11–14: **Project posting and blogging.** As students complete their projects, they upload them to the school server. All students review all story presentations and select at least five on which to post comments and suggestions. Students may revise their projects as they read the comments.

Day 15: **Project review and discussion.** The teacher leads a wrap-up discussion on what the students learned about character analysis from the project and how they might look at stories differently in the future. He asks students to vote on a "best-of-class" project to be placed on the school website for special recognition.

### Step 5: Prepare instructional environment.

Mr. Caruso did the following tasks to prepare for the project:

Select stories for student review. He reviewed a variety of stories students might like to use for their project and asked the librarian to make copies available on the days students needed them.

Schedule library. He scheduled the library for a two-day period and asked the library/media center director to be available to assist his students.

Computer preparation. He made sure the presentation software was available and working on each of his classroom tablets and set up a special blog area for this project.

Prepare assessments. He created a rubric for grading the assignments and a checklist for reviewing blog posts.

## PHASE 3  POST-INSTRUCTION ANALYSIS AND REVISIONS

### Step 6: Analyze results.

As Mr. Caruso reviewed the rubric scores, he realized he had met his objectives for the project. All but two students achieved a score of 80% or better. Most points were lost on criteria related to image use and copyright. As usual, students were most enthusiastic about blogging. Every student had commented on more than the required five projects, and each had posted at least one comment that reflected good insights about character portrayals. He knew he was on the right track with the project.

### Step 7: Make revisions.

Based on results from the projects, Mr. Caruso knew he would have to spend more time teaching students about effective and legal use of images. He decided to provide some good and bad examples of image use from the projects submitted by this group of students. He had also encountered an unexpected problem when students wanted to record narrations. The noise level in the classroom did not allow good, clear recordings, and he had to allow students to record in other rooms. He planned to provide for this ahead of time the next time he taught this unit. Finally, he decided to look for funding for his own classroom set of tablets so he could carry out this project and ones like it in the future.

*Source:* Based on a concept from the Hot Chalk Lesson Plans Page lesson, "What Really Did Happen?" at: http://www.lessonplanspage.com.

# CHAPTER 9 **BIG IDEAS OVERVIEW**

Before you begin reading the rest of this chapter, listen to the Chapter 9 Big Ideas Overview. It will give you a brief audio overview of main concepts to look for and help prepare you to work through information and exercises to achieve this chapter's outcomes.

# ISSUES AND CHALLENGES IN ENGLISH AND LANGUAGE ARTS

Reading, writing, speaking, listening, and critically analyzing written and oral language are considered fundamental skills for a literate person, and technologies have much to offer teachers as they help their students develop these skills. However, technologies have also brought about dramatic changes in the format and types of communications and activities that literate people must deal with, thus presenting an array of new challenges to English and language arts teachers. This section discusses the types of issues English and language arts teachers must confront when teaching literacy skills and integrating technology into literacy topics.

▲ To be able to teach the new literacies, teachers must become proficient in the new tools that help define literacy in the 21st century and develop possible strategies to teach it. (Photo courtesy W. Wiencke)

## Teachers' Changing Responsibilities for the "New Literacies"

The definition of *literacy* has changed dramatically in the United States over the course of its history, from being able to sign your name, to being familiar with certain canonical texts, to being able to read and write and make meaning from the written word, to being proficient in 21st-century literacies. The English and language arts discipline is guided by a prominent theory, **new literacies**, which describes an ever-shifting definition of literacy. Other terms, such as *21st-century skills, media literacy, digital literacy*, and *information literacy*, describe similar intersections of digital technologies and literacy and are prevalent terms used in general education contexts.

Leu, Kinzer, Coiro, Castek, and Henry (2013) explained how the forms and functions of literacy have always been changing and are shaped by current society. Currently, the global economy, the omnipresent Internet in society, and the co-mingling of literacy and the Internet in policy, such as national and state standards, are shaping the definition of literacy. While the core of new literacies rests upon the fact that literacy changes constantly, Leu et al. described the central principles that underlie the theory. The core technology underlying new literacies is the ubiquitous Internet (and technologies it supports) in our global society, which requires additional literacies. These literacies are always changing, are "multiple, multimodal, and multifaceted" (p. 1158), and require critical thinking. New strategic knowledge and social practices will be required, and finally, teachers' roles in New Literacy classrooms will be shifting and extremely important. For example, students will now need to seek meaning across a range of media, such as text, video, images, sounds, animations, and interactive elements, oftentimes presented simultaneously online or in apps. In addition, students will need to develop strategies to decipher and learn from global information sources that could introduce new social and cultural knowledge. Hypertextual structures and aesthetic differences in Internet-based technologies may require strategic knowledge for students to optimally seek, critique, and use information. New social practices include shifts in ways students can learn, express, share, and consume information. Students and teachers may take on new roles, such as those in a **distributed knowledge network**, in which some individuals are more expert than others on certain skills/knowledge but all participants in the classroom use social activities to maximize everyone's learning.

### Defining competencies and focus for 21st-century literacies.

The National Council of Teachers of English (NCTE, 2013) also recognizes these rapid changes in literacy and adopted in 2008 (and updated in 2013) a 21st Century Literacies Framework that says a literate person should have many kinds of literacy. Given our global society, NCTE aims for learners to:

1. Develop proficiency and fluency with the tools of technology;
2. Build intentional cross-cultural connections and relationships with others so to pose and solve problems collaboratively and strengthen independent thought;
3. Design and share information for global communities to meet a variety of purposes;
4. Manage, analyze, and synthesize multiple streams of simultaneous information;
5. Create, critique, analyze, and evaluate multimedia texts; and
6. Attend to the ethical responsibilities required by these complex environments (NCTE, 2013).

In this definition of 21st-century literacies, NCTE introduces six competencies that also reflect examples of the new strategic knowledge, social practices, and critical thinking that are required in New Literacies theory.

As described in Chapter 1, the terms **digital literacy** and **information literacy** are also widely used in general education contexts to describe the required skills in using technologies and information. According to the American Library Association (ALA), **information literacy** requires people to recognize when they need information, to know how to locate and evaluate it, and to be able to use it effectively. Because English and language arts focus on reading and writing, information literacy is inherent in the New Literacies theory and NCTE's 21st-century literacies. Information literacy involves critical thinking and analysis of online information, described later in this chapter as a key instructional strategy.

Regardless of the preferred "literacies" term used in your teaching context, a key understanding in new literacies or digital literacy is that these literacies capture more than the ability to use computer devices and software tools to locate and use information. These literacies call upon teachers to develop new instructional and learning strategies to assist students in finding, understanding, critiquing, and contributing to multimodal, global digital information using social learning practices. Patricia Edwards, when she was serving as president of the International Reading Association (IRA) in 2010, pointed out that students have to adapt the ways they read and write if they are to be successful socially, politically, and economically.

### Materials to develop literacy.

Information now comes to students via email and e-books; Web pages and podcasts; blogs, vlogs, and wikis; instant messages and Twitter feeds; curation apps like Pinterest; social knowledge management like Diigo; and movies and streaming video. The term **blog** is short for "Web log" and refers to a Web page that serves as a publicly accessible location for discussing a topic or issue. Blogs began as personal journals, but their use rapidly expanded to a public discussion forum in which anyone could post opinions on the topic. A **vlog**, a combination of video and blog is a video version of the blog in which posts are video clips instead of text entries. A **wiki**, on the other hand, is a collection of web pages located in an online community that encourages collaboration and communication of ideas by having users generate or modify content. Thus, wikis contain the ongoing work of many authors. **Twitter** is a social networking **microblog** technology that allows users to express 140-character micromessages (i.e., a Tweet) that may include links, video (e.g., Vine, an app that allows users to make and share six-second videos), or pictures (e.g., Instagram, an app that allows users to share photos and, if they wish, add filters to change the appearance of their photos). Users may create an identity, follow other users, and set privacy settings.

### Materials to organize information.

Other features like Replys, Favorites, Retweets, and Lists allow users to communicate more and organize people and information. **Pinterest** is a **curation tool** that allows users to collect (pin) and organize Internet-based information on boards into their account. Users create an identity, follow other boards or co-create boards, and set privacy settings. **Diigo** has developed from a social bookmarking technology towards a sophisticated knowledge management tool that supports work with Web-based information.

Diigo users have a library into which they can add links, screenshots, and pages during Web browsing. Annotation tools allow users to highlight or add sticky notes. Users can organize their information using tags or lists and can easily share any information using social networking tools (e.g., Twitter, Facebook). Again, users have privacy tools and collaboration features in which groups of people can contribute or subscribe to knowledge repositories.

Technologies such as those described above have been created through contemporary social forces within our global society. These ever-shifting technologies challenge teachers to constantly rethink the literacies they teach in order to make their 21st-century students truly literate. Edwards (2010) and Leu and Forzani (2012) remind us of the constant changes that will occur with technologies and literacy.

Research is starting to gauge the impact on comprehension of students reading digital text in e-books versus in print media. Connell, Bayliss, and Farmer (2012) found that college students tended to read faster in print environments, and studies by Schugar, Smith, and Schugar (2013) and Schugar and Schugar (2014) found that comprehension of K–6 students was significantly less in e-books when compared to print texts. These early findings point to the need for instructing students in optimal use of digital text. Based on their findings to date, Schugar and Schugar (2014) concluded that such instruction must become an essential component of today's digital literacy instruction.

## New Instructional Strategies to Address New Needs

Educational policy has begun to recognize the strength of the current societal forces, mainly globalization and the Internet, which are changing how people learn. National standards for English and language arts recognize integration of the Internet and digital technologies into curriculum and instruction. The National Council of Teachers of English (NCTE) and International Reading Association (IRA) Standards for the English and Language Arts (1996 and reaffirmed in 2013; see Figure 9.1) emphasize the importance of students having opportunities and resources to use technology to develop their language skills, as reflected in expectations that "Students read a wide range of print and nonprint texts . . ." (Standard 1), "Students apply knowledge of . . . media techniques . . . to create, critique, and discuss print and nonprint texts" (Standard 6), and "Students use a variety of technological and informational resources (e.g., libraries, databases, computer networks, video) to gather and synthesize information and to create and communicate knowledge" (Standard 8) (p. 3). The Common Core State Standards (Common Core, 2010) for English Language Arts & Literacy in History/Social Studies, Science, and Technical Subjects outline standards in reading, writing, speaking, listening, and language. Digital technologies are explicitly mentioned in five of the general, cross-disciplinary Common Core State Standards: College and Career Anchor Standards (see Table 9.1). Drew (2012) argued that the CCSS do not acknowledge sufficiently the changing nature of literacy and how the Internet has become "a central text" (p. 321). New literacies require a high level of critical sophistication from our students, and it is only through instruction and experiences with new technologies that they will develop these skills. However, teaching students to use new technologies calls for an array of new instructional strategies that are not prescribed by the NCTE/IRA or CCSS. Fortunately, many new tools are available to support these strategies, including the Top Ten Must-Have Apps for English and Language Arts.

### New strategies to foster reading and writing skills.
Many readers are now doing the majority of their reading online. Serafini (2012) explained how novice readers are challenged by multimodal texts that include a range of text, visual images, links, sounds, and other design features. He encourages teachers to shift from teaching readers to be only reader-decoders (of written texts) to be reader-viewers (of multimodal texts). This calls for them to employ four roles: (a) navigator, (b) interpreter, (c) designer, and (d) interrogator, as needed. Readers still need decoding skills but also will need skills to navigate and interpret multimodal texts that are frequently online and do not have linear paths. Readers are also called on to design their own (multi)paths through multimodal texts and actively construct meaning. Finally, readers can develop personal meanings and identify culturally-mediated public meanings—all of which may differ for each person. Texts that naturally position readers as reader-viewers of

## FIGURE 9.1 NCTE/IRA Standards for the English Language Arts

1. Students read a wide range of print and non-print texts to build an understanding of texts, of themselves, and of the cultures of the United States and the world; to acquire new information; to respond to the needs and demands of society and the workplace; and for personal fulfillment. Among these texts are fiction and nonfiction, classic and contemporary works.

2. Students read a wide range of literature from many periods in many genres to build an understanding of the many dimensions (e.g., philosophical, ethical, aesthetic) of human experience.

3. Students apply a wide range of strategies to comprehend, interpret, evaluate, and appreciate texts. They draw on their prior experience, their interactions with other readers and writers, their knowledge of word meaning and of other texts, their word identification strategies, and their understanding of textual features (e.g., sound-letter correspondence, sentence structure, context, graphics).

4. Students adjust their use of spoken, written, and visual language (e.g., conventions, style, vocabulary) to communicate effectively with a variety of audiences and for different purposes.

5. Students employ a wide range of strategies as they write and use different writing process elements appropriately to communicate with different audiences for a variety of purposes.

6. Students apply knowledge of language structure, language conventions (e.g., spelling and punctuation), media techniques, figurative language, and genre to create, critique, and discuss print and non-print texts.

7. Students conduct research on issues and interests by generating ideas and questions, and by posing problems. They gather, evaluate, and synthesize data from a variety of sources (e.g., print and non-print texts, artifacts, people) to communicate their discoveries in ways that suit their purpose and audience.

8. Students use a variety of technological and information resources (e.g., libraries, databases, computer networks, video) to gather and synthesize information and to create and communicate knowledge.

9. Students develop an understanding of and respect for diversity in language use, patterns, and dialects across cultures, ethnic groups, geographic regions, and social roles.

10. Students whose first language is not English make use of their first language to develop competency in the English language arts and to develop understanding of content across the curriculum.

11. Students participate as knowledgeable, reflective, creative, and critical members of a variety of literacy communities.

12. Students use spoken, written, and visual language to accomplish their own purposes (e.g., for learning, enjoyment, persuasion, and the exchange of information).

Source: *Standards for the English Language Arts*, by the International Reading Association and the National Council of Teachers of English, Copyright 1996 by the International Reading Association and the National Council of Teachers of English. Reprinted with permission.

## TABLE 9.1 Technology-Related Common Core State Standards (Common Core, 2010)

| Anchor Standards (A.S.) | Applicable to: | | |
| --- | --- | --- | --- |
| | K-5 | 6–12 | History/Social Studies, Science, and Technical Subjects |
| **Reading**: **A.S.** 7. Integrate and evaluate content presented in diverse media and formats, including visually and quantitatively, as well as in words. | ✓ | ✓ | ✓ |
| **Writing**: **A.S.** 6. Use technology, including the Internet, to produce and publish writing and collaborate with others. | ✓ | ✓ | ✓ |
| **Writing**: **A.S.** 8. Gather relevant information from multiple print and digital sources, assess the credibility and accuracy of each source, and integrate the information while avoiding plagiarism. | ✓ | ✓ | ✓ |
| **Speaking/Listening**: **A.S.** 2. Integrate and evaluate information presented in diverse media and formats, including visually, quantitatively, and orally. | ✓ | ✓ | |
| **Speaking/Listening**: **A.S.** 5. Make strategic use of digital media and visual displays of data to express information and enhance understanding of presentations. | ✓ | ✓ | |

▲ Teachers see the range of digital technology tools available to students as expanding opportunities for self-expression. **Pearson Education**

multimodal texts include postmodern picturebooks, such as *Black and White* (Macaulay, 1990) for children in grades K-3, graphic novels, such as *Anne Frank: The Anne Frank House Authorized Graphic Biography* (Jacobson & Colón, 2010) for children in grades 6–8, and web-based texts of all sorts to which children of all grades gravitate.

Likewise, print-centric texts and the dominant mode in schools of communicating ideas though writing are important but no longer sufficient for learners. Alvermann, Hutchins, and McDevitt (2012) described a range of digital literacy practices, including students writing and publishing a fan fiction prequel to *Of Mice and Men*, and said, "Multimodal texts that combine language, imagery, sounds, performance, and the like are what students deserve and expect, coming as they are from a world rich in multimedia" (p. 40). Teachers see the range of digital technology tools available to students as expanding opportunities for self-expression, increasing writing frequency and formats, and broadening the audiences for whom students write, yet these AP and National Writing Project teachers also highly value "formal writing," which they see as essential (Purcell, Buchanan, & Friedrich, 2013).

**New strategies for information literacies.** Beach (2012) said that informational/accessibility literacies allowed students to access, acquire, and evaluate the quality of online information, as well as using, synthesizing, and communicating what they find. The most common way of teaching these skills, a "one-shot" library session (Artman, Frisicaro-Pawlowski, & Monge, 2010), is not sufficient. Students often rely on simple Google searches (Jonker, 2011), which are inefficient. Teachers teach students how to use the most effective **keyword searches** to search educational online databases, such as InfoTrac Junior Edition or EBSCO Host, as well as in search engines.

As students find informational sources online, they need explicit instruction in how to think critically and evaluate what they find (Castek, 2012). Rheingold (n.d.) advised students to analyze critically the author, publisher, timeliness, audience, and argument structure of the material, as applicable. Rheingold (n.d.) provided grade-appropriate critical questions in each of the areas for analysis. When teachers select and vet the websites students will use, it is recommended that teachers model or review Rheingold's critical thinking steps to model how the sites were chosen. Next, students must employ critical thinking skills to determine the accuracy, reliability, and bias of the information sources. Roland Paris (n.d.) suggested students use the C-L-E-A-R model for critical reading, as shown in Figure 9.2. Learning these strategies will require more time than a one-shot library session. However, they are important activities to spend time on. This is because research shows that students have difficulty processing information once they have found it online (Salmerón & García, 2011). Also, they may read superficially, be paralyzed by information overload (Carr, 2011), or struggle with website text readability that is way above the grade level (Dalton & Smith, 2012).

### FIGURE 9.2 The CLEAR Model

1. **C**LAIMS: What are the main claims or arguments in the text? What is the author's main point?

2. **L**OGIC: How does the author reach these conclusions? What are the steps in the author's reasoning or logic? Is this logic sound?

3. **E**VIDENCE: What evidence does the author present to support the argument(s)? Does the author offer enough evidence? Is this evidence convincing? Can you think of any counter-evidence that would challenge the author's claims?

4. **A**SSUMPTIONS: Does the author rely on hidden assumptions? If so, are these assumptions correct?

5. **ALTERNATIVE A**RGUMENTS: Can you think of alternative arguments that the author has not considered?

*Source:* Reproduced with permission from the website of Professor Roland Paris, University of Ottawa: http://aix1.uottawa.ca/~rparis/critical.html.

**New strategies to address social interaction.** New literacies are much more contingent on social interactions with others than traditional literacies. According to the Standards for the English Language Arts (1996), teachers should begin "giving students the enjoyment and pride of sometimes being their teachers' teachers" (p. 40). Technology offers a natural setting in which students can be positioned as the experts, helping redefine the student–teacher and student–student relationships. The new forms of literacy and students becoming experts illustrate the power of people working together and are grounded in the social constructivist theory proposed by Vygotsky (Davydov, 1995), which asserts that learning occurs through interactions with others.

Another reason that new literacies demand a more social environment is that teaching and learning are no longer confined to a traditional classroom context. Today thanks to the Internet, the classroom is a worldwide location in which networked technologies for literacy enable us to communicate with people anywhere. We transmit and receive information in various formats and from many different people. These interactions provide a tremendous multicultural benefit to our classrooms that has never existed before. One strategy that makes use of this new social environment allows students to socially curate and bookmark online sources using apps such as Pinterest and Diigo. These social sites allow selective sharing that supports collaboration. Another strategy is having students share their work products with the world by publishing them online in blogs, wikis, Web pages, and e-books. By sharing their work, students to are able to comment on or annotate each other's posted works, thus engaging in a collaboration that makes them part of an ever-growing and changing community of learners.

Redesigning classroom spaces into learning commons or flipped/inverted classrooms is another type of instructional strategy. **Learning commons** are areas in a school that integrate school media centers and ELA classrooms around knowledge sharing and can even involve parents, student peers, counselors, administrators, and other teachers. **Flipped classrooms** invert individual instruction, lecture, and practice as homework while class time is reserved for collaborative creation, sharing, and discussion.

## Challenges of Working with Diverse Learners

Schools have more diverse student populations today than ever before. This cultural and linguistic diversity creates classrooms that are richer yet more complex. Although we value and celebrate the opportunity to interact with students of different nationalities, races, and ethnicities, this creates new challenges for English and language arts teachers. This is especially true when working with students who are learning English as a second or third language. It is also true when working with struggling readers. Often when students experience literacy problems at a young age, they continue to have reading difficulties throughout their schooling. Students who typically experience this problem include children who begin school without a solid literacy foundation, learn English as a second language, live in literacy-impoverished homes, have attention deficit/hyperactivity disorder, or do not receive appropriate instruction in school. Because many students need additional instruction in literacy, appropriate use of technology (e.g., audio books and e-books, websites, iPods/iPads, and software) can support their growth.

## Challenges of Motivating Students to Read and Write

The more students read, the better developed their language and writing skills become. However, teachers find it an ongoing challenge to motivate students to read—either for study or for pleasure. While youth aged 8–18 actually increased their leisure time spent reading print books from 21 to 25 minutes per day from 1999–2009, computer use, which methodologically included reading online, rose from 27 minutes to 73 minutes per day (Rideout, Foehr, & Roberts, 2010). Thus, teachers are turning to the interactive and visual qualities of software and websites to increase motivation for reading and writing. In fact, use of e-books on e-readers, which have interactive features, led to middle school boys who were reluctant readers to value reading more and increase their self-concept of reading ability (Miranda, Williams-Rossi, Johnson, & McKenzie, 2011). The Adapting for Special Needs feature provides information on how to support students who struggle with reading and writing.

# Adapting for Special Needs

## Reading and Writing Tools

### Writing Tools

Students with disabilities may struggle in many English and Language Arts classrooms because of the emphasis on reading and writing skills; these are common deficit areas for many students with disabilities. As a result, it is important to consider how technology might be used to scaffold and support each student's literacy development. One common approach for supporting diverse learners is to provide a specialized word processor specially designed with features that support poor writers. These include:

- Clicker5 (at the Crick software website)—Word processor with point-and-click access to whole words, phrases, and pictures to insert into writing.
- Co: Writer (at the Don Johnston website)—Word prediction software that assists a user during word processing by "predicting" and inserting a word the user intends to type.
- PixWriter (at the SunCastle Technology website)—Program that assists writing by allowing users to select text from pictured buttons.
- Read, Write Gold (at the Texthelp website)—A program with a toolbar that integrates with applications such as Microsoft Word, allowing students to access support tools that highlight and read aloud text from within these programs.

Another tactic is to compensate for poor writing and spelling skills by changing the writing production task from written drafting to dictation. Several tools are available that alter the nature of the text generation process and allow students to move into the revision phase of writing.

- Dragon Speech Recognition Software (software and app)— This software can be trained to recognize one's voice.
- iDictate (at the iDictate website) and Speak-Write (at the SpeakWrite website)—These are transcription services that accept voice recordings and email a text transcription.

### Reading Tools

When students struggle to read grade level content independently and fluently, text-to-speech products may be useful to allow students to listen to the information. They use these tools to play back any given text selection in a spoken voice. Free text-to-speech tools include the following:

- Natural Reader (at the NaturalReader website)
- Snap & Read (at the Don Johnston website)

*—Contributed by Dave Edyburn*

---

Teachers also find it an ongoing challenge to motivate students to express themselves in writing. Students especially resist the labor involved in revising research papers and compositions. In addition to word processing, which has been in use for many years, a variety of technology tools and strategies have emerged to spur students' desire to write, to improve the quality of their written products (e.g., email projects, blogs), to provide authentic publication sources (e.g., fan fiction), and to engage in purposeful, social communications (Dredger, Woods, Beach, & Sagstetter, 2010). Reviews of research have found the use of blogs and wikis have led to more student–student and student–teacher collaborative idea sharing, more consideration of audience in writing, and higher motivation and reading retention (Beach, 2012). Ultimately, writers need to see value in writing tasks.

## Teachers' Growth as Literacy Professionals and Leaders

The position statement published by the International Reading Association (2009) clearly states what literacy teachers need to know about integrating technology into the curriculum. According to the IRA, students have the right to have:

- Teachers who use information and communication technologies (ICTs) skillfully for teaching and learning
- Peers who use ICTs responsibly and who share their knowledge
- A literacy curriculum that offers opportunities for collaboration with peers around the world
- Instruction that embeds critical and culturally sensitive thinking into practice

- Standards and assessments that include new literacies
- Leaders and policymakers who are committed advocates of ICTs for teaching and learning
- Equal access to ICTs (Reprinted with permission of the International Reading Association.)

In our ever-shifting global society with changing expectations for literacy, 81.6% of U.S. literacy educators report a lack of professional development on technology integration (Hutchison & Reinking, 2011). This is not surprising given in 2011–2012, only 67.2% of public school teachers (U.S. DOE, 2011–12) and 55.2 % of private school teachers (U.S. DOE, 2011–12b) reported participating in professional development focused on using computers in instruction in the last twelve months. Literacy teachers identified four ways professional development about technology integration could be improved, including:

1. Time to learn, explore, and develop literacy lessons
2. Access to the technologies
3. Access to more knowledge and knowledgeable others
4. Continued, direct support (Hutchison, 2012)

When professional development is not provided or does not meet optimal conditions noted above, one solution is for teachers to grow as a literacy professional by developing themselves into a connected educator who interacts with professional educators around the world in order to construct new knowledge and deepen understanding (Wong, 2013). Nussbaum-Beach and Hall's (2013) informative book recommends teachers assume personal responsibility for professional learning through organized professional communities (e.g., at NCTE's Connected Community website), teacher-selected **personal learning communities**, and interest-based communities of practice (e.g., at the English Companion Ning site). Wong (2013) suggests Twitter, selective listservs, blogging, digital portfolios, and RSS feeds may be technologies that help educators identify new trends, connect with other educators, share and receive ideas, build relationships, and ultimately become connected educators that know both the affordances and challenges of using digital tools (Beach, 2012) and support the development of new literacies.

Begun in October 2012, the Office of Educational Technology's Connected Educators initiative sponsored "Connected Educator Month" which involved more than 300 online events, such as keynotes, panel discussions, courses, webinars, tours, chats, forums, and workshops that accounted for thousands of hours of online professional development. In October 2013, Connected Educators Month's online learning opportunities expanded beyond the USDOE to include events curated from existing sources. Becoming a connected educator allows you to join the online participatory culture from which you will gain valuable knowledge.

Finally, the connected educator must also know students' current digital literacy practices, as well how much high-speed access they have to the Internet (Alvermann et al., 2012). The latter is needed to facilitate the development of literacy activities that are of value to students. Wohlwend (2010) notes that though digital tools are increasingly being developed and used throughout society, U.S. schools are "clamping down rather than ramping up" (p. 144). Teachers who are in tune with the need for a revised definition of literacies can lead the way for new policies in schools, policies that embrace technologies, rather than fear them.

## QWERTY Keyboarding: To Teach or Not to Teach?

The most common way to write using a computer requires input through a regular **QWERTY keyboard**, so named because of the first six letters in the top letter line of a typewriter keyboard. There is an ongoing discussion of whether we should teach keyboarding instruction as a prerequisite to the use of computers for writing. Those in favor argue that students will learn bad habits if they use the keyboard without proper training, that these bad habits might become permanent, and that failure to learn proper fingering will inhibit fluent and speedy keyboarding. Those against requiring keyboarding instruction as a prerequisite argue that too much student time and computer resources are spent on getting students trained to type quickly, that students need only basic keyboard familiarization, and that keyboarding instruction would likely be a waste of time unless students have real-world applications in which to use the computer. Both

arguments are legitimate, and most teachers have resolved the issue, at least temporarily, by favoring keyboarding instruction if it is available and needed but not preventing students from using the computer if they do not yet have good keyboarding skills. It is important to note that the CCSS for ELA expect third through sixth grade students and older to be able to "demonstrate sufficient command of keyboarding skills to type a minimum of one page [in fourth grade] in a single setting" (Common Core, 2010, p. 21). Expectations for typed page length increase by one page each for fifth and sixth grade levels.

## The Cursive Writing Controversy

An issue that is related to questions about keyboarding is whether time spent teaching cursive writing would be better spent on other educational priorities. Critics of this long-taught skill argue that it is no longer used enough to justify its place in the elementary school curriculum. Some feel that this time would be better spent teaching writing with word processing. Supporters of cursive writing instruction point to its effect on shaping fine motor skills, its use in legal matters, and the need to be able to read historical handwritten documents. Some states (e.g., Tennessee) have responded to this controversy by introducing laws requiring cursive writing be taught. Read more about this issue in the Hot Topics for Debate feature.

**TECHNOLOGY LEARNING CHECK**

Complete **TLC 9.1** to review what you have learned from this section about issues that determine how technology is used in English and language arts education.

## TECHNOLOGY INTEGRATION STRATEGIES FOR ENGLISH AND LANGUAGE ARTS

Thanks in part to strong support for technologies by professional organizations such as the International Reading Association and the National Council of Teachers of English, the last decade has seen a growing emphasis on the use of technologies to support literacy instruction. This section focuses on integration strategies that support the following four English and language arts areas: word fluency and vocabulary development; comprehension and literacy development; the teaching of writing; and learning about literature. Strategies and resources under these four headings are summarized in Table 9.2.

**TABLE 9.2** Summary of Technology Integration Strategies for English and Language Arts

| Technology Integration Strategies | Benefits | Sample Resources and Activities |
|---|---|---|
| **Support for Word Fluency and Vocabulary Development** | | |
| Online practice in matching letters and sounds | Offers motivating environment for practice | International Reading Association (IRA) website |
| Online practice in matching words and meanings | Offers motivating environment for practice | Brainpop<br>PBS Kids |
| Online tools to engage students in vocabulary learning | Offers motivating environment for engaging students with words | Endless Alphabet & Endless Reader (see iTunes)<br>Wordle<br>Wordsift<br>Visual Thesaurus |
| **Support for Comprehension and Literacy Development** | | |
| Using digital text to encourage engaged reading | Allows more flexibility to interact with text; scaffolds emerging reading skills | E-books<br>Interactive stories<br>iBooks (see iTunes) |
| Supported reading with software and portable assistive devices | Devices and software read words aloud to students; especially helps struggling students | Talking word processors, such as Write: OutLoud (Don Johnston, Inc., and Kurzweil 300<br>Handheld devices such as Audiobooks (see iTunes) |
| **Support for Writing Instruction** | | |
| Strategies for preparing to write (prewriting) | Helps students organize their thoughts prior to writing | Electronic outlining<br>Concept mapping<br>Curation apps, such as<br>FlipBoard, Pinterest, and Diigo<br>Notetaking with Evernote |
| Strategies to encourage writing | Provides environments for modeling, supporting good writing | Websites such as the Academy of American Poets<br>Story starters<br>Blogs and wikis<br>Serious games, such as Dafur is Dying; Ayiti: The Cost of Life; and Quest Atlantis |
| Strategies to produce written drafts | Offers more flexibility to revise while writing | Various word processing software packages (e.g., Microsoft Word, GoogleDocs)<br>Speech to text: Dragon Dictation<br>Bibliography: Zotero |
| Modeling to support revising and editing written drafts | Provides environments for modeling editing process and offers more editing flexibility | Interactive whiteboards<br>Word processing features: spell-checkers and grammar checkers<br>Screencasting, such as ExplainEverything and ShowMe |
| Providing feedback with grammar, spell-check, and thesaurus features | Provides visual, immediate support and feedback during revision of drafts | Word processing features such as grammar-check, spell-check, and thesaurus |
| Providing feedback on student writing with editing tools | Provides supportive environment for demonstrating revision needs | Word processing features: autocorrect and track changes features<br>Annotation software, such as iAnnotate and Highlighter |
| Multimodal communication and publishing | Gives students an authentic purpose, audience for their multimodal works | Figment<br>Fan fiction sites<br>KidPub<br>Your Student News website<br>iBook Author<br>Center for Digital Storytelling<br>Celtx Script<br>Gamemaker: Studio (from YoYo Games)<br>GameStar Mechanic |

## TABLE 9.2 Summary of Technology Integration Strategies for English and Language Arts (continued)

| Technology Integration Strategies | Benefits | Sample Resources and Activities |
|---|---|---|
| **Support for Literature Learning** | | |
| Accessing online free copies of published works | Offers students free access to reading materials | International Children's Digital Library Free Books for Children (see iTunes)<br>OverDrive Media Console: Library e-books and audiobooks<br>Google Books Online<br>Project Gutenberg<br>Poets.org<br>Shakespeare Online<br>The Literature Page<br>The Literature Network<br>The Bible Gateway<br>Qur'an website |
| Accessing online background information on authors | Offers quick access to a wealth of information on authors | Famous People website<br>Poets.org<br>Biblio website |
| Support for literary analysis | Allows visual demonstrations, interactions to support analysis activities | Interactive whiteboards<br>E-readers<br>Ngram Viewer |

## Strategies to Support for Word Fluency and Vocabulary Development

Literacy begins at the word level, with fluency in decoding, reading, and understanding individual words. Several technology-enhanced strategies support student growth in these skills, including practice in matching letters and sounds, matching words with meanings, and vocabulary growth. Many strategies described here can be implemented with free websites, only a few of which are mentioned here as examples.

**Online practice in matching letters and sounds.** Phonemic awareness remains a foundational skill in learning to read, and many websites provide interactive practice in these important skills. For example, the ReadWriteThink website maintained by the IRA and NCTE offers a number of matching-letters-to-sounds exercises like the one shown in Figure 9.3. To make this practice more accessible to children outside of school, apps are available with this focus. Apps for iPhones and iPads can be downloaded from the iTunes store, and apps for the Android phones may be downloaded from numerous sites. For example, Little Stars – Toddler Games (available on iTunes) offers practice with first words, letter names, and letter sounds. It is customizable, including custom recording and adaptive play, which shows content that learners need to practice. See other apps to support English and language arts in the Must-Have Apps feature.

**Online practice in matching words with meanings.** As Glenberg, Goldberg, and Zhu (2011) remind us, many children, especially those learning English as a second or third language, can learn to sound out words, but without visual prompts, they may not connect these words to images from their own experience. Websites such as Brainpop are among those that offer exercises to give students practice in linking words and images so that emerging readers and new English language learners can begin to make those associations. See an example Brainpop exercise in Figure 9.4. PBS KIDS offers a range of online games and apps that target a range of literacy activities.

### FIGURE 9.3 Sample ReadWriteThink.org Letter-Sound Exercise

Source: ReadWriteThink.org is a nonprofit website maintained by the International Reading Association and the National Council of Teacher and English, with support from the Verizon Foundation. We publish free lesson plans, interactive student materials, Web resources, and standards for classroom teachers of reading and the English language arts. Retrieved from www.readwritethink.org/files/resources/interacitves/abcmatch/. Reprinted with permission.

## FIGURE 9.4 Brainpop Practice in Matching Words and Images

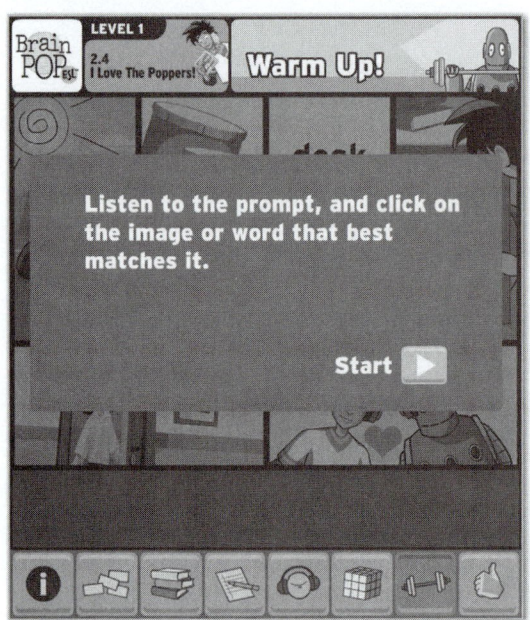

## FIGURE 9.5 Example Word Cloud Created with Wordle

**Online tools to engage students in vocabulary learning.** A growing number of innovative and fun sites are available for encouraging vocabulary growth. For early literacy, Endless Alphabet and Endless Reader helps build vocabulary and "sight words" through interactive puzzle games, talking letters, and definitional animations. Dalton and Grisham (2011) also offered some specific examples, such as Wordle, Wordsift, and Visual Thesaurus. One of these strategies calls for students to use Wordle to create a "word cloud" based on the frequency of words used in a text (see an example in Figure 9.5). These technologies are diverse in their approaches but all serve to engage students with words in motivating ways.

## Strategies to Support Reading Comprehension and Literacy Development

Technologies offer a variety of ways to support both traditional reading comprehension and emerging literacies. Those described in this section include encouraging engaged reading with digital text, collaborative reading, and supporting reading with portable assistive devices.

**Using digital text to encourage engaged reading.** E-books and interactive stories serve to engage readers by allowing them to notate and interact with digital versions of text as they read. In their review of research on using computer-assisted methods to support learning for struggling readers, Stetter and Hughes (2010) found that students profit most from supported use of text in digital tool such as e-books. They found that e-books and interactive versions of stories, especially those that offer audible reading on demand, offer students scaffolds for their emerging reading skills. The iBooks app allows downloading books, including children's picture books and classics, word search features, audio speaking of words, highlighting, notetaking, and sharing quotes/thoughts through social networking. Many books that are in the public domain (e.g., *Call of the Wild* by Jack London) may have singular apps created for the one text with special features. Students can also check out e-books and audiobooks from public or school libraries using the OverDrive Media Console app.

Collaborative reading that is facilitated in online spaces leads readers to share ideas and consider alternative perspectives on the reading topic. This contrasts with individual readers who focus on compiling facts (Leu et al., 2011). Such perspective broadening is important in new literacies.

However, as teachers encourage reading and foster these new literacies, they are also responsible for making sure that students are reading e-books and other digital formats in ways that best support reading comprehension. As research by Schugar and Schugar (2014) revealed, students have a tendency to skip over important passages in digital environments and, as a result, can have significantly lower comprehension than they would in print environments. Teachers must help students develop digital literacy skills that specifically address and counter this tendency.

**Supported reading with software and portable assistive devices.** To aid student reading, software is available to read passages aloud using handheld devices (e.g., smartphones, e-readers, tablets, iPod) are available to give definitions or to pronounce unfamiliar words aloud. These materials are particularly useful for students with reading difficulties or those for whom English is not a first language. Larson (2010) describes how e-book and e-reader reading behaviors differ from behaviors with print text. With e-books, students can make notes and

To aid student reading, software is available to read passages aloud using handheld devices. (Photo courtesy of W. Wiencke)

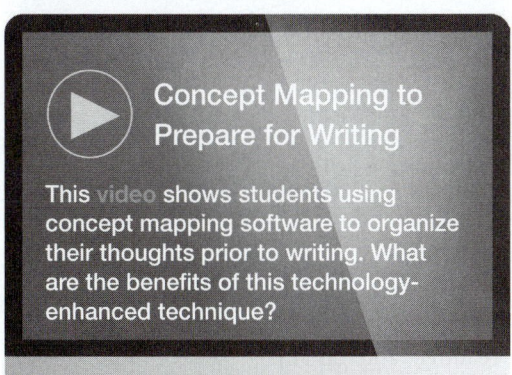

▶ Concept Mapping to Prepare for Writing

This video shows students using concept mapping software to organize their thoughts prior to writing. What are the benefits of this technology-enhanced technique?

comments directly on what they are reading, which helps them better comprehend its meaning. They can also adjust font size, access a built-in dictionary to examine word meanings and pronunciations, and use a text-to-speech feature to listen to or reread passages they find difficult. The device "reads" the word as the student points to it. Some devices and websites give a printed definition on the small screen or pop-up; others offer audio pronunciation. Still others are available to translate words to other languages. **Audiobooks** can be paired with print-based texts to support reading.

**Talking word processors** are software packages that read typed words aloud. They have proven especially useful for students with disabilities. Two examples of these are Write: OutLoud from Don Johnston, Inc., and the Kurzweil 300. Computer operating systems may also have built-in accessibility features for vision, hearing, physical and motor skill challenges that can be leveraged for support in reading and writing activities.

## Strategies to Support Teaching the Writing Process

A plethora of technologies offer unique capabilities to help writers prepare to write and to improve the quality of their written work and creation of multimodal texts. Strategies are described here for each phase in the writing process, including preparing to write (prewriting); drafting, revising, and editing; and publishing student work.

### Instructing students who are preparing to write (prewriting).

Getting started is often one of the most difficult aspects of writing, and young writers find it particularly onerous. During the prewriting stage, teachers communicate to students the format, audience, topic, purpose, and assessment method for the writing assignment. During this stage, students need to organize their thoughts graphically. For instance, if students are writing a fictional story, they need to brainstorm ideas for the story line, setting, and major characters; refine and organize those ideas; and generate a plan for presenting each story element in an intriguing manner. If the assignment is to write a report, then students need to gather information on the topic from a variety of sources; synthesize and arrange this information into categories or subtopics; and generate a plan for presenting the information in a logical way. All types of prewriting activities can be facilitated by using information organizing software, such as concept mapping, note-taking, content curation, and electronic outlining apps or features, and various strategies to encourage student writing.

- **Concept mapping.** Concept mapping software is popular as a prewriting planning tool, allowing students to produce an outline as a visual map (see Figure 9.6). The most popular concept mapping programs are Kidspiration for grades K–3 and Inspiration for grades 4 and above (Inspiration Software, Inc.); both products have electronic tools for both outlining and diagramming. (See an example concept map created with Inspiration in Figure 9.6.) The diagramming side of the program can be used to create a variety of graphic displays, all of which are useful for students who like to think and plan using visual representations of their ideas. For example, students can easily brainstorm a cluster map of ideas for a story and then rearrange or expand on the ideas for later development. Students can also use the program to generate a hierarchical map of key concepts to be explored for a research paper and link those concepts with labels that demonstrate their conceptual relationship. MindMeister is a powerful iPad collaborative mindmapping app that synchronizes with online MindMeister.

- **Note-taking.** Note-taking occurs during classtime as well as in preparation for larger writing projects. Many apps are available to support flexible note-taking online or mobiles. Evernote serves multiple computing platforms and allows users to easily type written notes, take photos, record audio, and save Web pages. It allows users to organize all these materials and share notes or collaborate with others.

## FIGURE 9.6 Concept Map for *To Kill a Mockingbird*

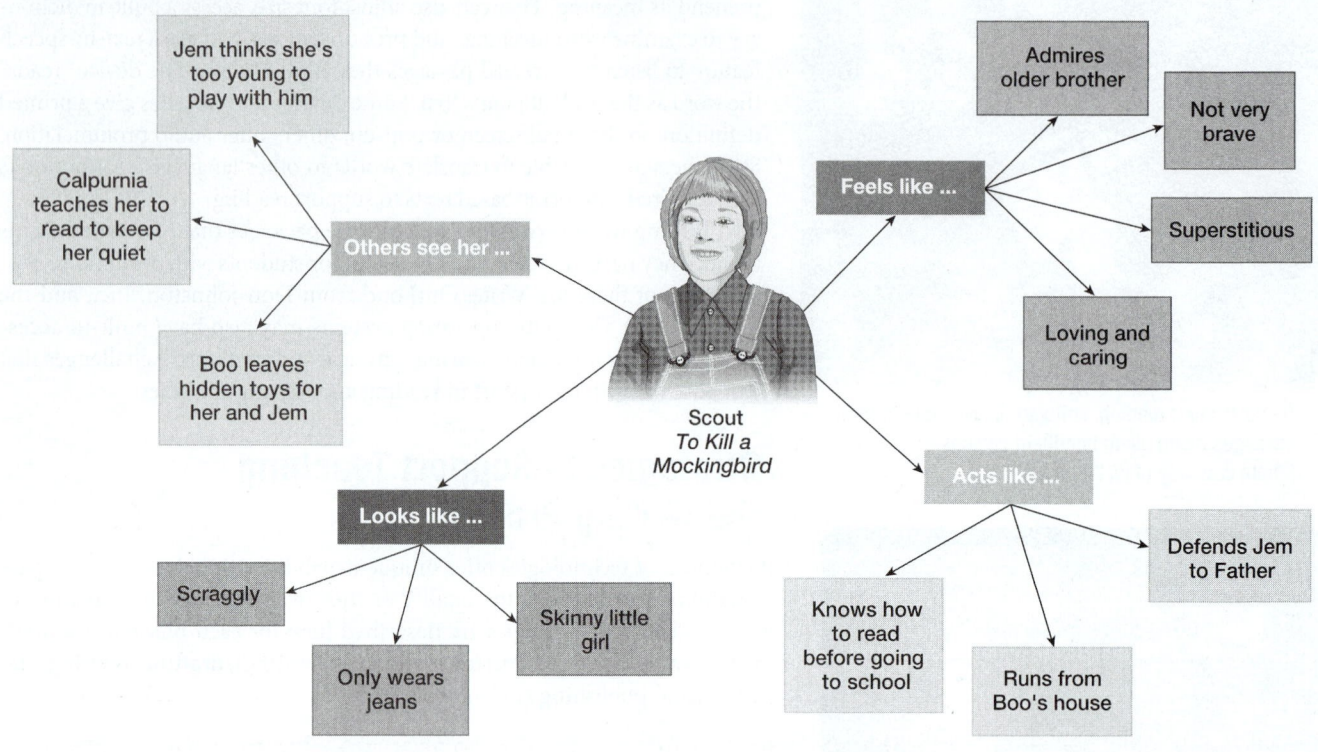

- **Curation.** Curation involves research, reading, and organization. For reports, students can curate their online resources using curation apps that were described earlier (e.g., Flipboard, Pinterest, or Diigo). These tools allow users to collect information that is pertinent to their writing project, organize it, and even share it with others. The sharing features support peer or teacher formative assessment during planning stages of a writing task.

- **Electronic outlining.** Electronic outlining is now integrated into almost all major word processing programs and is easily accessible as a planning tool. Electronic outliners automatically generate headings and subheadings from typed information. The advantages to using them are that new headings/subheadings can be easily inserted anywhere in the outline, headings/subheadings can be shifted around quickly to reflect a student's thinking and planning, and the prefixes serving as organizational clues are automatically changed to reflect revisions to the outline's organization.

**Using modeling, programs, and websites to encourage writing.** It is critical that teachers both model the type of writing expected and provide environments that motivate students to write. For modeling, Internet sites offer rich sources of poetry examples (e.g., the website of the Academy of American Poets) and examples of student writing (e.g., see student models at The Write Source website). In addition, several kinds of programs and websites are available to help the slow-to-write student get started, including story starters, like Scholastic's whiteboard-ready site Story Starters, and Scholastic's Poetry Idea Engine (both listed in the Open Source Options feature). Many language arts and writing teachers encourage student writing by assigning journaling. This assignment can be made more motivational by assigning blog posting, wiki interactions, or collaborative writing rather than on-paper journals. GoogleDocs and EtherPad support real-time collaborative writing and editing.

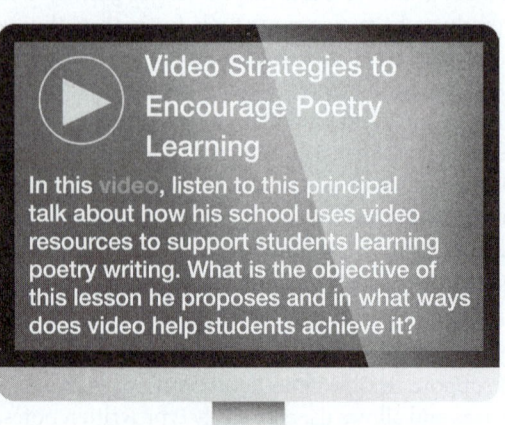

### Video Strategies to Encourage Poetry Learning

In this video, listen to this principal talk about how his school uses video resources to support students learning poetry writing. What is the objective of this lesson he proposes and in what ways does video help students achieve it?

# OPEN SOURCE OPTIONS for English and Language Arts

| TYPES | FREE SOURCES |
|---|---|
| **Free word processing software** | AbiWord: abisource.com<br>Google Docs WP: google.com/<br>Writer: openoffice.org/download/<br>Zoho Writer: writer.zoho.com |
| **Story starters** | Scholastic's Story Starter site: (search for the "Scholastic Story Starters" website) |
| **Blogs and wikis** | Blogger (now hosted by Google): blogger.com<br>Wikispaces: wikispaces.com |
| **Design Internet-based reading and research experiences** | CAST Strategy Tutor cast.org/learningtools/strategy_tutor/ |
| **Collaborate writing and editing** | Etherpad: etherpad.org |

See Technology Integration Example 9.1 for a variety of ways blogs can encourage student writing. Email and website projects are also a way to connect student writers with distant audiences. Electronic pen pal (sometimes called key pal) projects are popular and provide creative and authentic opportunities for communication. The ePALS Global Community connects millions of students and educators in 200 countries who want to work together. Finally, the use of game-based instruction may support writing. Barab, Pettyjohn, Gresalfi, Volk and Solomon's (2012) research indicated game-based instruction in argumentative writing led to

# TECHNOLOGY INTEGRATION

## Example 9.1

**TITLE:** "My Pet is Special" Blog

**CONTENT AREA/TOPIC:** Language arts, writing

**GRADE LEVELS:** All grades

**ISTE STANDARDS•S:** Standard 1—Creativity and Innovation; Standard 2—Communication and Collaboration; Standard 4—Critical Thinking, Problem Solving, and Decision Making; Standard 6—Technology Operations and Concepts

**CCSS:** CCSS.ELA-LITERACY.W.4.1, CCSS.ELA-LITERACY.W.4.3.B, CCSS.ELA-LITERACY.W.4.10, CCSS.ELA-LITERACY.W.8.2.A, CCSS.ELA-LITERACY.W.8.3.B

**DESCRIPTION:** Blogs are a popular way to help students engage with text and provide opportunities for an authentic writing experience. One way to encourage writing in this way is to set up a classroom blog in which students exchange information about their current or desired pet. The teacher models how to use the blog by writing about his or her own pet and what is so special about it. Then students are encouraged to submit daily or weekly updates, including images and/or videos, to their posting and respond to each other's posts.

*SOURCE:* Based on concepts from Lorrie Jackson's "This Bird Can Blog: Online Writing with a Twist" article on blogs at the Educational World website: http://www.educationworld.com.

better writing quality, more student engagement, and more on-task behavior, as compared with a story-based approach. However, Beach (2012) argued that digital games are not necessarily required to have the same impact; he advocates the use of online role-play to encourage writing.

Free sites to set up blogs and wikis are listed in the Open Source Options feature. With blogging and wiki exchanges, students have an audience for their writing and their posts become, as Bromley (2010) said, "dynamic sites for conversation" (p. 100) with their colleagues, rather than just products for a grade in school.

### Working with word-processed written drafts.

As students draft their papers, they continue to plan, rethink, and reorganize their work, even while producing more text. Word processing programs aid drafting by allowing students to make changes as they write, thus making drafting a more fluid process. It is preferable if students learn to draft directly into a digital format, rather than handwrite their drafts, since it facilitates later revision and editing. When computer access is a concern, teachers sometimes ask students to handwrite their drafts, then type them into the computer when a computer becomes available. However, this is not the most efficient approach to drafting and should be avoided, if possible, since it provides a poor model for future work using word processing. While it might be optimal for students to learn to draft directly in word processing, access to word processors may not always be available. Teachers need to support technologies that best support writing in their context. Students have used cell phone texting, instant-messaging, and email to write collaboratively. Speech-to-text technologies, such as Dragon Dictation, could support moving thoughts or writing into a digital format for flexible integration into digital works. For students completing research-based writing, Zotero will support citation of sources and automatic building of bibliographies within word processing programs.

### Modeling to support revising and editing written drafts.

Revising is the stage during which students make changes in content or structure that reflects decisions about how to improve overall quality. To revise well, students have to move from composing text to analyzing it, looking for what needs to be added, deleted, or rearranged. One of the best ways for teachers to assist in this process is to project a student's typed draft onto a screen or whiteboard and then model the thinking and decision making that goes into analyzing and revising the text. If projected in this way, students can make changes to the text as other students watch. Another strategy teachers can use is videoconferencing, audio recording, and archiving any of the above, along with subsequent student revisions, as examples on a wiki or other sharing site so students may access them for guidance at any time. They may also use **screencasting**, or capturing movements on a computer screen with a software like Camtasia. ExplainEverything or ShowMe apps may support the modeling and enable archiving.

Editing, as opposed to revising, is the process of refining a paper so that it adheres to standard conventions for spelling, syntax, punctuation, and style. Editing is a far more superficial task than revising but no less important. All word-processing programs have features that support the editing process, including spell-checkers and grammar-checkers, as well as electronic search capabilities to verify consistency of word usage, tone, and tense. Once again, the teacher can model the editing process, and students can then edit each other's papers. The teachers may ask students to use color to highlight elements, such as the thesis sentence, supporting sentences, and transition sentences within a passage. This makes the structure more visible and aids editing and revising.

### Providing feedback with grammar, spell-check, and thesaurus features.

Most word processing programs have automatic grammar- and spell-check features that flag problems in written text. For example, Microsoft Word underlines in red any words it perceives as misspelled and underlines passages in green to highlight possible grammar problems. Word-processing programs do not always offer correct "advice," but teachers can show students how to use these prompts to check for and correct mistakes in their writing. To improve written vocabulary use, students can also access the program's thesaurus, which offers a variety of alternative synonyms to given words.

### Providing feedback on student writing with editing tools.

Dunford and Fink (2011) offered advice on how to use three of Microsoft Word 's built-in revision and automation tools to give students useful feedback on their word-processed drafts. These tools include

- **Autocorrect.** This is a built-in feature that automatically detects and corrects misspelled words and incorrect capitalization. Dunford and Fink explained how to insert other automatic changes into the standard set that Word uses.
- **Track changes.** This is an editing command that can be turned on from one of the program's drop-down menus to show changes as they are made to an original document. Changes can either be accepted or rejected later.
- **Comments.** This is a feature that allows a teacher to insert notes for the student in "balloons." The comments appear in the margins of a document to remark on specific words or sentences. The use of the comments feature is preferable to handwritten comments because they are often easier to produce and read and because they stand out from text so that students can see them more clearly.

Each of these built-in features can save teachers editing time and make writing problems and mistakes more visible to students. Highlighter and iAnnotate apps support annotation and sharing features that can facilitate collaborative feedback and editing.

## Strategies to Support Literature Learning

The other area of traditional literacy after reading and writing instruction is learning about great works of literature and learning to read literature with a discerning, critical, and appreciative eye. Three strategies for using technologies to support literature learning are described in this section: accessing free copies of published works, accessing information about authors, and support for literary analysis.

### Accessing online copies of published works.
Many authored works whose copyrights have expired are now available free from online sources. In addition, Google has undertaken a project to digitize a large number of copyrighted and uncopyrighted texts of all kinds. Allowing students to access these digital versions of texts promotes reading by making texts less expensive and more easily accessible. Copyrighted books may be available to students by checking e-books out from public or school libraries using the OverDrive Media Console app, iMLS HD, or AccessMyLibrary: School Edition, depending on the library's adopted technologies. Many books in the iTunes bookstore are free; the iBooks, Google Play Books, or Kindle apps allow easy access with features that scaffold reading. As previously stated, many books that are in the public domain (e.g., *Call of the Wild* by Jack London) may have singular apps created for the one text with special features.

### Accessing background information on authors.
Since an author's life usually affects the choice of writing topics and may also affect his or her style, teachers often want students to learn about authors' backgrounds as a path for understanding the authors' written works. Again numerous websites are available. Teachers must choose these sites judiciously, since not all offer accurate or unbiased information. As with all websites, teachers and students can evaluate quality by noting the legitimacy of the sponsoring organization, how frequently the site is updated, if the site author can be contacted, and spot-checking the accuracy of information. Most contemporary writers have their own websites or blogs and may even offer online reading clubs or guest appearances.

### Accessing support for literary analysis.
When teachers want to engage students in reading and analyzing written works, they frequently ask students to focus on key words or phrases or look for patterns, such as meter. Two technology strategies support this kind of literary analysis:

- **Projecting text for analysis.** Projecting text onto an interactive whiteboard is a great way to demonstrate analysis for the whole class. For example, see Figure 9.7, which shows students indicating meter in Edgar Allan Poe's *The Raven*.

**FIGURE 9.7** Students Using Whiteboard for Literary Analysis

▲ Projecting text on an interactive whiteboard makes literary analysis exercises more interactive and visual. (Photo courtesy of W. Wiencke)

- **Using digital texts for analysis.** Using digital texts, such as on an e-reader device or a PDF file, students can do searches and count instances of words or phrases that indicate mood or metaphor (e.g., search for the word *dark* in Poe's works). Depending on the digital format capabilities, students can also make notations directly on the text or quantitatively analyze the patterns. A larger scope analysis is facilitated by Google's Ngram Viewer, which allows quantitative analysis of words or phrases in a historical corpus of books from 1500 to 2008 (Michel et al., 2010).

## Enabling Multimodal Communication and Digital Publishing

New literacies also lead students to engage in multimodal communication, which involves accessing, reading, listening, writing, creating, producing, and publishing written texts, digital portfolios, digital video/stories, podcasts or vodcasts, and video games. A major challenge for students who use multimodal communication is considering the aesthetic features of the digital materials (e.g., fonts and backgrounds) and thinking about how to use these features in ways that engage their audience.

Sharing multimodal texts.   As mentioned earlier, students find it more motivating to write when they know their work will be shared with others. Now students can share their written works in forums such as websites, Fan fiction sites, electronic books, multimedia slide shows, and news broadcasts. Students appear to be highly motivated when engaging in collaborative **relay writing** (a.k.a., **chain writing**) a novel, in which one student or group of students writes a part and sends it on to the next student or group to add to. They also find it motivating to construct hypermedia digital stories and e-zines. Each of these activities involve students extending and adding to each other's writing (Beach, 2012).

Teachers should look for sites set up especially for publishing student work (e.g., Figment, Fan Fiction, KidPub, and Your Student News). Students and teachers can also publish their own multimodal digital books using iBooks Author. To collect and maintain student work, teachers can facilitate the use of e-portfolios so that over time, they and their students can, analyze it and reflect on learning and identify ways to improve in the future. E-portfolios can be created in systems such as Three Ring or using Adobe Acrobat Professional, websites, blogs, and wikis.

Digital storytelling.   **Digital storytelling** is the process of using images and audio to tell the stories of lives, events, or eras. The Center for Digital Storytelling site says that a digital story is a narrative someone tells in the first person in video format. Thesen and Kira-Soteriou (2011) and Rule (2011) are among many teachers who advocate using digital storytelling with students in order to enrich their literacy development. Thesen and Kira-Soteriou (2011) also offered detailed advice on how to implement this strategy in a classroom. Students engage in scriptwriting (e.g., using Celtx Script app), storyboarding ideas, and video/photo production and publish their work often as videos in which they can distribute as vodcasts or audio podcasts. Many multimodal communication activities lead students to examine their identity or try alternative identities, contribute to diversifying students' views, examine authentic social or cultural issues, and are highly motivating. Further information and professional development opportunities are available at the Center for Digital Storytelling site. Also, see the Technology Integration Example 9.2 based on the approach described by Thesen and Kira-Soteriou (2011).

Video game design.   While some teachers are using game-based instruction, others are creating opportunities for students to design and create their own video games using software such as GameMaker: Studio, Gamestar Mechanic, Scratch, or Alice. Again, in the process, students engage in new literacies, such as script writing, drawing, and animating.

# TECHNOLOGY INTEGRATION

## Example 9.2

**TITLE:** Important Moments: A Narration

**CONTENT AREA/TOPIC:** Language arts, digital literacy

**GRADE LEVEL:** 2

**ISTE STANDARDS•S:** Standard 1—Creativity and Innovation; Standard 2—Communication and Collaboration; Standard 6—Technology Operations and Concepts

**CCSS:** CCSS.ELA-LITERACY.RF.2.3, CCSS.ELA-LITERACY.W.2.3, CSS.ELA-LITERACY.W.2.5, CCSS.ELA-LITERACY.W.2.6

**DESCRIPTION:** Students begin by viewing digital stories previously produced by other children and learning the elements of telling a story. After an introduction to the software they will use (PhotoStory 3), students choose a moment in their lives that was significant to them and write a short narrative about it. They learn how to put expression in their voices to convey emotions. They work with a partner to review their written narratives and give each other feedback. They record the narration, learning how to use tempo, rate, and silences. Finally, they put their stories together and create drawings to illustrate them. The movies "premier" in the classroom, complete with popcorn, and the teacher gives each student a digital copy of the stories to take home.

*SOURCE:* Based on concepts from Thesen, A., & Kira-Soteriou, J. (2011). Using digital storytelling to unlock student potential. *New England Reading Association Journal, 46*(2), 93–101.

**TECHNOLOGY LEARNING CHECK**

Complete TLC 9.2 to review what you have learned from this section about strategies for integrating technology into English and language arts education.

## TEACHING ENGLISH AND LANGUAGE ARTS TEACHERS TO INTEGRATE TECHNOLOGY

This section gives recommendations for how teachers can prepare to integrate technology effectively into instruction for English and language arts. Many teachers in this content area are faced with a significant amount of learning and relearning. The communications tools and social media technologies that arrived on the scene in the last dozen years have already had a revolutionary impact on English and language arts curriculum and practice, and teachers graduating from today's teacher education programs enter classrooms much transformed from those they would have encountered in 2000. Today's teachers are as likely to see students composing on blogs and wikis as on paper, and both teachers and students are more likely to get their information online as from any other medium. Today's technologies have not only offered new and distinctive capabilities that have changed the definition of what it means to be literate, they have also changed what it means to be an effective English or language arts teacher. As this chapter has demonstrated, teachers are continually challenged to keep up with the new requirements they must teach their students; often, teachers must first learn these new resources and skills themselves.

### Rubric to Measure Teacher Growth in English and Language Arts Technology Integration

Begin by reviewing the rubric in Figure 9.8 to measure teachers' progress in effectively integrating technology in English and language arts instruction. Part I of the rubric addresses knowledge of issues and challenges, and Part II addresses English and language arts technology integration strategies.

# FIGURE 9.8 Rubric to Measure Teacher Growth in English/Language Arts Technology Integration

| Part I: Teacher Knowledge of English/Language Arts Issues and Challenges | | | |
|---|---|---|---|
| | Basic Knowledge (1–2 points) | Intermediate Knowledge (3–4 points) | Advanced Knowledge (4–5 points) |
| Teachers' changing responsibilities for the new literacies | I can articulate the nature of the issue. | I can both articulate the nature of the issue and some of the possible ways to address it. | I can articulate my own plan for addressing the issue in my own teaching. |
| New instructional strategies to address new needs | I can articulate the nature of the issue. | I can both articulate the nature of the issue and some of the possible ways to address it. | I can articulate my own plan for addressing the issue in my own teaching. |
| Challenges of working with diverse learners | I can articulate the nature of the issue. | I can both articulate the nature of the issue and some of the possible ways to address it. | I can articulate my own plan for addressing the issue in my own teaching. |
| Challenges of motivating students to read and write | I can articulate the nature of the issue. | I can both articulate the nature of the issue and some of the possible ways to address it. | I can articulate my own plan for addressing the issue in my own teaching. |
| Teachers' growth as literacy professionals and leaders | I can articulate the nature of the issue. | I can both articulate the nature of the issue and some of the possible ways to address it. | I can articulate my own plan for addressing the issue in my own teaching. |
| QWERTY keyboarding: To teach or not to teach? | I can articulate the nature of the issue. | I can both articulate the nature of the issue and some of the possible ways to address it. | I can articulate my own plan for addressing the issue in my own teaching. |
| The cursive writing controversy | I can articulate the nature of the issue. | I can both articulate the nature of the issue and some of the possible ways to address it. | I can articulate my own plan for addressing the issue in my own teaching. |

| Part II: Teachers' Technology Integration Strategies for English and Language Arts | | | |
|---|---|---|---|
| | Basic Knowledge (1–2 points) | Intermediate Knowledge (3–4 points) | Advanced Knowledge (4–5 points) |
| Strategies to support for word fluency and vocabulary development | I can describe the strategies and identify technologies to carry them out. | I have designed at least 1–2 activities based on these strategies to enhance my teaching and my students' learning. | I have designed plans for how I will integrate these strategies throughout my curriculum to enhance my teaching and my students' learning. |
| Strategies to support reading comprehension and literacy development | I can describe the strategies and identify technologies to carry them out. | I have designed at least 1–2 activities based on these strategies to enhance my teaching and my students' learning. | I have designed plans for how I will integrate these strategies throughout my curriculum to enhance my teaching and my students' learning. |
| Strategies to support teaching the writing process | I can describe the strategies and identify technologies to carry them out. | I have designed at least 1–2 activities based on these strategies to enhance my teaching and my students' learning. | I have designed plans for how I will integrate these strategies throughout my curriculum to enhance my teaching and my students' learning. |
| Strategies to support literature learning | I can describe the strategies and identify technologies to carry them out. | I have designed at least 1–2 activities based on these strategies to enhance my teaching and my students' learning. | I have designed plans for how I will integrate these strategies throughout my curriculum to enhance my teaching and my students' learning. |
| Enabling multimodal communication and digital publishing | I can describe the strategies and identify technologies to carry them out. | I have designed at least 1–2 activities based on these strategies to enhance my teaching and my students' learning. | I have designed plans for how I will integrate these strategies throughout my curriculum to enhance my teaching and my students' learning. |

**Total points** _____ **of 60 possible points**

## Learning the Issues and Applications

The first step in technology integration is to become acquainted with the issues and challenges discussed in this chapter and how they shape teachers' uses and applications of technologies. Then teachers can begin developing capabilities to address instructional standards and curriculum goals. The following is a suggested sequence of learning activities.

- **Issues and challenges in English and language arts instruction.** After reviewing the information in this chapter, go to the websites of the English/language arts and reading professional organizations—the National Council for Teachers of English (NCTE) and the International Reading Association (IRA)—and review the standards. See professional development resources the sites offer, and decide on which can help you gain insight into the issues and challenges outlined in this chapter. Discuss and reflect on the two questions under the Collaborate, Discuss, Reflect feature at the end of the chapter. Complete Part I of the rubric in Figure 9.8 before you begin this sequence and again at various points in your progress.

- **English and language arts technology integration strategies.** After reviewing the information in this chapter, review examples of the technologies suggested in the Open Source Options feature and the websites and projects described under each section, and do the lesson evaluation and lesson development activities outlined in the Technology Integration Workshop at the end of this chapter. Reflect on how you will plan for implementing these strategies in your own classroom using the TIP model. Complete Part I of the rubric in Figure 9.8 before you begin this sequence and again at various points in your progress.

**TECHNOLOGY LEARNING CHECK**

Complete **TLC 9.3** to review what you have learned from this section about how English/language arts teachers can develop their knowledge and skills in technology integration.

# COLLABORATE, REFLECT, DISCUSS

Monkey Business/Fotolia

The following questions may be used either for in-class, small-group discussions or may be used to initiate discussions in blogs or online discussion boards:

1. In an article, "Will We Ever Allow Computers to Grade Students' Writing?" Berkowicz and Myers (2014) discuss the controversies arising from proposals to allow computer grading of students' written work. Programs to rate and give feedback on written text have advanced to the point that many assessment experts consider them reliable instruments. However, Berkowicz and Myers noted that while educators are almost unanimously opposed to the practice, increasingly greater loads encountered by teachers and others charged with assessment make it impossible to give meaningful feedback to every student's writing assignment, unless computer grading programs are employed. What evidence can you cite that this practice is growing? Has it proven a valid and reliable way to grade students' work and give them meaningful feedback? What are the arguments against the practice?

2. Many educators believe that budgeting for computer equipment, software, and infrastructure can be defended because digital and information literacy are as important—if not more important than—traditional reading-and-writing literacy. What evidence can you cite that this is true? What information and/or conditions in today's schools do you feel should inform policy makers on the relative priority of these "old and new" kinds of literacy?

# Summary

**The following is a summary of the main points covered in this chapter.**

1. **Issues and Challenges in English and Language Arts.** Each of these current issues has implications for how teachers can and should integrate technologies. These include: teachers' responsibilities for the new literacies, the need for new instructional strategies, challenges of working with diverse learners, challenges of motivating students to read and write, teachers' growth as literacy professionals and leaders, to teach or not to teach QWERTY keyboarding, and the cursive writing controversy.

2. **Technology Integration Strategies for English and Language Arts.** Integration strategies include the following activities to address language-learning needs:
   - To offer support for word fluency and vocabulary development support, teachers can use online practice in matching letters and sounds and matching words with meanings, and online tools to engage students in vocabulary learning.
   - To support comprehension and literacy development, teachers can use digital text to encourage engaged reading, support reading with software and portable assistive devices, and use talking word processors to scaffold reading development.
   - To support teaching the writing process, teachers can use the following: prewriting strategies that include concept mapping, note-taking, content curation, and electronic outlining apps or features; strategies to encourage writing that include story starters, word-processed written drafts; whiteboard modeling to support revising and editing written drafts, to provide feedback on student writing with editing tools, and to provide feedback with grammar, spell-check, and thesaurus features.
   - To meet needs for multimodal communication and digital publishing, teachers may employ strategies for sharing written texts such as using fan fiction sites, e-books, multimedia slide shows, and news broadcasts; and they may employ digital storytelling and video game design.
   - To meet needs for literature learning, teachers can access online copies of published works and get online background information on authors. They can also support literary analysis by projecting text on interactive whiteboards for analysis and use digital texts.

3. **Teaching English and Language Arts Teachers to Integrate Technology.** Teachers can begin by consulting the rubric provided in this chapter to measure their own growth in English and language arts technology integration. After that, they may review issues and challenges in English and language arts instruction and use chapter resources to learn technology integration strategies they will use to address the issues and challenges.

# TECHNOLOGY INTEGRATION **WORKSHOP**

## 1. APPLY WHAT YOU LEARNED

To apply the concepts and skills you've read about throughout this chapter, go to the Chapter 9 Technology Application Activity.

## 2. TECHNOLOGY INTEGRATION LESSON PLANNING: PART 1—EVALUATING AND CREATING LESSON PLANS

Complete the following exercise using the sample lesson plans found on any lesson planning site that you find on the Internet.

**a.** Locate lesson ideas—Identify three lesson plans that focus on any of the tools or strategies you learned about in this chapter. For example:

- Online practice in matching letters and sounds or matching words with meanings
- Supporting prewriting with concept mapping, note-taking, curation, or electronic outlining
- Using grammar, spell-check, and thesaurus features to provide students with feedback on their writing
- Digital storytelling
- Promoting literacy through video game design
- Using digital tools to carry out literary analysis

**b.** Evaluate the lessons—Use the Technology Lesson Plan Evaluation Checklist to evaluate each of the lessons you found.

**c.** Create your own lesson—After you have reviewed and evaluated some sample lessons, create one of your own using a lesson plan format of your choice (or one your instructor gives you). Be sure the lesson focuses on one of the technologies or strategies discussed in this chapter.

## 3. TECHNOLOGY INTEGRATION LESSON PLANNING: PART 2—IMPLEMENTING THE TIP MODEL

Review how to implement the TIP model in your classroom by doing the following activities with the lesson you created in the Technology Integration Lesson Planning exercise above.

**a.** Describe the Phase 1—Planning activities you would do to use this lesson in your classroom:

- What is the relative advantage of using the technology(ies) in this lesson?
- Do you have resources and skills you need to carry it out?

**b.** Describe the Phase 2—Implementation activities you would do to use this lesson in your classroom:

- What are the objectives of the lesson plan?
- How will you assess your students' accomplishment of the objectives?
- What integration strategies are used in this lesson plan?
- How would you prepare the learning environment?

**c.** Describe the Phase 3—Evaluation/Revision activities you would do to use this lesson in your classroom: What strategies and/or instruments would you use to evaluate the success of this lesson in your classroom in order to determine revision needs?

**d.** Add lesson descriptors—Create descriptors for your new lesson (e.g., grade level, content and topic areas, technologies used, ISTE standards, 21st Century Learning standards).

**e.** Save your new lesson—Save your lesson plan with all its descriptors and TIP model notes.

## 4. FOR YOUR TEACHING PORTFOLIO

Add the following to your Teaching Portfolio:

- Reflections on Hot Topic Debate.
- Summary notes from the Collaborate, Discuss, Reflect activity.
- Lesson plan evaluations, lesson plans, and products you created above.
- Your *Apply What You Learned* Product from Activity 1.

Phillip Hubbard and M. D. Roblyer

# 10

# Teaching and Learning with Technology for Foreign and Second Languages

## Learning Outcomes

After reading this chapter and completing the learning activities, you should be able to:

1. Identify implications for technology integration of each current issue faced by foreign/second language teachers. (ISTE Standards•T 4, 5)

2. Select technology integration strategies that can meet various needs for instruction in foreign/second language curricula. (ISTE Standards•T 2, 5)

3. Design a strategy for how to build teacher knowledge and skills in technology integration for foreign and second language instruction. (ISTE Standards•T 5)

Vladgrin/Shutterstock

# TECHNOLOGY INTEGRATION IN ACTION: WRITING IN BLOGS EN FRANÇAIS

GRADE LEVELS: 9–12 • CONTENT AREA/TOPIC: French, art • LENGTH OF TIME: One semester

## PHASE 1 ANALYSIS OF LEARNING AND TEACHING NEEDS

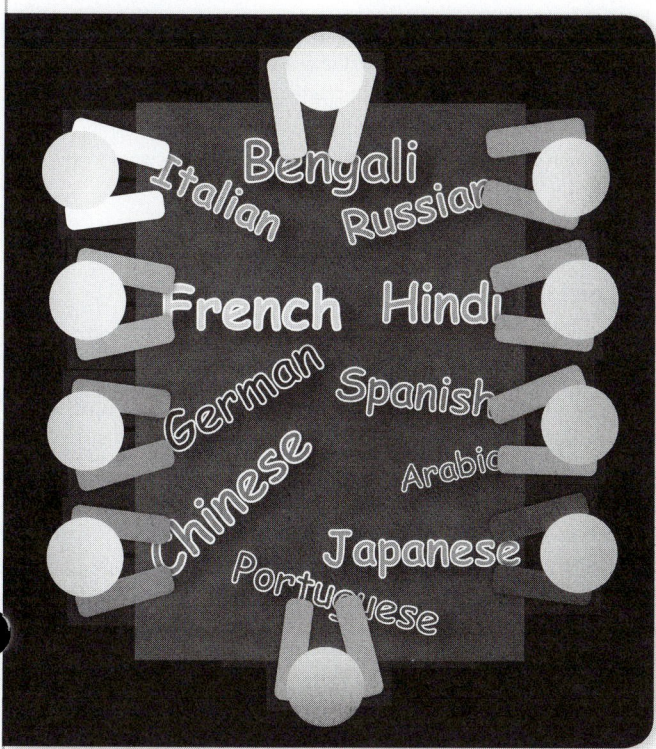

Carlosgardel/Fotolia

### Step 1: Determine relative advantage.

The French teachers at Sabine High School agreed that their students needed more practice writing in French. They had tried various kinds of writing assignments, but students always seemed to do the minimum required, and their fluency in writing the language remained low. The teachers agreed that students would be more motivated if assignments had greater purpose and a real audience. While visiting another school, one of the teachers saw a project for Spanish language students that seemed to fulfill all of these requirements. The teachers at that school held a Spanish art identification contest using an asynchronous online discussion board. They posted images of Spanish art, and students had to identify the pieces and discuss and describe the art en Español on the discussion board. Students who were the first to do these tasks earned points, and students who accumulated the most points won recognition and prizes. The Spanish teachers said that the strategy worked well for students learning English as well. Also, the project exposed students to some important artwork from the Spanish-speaking countries the students were learning about. Since students were already used to writing in blogs with their English classes, the French teachers decided to implement the project using these blogs.

### Step 2: Assess current resources and skills.

French teachers determined that the school technology support was sufficient for their needs. The students' previous experience with blogs meant that they had the technical facility to use them and understood their general nature. Additional training and discussion with students regarding the challenges in blogging in a foreign language would be added.

## PHASE 2 PLANNING FOR INTEGRATION

### Step 3: Decide on objectives and assessments.

The French teachers wanted to make sure the expectations for the project were clear to students and teachers alike, so they agreed on the following objectives and assessment methods to measure students' performance:

Outcome: Participate in blogs on artworks.
Objective: All students access each of the blogs and post all of the required descriptions.
Assessment: A checklist of items students were required to post about each artwork, with points for each posting and extra points for being first or second to identify and describe the artwork.

Outcome: Improved writing in French.
Objective: All students will demonstrate improved writing in French by achieving a 90% rubric score.
Assessment: A rubric to assess the quality and quantity of students' descriptive writing in French.

Outcome: Demonstrate knowledge of artworks.
Objective: Each student must score at least 80% on a short-answer test on art from French-speaking countries.
Assessment: A test consisting of questions on the art discussed in the blogs.

### Step 4: Design integration strategies.

The teachers knew that it would take some time to review students' French language skills, prepare content and procedures for the blogs, and get students used to working with them. They designed the following sequence of activities to prepare for and carry out the project:

**August–December:** Prepare artwork graphics to place on the school website and do administrative tasks to use blogs. Develop students' descriptive vocabulary related to art (e.g., *nature morte, paysage, croquis, aquarelle, gravure, toile*) and language to express their opinions about art (e.g., *J'aime vraiment cette peinture à l'huile*). Develop students' knowledge about the French-speaking countries and cultures from which the art originates.

**January:** Introduce the blogging and the art identification tasks. Assign the first blog as a practice to iron out any logistical problems. Review the items students are required to post about each artwork, and review assessment strategies. Remind students that they can see each other's postings and can complete the assignment requirements in the context of a reply to a classmate.

**February–April:** Introduce one blog for credit each month. Assess each, and review the answers to the blog at the end of the month.

**May:** Review points won, recognize students, and award prizes.

### Step 5: Prepare instructional environment.

The teachers knew that setting up the activity would require some concerted effort the first time they did it, so they divided the following tasks among themselves to lessen the load on each of them:

**Setting up blogs.** Teachers obtained the required information about how to create blogs and set up one blog for each month. Each student needed to have a unique sign-on, so they made a list of students, created usernames and passwords for them, and entered them into the system.

**Preparing content for assignments.** Teachers selected a set of paintings and sculptures for each blog, making sure they represented various French-speaking countries and cultures they had studied. For each blog, they wrote a set of questions to be answered about the pieces of art.

**Preparing assessments and handouts.** Teachers created the checklists and rubrics they would use to assess student progress. They also prepared a handout describing the project and giving the URLs for accessing the system. Finally, they provided examples of some exemplary posts and replies and discussed how the project could foster developing the students' written fluency in French.

**Ensuring student access.** Teachers had already confirmed that most students had Internet access at home. However, to make sure everyone had adequate time and access whenever they wanted it (so they all had equal chance to be first with the correct answers), the teachers designated times when students could get online in their classrooms and in the language lab.

## PHASE 3 POST-INSTRUCTION ANALYSIS AND REVISIONS

### Step 6: Analyze results.

Teachers observed that students posted increasingly faster for each blog and that most wrote more sentences each time. By having a clear purpose for writing that allowed for student choice, the project helped develop students' writing skills. Furthermore, the teachers noticed that there was more interaction between students with each successive blog, which speaks to the benefits of having an interested audience when writing in a foreign language, even if this audience includes students' classmates and other classes in the school. The test on students' knowledge of art and culture showed that students had learned a lot about art from the countries they were studying. When the teachers interviewed the students, it was apparent that all were enthusiastic about the project, with a few exceptions. Students who had no Internet access at home or had to share access with family members felt it was unfair that others had more opportunities to look up and post answers.

### Step 7: Make revisions.

The teachers decided to designate more time in each blog for lab work so that all students would have the access they needed. Students also suggested that the competition be by class instead of across classes, giving more students opportunities for winning awards. The teachers decided that the project had worked so well that they would expand it to include musical works by French-speaking musicians next time.

*Source:* Based on a concept from: DeLuca, A., and Hoffman, B. (2003). Vamos a darles algo a discutir (Let's give 'em something to talk about). *Learning and Leading with Technology, 30*(5), 36–41.

# CHAPTER 10 **BIG IDEAS OVERVIEW**

Before you begin reading the rest of this chapter, listen to the Chapter 10 Big Ideas Overview. It will give you a brief audio overview of main concepts to look for and help prepare you to work through information and exercises to achieve this chapter's outcomes.

## ISSUES AND CHALLENGES IN FOREIGN AND SECOND LANGUAGE LEARNING

There are two forms of language learning: second language learning and foreign language learning. When language learners are in a classroom with an English-speaking environment, English is the second (or additional) language for them and students are commonly referred to as **English language learners (ELLs)**. (This used to be called **English as a second language** or **ESL**, a term that is still widely used outside of the K–12 setting). However, when the language being studied is spoken mainly in other countries, it is referred to as **foreign language (FL) learning**. While the underlying processes of ELL and FL learning are similar, there are also many differences relevant to teaching and technology integration strategies. Key differences are the availability of the language input in the environment and opportunities for using the language in meaningful situations.

Unlike learners of a foreign language, ELLs have many more opportunities for learning English because it is a majority language that is being spoken all around them. This allows them to engage in field trips, assignments, and collaborations with native speakers in linguistically and culturally rich settings. They also have urgency to learn the language quickly because they need English for everyday tasks, employment, and educational purposes. Conversely, FL learners typically have fewer opportunities to practice the foreign language, and teachers often go to great lengths to find people and places with whom and where their students can use the target language. Technology is perhaps even more important for them as it allows a great variety of connections to people, places, and authentic language outside of the local environment. FL learning is different than ELL learning in that it is often seen as enrichment rather than a matter of crucial importance for academic success. This section introduces key problems of practice for learning in each setting.

Besides recognizing the differences between ELL and FL, teachers should be sensitive to the differences between using technology for content learning and for language learning. In evaluating tools, tasks, and activities, it is important to supplement a general evaluation procedure with one that considers the unique nature of language learning. The applied linguist Carol Chapelle has offered such an evaluation framework for technology-oriented language learning tasks that takes into account six key concepts from second language acquisition research. She claims that for both judging the suitability of the tasks initially and for evaluating outcomes, the following categories should be addressed: language learning potential, learner fit, meaning focus, authenticity, positive impact, and practicality. See Jamieson and Chapelle (2010) for an example of the framework in action.

## ELL Issue #1: Demands on Content Area Teachers

As the U.S. population becomes increasingly diverse and children from many different countries and cultures enter American schools in larger numbers, teachers face a continuing challenge to teach content to students with limited English proficiency to meet academic standards mandated by the state and by their local district. In addition, many states have discontinued funding for special classes or bilingual approaches and have begun placing these students into regular classroom settings in which instruction is entirely in English. Many ELL students are not literate in their first language, which compounds the problem. These students must be taught to read, so teachers must teach them to speak and read English at the same time. Teachers often have students in their classrooms with many different home languages. Technology tools give teachers some of the support they need to meet widely varying needs of ELL while still proceeding with regular classroom instruction for other students. For example, activities such as those on Brainpop are available to let students practice their vocabulary and English skills individually, both in the classroom and on their own. Also, many online translation sites are available that can scaffold students' current knowledge by providing on-the-spot translations of directions and classroom tasks. Mobile devices have made these aids more portable and easier to access from any location.

O'Dowd (2011) notes that providing more authentic experiences through intercultural exchanges is still just an add-on activity for most teachers of foreign languages. The same may be said of ELL classes. The pressures of preparing students to meet curriculum standards, in addition to the logistical issues in implementing what O'Dowd calls "telecollaborations," make it difficult for teachers to find classroom time for these valuable experiences. Increasingly, however, online sites like ePals (see Table 10.1) provide dedicated, secure platforms with support materials for projects linked to Common Core State Standards, making it easier to justify the class and preparation time spent.

## ELL Issue #2: Academic and Language Prerequisites for ELLs

Typical grade-level content materials are above the reading proficiency levels of ELL students. Technology offers some helpful solutions to a common problem faced by K–12 ELL teachers: developing their students' academic language and background knowledge sufficiently for them to participate in mainstream classes. For example, a high school English language learner who has a low level of proficiency but much knowledge of current events can make use of multimedia content on the websites of national and local newspapers, magazines from across the spectrum of pop culture such as *Sports Illustrated* or *People*, or television stations like ESPN and CNN. On these websites, students can look at photos with short captions, listen to podcasts, and watch videos on topics of their choice. In addition to lessening the reading load, these highly visual options give learners with lower levels of proficiency access to authentic information on high-interest, current topics. Initially, students may need guidance in navigating these kinds of websites. They need to learn what the icons mean, how to use the headings, and how to recognize the key vocabulary words—that is, acquire the basic media literacy needed to benefit from the tools. Another way to scaffold these experiences is to help students to find media on a current event or story of interest first in their native language. The resulting background knowledge will be useful when tackling the new English vocabulary.

It is often helpful for English language learners to read text designed for native English speakers who are younger than they are, if the materials are not too childish and the task assigned is age appropriate (e.g., compare and contrast three versions of the Cinderella story through literary and cultural lenses). One useful resource for finding books with relevant academic and cultural content for English language learners is the International Children's Digital Library, a searchable, multilingual children's library. The listed books are appropriate for children from 3 to 13 years of age, but they may also work well for older English language learners, particularly the nonfiction books. There are also many websites that have simplified language and interesting pictures and visuals, such as Desert USA and National Geographic.

## ELL Issue #3: The Need to Differentiate Instruction

In many ELL settings, teachers need to deliver instruction across a wide range of proficiency levels. Unlike FL classes, ELL teachers cannot assume their classes have been divided according to proficiency level. Older English language learners come with a range of print literacy skills in English and their native language as well as a wide range of prior formal schooling experiences. It is common at the elementary level to collaborate with a grade-level teacher to deliver ELL services; at the upper levels, students of different needs are sometimes served in stand-alone classes, sheltered content classes, and ELL classes. Technology can help the teacher differentiate

**TABLE 10.1** Summary of Technology Integration Strategies for ELL and FL Learning

| Technology Integration Strategies | Benefits | Sample Resources and Activities |
|---|---|---|
| Support for authentic oral language practice and assessment | • Helps provide individual help for students' different language levels<br>• Helps students internalize word meanings and gives additional practice in using new words.<br>• Gives practice in following oral English direction, and in reading and responding in written English<br>• Builds listening competence | • Scholastic interactive storybooks<br>• Leapfrog products<br>• Living Books<br>• Natural Reader<br>• Auralog's Tell Me More Series<br>• Rosetta Stone<br>• Transparent Language<br>• Penpower WorldpenScan Pro<br>• Radio broadcasts from NPR<br>• Radio broadcasts from Multilingual Books Online<br>• English Central |
| Virtual collaborations | • Helps motivate students to use new language skills<br>• Helps students learn more about cultural contexts of languages they are learning | • Global SchoolNet<br>• ePals Global Community<br>• My Language Exchange<br>• Global Friends Group<br>• The Mixxer |
| Virtual field trips for modified language immersion | • Offers expanded opportunities for language acquisition<br>• Allows students to "visit" locations and have experiences not available to them in person | • InterLingo Spanish<br>• Tramline Virtual Field Trips |
| Teletandem experiences for modified language immersion | • Gives students authentic practice in conversations with native speakers of other languages | • Teletandem Brasil<br>• Teletandem projects at various universities |
| Support for practice in language subskills | • Provides intense, targeted practice in specific language skills and vocabulary sets<br>• Provides immediate feedback to correct common errors students make<br>• Incorporates current vocabulary of specific classroom lessons | • Tower of English<br>• English Banana<br>• Pinyin Practice<br>• Quia |
| Presentation aids | • Helps reduce student stress and focus their presentations<br>• Teaches valuable skills in making effective presentations<br>• Makes classroom presentations more understandable and more enjoyable for both presenters and listeners | • PowerPoint<br>• Prezi<br>• Creative commons search |
| Support for text production | • Supports authentic use of language in creating documents (e.g., journals, reports)<br>• Helps correct students' written text through grammar and spelling checks | • NJStar Chinese word processor<br>• Volga-Writer Russian word processor<br>• Word processing in many languages |
| Productivity and lesson design support for teachers | • Saves teacher time in locating and preparing lesson ideas and materials<br>• Gives teachers access to a wealth of classroom-tested lesson ideas and strategies<br>• Provides models of effective technology integration | • Content-Based Language Teaching through Technology (CoBaLTT)<br>• Intercultural Development Research Association<br>• Global Friends Group<br>• 2Learn.ca |

instruction through software that assists in tracking individual students and can offer ways for students to work independently on developing their reading, writing, speaking, and listening skills. Oral and written language practice programs can offer individuals simulated authentic practice while the teacher is working with other students. With multimedia programs that include actual spoken models, ELL students can use the computer to help them practice their oral English language production. While these allow only practice for imitation and memorization and cannot yet handle open-ended, creative use of language, some can nevertheless provide useful feedback on whether a word or sentence is spoken accurately. One example is English Central, which incorporates speech recognition technology into its activities. In addition, grammar check programs allow students to receive instant feedback on their use of vocabulary and verb tenses as they practice their written English. However, these programs should be used with care as they do not consistently provide accurate results.

## ELL Issue #4: Challenges of Integrating the Students' Native Languages

Efforts to prepare students for mainstream classes in English often require building background knowledge in the content area so that when they are confronted with grade-level content instruction, students have a base upon which to acquire new knowledge. One of the easiest ways to do this is to use students' native languages. Based on Cummins' Linguistic Interdependence Hypothesis (Proctor, August, Snow, & Barr, 2010), use of students' native languages also serves to build students' skills in their native languages, which in turn facilitates skills in English. An additional benefit of using the students' native languages to help them gain access to grade-level content is that they come to see that their native languages are valued as a resource at school. This practice creates a more welcoming learning environment for immigrant children and youth.

Technology can assist teachers in using the students' native languages even when the student speaks a less common native language. Many new programs allow teachers to create vocabulary lists specific to their lessons. These can help prepare students who have few other scaffolds to be more successful in participating in grade-level and content classrooms. Using a computer program to translate from one language to another, or **machine translation**, can be helpful to teachers and students. For this translation, they can now use online websites, as well as handheld devices. However, both teachers and students need to be aware of the controversy surrounding online translation sites (see the Hot Topic for Debate feature). This seems particularly true for online searches. From their text-analysis study using translators before online searches, Dolamic and Savoy (2010) concluded that doing a search that begins with asking a search engine such as Google to translate it will have a negative impact on retrieval effectiveness (p. 2272). It is worth noting, however, that in language programs where translation is acceptable as a tool for comprehension, sites with parallel texts that humans have translated can be useful. These include multilingual websites where users click on flag icons to select the language and video sites with multilingual captions and transcripts, such as TED, (Technology, Entertainment, and Design). In these cases, students may see more accurate translation of words and phrases in context than is possible with machine translation, and may also see more conventional grammatical patterns in the language being learned.

Teachers can look up key content words in the students' native languages or translate some simple instructions on a project. For students, the tools function like bilingual dictionaries and help them unlock the meaning of a text both at the word level and the phrase level. Some of these tools are Babylon Online Translation, Google Translate, Bing Translator, and World Lingo. Though many of these tools offer translations only in common foreign languages (e.g., French, Spanish, Chinese, Korean), some are beginning to include languages less commonly seen in U.S. classrooms (e.g., Farsi, Hmong, Somali).

Another way to bring students' native languages into the ELL class is through electronic newspapers from around the world. It is possible to access newspapers in most languages found among English language learners on the Internet, as long as the computer is set up to read the fonts used in languages that do not use the Roman alphabet. Students can read about many topics relevant to their classes in newspapers in their native language.

## Hot Topic Debate
### What is the Role of Online (Machine) Translators When Learning a Foreign Language?

*Take a position for or against (based either on your own position or one assigned to you) on the following controversial statement. Discuss it in class or on an online discussion board, blog, or wiki, as assigned by your instructor. When the discussion is complete, write a summary of the main pros and cons that you and your classmates have stated, and put the summary document in your Teacher Portfolio.*

When it comes to the reliability of online translation sites (a.k.a., machine translation or web-based machine translation), articles from business and education alike tend to cite the Bill Murray movie *Lost in Translation*. A 2012 posting on the *Entrepreneur* website warns readers that relying on these translation "widgets" can result in unintended insults to your customers. In her study of German language learners' use of online resources, Larson-Guenette (2013) found that many students felt that though such sites were unreliable for pure translation purposes, they tended to use them anyway to check their work. This was true despite the fact they many of their instructors prohibited the use of online translators, saying it was academically dishonest practice. Do online translation sites have a place in language learning classrooms? What evidence can you cite that helps define an appropriate and helpful role that supports both instructors and students?

## FL Issue #1: The Need for Authentic Materials and Perspectives

Often FL teachers are nonnative speakers of the languages they teach and may have infrequent opportunities to spend extended periods of time in countries where their FL is spoken. Therefore, there is a need to find ways to expose students to both a range of native speakers of the FL, including varieties of the language not spoken by the teacher, and to up-to-date examples of how the language is currently used. Technologies are available to make these connections possible. Using websites and projects to connect students with speakers from around the world, students can also experience the cultural, political, and individual perspectives of those who speak the language of study. An increase in authentic perspectives and materials designed for native speakers of the language taps into high-quality teaching of culture using the standards set forth by the American Council on the Teaching of Foreign Languages (Standards for Foreign Language Learning, 1999). See their site to review these standards. The standards integrate perspectives, products, and practices to teach culture. When all three components are integrated into a FL curriculum, they work together to deepen students' cultural competency. Technology can bring insider voices and authentic materials into the FL classroom to teach culture through perspectives, products, and practices.

It used be a major challenge for language teachers to find authentic media for their students, but now such resources abound. However, it is often difficult and time consuming to identify material that it at the appropriate level. The European Commission has funded a project in the area of Content Integrated Language Learning (CLIL) that provides a repository of short videos on topics of interest that have been leveled according to the Common European Framework's six proficiency levels. Through the site, the videos can be browsed for topic and level and loaded into a player that includes transcripts with the words linked to bilingual dictionaries. Videos for English and other world languages as well as some less commonly taught ones are included, and the site is available worldwide free of charge.

## FL Issue #2: The Need for Creating Audience and Purpose

Another common problem related to practice opportunities for FL teachers and their students is creating a broader repertoire of individuals to talk with and audiences that wish to read their writing. Technology-based projects can assist with the need to provide both means and a reason to contact native language speakers. With online video and audio conferencing tools (e.g., Skype or Google Hangouts), students are now able to talk with peers in other countries and interact with presenters who visit their class via these inexpensive online tools (Bahrani, 2011). Blogging and wiki functions also offer a platform for writing to classmates and with students in other classes about collaborative projects or reviews of movies or music (Castleberry & Evers, 2010). Online publishing offers students an audience beyond their teachers and can give students an incentive to revise their work. There is a wide array of opportunities for sharing student writing with new audiences.

**TECHNOLOGY LEARNING CHECK**
Complete **TLC 10.1** to review what you have learned from this section about issues that determine how technology is used in FL and ELL.

# TECHNOLOGY INTEGRATION STRATEGIES FOR ELL AND FL INSTRUCTION

### Learning Foreign Languages Online

In this video, a virtual school principal talks about how online courses make foreign-language learning accessible for students who have no teachers available locally. How could this kind of program be useful in your current or future situation? What would your school or district have to do to decide which language(s) to offer?

**Computer-assisted language learning (CALL)**, an accepted term for using computers in language testing, teaching, and learning, has made great strides in offering students new ways to enhance their speaking and listening skills. There are now a variety of technology-based tools available to support both ELL and FL learners in and out of class. These strategies include support for authentic oral language practice, virtual collaborations, virtual field trip immersion experiences, language subskills practice, presentations, text production, and productivity and lesson design support for teachers. See a summary of these strategies and the resources to support them in Table 10.1.

Castleberry and Evers (2010) say that mediated formats are flexible enough to provide opportunities for learning that are not possible though traditional methods. Technology makes curriculum more accessible to students with diverse needs, and provides information about the languages and cultures they are studying. They offer 20 different ways to use technologies to support language learning, all of which are discussed in various parts of this section. See the Adapting for Special Needs feature with more tips for addressing these.

## Adapting for Special Needs

### English as a Second Language Learning

Students whose first language is not English sometimes participate rather slowly or do not respond to teacher questions due to the multilingual processing they must use. Teachers can support learning for these students by allowing adequate time for cognitive processing and by encouraging students to make connections between their first language and English. Here are some useful classroom resources for these students:

- Larry Ferlazzo's Websites of the Day: For Teaching ELL, ESL, & EFL – A classroom teacher who searches the Web to provide daily reports on the best resources he can find for busy teachers working with second language students.

- Book Box (at the Bookbox website)—View and listen to stories in one language along with second language captions.

- Simple English Wikipedia (at the Simple English Wikipedia website)—Articles are written explicitly in simple English to reduce the complexity and eliminate jargon. This feature is also found in the main Wikipedia and is offered as a language translation option on the left column of the page.

- VocabGrabber (at the VisualThesaurus website)—Paste in a section of text to have the vocabulary analyzed. Provides definitions, visualizations of synonyms, word frequency, and other resources.

*—Contributed by Dave Edyburn*

## Support for Authentic Oral Language Practice and Assessment

Several technologies are available to enhance and support a more authentic approach to language learning and assessment. These include the following:

**Videoconferencing.** New and inexpensive technologies help teachers connect FL students with native speakers in other countries. Quillen (2011) says that many FL teachers claim that, in addition to making interactions with native speakers more feasible logistically, they can make teaching and learning more effective than having conversations through other means.

**Multimedia software and interactive (electronic) storybooks.** These technologies, designed to support language acquisition and vocabulary development, have several strengths. First, they allow teachers to individualize instruction for students' differing language levels. Second, they give students an opportunity to interact in English authentically in a less stressful environment as compared to a face-to-face environment. Interactive books are a good example of using technology in this manner. These books appear on the screen, and the student can set the program to read the book aloud as he or she follows along, giving the reader the chance to see the word and the illustrations and to hear the words pronounced. The reader can opt to read the story unaided, touching a word with a stylus when a prompt is needed. Many of these programs have additional learning games attached, using the vocabulary and illustrations from the storybook.

Scholastic has a number of titles available in interactive (electronic) storybook format, including the Clifford series. Many of these interactive book programs emphasize vocabulary games to help students internalize word meanings and to give additional practice in using the new words encountered in the storybooks.

Software series for learning various languages continue to be popular, particularly with older language learners. Companies that offer these series include Rosetta Stone, Transparent Language, and Auralog. Refer back to Table 10.1 for a list of these and other resources.

**Learning games on handheld devices.** LeapFrog also has learning games appropriate for language learners of various ages. Its series of handheld devices is designed to give elementary, middle, and high school students practice in math, science, social studies, and languages using content from the most common textbooks across the country. Newer devices also have multimedia and ereader capabilities (see Figure 10.1).

**Language labs.** Though language labs have long been a mainstay in ELL and FL instruction, they have changed from strictly audio to more multimedia experiences for students. In the 1960s and 1970s, they consisted of audiotapes that students listened to and imitated. Since then, we have learned much about the importance of communication, authentic practice, monitoring, and feedback. Today's digital language labs look very different. They provide students with a computer, headset, and video monitor in each individual station, and activities are much more interactive. The teacher's station typically projects on a main screen in the lab and depending on the software and hardware, may allow control or monitoring of the student stations as well (see the SANS 21st Century Technology for Language Learning site and and the CAN-8 virtual language lab for examples). Activities such as recorded dialog journals, in which students speak about an assigned topic or a topic of their choice, give the teacher an opportunity for monitoring, feedback, and authentic verbal interaction. Listening instruction can be built into the lab setting by having students listen to oral instructions while building a project such as a paper airplane, Lego construction, or origami figure. Additional resources for building listening competence can be found at Randall's ESL Cyber Listening Lab. This site provides short (1–3 minute) and long (5–10 minute) listening exercises, as well as an array of other useful resources such as "culture videos." The English Language Listening Library Online offers over 2,000 free audio and video listening activities, including culturally rich examples of both native and non-native English speakers, often interacting through interviews.

**FIGURE 10.1** Leapster Handheld Personal Learning Tools

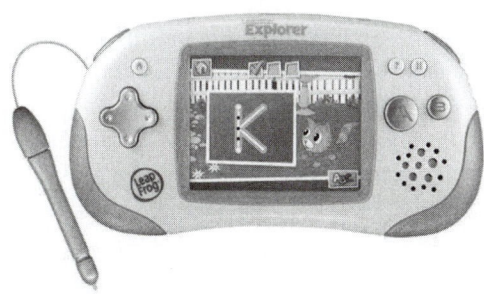

▲ Today's digital language labs provide students with a computer, headset, and video monitor at each station. **Andrey_Kuzmin/ Shutterstock**

**Radio and TV broadcasts.** For more advanced students, National Public Radio offers live radio broadcasts on the Internet that provide both news and drama from which teachers can create motivational activities to give the learner practice in oral and written language. Also, Multilingual Books Online provides links to radio stations in multiple languages around the world. CNN Student News has a 10-minute online program of news highlights for students weekdays with a transcript that can be valuable for ELLs for both comprehension and vocabulary development.

**Podcasts.** Teachers can now create their own podcasts for listening instruction and practice, but an even more innovative use for podcasts is assessment. Using Audacity or another free software tool, teachers can gather oral language samples from students. This use of podcasts gives teachers greater ease in assessing students' individual speaking skills, using a rubric or checklist they design specifically for the task. Student-produced digital files can be stored in an online portfolio to assess progress over time and for students' reflection on their own progress.

**FIGURE 10.2** The WorldPenScan by Penpower

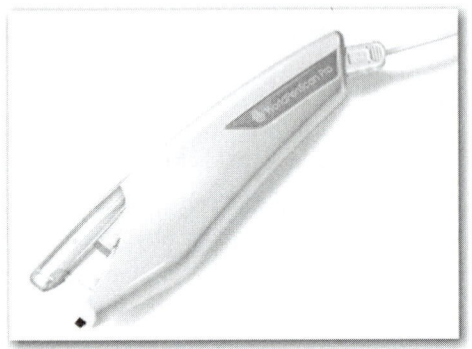

*Source:* Reprinted by permission of Penpower Technology Ltd.

**FIGURE 10.3** The Lingo Talking Translator by Lingo Travel

*Source:* Reprinted by permission of Lingo Corporation.

**Translation websites and handheld translation devices.** A variety of websites and portable devices are available to aid translation from one language to another. All these aids are considered forms of machine translation. (See the Hot Topic for Debate feature.) Handheld devices make translation more accessible. For example, the Penpower WorldPenScan Pro shown in Figure 10.2 is a text scanner that is integrated with Babylon dictionary and translation software. Using this "pen," students scan a word or phrase and get a spoken or written translation. The Lingo Talking Translator is another kind of handheld that provides on-the-spot translation (see Figure 10.3). Also look for free language learning communities and other free resources in the Open Source Options feature.

## Virtual Collaborations

Many teachers have found student collaborations to be effective in motivating students to use their emerging language skills. Using email, blogs, wikis, online chats, and other communication technologies, students can work with peers from other cultures to provide authentic writing and research experiences. O'Dowd (2011) says that these exchanges are called **blended intercultural telecollaborations**, or "international class-to-class partnerships in which projects and tasks are developed by the partner teachers in the collaborating institutions" (p. 3), and can be divided into three categories:

1. Information exchange tasks—Learners provide their long-distance partners with information about their personal biographies or aspects of their home cultures.

2. Comparison and analysis tasks—In addition to requiring learners to exchange information, they also carry out comparisons or critical analyses of cultural products from each culture (e.g., books, surveys, films, newspaper articles).

3. Collaborative tasks—Learners are required to work together to produce a joint product or conclusion.

O'Dowd says that these exchanges emphasize developing both better cultural awareness and greater linguistic competence. These collaborations are made possible when two teachers establish an email connection and begin an exchange of messages between their students. See sites such as the ePals Global

# OPEN SOURCE OPTIONS for ELL and FL Classrooms

| TYPES | FREE SOURCES |
|---|---|
| **Free online practice and translation** | Brainpop ELL: brainpopesl.com<br>Google Language Tools: google.com/language_tools<br>Multi-Language Words Memorizer: memorizer.codeplex.com |
| **Free language learning websites and software** | Busuu Language Learning Community: busuu.com<br>LiveMocha Language Learning Community: livemocha.com; (free for initial period only)<br>Hello-Hello Language Learning Community: hello-hello.com<br>BBC Audio-Video Courses: bbc.co.uk/languages<br>Byki Express: byki.com/fls/FLS.html<br>Trace Effects (online ESL game): americanenglish.state.gov/trace-effects |
| **Blogs and wikis** | Blogger (now hosted by Google): blogger.com<br>Wikispaces: wikispaces.com |

**FIGURE 10.4** The Mixxer Website

*Source:* Reprinted by permission of Todd Bryant, Dickinson College. http://www.language-exchanges.org.

Community, Global SchoolNet, and The Mixxer (Figure 10.4) for help on establishing contacts with distant students.

## Virtual Field Trips for Modified Language Immersion Experience

Field trips offer a wealth of opportunities for language acquisition but are being greatly limited by funding. Virtual field trips provide opportunities for students to go places that would be impossible for them to see otherwise (Castleberry & Evers, 2010). There are several ways to implement virtual field trips. The most common virtual field trip format is a webquest-like format that has students visit websites, answer questions, and produce a product of some kind in the target language, such as a poster, brochure, or menu (see Technology Integration Example 10.1). Examples of virtual tour support sites include InterLingo Spanish. Another kind of virtual field trip is when the teacher or a member of the class takes a field trip, video records it, and then adds a running commentary to share with the class. The narrator strives to make sure that there is a good match between what is being viewed and what is being said, and depending on the language level, the narration can be in either English or the target language. There are also professionally produced virtual-reality field trips in which the user can "walk around" in the site by pressing various keys on the keyboard. Many of the world's outstanding art museums have virtual tours of this kind.

As with any field trip, students should be prepared ahead of time for their experience, building background knowledge, vocabulary, and expectations. The virtual field trip should be

# TECHNOLOGY INTEGRATION

## Example 10.1

followed with activities that encourage students to use their experiences and to practice their oral and written language.

## Teletandem Experiences for Modified Language Immersion

Another way to immerse students in authentic language learning is **teletandem** (a.k.a., **telecollaboration**) experiences (Perez-Hernandez, 2014). These are when students use videoconferencing or other collaborative technologies to work together to learn each other's native language. The goal is to pair students of the same proficiency level so that each student can learn a language from the other through real-world communications. Abreu-Ellis et al. (2013) found that structuring communications requirements, having an array of ways to communicate, and the high degree of **social presence,** primarily between peers, all contributed to the overall success of teletandem experiences. Social presence is the perception of "connectedness" or actually being with someone in a virtual environment. On the other hand, factors that detracted from the experience were technical problems and failures in communications systems. Thus, Abreu-Ellis et al. say that having backups for these systems is also critical to the success of teletandem activities.

## Support for Practice in Language Subskills

Many websites provide intense practice in specific language skills and vocabulary sets. (See samples of these in Table 10.1.) Websites such as English Zone, English Banana, English Online, and Tower of English provide fun but in-depth practice in areas that often give students great difficulty. For FL teachers, websites allow students to practice speaking and writing the language. For example, the Quia site allows teachers to design exercises tailored to specific languages and textbooks, and many such exercises are already available and free to anyone. Pinyin Practice

▲ Teletandem experiences let students use videoconferencing or other collaborative technologies to work together to learn each other's native language.
**Phovoir/Imagestate**

▲ Websites allow students to practice speaking and writing the language they are learning. **Teressa/Fotolia**

offers Chinese tones online, and Kanji Practice offers an opportunity to practice reading and writing Japanese kanji. Students can even do traditional grammar drills in Spanish or other languages, but in a new and more engaging way.

One value of these types of websites is that the exercises provide models of activities that can be used by teachers to create similar activities to correct common errors being made by the students or to incorporate vocabulary currently being studied in class. Teachers can have students read exercises aloud after completing them to promote the connection between written and oral modalities to help balance skill development. Apps are also available to add anytime-anywhere practice on handheld devices and smart phones. See Top Ten Must-Have Apps for ELL/FL.

## Presentation Aids

Castleberry and Evers (2010) say that every FL classroom should have a DVD player so that teachers can display films in the target language with or without subtitles. These media help students link words they are hearing and reading to visual presentations of actions and objects. In schools with good broadband capabilities, streaming of movies and television shows from the target culture is also an option.

When students are asked to give oral presentations, they can use PowerPoint, Prezi, or Keynote software or homemade videos to assist them. Visuals, in addition to supporting the concepts being presented, help students using them learn valuable skills in making effective presentations. Visuals also help reduce students' stress and focus their presentations. The 2Learn website gives teachers links to lessons for interactive whiteboards.

In addition to the websites and programs available for creating good oral presentations, digital cameras and scanners can also help create visuals to make the presentations more understandable and interesting. Scanned or digital pictures can easily be imported into PowerPoint or Keynote slides and are very effective in supporting student learning. Many teachers of English learners have found it vital to create a file of images for use in their instruction. The slides can be alphabetized, grouped by topic, or organized in any other way that makes them accessible. The Internet serves as a valuable resource for photographs and other images to add to presentations. By showing students how to search for Creative Commons images (see Table 10.1), teachers can emphasize the importance of considering the original creator's wishes with respect to reuse. Within the foreign language classroom in particular, it is important that presentation assignments be designed in such a way that the learner engages frequently with the target language. It is easy for undirected students to spend hours selecting and arranging the graphics for their talk at the expense of the linguistic and cultural elements that are the learning focus of the task.

## Support for Text Production

In FL learning, students need experience in the process of reading and writing the new language. Most standard word processing programs, such as Microsoft Word, offer support for producing and/or proofreading text in languages other than English. These programs also allow symbols to be inserted (e.g., umlauted letters in German or accented letters in French). However, special programs can also be obtained for languages such as Chinese or Russian that require characters other than the standard English alphabet (see Table 10.1 for samples). In addition to the authentic use of language in creating journals, descriptions of experiences, oral reports, and research projects, word processing programs support correct usage with grammar checks, correct spelling (spell-checks), and reminders to employ good style (e.g., use active rather than passive voice). (See Technology Integration Example 10.2 for a sample classroom strategy that uses a word processing program and images from websites.)

## Example 10.2

**TITLE:** The ABCs of Learning (Language Name)!

**CONTENT AREA/TOPIC:** ELL or any foreign language with an alphabetic writing system

**GRADE LEVELS:** 5–8

**ISTE STANDARDS•S:** Standard 1—Creativity and Innovation; Standard 2—Communication and Collaboration; Standard 3—Research and Information Fluency; Standard 6—Technology Operations and Concepts

**SFLL:** Standard 1.1 Standard 1.2 Standard 4.1

**DESCRIPTION:** Students can work individually or in pairs and use a language-specific word processing program to create an alphabet book in the target language. They begin by looking up words for each letter on various websites. The teacher can give them some vocabulary sites to begin with, or they can locate their own. For each word, they put an oversized image of the letter, a word that begins with the letter, an image that represents the word, and one to three additional words that also begin with that letter. Encourage them to think creatively about how to display these elements on the page. They print the books or display them on a school website, along with the "author name(s)."

*SOURCE:* Based on a concept in the lesson plan by Joan Diez at the Lesson Plans Page website: http://www.lessonplanspage.com.

---

Spell-check and grammar-check are not foolproof, however, in any language, and this is especially true for second language writers. Grammar-checking software is programmed primarily to recognize native speaker errors rather than those of language learners. For example, the default setting for Microsoft Word 2010 accepts "I go to store yesterday and buy candy bar" as a good sentence but correctly tags the verb as an error if this is changed to "I goes . . ." Students should always be encouraged to read their writing aloud and to listen for clues that corrections or refinements should be made. Peer review is also a good strategy here, as students may notice errors and omissions in others' work more readily than in their own.

A valuable addition to the writing process is inviting student authors to read their writing aloud to a small group or developing an audio file with a program like Audacity to be posted online while structuring opportunities for questions and comments. These processes provide opportunities for oral English practice and listening practice while also giving authors some ideas for revisions. The use of word processors allows the student/author to revise easily without rewriting by hand. The finished, printed copy of the text is also very motivational to the writer because it is very readable in typed, rather than in handwritten, form.

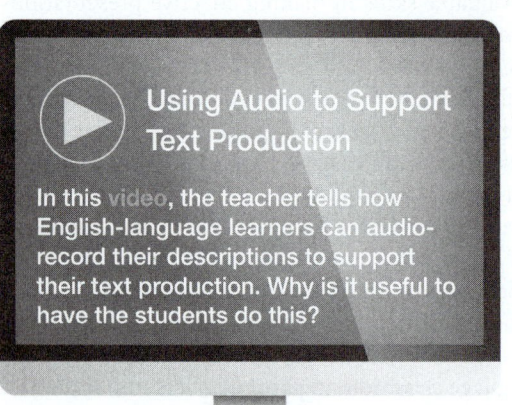

**Using Audio to Support Text Production**

In this video, the teacher tells how English-language learners can audio-record their descriptions to support their text production. Why is it useful to have the students do this?

## Use of Apps to Support Language Learning and Use

The prevalence of mobile devices like tablets and smartphones is growing, and both ELL and FL teachers need to be aware of both their strengths and limitations as learning devices. In 2013, the International Research Foundation (TIRF) released a set of commissioned articles providing an overview of mobile-assisted language learning (MALL) and made them freely available on the TIRF website. An important skill in integrating mobile language learning is the selection of appropriate apps for particular language learning tasks. Given the various language skills that apps can target and their wide range of uses for language learning, the Top Ten Must-Have Apps for ELL/FL in this list are divided across a number of subcategories. Teachers are therefore encouraged to see this as a representative rather than definitive selection. This is especially true given how rapidly apps are created and adopted.

A number of the apps have already been used creatively by language teachers both in and out of class. Try searching Google, Yahoo, or Bing for "language learning X" and "language teaching X" (without quotes), replacing X with the app name, for example "language learning Evernote."

## Productivity and Lesson Design Support for Teachers

The Internet holds an enormous range of resources to help ELL and FL teachers prepare for and carry out lessons. For example, the Intercultural Development Research Association offers a number of teaching resources and professional development opportunities, as do national foreign language resource centers such as CARLA (Center for Advanced Research in Language Acquisition) and LARC (Language Acquisition Resource Center). Some of these sites allow ELL teachers to network and share ideas and concerns in what are commonly referred to as communities of practice. For FL teachers, a wealth of lesson and unit ideas can be found across the Internet on sites hosted by commercial and private groups and university programs. See Table 10.1 for samples of all these sites.

This chapter has provided a number of technology-oriented strategies and resources for teachers engaged in helping students acquire proficiency in a second or foreign language. In addition to the previously mentioned ISTE standards, there is a complementary set specifically targeted to language teaching and learning, the TESOL Technology Standards for Teachers and Learners (TESOL, 2008).

The 14 standards for teachers are divided across four overarching goals related to foundational technological skills, integration of technology and language pedagogy, feedback and assessment, and communication and collaboration. The 11 learner standards similarly fall under three main goals: foundational technological skills, ethical and socially appropriate usage, and effective use of technology for language learning. At the time of this writing, the TESOL framework is available for free download at the TESOL website: search for the TESOL Technology Standards Framework. An expanded volume (Healey et al., 2011) that provides additional examples along with advice for teachers and teacher educators as well as a concordance to the ISTE standards is available through TESOL publications. Both the 2008 framework document and the 2011 volume include performance indicators for each standard, and the latter also has vignettes showing how each standard can be incorporated into an online or classroom situation consisting of high-, mid-, and low-technology–resource settings.

The existence of learner standards is evidence of an important aspect of technology for language learning that is often overlooked: learner training. Despite assumptions that so-called digital natives know how to use technology, it is clear that 1) there is significant variation in students' technology skills and knowledge, and 2) social uses of technology are not identical to their uses for learning. In a study of students in a hybrid Spanish course, Goertler, Bollen and Gaff (2012) reviewed a large-scale survey showing that language students at a midwestern university were unprepared in some areas to do the technology-based activities required of them in foreign language classes, such as typing diacritics and creating and editing audio and video files. According to Hubbard (2013), it is not only important to be sure that students have the technological skills and knowledge to work with their devices and tools, but also crucial that they have some pedagogical and strategic understanding of how to connect that knowledge to effective language learning.

To provide the best chance for reaching desired outcomes, language teachers should prepare students appropriately for new tasks and activities involving technology and monitor their progress to be sure they are doing what is expected. Reflect on what students need to know and be able to do, and then be sure to budget additional class time to train them as needed.

▲ An important skill in integrating mobile language learning is the selection of appropriate apps for particular language learning tasks
Kiko_Kiko/Shutterstock

**TECHNOLOGY LEARNING CHECK**
Complete **TLC 10.2** to review what you have learned from this section about technology integration strategies for FL and ELL instruction.

# TEACHING FOREIGN LANGUAGE AND SECOND LANGUAGE TEACHERS TO INTEGRATE TECHNOLOGY

This section gives recommendations for how teachers can prepare to integrate technology effectively into instruction for foreign and second language learning. Today's teachers of foreign and second languages have some of the same challenges with updating their teaching skills as teachers of English and language arts. Technologies offer so many new ways for students to express themselves in both writing and speaking that teachers must both learn how to use the technologies and find ways to take advantage of them to support student learning. But unlike English and language arts teachers, teachers of foreign and second languages may find new technologies do not place additional skills in the curriculum. Instead, they offer a variety of strategies that can make language learning more engaging and productive.

## Rubric to Measure Teacher Growth in Foreign and Second Language Technology Integration

Begin by reviewing the rubric in Figure 10.5 to measure teachers' progress in effectively integrating technology in foreign and second language instruction. Part I of the rubric addresses knowledge of issues and challenges, and Part II addresses foreign and second language technology integration strategies.

## Learning the Issues and Applications

The first step in technology integration is to become acquainted with the issues and challenges discussed in this chapter and how they shape teachers' uses and applications of technologies. Then teachers can begin developing capabilities to address instructional standards and curriculum goals. The following is a suggested sequence of learning activities.

- **Issues and challenges in foreign and second language instruction.** After reviewing the information in this chapter, go to the website of the American Council on the Teaching of Foreign Languages (ACTFL); also see the TESOL Technology Standards for Teachers and Learners. Review the standards at both sites. See professional development resources the sites offer, and decide on which can help you gain insight into the issues and challenges outlined in this chapter. Discuss and reflect on the two questions under the Collaborate, Discuss, Reflect feature at the end of the chapter. Complete Part I of the rubric in Figure 10.5 before you begin this sequence and again at various points in your progress.

- **Foreign and second language technology integration strategies.** After reviewing the information in this chapter, review examples of the technologies suggested in the Open Source Options feature and the websites and projects described under each section, and do the lesson evaluation and lesson development activities outlined in the Technology Integration Workshop at the end of this chapter. Reflect on how you will plan for implementing these strategies in your own classroom using the TIP model. Complete Part I of the rubric in Figure 10.5 before you begin this sequence and again at various points in your progress.

**TECHNOLOGY LEARNING CHECK**
Complete TLC 10.3 to review what you have learned from this section about how FL and ELL teachers can develop their knowledge and skills in technology integration.

**FIGURE 10.5** Rubric to Measure Teacher Growth in Foreign and Second Language Technology Integration

| Part I: Teacher Knowledge of Foreign and Second Language Issues and Challenges | | | |
|---|---|---|---|
| | **Basic knowledge** (1–2 points) | **Intermediate knowledge** (3–4 points) | **Advanced knowledge** (4–5 points) |
| ELL Issue #1: Demands on content area teachers | I can articulate the nature of the issue. | I can both articulate the nature of the issue and some of the possible ways to address it. | I can articulate my own plan for addressing the issue in my own teaching. |
| ELL Issue #2: Academic and language prerequisites for ELLs | I can articulate the nature of the issue. | I can both articulate the nature of the issue and some of the possible ways to address it. | I can articulate my own plan for addressing the issue in my own teaching. |
| ELL Issue #3: The need to differentiate instruction | I can articulate the nature of the issue. | I can both articulate the nature of the issue and some of the possible ways to address it. | I can articulate my own plan for addressing the issue in my own teaching. |
| ELL Issue #4: Challenges of integrating the students' native languages | I can articulate the nature of the issue. | I can both articulate the nature of the issue and some of the possible ways to address it. | I can articulate my own plan for addressing the issue in my own teaching. |
| FL Issue #1: The need for authentic materials and perspectives | I can articulate the nature of the issue. | I can both articulate the nature of the issue and some of the possible ways to address it. | I can articulate my own plan for addressing the issue in my own teaching. |
| FL Issue #2: The need for creating audience and purpose | I can articulate the nature of the issue. | I can both articulate the nature of the issue and some of the possible ways to address it. | I can articulate my own plan for addressing the issue in my own teaching. |

| Part II: Teachers' Technology Integration Strategies for Foreign and Second language Learning | | | |
|---|---|---|---|
| | **Basic knowledge** (1–2 points) | **Intermediate knowledge** (3–4 points) | **Advanced knowledge** (4–5 points) |
| Support for authentic oral language practice and assessment | I can describe the strategies and identify technologies to carry them out. | I have designed at least 1–2 activities based on these strategies to enhance my teaching and my students' learning. | I have designed plans for how I will integrate these strategies throughout my curriculum to enhance my teaching and my students' learning. |
| Virtual collaborations | I can describe the strategies and identify technologies to carry them out. | I have designed at least 1–2 activities based on these strategies to enhance my teaching and my students' learning. | I have designed plans for how I will integrate these strategies throughout my curriculum to enhance my teaching and my students' learning. |
| Virtual field trips for modified language immersion experience | I can describe the strategies and identify technologies to carry them out. | I have designed at least 1–2 activities based on these strategies to enhance my teaching and my students' learning. | I have designed plans for how I will integrate these strategies throughout my curriculum to enhance my teaching and my students' learning. |
| Teletandem experiences for modified language immersion | I can describe the strategies and identify technologies to carry them out. | I have designed at least 1–2 activities based on these strategies to enhance my teaching and my students' learning. | I have designed plans for how I will integrate these strategies throughout my curriculum to enhance my teaching and my students' learning. |
| Support for practice in language subskills | I can describe the strategies and identify technologies to carry them out. | I have designed at least 1–2 activities based on these strategies to enhance my teaching and my students' learning. | I have designed plans for how I will integrate these strategies throughout my curriculum to enhance my teaching and my students' learning. |

*(Continued)*

| Part II: Teachers' Technology Integration Strategies for Foreign and Second language Learning | | | |
|---|---|---|---|
| | **Basic knowledge** (1–2 points) | **Intermediate knowledge** (3–4 points) | **Advanced knowledge** (4–5 points) |
| Presentation aids | I can describe the strategies and identify technologies to carry them out. | I have designed at least 1–2 activities based on these strategies to enhance my teaching and my students' learning. | I have designed plans for how I will integrate these strategies throughout my curriculum to enhance my teaching and my students' learning. |
| Support for text production | I can describe the strategies and identify technologies to carry them out. | I have designed at least 1–2 activities based on these strategies to enhance my teaching and my students' learning. | I have designed plans for how I will integrate these strategies throughout my curriculum to enhance my teaching and my students' learning. |
| Use of apps to support language learning and use | I can describe the strategies and identify technologies to carry them out. | I have designed at least 1–2 activities based on these strategies to enhance my teaching and my students' learning. | I have designed plans for how I will integrate these strategies throughout my curriculum to enhance my teaching and my students' learning. |
| Productivity and lesson design support for teachers | I can describe the strategies and identify technologies to carry them out. | I have designed at least 1–2 activities based on these strategies to enhance my teaching and my students' learning. | I have designed plans for how I will integrate these strategies throughout my curriculum to enhance my teaching and my students' learning. |
| **Total points** | _____ of 75 possible points | | |

# COLLABORATE, DISCUSS, REFLECT

Monkey Business/Fotolia

**The following questions may be used either for in-class, small-group discussions or may be used to initiate discussions in blogs or online discussion boards:**

1. In one of the 2012 opinion editorials for the *Los Angeles Times* entitled "The Spanish Road to English," Fuller discussed the issue of whether students who come to school in the United States unable to speak English should be taught via bilingual methods or by English immersion. He characterized it as a "polarizing debate." According to Fuller, research shows that the critical factor is not which way students learn English but teachers who engage and motivate students. The number of nonnative speakers of English in U.S. classrooms continues to grow. How can the technology tools and resources described in this chapter help make teachers equal to the challenge of providing motivating classroom activities?

2. Globalization and multicultural awareness are both concerns that make FL teaching and learning a critical need in 21st-century classrooms. Yet K–12 language classes are in short supply due to economic constraints, such as teacher availability and too few students to justify hiring a teacher in every language that students want to take. What are some possible technological solutions to this problem? What does research show about the benefits and limitations/constraints of each proposed solution?

The following is a summary of the main points covered in this chapter.

1. **Issues and Challenges in ELL and Foreign Language Learning.** Each of these current issues has implications for how teachers can and should integrate technologies.
   - For ELL, these include demands on content area teachers, academic and language prerequisites for ELLs, the need to differentiate instruction for various learners, and challenges of integrating the students' native languages.
   - For FL, these include the need for authentic materials and perspectives, and the need for creating audience and purpose.

2. **Technology Integration Strategies for ELL and FL Learning.** Integration strategies include the following activities to address second-language and English language learning needs:
   - Support for authentic oral language practice and assessment that includes videoconferencing, multimedia software and interactive (electronic) storybooks, learning games on handheld devices, use of language labs and radio and TV broadcasts, podcasts, and translation websites and handheld translation devices.
   - Virtual collaborations that include information exchange tasks, comparison and analysis tasks, and collaborative tasks.
   - Virtual field trips for modified language immersion experience that provide opportunities for students to go places that would be impossible for them to see otherwise.
   - Teletandem learning experiences for modified language immersion.
   - Support for practice in language subskills.
   - Presentation aids so that teachers can help students link words they are hearing and reading to visual presentations of actions and objects.
   - Support for text production for producing and/or proofreading text in languages other than English.
   - Use of apps to support language learning and use.
   - Productivity and lesson design support for teachers in the form of websites with teaching resources and professional development opportunities.

3. **Teaching Foreign Language and Second Language Teachers to Integrate Technology.** Teachers can begin by consulting the rubric provided in this chapter to measure their own growth in foreign and second language technology integration. After that, they may review issues and challenges in foreign and second language instruction and use chapter resources to learn technology integration strategies they will use to address the issues and challenges.

# TECHNOLOGY INTEGRATION **WORKSHOP**

## 1. APPLY WHAT YOU LEARNED

To apply the concepts and skills you've read about throughout this chapter, go to the Chapter 10 Technology Application Activity.

## 2. TECHNOLOGY INTEGRATION LESSON PLANNING: PART 1—EVALUATING AND CREATING LESSON PLANS

Complete the following exercise using the sample lesson plans found on any lesson planning site that you find on the Internet.

a. Locate lesson ideas—Identify three lesson plans that focus on any of the tools or strategies you learned about in this chapter. For example:
   - Videoconferencing
   - Interactive or electronic storybooks

- Learning games on handheld devices
- Use of language labs
- Radio and TV broadcasts and podcasts
- Use of translation websites
- Handheld translation devices
- Virtual collaborations
- Virtual field trips

**b.** Evaluate the lessons—Use the Technology Lesson Plan Evaluation Checklist to evaluate each of the lessons you found.

**c.** Create your own lesson—After you have reviewed and evaluated some sample lessons, create one of your own using a lesson plan format of your choice (or one your instructor gives you). Be sure the lesson focuses on one of the technologies or strategies discussed in this chapter.

## 3. TECHNOLOGY INTEGRATION LESSON PLANNING: PART 2—IMPLEMENTING THE TIP MODEL

Review how to implement the TIP model in your classroom by doing the following activities with the lesson you created in the Technology Integration Lesson Planning exercise above.

**a.** Describe the Phase 1—Planning activities you would do to use this lesson in your classroom:
- What is the relative advantage of using the technology(ies) in this lesson?
- Do you have resources and skills you need to carry it out?

**b.** Describe the Phase 2—Implementation activities you would do to use this lesson in your classroom:
- What are the objectives of the lesson plan?
- How will you assess your students' accomplishment of the objectives?
- What integration strategies are used in this lesson plan?
- How would you prepare the learning environment?

**c.** Describe the Phase 3—Evaluation/Revision activities you would do to use this lesson in your classroom: What strategies and/or instruments would you use to evaluate the success of this lesson in your classroom in order to determine revision needs?

**d.** Add lesson descriptors—Create descriptors for your new lesson (e.g., grade level, content and topic areas, technologies used, ISTE standards, 21st Century Learning standards).

**e.** Save your new lesson—Save your lesson plan with all its descriptors and TIP model notes.

## 4. FOR YOUR TEACHING PORTFOLIO

Add the following to your Teaching Portfolio:
- Reflections on Hot Topic Debate.
- Summary notes from the Collaborate, Discuss, Reflect activity.
- Lesson plan evaluations, lesson plans, and products you created above.
- Your *Apply What You Learned* Product from Activity 1.

## 11

Margaret L. Niess and M. D. Roblyer

# Teaching and Learning with Technology in Mathematics and Science

## Learning Outcomes

After reading this chapter and completing the learning activities, you should be able to:

1. Identify implications for technology integration of each current issue that mathematics teachers face. (ISTE Standards•T 4, 5)

2. Select technology integration strategies that can meet various needs for instruction in mathematics curricula. (ISTE Standards•T 2, 5)

3. Identify implications for technology integration of each current issue that science teachers face. (ISTE Standards•T 4, 5)

4. Select technology integration strategies that can meet various needs for instruction in science curricula. (ISTE Standards•T 2, 5)

5. Design a strategy for how to build teacher knowledge and skills in technology integration for mathematics or science instruction. (ISTE Standards•T 5)

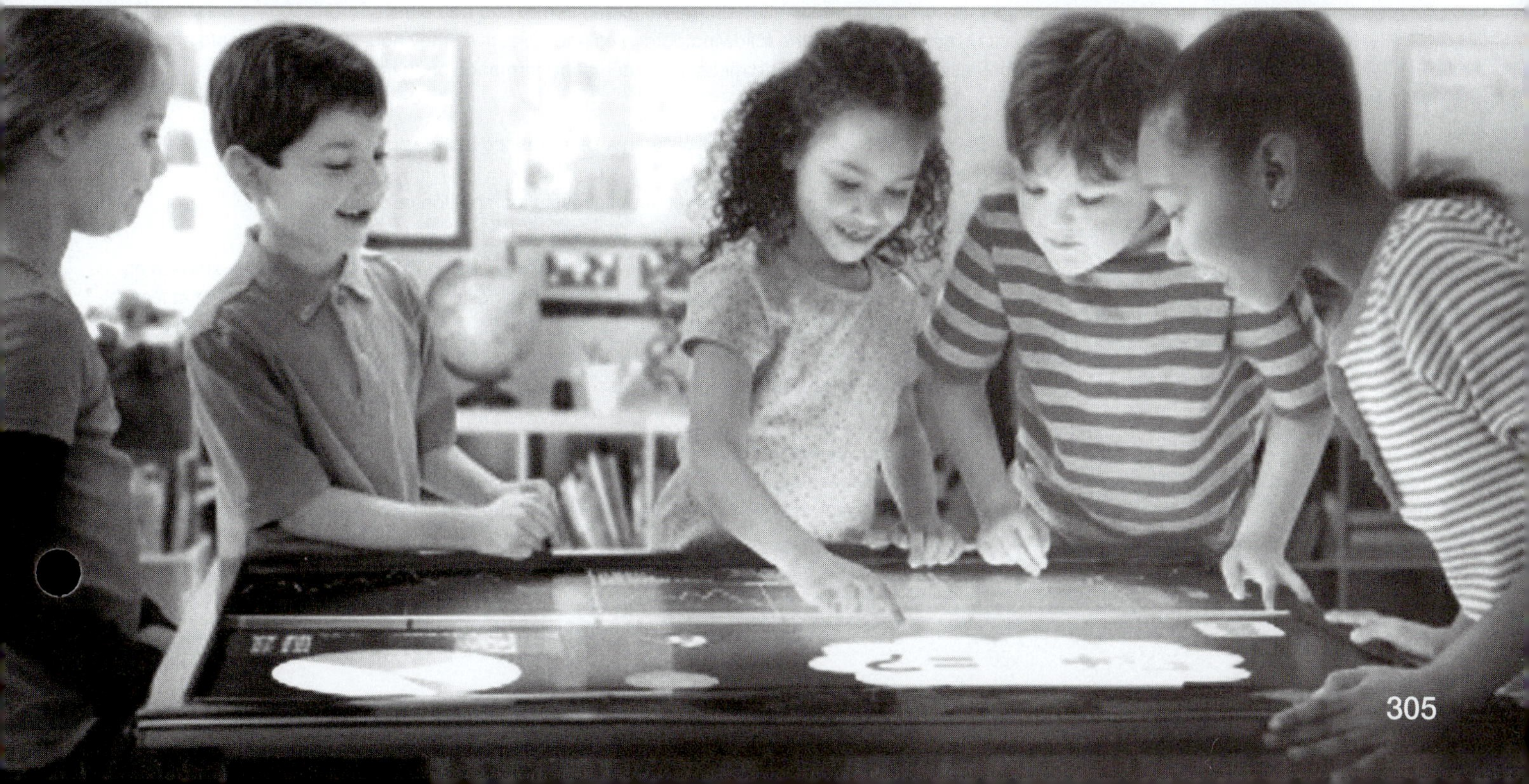

# TECHNOLOGY INTEGRATION IN ACTION
# HOT AND COLD DATA

GRADE LEVELS: 7-9 • CONTENT AREA/TOPIC: Physical science, mathematics • LENGTH OF TIME: Three weeks

## PHASE 1  ANALYSIS OF LEARNING AND TEACHING NEEDS

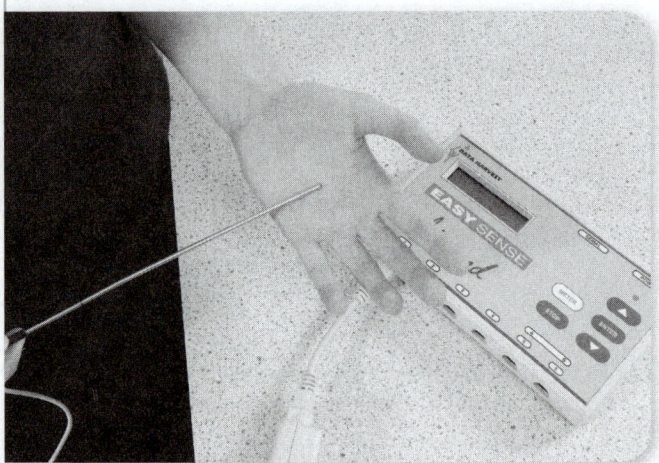

Trevor Clifford/Pearson Education

### Step 1: Determine relative advantage.

Ms. Belt and Mr. Alter, the physical science teacher and mathematics teacher, respectively, at Pinnacle Middle School, were excited about the new calculator-based laboratories (CBLs) that had just arrived. As they learned about how CBLs can "grab" temperature data and display it in graphs and spreadsheets, they realized that activities with CBLs provide a natural link between science and mathematics studies. Having students use CBLs would be an ideal way to give them hands-on insights into the relationship between these two important skill areas. They also agreed that CBL activities would address the ongoing challenge of making abstract science and math concepts more concrete and visual. Having students collect and analyze their own data, they felt, would give students authentic, hands-on application of these concepts. They decided that a unit on heating and cooling experiments would be a good first activity. Students could take temperature measurements with the CBL probes and then use mathematical procedures to graph and analyze the resulting data.

### Step 2: Review required skills and resources.

Both teachers had a good bit of experience with various technologies and knew they would not have trouble learning how to use the new CBL resources. Each had also experimented with small-group collaborative projects in their classrooms, though they knew that a collaboration across classrooms would involve more time for planning and coordination.

## PHASE 2  PLANNING FOR INTEGRATION

### Step 3: Decide on objectives and assessments.

The teachers decided they would assess student progress in four areas: CBL performance tasks, conducting scientific experiments, interpreting data from experiments, and completing and reporting on scientific experiments. They decided on the following outcomes and objectives they hoped students would achieve and outlined assessment methods to measure students' performance on them:

Outcome: CBL procedures.
Objective: Each student will score at least 85% on a performance test designed to measure competence with CBL procedures.
Assessment: A checklist with points assigned for successful completion of each task.

Outcome: Completing and reporting on scientific experiments, with teacher assistance.
Objective: All students will demonstrate they can work in collaborative groups to complete the steps in an assigned experiment and write individual summaries of their findings by achieving a rubric score of at least 85% on their work.
Assessment: A checklist with points assigned for each step done correctly; a rubric to assess the collaborative group PowerPoint presentation; a rubric to assess the quality of individually written summaries.

Outcome: Interpreting data from experiments.
Objective: All students will demonstrate the ability to review and interpret data derived from experiments by correctly answering at least eight of ten questions requiring data interpretation.
Assessment: A mid-unit test in which each student reviews example charts and answers questions on how to interpret the data.

**Outcome:** Completing and reporting on scientific experiments, without teacher assistance.
**Objective:** All students will demonstrate they can replicate and interpret data from a CBL experiment by working in pairs to complete the required tasks without assistance.
**Assessment:** A checklist with points assigned for each step done correctly; a rubric to assess the quality of written summaries.

### Step 4: Design integration strategies.

The teachers decided to team-teach the unit to emphasize important links between the two content areas. Working together, they designed the following sequence of activities:

**Week 1:** Introduce unit activities and CBLs, and provide hands-on practice. Introduce the unit with a Consumer Reports–type scenario. Makers of camp stoves each claim their product heats water faster than their competitors' do. The various stoves used three different fuels: white gas, kerosene, and butane. The students have to establish which manufacturer is correct and write up their findings for the "Consumer Reports" (CR) magazine. Show the YouTube videos: "Eureka! Episode 20 Measuring Temperature" and "Eureka! Episode 21 Temperature vs. Heat." Demonstrate how students can use the CBL to grab data and how it displays temperatures in graph form. Demonstrate how to calibrate a CBL and discuss how to interpret CBL data.

**Week 2:** To set the stage for the main experiment, have students carry out initial heating/cooling experiments and present findings. As Ms. Belt helps small collaborative groups prepare materials for the next set of experiments, Mr. Alter has students do individual performance checks on CBL procedures and provides additional instruction as needed. Each small collaborative group is assigned a heating/cooling experiment. For example, have them heat bolts of various sizes and add them to beakers of water. Ask, for example: Does water temperature in a beaker increase more when two smaller metal bolts are added or when one large bolt is added? Each group completes its assigned experiment, answers the question, writes up its findings, and presents the findings to the class by inserting spreadsheet and graphed data into a PowerPoint presentation. Each student in the class individually prepares a final summary of all the experiments based on the presentations.

**Week 3:** Students carry out the final experiment in three large groups. Using camp stoves borrowed from a local sporting goods store, they use the CBLs to heat water to boiling. They collaboratively conduct the step-by-step procedures for hands-on experiments, write up their findings, present them to the whole class, hold a whole-class discussion to interpret results, and write up a summary for credit. Each group works with the data to explore linear, quadratic, and exponential functions of graphed data. Finally, students work in pairs to answer questions on the meaning of the graphs. They complete the mathematical analyses and presentations. Finally, they take end-of-unit tests.

### Step 5: Prepare instructional environment.

The teachers prepared the classroom by setting up beakers, hot plates, and CBLs. They got a local sporting goods store to loan them three different camp stoves for the experiments. They tested each of the CBLs and made sure they worked. They designed and copied each of the performance measures and made copies of lab sheets needed during the experiments. Finally, they bookmarked the YouTube sites with videos they wanted to show so they could get to them quickly.

## PHASE 3 POST-INSTRUCTION ANALYSIS AND REVISIONS

### Step 6: Analyze results.

At the end of the unit, the teachers reviewed students' products and discussed how the unit had worked. Mr. Alter and Ms. Belt were happy with the overall performance of the class. They were impressed by how engaged students had become in using the CBLs to gather and analyze data and pleased with the level of collaboration they observed while the small groups were conducting experiments. Perhaps most encouraging, two female students seemed especially excited by the work they had done on the scientific experiments; they asked the teachers to give them information on careers in science and mathematics.

### Step 7: Make revisions.

The teachers concluded that this kind of multidisciplinary unit worked very well. They decided to plan other CBL experiments, to be carried out on a long-term basis and at locations outside the classroom.

*Source:* Based on concepts from: *The Heat is On! Using the Calculator-based laboratory to Integrate Math, Science, and Technology* by Joanne Caniglia and *Heat vs. Temperature: What's the Difference?* by Karen Campbell.

# CHAPTER 11 BIG IDEAS OVERVIEW

Before you begin reading the rest of this chapter, listen to the Chapter 11 Big Ideas Overview. It will give you a two-minute audio overview of main concepts to look for and help prepare you to work through information and exercises to achieve this chapter's outcomes.

# ISSUES AND CHALLENGES IN MATHEMATICS INSTRUCTION

The growing national concern that the United States is not adequately preparing students, teachers, and professionals in science, technology, engineering, and mathematics (STEM) areas has resulted in new standards and recommendations for revising the mathematics curriculum. The appropriate role for technology in helping to meet these new requirements is the focus of this section.

## Accountability for Standards in Mathematics

Mathematics and technology have a unique relationship as highlighted in the National Council of Teachers of Mathematics *Technology Principle* in the *Principles and Standards for School Mathematics (2000)* document emphasizes the essential role of technology in teaching and learning mathematics. "The existence, versatility, and power of technology make it possible and necessary to reexamine what mathematics students should learn as well as how they can best learn it" (from the Executive Summary of NCTM Standards). The Association of Mathematics Teacher Educators (AMTE) in their position statement on technology added that students have to be better prepared to use technology efficiently and fluently both so they can learn mathematics better and apply what they learn in the workplace. Thus, it is not surprising that efforts to reform teaching and learning in mathematics has been at the center of the national standards movement. Technology provides many opportunities to build students' conceptual knowledge of mathematics as well as to connect their learning to problems found in our world. This section highlights current issues and challenges in mathematics education that shape technology integration strategies for these areas.

Currently, the Common Core State Standards for Mathematics (CCSS-M, National Governors Association Center for Best Practices & Council of Chief State School Officers, 2010) are redirecting the curriculum description for what students should know and be able to do in mathematics. In accordance with this move, NCTM noted that the Common Core State Standards provide a foundation to develop mathematics curricula, instruction, and assessments that strengthen understanding, reasoning, and skill fluency and ultimately better prepare students for college and careers. (from NCTM's position statement *Supporting the Common Core State Standards for Mathematics*). The CCSS-M standards begin with eight Mathematical Practices (MP) for all grades K–12, describing what mathematically proficient students are able to do:

- MP 1. Make sense of problems and persevere in solving them.
- MP 2. Reason abstractly and quantitatively.
- MP 3. Construct viable arguments and critique the reasoning of others.
- MP 4. Model with mathematics.
- MP 5. Use appropriate tools strategically.
- MP 6. Attend to precision.
- MP 7. Look for and make use of structure.
- MP 8. Look for and express regularity in repeated reasoning.

Focusing on these recommendations for student engagement in mathematical practices, teachers are challenged to redesign their mathematics lessons around at least one if not more of these practices as students explore and learn mathematical ideas. For example, when students design a spreadsheet for solving a mathematics problem, they are engaged in the following: reasoning abstractly as they enter formulas (MP2); constructing viable arguments (MP3) in defense of their spreadsheet designs; accurately displaying the mathematics of the problem (MP1) as they make use of the structure in the spreadsheet design (MP7) that uses repeated reasoning (MP8); and ultimately defending their use of the spreadsheet as an appropriate tool for solving the problems (MP5) as they model the ideas using mathematics (MP4).

The CCSS-M serves as a primary resource and guide for those making decisions that affect the mathematics education of students. The standards add to the Mathematical Practices by describing the mathematics content that students should understand in their study at each grade level kindergarten through high school. The standards are organized in multiple domains for each grade level through grade 8. High school standards are then organized in conceptual categories providing a comprehensive view for high school mathematics. The content domains and conceptual categories are described in Table 11.1.

NCTM states that when the CCS are properly implemented, they will both support students' access to mathematics skills and enhance their learning of them. The ultimate goal is to be able to apply mathematical concepts in both their workplace and everyday activities. NCTM's support continues to direct educators' attention to their *Principles and Standards* document (2000) for prekindergarten through grade 12. Their content standards are described in five categories from which most of the domains/conceptual categories of the CCSS-M have been drawn:

1. Numbers and Operations
2. Algebra
3. Geometry
4. Measurement
5. Data Analysis

NCTM also recommends five process standards that are reasonably linked with the Common Core Mathematical Practices as shown in Table 11.2.

## TABLE 11.1 Domains and Conceptual Categories for CCSS-M

| Domain/Conceptual Category | K | 1 | 2 | 3 | 4 | 5 | 6 | 7 | 8 | High School |
|---|---|---|---|---|---|---|---|---|---|---|
| Counting and Cardinality | X | | | | | | | | | |
| Operations and Algebraic Thinking | X | X | X | X | X | X | | | | |
| Number and Operations in Base Ten | X | X | X | X | X | X | | | | |
| Number and Operations—Fractions | | | | X | X | X | | | | |
| Ratios and Proportional Relationships | | | | | | | X | X | | |
| Measurement and Data | X | X | X | X | X | X | | | | |
| The Number System | | | | | | | X | X | X | |
| Expressions and Equations | | | | | | | X | X | X | |
| Number and Quantity | | | | | | | | | | X |
| Algebra | | | | | | | | | | X |
| Functions | | | | | | | | | X | X |
| Modeling | | | | | | | | | | X |
| Geometry | X | X | X | X | X | X | X | X | X | X |
| Statistics and Probability | | | | | | | X | X | | X |

## TABLE 11.2 Linking the NCTM Process Standards with the CCSS-M Mathematical Practices

| NCTM Process Standards | Linked with CCSS-M Mathematical Practices |
| --- | --- |
| Problem Solving | MP1. Make sense of problems and persevere in solving them. |
| Reasoning and Proof | MP2. Reason abstractly and quantitatively.<br>MP3. Construct viable arguments and critique the reasoning of others.<br>MP7. Look for and make use of structure.<br>MP8. Look for and express regularity in repeated reasoning. |
| Communication | MP3. Construct viable arguments and critique the reasoning of others.<br>MP6. Attend to precision. |
| Connections | MP7. Look for and make use of structure. |
| Representations | MP4. Model with mathematics.<br>MP5. Use appropriate tools strategically. |

## Challenges in Implementing the Common Core State Standards for School Mathematics

The mathematics education community has actively supported the implementation of the NCTM *Principles and Standards* since 2000, effectively influencing the majority of the current textbooks. Yet, critics have challenged the current curriculum is a mile wide and an inch deep; that is, it is broad in scope of topics but demands minimal performance in any one topic. Critics say this results in lower math performance of U.S. students on internationally benchmarked assessments. The CCSS-M hopes to provide a more focused and coherent set of mathematics standards that results in improving mathematics achievement of all students. Helping teachers change their teaching styles to meet this vision is not an easy task since the standards seek a fundamental shift in the way many teachers have learned mathematics and have been taught to teach.

Digital technologies with advanced computational, graphical, and symbolic capabilities have changed how mathematicians are able to think and do mathematics. The question is whether this change has shifted how students should learn and do mathematics. These technologies provide students with the opportunity to visualize and make more concrete the abstract world of mathematics. Technologies can also serve as a catalyst to move teachers toward an instructional style that is more student-centered, active, and relevant to the world in which they live. The challenge for teachers is to determine:

1. Which technologies are best for developing student thinking?
2. How should these technologies serve as mathematics learning tools?
3. When in the course of the mathematics content development should these technologies be incorporated?

One way to accomplish these goals is to use technology applications that can be extended for long periods of time across topics to engage students in meaningful problems and projects rather than providing a variety of applications with no internal coherence.

▲ Digital technologies with advanced computational, graphical, and symbolic capabilities have changed how mathematicians are able to think and do mathematics. **Pearson Education**

### Directed versus Social-Constructivist Teaching Strategies: Ongoing "Math Wars"

In Sparks's 2010 article reporting results of studies of early math curricula, she observed that the "math wars" battling traditional versus reform-based mathematics curriculum and instruction remain unresolved. Do students learn mathematics best from explicit, teacher-directed explanations followed by individual practice? Do they learn best when they are engaged in student-centered learning where they construct the conceptual ideas through hands-on activities that help them build their personal understandings as in the constructivist approach? Or, do they learn best when they are involved in group work and discussions with other students using a more social-constructivist approach? In support of the question on constructivism, Cobb and Yackel (1996) describe the social and constructivist ideas as reflexive rather than in conflict, thus influencing the movement toward a social-constructivist approach. Their research has influenced the discussions on learning mathematics with the recognition that the social context in which the students are learning impacts their personal understandings. Technologies are available to support many of these methods, but the approach teachers use to teach math definitely determines the kind of integration strategies they would consider appropriate. See the Hot Topic Debate feature for one of the "battles" in these "math wars."

▲ The debate over the role of calculators is one reflection of the curricular "war" over whether students should memorize certain basic math or focus on deeper conceptual mathematical knowledge and insights. (Photo courtesy W. Wiencke)

**TECHNOLOGY LEARNING CHECK**

Complete **TLC 11.1** to review what you have learned from this section about issues that affect how technology may be integrated into mathematics education.

## ◉ TECHNOLOGY INTEGRATION STRATEGIES FOR MATHEMATICS INSTRUCTION

Technology resources have made possible a variety of teaching and learning strategies to help address the Common Core State Standards in Mathematics. This section describes those strategies, and Table 11.3 summarizes them and gives examples of some of the technology resources that make them possible.

## TABLE 11.3 Summary of Technology Integration Strategies for Mathematics

| Technology Integration Strategies | Benefits | Sample Resources and Activities |
|---|---|---|
| Bridging the gap between abstract and concrete with virtual manipulatives | • Helps make abstract mathematics concepts more concrete to young students<br>• Offers flexible environments that allow students to explore complex concepts<br>• Provides concrete representations of abstract concepts | • National Library of Virtual Manipulatives—a database of Java applets and interactive, hands-on activities for K–12 mathematics |
| Allowing representation of mathematical principles | • Allows a visual depiction of abstract math concepts<br>• Gives students environments to explore conjectures and make discoveries about geometry concepts | • Geometer's Sketchpad from Keypress, Inc.—an interactive geometry software program that uses Euclidean tools for exploring geometry, algebra, and other K–12 mathematics<br>• Maple software from Maplesoft—a computer algebra system with capabilities for symbolic computation in secondary and higher levels of mathematics.<br>• Derive from Texas Instruments—a computer algebra system for symbolic and numeric mathematics. |
| Supporting mathematical problem solving | • Helps students gather data to use in problem solving<br>• Provides rich, motivating, problem-solving environments<br>• Gives students opportunities to apply mathematical knowledge and skills in authentic contexts | • Geometer's Sketchpad from Keypress Inc.—an interactive geometry software program that uses Euclidean tools for exploring geometry, algebra, and other K–12 mathematics<br>• Vernier data collection systems—provides active hands-on science through a combination of multiple probeware sensors and data loggers for gathering real-time data for experiments and graphical analysis.<br>• Texas Instruments graphing calculators and TI-NspireCAS from Texas Instruments—handheld devices providing algebraic manipulation capabilities for mathematical explorations in middle and secondary classes. |
| Implementing data-driven curricula | • Provides easy access to many data sets<br>• Provides real data and statistics to support investigations<br>• Helps students develop skills in data analysis<br>• Allows students to explore and present data in graphical form | • Fathom from Keypress—dynamic data and statistical software package for secondary and higher-level mathematics<br>• Spreadsheets such as Microsoft Excel—data analysis tool for supporting algebraic reasoning and thinking in K–12 mathematics<br>• Data from the U.S. Census<br>• SPSS statistical software from IBM—data analysis statistical package for college level and above. |
| Supporting math-related communications | • Allows easy contact with math experts for help on math problems<br>• Promotes social interaction and discussion of math topics<br>• Allows teachers to connect with each other and exchange ideas | • Math Forum at Drexel: Ask Dr. Math—an Internet resource for K–12 mathematics where students submit questions to be answered by mathematics experts<br>• Student-developed websites |
| Motivating skill building and practice | • Provides motivating practice in foundation skills required for higher-level learning<br>• Provides guided instruction in a structured learning environment | • Carnegie's Cognitive Tutor software—relies on an artificial intelligence model for diagnosing student's mastery of mathematics ideas<br>• Waterford's Early Learning Series—a comprehensive computer-based preK-12 curriculum<br>• PLATO's Achieve Now program—computer-based curriculum for elementary and middle school<br>• Leapfrog's Didj—a handheld gaming system for teaching skills in a range of subjects, such as language arts, spelling, math and math facts |

## TABLE 11.3 Summary of Technology Integration Strategies for Mathematics (continued)

| Technology Integration Strategies | Benefits | Sample Resources and Activities |
|---|---|---|
| Other mathematics resource websites for teachers | • Offers sources of information, lesson plans on mathematics topics | • National Council of Teachers of Mathematics<br>• Math Forum at Drexel—Internet Math Library<br>• Texas Instruments Resources for Educators<br>• Math World from Wolkfram—a Web-based glossary of mathematical terms<br>• PBS Mathline contains lesson plans with video for grades preK–2 |

## Bridging the Gap Between Abstract and Concrete with Virtual Manipulatives

Physical manipulatives are real objects such as blocks, Cuisenaire rods, and coins. They are a mainstay of the elementary school classroom because they help students bridge the conceptual distance between concrete and abstract mathematical concepts. **Virtual manipulatives** are replicas of real manipulatives that are accessed via the Internet and can be manipulated through a keyboard or other input device. According to Li and Ma (2010), research has found that virtual manipulatives have a positive impact on both attitudes toward mathematics and student achievement. For example, Burris (2013) compared third graders' mathematical thinking using virtual versus concrete base-10 blocks to learn place-value concepts. The study found that the students were able to manipulate the virtual blocks in much the same way as the concrete blocks, but that the virtual models were advantageous for students in generating nonstandard numbers connected with addition and subtraction. While many of these virtual tools are mentioned most often for lessons at the elementary level, Lee and Chen (2010) also report that virtual manipulatives can improve high school students' attitudes toward mathematics. These simulated activities are popular because they offer more flexibility than activities using actual objects in the way teachers can use them to illustrate concepts.

Sarama and Clements (2009) say that virtual manipulatives may actually be better than physical ones for young children who are learning to connect concrete and abstract number concepts. They characterize virtual manipulatives as more "manageable, flexible, extensible, and 'clean' (i.e., free of potentially distracting features)" (p. 147). To support this assertion, they describe "affordances" or unique characteristics that virtual manipulatives have for supporting learning, along with research that supports each one.

Rosen and Hoffman (2009) illustrate how real and virtual manipulatives can be used to enhance mathematics learning at the elementary level. Niess (2012) describes advantages of virtual algebra tiles with sliders for changing the lengths of the tiles when modeling variable lengths. Thus the virtual manipulatives provide a clearer vision of the variable ideas than that provided with the handheld blocks. Utah State University maintains a library of virtual manipulatives for all grade levels that are tied to each of the mathematics standards' content strands. For examples of virtual manipulatives, see the websites listed in Table 11.3. Also see Technology Integration Example 11.1 for a lesson that uses these tools.

## Allowing Representation of Mathematical Principles

Mathematics is an abstract subject. Our understanding of mathematical ideas and concepts is closely tied to how we represent the abstractions of mathematics. To some, the concept of "five" is literally five objects (apples, pennies, and so on); to others, it is the numeral 5; to the ancient Romans, it was represented by the numeral V. Technology has greatly enriched the way the abstractions of mathematics can be represented, and today students must learn mathematics using several representations: symbolic (with numerals, variables, equations, and so on), verbal (with words such as "What percent increase is needed to reach $32,000?"), graphical (using two- or three-dimensional graphs), or numerical (using tables of numbers or spreadsheets). For each

# TECHNOLOGY INTEGRATION

## Example 11.1

**TITLE:** Virtual Manipulatives Help Teach Platonic Solids

**CONTENT AREA/TOPIC:** Mathematics, geometry

**GRADE LEVELS:** Middle school

**ISTE STANDARDS•S:** Standard 1—Creativity and Innovation; Standard 2—Communication and Collaboration; Standard 3—Research and Information Fluency; Standard 6—Technology Operations and Concepts

**CCSS:** CCSS.MATH.PRACTICE.MP5, CCSS.MATH.CONTENT.6.G.A.4, CCSS.MATH.CONTENT.7.G.A.3

**MATHEMATICAL PRACTICES:** Make sense of problems (MP1); construct viable arguments (MP3); model with mathematics (MP4); use appropriate tools strategically (MP5); look for and express regularity in repeated reasoning (MP8).

**DESCRIPTION:** Use 3D manipulatives online at the National Center for Virtual Manipulatives to help students learn about the five Platonic solids. Introduce or reinforce the terms "vertices, edges, and faces" and review Euler's formula. Encourage students to describe attributes of the five solids as they view them. For each form, let students use the virtual tools to rotate the form and color each of the planes. Have them count the edges, vertices, and faces. Then have them use Euler's formula to confirm it holds for each solid. Follow up with student construction of other solids using clay or paper. Ask inquiry questions such as, "What is the minimum number of colors required if no two faces of the same color can share an edge? Which of the Platonic solids have faces that could reasonably be considered "opposite one another?"

*SOURCE:* Based on a concept from instructor information at the National Library of Virtual Manipulatives at http://nlvm.usu.edu.

---

of these representations, technology resources have been developed to allow learners to explore mathematics within that representation—and to explore the interaction among representations. For example, Obara (2010a) says that students have a hard time visualizing three-dimensional solids; however, by using physical models in conjunction with appropriate software, they can develop the required spatial sense.

**Graphing calculators** are advanced calculators that can graph equations as well as perform calculation functions involved in higher-level math and science problems (see a sample graphing calculator in Figure 11.1). Research has shown that these tools can improve students' understanding of functions and graphs as well as the interconnections among the symbolic, graphical, and numerical representations of problems. Browning and Garza-Kling (2010) review four different ways to use graphing calculators: (1) collecting or generating raw data, (2) examining multiple cases, (3) providing immediate feedback, and (4) showing graphical and numerical displays. Without technology, it is difficult, if not impossible, for students to move from the symbolic realm of $f(x) = x2-3$ to the equivalent graphical rendering on an x-y coordinate to its accompanying numerical representation.

A number of materials are designed to help students with special needs with calculations and other tasks involved in representing math concepts. See the Adapting for Special Needs feature to see some recommendations for selecting these.

In addition to calculators, many computer-based programs such as Derive (Chartwell-Yorke Ltd.) and TI Interactive! (Texas Instruments) provide learning environments across various mathematical realms. **Interactive or dynamic geometry software** refers to programs that allow users to create and manipulate geometric constructions. They provide students with an environment in which to make discoveries and conjectures related to geometry concepts and objects. Here abstract ideas can be played out on a computer screen, making concepts more real and providing a doorway into mathematical reasoning and proof. Internet resources also can help students make connections between abstract geometry and real objects in the world around them. Instead of memorizing geometric facts or concepts, students can explore proofs and arrive at conclusions on their own.

Geometer's Sketchpad is among the most popular of these geometry programs (Graf, 2010; Muller, 2010; Obara, 2010b). Graf (2010) recommends using real manipulatives first, followed by Geometer's Sketchpad. Obara (2010b) recommends both this tool and Maple computer algebra

**FIGURE 11.1** TI-Nspire Graphing Calculator

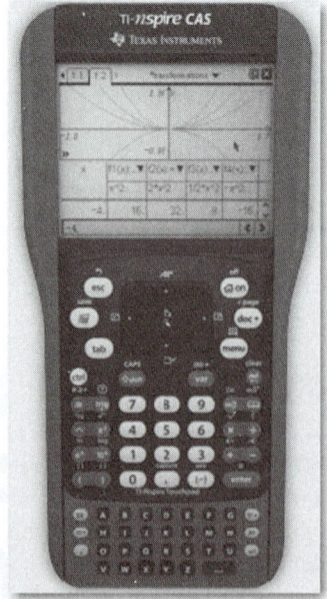

*Source:* Image used with permission of Texas Instruments Inc.

# Adapting for Special Needs

## Problem-Solving Aids, Simulations, and Games for Mathematics and Science

Some students with learning disabilities become discouraged in mathematics when they make mistakes in basic calculations involved in solving problems. In these cases, they lose sight of the overall purpose of inquiry and problem solving, and their experience with these subjects suffers. The tools described below offer support that can be provided to an individual student or, better yet, provided to the entire class to support their problem-solving efforts as they pursue big ideas.

- Google Calculator (at the Google website)—Complete calculations quickly and easily right within the browser.
- Web Math (at the Discovery Education website)—Enter a problem and view the step-by-step procedure for how the answer is derived.
- Wolfram Alpha (at the Wolfram Alpha website)—A knowledge engine that not only computes simple and complex calculations but also contains links to related problem sets as might be found in a search engine.

Marino, Tsurusaki, and Basham (2011) say that "appropriate technology-enhanced curricular materials, such as simulation and gaming software, can help students with disabilities (SD) be successful in science. These products engage students in the learning process and are fun and easy to use" (p. 70). They recommend websites like the following that provide interactive, highly motivating science activities. They allow students to repeat experiments quickly and efficiently and help students manipulate complex data.

- Filament Games (at the Filament Games website)—With support from the Institute of Education Sciences (IES) in the U.S. Department of Education, this group is developing a series of middle school life science games informed by current evidence-based educational practices and the Universal Design for Learning framework. These materials are especially intended to meet the needs of students with learning disabilities and other reading difficulties.
- Explore Learning's Gizmos (at the Explorelearning website)—This website offers over 450 highly interactive simulations for students in grades 3–12.

*—Contributed by Dave Edyburn*

---

system (CAS) software. Maple is a multipurpose **computer algebra system (CAS)**. A CAS can be either software or devices with software that help carry out complex numeric calculations involved in higher-level math problems. Maple has its own built-in programming language that is similar to Pascal and allows flexibility to design other algebra applications. See an example product from Maple in Figure 11.2.

Software capable of depicting solid or three-dimensional objects on a screen provides learners with a way to visualize objects that are difficult to imagine. Understanding the nature and properties of transformations and symmetry has become increasingly important and can be found in nearly all state mathematics standards. Bucher and Edwards (2011) and Garber and Picking (2010) recommend the free GeoGebra dynamic geometry software (shown with other free programs in the Open Source Options feature) for this purpose.

## Supporting Mathematical Problem Solving

NCTM defines problem solving as "engaging in a task for which the solution method is not known in advance." In order to find a solution, students must draw on their knowledge, and through this process, they will often develop new mathematical understandings. The NCTM standards indicate that solving problems is both a goal of learning mathematics and provides methods for meeting out the goal. Regardless of

**FIGURE 11.2  Product of Maple Algebra Software**

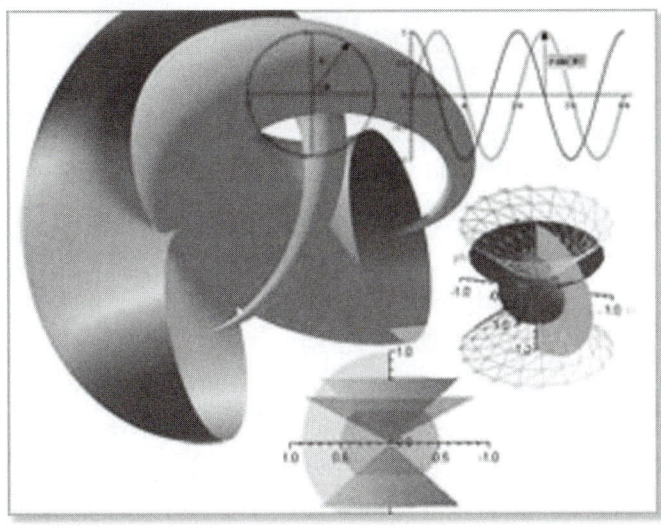

*Source: Maple* is a trademark of Waterloo Maple Inc. Reprinted by permission.

# OPEN SOURCE
## OPTIONS *for Mathematics and Science Classrooms*

| TYPES | FREE SOURCES |
|---|---|
| **Free library of virtual manipulatives** | National Library of Virtual Manipulatives: nlvm.usu.edu/en/nav/vlibrary.html<br>Manipula Math with Java: ies-math.com/math/java/ |
| **Free online software** | GeoGebra geometry software: geogebra.org<br>Graph mathematical graphing software: padowan.dk/graph<br>Mathomatic computer algebra system: mathomatic.org/<br>Listing of free statistical software: freestatistics.altervista.org/en/stat.php |
| **Free science tutorials and games** | Sheppard Software: sheppardsoftware.com/science.htm |
| **Free videos and books** | YouTube science videos, for example: "Eureka! #Episode 20, Measuring Temperature" and "Eureka! #Episode 21, Temperature vs. Heat"<br>National Academy Press (NAP): nap.edu |

**FIGURE 11.3** Sample Vernier LabQuest Probeware System

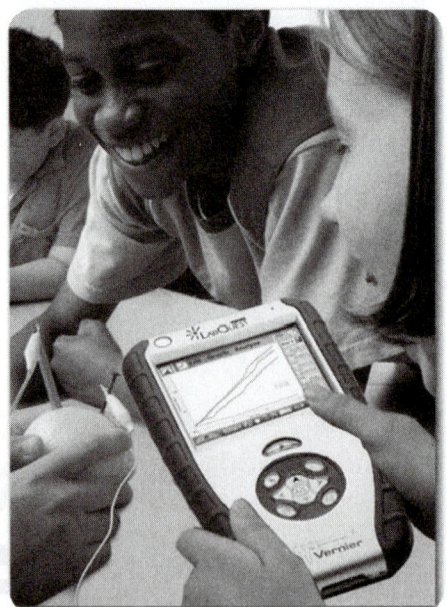

*Source:* Photo courtesy of Vernier Software & Technology.

how many mathematical facts, skills, or procedures students learn, the true value of mathematics is realized only when they can apply their knowledge to solve problems. Technology, by its definition, is a tool for solving problems. To prepare mathematically powerful citizens for the future, learning to solve problems using mathematics and appropriate technological tools is essential to education at all levels.

As students acquire number sense, they can begin to make generalizations that lead them to concepts in algebra. Technology tools provide students with a variety of means for exploring the critical concept of functions. Using CAS or graphing calculators, students can graph functions accurately, explore mathematical models of real-life phenomena, and explore symbolic representations and patterns. **Calculator-based laboratories (CBLs,** a.k.a. **probeware)** provide a means to link either calculators or computers to scientific data–gathering instruments, such as thermometers or pH meters, which allow students to gather data and then analyze it. Probes are also available for handheld devices. Texas Instruments and Vernier Inc. are companies that produce many of these tools and they often collaborate on products for both companies to market. See Figures 11.3 and 11.4 for examples of their products.

Although data-collection devices are available for purchase, Sory, Willard, and Kim (2010) describe a lesson in which students create their own low-cost digital thermometers and use a graphing calculator to calibrate them. Doe (2009) points out that handheld devices like mobile phones make technologies such as probeware an even more versatile tool for problem-solving lessons.

Finally, spreadsheets have long been considered a powerful means of supporting problem-solving activities. Niess, van Zee, and Gillow-Wiles (2010–2011) say that spreadsheets provide tools for problem solving that relies on both "science and mathematics concepts and processes for accurate analysis" (p. 42).

**FIGURE 11.4** Texas Instruments TI-Nspire Handheld Data Collection System

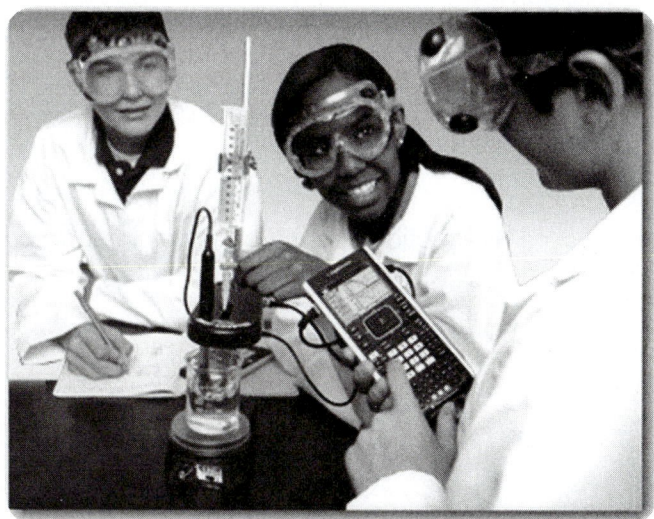

**FIGURE 11.5** The Math Forum @ Drexel's Ask Dr. Math

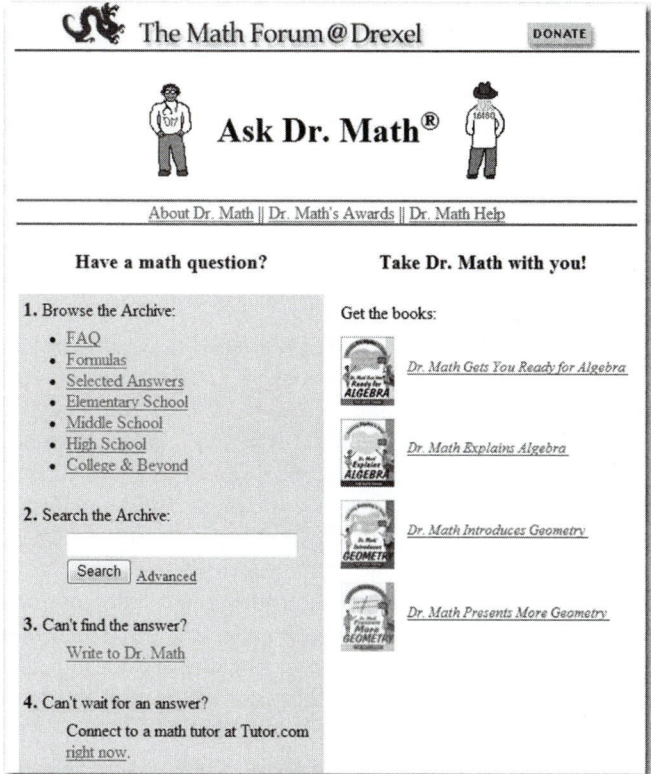

## Implementing Data-Driven Curricula

The importance of statistical inference and probability has already had an impact in U.S. schools. Technology provides an ideal means of developing student knowledge and skill related to data analysis. Fathom is a comprehensive package designed for schools that helps analyze and represent statistical data in a wide range of forms. Edwards and Phelps (2008) describe how Fathom can help students explore common geometry and algebra topics, and Shafer (2010) illustrates its use in teaching hypothesis testing.

Computer spreadsheets also provide environments in which children can explore number concepts, operations, and patterns with data they obtain from various sources. Students can work with basic operations, explore "what if" problems, and build a foundation for algebraic thinking. As noted by Niess, et al. (2010–2011), spreadsheet features permit modeling situations and analyzing the impact of changes. Presentation of tables and charts to display variables offers "dynamic environments that afford opportunities to engage in algebraic reasoning even in elementary grades" (p. 52). Spreadsheets can facilitate activities such as planning a fund-raising activity or analyzing data from students' counts of colors in a bag of M&Ms or other candies; both are much-used strategies for helping to build students' number sense. Students at later grade levels often use statistical software such as SPSS for this purpose. From sites such as the U.S. Census Bureau, students can download sample data sets to use in their math explorations.

## Supporting Math-Related Communications

Expressing numerical ideas in textual form is essential; therefore, students must be able to convert their mathematical thinking into words. Projects such as those found at the Math Forum @ Drexel's Problems of the Week allow teachers to pose problems that their students must solve and then communicate about. Ask Dr. Math (also on the Math Forum) lets students contact math experts who can answer a question (see Figure 11.5).

Student-created websites can be a valuable form of communication for student projects. Using computers and calculators in small-group settings also promotes social interaction and discourse. Teachers often find that grouping students in pairs enhances learning, augmenting communication from teacher-to-student or computer-to-student to a richer student-to-student-to-computer type of communication.

## Motivating Skill Building and Practice

Computer-based tutoring systems for mathematics have been available for some time. One such product is Cognitive Tutor, developed by professors at the Carnegie Mellon University. It has been adopted in over 2,600 schools throughout the country (Bhattacharjee, 2009). Brown (2013) reported that a large-scale, randomized study conducted by the Rand Corporation on behalf of the U.S. Department of Education showed that students using the program achieved significantly more than a control group using other curricula.

Although the current emphasis in mathematics instruction is on learning higher-order mathematics skills, students often need more resources to support the practice of basic skills. These skills provide an important foundation on which they can build more advanced skills. Some technology resources that can support this practice are listed in Table 11.3.

**TECHNOLOGY LEARNING CHECK**
Complete TLC 11.2 to review what you have learned from this section about technology integration strategies for mathematics.

## ◉ ISSUES AND CHALLENGES IN SCIENCE INSTRUCTION

Issues that impact technology integration in science are similar to those for mathematics. The appropriate role for technology in helping to meet science education needs is the focus of this section.

## Accountability for Standards in Science

The National Science Education Standards (NSES), published in 1996 by the National Research Council (NRC), outlined the content that all students should know and be able to do; it also provided guidelines for assessing student learning in science. Since that time, the NSES provided guidance for science teaching strategies, science teacher professional development, and the support necessary to deliver high-quality science education. The NSES also described the policies to bring coordination, consistency, and coherence to science education programs. Many of the current state standards documents have drawn their content from the *Benchmarks for Science Literacy*, published by the influential American Association for the Advancement of Science (AAAS), and/or the NSES.

As of 2012, the NRC released a new framework for science standards to be designed in its document titled *A Framework for K–12 Science Education: Practices, Crosscutting Concepts and Core Ideas*. Achieve (an education reform organization created in 1996 by group of governors and business leaders) has worked in partnership with the NRC, the National Science Teachers Association (NSTA), and the American Association for the Advancement of Science (AAAS) to create the foundation for the development of the CCSS in Science in the document titled *Next Generation Science Standards for Today's Students and Tomorrow's Workforce*. These K–12 science standards highlight NRC's *Framework* in three dimensions.

These dimensions and the resulting standards are intended for leading toward the Common Core State Science Standards (CCSS-S). A new emphasis in these standards is the recognition of engineering as a result of the STEM initiative that links science, technology, engineering, and mathematics. In these new directions Achieve describes Scientific and Engineering Practices (S&EP) similar in nature to those in the Mathematical Practices.

With these practices in mind, teachers are challenged to design their science lessons around at least one if not more of these practices as students explore and learn scientific and/or engineering ideas. For example, in the "Hot and Cold Data" Technology Integration In Action example, Ms. Bell and Mr. Alter designed a three-week unit around the integration of CBL probeware. They challenged the students to ask questions about the water temperature when two smaller bolts were added versus adding only one larger bolt (S&EP1). They challenged the students to carry out experiments (S&PE3), analyze the results (S&PE4), use spreadsheets for graphing data (S&PE2 and S&PE5), and present their findings to the whole class (S&EP6 and S&EP7)

using a PowerPoint presentation for communicating their results (S&EP8). The crosscutting concepts of the *Framework* include:

- Patterns
- Cause and effect: mechanism and explanation
- Science, proportion, and quantity
- Systems and system models
- Energy and matter: flows, cycles, and conservation
- Structure and function
- Stability and change

Moreover, the four disciplinary core ideas include: physical sciences, life sciences, earth and space sciences, and engineering, technology, and applications of science.

The U. S. Department of Education and the National Science Foundation endorsed the mathematics and science curricula that focused on motivating students through active learning, inquiry, problem solving, cooperative learning, and other instructional methods (NRC, 1996).

The National Science Education Standards also called for "a vision of science education that will make scientific literacy for all a reality in the 21st century" (NRC, 1996, p. 10). The basis for inquiry-oriented science instruction is developing varied opportunities for students to learn science process skills, such as collecting, sorting, and cataloging; observing, note taking, and sketching; and interviewing, polling, and surveying. In addition, research shows that inquiry-related teaching is effective in developing scientific literacy and the understanding of science processes, vocabulary knowledge, conceptual understanding, critical thinking, positive attitudes toward science, and construction of logico-mathematical knowledge.

Technology provides powerful learning tools for engaging students in investigating more complex ideas and problem solving to reveal important interactions among the disciplines while engaging students in an inquiry-oriented science instruction. Harris and Rooks (2010) found that these tools allow classrooms to become more inquiry-oriented. Students "engage in real-world investigations and communicate findings" (p. 144) by searching Internet databases and using model-building software and tools to collect data and describe findings. In fact, students are using the same tools as professionals in the field. Owston (2009) also found an important role for technology in science inquiry learning in programs that sought to improve mathematics and science teaching at the high school, middle school, and upper elementary levels: all "emphasized teachers' use of student-centered, inquiry-based approaches in their classrooms that involved all students regardless of ability. All made use of . . . blogs, webcasting, podcasting, and live video sessions" (p. 271).

To integrate technology in the science classroom on a regular basis, one must understand the meaning of technology in the context of science teaching and learning. The NSES explained the difference between science and technology. "The goal of science is to understand the natural world, and the goal of technology is to make modifications in the world to meet human needs. Technology as design is . . . parallel to science as inquiry. . . . The need to answer questions in the natural world drives the development of technological products" (NRC, 1996, p. 24). The parallelism is represented in the recognition that technology results from the design process, much as science results from the inquiry process.

## The Narrowing Pipeline of Scientific Talent

Of particular importance throughout the *Framework* is supporting a science, technology, engineering, and mathematics (STEM) curriculum that engages students in the power of the integration of these multiple disciplinary areas. For years now, concern has been growing about America's future ability to compete in science, technology, engineering, and mathematics. Achievement gaps in science are well documented with particular recognition of a continued underrepresentation of female and minority science professionals. When compared with boys, girls' interest in science decreases as they enter middle school. Thus, women continue to be underrepresented in STEM fields. With the declining number of students—especially female and minority students—pursuing studies in the science, technology, engineering, and mathematics fields, America faces a growing crisis in leadership for much-needed STEM initiatives.

▲ The declining number of female and minority students pursuing studies in the math, science, and engineering fields challenges the United States to provide leadership for much-needed STEM initiatives. (Photo by W. Wiencke)

This trend could have serious consequences for the long-term economic and national security of our country. One of the first reports on the issue was presented by EMC Corporation's (2003) *Fueling the Pipeline: Attracting and Educating Math and Science Students*. Since the publication of this seminal report, other organizations—both private and public—have continued to explore the problem. Bayer's Facts of Science Education survey (2010) and the 2011 report by the Committee on Science, Engineering, and Public Policy (COSEPUP) confirm this is an ongoing issue. Providing all students with access to quality education in the STEM disciplines is important to our nation's competitiveness. However, it is challenging to identify the most successful approaches in the STEM disciplines. The reality is that success for all students lies in integrating the four disciplines, rather than segregating them.

## Increasing Need for Scientific Literacy

As the science framework emphasizes the importance of students learning about science and engineering through "integration of the knowledge of scientific explanations (i.e., content knowledge) and the practices needed to engage in scientific inquiry and engineering design" (NRC, 2012, p. 26). There is a need for all citizens to be scientifically literate in order to make informed decisions that affect our country's future. More than ever before, America's economic and environmental progress depends on the character and quality of the science education that the nation's schools provide. The NRC's *Framework* position (2012) emphasizes the need for students to directly experience scientific practices for themselves in order to fully appreciate the nature of scientific knowledge. Thus, the *Framework* recommends scientific inquiry for the primary scientific and engineering practices.

## Difficulties in Teaching K–8 Science

Science is a rapidly changing area, and teachers are constantly challenged to keep up with new developments in science content, tools, and methods. Elementary education teachers face an even greater challenge, since they are typically required to have much less initial preparation in mathematics and science content than secondary science teachers. As a result, teaching science for understanding at an early level becomes difficult due to teachers' lack of deep understanding of the discipline. One way to assist teachers in science is through increased professional development (PD). Online PD opportunities increase access for elementary teachers to this important area. For example, the Annenberg Foundation offers a collection of materials that can be used for a distance-education science PD program (see Distance Learning at the Annenberg Foundation website. Moreno and Erdmann (2010) offer BioEd Online and K8 Science, both

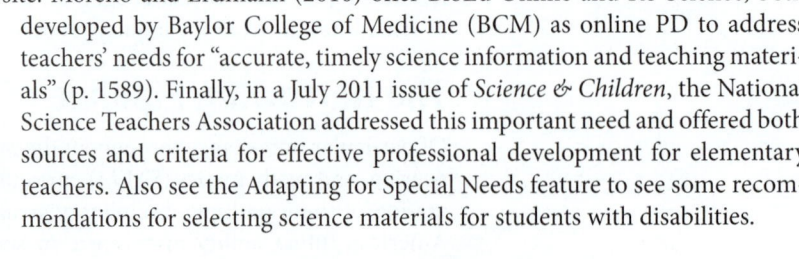

**The Benefits of Virtual Science Labs**

In this video, a virtual school principal tells how some schools use virtual science labs to enhance learning opportunities for their students. What are the benefits she cites for doing this kind of lab?

developed by Baylor College of Medicine (BCM) as online PD to address teachers' needs for "accurate, timely science information and teaching materials" (p. 1589). Finally, in a July 2011 issue of *Science & Children*, the National Science Teachers Association addressed this important need and offered both sources and criteria for effective professional development for elementary teachers. Also see the Adapting for Special Needs feature to see some recommendations for selecting science materials for students with disabilities.

## Objections to Virtual Science Labs

When science reform efforts began taking shape in the early 1990s, the American Association for the Advancement of Science called on teachers and schools to engage students in doing science rather than just hearing about it or seeing a demonstration. "Hands-on/minds-on" science became a common term in science reform, synonymous with immersing students in authentic learning

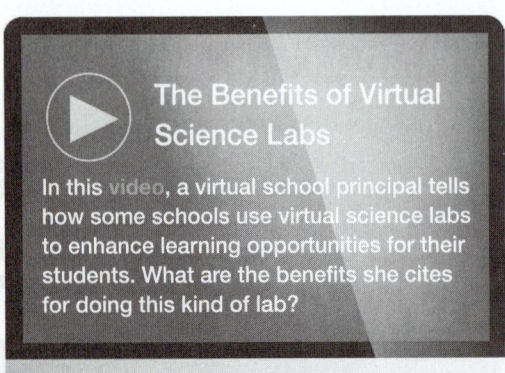

experiences. According to Haury and Rillero (1994), Karen Worth, noted science reformer, defined **hands-on/minds-on science** as "engaging in in-depth investigations with objects, materials, phenomena, and ideas and drawing meaning and understanding from those experiences."

Virtual schools, among others, have proposed that simulated labs for activities such as experiments with chemical compounds and animal dissections in biology are very much in keeping with the idea of hands-on learning. They maintain that students can spend more time focusing on the "science" of the activities when danger and sensory unpleasantness are removed. However, the National Science Teachers Association (2007) and the American Chemical Society (2008) take issue with this view, saying that "hands-on" means that students must touch the materials rather than "do" science on a computer. Both organizations have issued position statements arguing against the acceptance of computer simulations as a substitute for real-life laboratory experiences.

At this writing, the College Board requires virtual schools and others who provide distance education courses in biology and chemistry to provide school-lab experiences in order to retain its endorsement as an Advance Placement (AP) course. This policy is under review pending sufficient research comparing learning outcomes from simulated and lab experiences. At this time, research results are inconsistent. For example, in their study comparing learning from simulated and in-person frog dissection, Akpan and Strayer (2010) found that the simulation group had higher achievement gains and better attitudes than the group that did a conventional dissection. But they note that these results contradict results of past studies. Clearly, this is an area in need of further research.

**TECHNOLOGY LEARNING CHECK**

Complete **TLC 11.3** to review what you have learned from this section about issues that affect how technology may be integrated into science education.

## 🔘 TECHNOLOGY INTEGRATION STRATEGIES FOR SCIENCE INSTRUCTION

The Biological Sciences Curriculum Studies (BSCS) 5E instructional model focuses on development of key cognitive 21st-century skills by engaging in scientific inquiry explorations and provides a framework for how technology can enhance science instruction. The models five phases are (Duran, Duran, Haney, & Scheuermann, 2009):

- **Engagement:** Confront students with specific questions for the future inquiry
- **Exploration:** Engage students in experiences where they generate new ideas as they examine and explore the questions
- **Explanation:** Provide teachers with opportunities to directly introduce the topic and for students to explain their understandings
- **Elaboration:** Offer students with opportunities to develop deeper understandings and apply the ideas to additional activities
- **Evaluation:** Encourage students to assess their understandings and teachers opportunities to evaluate student progress.

Duran et al. said that "the standards are designed to provide a vision of scientific literacy for all students—regardless of age, race, ethnic background, English-language proficiency, socioeconomic status, disability, or giftedness" (p. 57).

Polly (2011) said technologies are more effective when students engage in higher-order thinking skills. During engagement in technology-rich and learner-centered activities, students analyze and synthesize results from their inquiries in ways that deepen their understandings and helps them make connections among the multiple disciplines. Multiple technology resources support the higher-order thinking engagement that characterizes the emerging science CCSS. Table 11.4 highlights some additional teaching and learning strategies with potential for student engagement in higher-order thinking skills and gives examples of some of the technology resources that make them possible.

# TABLE 11.4 Summary of Technology Integration Strategies for Science

| Technology Integration Strategies | Benefits | Sample Resources and Activities |
|---|---|---|
| Involving students in scientific inquiry through authentic online projects | • Internet projects provide environments that support all phases of an authentic scientific inquiry experience | • Globe Project—GLOBE Program http://globe.gov)<br>• Journey North—global study of wildlife migration and seasonal change<br>• Project FeederWatch at Cornell University—winter-long survey of birds that visit multiple feeders from volunteer locations in North America |
| Support for specific processes in scientific inquiry | • Helps students locate and obtain information to support inquiry<br>• Makes data collection and analysis more manageable<br>• Makes phenomena easier to visualize and understand<br>• Helps students communicate results of inquiries | • CBLs and spreadsheets—a computer based laboratory for simulating science experiments<br>• The Exploratorium Museum—hands-on museum in San Francisco that provides interactive online exhibits and exhibitions<br>• National Science Digital Library (NSDL) an online resource for science, technology, engineering and mathematics education funded by the National Science Foundation<br>• Digital Library for Earth System Education—an online library resource funded by the National Science Foundation featuring among agricultural, geographical, oceanography and other earth sciences<br>• PhET Independent Simulations at the University of Colorado—provides simulations for physics, biology, chemistry, earth science, and mathematics learning in elementary, middle school, high school and college grade levels<br>• ReciprocalNet: a distributed crystallography network for researchers, students and teachers |
| Supporting science skills and concept learning | • Allows students to simulate and model various scientific processes<br>• Provides opportunities to engage in problem solving | • Poll Everywhere—a text message polling service that allows students to use their cell phones as "clicker" devices to participate in polls |
| Engaging students in engineering topics through robotics | • Gives students experience with engineering principles<br>• Gets students thinking about engineering careers | • NASA's Robotics Alliance project (http://robotics.nasa.gov)<br>• International Technology and Engineering Educators Association—a professional association for technology education teachers who teach a curriculum focused on engineering and design |
| Accessing science information and tools | • Offers sources of information, lesson plans on science topics | • National Academy Press (NAP)—provides publications that address key issues in science<br>• Telescopes that educators and students may use:<br>  - Telescopes in Education website<br>  - British telescope system with observatories in Hawaii and Australia<br>  - National Optical Astronomy Observatory<br>  - Bradford robotic telescope in Canary Islands<br>• San Diego Astronomy Association—a non profit educational association focused on furthering astronomy, space and physical science<br>• Night Skies Network—for amateur astronomers to view the nighttime skies |
| Other science resource websites for teachers | • Offers sources of information, lesson plans on science topics | • National Science Education Standards<br>• National Science Teachers Association (NSTA, http://www.nsta.org<br>• American Association for the Advancement of Science (AAAS)<br>• National Aeronautical and Space Administration (NASA, http://www.nasa.gov)<br>• National Science Education Standards<br>• National Oceanic and Atmospheric Administration (NOAA, http://www.noaa.gov) |

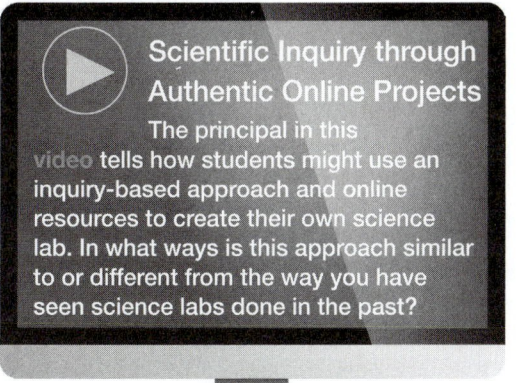

**Scientific Inquiry through Authentic Online Projects**

The principal in this video tells how students might use an inquiry-based approach and online resources to create their own science lab. In what ways is this approach similar to or different from the way you have seen science labs done in the past?

# Involving Students in Scientific Inquiry Through Authentic Online Projects

Authentic science not only involves having students "do" science, it also includes connecting science to students' lives and life experiences. Involving students in active scientific investigations can improve their attitude toward science as well as their understanding of scientific concepts. The BSCS 5E's instructional model supports the design of units that involve these scientific investigations. Some online projects are available that can engage students by making them partners in scientific investigations. These projects give them experience with all aspects of the scientific approach: asking new and novel questions, setting up researchable hypotheses, collecting and analyzing data, communicating the results, and getting feedback to help interpret and refine results. Scientists use a variety of technologies in their own work, and these projects use many of the same tools to teach the scientific process. Three such projects are: the Global Learning and Observations to Benefit the Environment (GLOBE) Program, Project FeederWatch, and Journey North.

The GLOBE Program is an excellent example of this kind of all-purpose project. GLOBE is an environmental science project that has students investigate the weather, land cover, soil, and hydrology, and record their observations at the GLOBE site. In effect, they become collaborators in a real scientific investigation.

First, they take ground observations using state-of-the-art technologies such as temperature **data loggers**, which are devices that record data over time with sensors, and global positioning systems (GPS), as well as traditional technologies such as a weather shelter and a U-tube thermometer. They record their data in a notebook and enter it into a database at the GLOBE site. Then they manipulate data with online graphing and visualization tools. The data can also be displayed in a graphical form, allowing students to look for patterns over time. To complete the process, students write up their results and post them to the GLOBE Student Research website. In the write-up, students report on their research questions, discuss their procedures, communicate their results using graphs and charts, and make conclusions. Once posted on the website, the report is peer reviewed by GLOBE participants.

Another such multipurpose site that involves students in real scientific investigations is Project FeederWatch from Cornell University, which provides teachers with a bird identification key and instructions for stocking a bird feeder, gathering data, and submitting the information to the site. This project provides numerous opportunities for using spreadsheet data and carrying out geographic information system analyses.

Finally, Journey North projects connect students and scientists in real-life science research. The project identifies itself as the "citizen science" project for children. It engages students in a global study of wildlife migration and seasonal change. K–12 students share their own field observations with classmates across North America. They track the coming of spring through the migration patterns of monarch butterflies, robins, hummingbirds, whooping cranes, gray whales, bald eagles, and other birds and mammals; the budding of plants; changing sunlight; and other natural events. The database they help create can be used to study factors such as climate change, migration, and soil and water conditions. All Journey North projects correlate directly to National Science Education Standards, with an emphasis on science inquiry. The site also offers teachers dozens of lesson plans and activities to use with their students.

## Support for Specific Processes in Scientific Inquiry

Teachers do not always have time to commit to long-term projects that encompass the entire scientific process. However, various technologies can provide support for specific elements of the scientific inquiry process. Some of these are described here. Also see Technology Integration Example 11.2 for an illustration of these principles in action.

**Locating information to investigate scientific issues and questions.** The Internet has become an indispensable tool for investigating important scientific questions. Science teachers and students have access to a number of exciting resources for teaching and

# TECHNOLOGY INTEGRATION

## Example 11.2

**TITLE:** Think Before You Drink!

**CONTENT AREA/TOPIC:** Science

**GRADE LEVELS:** 4–6

**ISTE STANDARDS•S:** Standard 2—Communication and Collaboration; Standard 3—Research and Information Fluency; Standard 4—Critical Thinking, Problem Solving and Decision Making; Standard 6—Technology Operations and Concepts

**SCIENTIFIC AND ENGINEERING PRACTICES:** Ask questions (S&EP1); plan and carry out investigations (S&EP3); analyze and interpret data (S&EP4); construct explanations (S&EP6; communicate information (S&EP8).

**DESCRIPTION:** Students work in small groups to gather water samples from various locations that have consumable drinking water and make predictions about whether they are safe to drink. They use probeware to gather data on various aspects of water quality and enter the data into a spreadsheet for analysis. Each group presents results in a PowerPoint presentation to the rest of the class. If any water proves to be unsafe or of questionable quality, the students work as a whole class on a letter to the business or city about what needs to be changed to improve the water quality.

*SOURCE:* Based on a concept in the Vernier lesson plan by Erin Van Lue, Lesley Drinkwine, and Mark Alexander at http://www.nd.edu/~nismec/vernier.htm.

---

learning science. For many of the science areas, teachers and students can access information from sources, such as NASA, or museums, such as the Exploratorium (see Figure 11.6).

The National Science Foundation (NSF) has funded the creation of digital libraries for science topics, as well as an online portal to education and research on learning in STEM topics called the National Science Digital Library (NSDL). One of the NSF-funded libraries is the Digital Library for Earth System Education (DLESE). The DLESE is a community of educators, students, and scientists working to improve the teaching of and learning about the earth system at all levels. DLESE provides access to a number of collections of educational and scientific resources. Digital libraries provide a starting point for the investigation of scientific questions.

Collecting data.    Data collection and archiving are important parts of the scientific inquiry process. Science bases its conclusions on data, and a number of tools are available for students' data collection and archiving. The calculator or computer-based laboratory (CBL or probeware) is an ideal tool for middle school through high school science. CBL sensors collect data, and the data can be downloaded into a computer or calculator and then manipulated in a spreadsheet. By archiving data in a spreadsheet, the data can be used at another time or compiled for long-term investigations. Using today's tools, students do not even have to be in the same location as the data being collected. They can collect data from remote sensors or from webcams set up to observe phenomena. Quillen (2011) describes one such activity where students operate a Geiger counter in Queensland, Australia, to measure how the intensity of radiation changes with distance.

Visualizing data and phenomena.    A number of visualization tools exist that allow students to see representations of data and phenomena that may be difficult to observe directly. These include simulations that help students see illustrations of macroscopic phenomena (e.g., phases of the moon or butterfly metamorphoses), which usually occur too slowly to observe processes, and microscopic or other phenomena that would otherwise be difficult or impossible to observe (e.g., molecular structure or parts of cells). In the past, students have learned from images or sped-up videos of some of these phenomena. Computer simulations differ from illustrations or videos in that students can manipulate elements in them and see the result. One resource for simulations is the Physics Education

**FIGURE 11.6  Exploratorium Website**

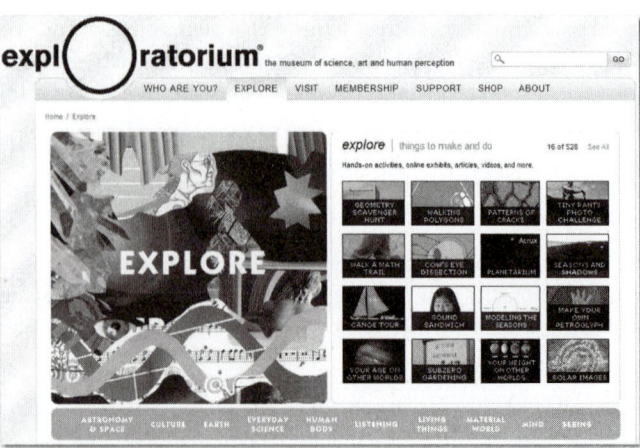

*Source:* © Exploratorium, www.exploratorium.edu. Reprinted by permission.

## FIGURE 11.7 Sheppard Software's Science Website

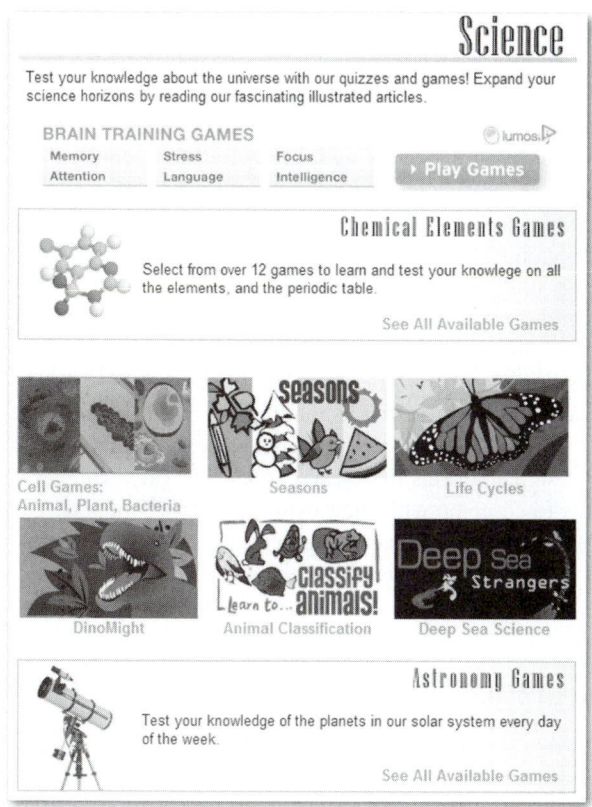

*Source:* From Sheppard Software http://www.sheppardsoftware.com. Reprinted by permission.

Technology (PhET) Independent Simulations project at the University of Colorado at Boulder. It offers more than 100 models to teach concepts in physics, chemistry, biology, and calculus; all are free for teachers' and students' use (Quillen, 2011).

Modeling tools make it possible to rotate and examine structures from multiple viewpoints to help students understand them. These tools also emulate the way scientists work in real environments. For example, meteorologists regularly show computer-generated visualizations on television to help explain weather phenomena. City planners use GIS modeling to plot population growth. One such modeling tool for use in physics is ReciprocalNet. It offers a digital collection of molecular structures, as well as software tools for visualizing, interacting with, and rendering printable images of the structures.

**Analyzing data.** Analyzing data can be done with a number of existing programs that come standard on computers. Spreadsheets allow data to be entered and analyzed using simple statistics or algorithms supplied by the students. In the GLOBE project, MultiSpec software provides students with the ability to identify land cover types on a LandSat image. GIS software allows students to analyze factors in an image by removing or adding attributes and looking for connections among attributes.

**Communicating results.** Once data are analyzed, scientists write up the results and submit them for publication using standard productivity software (e.g., word processing). Scientists collaborate on scientific problems, and the Internet facilitates the communication process. In addition to graphs and visualizations, scientists use images from digital cameras and other digital instruments to record data and compare and contrast data over time. This is especially useful in land cover investigations and in astronomy. The Internet also provides a medium for communication among scientists. Data can be emailed to researchers around the globe. Classroom teachers can also have scientists interact with students in their classroom via email, blogs, or by participating in **webcasts**, which are live video broadcasts of an event sent over the Internet.

## Supporting Science Skills and Concept Learning

Though hands-on science remains the major science instructional strategy, online science lessons and games can provide motivational ways to supplement this instruction. For example, Sheppard Software has well-designed, free science tutorials and games (see Figure 11.7 for samples of these games, and the Open Source feature for a link to their site). A search for "science games" yields a number of other good activities.

Tremblay (2010) discusses an innovative way to check students' concept learning after a science lesson by turning students' cell phones into student response systems (SRS, a.k.a., clickers). The teacher sets up a set of questions over lesson content in an online survey format on the Poll Everywhere (PE) website. Students respond to the questions by sending a text message from their cell phone to the number provided by the PE service or by going to the PE website using the browser on their phone. As answers come in, the website also updates a graph showing the number of responses to each option.

## Engaging Students in Engineering Topics through Robotics

Technology and engineering topics are often called "the missing T and E" in STEM education. One wry observer said that in STEM, the "T is lowercase and the E is silent." In fact, the lack of emphasis on these important areas was

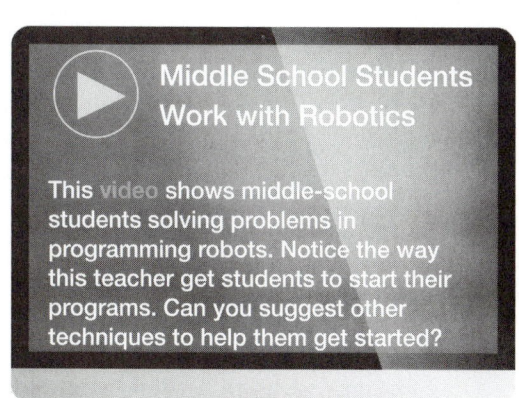

Middle School Students Work with Robotics

This video shows middle-school students solving problems in programming robots. Notice the way this teacher get students to start their programs. Can you suggest other techniques to help them get started?

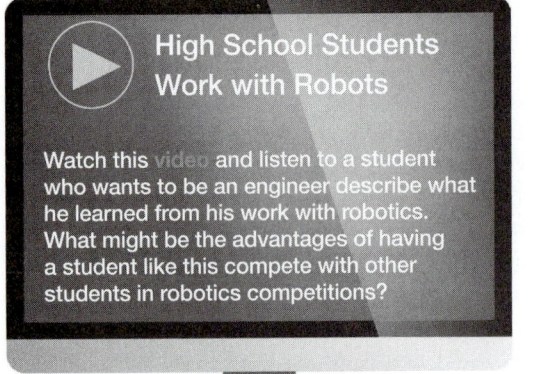

**High School Students Work with Robots**

Watch this video and listen to a student who wants to be an engineer describe what he learned from his work with robotics. What might be the advantages of having a student like this compete with other students in robotics competitions?

the driving force behind the International Technology Education Association (ITEA) changing its name to the International Technology and Engineering Educators Association in 2010.

The ITEEA has information and publications at its website on how to combine and emphasize these topics. One of these ways is through robotics curriculum, which has become an increasingly popular strategy for engaging students in problem solving and getting them interested in engineering principles and careers. Nugent, Barker, Grandgenett, and Adamchuk (2010) found that an intensive 40-hour robotics/GPS/GIS camp had great impact on students' learning of science content, but even a three-hour experience modeled on the same camp had great effect on improved attitudes toward science and technology and made kids excited about learning more.

Robotics camps and competitions sponsored by companies, universities, and professional organizations are plentiful; an Internet search under "robotics competitions" lists events at every grade level and region of the country. Many schools sponsor students to prepare products to enter in robotics competitions as a part of their science curriculum. The focus of competitions varies: some set a common problem for all participants and ask for innovative design solutions (e.g., build an electric car), while others set general goals and ask participants to come up with their own innovative products. The number of these contests speaks to their perceived impact on generating student interest in STEM content. NASA provides information on these contests as well as a collection of robotics information and materials at its website.

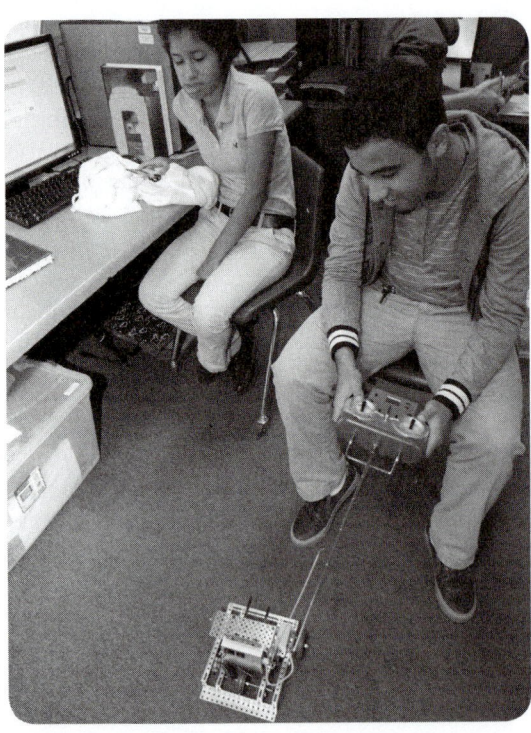

▲ Robotics projects like this helps supply the "missing E" in STEM education (Photo courtesy of W. Wiencke)

## Accessing Science Information and Tools

The Internet has opened up a world of tools and materials for use by teachers and students. One example of the opportunities provided by these unique tools is the ability for teachers and students to get time to use a remote online telescope to carry out various investigations. A few of the remote telescopes are given in Table 11.4.

The Internet is also an unlimited source of data for classroom experiments and investigations, camps and competitions, and up-to-date science information. Science knowledge changes faster than most school libraries can keep up. For the latest information on space, students can access National Aeronautics and Space Administration (NASA); for the weather, National Oceanic and Atmospheric Administration (NOAA); and for medicine, the National Institute of Health (NIH). Most of these sites provide content targeted for teachers and students. As of June 2011, anyone can download new publications from the National Academy Press (NAP) website free of charge. The NAP has a wide variety of current, useful publications in science and science education. Teachers can also use the Internet for assistance with content knowledge and for professional development opportunities that may not be available locally. They can also exchange ideas and teaching strategies with other teachers in learning communities. See a general list of helpful information sources under Other Science Resource Websites in Table 11.4 and the Top Ten Must-Have Apps for Science and Mathematics.

**TECHNOLOGY LEARNING CHECK**

Complete TLC 11.4 to review what you have learned from this section about technology integration strategies for science.

# TEACHING MATHEMATICS AND SCIENCE TEACHERS TO INTEGRATE TECHNOLOGY

This section gives recommendations for how teachers can prepare to integrate technology effectively into instruction for mathematics and science learning. Because technological advances change the tools and language of scientific methods, teachers of mathematics and science have found that they must reflect those changes in their teaching. Their challenge is keeping pace with the speed at which these changes are occurring and using new technologies to enhance their methods in ways that address the nation's primary concern in this area: to increase the number of students interested in pursuing STEM careers.

## Rubric to Measure Teacher Growth in Mathematics and Science Technology Integration

Begin by reviewing the rubric in Figure 11.8 or Figure 11.9 to measure teachers' progress in effectively integrating technology in mathematics and science instruction. Part I of the rubric addresses knowledge of issues and challenges, and Part II addresses mathematics and science technology integration strategies.

## Learning the Issues and Applications

The first step in technology integration is to become acquainted with the issues and challenges discussed in this chapter and how they shape teachers' uses and applications of technologies. Then teachers can begin developing capabilities to address instructional standards and curriculum goals. The following is a suggested sequence of learning activities.

- **Issues and challenges in mathematics and science instruction.** After reviewing the information in this chapter, go to the website of the science and mathematics professional organizations: the National Council of Teachers of Mathematics (NCTM), and the National Science Teachers Association (NSTA); review the standards at both sites. See professional development resources the sites offer, and decide on which can help you gain insight into the issues and challenges outlined in this chapter. Discuss and reflect on the two questions under the Collaborate, Discuss, Reflect feature at the end of the chapter. Complete Part I of the rubric in Figure 11.8 or Figure 11.9 before you begin this sequence and again at various points in your progress.

- **Mathematics and science technology integration strategies.** After reviewing the information in this chapter, review examples of the technologies suggested in the Open Source Options feature and the websites and projects described under each section, and do the lesson evaluation and lesson development activities outlined in the Technology Integration Workshop at the end of this chapter. Reflect on how you will plan for implementing these strategies in your own classroom using the TIP model. Complete Part I of the rubric in Figure 11.8 or Figure 11.9 before you begin this sequence and again at various points in your progress.

**TECHNOLOGY LEARNING CHECK**

Complete TLC 11.5 to review what you have learned from this section about how mathematics and science teachers can develop their knowledge and skills in technology integration.

# FIGURE 11.8 Rubric to Measure Teacher Growth in Mathematics Technology Integration

| Part I: Teacher Knowledge of Mathematics Issues and Challenges | | | |
|---|---|---|---|
| | **Basic knowledge (1–2 points)** | **Intermediate knowledge (3–4 points)** | **Advanced knowledge (4–5 points)** |
| Accountability for standards in mathematics | I can articulate the nature of the issue. | I can both articulate the nature of the issue and some of the possible ways to address it. | I can articulate my own plan for addressing the issue in my own teaching. |
| Challenges in implementing the common core state standards for school mathematics | I can articulate the nature of the issue. | I can both articulate the nature of the issue and some of the possible ways to address it. | I can articulate my own plan for addressing the issue in my own teaching. |
| Directed vs. Social-Constructivist teaching strategies: ongoing "math wars" | I can articulate the nature of the issue. | I can both articulate the nature of the issue and some of the possible ways to address it. | I can articulate my own plan for addressing the issue in my own teaching. |

| Part II: Teachers' Technology Integration Strategies for Mathematics Instruction | | | |
|---|---|---|---|
| | **Basic knowledge (1–2 points)** | **Intermediate knowledge (3–4 points)** | **Advanced knowledge (4–5 points)** |
| Bridging the gap between abstract and concrete with virtual manipulatives | I can describe the strategies and identify technologies to carry them out. | I have designed at least 1–2 activities based on these strategies to enhance my teaching and my students' learning. | I have designed plans for how I will integrate these strategies throughout my curriculum to enhance my teaching and my students' learning. |
| Allowing representation of mathematical principles | I can describe the strategies and identify technologies to carry them out. | I have designed at least 1–2 activities based on these strategies to enhance my teaching and my students' learning. | I have designed plans for how I will integrate these strategies throughout my curriculum to enhance my teaching and my students' learning. |
| Supporting mathematical problem solving | I can describe the strategies and identify technologies to carry them out. | I have designed at least 1–2 activities based on these strategies to enhance my teaching and my students' learning. | I have designed plans for how I will integrate these strategies throughout my curriculum to enhance my teaching and my students' learning. |
| Implementing data-driven curricula | I can describe the strategies and identify technologies to carry them out. | I have designed at least 1–2 activities based on these strategies to enhance my teaching and my students' learning. | I have designed plans for how I will integrate these strategies throughout my curriculum to enhance my teaching and my students' learning. |
| Supporting math-related communications | I can describe the strategies and identify technologies to carry them out. | I have designed at least 1–2 activities based on these strategies to enhance my teaching and my students' learning. | I have designed plans for how I will integrate these strategies throughout my curriculum to enhance my teaching and my students' learning. |
| Motivating skill building and practice | I can describe the strategies and identify technologies to carry them out. | I have designed at least 1–2 activities based on these strategies to enhance my teaching and my students' learning. | I have designed plans for how I will integrate these strategies throughout my curriculum to enhance my teaching and my students' learning. |
| **Total points** | _____ of 45 possible points | | |

**FIGURE 11.9** Rubric to Measure Teacher Growth in Science Technology Integration

| Part I: Teacher Knowledge of Science Issues and Challenges | | | |
|---|---|---|---|
| | **Basic knowledge (1–2 points)** | **Intermediate knowledge (3–4 points)** | **Advanced knowledge (4–5 points)** |
| Accountability for standards in science | I can articulate the nature of the issue. | I can both articulate the nature of the issue and some of the possible ways to address it. | I can articulate my own plan for addressing the issue in my own teaching. |
| The narrowing pipeline of scientific talent | I can articulate the nature of the issue. | I can both articulate the nature of the issue and some of the possible ways to address it. | I can articulate my own plan for addressing the issue in my own teaching. |
| Increasing need for scientific literacy | I can articulate the nature of the issue. | I can both articulate the nature of the issue and some of the possible ways to address it. | I can articulate my own plan for addressing the issue in my own teaching. |
| Difficulties in teaching K–8 science | I can articulate the nature of the issue. | I can both articulate the nature of the issue and some of the possible ways to address it. | I can articulate my own plan for addressing the issue in my own teaching. |
| Objections to virtual science labs | I can articulate the nature of the issue. | I can both articulate the nature of the issue and some of the possible ways to address it. | I can articulate my own plan for addressing the issue in my own teaching. |
| Part II: Teachers' Technology Integration Strategies for Science Instruction | | | |
| | **Basic knowledge (1–2 points)** | **Intermediate knowledge (3–4 points)** | **Advanced knowledge (4–5 points)** |
| Involving students in scientific inquiry through authentic online projects | I can describe the strategies and identify technologies to carry them out. | I have designed at least 1–2 activities based on these strategies to enhance my teaching and my students' learning. | I have designed plans for how I will integrate these strategies throughout my curriculum to enhance my teaching and my students' learning. |
| Support for specific processes in scientific inquiry | I can describe the strategies and identify technologies to carry them out. | I have designed at least 1–2 activities based on these strategies to enhance my teaching and my students' learning. | I have designed plans for how I will integrate these strategies throughout my curriculum to enhance my teaching and my students' learning. |
| Supporting science skills and concept learning | I can describe the strategies and identify technologies to carry them out. | I have designed at least 1–2 activities based on these strategies to enhance my teaching and my students' learning. | I have designed plans for how I will integrate these strategies throughout my curriculum to enhance my teaching and my students' learning. |
| Engaging students in engineering topics through robotics | I can describe the strategies and identify technologies to carry them out. | I have designed at least 1–2 activities based on these strategies to enhance my teaching and my students' learning. | I have designed plans for how I will integrate these strategies throughout my curriculum to enhance my teaching and my students' learning. |
| Accessing science information and tools | I can describe the strategies and identify technologies to carry them out. | I have designed at least 1–2 activities based on these strategies to enhance my teaching and my students' learning. | I have designed plans for how I will integrate these strategies throughout my curriculum to enhance my teaching and my students' learning. |
| **Total points** | _____ of 50 possible points | | |

Monkey Business/Fotolia

**The following questions may be used either for in-class, small-group discussions or may be used to initiate discussions in blogs or online discussion boards:**

1. As noted in this chapter, the "math wars" continue between those who believe math should be explicit and teacher-directed and those who advocate a more social-constructivist approach. How do technology integration strategies differ between these two positions? Are there ways to combine them that address the recommendations of both sides?

2. As noted in this chapter, the National Science Teachers Association (NSTA) and the American Chemical Society (ACS) have taken the position that "hands-on" means that students must physically touch the materials rather than "do" science on a computer. Both organizations have issued position statements arguing against using computer simulations as a substitute for in-person, in-school laboratory experiences. Can you cite evidence that some science skills cannot be learned from a virtual lab experience? If so, what are they?

3. In the U.S. government's 2010 report, *Rising Above the Gathering Storm, Revisited: Rapidly Approaching Category 5*, the authors make the case that the country is not making the necessary investments in science and technology to remain globally competitive. Go to the National Academies Press website and download and read a free copy of the report. What role does educational technology play in their recommendations to address this need?

## Chapter 11 Summary

**The following is a summary of the main points covered in this chapter.**

1. **Issues and challenges in Mathematics Instruction.** These issues include accountability for standards in mathematics, challenges in implementing the common core state standards for school mathematics, and directed versus social-constructivist teaching strategies (the ongoing "math wars").

2. **Technology Integration Strategies for Mathematics Instruction.** Integration strategies include:
   - Bridging the gap between abstract and concrete with virtual manipulatives
   - Allowing representation of mathematical principles
   - Supporting mathematical problem solving
   - Implementing data-driven curricula
   - Supporting math-related communications
   - Motivating skill building and practice

3. **Issues and Challenges in Science Instruction.** Issues include accountability for standards in science, the narrowing pipeline of scientific talent, increasing need for scientific literacy, difficulties in teaching K–8 science, and objections to virtual science labs.

4. **Technology Integration Strategies for Science Instruction.** Integration strategies are based on the BSCS 5e framework (engagement, exploration, explanation, elaboration, and evaluation) and include:
   - Involving students in scientific inquiry through authentic online projects
   - Support for specific processes in scientific inquiry, including: locating information to investigate scientific issues and questions, collecting data, visualizing data and phenomena, analyzing data, and communicating results
   - Supporting science skills and concept learning
   - Engaging students in engineering topics through robotics
   - Accessing science information and tools

5. **Teaching Mathematics and Science Teachers to Integrate Technology.** Teachers can begin by consulting the rubrics provided in this chapter to measure their own growth in mathematics and science technology integration. After that, they may review issues and challenges in mathematics and science instruction and use chapter resources to learn technology integration strategies they can use to address the issues and challenges.

# TECHNOLOGY INTEGRATION **WORKSHOP**

## 1. APPLY WHAT YOU LEARNED

To apply the concepts and skills you've read about throughout this chapter, go to the Chapter 11 Technology Application Activity.

## 2. TECHNOLOGY INTEGRATION LESSON PLANNING: PART 1—EVALUATING AND CREATING LESSON PLANS

Complete the following exercise using the sample lesson plans found on any lesson planning site that you find on the Internet.

**a.** Locate lesson ideas—Identify three lesson plans that focus on any of the tools or strategies you learned about in this chapter. For example:

- Using virtual manipulatives
- Mathematical problem solving
- Online scientific inquiry
- Engaging students in engineering topics through robotics

**b.** Evaluate the lessons—Use the Technology Lesson Plan Evaluation Checklist to evaluate each of the lessons you found.

**c.** Create your own lesson—After you have reviewed and evaluated some sample lessons, create one of your own using a lesson plan format of your choice (or one your instructor gives you). Be sure the lesson focuses on one of the technologies or strategies discussed in this chapter.

## 3. TECHNOLOGY INTEGRATION LESSON PLANNING: PART 2—IMPLEMENTING THE TIP MODEL

Review how to implement the TIP model in your classroom by doing the following activities with the lesson you created in the Technology Integration Lesson Planning exercise above.

**a.** Describe the Phase 1—Planning activities you would do to use this lesson in your classroom:

- What is the relative advantage of using the technology(ies) in this lesson?
- Do you have resources and skills you need to carry it out?

**b.** Describe the Phase 2—Implementation activities you would do to use this lesson in your classroom:

- What are the objectives of the lesson plan?
- How will you assess your students' accomplishment of the objectives?
- What integration strategies are used in this lesson plan?
- How would you prepare the learning environment?

**c.** Describe the Phase 3—Evaluation/Revision activities you would do to use this lesson in your classroom: What strategies and/or instruments would you use to evaluate the success of this lesson in your classroom in order to determine revision needs?

**d.** Add lesson descriptors—Create descriptors for your new lesson (e.g., grade level, content and topic areas, technologies used, ISTE standards, 21st Century Learning standards).

**e.** Save your new lesson—Save your lesson plan with all its descriptors and TIP model notes.

## 4. FOR YOUR TEACHING PORTFOLIO

Add the following to your Teaching Portfolio:

- Reflections on Hot Topic Debate.
- Summary notes from the Collaborate, Discuss, Reflect activity.
- Lesson plan evaluations, lesson plans, and products you created above.
- Your *Apply What You Learned* Product from Activity 1.

By Michael Berson and M. D. Roblyer

# 12

# Teaching and Learning with Technology in Social Studies

## Learning Outcomes

After reading this chapter and completing the learning activities, you should be able to:

1. Identify implications for technology integration of each current issue that social studies teachers face. (ISTE Standards•T 4, 5)

2. Select technology integration strategies that can meet various needs for instruction in social studies. (ISTE Standards•T 2, 5)

3. Design a strategy for how to build teacher knowledge and skills in technology integration for social studies. (ISTE Standards•T 5)

Vladgrin/Shutterstock

# TECHNOLOGY INTEGRATION IN ACTION
# I WITNESS ACCOUNTS – SURVIVOR VIDEOS

GRADE LEVEL: 8–12 • CONTENT AREA/TOPIC: American history, civics • LENGTH OF TIME: Two weeks

## PHASE 1 ANALYSIS OF LEARNING AND TEACHING NEEDS

Benjamin Haas/Shutterstock

### Step 1: Determine relative advantage.

Like many history teachers, Mr. Kinsella struggled to make the study of American history meaningful and interesting to his students. Through a workshop at the regional social studies conference, he became acquainted with the IWitness website, where he saw a collection of video interviews in which survivors of various catastrophic events (e.g., wars, Holocaust, deportations) tell their stories. He found the videos so compelling, he immediately began thinking of how students could use video to connect with some of our country's recent history. He decided on the strategy of students creating their own video "survival stories" of people in the community who had survived catastrophic events such as wars, civil rights conflicts, and terrorist attacks such as the ones in New York and Colorado.

### Step 2: Assess required skills and resources.

Mr. Kinsella decided to introduce the IWitness site when his history class covered the years from 1940 to the present. He would assign his students to view several IWitness videos as an outside-class assignment (a kind of flipped-classroom activity) to develop an understanding of the use of testimony from Holocaust survivors. For student-created videos, he realized that though he had used digital cameras to capture home videos, he knew little about video editing and features like screen effects and captioning. He asked Ms. Lorde, the technology education teacher, to recommend video software that was both free and easy to learn. Ms. Lorde recommended Windows Moviemaker; she also offered to help Mr. Kinsella learn the software and assist students with their video projects. With the help of the school district office, he managed to obtain three digital cameras, and students were able to borrow others from their parents. He also knew he could use the class's Edmodo site to post assignments and directions and to communicate with students about the project. The final resource he needed was a list of people to interview. Through his classroom blog, Mr. Kinsella identified veterans from the Vietnam War, the Korean Conflict, Desert Storm, and Afghanistan who were willing to tell their stories. Students' grandparents who grew up in the segregated South offered to tell their stories of struggle, and a Jewish great-grandparent offered to share a story of survival in France during World War II. Finally, one student had an uncle who was a survivor of the 2001 terrorist attack in New York.

## PHASE 2 PLANNING FOR INTEGRATION

### Step 3: Decide on objectives and assessments.

Though students were very excited about the idea of doing video interviews, Mr. Kinsella had to think carefully about outcomes he wanted to achieve with this unit—outcomes beyond generating excitement about doing their own video. He decided he wanted to achieve the following outcomes, objectives, and assessment strategies:

Outcome: History achievement.
Objective: At least 85% of students will make an 80% or better on the history unit test for the period 1940–present.
Assessment: Benchmark state-created test.

Outcome: History attitudes.
Objective: Students will demonstrate improved attitudes toward the relevance and appeal of studying history.
Assessment: Teacher-designed Likert scale.

Outcome: Video quality.
Objective: Students will score at least 80% on a video quality rubric.
Assessment: Video rubric modified from one located online.

### Step 4: Design integration strategies.

Mr. Kinsella planned the following sequence of activities to carry out the unit:

Introduce unit and I Witness website: Introduce the project at the beginning of the unit and use an interactive whiteboard to demonstrate the website and show one of the survivor videos.

Students watch videos: Tell students to access the class's Edmodo site to get a Viewing Assignment sheet and a Video Project assignment outline. They will select and watch at least three videos, complete the assignment sheet to show those which they viewed, and post the completed sheet to the Edmodo site.

Review assignment in class: To make sure students understand how to proceed, a class discussion will allow students to ask questions.

Students decide on a video subject: Students may work individually or in pairs or threes to select a subject to interview, create video questions, and complete their interviews.

Students work on video editing: Ms. Lorde demonstrates how to use the movie-making software, and each student or group works on editing and placing effects in the video interview.

Students research historical period: With Mr. Kinsella's guidance, the students use classroom and online resources to research the time period in which their survival story is set. The assignment sheet lists the items they are to find out and be prepared to report on.

Student presentations: The students place their videos on the Edmodo site, view each other's videos, and give their reports in class on the historical period. After all reports are given, Mr. Kinsella facilitates a class discussion in which students comment on each other's videos and the history surrounding them.

### Step 5: Prepare instructional environment.

Mr. Kinsella created the needed assignment and directions documents and set up the Edmodo site with the required areas to support the project.

## PHASE 3  POST-INSTRUCTION ANALYSIS AND REVISIONS

### Step 6: Analyze results.

At the end of the unit, Mr. Kinsella gave the unit test and reviewed the results from the attitude surveys and video rubrics. He had met his target criterion for success in improved student attitudes about studying history, and the video rubrics all reflected passing results. Some students still could not pass the end-of-unit test on the history of the period, but on parts pertaining to the time periods on which students reported, results were generally much better. An unexpected outcome was the attention the project drew from the community. The local TV channel did a special on the project, featuring clips from some of the videos. Mr. Kinsella received many emails and blog-posted messages from parents and community leaders applauding his work. A local veterans group offered financial assistance to expand the scope of the project to any local veteran who wanted to share a survivor story.

### Step 7: Make revisions.

To improve results on the required unit tests, Mr. Kinsella made plans to do "mini-reviews" of information from each decade before students took the test. Also, some students had complained that they needed more time to work on videos and wanted more assistance creating various video effects, so Mr. Kinsella revised the project schedule to allow for more in-class time and after-school assistance to work on videos.

*Source:* Based on ideas from the iWitness website's lesson plan iWitness Video Challenge at http://iwitness.usc.edu/SFI/Activity/.

# CHAPTER 12 BIG IDEAS OVERVIEW

Before you begin reading the rest of this chapter, listen to the Chapter 12 Big Ideas Overview. It will give you a two-minute audio overview of main concepts to look for and help prepare you to work through information and exercises to achieve this chapter's outcomes.

# ISSUES AND CHALLENGES IN SOCIAL STUDIES INSTRUCTION

Since the Industrial Revolution, science and technology have shaped the world in fundamental ways, but in the 1990s the Internet accelerated this influence. Better, faster worldwide communications have made the world at once smaller and more complex. Life was simpler—and less informed—when people were not able to know so much about themselves and others so quickly. Social studies instruction is designed to help us discover and better understand our world and its people, and technology-based strategies have become integral to this instruction (Diem & Berson, 2010).

Various issues shape the technologies that social studies teachers choose and the strategies they create with them. This section reviews these issues, which include challenges presented by social studies standards, challenges inherent in social studies instruction, debates about how best to teach social studies content, and the impact of the "information explosion" on social studies content and methods.

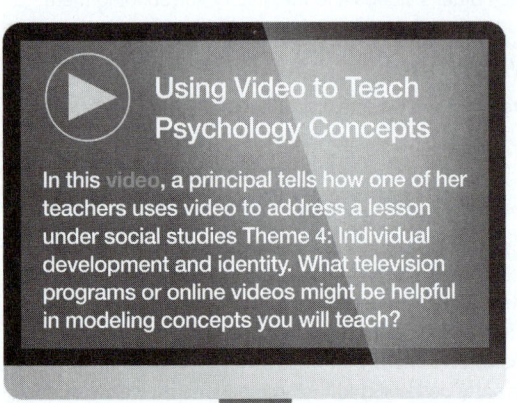

**Using Video to Teach Psychology Concepts**

In this video, a principal tells how one of her teachers uses video to address a lesson under social studies Theme 4: Individual development and identity. What television programs or online videos might be helpful in modeling concepts you will teach?

## Meeting Standards Across Social Studies Areas

The National Social Studies Standards, released in 2004 and revised in 2010, address overall curriculum design and comprehensive student performance expectations. However, standards also exist for each of the social studies disciplines—such as civics, economics, geography, government, and history—which provide more specific content detail for each discipline. The intent of the NCSS standards is to encourage curriculum designers to use the NCSS social studies standards for creating the overall framework and then fill in the detail using the discipline standards. The National Council for the Social Studies (NCSS) has adopted the following formal definition of **social studies**:

Social studies is the integrated study of the social sciences and humanities to promote civic competence. Within the school program, social studies provides coordinated, systemic study drawing upon such disciplines as anthropology, archaeology, economics, geography, history, law, philosophy, political science, psychology, religion, and sociology, as well as appropriate content from the humanities, mathematics, and the natural sciences. The primary purpose of social studies is to help young people develop the ability to make informed and reasoned decisions for the public good as citizens of a culturally diverse, democratic society in an interdependent world (National Council for the Social Studies, 2010, p. 3; reprinted by permission).

Ten themes form the framework of the social studies standards; those, along with a brief description of each, are presented next (NCSS, 2010). At the elementary and middle school levels, school systems usually address the social studies curriculum by teaching a variety of topics from these strands. In high school, social studies tends to become divided into more specific areas, such as history and civics. Thus, when referring to a course, the term social studies is more commonly used to describe K–8 classes than high school classes. The themes are summarized below.

**Theme 1: Culture.** This focuses on the characteristics of cultures and how belief systems from religion or politics influence culture. Instruction on this theme is covered in geography, history, sociology, and anthropology, and multicultural topics of various courses.

▲ Technology plays an important role in addressing social studies Theme 1, which addresses the characteristics of cultures and how belief systems from religion or politics influence culture. **Dboystudio/Shutterstock**

**Theme 2: Time, continuity, and change.** Instruction on this theme is usually in history courses and helps students answer questions such as: "Who am I? What happened in the past? How am I connected to those in the past? How has the world changed, and how might it change in the future? Why does our personal sense of relatedness to the past change?" (Social Studies Standards, 2010).

**Theme 3: People, places, and environments.** This theme is covered in geography courses and studies of local areas to help students create "geographic perspectives of the world beyond their personal locations" (Social Studies Standards, 2010). They gain knowledge about how things are located, how landforms change, and how these changes affect people.

**Theme 4: Individual development and identity.** This theme usually appears in psychology and anthropology courses to help students learn about how their identity is shaped by their membership in a culture, groups, or institutions. They also come to understand how people learn and behave as they do and how they develop from youth to adulthood.

**Theme 5: Individuals, groups, and institutions.** This theme is covered in sociology, anthropology, psychology, political science, and history courses. It focuses on the roles that schools, houses of worship, families, government agencies, and the courts play in our lives and how these entities control or influence them.

**Theme 6: Power, authority, and governance.** Courses in government, politics, political science, history, and law cover this theme and help students understand how power, authority, and governance function in the United States and other parts of the world. Such understanding is seen as integral to students developing civic competence.

**Theme 7: Production, distribution, and consumption.** This theme is usually seen in economics courses. Instruction on this theme addresses topics in the production and distribution of goods and services and how land, labor, capital, and management are involved in them.

**Theme 8: Science, technology, and society.** This is the one social studies theme that directly addresses technology and is covered in many different social studies courses, including history, geography, economics, civics, and government. It focuses on the nature of change, how technology helps bring it about, and how we can preserve our fundamental values and beliefs in the midst of this change.

**Theme 9: Global connections.** Though usually covered in courses dealing with geography, culture, and economics, this theme also shares information from natural and physical sciences and the humanities. It seeks to show students that though national and global goals sometimes conflict, these goals also connect and depend on each other. Topics include "health care, the environment, human rights, economic competition and interdependence, age-old ethnic hostilities, and political and military alliances" (Social Studies Standards, 2010).

**Theme 10: Civic ideals and practices.** This theme appears in history, political science, and cultural anthropology courses, and in fields such as global studies, law education, and the humanities. It addresses ideals and practices that enable students to be informed citizens and participants in their community, country, and the world at large.

**College, Career, and Civic Life (C3) Framework.** In addition to the 2010 social studies standards, the National Council for the Social Studies (NCSS, 2013) published the College, Career, and Civic Life (C3) Framework for Social Studies. This framework helps states upgrade their state social studies standards and assist school districts, schools, teacher,s and curriculum writers in strengthening their local social studies programs. C3's four dimensions are designed to be used across all 10 social studies themes and include:

1. Developing Questions and Planning Inquiries
2. Applying Disciplinary Concepts and Tools
3. Evaluating Sources and Using Evidence
4. Communicating Conclusions and Taking Informed Action

Despite guidance provided by the standards and framework, the social studies teacher is challenged to have sufficient background to teach such diverse topics. The typical social studies teacher is often called on to be a "jack of all trades" and, hopefully, a master of more than one of the social studies content areas. Unfortunately, many preservice teachers with social studies majors go into specific areas such as history where they feel they are most likely to get a job, leaving courses in content areas such as economics and geography last on their list. Depending on the teaching position teachers take, they must look to available resources such as those found online to help them meet the needs of content areas in which they may lack background (Berson & Berson, 2013).

## Challenges in Teaching Social Studies

Despite their obvious value and relevance to future citizens, social studies themes and topics are not usually among those included in statewide assessments. Many states limit their graduation tests to language arts (i.e., reading and writing) and mathematics. Since schools tend to focus instruction and resources primarily on tested topics, social studies areas are often placed on the back burner (Passe & Fitchett, 2013). Consequently, technology materials tend to be directed toward other content areas. This means that teachers have to look for inexpensive or free sources such as those shown in the Open Sources Options for Social Studies. There are also many options available to help teachers meet diverse needs when teaching social studies, as shown in the Adapting for Special Needs feature.

The sheer amount of material to review in many social studies topic areas is also a challenge. A good example is a world history course, which often covers the period from the dawn of civilization to the present day. The amount of content, coupled with the de-emphasis on social studies topics, creates an ongoing challenge to teachers and schools to address social studies in a meaningful way.

# OPEN SOURCE
## OPTIONS for Software in Social Studies Classrooms

| TYPES | FREE SOURCES |
| --- | --- |
| **Polling students** | Poll Everywhere: polleverywhere.com/# |
| **Brainstorming** | Bubbl: bubbl.us/ |
| **Poster creation** | Glogster: glogster.com/ |
| **Timelines** | Dipity: dipity.com/<br>Timetoast: timetoast.com/ |
| **Dynamic presentations** | Prezi: prezi.com/ |
| **Graphing** | National Center for Education Statistics: nces.ed.gov/nceskids/createagraph/ |

# Adapting for Special Needs

## Social Studies

Social studies topics can be challenging for some students with disabilities because of the significant amount of grade level reading required. As a result, educators should consider how to provide multiple means of accessing information such as photos, movies, audio, and simplified text. A strategy that incorporates a variety of media in a meaningful, enjoyable activity is to use technologies that allow students to follow news stories and create their own, personalized newspaper. The value to students is that they take responsibility for deciding which stories they want to follow, which engages them more in reading, and also create a professional-looking product they can be proud of. The following are several resources that can help carry out this kind of activity:

- Tween Times Tribune (at the Tween Tribune website)—Students can read the same current event news article at multiple grade levels.
- Newsela (at the Newsela website)—Current events news articles are available at multiple Lexile levels.

- The Big Picture (at Boston.com's Big Picture website)—Major news stories in photographs.
- Newsmap (at the Newsmap website)—Summarizes major stories in short paragraphs and provides links to full stories.
- Social Studies for Kids (at the Social Studies for Kids website)—Current events written at low readability levels.
- News-2-You (at the News-2-you website)—This subscription-based service prepares a weekly, downloadable current-events reader that teachers may copy and distribute to students. For students with mild or moderate cognitive impairments, this specially designed newspaper keeps them in touch with the news using high-interest, low-vocabulary stories with each word accompanied by a rebus image.

*—Contributed by Dave Edyburn*

## The "History Wars" and Other Debates on the Content and Focus of Social Studies

Social studies has attracted more debate and criticism than perhaps any other content area, and much of this discussion centers around the appropriate role of history in the curriculum. In recent years, leaders in the field of social studies have made the case that students should be aware of the broad array of influences that have shaped our country's history. Critics of this approach feel that the content of history courses has become diluted—that courses focus too much on topics they consider to be outside the mainstream, traditional historical themes and important events that shaped the United States (Lanius, 2013). These critics feel that teachers are ill-equipped to teach history effectively (Halvorsen, 2012). As a result, the disciplines within the social studies each have their own camps that are fighting for more coverage within the schools and financial support to prepare teachers effectively.

## Perils of the Information Explosion

The ready availability of information on the Internet has created several concerns for social studies educators. Some believe that Internet information has the potential to alter the traditional relationship between student and teacher, since teachers are no longer the primary source of facts or opinions. Teachers tell of students bringing printed Web pages to school to contradict what the textbook and/or teacher says. In the past, most information that students received was sifted through a reliable filter; today, those filters often are nonexistent. Students can find sites that profess Nazi and Ku Klux Klan ideology, treat rumor as fact, and promote conspiracy theories that range from UFO landings in Roswell, New Mexico, to the CIA selling drugs in American cities.

Many students have been drawn to online sites without questioning their accuracy. Many educators believe we should use such controversial websites as demonstration tools to teach our students how to become critical consumers of information, and others believe students need digital literacy skills now more than ever.

**TECHNOLOGY LEARNING CHECK**

Complete **TLC 12.1** to review what you have learned from this section about issues that affect how technology may be integrated into social studies.

## TECHNOLOGY INTEGRATION STRATEGIES FOR SOCIAL STUDIES

Technology tools make possible a variety of strategies to enhance learning for the diverse topics and concepts that comprise social studies content. The strategies described here support both traditional, directed approaches to teaching social studies topics as well as constructivist ones. The following integration strategies suggest activities to address each of the 10 themes in the NCSS National Social Studies Standards, as well as the C3 Framework dimensions. Also see the **Top Ten Must-Have Apps for Social Studies**. Berson, Berson, and Manfra (2012) call for bundling multiple apps together to support innovative teaching and learning.

### Using Simulations and Problem-Solving Environments

Many social studies topics present issues, concepts, or procedures that may be complex and confusing to students. **Simulations**, or software that allows users to work with a computerized model of a real or imagined system, can help make these concepts more clear and meaningful. Some simulations allow students to take an active part in historical situations that would not otherwise be possible due to historical or physical distance. Other problem-solving environments situate learning in authentic situations using real-world data and situated movies to motivate students. These products are designed to immerse students in problem-solving scenarios where they must make decisions and apply information they have learned. For example, Muzzy Lane's Making History places students in the role of decision makers by assuming the role of a country's leader during World War II. Some of the best simulation and problem-solving resources for social studies topics are shown in Figure 12.1

**FIGURE 12.1** Simulations and Problem-Solving Resources for Social Studies

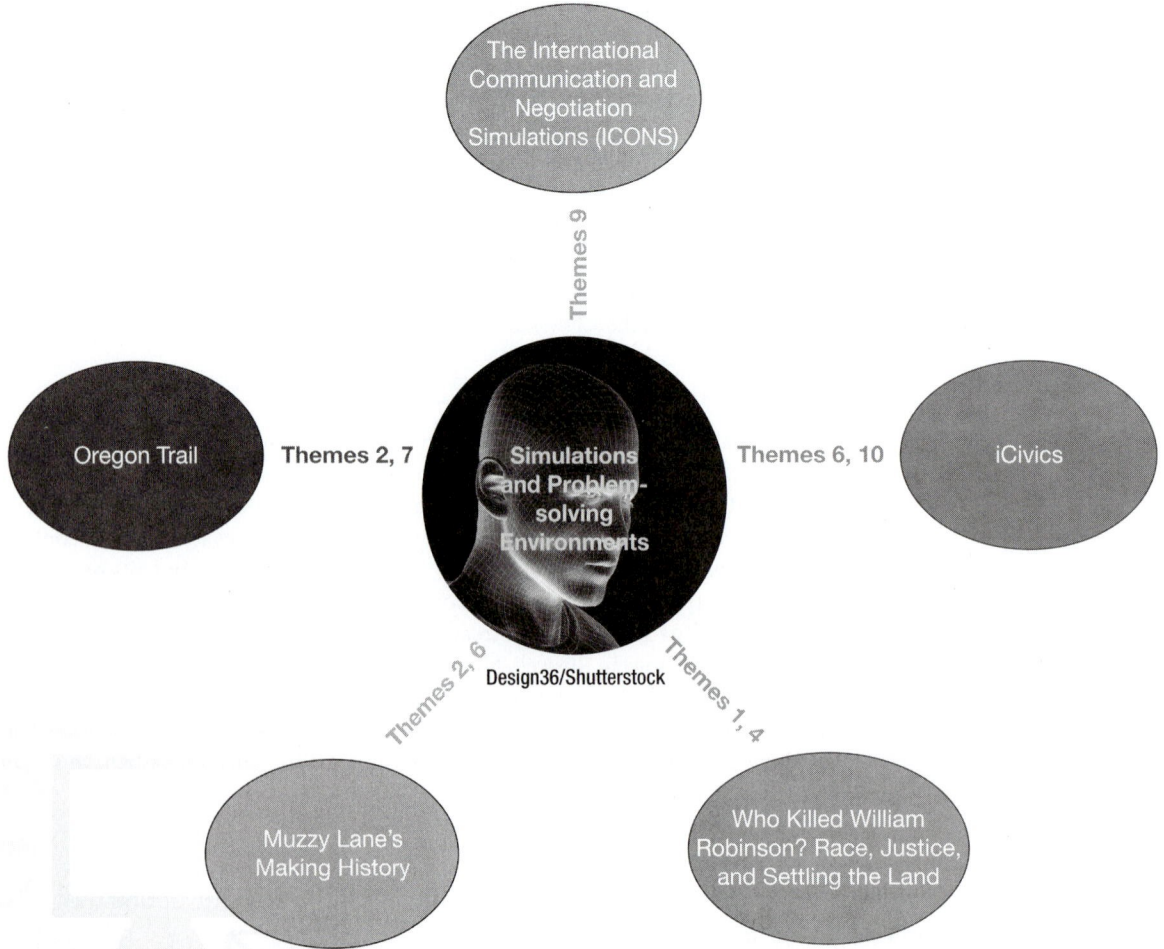

Also see these website simulations: JA Finance Park, A Sailor's Life for Me! (at the USS Constitution Museum website), and Quandary.

## Accessing Primary Sources

The power of integrating primary sources into social studies has long been documented in research. Through primary sources teachers may use familiar objects, images, and sounds to represent distinct time periods and cultural traditions. Primary sources foster the visual literacy and historical inquiry of students by making academic content meaningful and building on prior experiences. Moreover, they capitalize on the active and social nature of children's learning when teachers engage students in sifting, questioning, comparing, evaluating, and constructing their own interpretations of the primary sources (Berson & Berson, 2013, 2014). The following resources represent some of the very best primary source digital databases:

- Library of Congress (http://www.loc.gov)—Print, pictorial, audio-visual, and other digital collections that record the documented history of the American people
- National Archives and Records Administration (http://www.archives.gov)—Important documents from the U.S. federal government
- Our Documents (http://www.ourdocuments.gov)—Compilation of 100 milestone documents from the National Archives that chronicle U.S. history from 1776 to 1965
- The Oyez Project—Multimedia archive of cases from the U.S. Supreme Court
- Project Gutenberg—Freely accessible historical books in digital form

## Digital Information Critiques

History has many examples of using manipulated images to control people's impressions and opinions. As informed digital citizens, students need to develop skills in evaluating digital information critically. These skills include analyzing images for hidden meaning and telling fact from fiction in articles, reports, and websites. Social studies activities provide a context for simultaneously exploring the social impact of images and developing digital literacy skills. (See Figure 12.2. See also the Hot Topic Debate on this area.)

## Electronic Research Strategies

As students study areas such as politics, economics, and current events, information is likely to change quickly and frequently. Accessing Internet sources give students and teachers up-to-date information they could not obtain easily from other sources. Also, access to information summaries and examples of data "pictures" on the Internet help students learn to analyze information in

**FIGURE 12.2** Critiquing Digital Information Resources for Social Studies

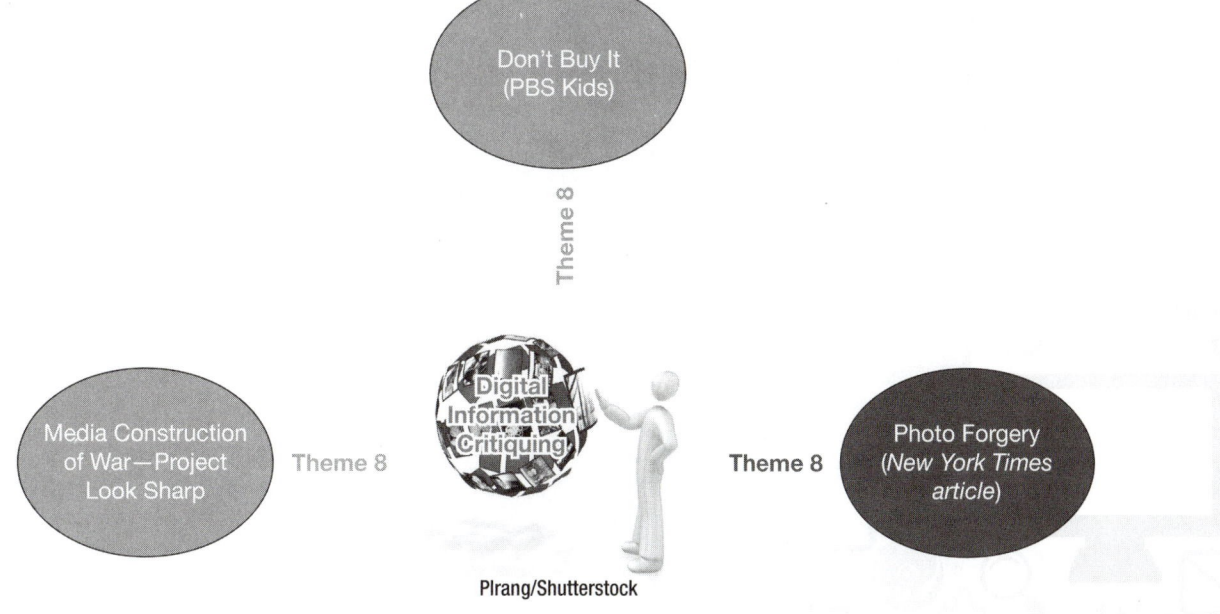

PIrang/Shutterstock

## Hot Topic Debate
### Should Wikipedia be Forbidden in Students' Social Studies Research?

*Take a position for or against (based either on your own position or one assigned to you) on the following controversial statement. Discuss it in class or on an online discussion board, blog, or wiki, as assigned by your instructor. When the discussion is complete, write a summary of the main pros and cons that you and your classmates have stated, and put the summary document in your Teacher Portfolio.*

In his 2009 article "High School Research and Critical Literacy: Social Studies With and Despite Wikipedia," Harouni found that Wikipedia had become an obstacle to his students learning that "defined my students' experience with research" (p. 473). He noticed his students' dependence on Wikipedia as a source for their social studies reports, but realized that they neither understood well what they had quoted nor checked it for accuracy. However, he still felt Wikipedia had a role to play as a tool for making students more aware of critical evaluation of sources. Other social studies educators are not so tolerant, viewing Wikipedia as an unreliable source that should be forbidden in student work. Even Wikipedia creator Jimmy Wales said that Wikipedia is not what history students should be citing, because they should be citing history books, rather than any encyclopedia. Do Wikipedia and other social sources like blogs have a role to play in student research? If so, what should that role be? Or should such sources be forbidden and, if so, why?

both graphic and text forms. Since we are relying more and more on Internet sources for reliable, up-to-date information, students must learn where they can look for various kinds of data and facts they need to complete research in school and, later, at work. See Figure 12.3 for a summary of these strategies.

## FIGURE 12.3 Electronic Research Resources for Social Studies

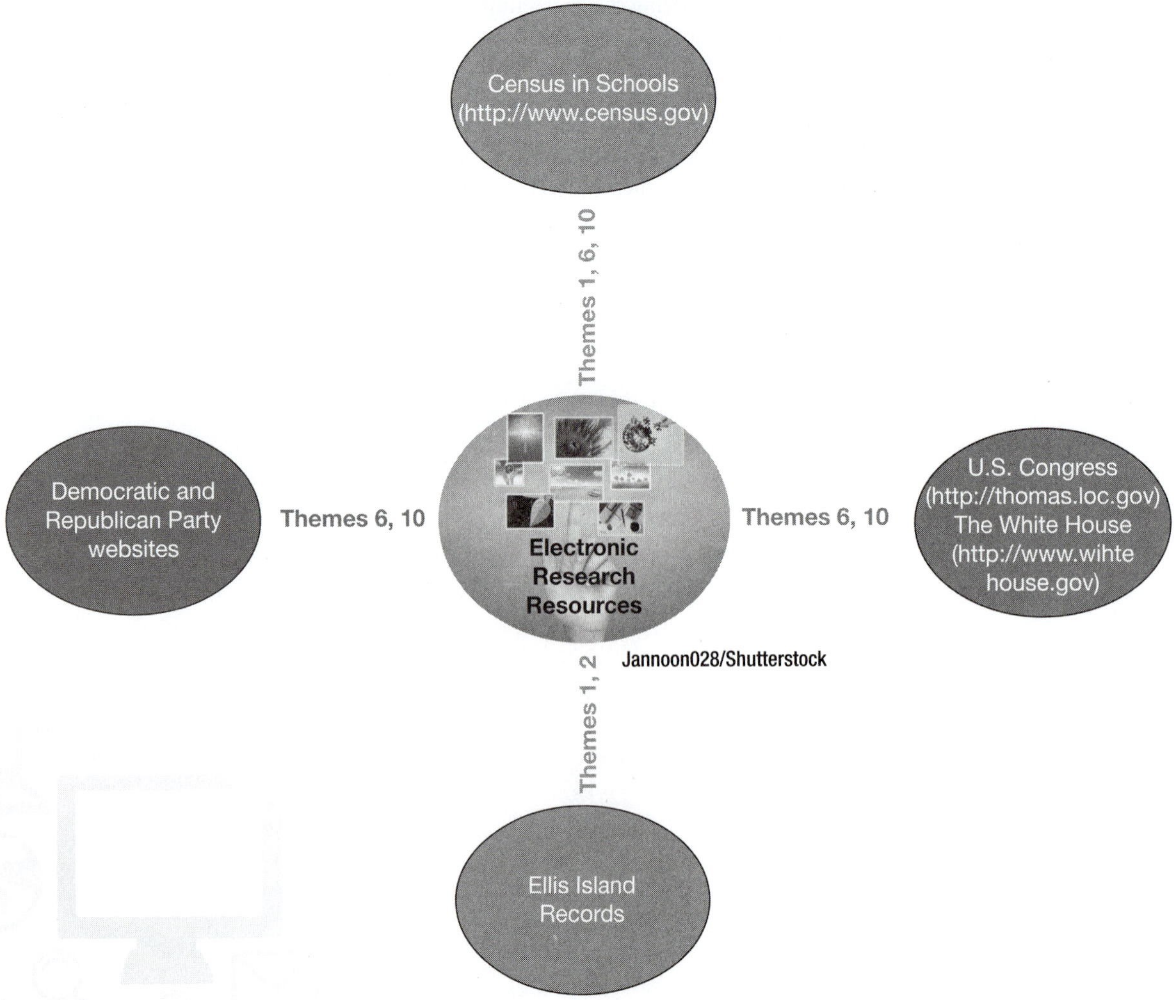

Census in Schools (http://www.census.gov)

Themes 1, 6, 10

Democratic and Republican Party websites

Themes 6, 10

Electronic Research Resources

Themes 6, 10

U.S. Congress (http://thomas.loc.gov) The White House (http://www.wihte house.gov)

Jannoon028/Shutterstock

Themes 1, 2

Ellis Island Records

## Information Visualization Strategies

Students often have problems visualizing abstract concepts and data. The availability of large data sets combined with exponential growth in hardware and software capability creates the potential to improve communication through the use of enhanced visualization techniques (Berson & Berson, 2009). In the past, teachers strove to use various technologies to represent concepts and data graphically, which can help novices understand and apply them. Today, even students can use products such as graphing software, spreadsheets, and numerous online information visualization sites to put data into a concrete form for easier analysis and representation of concepts, allowing concepts to be depicted visually. Information visualization products (see Figure 12.4) allow students to understand time sequences, track change over time, and represent complex data in ways that can be readily understood.

## Virtual Field Trips

**Virtual field trips** are "visits" students make with online sites to see places they could not easily go to in real life or that can help them get more out of trips they are able to take. For example, visiting foreign locations online gives students a richer, more comprehensive perspective on the world around them and makes the world a living part of their classroom. For students who may travel little, the wealth of images and information from virtual field trips helps them see and understand the variety of cultures, sights, and events outside their own communities. Virtual field trips also offer budget-friendly opportunities for schools and students who are not able to afford the expenses of physical field trips, while at the same time reaching an unlimited number of students. See Figure 12.5 for some good field-trip resources for social studies classrooms.

**FIGURE 12.4** Information Visualization Resources

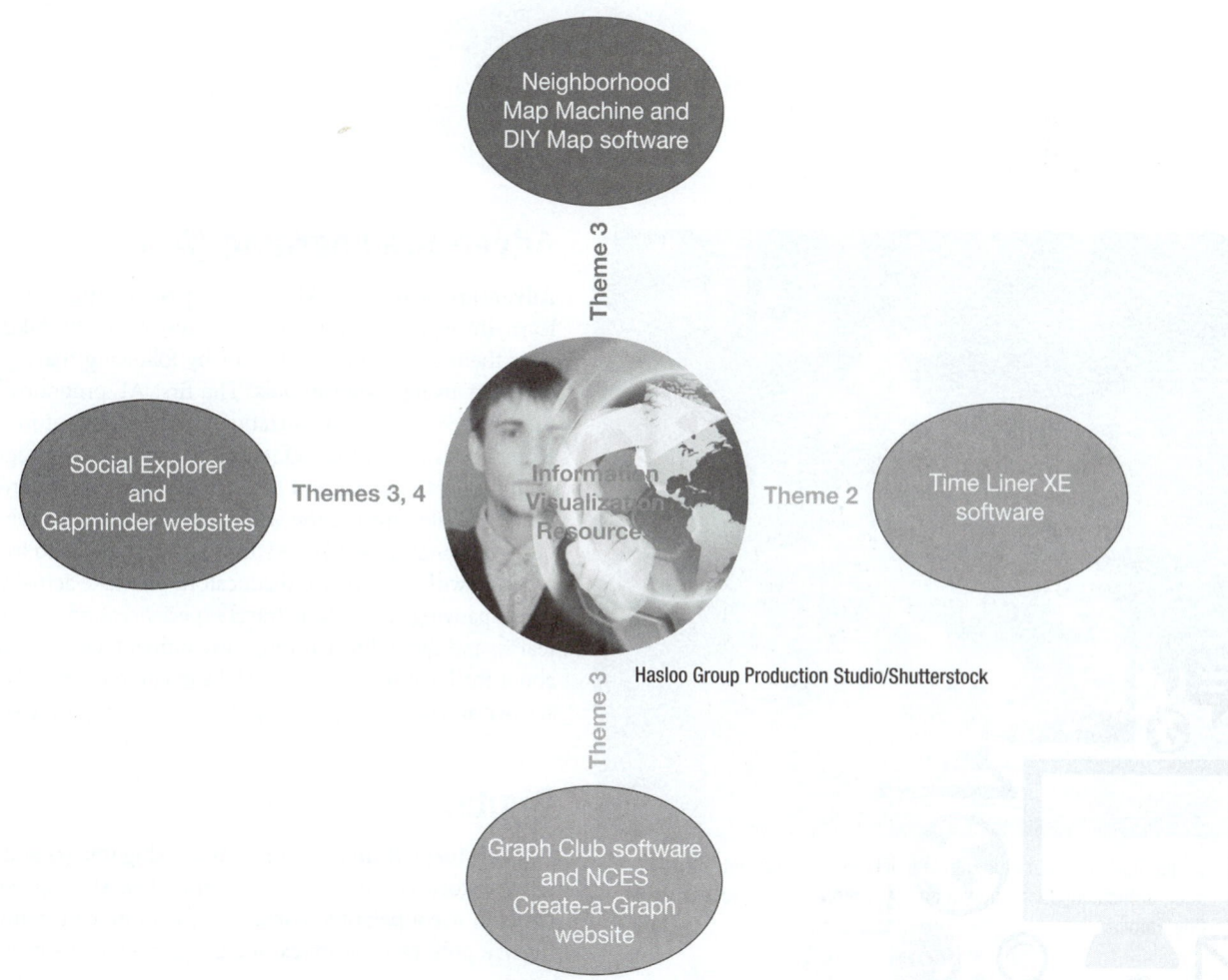

Hasloo Group Production Studio/Shutterstock

**FIGURE 12.5** Virtual Field Trip Resources for Social Studies

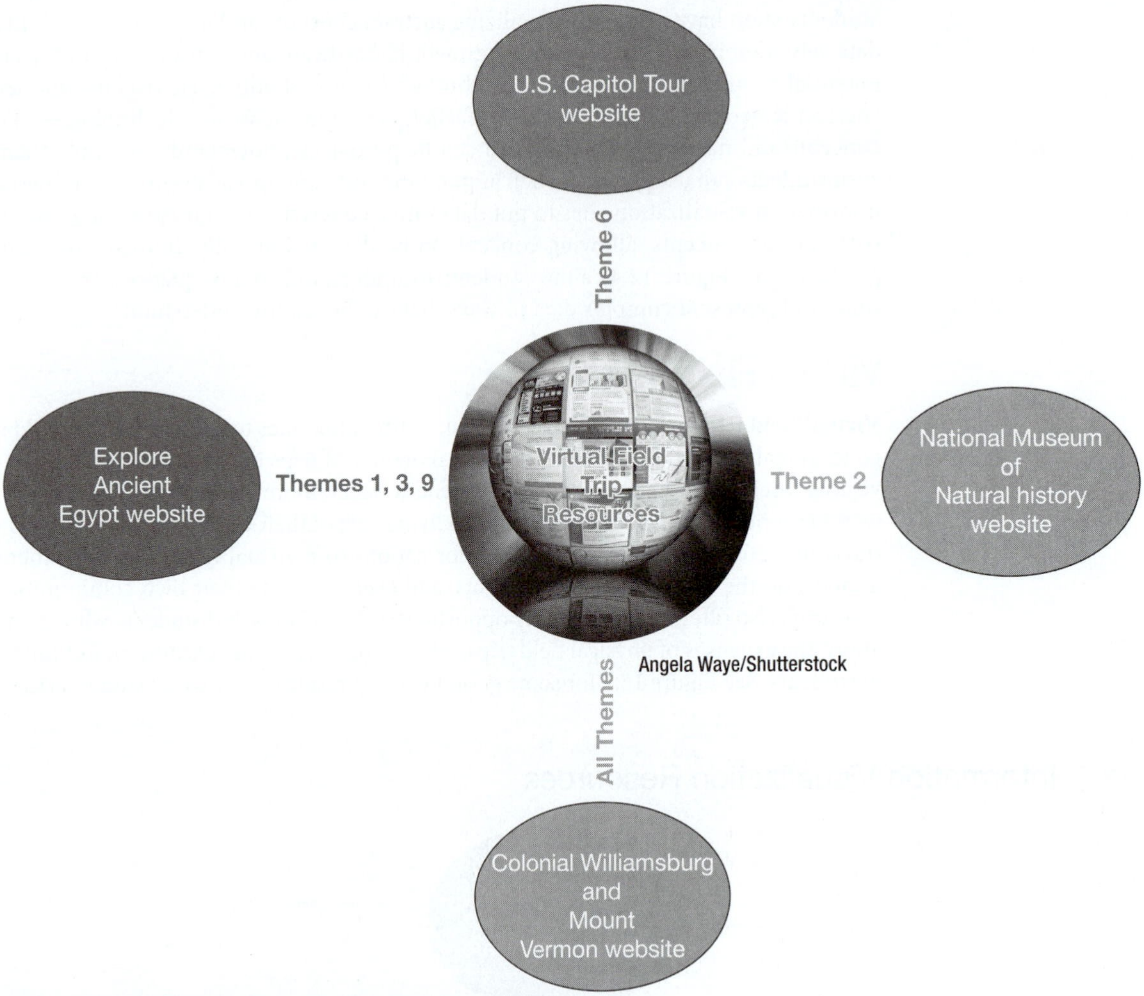

U.S. Capitol Tour website

Theme 6

Explore Ancient Egypt website

Themes 1, 3, 9

Virtual Field Trip Resources

Angela Waye/Shutterstock

All Themes

Theme 2

National Museum of Natural history website

Colonial Williamsburg and Mount Vermon website

▲ Virtual field trips put students in touch with people and with geographical locations they may not otherwise have access to. Olly/Fotolia

## Adventure Learning (AL)

**Adventure learning (AL)** is an approach that lets students learn through real-world experiences, either by taking actual trips themselves with mentors or by following the explorations of others using distance tools. The first AL programs began in the mid-1990's with organizations such as Adventure Learning Experiences in Toronto, Ontario, Canada. These programs use online sites to recruit and register students and organize expeditions to sites around the world. Veletsianos & Doering (2010) described another kind of AL that allows students to travel along virtually with explorers and educators who take actual trips. The accompanying curriculum, travel experiences and observations of teams, and the online learning environment allow them to learn about the locations, as well as skills in content areas that include science and geography. See Figure 12.6 for sample AL sites.

## Digital Storytelling

**Digital storytelling** is the process of using images and audio to tell the stories of lives, events, or eras. This strategy allows students to use a personal narrative to explore community-based history, politics, economics, and geography. These projects offer

# FIGURE 12.6 Adventure Learning Resources for Social Studies

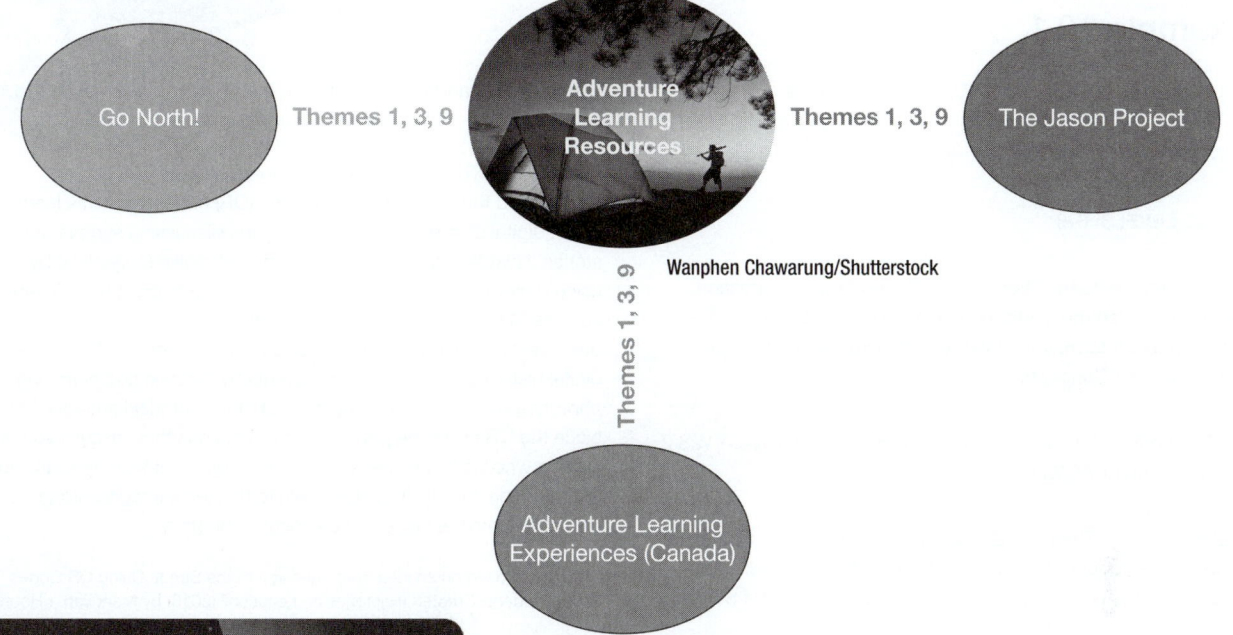

Go North! — Themes 1, 3, 9 — Adventure Learning Resources — Themes 1, 3, 9 — The Jason Project

Wanphen Chawarung/Shutterstock

Themes 1, 3, 9

Adventure Learning Experiences (Canada)

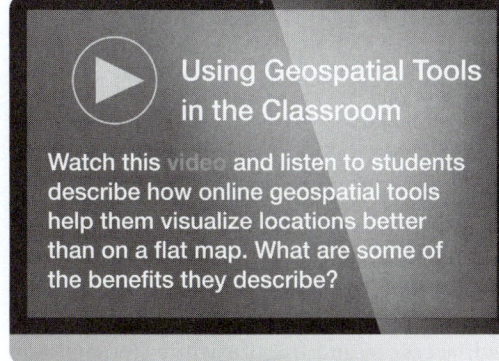

## Using Geospatial Tools in the Classroom

Watch this video and listen to students describe how online geospatial tools help them visualize locations better than on a flat map. What are some of the benefits they describe?

students the opportunity to make their own lives a part of their scholarly research. Using technologies such as movie-editing software, camcorders, digital cameras, and voice recorders, or even their own smartphones, students can create their own digital stories. By sending students into their world with a digital camera in hand, teachers provide opportunities for them to bring their lives into the classroom, creating a rich, authentic authoring space. Writing text and arranging pictures as artifacts within a digital space allows students to explore events from multiple perspectives. As an extension or adaptation, students might create digital movies about an event, place, or person, using the camera to capture scenes and artifacts that could be woven together to tell a particular story. After creating the digital story, the student can post it onto the class website for other students to watch. Figure 12.7 suggests resources

# FIGURE 12.7 Digital Storytelling Resources for Social Studies

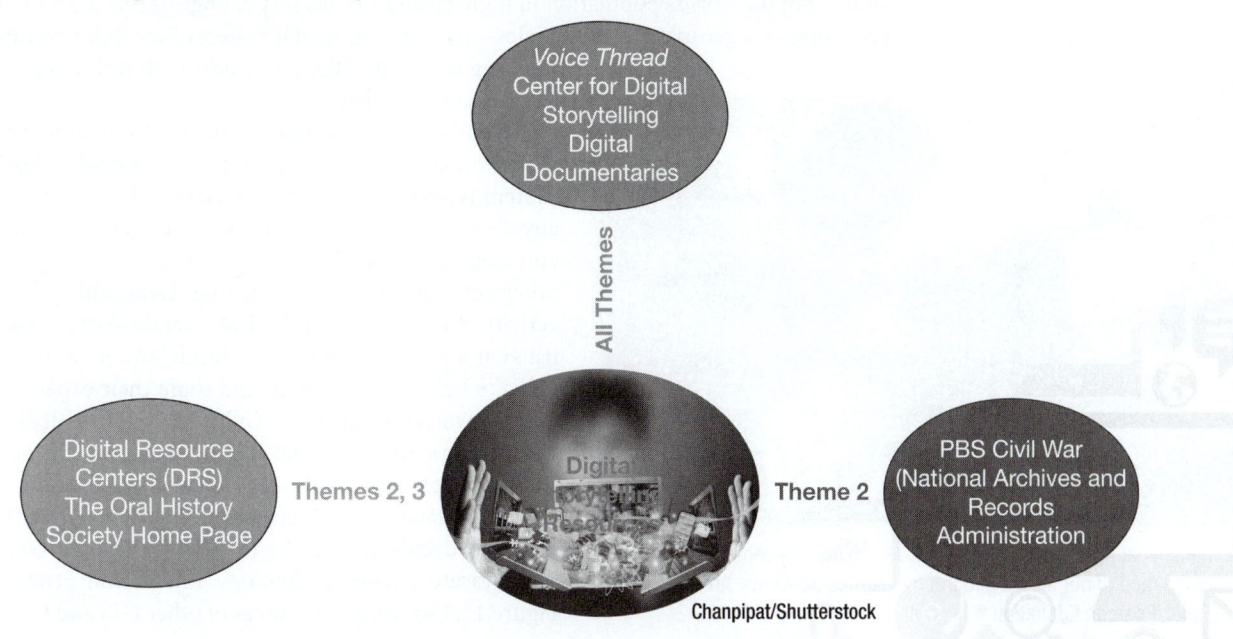

*Voice Thread* Center for Digital Storytelling Digital Documentaries

All Themes

Digital Resource Centers (DRS) The Oral History Society Home Page — Themes 2, 3 — Digital Storytelling Resources — Theme 2 — PBS Civil War (National Archives and Records Administration)

Chanpipat/Shutterstock

# TECHNOLOGY INTEGRATION

## Example 12.1

**TITLE:** Using QR Codes to Tell Our Digital Histories

**CONTENT AREA/TOPIC:** History

**GRADE LEVELS:** 6–8

**ISTE STANDARDS•S:** Standard 1—Creativity and Innovation; Standard 2—Communication and Collaboration; Standard 3—Research and Information Fluency; Standard 6—Technology Operations and Concepts

**CCSS:** CCSS.ELA-LITERACY.W.8.6, CCSS.ELA-LITERACY.W.8.2, CCSS.ELA-LITERACY.W.8.3

**NCSS THEMES:** Thematic Standards: 1 – Culture and Cultural Diversity, 3 – People, Places, and Environments, 5 – Individual Development and Identity; 8 – Science, Technology, and Society;

**Disciplinary Standards:** 1 – History, 2 – Geography, 3 – Civics and Government

**DESCRIPTION:** Following a brief introduction to the unit and the use of quick response (QR) codes, students learn about digital storytelling by looking at and discussing sample digital stories. Next they practice the technique of digital storytelling by using digital cameras, scanners, and digital story creation software such as Microsoft's PhotoStory to create brief histories about their own lives, which they share with classmates for review. They create digital histories of local sites and events by locating and analyzing photographs, videos, documents, and other historical artifacts. They place the QR codes on plaques at the locations they discuss so that anyone who visits the sites can read their digital stories by scanning the QR code. Finally, they use a wiki to house their digital stories to be shared with the class and the local community.

*SOURCE:* Based on an idea from "Taking It to the Street: Using QR Codes to Tell Student- Created (Hi)stories on Location" (2013) by Mark van 't Hooft.

that support digital storytelling, and Technology Integration Example 12.1 shows how to use technology in innovative ways to construct these stories.

## Geospatial Analysis Strategies

**Geospatial technologies,** the use of technology for visualization, analysis, and measurement of features and phenomena, are being written into U.S. social studies standards. The use of geospatial technologies such as Google Earth and ArcGIS allow individuals to view and examine the world through multiple layering of data sets (population density, roads, earthquake activity) within a spatial environment. Although access to and use of such technology was previously limited by steep costs and demanding hardware, that is no longer the case, and recently geospatial technologies have become increasingly popular with the general public. Google Earth is free and has become the foundation of numerous geography learning activities. It is now available in 13 languages and has more than a third of the world's land surface and half of the world's population in high-resolution imagery. Google is not the only company providing new geospatial technologies—the Environmental Systems Research Institute (ESRI) has long dominated the GIS world with technologies such as ArcGIS and ArcView.

Another tool that allows students to look at social studies from many different perspectives is a **Global Positioning System (GPS).** A GPS provides users with a location and time anywhere on Earth and is commonplace in today's automobiles and smart phones. However, GPS is also used for numerous other activities such as geocaching. **Geocaching** is an online activity in which students look at a database of caches or items listed at a geocaching website, decide on one to hunt for, use GPSs to help them locate it, and share their experiences with others involved in the hunt. Gillin and Gillin (2010) note that geocaching's appeal is that it gets people out in nature and examining physical locations firsthand. In education, students look at a database of caches at numerous geocaching websites and decide on a cache to hunt for using a GPS to help them locate it (see Technology Integration Strategy 12.2). Figure 12.8 shows good sources of other GIS and GPS lessons.

▲ Geospatial technologies like Google Earth have become the foundation of numerous geography learning activities. **Annie Pickert Fuller/Pearson Education**

# TECHNOLOGY INTEGRATION

## Example 12.2

**TITLE:** Are We There yet?

**CONTENT AREA/TOPIC:** Geography

**GRADE LEVELS:** 6–12

**ISTE STANDARDS•S:** Standard 3—Research and Information Fluency; Standard 4—Critical Thinking, Problem Solving, and Decision Making; Standard 6—Technology Operations and Concepts

**NCSS THEMES:** Thematic Standards: 8 – Science, Technology, and Society; Disciplinary Standard: 2 – Geography

**DESCRIPTION:** Students go in small groups on a geocaching adventure that the teacher sets up ahead of time in the local area by hiding caches of three plastic containers or other waterproof boxes. The first contains a copy of a handout on how the GPS works. The second cache has navigational tools such as maps and compass. The third has a toy or model representing the treasure students are seeking. The teacher numbers the boxes and hides each on the school grounds. Finally, the teacher gives students one GPS per group, a handout with "X Marks the Spot," and the GPS coordinates of the three caches; students write the coordinates on their handouts. As they locate the boxes, they answer clues to the "treasure" on their handout.

*SOURCE:* Based on an idea from the lesson "Are We There Yet" by Catherine Hutchings at The Learning Network website: http://learning.blogs.nytimes.com.

## FIGURE 12.8 Geospatial Technology Resources for Social Studies

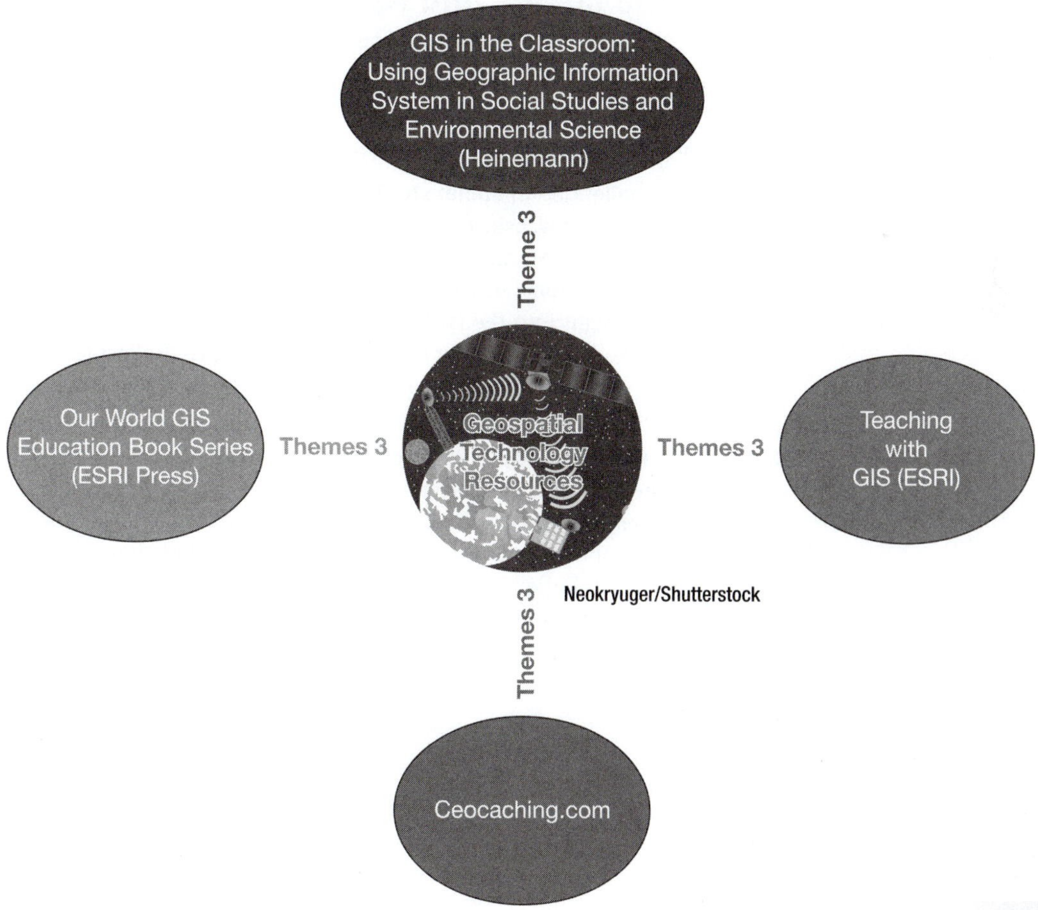

GIS in the Classroom: Using Geographic Information System in Social Studies and Environmental Science (Heinemann)

Theme 3

Our World GIS Education Book Series (ESRI Press)

Themes 3

Geospatial Technology Resources

Themes 3

Teaching with GIS (ESRI)

Neokryuger/Shutterstock

Themes 3

Ceocaching.com

**TECHNOLOGY LEARNING CHECK**

Complete **TLC 12.2** to review what you have learned from this section about technology integration strategies for social studies.

# TEACHING SOCIAL STUDIES TEACHERS TO INTEGRATE TECHNOLOGY

This section gives recommendations for how teachers can prepare to integrate technology effectively into instruction for the various social studies topics. As discussed earlier in this chapter, it is difficult for a teacher to be equally well-prepared to teach all content topics that fall under the general heading of "the social studies." They will likely become proficient in only one or two. Therefore, teachers must tailor skills and strategies described here to their own area(s) of expertise. For example, a history teacher may not need to know and apply GIS or mapping software in the same way as one who teaches geography, but every social studies teacher should be able to use information visualization tools and strategies to enhance instruction.

## Rubric to Measure Teacher Growth in Social Studies Technology Integration

Begin by reviewing the rubric in Figure 12.9 to measure teachers' progress in effectively integrating technology in social studies instruction. Part I of the rubric addresses knowledge of issues and challenges, and Part II addresses social studies technology integration strategies.

## Learning the Issues and Applications

The first step in technology integration is to become acquainted with the issues and challenges discussed in this chapter and how they shape teachers' uses and applications of technologies. Then teachers can begin developing capabilities to address instructional standards and curriculum goals. The following is a suggested sequence of learning activities:

- **Issues and challenges in social studies instruction.** After reviewing the information in this chapter, go to the website of the social studies professional organization—the National Council for the Social Studies (NCSS)—and review both the standards and the C3 framework. See the professional development resources the site offers, and decide on which can help you gain insight into the issues and challenges outlined in this chapter. Discuss and reflect on the two questions under the Collaborate, Discuss, Reflect feature at the end of the chapter. Complete Part I of the rubric in Figure 12.9 before you begin this sequence and again at various points in your progress.

- **Social studies technology integration strategies.** After reviewing the information in this chapter, review examples of the technologies suggested in the Open Source Options feature and the websites and projects described under each section, and do the lesson evaluation and lesson development activities outlined in the Technology Integration Workshop at the end of this chapter. Reflect on how you will plan for implementing these strategies in your own classroom using the TIP model. Complete Part I of the rubric in Figure 12.9 before you begin this sequence and again at various points in your progress.

**TECHNOLOGY LEARNING CHECK**
Complete TLC 12.3 to review what you have learned from this section about how social studies teachers can develop their knowledge and skills in technology integration.

# FIGURE 12.9 Rubric to Measure Teacher Growth in Social Studies Technology Integration

| Part I: Teacher Knowledge of Social Studies Issues and Challenges | | | |
|---|---|---|---|
| | **Basic knowledge (1–2 points)** | **Intermediate knowledge (3–4 points)** | **Advanced knowledge (4–5 points)** |
| Meeting standards across the social studies | I can articulate the nature of the issue. | I can both articulate the nature of the issue and some of the possible ways to address it. | I can articulate my own plan for addressing the issue in my own teaching. |
| Challenges in teaching social studies | I can articulate the nature of the issue. | I can both articulate the nature of the issue and some of the possible ways to address it. | I can articulate my own plan for addressing the issue in my own teaching. |
| The history wars | I can articulate the nature of the issue. | I can both articulate the nature of the issue and some of the possible ways to address it. | I can articulate my own plan for addressing the issue in my own teaching. |
| Perils of the information explosion | I can articulate the nature of the issue. | I can both articulate the nature of the issue and some of the possible ways to address it. | I can articulate my own plan for addressing the issue in my own teaching. |

| Part II: Teachers' Technology Integration Strategies for Social Studies | | | |
|---|---|---|---|
| | **Basic knowledge (1–2 points)** | **Intermediate knowledge (3–4 points)** | **Advanced knowledge (4–5 points)** |
| Using simulations and problem-solving environments | I can describe the strategy and identify technologies to carry it out. | I have designed at least 1–2 activities based on this strategy to enhance my teaching and my students' learning. | I have designed plans for how I will integrate this strategy throughout my curriculum to enhance my teaching and my students' learning. |
| Digital information critiques | I can describe the strategy and identify technologies to carry it out. | I have designed at least 1–2 activities based on this strategy to enhance my teaching and my students' learning. | I have designed plans for how I will integrate this strategy throughout my curriculum to enhance my teaching and my students' learning. |
| Electronic research strategies | I can describe the strategy and identify technologies to carry it out. | I have designed at least 1–2 activities based on this strategy to enhance my teaching and my students' learning. | I have designed plans for how I will integrate this strategy throughout my curriculum to enhance my teaching and my students' learning. |
| Information visualization strategies | I can describe the strategy and identify technologies to carry it out. | I have designed at least 1–2 activities based on this strategy to enhance my teaching and my students' learning. | I have designed plans for how I will integrate this strategy throughout my curriculum to enhance my teaching and my students' learning. |
| Virtual field trips | I can describe the strategy and identify technologies to carry it out. | I have designed at least 1–2 activities based on this strategy to enhance my teaching and my students' learning. | I have designed plans for how I will integrate this strategy throughout my curriculum to enhance my teaching and my students' learning. |
| Adventure learning | I can describe the strategy and identify technologies to carry it out. | I have designed at least 1–2 activities based on this strategy to enhance my teaching and my students' learning. | I have designed plans for how I will integrate this strategy throughout my curriculum to enhance my teaching and my students' learning. |
| Digital storytelling | I can describe the strategy and identify technologies to carry it out. | I have designed at least 1–2 activities based on this strategy to enhance my teaching and my students' learning. | I have designed plans for how I will integrate this strategy throughout my curriculum to enhance my teaching and my students' learning. |
| Geospatial analysis strategies | I can describe the strategy and identify technologies to carry it out. | I have designed at least 1–2 activities based on this strategy to enhance my teaching and my students' learning. | I have designed plans for how I will integrate this strategy throughout my curriculum to enhance my teaching and my students' learning. |
| **Total points** | _____ of 60 possible points | | |

Monkey Business/Fotolia

**The following questions may be used either for in-class, small-group discussions or may be used to initiate discussions in blogs or online discussion boards:**

1. In 2013, the NCSS Board of Directors drafted a Technology Position Statement and Guidelines that articulated the role of emerging technologies in shaping social studies content and curriculum. Saying that the explosion of online data and blended settings for learning "are reshaping how children and youth are able to act as citizens and consumers" (NCSS, 2013), one of the guidelines encourages teachers to draw parallels between the "growth of Wikipedia and the democratization of knowledge" with the advent of movable type and the mechanical printing press in the 1550s. Do you feel this is an accurate comparison? What information could you cite to support or question this connection?

2. Another recommendation of the NCSS Technology Position Statement is to "establish guidelines for the promotion of media literacy and related research skills in social studies." What specific guidelines should teachers encourage or require students to use when they use online sources to research assignments in social studies topics?

---

Chapter **12** ## Summary

**The following is a summary of the main points covered in this chapter.**

1. **Issues and Challenges in Social Studies.** Issues include challenges of meeting standards across social studies areas, challenges when teaching social studies, the "history wars" and other debates on the content and focus of social studies, and the perils of the information explosion.

2. **Technology Integration Strategies for Social Studies Instruction.** Technology integration strategies include:
   - Using simulations and problem-solving environments
   - Digital information critiques
   - Electronic research strategies
   - Information visualization strategies
   - Virtual field trips
   - Adventure learning
   - Digital storytelling
   - Geospatial analysis strategies

3. **Teaching Social Studies Teachers to Integrate Technology.** Teachers can begin by consulting the rubric provided in this chapter to measure their own growth in social studies technology integration. After that, they may review issues and challenges in social studies instruction and use chapter resources to learn technology integration strategies they can use to address the issues and challenges.

# TECHNOLOGY INTEGRATION **WORKSHOP**

## 1. APPLY WHAT YOU LEARNED

To apply the concepts and skills you've read about throughout this chapter, go to the Chapter 12 Technology Application Activity.

## 2. TECHNOLOGY INTEGRATION LESSON PLANNING: PART 1—EVALUATING AND CREATING LESSON PLANS

Complete the following exercise using the sample lesson plans found on any lesson planning site that you find on the Internet.

**a.** Locate lesson ideas—Identify three lesson plans that focus on any of the tools or strategies you learned about in this chapter. For example:

- Digital storytelling
- Geocaching
- Geospatial analysis
- Virtual field trips

**b.** Evaluate the lessons—Use the Technology Lesson Plan Evaluation Checklist to evaluate each of the lessons you found.

**c.** Create your own lesson—After you have reviewed and evaluated some sample lessons, create one of your own using a lesson plan format of your choice (or one your instructor gives you). Be sure the lesson focuses on one of the technologies or strategies discussed in this chapter.

## 3. TECHNOLOGY INTEGRATION LESSON PLANNING: PART 2—IMPLEMENTING THE TIP MODEL

Review how to implement the TIP model in your classroom by doing the following activities with the lesson you created in the Technology Integration Lesson Planning exercise above.

**a.** Describe the Phase 1—Planning activities you would do to use this lesson in your classroom:

- What is the relative advantage of using the technology(ies) in this lesson?
- Do you have resources and skills you need to carry it out?

**b.** Describe the Phase 2—Implementation activities you would do to use this lesson in your classroom:

- What are the objectives of the lesson plan?
- How will you assess your students' accomplishment of the objectives?
- What integration strategies are used in this lesson plan?
- How would you prepare the learning environment?

**c.** Describe the Phase 3—Evaluation/Revision activities you would do to use this lesson in your classroom: What strategies and/or instruments would you use to evaluate the success of this lesson in your classroom in order to determine revision needs?

**d.** Add lesson descriptors—Create descriptors for your new lesson (e.g., grade level, content and topic areas, technologies used, ISTE standards, 21st Century Learning standards).

**e.** Save your new lesson—Save your lesson plan with all its descriptors and TIP model notes.

## 4. FOR YOUR TEACHING PORTFOLIO

Add the following to your Teaching Portfolio:

- Reflections on Hot Topic Debate
- Summary notes from the Collaborate, Discuss, Reflect activity.
- Lesson plan evaluations, lesson plans, and products you created above.
- Your *Apply What You Learned* Product from Activity 1.

By Jay Dorfman and M. D. Roblyer

# 13

# Teaching and Learning with Technology in Music and Art

## Learning Outcomes

After reading this chapter and completing the learning activities, you should be able to:

1. Articulate a rationale for including technology in curriculum for arts education. (ISTE Standards•T 1, 5)

2. Identify implications for technology integration for each current issue that music teachers face. (ISTE Standards•T 4, 5)

3. Select technology integration strategies that can meet various needs for instruction in music curricula. (ISTE Standards•T 2, 5)

4. Identify implications for technology integration for each current issue that art teachers face. (ISTE Standards•T 4, 5)

5. Select technology integration strategies that can meet various needs for instruction in art curricula. (ISTE Standards•T 2, 5)

6. Design a strategy for how to build teacher knowledge and skills in technology integration for music or art instruction. (ISTE Standards•T 5)

Vladgrin/Shutterstock

# TECHNOLOGY INTEGRATION IN ACTION
# THE FINE ART OF ELECTRONIC PORTFOLIOS

**GRADE LEVELS:** Middle to high school • **CONTENT AREA/TOPIC:** Music and art composition, technology • **LENGTH OF TIME:** Ongoing

## PHASE 1  ANALYSIS OF LEARNING AND TEACHING NEEDS

Angela Waye/Shutterstock

### Step 1: Determine relative advantage.

The music, arts, and technology resource teachers at Eureka High School were discussing the new block scheduling plan in which music, art, and technology credits would share one of the four 90-minute units students would attend each day. The teachers realized that a logical thread among these three curricula would be to have students develop a Web-based portfolio of their musical and artistic work. They felt this would meet several needs. First, it would be a way of working with each student at individual levels of musical and artistic expertise. This was important because students in their classes would range from beginners at musical composition or art skills to advanced musicians or artists. Second, it had always been difficult to find an audience for student work; the teachers knew that having others listen to or view their work was motivating and provided helpful feedback to students at all levels. A Web-based format would make it easier to share students' works. Third, it would be easy to create projects that linked skills across the disciplines—for example, having students use a **Musical Instrument Digital Interface (MIDI)** keyboard and music editor to prepare a musical composition expressing the feeling or mood of a painting. (MIDI refers to a protocol that has been adopted by the electronic music industry for communication between devices, such as synthesizers and sound cards.) Finally, the teachers realized that an electronic portfolio could serve as a valuable, ongoing assessment tool for students' art, music, technology, and language development, and would help students develop skills in using technology to present their work and to communicate and share information with others.

### Step 2: Assess required skills and resources.

The teachers explored the available Web-based tools for constructing portfolios. They each examined several online platforms ranging from free or low-cost to pay-per-use; they also tried using portfolio systems that ranged from prescriptive to extremely flexible. They eventually settled on a Web-based tool that was flexible in that it allowed for many types of media to be displayed, but it was limited in that the overall design of each student portfolio would be the same. However, since the tool fit within their budget and would be easier to implement across classes, they decided it was the best choice. The technology teacher prepared a handout on how to use it and shortcuts for performing each required operation; this would be useful for both teachers and their students.

## PHASE 2  PLANNING FOR INTEGRATION

### Step 3: Decide on objectives and assessments.

The teachers decided they each would use a component of the portfolio as the basis of student assessment for each grading period. The art and music teachers would assign each student individual benchmarks to achieve in their composition and skill development, and the technology teacher would use the electronic portfolios the students produced to assess their production skills. Students' grades would be a combination of the three assessments, with each content area weighted according to which one was being emphasized during the grading period. They decided on the following outcomes, objectives, and assessment strategies:

**Outcome:** Progress in art.
**Objective:** Students will meet their assigned benchmark for progress in art skills.
**Assessment:** Rubric to assess this portfolio component.

**Outcome:** Progress in music.
**Objective:** Students will meet their assigned benchmark for progress in music skills.
**Assessment:** Rubric to assess this portfolio component.

Outcome: Progress in language expression.
Objective: Students will meet their assigned benchmark for development in written expression.
Assessment: Rubric to assess this portfolio component.

Outcome: Technology skills.
Objective: Students will demonstrate competence in each required Web page development skill by completing assigned tasks.
Assessment: Web production checklist.

### Step 4: Design integration strategies.

The teachers decided they would follow the same sequence of activities for each grading period:

Review skill levels and set benchmarks. The art and music teachers meet with each student, review accomplishments to date, and set benchmarks for individual skill development. Some students with lower skill levels are placed in small groups so that teachers can spend more time working with them.

Review portfolio requirements. The technology teacher meets with each student, reviews the requirements for the portfolio, and sets tasks and expectations to assist students in developing a more clear and aesthetically pleasing presentation.

Decide on projects. A different project is set for each grading period. For example, for the first project, the teachers decide to have students use their MIDI keyboards and notation software to write a musical composition based on the music of a period they have been studying in their history classes. Then the students use image manipulation software to create a collage of colors and images that come to mind as they listen to the music composition they or their fellow students have created. The technology teacher helps them add their sound and graphics creations to their portfolios.

Determine group presentations. Each teacher identifies whole-group presentations that they need to offer. For example, the music teacher needs to demonstrate techniques with the MIDI keyboard and music notation software. The art teacher designs a presentation on how to use layering techniques in Adobe Photoshop to create a graphic collage. The technology teacher develops demonstrations of video and audio editing techniques. After their group presentations, the teachers work with each student as needed to complete the required products.

Arrange reviews and final presentations. The teachers arrange for various experts in other locations to do online reviews of the students' creations and to give them feedback. Students will revise their products as time permits and as they feel appropriate. The teachers arrange for an "Evening at Eureka" to be given at the end of the grading period, at which computers would be set up in a lab to display each student's work. Parents and friends are to be invited via the school website and via desktop-published invitations created by the art students.

### Step 5: Prepare instructional environment.

The technology teacher created a main page for the student portfolios, with links to each student's work. He also created a link from the school's main page to the portfolio section. The music teacher had a MIDI keyboard classroom, but there were not enough keyboards for each student to have one for a whole period. The teachers arranged the schedule so that half the class attended band, choir, or orchestra rehearsal, worked in the art studio, or worked on their individual portfolios in the computer lab, while the other half worked on composition.

## PHASE 3 POST-INSTRUCTION ANALYSIS AND REVISIONS

### Step 6: Analyze results.

At the end of each grading period, the teachers reviewed the students' portfolios, assessed progress, and discussed ways to make the work go more smoothly. Some of the questions they asked were:

- Did most students meet the individual benchmarks set for them?
- Were students actively engaged in the project work?
- Did the group demonstrations provide adequate initial instruction before students began work on their own?
- Were the classrooms and lab times organized for efficient work?
- Did the Web-based tool that the teachers chose provide appropriate amounts of flexibility and structure for the students to create well-designed, functional portfolios?

## Step 7: Make revisions.

The teachers were gratified to see that most students seemed motivated by the idea of using a multimedia Web format to display their work and were making good progress on their benchmarks. However, it was apparent that many students needed more individual instruction than the demonstrations could provide. The teachers decided to record a series of short demos so that students could view them individually or in small groups, as needed, after the initial presentation. They agreed that the scheduling proved to be a challenge. They decided to request that additional MIDI keyboards and software be obtained to support this work. Also, English and history teachers approached them about coordinating the portfolio work with students' writing and research projects. The teachers agreed to work together to merge these skill areas into students' portfolio assessments.

*Source:* Based on concepts from Duxbury's article "Make Sweet Music with Electronic Portfolios" in *Learning and Leading with Technology.*

# CHAPTER 13 **BIG IDEAS OVERVIEW**

Before you begin reading the rest of this chapter, listen to the Chapter 13 Big Ideas Overview. It will give you a two-minute audio overview of main concepts to look for and help prepare you to work through information and exercises to achieve this chapter's outcomes.

# A RATIONALE FOR INCLUDING TECHNOLOGY IN THE ARTS

Technology has always played a part in the arts, providing tools, materials, and processes that aided artists' creative expression. In more recent times, electronic devices in the making and recoding of music and the digital camera in visual arts have changed people's definitions of art. While technology integration in the arts can be difficult because of the traditional ways in which arts instruction is often approached, integration of computers and other forms of electronic technology represents a logical evolution of the arts and arts education.

Many educators and members of the community question the need for instructional technology in the arts curriculum. Peppler (2010) observed that arts education curriculum do not emphasize the use of new technologies, despite the opportunities they offer to "address arts integration, equity, and the technological prerequisites of an increasingly digital age" (p. 2118). Peppler felt that this omission represented a "missed opportunity" (p. 2148). She argued that media arts should be included more extensively in school curriculum. This new form of literacy is especially important for those youths who have been traditionally marginalized in our society, since messages are increasingly being displayed in visual, auditory, or kinesthetic formats, as well as print ones.

Thus, immersion in media arts represents a path to greater participation in the life of our society. The National Standards for Arts Education also make it clear that technologies offer new and powerful means to accomplish artistic, scholarly, production, and performance goals. Clearly, the place of technologies in arts education has never been more relevant.

**TECHNOLOGY LEARNING CHECK**

Complete TLC 13.1 to review what you have learned from this section about a rationale for including technology in arts education.

# ISSUES AND CHALLENGES IN MUSIC INSTRUCTION

Music and technology have always had a unique relationship. Throughout the history of music, technological tools have been developed that afford musicians, teachers, and students the opportunity to experience music through creating, performing, and responding to it. However, there are several issues and challenges related to music education in general, as well as the use of technology in the classroom for teaching music. These issues and challenges are explored in this section.

## A Changing Definition for Music Literacy

In music education, the term *music literacy* usually means an ability to read standard music notation. But the computer enables—if not encourages—experimentation with alternative ways to represent music. The earliest **music sequencers**, even those with notation capability, have always included a "graphic" or "matrix" editor, a window in which the user could edit music by dragging, deleting, or expanding small rectangles on a grid. Touchscreen interfaces such as those found on tablets have also led to apps that use similar drawing metaphors for creating music. These include apps such as Beatwave, Kaossilator, and Musyc, among others. See a list of the Top Ten Must-Have Apps for Music.

Today, the desktop music production software industry is helping accelerate a trend away from reliance on printed sheets and toward an audio artifact. This means that many students who are discouraged by a requirement to learn notation-based theory can now participate in the school music program as both composers and performers without solely relying on standard notation to perform or compose music. Electronically-produced music is also playing an increasing role in in music production, as noted in the Hot Topic Debate. When the definition of *music literacy* is expanded to include nontraditional performance and composition, music education may be more accessible for the approximately 80% of American high school students who do not participate in band, orchestra or chorus activities (Dammers, 2010, 2012).

## Training Teachers to Meet Music Standards

Until states begin requiring that teacher candidates demonstrate proficiency with technology, teacher preparation programs will have a difficult time making a case for including required technology courses in music curricula. Such programs, already overloaded with content, would be reluctant to displace a more traditional course with one whose skills remain in the "optional" category with respect to licensure. Still, most teacher training programs in music include experiences with technology, if not as a full class then as a strand of components in other classes.

The National Association of Schools of Music, which accredits schools of music, recommends that students have opportunities to explore "areas of individual interest" (NASM, 2013, p. 101)

## Hot Topic Debate
### Can an Electronic Music Ensemble Supplant a Traditional One?

*Take a position for or against (based either on your own position or one assigned to you) on the following controversial statement. Discuss it in class or on an online discussion board, blog, or wiki, as assigned by your instructor. When the discussion is complete, write a summary of the main pros and cons that you and your classmates have stated, and put the summary document in your Teacher Portfolio.*

Many schools, including some that do not offer traditional ensembles, are starting to organize groups of students to play electronic instruments. These ensembles may not include any instruments that could be considered traditional; they instead use iPads, laptops, and other kinds of technological devices to produce sound. Electronic ensembles also might not perform in public. Do these types of ensembles have a place in the school music program? Can these ensemble experiences help students to develop musicianship? What should be the role of the teacher in an electronic ensemble, especially if the music is largely improvised?

# TABLE 13.1 Standards in Music Technology and Music Education

| Areas of Competency in Music Technology | MENC Standards |
| --- | --- |
| 1. Electronic musical instruments (keyboards, controllers, synthesizers, samplers, sound reinforcement equipment)<br>2. Music production: data types (MIDI, digital audio); processes (sequencing, looping, signal processing, sound design)<br>3. Music notation software<br>4. Technology assisted learning (instructional software, accompaniment/practice tools, Internet-based learning)<br>5. Multimedia: authoring (Web pages, presentations, digital video); digital image capturing (scanning, still/video camera); Internet; electronic portfolios<br>6. Productivity tools, classroom and lab management: productivity tools (word processing, spreadsheet, database); computer systems (CPU, I/O devices, storage devices/media); lab management systems; networks | 1. Singing, alone and with others, a varied repertoire of music<br>2. Performing on instruments, alone and with others, a varied repertoire of music<br>3. Improvising melodies, variations, and accompaniments<br>4. Composing and arranging music within specified guidelines<br>5. Reading and notating music<br>6. Listening to, analyzing, and describing music<br>7. Evaluating music and music performances<br>8. Understanding relationships between music, the other arts, and disciplines outside the arts<br>9. Understanding music in relation to history and culture |

*Source:* Areas of Competency in Music Technology: Reprinted by permission. Copyright © by Technology in Music Education (TI:ME - www.ti-me.org). MENC Standards: From National Standards for Arts Education. Copyright © 1994 by National Association for Music Education, www.nafme.org. Used by permission. Areas of Competency in Music Technology: Reprinted by permission. Copyright © by Technology in Music Education (TI:ME - www.ti-me.org). MENC Standards: From National Standards for Arts Education. Copyright © 1994 by National Association for Music Education, www.nafme.org. Used by permission.

such as technology. Professional organizations are working hard to develop standards to guide teacher development with the hope that these standards will provide the guidelines needed for uniformity. Table 13.1 lists the Areas of Music Technology Competency developed by the Technology Institute for Music Educators (**TI:ME**), a professional organization for technology-using music educators, and the music education national standards published by the National Association for Music Education or **MENC**, formerly called the National Association for Music Education or **NAfME**, the professional organization for music educators.

## Downloading of Music Illegally

Since the days of bulletin board services and software like Napster, Pirate Bay, and LimeWire (currently under a court-ordered injunction to stop distributing their software) that allow peer-to-peer sharing of files, downloading music illegally has been a concern of the music industry. The sharing of files was extremely popular in the late 1990s and early 2000s, and numerous court cases have surrounded this issue. According to the Recording Industry Association of America (RIAA) website, since file downloads through Napster became prominent in 1999, U.S. music sales have dropped by more than half. The sharing of files is so readily available today that many students do not view the downloading of music as illegal.

Recent data (The Nielsen Company, 2013) show some interesting trends. While overall music sales decreased 6.3% and physical sales (of CDs, LPs, and cassettes) decreased by 13% between 2012 and 2013, music streaming increased by 32% during that same period. In essence, people are still consuming music, but are showing a strong preference for online music streaming services such as Pandora, Spotify, r.dio, and iTunes Radio over physical purchases. It is possible that online musical engagement could make illegal capture of music even more prevalent. The topic of illegal use of copyrighted works such as music has become an essential part of the digital literacy that schools must address, as shown in Technology Integration Example 13.1.

## The Intersection of Popular Music, Technology, and Music Instruction

The National Association for Music Education (NAfME, formerly MENC) published a collection of landmark essays addressing the issue of popular music, but "Bridging the Gap: Popular Music and Music Education" made very little mention of popular music's heavy reliance on technology for both production (composition) and live performance (Rodriguez, 2004). Some

# TECHNOLOGY INTEGRATION

## Example 13.1

**TITLE:** Why is Downloading Music Illegal?

**CONTENT AREA/TOPIC:** Art

**GRADE LEVELS:** 9–12

**ISTE STANDARDS•S:** Standard 1—Creativity and Innovation; Standard 2—Communication and Collaboration; Standard 3—Research and Information Fluency; Standard 4—Critical Thinking, Problem Solving, and Decision Making; Standard 6—Technology Operations and Concepts

**CCSS:** CCSS.ELA-LITERACY.SL.9-10.2, CCSS.ELA-LITERACY.SL.9-10.3, CCSS.ELA-LITERACY.SL.9-10.5, CCSS.ELA-LITERACY.RH.11-12.1, CCSS.ELA-LITERACY.SL.11-12.1

**DESCRIPTION:** In this lesson, students work in small groups and use websites to learn the history of copyright infringement as it relates to audio files and review the applicable laws and issues that arise from violations of them. They discuss their own practices and compare them to the legal standards. Finally these use Web resources to create a presentation in which they take a position on the controversy and use information they have found to make a persuasive argument to defend their position.

*SOURCE:* Based on an idea from the lesson plan *Copyright Infringement or Not? The Debate over Downloading Music* by Suzanne Taylor at http://www.readwritethink.org/classroom-resources/lesson-plans/copyright-infringement-debate-over-855.html.

---

recent publications include descriptions of many kinds of alternative music programs including those that focus on popular music styles (Clements, 2010; Smith, 2013). Any music teacher seeking to start and sustain a program component dedicated to rock, hip hop, rap, or other pop genres must have (or have access to) extensive knowledge of desktop music production and live sound reinforcement—not to mention a credible familiarity with pop music's complex web of music, culture, and traditions.

## The Music Director as Small Business Administrator

Typical secondary school music programs may involve hundreds of students, rooms full of instruments and other equipment, wardrobes of uniforms and choral robes, libraries of sheet music, methods books and other print resources, and large budgets. The music director usually oversees the largest inventory of physical assets outside the athletic department. The music director is responsible for tracking students' academic progress and other duties common to all classroom teachers. In addition, the music director must be his or her own director of development, constantly on the lookout for continuing or increased funding. All of these issues make knowledge of information management software a high priority—if not a stated requirement—for the efficient operation of a successful music program.

**TECHNOLOGY LEARNING CHECK**

Complete **TLC 13.2** to review what you have learned from this section about issues in music education that affect how technology is integrated.

## TECHNOLOGY INTEGRATION STRATEGIES FOR MUSIC INSTRUCTION

In a superb review of research related to technology and music learning, Webster (2002) identified several categories of music experience that have been the focus of technology integration and are still excellent guidelines today, including music listening, performance, and composition. He also acknowledged the crucial role that technology plays in research and assessment within the educational environment. In addition to general-purpose software (e.g., word processing, spreadsheet, Web authoring), two broad categories of computer-based tools play a primary role in serving the needs of music teachers: instructional software (programs developed primarily for teaching music skills) and music production software (programs that facilitate music composition, recording, and performance). More recently, Bauer, Harris and Hofer (2012) explained how musical activities can be associated with particular technologies in accord with the TechPACK model.

The first step in the process of integrating music technology may well be the purchase of electronic keyboards or synthesizers. For financial reasons, many schools that have to choose between a computer lab and a keyboard lab for their music programs choose the latter. Another relatively recent entry into the music performance realm is the "intelligent" accompaniment system (SmartMusic). With a library of over 80,000 compositions at the time of this writing, students can select a piece from either the ensemble or solo literature and practice with an accompaniment system that follows their performance as tempo is varied for expressive purposes. Perhaps the greatest contribution that SmartMusic can make to the broad goals of music education is that it helps teachers assess students' progress through automated means; it checks students' performances for correct pitches and rhythms and provides assessment data. In a school or university with little or no budget to provide accompanists, such technologies provide significant opportunity. Strategies that make use of all these resources include support for music composition and production, music performance, self-paced learning and practice, teaching music history, and interdisciplinary strategies. These are summarized in Table 13.2 and discussed next.

▲ The first step in the process of integrating music technology may well be the purchase of electronic keyboards or synthesizers. (Photo courtesy of Jay Dorfman)

## TABLE 13.2 Summary of Technology Integration Strategies for Music

| Technology Integration Strategies | Benefits | Sample Resources and Activities |
|---|---|---|
| Support for music composition and production | • Offers a range of mixing and sound design options to support composition for students of any age<br>• Supports both traditional and nontraditional composition<br>• Offers teachers maximum flexibility in designing music curriculum | • Apple/Emagic Logic<br>• Apple's GarageBand<br>• Reason (Propellerhead) Software<br>• BubbleMachine |
| Support for music performance | • Expedites preparation for performance (e.g., rearranging music for alternate instrumentations, re-creating lost or missing parts from the score, transposing parts, and simplifying difficult passages)<br>• Helps teachers with theory lessons, quizzes, and other handouts to aid student performance | • Sibelius<br>• Finale and Print Music software<br>• MidiNotate |
| Support for self-paced learning and practice | • Offers individual, personal help with needed skills, ear training, or music theory | • Practice Musica |
| Support for teaching music history | • Internet sites provide easy-to-access background information on composers and musical periods/compositions<br>• Website generation offers a venue for students to share their research | • Classic Motown timeline<br>• Internet Public Library 2<br>• See also pbs.org for other interactive and educational timelines and music history resources |
| Support for interdisciplinary strategies | • Builds on natural relationships between music and other topics (e.g., physics)<br>• Helps promote musical literacy while teaching related concepts | • Math & Music |

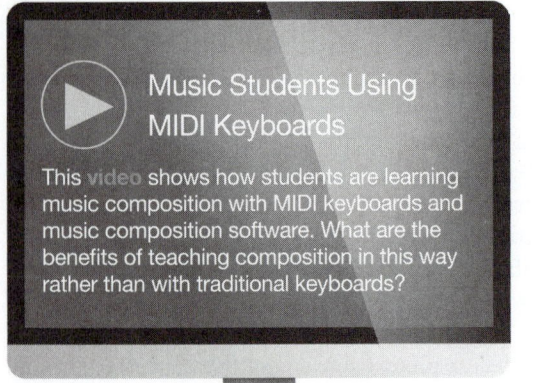

**Music Students Using MIDI Keyboards**

This video shows how students are learning music composition with MIDI keyboards and music composition software. What are the benefits of teaching composition in this way rather than with traditional keyboards?

## Support for Music Composition and Production

For the purposes of this chapter, music production and music composition mean the same thing. The three essential tools in this process are sequencers, **notation software**, and **vocal processing software**, and each can contribute substantially to teaching both production and performance. Sequencers allow the user to record, edit, and play back digital audio and MIDI data. Notation programs concentrate music production on the traditional realm of composition with standard notation. They focus on score and page setup, part extraction, text formatting, and other print-related issues. In other words, a sequencer facilitates music making in the aural domain, whereas notation facilitates music making in the visual domain. Vocal processing software is to voice audio what word processing software is to text. It allows users to make changes to the pitch and create interesting vocal distortions. Auto-Tune by Antares is the premier software of this kind. It was created by Andy Hildebrand, an engineer working on seismic data, who suddenly realized this type of software had vocal-editing potential. This software allows a unique vocal distortion technique called **auto-tuning**.

All three of these types of programs allow students to compose music in both traditional and nontraditional ways. With these tools, they can enter music with the mouse, play it with a MIDI-equipped keyboard or other input device (e.g., guitar or wind controller), or import it by opening standard MIDI files created by others (e.g., their fellow students, their teachers, or files found on the Internet). Designed primarily for desktop music production, the sequencer typically offers more options for creating a sonic artifact: more sophisticated mixing and sound design features. New types of sequencers such as Ableton's Live also offer new paradigms within the realm of sequencing software. Notation software is designed primarily to facilitate the production of music as a visual artifact, music on paper or on screen that can then be performed by a live musician. A recent entry into the notation software market is NoteFlight, an online notation program that adds social, collaborative functions so that teachers and students can work on projects together and receive feedback from others across the Internet.

Music production software includes sequencing (MIDI and digital audio), digital audio editing (often a component of a sequencing program), and music notation. Although these programs offer teachers maximum flexibility in designing curriculum, they may require the teacher to have more specialized knowledge of the individual software package because each product operates with different functions.

While hardware sequencers can still be found, often as components of sophisticated workstation keyboards, most sequencing platforms are computer applications. Computer-based sequencers require a more complete MIDI workstation. Modern computers all contain the sound card required to use a sequencer, and most external MIDI equipment can interface with the computer through common USB connections. Computer sequencing software is very powerful, requiring increased processing speed, storage capacity, and a bigger screen on which to display data as compared to hardware workstations.

Most sequencing programs simulate the functions of the physical recording studio. Many applications even include graphics that are designed to look like physical studio gear (for an interesting example, see Reason from Propellerhead, which can also be used to teach students correct cabling of studio components with virtual cables). Music is recorded on tracks and assigned to channels for playback and editing. Software plug-ins are digital equivalents of outboard (hardware) signal modifiers such as echo chambers and compressors and, depending on the processing power of the computer being used, provide the composer with a desktop recording studio equipped with virtually unlimited mixing options. Many sequencers offer the ability to record sound directly onto the computer's hard drive with the use of a microphone. Live, simultaneous multichannel recording is possible with an external digital audio interface. After recording, digital audio data, as represented by a wave shape, can be manipulated (edited) with the ease and precision of text in a word processor.

With very few exceptions, all sequencers support both step- and real-time recording of MIDI data. Once MIDI notes are entered, they can be edited like any other data on the computer:

cut, copied, and pasted. All performance parameters of MIDI data can be controlled by the user independently of one another—including pitch, tempo, volume, and dynamics.

Some programs designed for young children have sequencing components that enable composition. The "Doodle Pad" component of Music Ace, for example, allows the user to drag different-shaped happy faces (representing notes of different rhythmic values) onto a staff. In addition, the user can assign each note to one of several different sounds (e.g., piano, violin) as represented by a different color. Similar functions are available in Hyperscore. With proper direction, however, elementary school students can be taught the basic operations of even the most sophisticated professional software (see Technology Integration Example 13.2).

Projects that begin at a computer workstation in a lab can be used in other situations throughout the music program. Students can create notation files that are then used to facilitate performance in the rehearsal room or at a concert. Students who are especially proficient on an instrument (including voice) can create a sequenced instrumental "bed" to accompany a live performance or group or individual rehearsal. While this may not be the goal of all composition activities, this technique can be used in circumstances in which students are proficient in traditional performance on instruments or voice.

Desktop music systems (e.g., the MIDI sequencer) have prompted new definitions of musicianship that recognize alternative tracks to musical creativity, in addition to the traditional conservatory model of preparation. As suggested earlier, students with little or no "formal" musical training can create and edit compositions using a sequencing program with step-entry capability. Students can also perform analyses of music using preexisting MIDI files and/or digital audio. Once the pieces have been imported into a sequencer, students can explore all aspects of musical form, harmony, orchestration, and other parameters. Sequencers and audio editing software offer students the ability not only to listen to prerecorded music but also to manipulate it. Students can demonstrate their understanding of musical form by literally separating a piece of recorded music into its structural components. In this way, expositions, recapitulations, second choruses, guitar solos and other sectional form elements all become discrete audio events, which in turn can be rearranged—resequenced—into new formal configurations.

Apple's GarageBand has become popular among young people for mixing and playing their own music, and its app counterpart has made these activities even more accessible. Multimedia authoring programs like Flash and Director exemplify another type of technological tool that can be used to facilitate the understanding and exploration of musical form. BubbleMachine, a Flash-based program developed by Scott Lipscomb and Marc Jacoby, is available for free download to educators and allows the user to create interactive listening guides for any audio

# TECHNOLOGY INTEGRATION

## Example 13.2

TITLE: Organize and Create Music

CONTENT AREA/TOPIC: Music composition

GRADE LEVELS: 2–8

ISTE STANDARDS•S: Standard 1—Creativity and Innovation; Standard 6—Technology Operations and Concepts

MENC: 4, 5

TI:ME: 3, 4, 6

DESCRIPTION: Hyperscore is software designed by developers at the M.I.T. Media Lab that enables students of all ages to compose music. The software is entirely graphical—no standard music notation is used, so the complexity of notation is removed from the composition process. In the Hyperscore environment, students compose by drawing on the screen. Musical elements such as melody and timbre are represented on the "score" with objects of varying shapes, textures, and colors. Pieces can also take on sectional forms by grouping chunks of symbols together. A visual grid represents time, so there is a recognizable element of the visual elements flowing from left to right. Using this software, teachers can encourage students to be creative with composing their own music without the normal conventions of music notation.

MP3 file. Also available from this same website are a variety of template files that can be used to create interactive listening guides for any composition falling into the following established musical forms: sonata form, AABA, and 12-bar blues.

Students can record MIDI data over their favorite audio recordings using different kinds of MIDI controllers. More advanced analysis projects, such as those that might take place in an Advanced Placement music theory class, can now be undertaken using music software as a presentation tool. Consequently, the general music class can accomplish a great deal more than simply providing those students who are supposed to be unmusical or at least untrained with a passive listening experience.

While the preceding scenarios lend themselves best to a lab environment with multiple computers, even a single computer can provide valuable support for a general music curriculum. According to Smith (2010), creative pedagogy, free software tools, and a single computer classroom can be combined to effectively engage students in group composition and analysis of music as they learn collaboratively. Smith (2010) said that when educational resources are limited, using a free **audio recording and editing program** like Audacity can be a powerful educational tool for collaborative work composing, performing, and recording music or manipulating elements such as pitch and tempo in order to deconstruct and analyze the dynamic elements of music as well. The integration of technology like this also provides a medium for the formative and summative assessment of students' creative products and performances, as well as their understanding of fundamental music concepts (Bauer, 2010). There are numerous open-source software options for music production that make it more and more viable in the K–12 classroom (see Open-Source Options).

## Support for Music Performance

Software like Finale and Sibelius offers all of the power and flexibility of word processing applied to music notation. In a school music program, this category of software lets teachers rearrange music for alternate instrumentations, transpose parts into more accessible keys for performance, and simplify difficult passages. When printed, notation documents are legible and have a professional look, eliminating the lack of clarity and potential confusion that can result from hand-written parts. And, as is the case with all computer-generated data, existing documents can be

# OPEN SOURCE
## OPTIONS for Software in Art and Music Classrooms

| TYPES | FREE SOURCES |
|---|---|
| **Free audio editing and recording software** | Audacity: audacity.sourceforge.net<br>Power Sound Editor: free-sound-editor.com |
| **Free music notation software** | MuseScore: musescore.org<br>NoteFlight: noteflight.com<br>Canorus: sourceforge.net/apps/mediawiki/canorus/index.php?title=Main_Page |
| **Free drawing, photo editing, and graphic design software** | Gimp (photo editing): gimp.org<br>Google SketchUp (3-D modeling): sketchup.google.com<br>Inkscape (vector drawing): inkscape.org<br>Sumo Paint (online drawing and photo editing): sumopaint.com/home |

corrected and/or revised without having to reenter the music from scratch. Notation files are small in comparison to digital audio, video, and graphics files, so entire libraries (hundreds of scores, parts, and handouts) can be stored using an insignificant amount of disk space. Teachers must exercise caution when using notation software to rearrange music in cases where copyright laws prohibit that practice.

With notation software, teachers can create theory lessons, quizzes, and other handouts that combine notation with text and other graphics. The most recent versions of these programs often include templates or wizards to facilitate creating such informational documents and assessments. The capability of exporting sections of a musical score in a graphic format (GIF, JPG, or EPS) makes inserting images into word processing documents very easy to accomplish. Even when such capabilities are not built into the notation software, screen captures of short passages can be created from the notation document and then inserted into a word processing document.

The distinction between the functions of modern notation and sequencing programs is easily blurred; this is because newer sequencing software often contains scoring functions, and notation software includes mixing and other playback functions generally associated with sequencers. To clarify the roles of the sequencer and the notation program in the teaching of music performance, analysis, and composition, it is helpful to consider the hypothetical scenario of an ensemble class. To support sectional or individual practice, the teacher could enter the score of a piece into a sequencer. Once the music had been entered, the student or teacher could choose which parts needed to be heard, creating a "music-minus-one" type of accompaniment. In this way, for instance, the clarinet section could rehearse to a sequence consisting of the entire ensemble minus the clarinets. Or the second clarinet player could practice sectional passages by selecting only the clarinet parts for playback, but muting the second clarinet part. Meanwhile, the notation program could be used to edit any parts that need to be revised in order to better match the performance level of the students. Notation software is generally more flexible, powerful, and appropriate when the end goal is a printed score; when audio files are the aim, sequencing software is the more suitable choice. See the Open Source Options feature for free software to support music education.

During the past decade, the piano lab has given way to the electronic keyboard lab, where students can develop much more than keyboard skills. Demski (2010) describes how electronic keyboard labs can be used to help students learn about music theory as well as fundamental music elements such as melody, rhythm, and harmony. Keyboard labs can now be networked with devices such as the Korg GEC-III or the Yamaha LC3+ that allow the teacher to communicate with individual students or groups of students by means of a microphone and headphones. This allows instructional guidance as students are afforded the freedom to explore, experiment with, and compose music. Developing composition skills also provides an outlet for creative expression (Demski, 2010). Southcott and Crawford (2011) advocate for pedagogical strategies that encourage using music technology as more than just a technical tool. Also see how to help all students have access to this tool in the Adapting for Special Needs feature.

Teachers should also consider technology for performance beyond traditional instruments. Electronic devices and computers can offer students creative outlets. Intuitive surface interfaces, such as the Native Instruments Maschine and Launch Control and the Ableton Push, allow for control of complex software without knowledge of a keyboard or other traditional musical instruments. Students with access to these kinds of instruments can take part in new and different musical experiences unique to the world of technology. Dorfman (2013) provides profiles of students and teachers taking part in nontraditional ensembles, and shows their benefit to students' musical learning.

## Support for Self-Paced Learning and Practice

Instructional software is available to help students learn new skills (tutorials) or practice skills introduced by a teacher (drill and practice). Practica Musica, for example, can be used as a tutorial in music fundamentals with little or no input from the teacher. It can also serve as a drill program when a student needs help with a particular topic related to ear training or music theory. Some of these software packages, such as Auralia, have moved from installing on desktops to cloud-based deployment, allowing students to access the software from any location. Almost all music instructional software packages either have a designated drill component, and many have the capability of maintaining assessment information and other important data for

## Music and the Arts

Students with disabilities need to participate in music and art just as other students do. In some cases, some accommodations are necessary to ensure opportunities for access and engagement. The resources below describe some resources that may be useful.

### For Music

- *Assistive Technology in Education/Music* (at the Wikibooks website)—An overview of strategies and tools for using assistive technology to provide access to music for students with disabilities.

- *Meet Carly W. and Learn About Her Successful Use of Assistive Technology* (at the Family Center on Technology and Disability website)—This is a profile of a student and the efforts of her teachers to help her learn to use assistive technology to enhance her access and engagement with music.

### For Art

- Art for Children and Adults with Disabilities (at the Kinder Art website)—Resources and art activity ideas for children and adults.

- Design and Art (look under the Accommodations and Universal Design topic on "The Faculty Room," a faculty forum on design of classroom environments at the University of Washington website)—Suggestions for teachers and college instructors on how to make art more accessible for students with disabilities.

- Very Special Arts (at the Kennedy Center website)—An international organization devoted to promoting participation in the arts by individuals with disabilities.

*—Contributed by Dave Edyburn*

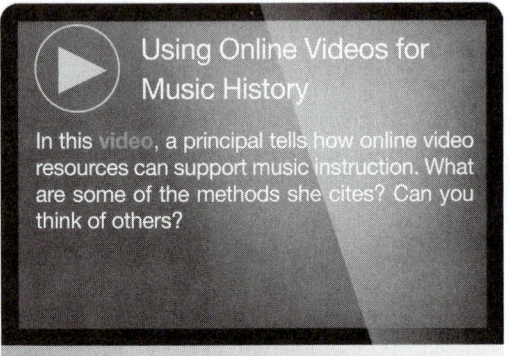

**Using Online Videos for Music History**

In this video, a principal tells how online video resources can support music instruction. What are some of the methods she cites? Can you think of others?

multiple students on the same computer, accessible only to the instructor through use of a password-protected account. This capability helps teachers track students' progress on music skills.

## Support for Teaching Music History

Of the nine national standards for music education, the only one that refers specifically to music history is the last one: "Understanding music in relation to history and culture." General music teachers have long sought to foster a deep understanding of musical works by situating them in their social and historical context. This is an excellent way to introduce young students to the practice of research while offering more mature students unlimited opportunities for independent projects. The Internet has become the most powerful research tool available to students and teachers at all levels of education. Students and teachers can access online databases, electronic books, online journals, archived and current newspaper articles, audio and MIDI files, video clips, thousands of out-of-print books, and discussion groups on almost any music topic imaginable. Online music archives such as the Naxos Music Library, the National Jukebox of the Library of Congress, and archive.org can be especially useful for teachers who cannot afford to buy recordings of historical music examples. Productive educational use of the Internet is limited only by the user and, to some extent, the connection speed and processing power of the computer. The effective use of such powerful tools requires clear instruction, guidance, and supervision by the teacher.

Building a website can be a perfect culminating activity for a general music class. Students can do much of the planning in groups—even offline, if computer access is limited. Within each group, students can assign themselves areas of the site according to individual strengths and literacies: A student who can't read music may be proficient with a Web page authoring tool; some students can search the Internet for relevant graphics while others look for text or sound. Videos and DVDs continue to be a source of valuable historical reference material, many in the form of informative documentaries. Excerpts from these media can be captured on a computer's hard drive or embedded using provided code from many media sharing sites and then incorporated into a student- or teacher-authored Web page or software presentation as long as care is taken to clearly understand and follow existing copyright laws. With the advent of digital music files, the understanding of the copyright law as it relates to digital media is a very important aspect of a student's education. Finished projects can be viewed locally on a single computer, burned to a disc for multiple computers, posted on a school network, or uploaded to an Internet site so that parents or other students around the world can see them, link to them, and perhaps even contribute their own material.

Finally, compelling music classes have the potential to be highly effective recruiting tools. Students who initially feel out of place in their school's traditional music program dominated by instrumental and/or choral ensembles may find an exciting and challenging alternative role for themselves by enrolling in a technology-enhanced general music class or a new music class focusing on digital music creation and audio engineering. Often, it is access to music technology that attracts these students, who typically constitute 80–85% of the secondary school population, and provokes in them a new interest in music. In addition to gaining the attention of nontraditional music students, Olson (2010) maintains that technology holds particular promise for music education in the areas of collaborative and interdisciplinary learning.

## Support for Interdisciplinary Strategies

Beyond the opportunities for interdisciplinary study that present themselves in a general music class, student-produced music and research can enhance a variety of other aspects of school life. Multimedia-based research projects in the humanities can easily include music that underscores a presentation or that is itself the object of study. A sequencer can facilitate the work of student composers who want to supply music for dance projects or video footage of athletic events. The close relationship between music and physics calls for projects that examine the science of sound by exploring elements such as vibration, pitch, and amplification. Identifying the existence of shared fundamental concepts across disciplines (e.g., ratios represented in math as fractions and in music as note durations) opens the door to a new world of learning potential within which multiple representations of these basic concepts and their connections are used to deepen student understanding (An, Ma, & Capraro, 2011). In music—as in other disciplines such as science or mathematics—creativity, innovation, and knowledge production are inextricably linked (Ghassib, 2010).

**TECHNOLOGY LEARNING CHECK**
Complete TLC 13.3 to review what you have learned from this section about strategies for integrating technology into in music education.

# ISSUES AND CHALLENGES IN ART INSTRUCTION

Like music instruction, art instruction faces many classroom challenges that intersect with technology integration. Some teachers are not adequately prepared to produce digital art, much less to teach their students to do so. Technology appropriate for the art classroom changes rapidly, and staying up to date with the latest software and hardware can be challenging. This section addresses some of these important issues.

## Funding for Art Instruction

As a result of lean economic times and the ever-increasing emphasis on accountability in mathematics and reading as reflected in standardized testing related to the No Child Left Behind Act, funding for arts education is at an all-time low (Ellerson, 2010). Public funding of the arts from local, state, and federal governments decreased during 2012 by 3–5% (Stubbs, 2012). Teachers and school administrators must increasingly find ways to stretch funds available for arts education. In light of this reality, funding for technology in art is especially difficult; updating technology resources and buying electronic supplies present continuing problems. For example, production of graphics is a popular art activity, but the cost of expensive ink for printers and specialized paper supplies quickly depletes an annual budget. Teachers are forced to take measures such as password-protecting printers and putting software print controls in place to limit the number of pages a student may print for free.

## Ethical Issues Associated with the Use of Images and Other Materials

Since it is easy to use images from the Internet and other sources, it is increasingly important to teach students that they must cite sources and request permission to use information, images, or other sourced materials. When students are carrying out research or creating artwork on computers for websites or graphic design or other art projects, they must also learn issues of appropriation and repurposing of images and how this use intersects with plagiarism. Discussions should take place about issues of copyright law and what constitutes infringement. Perhaps a short assignment early in the term could require students to identify the specific issues and how they feel about copying someone else's work, whether text, image, or sound. Consider using electronic resources such as the free activities at the Library of Congress website or from the Duke School of Law to help students understand the rules and implications of copyright in fun, interactive ways.

## Accessing Images Used in Art Instruction

If schools use filtering software on computers to protect students from unsavory materials (e.g., pornography), many great works of art are also likely to be filtered out, unless the filter is carefully constructed. Take care to allow these important artworks to be visible and accessible to students. The works of lesser-known contemporary artists can sometimes blur the line between what is generally considered to be art and what is not. In photography, the nude figure has been a common subject. Great artists throughout history have used the nude as metaphor for beauty, nature, and life. Limiting access by allowing only the names of the most famous artists to pass through a filter will not solve the problem. Strategies must be designed for allowing complete access to images of artworks for students to use. If all else fails, teachers must make sure the school library has a good collection of art and art history books. Also, many museums have images from their collections available on CD or DVD for purchase.

## The Challenge of Meeting Standards in Arts Instruction

Art teachers look to several sets of standards to guide their preparation and classroom work. The National Art Education Association (NAEA, 2009a) offers standards for art teacher preparation, including one (Standard V) that calls for teachers to use current and emerging technologies in their teaching. The **NAEC** also offers Professional Standards for Visual Arts Educators (2009b); Standard VI calls for teachers to use technology to enhance their teaching methods. A group of professional organizations joined with the Consortium of National Arts Education Associations to promote a vision of K–12 arts education as described in the National Standards for Arts Education (at the Kennedy center's ArtsEdge website). The standards suggest that students know and be able to do the following by the time they have completed secondary school:

1. Be able to communicate at a basic level in the four arts disciplines—dance, music, theatre, and the visual arts. This includes knowledge and skills in the use of the basic vocabularies, materials, tools, techniques, and intellectual methods of each arts discipline.

2. Be able to communicate proficiently in at least one art form, including the ability to define and solve artistic problems with insight, reason, and technical proficiency.

3. Be able to develop and present basic analyses of works of art from structural, historical, and cultural perspectives, and from combinations of those perspectives. This includes the ability to understand and evaluate work in the various arts disciplines.

4. Have an informed acquaintance with exemplary works of art from a variety of cultures and historical periods, and a basic understanding of historical development in the arts disciplines, across the arts as a whole and within cultures.

5. Be able to relate various types of arts knowledge and skills within and across the arts disciplines. This includes mixing and matching competencies and understandings in art making, history and culture, and analysis in any arts-related project.

Schools are challenged to find ways of meeting these standards in an educational climate in which the role of the arts is often not a priority. The limited time and resources available for arts instruction often results in these standards being interpreted as *ideals* that may never actually be reached in most schooling scenarios. New technologies can both help and exacerbate this challenge for arts educators. They help by providing access to examples and free resources not available locally. But access to the technologies themselves may be beyond the reach of already-underserved schools, thus further widening the gap between those who are and are not likely to meet the standards.

**TECHNOLOGY LEARNING CHECK**

Complete **TLC 13.4** to review what you have learned from this section about issues in art education that affect how technology is integrated.

# TECHNOLOGY INTEGRATION STRATEGIES FOR ART INSTRUCTION

As with music instruction, technology resources in art instruction support a variety of classroom strategies—from simple demonstrations of materials to student production techniques. These are described here and summarized in Table 13.3.

## Accessing Art Examples for Classroom Use

Internet sites and DVD collections are rich sources of artwork that students can use as illustrations of artists' work and as models for their own work. Teachers can generate a set of sites to bookmark for regular use in classes. (For examples, see Table 13.3.) They can also get students involved in these searches. For example, they might give students an assignment that asks them to find sources for paintings that use still life as subject matter, that use the technique of chiaroscuro, or that are 15th-century Florentine. Learning may result from the act of collaboratively searching for these types of artifacts. Other example activities include:

- Have students use the school library to find specific works of art, and then challenge them to locate on the Internet other examples of the artist's work or work from the same period.
- To teach about the work of contemporary artists, have students look at galleries and exhibitions online to see the new work.
- For instructional reinforcement, use DVD or Web-based collections on art techniques.
- Create a digital library to use for slide shows and presentations. Assign students who are traveling during the school year or during the summer to visit galleries and museums and bring back pamphlets, postcards, or examples of artwork they see. Scan the examples to create images for the classroom digital library.

## Using Teaching Examples and Materials

Teachers can use presentation software such as PowerPoint or Keynote to create lecture slides. Slides are especially helpful when they contain example images inserted after they are scanned or photographed with a digital camera, or downloaded from the Internet. Also, teachers can create interactive websites to help students learn color theory, design theory, and photography techniques. See a list of the Top Ten Must-Have Apps for Art.

## Producing and Manipulating Digitized Images

The most common type of hardware resource in art instruction is image-digitizing equipment. Graphic scanners are computer peripherals that create digital versions of images in a variety of formats (e.g., GIF, JPEG, BMP, TIFF). Artists can also capture an image from a video

# TABLE 13.3 Summary of Technology Integration Strategies for Art

| Technology Integration Strategies | Benefits | Sample Resources and Activities |
|---|---|---|
| Accessing art examples for classroom use | • Internet collections provide ready access to works of art to use as samples, illustrations, and models | • Masters of Photography CD<br>• World Wide Arts resources art history section<br>• Kinder Art's Multicultural Art resources |
| Using teaching examples and materials | • Multimedia slide lectures are easier to use than slides and allow quick, random access to examples, illustrations<br>• Teacher-created websites can provide easy-to-access exercises in color theory, design theory, and photography techniques | • *Microsoft* Powerpoint<br>• Apple's Keynote<br>• Google Drive Presentations app |
| Producing and manipulating digitized images | • Offers an easy, flexible system for creating images<br>• Lets novice artists create high-quality products<br>• Lets novice artists scan found objects to use in compositions | • Camcorders, VCRs, digital cameras, scanners<br>• Paint programs, e.g., Mackiev's Kidpix<br>• Adobe's Photoshop Elements<br>• Hardware drawing devices such as Wacom tablets or Apple iPads |
| Supporting graphic design and 3-D modeling | • Makes possible graphic techniques that can be done only on the computer with this software<br>• Offers many opportunities for artistic expression<br>• Demonstrates how easily images can be altered, thus fostering visual literacy skills | • Image manipulation software, e.g., Adobe *Photoshop*<br>• Morphing software, e.g., Morpheus<br>• 3-D modeling software, e.g., Ulead COOL 31, Blender, or Google SketchUp |
| Supporting student development of publications | • Lets students illustrate their brochures, newsletters, and other documents with high-quality graphics | • Desktop publishing software<br>• Image manipulation software such as Adobe Photoshop |
| Virtual field trips to art museums | • Allows students to see models and examples of artworks not locally available<br>• Makes possible multicultural "field trips" to gather examples of art and music from around the world | Virtual Tours of:<br>• Louvre Museum<br>• Art Institute of Chicago<br>• Museum of Modern Art<br>• Metropolitan Museum of Art<br>• Smithsonian museums<br>• National Gallery of Art |
| Creating movies as an art form | • Students can produce their own creative works for research, reports, assignments, and entertainment | • Apple iMovie and GarageBand<br>• ArcSoft's ShowBiz<br>• Microsoft's Windows Live Movie Maker |
| Sharing students creative and research works | • Allows students to share and get feedback on their work and see example products of others | • Art Education 2.0: Connecting Art Educators Around the Globe |

source (camcorder or VCR) using digitizing software like iMovie, Final Cut, or Premiere. This equipment and software provides users with flexible systems for capturing and manipulating digital images, which can then be edited using software like Photoshop. The ability to digitize still images and video has opened up a whole new genre of art. See Technology Integration Example 13.3.

# TECHNOLOGY INTEGRATION

## Example 13.3

**TITLE:** Visual Biography

**CONTENT AREA/TOPIC:** Art

**GRADE LEVELS:** 6–12

**ISTE STANDARDS•S:** Standard 1—Creativity and Innovation; Standard 2—Communication and Collaboration; Standard 3—Research and Information Fluency; Standard 6—Technology Operations and Concepts

**NATIONAL STANDARDS FOR ARTS EDUCATION:** Content & Achievement Standard: Grade 5–8 Visual Arts Standard 1, Content & Achievement Standard: Grade 5–8 Visual Arts Standard 6, Content & Achievement Standard: Grade 5–8 Visual Arts Standard 3, Content & Achievement Standard: Grade

9–12 Visual Arts Standard 6, Content & Achievement Standard: Grade 9–12 Visual Arts Standard 1, Content & Achievement Standard: Grade 9–12 Visual Arts Standard 3

**DESCRIPTION:** Students can use digital art tools to explore and express a sense of their own identities. Using digital cameras, students search for found objects that represent important parts of their lives. They can also search online and print media, and capture or scan those media. Depending on the students' ages and levels of sophistication, they can make a digital collage of these images using PhotoShop (or similar software), or use movie-making software (such as iMovie) to make a short film. Adding music to the film is a great way to cross disciplinary lines, especially if the students compose original music for their films.

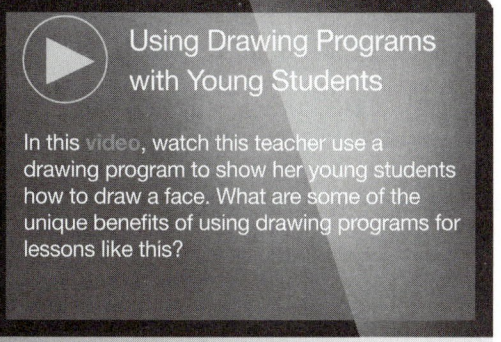

### Using Drawing Programs with Young Students

In this video, watch this teacher use a drawing program to show her young students how to draw a face. What are some of the unique benefits of using drawing programs for lessons like this?

A wide variety of software is available to teachers and students who are interested in producing computer art. Simple paint programs (Paintbrush, KidPix) are available for very young students; in fact, teachers often use these types of programs when first introducing students to the computer. Integrated software and multimedia authoring programs (Flash or Director) always include fairly sophisticated drawing and painting tools; these might be good intermediate tools for the developing computer artist. High-level programs (Photoshop) suitable to the advanced artist would be used primarily at the high school level. Teachers should also explore the wide variety of mobile apps available for editing images. These include the mobile version of iPhoto, Photo Editor by Aviary, PhotoShop Express, and the artistic filters available in application services such as Instagram.

## Supporting Graphic Design and 3-D Modeling

Art educators can choose from among a number of software options to let students explore graphic design. A range of animation programs is available, from simple cell-type animation to more advanced programs that offer features like **tweening** or morphing,

▲ A wide variety of software is available to teachers and students who are interested in producing computer art. (Photos courtesy of W. Wiencke)

graphic techniques that can be done only with computer software. Other programs are specifically geared toward cartoon production and allow artists to add music and sound.

An art studio would not be complete without an image manipulation program like Adobe Photoshop, which enables students to edit clip art or digital photos. High-end programs provide hundreds of options and special effects for altering images. Morphing software enables the user to transform images smoothly from one shape or image to another. This technique offers tremendous potential for artistic expression and, by demonstrating how easily images can be altered, helps foster the development of visual literacy skills.

Finally, as Davenport and Gunn (2009) and Bryant (2010) contend, students can use 3-D, modeling, and animation software to communicate ideas visually through computer-generated models, animation, and imagery. Davenport and Gunn (2009) describe a powerful example of the use of these tools in a high school media literacy program they developed to serve indigenous youth from underrepresented populations throughout remote areas of rural Mexico. Students used digital images and video cameras, as well as 3-D and animation software, to visually communicate images and stories about their cultures and traditions. The integration of technology as a medium to design and create not only aided in the opportunity for these students to explore their own identity, but also aided in their empowerment by giving them a voice to share their unique backgrounds and experiences through artistic and cultural expression. Bryant (2010) confirmed that such transformative learning experiences may also occur in traditional art classrooms as students' creativity, engagement, and collaborative problem-solving skills are fostered by the use of 3-D animation and visual imagery to create captivating artwork that holds personal meaning.

## Supporting Student Development of Publications

Many schools look to their own graphic arts programs for the creation of brochures and newsletters as part of student learning activities. Because students gain valuable experience through creating and producing these publications, the activities can be considered a kind of internship to prepare for actual jobs as graphic artists for newspapers or other companies. This strategy requires schools to provide both desktop publishing software and access to image manipulation program such as Adobe PhotoShop.

## Virtual Field Trips to Art Museums

Many museums around the world have sites that allow a virtual tour through the museum. Although clearly this is not the same as viewing the works in person, virtual tours offer a way for students to explore and experience masterworks. With the development of new 3-D imagery, many museums are exploring ways in which this technology can be used to provide virtual visitors with a more compelling, visceral experience by creating illusions that make the tour, as well as museum artifacts, seem even more realistic (Steinbach, 2011). To support classroom learning, some museum sites even make their server available for students to post their own creations and to learn to create art using a certain medium like papier mâché, batik, or origami. These sites also can be the basis for multicultural "field trips" to gather examples of art and music from around the world (Risinger, 2010). When using the Internet for arts instruction, it is important to remember that the images are reproductions; students will need to be made aware of the idea of scale and be reminded that they need to keep in mind the limitations of digital imagery. Check out the Hot Topic Debate feature for this chapter related to virtual field trips. Can a virtual tour of a museum supplant the actual museum field trip?

## Creating Movies as an Art Form

Students can now make short or full-length digital movies with software that often comes with the computer. For example, Macintosh computers come with iMovie, and Windows computers come with Windows Live Movie Maker, both of which allow students to produce their own creative works using images, digital video, and sound for the purpose of reports, assignments, and entertainment. These movies can be shared across platforms by saving them in universal

**FIGURE 13.1** Collaboration Opportunities for Arts Educators

**FIGURE 13.1** Collaboration Opportunities for Arts Educators

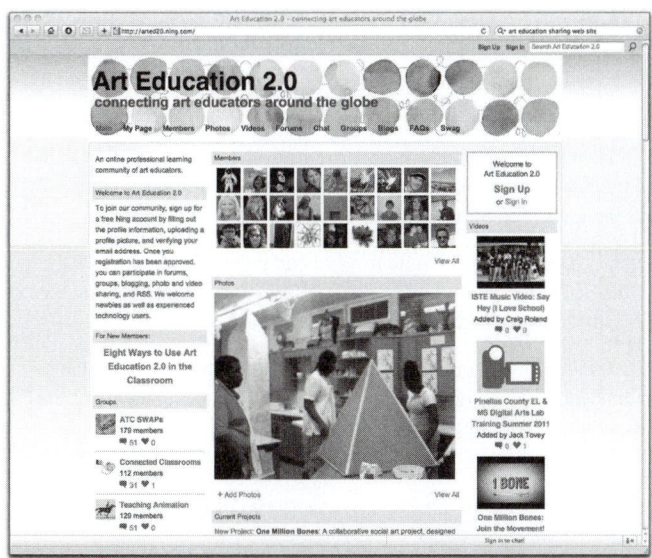

Attribution CC by Craig Roland 2011. Some Rights Reserved.

formats. When combined with technologies for capturing images such as digital cameras and scanners, and when students accompany visuals with sound, this relatively easy-to-use type of software can assist in producing powerful demonstrations of students' work.

## Sharing Students' Creative and Research Works

Through electronic publishing, videos, and presentation software, students can share their art creations with others (see Figure 13.1). Portfolios have long been a way for art students to demonstrate their achievements and abilities, and electronic portfolios are a natural extension of this strategy. Students can create PowerPoint presentations, videos, electronic books, blogs, and websites to show their research and creative work. Artists' books can be created and printed using desktop publishing and color inkjet printers. For higher quality output, students might use paid services that create photo books and projects, such as Shutterfly, Picasa, or iPhoto.

**TECHNOLOGY LEARNING CHECK**

Complete TLC 13.5 to review what you have learned from this section about strategies for integrating technology into art education.

## TEACHING MUSIC AND ART TEACHERS TO INTEGRATE TECHNOLOGY

This section gives recommendations for how teachers can prepare to integrate technology effectively into instruction for music and art learning. Although the Common Core State Standards (CCSS) did not specifically address standards for arts education and K–12 funding for the arts has often been channeled to CCSS subjects, several efforts have focused on aligning CCSS with the arts so that both may be addressed. The College Board released a report entitled *The Arts and the Common Core: A Review of Connections Between the Common Core State Standards and the National Core Arts Standards Conceptual Framework* (2012). Also, the National Coalition for Core Arts Standards (NCCAS) is a group of educators and organizations who seek to document the connection between CCSS and arts standards. The NCCAS website calls for teachers to "integrate new technology in ways that truly engage and energize learners" as part of the mission to align CCSS and the arts. For teachers, the challenge is to explore the intersection between CCSS, arts standards, and technology and prepare to teach in ways that combine them most effectively.

### Rubric to Measure Teacher Growth in Music and Art Technology Integration

Begin by reviewing the rubric in Figure 13.2 or Figure 13.3 to measure teachers' progress in effectively integrating technology in music and art instruction. Part I of each rubric addresses knowledge of issues and challenges, and Part II addresses music and art technology integration strategies.

**FIGURE 13.2** Rubric to Measure Teacher Growth in Technology Integration for Music Instruction

| Part I: Teacher Knowledge of Music Issues and Challenges | | | |
|---|---|---|---|
| | **Basic knowledge (1–2 points)** | **Intermediate knowledge (3–4 points)** | **Advanced knowledge (4–5 points)** |
| A changing definition for music literacy | I can articulate the nature of the issue. | I can both articulate the nature of the issue and some of the possible ways to address it. | I can articulate my own plan for addressing the issue in my own teaching. |
| Training teachers to meet music standards | I can articulate the nature of the issue. | I can both articulate the nature of the issue and some of the possible ways to address it. | I can articulate my own plan for addressing the issue in my own teaching. |
| Downloading of music illegally | I can articulate the nature of the issue. | I can both articulate the nature of the issue and some of the possible ways to address it. | I can articulate my own plan for addressing the issue in my own teaching. |
| The intersection of popular music, technology, and music instruction | I can articulate the nature of the issue. | I can both articulate the nature of the issue and some of the possible ways to address it. | I can articulate my own plan for addressing the issue in my own teaching. |
| The music director as small business administrator | I can articulate the nature of the issue. | I can both articulate the nature of the issue and some of the possible ways to address it. | I can articulate my own plan for addressing the issue in my own teaching. |

| Part II: Teachers' Technology Integration Strategies for Music Instruction | | | |
|---|---|---|---|
| | **Basic knowledge (1–2 points)** | **Intermediate knowledge (3–4 points)** | **Advanced knowledge (4–5 points)** |
| Support for music composition and production | I can describe the strategies and identify technologies to carry them out. | I have designed at least 1–2 activities based on these strategies to enhance my teaching and my students' learning. | I have designed plans for how I will integrate these strategies throughout my curriculum to enhance my teaching and my students' learning. |
| Support for music performance | I can describe the strategies and identify technologies to carry them out. | I have designed at least 1–2 activities based on these strategies to enhance my teaching and my students' learning. | I have designed plans for how I will integrate these strategies throughout my curriculum to enhance my teaching and my students' learning. |
| Support for self-paced learning and practice | I can describe the strategies and identify technologies to carry them out. | I have designed at least 1–2 activities based on these strategies to enhance my teaching and my students' learning. | I have designed plans for how I will integrate these strategies throughout my curriculum to enhance my teaching and my students' learning. |
| Support for teaching music history | I can describe the strategies and identify technologies to carry them out. | I have designed at least 1–2 activities based on these strategies to enhance my teaching and my students' learning. | I have designed plans for how I will integrate these strategies throughout my curriculum to enhance my teaching and my students' learning. |
| Support for interdisciplinary strategies | I can describe the strategies and identify technologies to carry them out. | I have designed at least 1–2 activities based on these strategies to enhance my teaching and my students' learning. | I have designed plans for how I will integrate these strategies throughout my curriculum to enhance my teaching and my students' learning. |
| **Total points** | _____ **of 50 possible points** | | |

**FIGURE 13.3** Rubric to Measure Teacher Growth in Technology Integration for Art Instruction

| Part I: Teacher Knowledge of Art Issues and Challenges | | |
|---|---|---|
| | **Basic knowledge (1–2 points)** | **Intermediate knowledge (3–4 points)** | **Advanced knowledge (4–5 points)** |
| Funding for art instruction | I can articulate the nature of the issue. | I can both articulate the nature of the issue and some of the possible ways to address it. | I can articulate my own plan for addressing the issue in my own teaching. |
| Ethical issues associated with the use of images and other materials | I can articulate the nature of the issue. | I can both articulate the nature of the issue and some of the possible ways to address it. | I can articulate my own plan for addressing the issue in my own teaching. |
| Accessing images used in art instruction | I can articulate the nature of the issue. | I can both articulate the nature of the issue and some of the possible ways to address it. | I can articulate my own plan for addressing the issue in my own teaching. |
| The challenge of meeting standards in arts instruction | I can articulate the nature of the issue. | I can both articulate the nature of the issue and some of the possible ways to address it. | I can articulate my own plan for addressing the issue in my own teaching. |

| Part II: Teachers' Technology Integration Strategies for Art Instruction | | |
|---|---|---|
| | **Basic knowledge (1–2 points)** | **Intermediate knowledge (3–4 points)** | **Advanced knowledge (4–5 points)** |
| Accessing art examples for classroom use | I can describe the strategies and identify technologies to carry them out. | I have designed at least 1–2 activities based on these strategies to enhance my teaching and my students' learning. | I have designed plans for how I will integrate these strategies throughout my curriculum to enhance my teaching and my students' learning. |
| Using teaching examples and materials | I can describe the strategies and identify technologies to carry them out. | I have designed at least 1–2 activities based on these strategies to enhance my teaching and my students' learning. | I have designed plans for how I will integrate these strategies throughout my curriculum to enhance my teaching and my students' learning. |
| Producing and manipulating digitized images | I can describe the strategies and identify technologies to carry them out. | I have designed at least 1–2 activities based on these strategies to enhance my teaching and my students' learning. | I have designed plans for how I will integrate these strategies throughout my curriculum to enhance my teaching and my students' learning. |
| Supporting graphic design and 3-D modeling | I can describe the strategies and identify technologies to carry them out. | I have designed at least 1–2 activities based on these strategies to enhance my teaching and my students' learning. | I have designed plans for how I will integrate these strategies throughout my curriculum to enhance my teaching and my students' learning. |
| Supporting student development of publications | I can describe the strategies and identify technologies to carry them out. | I have designed at least 1–2 activities based on these strategies to enhance my teaching and my students' learning. | I have designed plans for how I will integrate these strategies throughout my curriculum to enhance my teaching and my students' learning. |
| Virtual field trips to art museums | I can describe the strategies and identify technologies to carry them out. | I have designed at least 1–2 activities based on these strategies to enhance my teaching and my students' learning. | I have designed plans for how I will integrate these strategies throughout my curriculum to enhance my teaching and my students' learning. |

*(Continued)*

**FIGURE 13.3** Rubric to Measure Teacher Growth in Technology Integration for Art Instruction (continued)

| Part II: Teachers' Technology Integration Strategies for Art Instruction | | | |
|---|---|---|---|
| | **Basic knowledge (1–2 points)** | **Intermediate knowledge (3–4 points)** | **Advanced knowledge (4–5 points)** |
| Creating movies as an art form | I can describe the strategies and identify technologies to carry them out. | I have designed at least 1–2 activities based on these strategies to enhance my teaching and my students' learning. | I have designed plans for how I will integrate these strategies throughout my curriculum to enhance my teaching and my students' learning. |
| Sharing students' creative and research works | I can describe the strategies and identify technologies to carry them out. | I have designed at least 1–2 activities based on these strategies to enhance my teaching and my students' learning. | I have designed plans for how I will integrate these strategies throughout my curriculum to enhance my teaching and my students' learning. |
| **Total points** | _____ of 60 possible points | | |

## Learning the Issues and Applications

The first step in technology integration is to become acquainted with the issues and challenges discussed in this chapter and how they shape teachers' uses and applications of technologies. Then teachers can begin developing capabilities to address instructional standards and curriculum goals. The following is a suggested sequence of learning activities.

1. **Issues and challenges in music and art instruction.** After reviewing the information in this chapter, go to the website of the music and art professional organizations. For music, visit the National Association for Music Education (NAfME) and the Technology in Music Education (TI:ME) sites; for art, visit the National Arts Education Association (NAEC) and the ArtsEdge section of the Kennedy Center website. Review the standards at both sites. See professional development resources the sites offer, and decide on which can help you gain insight into the issues and challenges outlined in this chapter. Discuss and reflect on the two questions under the Collaborate, Discuss, Reflect feature at the end of the chapter. Complete Part I of the rubric in Figure 13.2 or Figure 13.3 before you begin this sequence and again at various points in your progress.

2. **Music and art technology integration strategies.** After reviewing the information in this chapter, review examples of the technologies suggested in the Open Source Options feature and the websites and projects described under each section, and do the lesson evaluation and lesson development activities outlined in the Technology Integration Workshop at the end of this chapter. Reflect on how you will plan for implementing these strategies in your own classroom using the TIP model. Complete Part I of the rubric in Figure 13.2 or Figure 13.3 before you begin this sequence and again at various points in your progress.

**TECHNOLOGY LEARNING CHECK**
Complete TLC 13.6 to review what you have learned from this section about how music and art teachers can develop their knowledge and skills in technology integration.

The following questions may be used either for in-class, small-group discussions or may be used to initiate discussions in blogs or online discussion boards:

1. Digital rights management (DRM) is a term used to describe the use of technologies that limit what a person can do with downloaded content after they buy it. DRM prevents users from copying, printing, and altering the content or saving it to other formats. Music distributors maintain that DRM is necessary in order to fight copyright infringement and help copyright holders maintain artistic control and ensure they make money from future purchases. However, many people object to DRM, saying that they should have the right to do what they want with content they have legitimately purchased. Research the opinions on each side of this controversy and identify arguments that can be made for each side. How would DRM affect music teachers and their students?

2. Using software to manipulate images has long been possible, but it is becoming increasingly problematic in a number of settings. In his 2008 article "Journals Find Many Images in Research Are Faked," Young reported an upsurge in the number of research reports with doctored images. The 2013 World Press Photo of the Year, an image of a burial in Gaza, was denounced as being a composite of several images. However, the *Huffington Post* reported that after careful examination by a team of experts, it was concluded that the photo was "real." The photographer told the *Huffington Post* that the photo was not a composite, but that he had used software to improve its quality. What does it mean to "photoshop" an image? What guidelines should students be taught about how someone should and should not be able to use technology to alter a photograph presented to the public?

## Chapter **13** Summary

**The following is a summary of the main points covered in this chapter.**

1. **A Rationale for Teaching Arts in the Information Age.** Four parts of the justification for including art and music in school curriculum are: expanded modes of expression; literacies for an information age; creative approaches to modern problems; and arts as aesthetic balance.

2. **Issues and challenges in Music Instruction.** These include issues such as the changing definition for music literacy; the need to train teachers to meet music standards; problems with illegal downloading of music; the intersection of popular music, technology, and music instruction; and the music director as small business administrator.

3. **Integration Strategies for Music Education.** Strategies include:
   - Support for music composition and production through using sequencers, notation, and vocal processing software.
   - Support for music performance with notation software.
   - Support for self-paced learning and practice with instructional software to help students learn new skills (tutorials) or practice skills introduced by a teacher (drill and practice).
   - Support for teaching music history with online databases, electronic books, online journals, archived and current newspaper articles, audio and MIDI files, video clips, out-of-print books, and online discussion groups.
   - Support for interdisciplinary strategies through multimedia-based research projects, creating music or video footage of school events, and the study of the science of music.

4. **Issues and challenges in Art Instruction.** These include issues such as funding for art instruction, ethical issues associated with the use of images and other materials, issues involved in accessing images used in art instruction, and the challenge of meeting standards in arts instruction.

5. **Integration Strategies for Art Instruction.** Strategies include:
   - Accessing online art examples for classroom use.
   - Using teaching examples and materials in presentation software.
   - Producing and manipulating digitized images with software.
   - Supporting graphic design and 3-D modeling with animal and image manipulation software.
   - Supporting student development of publications.

- Virtual field trips to art museums.
- Creating movies as an art form with digital cameras movie-editing software.
- Sharing students' creative and research works in various online formats.

6. Teaching Music and Art Teachers to Integrate Technology. Teachers can begin by consulting the rubrics provided in this chapter to measure their own growth in music and art technology integration. After that, they may review issues and challenges in music and art instruction and use chapter resources to learn technology integration strategies they can use to address the issues and challenges.

# TECHNOLOGY INTEGRATION **WORKSHOP**

## 1. APPLY WHAT YOU LEARNED

To apply the concepts and skills you've read about throughout this chapter, go to the Chapter 13 Technology Application Activity.

## 2. TECHNOLOGY INTEGRATION LESSON PLANNING: PART 1—EVALUATING AND CREATING LESSON PLANS

Complete the following exercise using the sample lesson plans found on any lesson planning site that you find on the Internet.

**a.** Locate lesson ideas—Identify three lesson plans that focus on any of the tools or strategies you learned about in this chapter. For example:

- Using sequencers and software for music composition and production, music performance, self-paced learning and practice, teaching music history, or interdisciplinary strategies.
- Accessing art examples for classroom use, using teaching examples and materials, producing and manipulating digitized images, supporting graphic design and 3-D modeling, supporting desktop publishing with graphics, taking virtual field trips to art museums, creating movies as an art form, and sharing students' creative and research works.

**b.** Evaluate the lessons—Use the Technology Lesson Plan Evaluation Checklist to evaluate each of the lessons you found.

**c.** Create your own lesson—After you have reviewed and evaluated some sample lessons, create one of your own using a lesson plan format of your choice (or one your instructor gives you). Be sure the lesson focuses on one of the technologies or strategies discussed in this chapter.

## 3. TECHNOLOGY INTEGRATION LESSON PLANNING: PART 2—IMPLEMENTING THE TIP MODEL

Review how to implement the TIP model in your classroom by doing the following activities with the lesson you created in the Technology Integration Lesson Planning exercise above.

**a.** Describe the Phase 1—Planning activities you would do to use this lesson in your classroom:

- What is the relative advantage of using the technology(ies) in this lesson?
- Do you have resources and skills you need to carry it out?

**b.** Describe the Phase 2—Implementation activities you would do to use this lesson in your classroom:

- What are the objectives of the lesson plan?
- How will you assess your students' accomplishment of the objectives?
- What integration strategies are used in this lesson plan?
- How would you prepare the learning environment?

**c.** Describe the Phase 3—Evaluation/Revision activities you would do to use this lesson in your classroom: What strategies and/or instruments would you use to evaluate the success of this lesson in your classroom in order to determine revision needs?

**d.** Add lesson descriptors—Create descriptors for your new lesson (e.g., grade level, content and topic areas, technologies used, ISTE standards, 21st Century Learning standards).

**e.** Save your new lesson—Save your lesson plan with all its descriptors and TIP model notes.

## 4. FOR YOUR TEACHING PORTFOLIO

Add the following to your Teaching Portfolio:

- Reflections on Hot Topic Debate.
- Summary notes from the Collaborate, Discuss, Reflect activity.
- Lesson plan evaluations, lesson plans, and products you created above.
- Your *Apply What You Learned* Product from Activity 1.

Derrick Mears and M. D. Roblyer

# 14

# Teaching and Learning with Technology in Health and Physical Education

## Learning Outcomes

After reading this chapter and completing the learning activities, you should be able to:

1. Identify implications for technology integration of each current issue faced by health and physical education teachers. (ISTE Standards•T 4, 5)

2. Select technology integration strategies that can meet various needs for instruction in health and physical education. (ISTE Standards•T 2, 5)

3. Design a strategy for how to build teacher knowledge and skills in technology integration for health or physical education. (ISTE Standards•T 5)

Vladgrin/Shutterstock

# TECHNOLOGY INTEGRATION IN ACTION DEVELOPING A PERSONAL FITNESS AND NUTRITION PLAN

GRADE LEVELS: 9–12 • CONTENT AREA/TOPIC: Biology, health, physical education, technology • LENGTH OF TIME: Three weeks

## PHASE 1   ANALYSIS OF LEARNING AND TEACHING NEEDS

Horst Petzold/Shutterstock

### Step 1: Determine relative advantage.

Mr. Martinez, a high school health/physical education teacher, was concerned that data from national studies of physical activity and nutrition have indicated that the majority of high school students do not participate in adequate levels of physical activity, and many struggle to make appropriate nutritional choices. To address his concerns, he talked to a biology teacher and technology education (TE) teacher in his school about an interdisciplinary project that would meet academic learning requirements for courses in physical education, health, biology, and technology. They decided that the project would have more impact if it could be presented in the form of instructional video and involve self-analysis. Video would allow the content to be presented easily in a visually compelling format and serve as a resource for future classes. Self-analysis would also give students a basis for making informed personal choices concerning physical activity and nutrition.

The teachers decide to use a combination of physical activity monitoring devices, Web-based applications, and video design for the project. Students will apply knowledge of the musculoskeletal system and nutrition gained from the biology course in conjunction with exercise program design principles learned in physical education to design, choreograph, and record a 10-minute exercise video during their technology class. Mr. Martinez plans to use physical activity simulations to increase students' understanding of fitness and nutritional concepts as well as pedometers to monitor students' physical activity levels, activity intensity, and calories burned over a two-week period. In addition, he will have students use the MyFitnessPal website or mobile application to record and track their progress and document caloric intake and nutrient values.

### Step 2: Review required resources and skills.

Mr. Martinez has good background knowledge of technology interventions for health and physical education. He has been a leader in implementing physical activity monitoring devices and using Web applications to enhance student learning. However, he still searches for ways to connect and integrate his subject with other content areas. The technology teacher is a relatively new practitioner with limited knowledge of health, physical education, or biology curriculum, but is eager to explore ways to assist other teachers with integrating technology in their classrooms. The biology teacher has extensive teaching experience but is just beginning to explore the integration of technology into courses. All three teachers, therefore, saw this project as a great opportunity to improve instruction and develop their own teaching skills.

In order to familiarize the biology teacher and technology teacher with the content-specific technology in physical education, Mr. Martinez issued the other two teachers an activity monitor to wear as they went through the project to facilitate their knowledge of their use. He also introduced them to the MyFitnessPal website and mobile application the students would be using to track and monitor their dietary intakes. The biology teacher provided an overview of the specific content related to the musculoskeletal system and nutrition that would be presented as part of the biology curriculum, and the technology teacher provided training to the other two teachers on the software that would be used to develop the exercise videos, including iMovie from Apple and Camtasia Studio from TechSmith.

### Step 3: Decide on objectives and assessments.

The teachers decided on three outcomes and assessments:

Outcome: Development of exercise routine instructional video.
Objective: Students will demonstrate audio/video production and collaboration skills by choreographing and producing an instructional exercise performance video, achieving at least an 85% rubric score.
Assessment: Student learning will be assessed using a rubric for components of the instructional video and collaboration skills.

Outcome: Knowledge of the function of the musculoskeletal system and nutritional concepts.
Objective: All students will demonstrate knowledge of the structure and function of the musculoskeletal system and nutritional concepts by achieving at least 90% on a written assessment of content knowledge.
Assessment: Series of questions reviewing musculoskeletal system content presented in instructional sessions.

Outcome: Personal fitness and nutritional levels
Objective: Students will achieve at least an 85% on their plan with specific and appropriate recommendations for lifestyle changes, exercises, and eating habits.
Assessment: Rubric to assess appropriateness of activity levels and plan details.

### Step 4: Design integration strategies.

The three teachers agreed on the following sequence of instruction and activities:

- Week 1: Assign the project and collect information. In each class, the teacher describes and discusses the requirements for the project and the learning activities that will take place.
  Biology class: Assign readings and hold class discussions about body systems. To review concepts, use assignment sheets for the InnerBody Works website and the 3D Muscle System Pro and iMuscle (online and/or mobile applications) to assist students in selecting appropriate exercises for each muscle group.
  Physical Education/Health class: Show the video *Personal Fitness: Looking Good/Feeling Good* (Kendall-Hunt). Review concepts about diet and exercise. Introduce activity monitors and the online MyFitnessPal application for recording and tracking data from exercise sessions. Students begin daily recording their activity levels and dietary intake utilizing application.
  Technology class: The teacher works with the whole class to design and choreograph the exercise videos and then forms small groups with each group given the task of developing a video.

- Week 2: Prepare information and materials.
  Biology class: The teacher assists as students finish working on their simulation assignments and as they take notes and gather materials to answer the biology and nutrition questions.
  Physical Education/Health class: Students continue to engage in their physical activity simulations monitoring and tracking their data on their pedometers. They also document and record their caloric intake for week two of the project and begin to analyze their results and prepare fitness plans using health-related fitness software (Mohnsen, 2013).
  Technology class: The small groups work on video production techniques and learning the video editing software.

- Week 3: Prepare and display video products.
  Technology class: The small groups storyboard their videos and prepare scripts based on information obtained from their study of systems and selection of exercises. They complete work on their videos and edit them as needed. Students present their videos to each of the classes, and teachers use their checklists and rubrics to assess the work.
  Physical Education/Health Class: Students develop their health-related fitness plans based on the results of their activity and caloric intake tracking from the two-week simulation.

### Step 5: Prepare instructional environment.

The teachers checked out the software and videos from the media center and gathered assignment sheets to be used with them. Each teacher prepared copies of the rubrics and checklists. The TE teacher agreed to put these on the website so that students can look at them online. The biology teacher placed simulations at the computer lab and scheduled times for it. Mr. Martinez coordinated which students can work in pairs or small groups and prepared materials to communicate this information to the students.

## PHASE 3 POST-INSTRUCTION ANALYSIS AND REVISIONS

### Step 6: Analyze results.

After they completed the unit, the three teachers reviewed the exercise videos, looked at summary data from the checklists and rubrics, and discussed how the activities progressed.

### Step 7: Make revisions.

The teachers agreed that the project worked well and discussed how they might share class time in the future to make the work easier to coordinate. They also found that some groups took more time with script writing than was originally planned, so their videos took more than a week to complete; this would need to be built into the plan for next time.

## CHAPTER 14 BIG IDEAS OVERVIEW

Before you begin reading the rest of this chapter, listen to the Chapter 14 Big Ideas Overview. It will give you a two-minute audio overview of main concepts to look for and help prepare you to work through information and exercises to achieve this chapter's outcomes.

## ISSUES AND CHALLENGES IN PHYSICAL AND HEALTH EDUCATION

Increasing evidence indicates that the health-related behaviors that children and adolescents choose to adopt can have an impact on their health and well-being as adults (Biro & Wein, 2010). It is estimated that fewer than 30% of students participate in recommended levels of physical activity and nearly 14% are considered sedentary. Only one-half of U.S. students attend physical education classes; only 31.5% attend daily. Over 30% of U.S. students use computers and watch television more than three hours per day, sedentary activities that have been suggested to contribute to childhood obesity. Currently, it is estimated that 13% of adolescents are considered obese and over 15% overweight (Centers for Disease Control and Prevention, 2012a).

These statistics are more an indication of the U.S. population overall. As of 2010, there was not a state in the country with less than 20% of its population classified as obese (Centers for Disease Control and Prevention, 2010b), and statistics have indicated that obese children are more likely to become obese adults (Biro & Wein, 2010). Because strong evidence exists that participation in health and physical education can facilitate healthy behavioral choices, many schools are trying to find ways to engage all students in school-related physical education and integrate health and physical education content across the curriculum. As the chapter-opening example shows, technologies are available that can help teachers inform and empower students to make appropriate health choices. In addition, new gaming technologies are integrating entertainment with activity requiring players to actively participate in the games challenges. Due to the unique environment of health and physical education, K–12 teachers in these and related areas face vastly different challenges than other subject areas when integrating technology. These issues will be further discussed in the sections that follow.

## Instructional Time and Quality Physical Education Programs

Appropriate physical education courses are those that have a clear learning sequence and are taught by certified professionals who focus upon developing student skills and knowledge to help students become physically literate (American Alliance for Health, Physical Education, Recreation, and Dance, 2013; National Association for Sport and Physical Education, 2012; American Heart Association, 2012). Various demands placed on schools are having an impact on the instructional priority of physical education and the ability of schools to offer programs that meet these outcomes. In some areas, the status of physical education in public schools is improving. There has been a slight increase since 2010 in the number of middle schools nationally requiring physical education courses. Currently, nearly 85% of elementary schools have state mandates for physical education. However, requirements for high school physical education have shown a 4% decrease, with fewer states requiring physical education courses to be completed for graduation.

The number of instructional minutes offered by schools varies widely ranging from 30–150 minutes per week at the elementary level to between 45 and 225 minutes at middle and high school levels (National Association for Sport and Physical Education, 2012). Over 64% of school districts allow students to substitute other activities for physical education and over half allow students to waive coursework entirely (National Association for Sport and Physical Education, 2012; American Heart Association, 2012). These trends seem in contrast with current initiatives. The "Let's Move" campaign spearheaded by First Lady Michelle Obama refocused attempts to improve physical education and nutrition programs in public schools (White House Task Force on Childhood Obesity, 2010). The American Academy of Pediatrics, the U.S Department of Health and Human Services, the U.S. Department of Education, President's Council on Physical Fitness and Sport, and the Centers for Disease Control and Prevention (CDC) have indicated the need for more physical education in public schools. In recent years, instructional time for physical education was reduced in public schools to provide additional instruction for other academic subjects with the goal of increasing student test scores (Center on Educational Policy, 2007; Trost & Van Der Mars, 2009). However, the results of this movement may have not been successful. Results from the Trends in International Mathematics and Science Study (TIMSS) have shown a decrease in the performance of U.S. students in math and science, dropping from 19th to 37th place and from 18th to 35th place, respectively, in the rankings of countries in the last 10 years (National Center for Educational Statistics, 2008). The trend of decreasing physical education time in schools is also in contrast to the growing body of research showing positive associations between school-based physical education programs and academic achievement (Centers for Disease Control and Prevention, 2010a; Center on Educational Policy, 2007; Trost & Van Der Mars, 2009).

## The Link Between Physical Inactivity and Obesity

It has been estimated that childhood obesity levels could reach the 30% level by 2030 if current trends continue (Wang, Beydoun, Laiang, Caballero, & Kumanyika, 2008). The treatment of obesity-related conditions has placed a huge burden on the U.S. medical system, with an estimated $344 billion dollars to be spent on its treatment by 2018 and projected to attribute to approximately 21% of health care spending (United Health Foundation, American Public Health Association, & Partnership for Prevention, 2009). An increasingly greater proportion of these dollars are beginning to be spent on treatment of conditions in children and adolescents. The rates of obesity among children ages 2–19 reached 17% by the time Ogden, Carroll, Curtin, Lamb, and Flegal wrote about the problem. Data from the Pediatric Nutrition Surveillance reveals that obesity levels for children under the age of five reached 12% by 2012 (Dalenius, Boreland, Smith, Polhamus, & Grummer-Strawn, 2012).

One cannot discuss childhood obesity without considering the technology use of children and the potential contribution it makes to sedentary behaviors. By the time today's group of students enter kindergarten, they are spending five to nine hours per day using some form of technology, with the average middle school student using technology forms for over 15 hours per day through multitasking activities (Mears, 2012; Rosen, 2010). In addition, it has been estimated that 25% of adolescents use a computer and/or play video games for over three hours per day (Centers for Disease Control & Prevention, 2010c; Hersey & Jordan, 2007; Mears, 2012).

Though technology use has not been identified as the primary cause of childhood obesity, it has been determined to have a potential effect related to two key factors. The first factor is that screen time, be it using a computer, watching television, or playing video games, is replacing more active pursuits in which the child could engage. The second factor is that children and adolescents have been shown to consume more calories while engaging in technology use and tend to make poor food choices (Crespo et al., 2001; Gortmaker et al., 1996; Mears, 2012; Robinson, 1999).

However, technology integration can also be effective for enhancing physical education. The Society of Health and Physical Educators (SHAPE) (formally known as the National Association of Sport and Physical Education, NASPE) developed appropriate practice guidelines to ensure technology is effectively integrated into physical education settings. These guidelines indicate that technology: 1) can be an effective tool for enhancing instruction; 2) should not replace but provide a supplement to instruction; 3) should provide opportunities for all students to receive equal exposure and benefits to the technology; 4) can be a valuable tool for maintaining student data and documenting progress (Mears, Hansen, Fine, Lawler & Mason, 2009). Thus, even though technology use has been postulated as a potential contributor to childhood obesity, it can effectively enhance instruction and provide rich learning experiences for students in physical education settings.

## Accuracy of Internet Information on Health and Physical Education

When young people search for information related to health and physical education topics, they must have a sufficient level of technological literacy to know how to locate, evaluate, and use the information obtained. The National Health Education Standards indicate that students should be able to identify valid health information, products, and services, and for today's "iGeneration" a great deal of this information comes via the Internet (Joint Committee on National Health Education Standards, 2007; Rosen, 2010). The Common Core State Standards reinforce this need indicating that students should be able to use the Internet for obtaining information when producing and publishing writing as well as for collaboration (Common Core State Standards Inititative, 2012). Because anyone can post anything on the Web, students need to become good consumers of health and fitness products and information. Specifically, they must be able to differentiate between accurate and inaccurate information. Without this ability, they are unsuspecting consumers of misleading and potentially harmful advice.

## Addressing Physical Education and Health Standards

School physical education has come far from its early emphasis on physical training and calisthenics. The subject area has evolved into an academic discipline with the goal of producing "physically literate" individuals. Students who demonstrate physical literacy have learned the skills to participate, know the benefits of participating, and value physical activity and its contribution to living a healthy lifestyle (American Alliance for Health, Physical Education Recreation, and Dance, 2013). This shift is evident with the 2013 release of the new *National Standards and Grade Level Outcomes for K-12 Physical Education*. These provide a sequential curricular focus for what students should know and be able to do in physical education and outline student learning outcomes in cognitive, psychomotor, and affective domains (American Alliance for Health, Physical Education Recreation, and Dance, 2013). This has been coupled with the release of *Appropriate Practice Guidelines* that outline acceptable instructional practice parameters for practitioners and the *Physical Education Teacher Evaluation Tool* for school administrators (National Association for Sport and Physical Education, 2007, 2009). A system of standardized assessments entitled "PE Metrics" has also provided extensive guidance for K-12 practitioners for evaluating student learning (National Association for Sport and Physical Education, 2008, 2010). The National Health Education Standards (Joint Committee on National Health Education Standards, 2007) have also established a scope and sequence for health education focusing upon the development of health literacy—the capacity of individuals to obtain, interpret, and understand basic health information along with the competence to use such information to enhance health.

## Handling Controversial Health Issues

Coordinated school health education programs consist of eight components: health education; physical education; health services; nutrition services; counseling, psychological, and social services; healthy and safe school environment; health promotion for staff; and family and community involvement (Centers for Disease Control and Prevention, 2014b). At the core of this program is a curriculum aligned to the National Health Education Standards (Joint Committee on National Health Education Standards, 2007), which outlines curricular content strands for K–12 health education programs. These consist of content related to helping students understand ways to promote their personal health and prevent disease; understand the influence that family, peers, culture, media, and technology have on health behaviors; develop skills to access valid health information, products, and services; develop and use interpersonal communication skills to enhance health and avoid health risks; use goal setting skills to enhance health; practice health-enhancing behaviors and avoid risks; and advocate for personal, family, and community health. At the core of this program is a recommendation for adequate time and effective instruction provided by instructors who are knowledgeable about health education curriculum and have effective instructional strategies to facilitate student learning (Centers for Disease Control and Prevention, 2014a).

The variability between state and national policies and perceptions of the controversial nature of some subject matter has proven a challenge for health education programs. Over the years, special interest groups have pressed for either the inclusion of particular content strands or the elimination of topics based upon the group's individual moral and/or value systems. A topic that has faced substantial scrutiny is human sexuality. It is currently estimated that 22 states require sexual education in schools, with 20 of those states mandating instruction in sexuality as well as HIV/AIDS. Policies for states vary widely, making the adoption of the National Health Education Standards difficult (National Conference of State Legislatures, 2013). Topics such as rape, suicide, drugs use and abuse, violence, and character education have also been questioned. Health educators are constantly faced with the challenge of how to provide valid and reliable content information to students while staying within the legal parameters of their state or individual school districts. Directing students to valid Web-based sources can assist in this area.

**TECHNOLOGY LEARNING CHECK**

Complete TLC 14.1 to review what you have learned from this section about issues in health and physical education that determine how technology is integrated.

## TECHNOLOGY INTEGRATION STRATEGIES FOR HEALTH AND PHYSICAL EDUCATION

As discussed previously, the high degree of technology use by children adolescents has been identified as a potential contributing factor to sedentary behavior and the level of childhood obesity (Hersey & Jordan, 2007; Mears, 2012; Rosen, 2010). However, technology can also enrich instruction in health and physical education. In order to effectively address the changing learning styles of a new generation of learners entering today's public schools, physical educators must integrate technology throughout the curriculum (Mears, 2012b; Rosen, 2010). Technology can enhance instruction by providing strategies for assisting in the development of physical fitness, improving motor skill performance, supporting students' development of rhythmic movement skills, helping students assess and enhance personal their personal development, helping students obtain valid health information, and supporting interdisciplinary instruction. Table 14.1 summarizes some potential strategies and benefits of integrating technology into health and physical education, as well as resources to assist the practitioner with implementation. Technology Integration Example 14.1 also describes how these strategies can be implemented in a classroom.

**TABLE 14.1** Summary of Technology Integration Strategies for Physical Education and Health Education

| Technology Integration Strategies | Benefits | Sample Resources and Activities |
|---|---|---|
| Supporting improved physical fitness | • Physical activity monitoring devices help provide data for analyzing, monitoring, and improving fitness<br>• Exercise equipment offers exercise options while providing feedback on performance<br>• Computer-based fitness planning and portfolios and nutrition programs help students set health and fitness goals and track achievement<br>• Synchronization of computer-based applications with physical activity–monitoring devices integrate nutrition with physical activity interventions<br>• Exergaming provides low-intensity fitness development and skill acquisition | • Heart rate monitors<br>• Blood pressure devices<br>• Pedometers/Accelerometers<br>• Spirometers<br>• Treadmills<br>• Stair steppers<br>• Stationary bikes<br>• Portfolio programs and websites<br>• Nutritional analysis programs such as DINE Healthy (http://www.dinesystems.com), FitBit, Jawbone<br>• Nintendo Wii, Sony PS3 iMove; Xbox Kinect |
| Developing and improving motor skill performance | • Tablets assist with monitoring students' progress in the field<br>• Recording and analyzing performance via digital video<br>• Instructional video providing exercise performance guidance and/or models of performance | • Tablet PCs<br>• Digital video cameras Ubersense and CoachMy Video mobile applications<br>• Video editing software<br>• SportsCAD motion analysis program (http://www.sportscad .com/)<br>• Dartfish Video Analysis software |
| Assessing student learning in the context of teaching | • Allows students and teachers immediate feedback on performance; allows assessment of all students to be performed efficiently without reducing time for the participation in physical activities<br>• Allows teachers to record and manage student data quickly and easily; allows immediate feedback to students on performance | • PollEverywhere.com or TopHat.com allows teachers to design and assess student learning with polls and short-response and multiple-choice questions through the use of smartphones, laptops or tablet devices<br>• Student response systems provide student remote controls for answering questions and track data using learning analytics<br>• Google Forms for assessment<br>• Wufoo.com form builder with Pico mobile application<br>• Numbers or Microsoft Excel data sheets |
| Supporting student work in dance | • Streaming video, mobile applications, MP3 players, digital video recorders, and other types of technology can enhance dance instruction and the development of chorography | • Mobile apps such as Tap, Salsa, Ballet for Beginners, Dance Choreography |
| Shaping students' beliefs and interactions related to physical activity | • Instructional video via the Web can provide prompts to facilitate students' writing and discussions about healthy behaviors to assist with meeting Common Core State Standards in English and Language Arts<br>• Websites such as the ePals Global Community offer ways for students in various locations to do joint projects on health issues | • KidsHealth website (look for movies under Kids and Teenagers buttons)<br>• ePals Global Community |

*(Continued)*

## TABLE 14.1 Summary of Technology Integration Strategies for Physical Education and Health Education (continued)

| Technology Integration Strategies | Benefits | Sample Resources and Activities |
|---|---|---|
| Helping students assess and enhance personal health | • Websites offer teenagers compelling tutorials to increase social-emotional learning<br>• Nutritional analysis programs such as DINE Healthy or mobile applications such as MyFitnessPal and Fat 2 Fit assist students with assessing dietary intake and goal setting | • Ripple Effects<br>• DINE Healthy nutritional analysis software<br>• Fat 2 Fit App calculates body mass index, basal metabolic rate, and other calculations to assist with tracking and goal setting |
| Helping students obtain valid health information | • Websites offer up-to-date information to aid student research on health issues<br>• Instructional media offers a variety of formats to match any student's interests and preferred learning format | • KidsHeath website<br>• Core Learning Family Health and Health for Kids series (under Health on menu)<br>• BARN DVD series on health topics |
| Influencing health behaviors | • Videos and collaborative projects allow students to see health issues in real-life settings and view models of healthy behaviors<br>• Internet sites provide helpful information to children and teens | • Webquests (search on addiction and other keywords)<br>• KidsHealth website (look for movies under Kids and Teenagers buttons) |
| Supporting interdisciplinary instruction | • Shows links between physical education/health topics and other content areas<br>• Sources to connect physical education to Common Core State Standards | • Technology Integration Example 14.1 Society of Health and Physical Educators webinar series |
| Offering physical education and health education online | • Provides materials to support flexible learning schedules<br>• Offers information in a highly visual format | • Distance courses<br>• WikisCourse Management Systems—Edmodo, Canvas, Blackboard<br>• Vodcasts |

# TECHNOLOGY INTEGRATION

## Example 14.1

TITLE: Interdisciplinary Activities for Physical Education Concepts

CONTENT AREA/TOPIC: Physical education in content areas: mathematics, biology, history, geography

GRADE LEVELS: 6–8

ISTE STANDARDS•S: Standard 2—Communication and Collaboration; Standard 4—Critical Thinking, Problem Solving, and Decision Making; Standard 6—Technology Operations and Concepts

CCSS: Mathematics-6.NS.B.3,—7.RP.A.3,—Language Arts-RI.6.1,—W.7.2,—W.8.4—(This is a sampling of potential standards and not all inclusive.)

DESCRIPTION: Technology-based strategies can help teachers integrate other content areas into physical education to create interdisciplinary lessons. Students can monitor and evaluate progress towards personal fitness goals and achievements as part of electronic portfolios; analyze and graph data from their use of heart monitors and/or pedometers (mathematics); log participation and skill acquisition scores achieved while participating in exergaming; use tablets to video record and analyze individual and peer performance, develop instructional video projects, read QR codes to complete exercise circuits, or participate in orienteering or geocaching activities; view videos that demonstrate model performances, various sports, and other motor activities to learn more about how the body works (biology); use the Internet to research sports and physical activities in other countries and historical periods (history).

SOURCE: Based on Mohnsen, B. (2000). Vaughn, Nekomi, and Luis: What they were doing in middle school physical education. *Learning and Leading with Technology, 27*(5), 22–27. Also see Mears, 2010, 2012a; Mears & Hansen, 2010; Witherspoon, 2012.

## FIGURE 14.1 Heart Rate Monitor

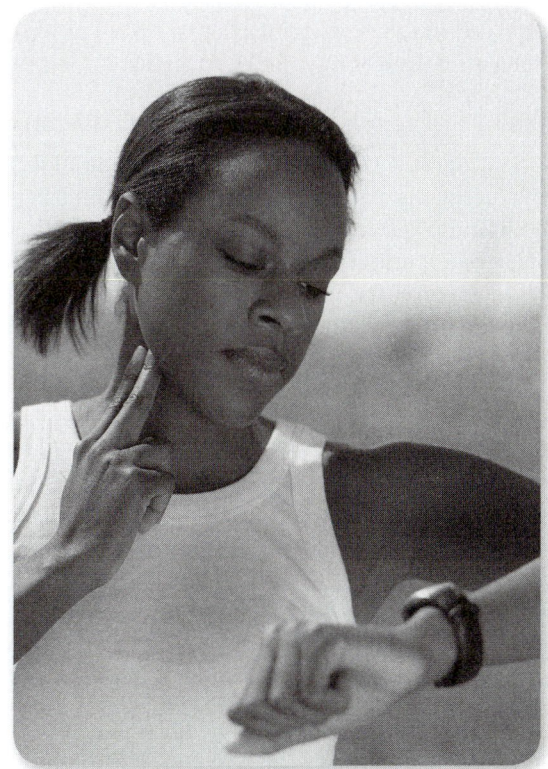

Russell Sadur/Dorling Kindersley, Ltd

## FIGURE 14.2 Example Pedometer

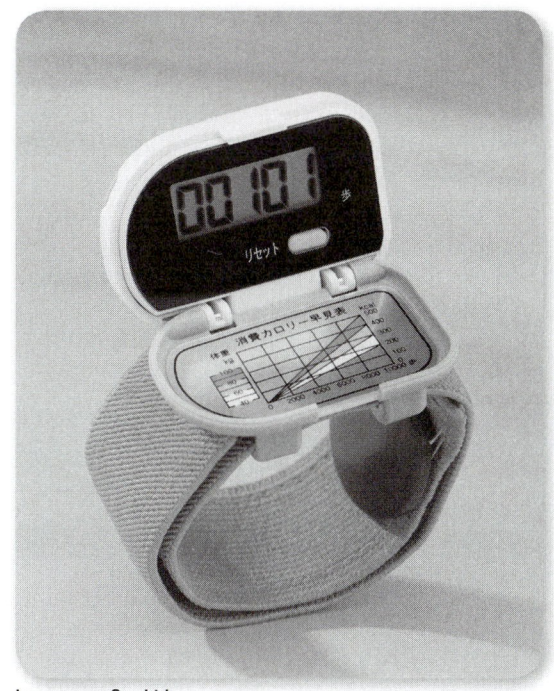

Imagemore Co., Ltd

# Supporting Improved Physical Fitness

Several technologies support interventions to assist and motivate youngsters to increase their levels of physical activity. Several of these strategies are described here.

### Physical activity monitoring devices.
Mears (2010) reviews devices to monitor body functions during sport and exercise activities. These include heart rate monitors (see Figure 14.1), **accelerometers,** which are devices for measuring rate of acceleration, and **pedometers** (see Figure 14.2), which are devices that count the number of steps one takes, calories burned, and exercise intensity minutes (New Lifestyles, 2013). Heart rate monitors are especially effective for providing students with feedback as to whether they are in their target heart rate zones and benefiting from the training effect for cardiorespiratory endurance (Nichols, Davis, McCord, Schmidt, & Slezak, 2009). Other monitoring devices students can use include electronic **blood pressure devices** (to monitor blood pressure), **body composition analyzers** (devices to determine the percent of body fat), and **spirometers** (devices to measure lung volume). Each device measures a different aspect of health and fitness, allowing students to use their own bodies for data collection and analysis.

### Exercising with equipment and monitoring software.
Technology devices and software are available to help analyze, monitor, and improve fitness. Exercise equipment, such as treadmills, stair steppers, and stationary bikes, are all technology devices designed to improve fitness. Used in combination with (usually built-in) monitors, these devices can show students the results of their efforts in terms of heart rate, speed, and power. Applications available on smartphones or Web-connected MP3 players allow for the use of GPS technology to track distance traveled or provide auditory cues for intervals.

### Fitness plans and portfolios.
Students also can be put in charge of their own learning along with the development of fitness goals and plans. For example, the Health-Related Fitness Tutorial/Portfolio (Bonnie's Fitware) guides students through the five areas of health-related fitness: flexibility, muscular strength, muscular endurance, body composition, and cardiorespiratory endurance. The electronic portfolio portion of this software allows students to enter fitness plans, exercises, drawings or video clips, journal entries, caloric input/output, and fitness scores, which are then analyzed by the software. **Nutritional analysis programs** (software that analyzes calorie intake and monitors portions of required food groups), fitness analysis programs, and spreadsheet applications can also be used to calculate and graph individual nutrition and fitness goals. These programs now integrate with many physical activity monitoring devices allowing the merging of nutrition data with caloric expenditure data to facilitate personal fitness development.

### Exergaming.
Mears and Hansen (2009) say that **exergaming** is "video games that provide physical activity or exercise through interactive play" (p. 29). Popular games such as Dance Dance Revolution and game systems such as Nintendo Wii, Xbox Kinect, and Sony PS3 with the iMove interface require participants to be physically active and engaged (see Figure 14.3). Active gaming is seeking to replace the more traditional video games, which use merely a finger/thumb activated controller, and provide an avenue for physical activity interventions. Many new game forms are being merged with exercise machines such as "exerbikes" or "exersteppers" which use traditional fitness machines with gaming. While exergaming will not provide a replacement for quality instruction in physical education, studies have shown that it can have a positive impact on motivation to engage in physical activity (Cordero, 2013; Shayne, Fogel, Miltenberger, & Koehler, 2012). Many physical education educators are beginning to find it to be a useful addition to their repertoire of tools (Hicks & Higgins, 2010). Companies are also developing

## FIGURE 14.3 Example of Exergaming

Shutterstock

commercial grade machines designed to allow multiple players to simultaneously participate. Questions remain, however, about how to appropriately integrate exergaming into the physical education curriculum (see the Hot Topic for Debate feature).

### Exercise and sport opportunities for students with special needs.

The Special Olympics has long been a way to meet the needs of students whose disability requires modifications and adaptations be provided to facilitate their participation in sports and activities. Information on how to join this program is on the Special Olympics website shown in the Adapting for Special Needs feature. Many specialized pieces of hardware and software allow the practitioner to modify instruction to meet the individual needs of students. Mobile apps such as Tap To Talk (Assistyx, 2013) allow students who have oral communication disabilities to communicate via tablet devices. Multiple research inquiries are exploring the concept of exergaming as a form of therapeutic intervention for children with disabilities as well (Foulds, Adamovich,Gordon & Okita, 2010; Gasperetti et al., 2010; Hilton, et al., 2014; Morelli, Folmer, Foley & Lieberman, 2011; Taylor, McCormick, Shawis, Impson, & Griffin, 2011).

## Developing and Improving Motor Skill Performance

Technology-based strategies are available to help students develop their motor skills. Types of strategies include those for monitoring, providing feedback, and self-analyzing performance. These include the use of video recording applications such as Ubersense and CoachMyVideo, which allow immediate review of skill performance and annotation. The use of digital video recorders combined with video cameras can also allow the student to perform a skill and watch immediate looped feedback and assess their performance using teacher designed scoring guides and rubrics.

### Monitoring performance.

Asking students to set personal goals and monitor progress is motivational to the student but can be a difficult management task for the physical educator. Tablets can assist in this task by helping the physical educator organize student performance data (e.g., grades, attendance, fitness scores) (Gubacs-Collins & Juniu, 2009). The influx of tablets including the iPad and other devices is a rapidly growing trend. Tablets have been referred to as the "physical educator's new clipboard" (Nye 2010, p. 21). When combined with mobile sites and applications such as Edmodo, Wufoo, or Google Forms, the practitioner can design customized assessment instruments which can be used to record data in the context of teaching with feedback being immediate and easily accessible to the student. Digital portfolios can also put students in charge of collecting, recording, and analyzing

## Hot Topic Debate
### Should Exergaming be Included in Physical Education Programs?

*Take a position for or against (based either on your own position or one assigned to you) on the following controversial statement. Discuss it in class or on an online discussion board, blog, or wiki, as assigned by your instructor. When the discussion is complete, write a summary of the main pros and cons that you and your classmates have stated, and put the summary document in your Teacher Portfolio.*

Technology use by children and adolescents has been cited as a potential contributor to physical inactivity and resulting obesity

(Centers for Disease Control and Prevention, 2012). Interactive "exergames" like Dance Dance Revolution and gaming systems such as Nintendo Wii, X-Box Kinect, and Sony PS3 iMove are increasingly popular and have been offered as a potential avenue for accumulating physical activity (Bidiss & Irwin, 2010). However, including exergaming in physical education curriculum remains controversial. Is there evidence that shows benefits of including exergaming? Would they outweigh the negatives?

# Adapting for Special Needs

## Physical Education and Health Education

Students with disabilities require exercise just as any other student. However, in some cases, special considerations must be made for specific disabling conditions. School personnel should always coordinate physical education activities with the student's family, physician, and the child's physical therapist. Below are some resources that can be used with all students as teachers explore the intersection of fitness, health, wellness, and technology.

- Adapted Physical Education (at the PE Central website)– Provides resources for teachers on how to engage students with disabilities in adapted physical activities.
- Adapted Physical Education National Standards (at the APENS website)– Provides national standards for adapted PE.

- Centers for Disease Control (at the LifeStages topic on the CDC website)—Information on health and wellness for all ages
- Family Center on Technology and Disability (2007). Adapted physical education & AT: To play or not to play (at the FCTD website) – A comprehensive examination of the relationship between assistive technology and participation in physical education.
- Special Olympics (at the Special Olympics website)— Information on sports opportunities for kids with physical and mental disabilities

—*Contributed by Dave Edyburn*

▲ Digital portfolios can help students keep track of their nutrition and fitness goals. **John Foxx Collection/Imagestate**

▲ Videos can be helpful for analyzing students' movements in sport or dance and providing helpful feedback on how to improve their performance. **Rick Becker-Leckrone/Shutterstock**

their learning in psychomotor and cognitive domains, their fitness performance, and their social interactions.

### Providing feedback on performance.

Once students begin to practice motor skills, providing feedback becomes necessary for improving performance. Research in the field has indicated that providing students' feedback using instructional video can increase the ability to perform motor skills (Banville & Polifko, 2009). The use of video is most effective when it is shown to the student immediately after the performance, along with external verbal feedback and cues. This is where mobile applications such as Ubersense become very valuable as they allow the instructor to view video and annotate and record voice-over feedback of performance, which can be sent to the student via YouTube or other cloud-based Web storage sites. Video replay is best used with students beyond a beginner skill level. Students need some knowledge of correct skill performance in order to use the information these images provide. For students with advanced skills, replay also is useful for strategy and tactics. Video software such as Dartfish Video Analysis can be helpful for analyzing movement and giving students helpful feedback; other programs that provide similar analysis and feedback are available. Lim, Pellett, and Pellett (2009) point out that video editing software can also be used to clip parts of sequences to focus on desired movements (see free editing programs listed in the Open Source Options feature).

Video footage allows a teacher, coach, or the individual to go back and review a performance and break down stages in the skill.

### Self-assessment of student learning.

Students can also use technology for self- and peer-assessment to facilitate engagement in their learning. For example, digital video cameras can be placed at stations or students can use mobile technology such as iPad, Flip cameras, or other types of video recording devices to self and peer assess. Tablets provide the ability to record and immediately review performance. Various phases of skill performance can be recorded and students can work in small groups to identify critical features, patterns, and concepts associated with the skill. In preparation, the teacher develops a skill evaluation checklist or rubric, which evaluates the critical elements of the skill. Then students rotate through stations in small groups. For example, students can work in a group of three

# OPEN SOURCE
## OPTIONS for Health and Physical Education

| TYPES | FREE SOURCES |
|---|---|
| **Dance software** | Labanwriter: dance.osu.edu/3_research_gallery/laban_writer.html |
| **Audio/Video editing software** | Open Movie Editor: openmovieeditor.org<br>VideoPad video editing software: nchsoftware.com/software/ video.html<br>Wax video editing software: debugmode.com/wax<br>Audacity audio recording and editing software: audacity.sourceforge.net/ |
| **Free health software** | Sheppard Software health games: sheppardsoftware.com/health.htm |

with one student performing the skill, the second providing feedback using the checklist/rubric provided, and the third student recording the performance. The ability to integrate cameras with digital video recorders (which have an auto-playback function) allows students to perform the skill at one station and then self-assess at the following station by watching the video as it replays.

### Facilitating skill acquisition.

Projects can be designed to assess and assist in the development and understanding of motor skills. Motor skills are classified into movement patterns (e.g., overhand pattern, kicking pattern). Understanding the relationship between skills using the same movement pattern helps with the transfer of knowledge and motor skills from one activity to another (e.g., overhand throw to volleyball serve). Students working in small groups can compare and contrast movement patterns using video to compare the similarities and differences between the patterns. They can also use mobile applications such as Inspiration Maps (from Inspiration Software) or WhiteBoard from GreenGarStudios to diagram and present their findings from the skill comparison.

Software packages, such as Biomechanics Made Easy and SimAthlete (Bonnie's Fitware), provide reference information on the important biomechanical and motor learning concepts (e.g., goal setting, feedback, stability, force production). Biomechanics Made Easy then quizzes students on their understanding and application of the concepts, whereas SimAthlete goes a step further by asking students to create a practice plan for different athletes. The better the practice plan, the better the athlete performs during competition. Measurement in Motion (Learning in Motion) and Dart Trainer (Dartfish) take biomechanical analysis to another level by encouraging open-ended exploration. These software packages use video clips (supplied by the teacher or captured using student subjects) and allow for ease of measurement and analysis of movement performance (e.g., ball rotation, limb speed). Similar applications can be performed using mobile devices with applications such as Ubersense and CoachMyVideo, described earlier. Voice-over feedback can be sent to the student via video server networks such as YouTube or Vimeo for students to view or self-assess. All of these resources can then be placed in one location for delivery using course management systems such as Edmodo or Canvas from Instructure or on a wiki such as PBWorks, all of which provide free course management system options for K–12 teachers.

## Assessing Student Learning in the Context of Teaching

Many technology options have been recently developed that allow teachers to assess student learning in the context of teaching quickly and easily. Student response systems such as iClicker or Got It systems by Califone allow the teacher to quickly and effectively quiz every student on cognitive concepts presented during lessons. Sites such as PollEverywhere.com or TopHat.com

▲ Mobile apps allow learners to take dance instruction and practice anywhere. **Erics/Shutterstock**

allow the teacher to perform similar functions using tablets, smartphones, Wi-Fi-capable MP3 players, or computers to assess learning. Assessment can also be performed using course management systems that have exam capabilities such as Canvas or Edmodo. These systems also allow the teacher to perform learning analytics to identify gaps in student learning or performance that can be readdressed during instructional sessions.

## Supporting Students' Work in Dance

Dania, Hatziharistos, Koutsouba and Tyrovola (2011) discussed various ways technologies can assist students as they learn and practice dance movements. Web-based digital video streaming allows the merging of choreography with performance, permitting multiple practitioners to work together. YouTube has become a way for dance students to research and view models of various dances. IPods and smartphones make music private so that several students can play music individually and work on their choreography without disturbing others. Mobile applications such as Dance Choreography (Pohl, 2014), Tap, Salsa, Ballet for Beginners, and the Dance App also allow learners to take dance instruction anywhere through smartphones and tablet devices (Obaiduzzaman, 2010).

## Shaping Students' Beliefs and Interactions Related to Physical Activity

Standards four and five of the National Standards and Grade Level Outcomes for Physical Education (American Alliance for Health Physical Education Recreation and Dance, 2013) primarily address learning outcomes in the affective domain. Assessing these areas as well as providing instruction can be enhanced through the use of technology. Spreadsheets and checklists can be used with tablets to assess attributes in the context of teaching, examining variables such as attendance, punctuality, participation levels, leadership, empathy, listening and applying criticism, as well as others (Mears, 2009). Videos and online materials can also provide opportunities to assist instruction in these areas. Physical educators can use portions of applicable TV programs as prompts for journal writing. For example, prompts might ask students how they would feel if presented with the situation addressed in the recording.

Web-based tools can be an ideal medium for connecting students of various backgrounds and providing them with the opportunities for interactions related to physical education content. In today's digital world ePals or key pals are newly evolved pen pals where students can connect via email, blog, chat, or through social media such as Facebook and Twitter. They can share ideas, concerns, physical education experiences, information, written assignments, and research. Combining these interactions through course management systems such as Canvas or Edmodo creates a safe environment for student to share information versus using open content sources. By using these sites, only designated participants are given permission to access assignments that can be uploaded and exchanged for peer review, editing, and collaboration. Through these connections, they learn to accept individuals from other communities and cultures. Sites such as the ePals Global Community help teachers get started with collaborative activities. They can visit one of the sites to find other physical educators interested in teaming for class projects.

Another option to connect students with others for collaboration on personal fitness goals is MyFitnessPal, an app shown in the Top Ten Must-Have Apps for Health and Physical Education feature, or through various types of physical activity monitoring devices such as FitBit. FitBit has software and mobile applications allowing students to form collaborative connections for sharing physical activity and nutritional data with each other and establishing support groups to compare activity levels, nutritional intake, and weight loss if desired.

**Helping Students Assess and Enhance Personal Health.** When attempting to motivate individuals to change their lifestyles and adopt a wellness approach toward improving their health, information alone is not enough. Fortunately, online sites are available to guide students through the process of making changes. One of these is the Ripple Effects website,

# TECHNOLOGY INTEGRATION

## Example 14.2

**TITLE:** What's the Buzz? Exploring Concepts About Caffeine

**CONTENT AREA/TOPIC:** Health, biology

**GRADE LEVELS:** 8–12

**ISTE STANDARDS•S:** Standard 1—Creativity and Innovation; Standard 2—Communication and Collaboration; Standard 4—Critical Thinking, Problem Solving, and Decision Making; Standard 6—Technology Operations and Concepts

**CCSS:** Reading: Informational Text-Key Ideas and Details (RI.9–10.1)—Reading: Informational Text-Integration of Knowledge and Ideas (RI.9–10.8)

**DESCRIPTION:** Before the lesson begins, have students collect and bring in containers from drinks that have caffeine. Discuss how much caffeine each student has consumed in the past three days and the effect caffeine has on the human body. Read and discuss website information on the effects of caffeine (e.g., the *New York Times* online article, "A Century Later, Jury's Still Out on Caffeine Limits"). Tell the class that they will work in groups to explore how caffeine affects the body, how common it is in various consumer products, and whether its use in consumer products is regulated in any way. Then each group will be assigned a focus question and will put together a dramatic skit intended to teach their peers about their specific question. Have students use video cameras to record the skits to post on SchoolTube.

*SOURCE:* Based on concepts from "The Buzz About the Buzz: Learning How Caffeine Affects the Body," a lesson plan at the Learning Network: Teaching and Learning with the New York Times, http://learning.blogs.nytimes.com.

which offers video-based scenarios and advice on behavior issues such as bullying. The activities it provides allow students to apply their knowledge to problem-solving situations. The U.S. Department of Health and Human Services has developed several websites that provide information for kids and teens related to healthy lifestyles and refraining from unhealthy behaviors.

Many nutritional analysis programs and mobile applications are currently available. These programs (e.g., DINE Systems' DINE Healthy; ChooseMyPlate.gov; MyFitnessPal) ask the user for data on age, weight, height, gender, and amount of physical activity, and then calculate the individual's nutritional needs. The U.S. Department of Agriculture's Choose My Plate.gov resource provides various calculators as part of their SuperTracker application, which allows children and adolescents to create a profile and monitor and track dietary intake with analysis tools (United States Department Agriculture, 2013). These sites allow the user to record the types and amounts of foods eaten daily, and the programs create reports that lists the calories ingested, the nutrient values for all foods, and the total of all nutrients ingested. These reports then are used to determine if the student has met the recommended dietary allowances and whether the number of calories ingested was excessive. These programs expose poor nutritional and fitness behaviors through their analysis of daily food intake and physical activity. Appropriate menus and exercises are recommended for a healthier lifestyle. The software packages can also serve as personal trainers for fitness and nutrition. Many of these sites also have calculators that determine body mass index, basal metabolic rate, and other information to assist in determine appropriate caloric intake and nutrient content. The CDC also has launched an interactive site for children that provides education on various health topics such as disease, food and nutrition, physical activity, and safety as well as other topics. Content is presented via interactive games and video. Also see Technology Integration Example 14.2 for a useful lesson on the effects of caffeine.

Health risk assessments are another type of useful tool. These electronic questionnaires ask the user to input data regarding his or her lifestyle. Questions include height, weight, gender, age, cholesterol level, blood pressure, smoking habits, alcohol usage, physical activity habits, family medical history, nutritional information, and use of seat belts. Based on the data received, the program determines the individual's life expectancy, cardiovascular disease risk, and/or cancer risk. Some examples of these include the weight and health risk, heart attack risk assessment, and diabetes risk assessment.

## Helping Students Obtain Valid Health Information

Historically, the health education textbook has been the primary source of information and reading material in health education classes. Today, the Internet and various software packages

## FIGURE 14.4  KidsHealth Website

*Source:* © The Nemours Foundation/KidsHealth. Reprinted by permission.

## FIGURE 14.5  CDC Body and Mind Website

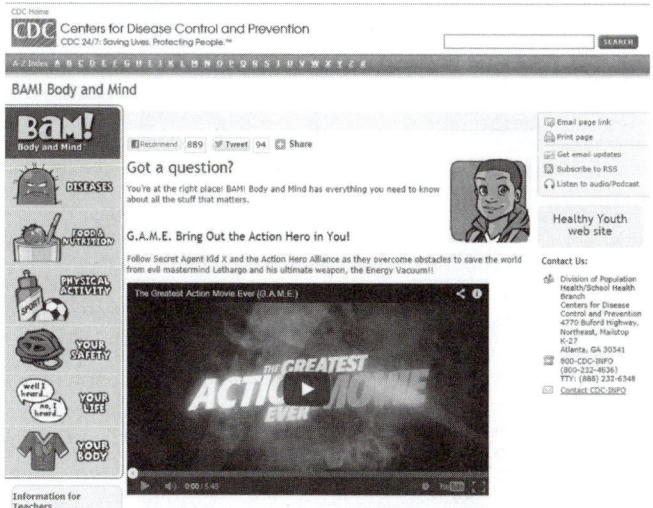

Copyright © Centers for Disease Control and Prevention, http:// www.cdc.gov/bam/

## FIGURE 14.6  From Explore Your Body Software

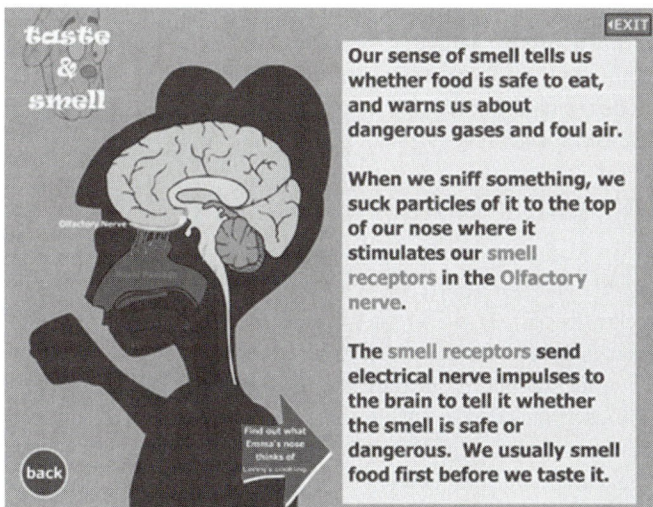

Software can help promote health awareness in young children.
*Source:* Interactive health lesson from Core Health I Course, published by Core Learning: www.core-learning.com. Reprinted by permission.

provide students with access to a rich variety of additional materials. KidsHealth (see Figure 14.4) is an example of a health-related site targeted at K–12 students. Another good source is the CDC (see Figure 14.5), which has information and materials designed for people of all ages and for special populations (see a link to the site in the Adapting for Special Needs feature). High-quality software includes the BARNS Multimedia Series I and II (Learning Multi-Systems) for middle and high school students, and the Core Learning series on health that has an appealing format and engaging activities on a variety of topics (menu items on the site include The Body, Illnesses and Injuries, Staying Healthy, Becoming an Adult, and Emotional Health; see Figure 14.6 for an example from The Body). Children and teenagers can use these and other resources to research health topics, including the side effects of commonly used medicines or symptoms of major medical illnesses.

Computer-mediated and online formats are also a good way for young people to obtain reliable information on topics that, due to their controversial nature, teachers may not be able to discuss through direct classroom instruction. For example, Goldsworthy and Schwartz (2008) describe an effective multimedia curriculum for sex education. Noar, Pierce, and Black (2010) reported a meta-analysis of studies on computer-based interventions in sex education that indicated these kinds of materials have the desired impact on attitudes and behaviors.

Buhi, Daley, Fuhrmann, and Smith (2009) say that "The Internet has become the leading source for sexual health information" (p. 101). However, as noted earlier, students need instruction on how to distinguish between accurate and inaccurate information, so these sources must be carefully vetted before teachers recommend that young people use them.

## Influencing Health Behaviors

When evaluating all of the complex issues related to health education, students frequently look for models of appropriate behavior. One way to provide these models is through working with

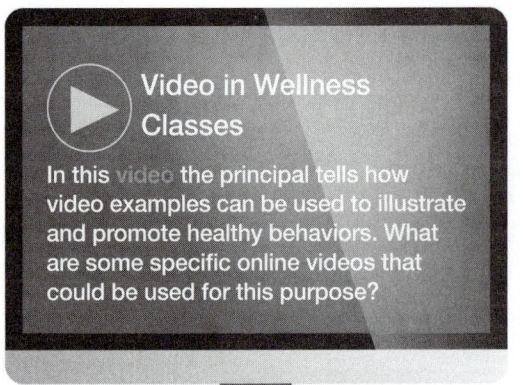

**Video in Wellness Classes**

In this *video* the principal tells how video examples can be used to illustrate and promote healthy behaviors. What are some specific online videos that could be used for this purpose?

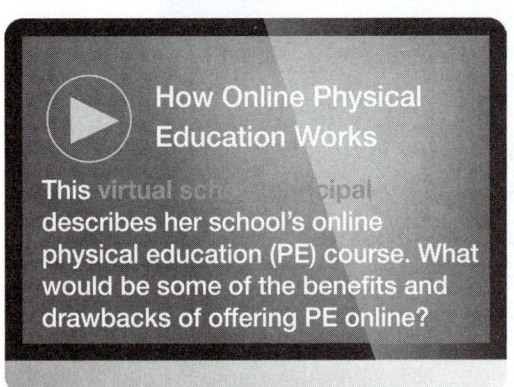

**How Online Physical Education Works**

This *virtual sch...cipal* describes her school's online physical education (PE) course. What would be some of the benefits and drawbacks of offering PE online?

other students like themselves who face the same kinds of problems and decisions. Classes in various parts of the world can collaborate on projects such as studying local safety or behavior issues. When they complete their research, they work together on developing a Web page or other product that documents healthy behaviors. Students also are able to discuss the differences between various cultures with regard to subjects such as drug use or government-sponsored health care.

Video resources are an efficient way to remove logistical hurdles when teaching health-related issues. They allow students to hear information and advice from a voice other than the teacher's. They also allow students to see health issues in real-life settings and view models of healthy behaviors.

## Supporting Interdisciplinary Instruction

The popular opinion regarding interdisciplinary instruction for health and physical education is that these subject areas support learning in other subjects. However, the perspective of health and physical educators is that interdisciplinary instruction requires a symbiotic relationship: subject areas support each other. The adoption of the Common Core State Standards (2012) by the majority of states nationwide has as its key objective the integration of multiple content areas in preparing students to become college and career ready. The website PE Central provides a section of peer-reviewed lesson ideas for integrating physical education content into other subject areas. SPARKPE has developed a series of lessons and activities aligned to Common Core State Standards, which merge physical education content with literacy and language arts instruction (SPARKPE, 2014a, 2014b). See Technology Integration Example 14.1, provided earlier in this chapter, for an example of an interdisciplinary lesson that integrates physical education, science, and math, along with the use of computers. Technology teachers can help with these interdisciplinary units by providing Internet research support and multimedia project development tools that let students demonstrate their health and physical education learning.

## Offering Online Health and Physical Education

A recent trend is for physical education and health education courses to be taught online. One might wonder what an online physical education course looks like. As with any course, the design and pedagogy differ greatly from class to class. However, they often state a goal, such as walking four miles a day, that students must accomplish for each week. Students keep a log of their physical activity, sharing their data with other students while they keep a journal of their experiences. However, more complex interventions are needed to ensure that students demonstrate mastery of cognitive, affective, and psychomotor domains of all applicable content areas versus merely physical activity to meet the National Standards and Grade Level Outcomes (American Alliance for Health Physical Education Recreation and Dance, 2013). Mears (2009) reviews how podcasts and wikis can help with learning at a distance, and Shumack and Reilly (2011) feel that video podcasting (**vodcasting**) can help get needed physical education information out to students in a highly visual format. Vodcasts are simply videos posted on a course site or other website, such as YouTube, a practice that is also referred to as video sharing. The Society of Health and Physical Educators (SHAPE America, formerly the American Alliance for Health, Physical Education, Recreation and Dance or AAHPERD) has developed appropriate practice guidelines for offering physical education online to ensure it meets national standards and appropriate practice guidelines. These guidelines are available at the SHAPE America website.

**TECHNOLOGY LEARNING CHECK**

Complete **TLC 14.2** to review what you have learned from this section about strategies for integrating technology into health and physical education.

# TEACHING HEALTH AND PHYSICAL EDUCATION TEACHERS TO INTEGRATE TECHNOLOGY

This section gives recommendations for how teachers can prepare to integrate technology effectively into instruction for health and physical education. Teachers in this area are challenged to use young people's natural fascination with technology to enhance and increase active and healthy behaviors. But these are also content areas where students' ready access to technologies has made it necessary to place additional skills in the curriculum. Health and physical education teachers are tasked with making students more savvy consumers of health-related information and encouraging them to take responsibility for their own health and wellness. This is also a content area that often includes instruction to reduce bullying behaviors. Fortunately, many new lesson plans and resources are available online to support instruction on these topics.

## Rubric to Measure Teacher Growth in Health and Physical Education Technology Integration

Begin by reviewing the rubric in Figure 14.7 to measure teachers' progress in effectively integrating technology in health and physical education. Part I of the rubric addresses knowledge of issues and challenges, and Part II addresses health and physical education integration strategies.

**FIGURE 14.7** Rubric to Measure Teacher Growth in Technology Integration for Health and Physical Education

| Part I: Teacher Knowledge of Health and Physical Education Issues and Challenges | | | |
|---|---|---|---|
| | Basic knowledge (1–2 points) | Intermediate knowledge (3–4 points) | Advanced knowledge (4–5 points) |
| Instructional time and quality physical education programs | I can articulate the nature of the issue. | I can both articulate the nature of the issue and some of the possible ways to address it. | I can articulate my own plan for addressing the issue in my own teaching. |
| The link between physical inactivity and obesity | I can articulate the nature of the issue. | I can both articulate the nature of the issue and some of the possible ways to address it. | I can articulate my own plan for addressing the issue in my own teaching. |
| Accuracy of Internet information on health and physical education | I can articulate the nature of the issue. | I can both articulate the nature of the issue and some of the possible ways to address it. | I can articulate my own plan for addressing the issue in my own teaching. |
| Addressing physical education and health standards | I can articulate the nature of the issue. | I can both articulate the nature of the issue and some of the possible ways to address it. | I can articulate my own plan for addressing the issue in my own teaching. |
| Handling controversial health issues | I can articulate the nature of the issue. | I can both articulate the nature of the issue and some of the possible ways to address it. | I can articulate my own plan for addressing the issue in my own teaching. |
| Part II: Teachers' Technology Integration Strategies for Health and Physical Education | | | |
| | Basic knowledge (1–2 points) | Intermediate knowledge (3–4 points) | Advanced knowledge (4–5 points) |
| Supporting improved physical fitness | I can describe the strategies and identify technologies to carry them out. | I have designed at least 1–2 activities based on these strategies to enhance my teaching and my students' learning. | I have designed plans for how I will integrate these strategies throughout my curriculum to enhance my teaching and my students' learning. |

*(Continued)*

| Developing and improving motor skill performance | I can describe the strategies and identify technologies to carry them out. | I have designed at least 1–2 activities based on these strategies to enhance my teaching and my students' learning. | I have designed plans for how I will integrate these strategies throughout my curriculum to enhance my teaching and my students' learning. |
|---|---|---|---|
| Assessing student learning in the context of teaching | I can describe the strategies and identify technologies to carry them out. | I have designed at least 1–2 activities based on these strategies to enhance my teaching and my students' learning. | I have designed plans for how I will integrate these strategies throughout my curriculum to enhance my teaching and my students' learning. |
| Supporting student work in dance | I can describe the strategies and identify technologies to carry them out. | I have designed at least 1–2 activities based on these strategies to enhance my teaching and my students' learning. | I have designed plans for how I will integrate these strategies throughout my curriculum to enhance my teaching and my students' learning. |
| Shaping students' beliefs and interactions related to physical activity | I can describe the strategies and identify technologies to carry them out. | I have designed at least 1–2 activities based on these strategies to enhance my teaching and my students' learning. | I have designed plans for how I will integrate these strategies throughout my curriculum to enhance my teaching and my students' learning. |
| Helping students assess and enhance personal health | I can describe the strategies and identify technologies to carry them out. | I have designed at least 1–2 activities based on these strategies to enhance my teaching and my students' learning. | I have designed plans for how I will integrate these strategies throughout my curriculum to enhance my teaching and my students' learning. |

| **Part II: Teachers' Technology Integration Strategies for Health and Physical Education** | | | |
|---|---|---|---|
| | **Basic knowledge (1–2 points)** | **Intermediate knowledge (3–4 points)** | **Advanced knowledge (4–5 points)** |
| Helping students obtain valid health information | I can describe the strategies and identify technologies to carry them out. | I have designed at least 1–2 activities based on these strategies to enhance my teaching and my students' learning. | I have designed plans for how I will integrate these strategies throughout my curriculum to enhance my teaching and my students' learning. |
| Influencing health behaviors | I can describe the strategies and identify technologies to carry them out. | I have designed at least 1–2 activities based on these strategies to enhance my teaching and my students' learning. | I have designed plans for how I will integrate these strategies throughout my curriculum to enhance my teaching and my students' learning. |
| Supporting interdisciplinary instruction | I can describe the strategies and identify technologies to carry them out. | I have designed at least 1–2 activities based on these strategies to enhance my teaching and my students' learning. | I have designed plans for how I will integrate these strategies throughout my curriculum to enhance my teaching and my students' learning. |
| Offering physical education and health education online | I can describe the strategies and identify technologies to carry them out. | I have designed at least 1–2 activities based on these strategies to enhance my teaching and my students' learning. | I have designed plans for how I will integrate these strategies throughout my curriculum to enhance my teaching and my students' learning. |
| **Total points** | _____ of 75 possible points | | |

## Learning the Issues and Applications

The first step in technology integration is to become acquainted with the issues and challenges discussed in this chapter and how they shape teachers' uses and applications of technologies. Then teachers can begin developing capabilities to address instructional standards and curriculum goals. The following is a suggested sequence of learning activities.

- **Issues and challenges in health and physical education.** After reviewing the information in this chapter, go to the SHAPE America website and the National Health Education Standards section of the CDC website. Review the standards at both sites. See professional development resources the sites offer, and decide on which can help you gain insight into the issues and challenges outlined in this chapter. Discuss and reflect on the two questions under the Collaborate, Discuss, Reflect feature at the end of the chapter. Complete Part I of the rubric in Figure 14.7 before you begin this sequence and again at various points in your progress.

- **Health and physical education technology integration strategies.** After reviewing the information in this chapter, review examples of the technologies suggested in the Open Source Options feature and the websites and projects described under each section, and do the lesson evaluation and lesson development activities outlined in the Technology Integration Workshop at the end of this chapter. Reflect on how you will plan for implementing these strategies in your own classroom using the TIP model. Complete Part I of the rubric in Figure 14.7 before you begin this sequence and again at various points in your progress.

**TECHNOLOGY LEARNING CHECK**

Complete TLC 14.3 to review what you have learned from this section about how health and physical education teachers can develop their knowledge and skills in technology integration.

## COLLABORATE, DISCUSS, REFLECT

Monkey Business/Fotolia

**The following questions may be used either for in-class, small-group discussions or may be used to initiate discussions in blogs or online discussion boards:**

1. In this chapter, you've read some of the ways technologies can help address what has often been referred to as the "childhood obesity crisis." Can you cite authority or evidence that these technology-based strategies will be sufficient to counter the contributions to obesity caused by the other technologies mentioned? What conditions will have to be in place for these positive strategies to make a difference?

2. Although physical education courses can be (and are being) taught online, what are the issues and problems you see associated with these kinds of courses? How would you recommend teachers address each of these issues and problems?

**Chapter 14** Summary

**The following is a summary of the main points covered in this chapter.**

1. **Issues and Challenges in Physical Education and Health Education.** Each of these current issues has implications for how teachers can and should integrate technologies. These include instructional time and quality physical education programs, the link between physical inactivity and obesity, accuracy of Internet information on health and physical education, addressing physical education and health standards, and handling controversial health issues.

2. **Technology Integration Strategies for Physical Education and Health Education.** Technology-enabled strategies in these areas include:
   - Supporting improved physical fitness (with physical activity monitoring devices, exercising with equipment and monitoring software, fitness plans and portfolios, exergaming, and exercise and sport opportunities for students with special needs).
   - Developing and improving motor skill performance (with monitoring performance, providing feedback on performance, self-assessment of student learning, and facilitating skill acquisition).
   - Assessing student learning in the context of teaching.
   - Supporting students' work in dance.
   - Shaping students' beliefs and interactions related to physical activity.
   - Helping students assess and enhance personal health.
   - Helping students obtain valid health information.
   - Influencing health behaviors.
   - Supporting interdisciplinary instruction.
   - Offering online health and physical education.

3. **Teaching Health and Physical Education Teachers to Integrate Technology.** Teachers can begin by consulting the rubric provided in this chapter to measure their own growth in health and physical education technology integration. After that, they may review issues and challenges in health and physical education and use chapter resources to learn technology integration strategies they can use to address the issues and challenges.

# TECHNOLOGY INTEGRATION **WORKSHOP**

## 1. APPLY WHAT YOU LEARNED

To apply the concepts and skills you've read about throughout this chapter, go to the **Chapter 14 Technology Application Activity**.

## 2. TECHNOLOGY INTEGRATION LESSON PLANNING: PART 1—EVALUATING AND CREATING LESSON PLANS

Complete the following exercise using the sample lesson plans found on any lesson planning site that you find on the Internet.

**a.** Locate lesson ideas—Identify three lesson plans that focus on any of the tools or strategies you learned about in this chapter. For example:

- Use of physical activity monitoring devices
- Use of software and/or websites for fitness planning
- Exergaming
- Joint student projects using sites such as ePals
- Videos to influence health behaviors
- Videos as models for sports and dance skills and to demonstrate needs for improvement
- Use of polling for immediate feedback on performances

**b.** Evaluate the lessons—Use the Technology Lesson Plan Evaluation Checklist to evaluate each of the lessons you found.

**c.** Create your own lesson—After you have reviewed and evaluated some sample lessons, create one of your own using a lesson plan format of your choice (or one your instructor gives you). Be sure the lesson focuses on one of the technologies or strategies discussed in this chapter.

## 3. TECHNOLOGY INTEGRATION LESSON PLANNING: PART 2—IMPLEMENTING THE TIP MODEL

Review how to implement the TIP model in your classroom by doing the following activities with the lesson you created in the Technology Integration Lesson Planning exercise above.

**a.** Describe the Phase 1—Planning activities you would do to use this lesson in your classroom:
- What is the relative advantage of using the technology(ies) in this lesson?
- Do you have resources and skills you need to carry it out?

**b.** Describe the Phase 2—Implementation activities you would do to use this lesson in your classroom:
- What are the objectives of the lesson plan?
- How will you assess your students' accomplishment of the objectives?
- What integration strategies are used in this lesson plan?
- How would you prepare the learning environment?

**c.** Describe the Phase 3—Evaluation/Revision activities you would do to use this lesson in your classroom: What strategies and/or instruments would you use to evaluate the success of this lesson in your classroom in order to determine revision needs?

**d.** Add lesson descriptors—Create descriptors for your new lesson (e.g., grade level, content and topic areas, technologies used, ISTE standards, 21st Century Learning standards).

**e.** Save your new lesson—Save your lesson plan with all its descriptors and TIP model notes.

## 4. FOR YOUR TEACHING PORTFOLIO

Add the following to your Teaching Portfolio:
- Reflections on Hot Topic Debates.
- Summary notes from the Collaborate, Discuss, Reflect activity.
- Lesson plan evaluations, lesson plans, and products you created above.
- Your *Apply What You Learned* Product from Activity 1.

# 15

## Dave Edyburn and M. D. Roblyer

# Teaching and Learning with Technology in Special Education

## Learning Outcomes

After reading this chapter and completing the learning activities, you should be able to:

1. Identify basic special education concepts teachers should know in order to make best use of technology to meet special needs of students. (ISTE Standards•T 4, 5)

2. Identify implications for technology integration of each current issue faced by teachers of students with special needs. (ISTE Standards•T 4, 5)

3. Select technology integration strategies that can meet various needs for instruction in special education. (ISTE Standards•T 2, 5)

4. Design a strategy for how to build teacher knowledge and skills in technology integration for special education. (ISTE Standards•T 5)

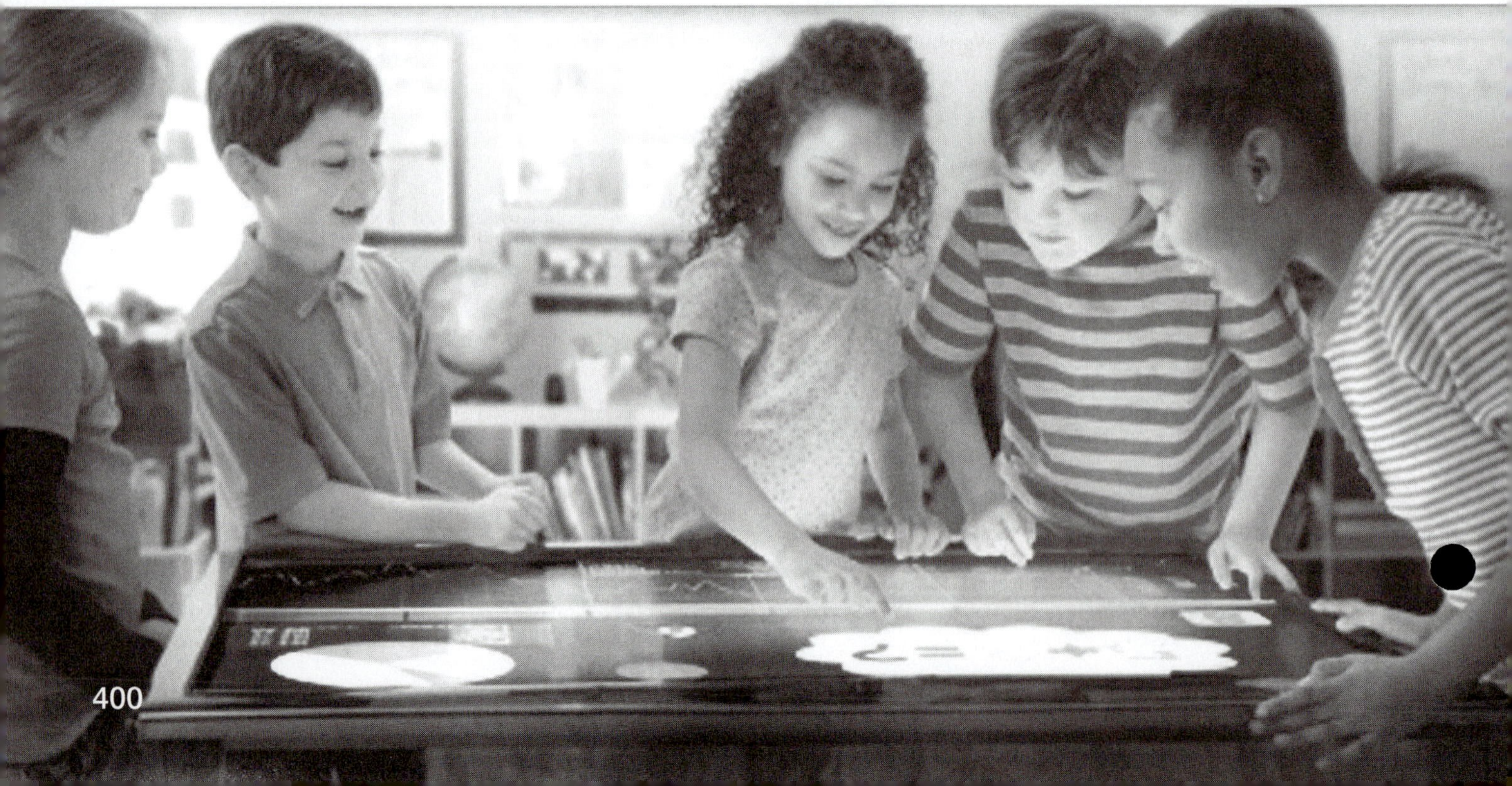

# TECHNOLOGY INTEGRATION IN ACTION
# CO-TEACHING TO MEET DIVERSE NEEDS

GRADE LEVELS: Middle school • CONTENT AREA/TOPIC: Disciplinary Literacy (Reading in Science) •
LENGTH OF TIME: One nine-week period

## PHASE 1 ANALYSIS OF LEARNING AND TEACHING NEEDS

Jules Selmes/Pearson Education

### Step 1: Determine relative advantage.

Ms. Ethelbart, the special education resource teacher for her middle school, was seeing a growing problem among the students she served. Most were now being included in general education classrooms, but many fared poorly on content-area tests in comparison with the rest of the class. Teachers expressed frustration, both because strategies that worked with other students did not always work as well with students who had cognitive and physical disabilities, and because there was insufficient time to provide personal assistance the students needed. Ms. Ethelbart had been researching co-teaching strategies, or those in which special education teachers and content-area teachers work together to plan and carry out instruction. These strategies have been found to result in better outcomes for students with special needs because they capitalize on the strengths and specialized knowledge of both teachers. She found that this model could be implemented in several different ways and had improved outcomes for many students with special needs. She also saw that online resources and assistive technologies could play a key role in making this kind of teaching possible.

She and the science teacher, Mr. Ardmore, agreed to try out the strategy with a unit on science reading. If the strategy proved successful, Ms. Ethelbart felt she could get support for expanding it to other science skills and to other content areas.

### Step 2: Review required skills and resources.

The teachers proposed to work on students' reading outcomes by having them locate, read, and present current-events articles that addressed a science topic discussed in class. They decided this would work best using two different co-teaching strategies: parallel teaching and station teaching. Parallel teaching, in which both teachers taught the same topics but to different parts of the class, would help address the special needs of two students who had more severe learning disabilities. The special education teacher would assist them with understanding what would be expected of them and with completing their online article searches, analyzing their articles, and creating their presentations. That strategy would be interspersed through the nine-week period with station teaching, in which small groups would use different learning stations to address the same topic in different ways. This would be especially useful for students who had physical disabilities such as motor coordination and hearing impairments, since a special station could be set up for them with assistive technologies. Though the teachers had never co-taught in just these ways, they were eager to try it and felt they would get better at it with practice.

## PHASE 2 PLANNING FOR INTEGRATION

### Step 3: Decide on objectives and assessments.

The teachers based their objectives on Common Core Standards in reading for grades 6–8 students and on reading in content areas such as science:

Outcome: Reading comprehension: Identify the author's purpose in a given text, determine the central ideas or conclusions of the text, and be able to present an accurate summary of the text.
Objective: At least 95% of the students will achieve at least an 80% on their verbal or written summary of a science article, scored by teacher checklist.
Assessment: Checklist of component comprehension skills.

Outcome: Analysis of scientific texts: Cite evidence to support analysis of text.
Objective: At least 95% of the students will achieve at least an 80% on the analysis of their science article, scored by teacher checklist.
Assessment: Checklist of component analysis requirements.

Outcome: Final presentations: Integrate technical information expressed in words with a visual version of the same information.

Objective: At least 95% of the students will achieve at least an 80% rubric score on their final presentation.

Assessment: Presentation software rubric.

## Step 4: Design integration strategies.

The teachers decided they would intersperse the co-teaching strategies in the following way and work to have students complete two complete cycles of article searches, analyses, and presentations:

Week 1: Introduce the unit, checklists and rubric assessments, and parallel teach the product requirements.

Week 2: Introduce online search strategies and resources for locating science articles at reading levels appropriate for various students. Implement learning stations to begin searches.

Week 3: Continue online searches in learning stations. Use parallel teaching to teach and model analysis methods.

Week 4: Work on analyses and final presentations. (Special education teacher works to meet needs of students with special needs. For example, students with physical disabilities that impair traditional keyboard use need help with switches and other means to input information to a computer.)

Week 5: Complete work on analyses and final presentations. Upload presentations to class site for individual review as homework.

Weeks 6–9: Repeat Weeks 2–5 cycle. Do summative assessment on final products.

## Step 5: Prepare instructional environment.

The key to the unit's success was setting up the environment with appropriate materials, so teachers divided the tasks of searching for sites students could use and setting up stations with appropriate materials and assistive technologies. The special education teacher made bookmarked lists of sites with science articles at various reading levels (e.g., Today's Front Pages; Newsmap, 10 by 10, 100 Words and Pictures; News 2 You), prepared presentations to review the rubric, and set up two stations with the assistive technologies students would need (e.g., text-to-speech tools, adaptive keyboard). The science teacher prepared the other learning stations and became familiar with sites the other teacher provided. They uploaded an explanation of the unit to the classroom website so that parents would see the unit goals and activities for all students.

# PHASE 3   POST-INSTRUCTION ANALYSIS AND REVISIONS

## Step 6: Analyze results.

At the end of the nine-week period, the teachers reviewed the overall checklist and rubric scores of each class. Mr. Ardmore found that results for most of his science students were at or above those in previous years for the same goals. However, results for the students with special needs were much improved as compared with past years. Ms. Ethelbart found that all her students with learning disabilities demonstrated they were able to locate articles, though they still had difficulties analyzing them and creating a presentation that met the minimum criteria.

## Step 7: Make revisions.

The teachers felt that it would help students with learning disabilities make faster progress if there was a more structured sequence of steps these students could complete at learning stations to lead them through the analysis process. Also, they needed a presentation template so they could focus more on presenting their results and less on the logistics of creating the graphs and slides. They decided to do the unit again to see the impact of these modifications on their outcomes.

Source: Based on ideas from Sileo, J.M., & van Garderen, D. (2010). Creating optimal opportunities to learn mathematics: Blending co-teaching structures with research-based practices. Teaching Exceptional Children, 42(3), 14–21.

# CHAPTER 15 **BIG IDEAS OVERVIEW**

Before you begin reading the rest of this chapter, listen to the **Chapter 15 Big Ideas Overview**. It will give you a two-minute audio overview of main concepts to look for and help prepare you to work through information and exercises to achieve this chapter's outcomes.

# INTRODUCTION TO SPECIAL EDUCATION

Educators who understand diversity in academic settings recognize that some students will learn quickly and others more slowly. For example, some are capable independent readers, but students who are blind will need special assistance to be able to extract meaning from print by using assistive technologies that convert text to speech. As a result, educators need to be prepared to use technology that supports learners who have a wide array of physical, sensory, and cognitive abilities and challenges. The purpose of this chapter is to introduce concepts and tools that will help educators use technology to meet these challenges.

While the terms *impairment*, *disability*, and *handicap* are often used synonymously, differences among these concepts have important implications for the use of technology in classrooms. An **impairment** involves an abnormality or loss of function in a physical, anatomical, or psychological structure. Impairments to human function may be congenital (present at birth) or acquired through accident or disease. It is important not to make assumptions concerning a person's ability or limitations simply because he or she has an impairment.

When an impairment limits an individual from performing an activity (communicating with others, hearing, movement, manipulating objects, and so on) in a manner normally expected for human beings, we refer to this as a **disability**. A student who has lost the function of his right arm has an impairment; this condition may have little or no impact on a variety of life functions. However, this student may encounter situations where the inability to use two arms places him at a disadvantage with others. A **handicap** arises when an individual is unable to fulfill a role due to a disability. It is critical to understand that a handicap is not a characteristic of an individual, and thus, the term is neither used to describe an individual nor the condition of a disability or impairment. Instead, its use is restricted to identifying the impact or consequence of the disability within the individual (Gargiulo, 2012). A handicap is the "negative consequence of an impairment. It may be a problem with access to certain buildings and facilities caused by poor walking, it may be difficulties in conversations caused by poor speech, or it may be difficulties in an education caused by poor reading ability" (Elbro, 2010, p. 470). This chapter is concerned primarily with technologies that can address disabilities through augmentation or through bypassing or compensating for impairments.

**TECHNOLOGY LEARNING CHECK**

Complete TLC 15.1 to review what you have learned from this section about background concepts required for using technology to meet special needs.

# ISSUES AND CHALLENGES IN SPECIAL EDUCATION

In the sections that follow, issues that have an ongoing influence on how, when, and why technology is used in special education will be introduced. These will provide a context for understanding how current trends and historical issues affect the use of technology in schools by students with disabilities and their teachers.

# Special Education and Inclusion Requirements

Before the passage of **Public Law 94-142** in 1975, students with disabilities were typically excluded from public schools. As special education programs began to take root in American public schools in the late 1970s and early 1980s, specialized instructional services for students with disabilities were provided in separate special education classrooms (West & Whitby, 2008). However, by the mid-to-late 1980s, experts called on special education to "mainstream" students with disabilities into appropriate classes within the general curriculum (McLeskey, Waldron, Spooner, & Algozzine, 2014).

By the time the Individuals with **Disabilities Education Act (IDEA, PL 101-476)** was reauthorized in 1990, the mainstreaming argument had evolved into advocacy for **inclusion** that resulted in the following clarification in U.S. federal special education law:

- To the maximum extent appropriate, children with disabilities, including children in public or private institutions or other care facilities, are educated with children who are non-disabled;

- Special classes, separate schooling or other removal of children with disabilities from the regular educational environment occur only when the nature or severity of the disability is such that education in regular classes with the use of supplementary aids and services cannot be achieved satisfactorily; and

- The educational placement of each child with a disability is as close as possible to the child's home (Individuals with Disabilities Education Act of 1990, §300.550, §300.552, 20 U.S.C. §1412 & 1414).

In accordance with federal law, inclusion was the norm by the early 2000s, and over 90% of students with disabilities spent the majority of their day in general education classrooms (Williamson, McLeskey, Hoppey, & Rentz, 2006). Thus, the history of special education has been described as a journey of helping students with disabilities gain access to educational opportunity through three stages: isolation, integration, and inclusion (Winzer, 2009).

One of the core principles of inclusion is the concept that individuals with disabilities should be included as valued, active participants in mainstream society and classrooms (McLeskey, Rosenberg, & Westling, 2013). Rather than treating differences as something that need to be addressed in segregated environments, the premise is that individual differences should be considered an ordinary feature of inclusive classrooms and addressed in ways that are a typical part of classroom instruction (McLeskey, Waldron, & Redd, 2012; Tomlinson, 2013).

Efforts to include students with disabilities over the past 20 years have generally been successful, as most students with disabilities are now included in general education classrooms for much of the school day (McLeskey, Landers, Williamson, & Hoppey, 2012). One consequence of this change is that, as a practical matter, special education is largely no longer under the sole control of the profession, but rather is embodied in the larger context of the educational reform efforts.

A comment by Judy Heumann, who was at the time assistant secretary, Office of Special Education Programs, U.S. Department of Education, captures the critical need for the specialized technologies used by individuals with disabilities: "For most of us, technology makes things easier. For a person with a disability, it makes things possible" (Edyburn, Higgins, & Boone, 2005, p. xiii). Within Heumann's statement are the five essential variables associated with special education technology: (1) The person, (2) the task, (3) the context/environment, (4) the technology tool, and (5) the outcome. In order to determine the best solution for an individual, educators and specialists are challenged to optimize the complex inter-play between the variables. When successful, the result is that an individual is able to complete a task that they previously could not complete, did so slowly, or did so poorly. Thus, the entire work of the field of special education technology can be summarized as searching, trialing, selecting, implementing, and evaluating technologies that augment, bypass, or compensate for a disability.

During the mid to late 1980s when computers began arriving in K–12 schools, they were initially placed in labs for whole class instruction. From the beginning it is easy to trace two sets of technology service delivery systems within schools: (1) for students in general education under the direction of a school-based computer coordinator and (2) assistive technology services for students with disabilities who may need adapted hardware and/or special software. Since the two groups of students were educated separately, there was little initial concern about the inequity of this model. Unfortunately, the legacy of this historical divide persists today in most schools.

As computers became commonplace in schools, individuals with disabilities encountered access problems (usually involving the keyboard, mouse, or monitor), thereby creating an obvious need for assistive technology. By the mid-1990s, the computer manufacturing industry began to install accessibility control panels on every computer shipped in the United States. This development marks the beginning of the accessible mainstream technology movement. That is, technology developers began to explore the intrinsic barriers encountered by individuals with disabilities and sought solutions that could be built into hardware and software (e.g., keyboard shortcuts, text enlargement, text-to-speech) that would help an even wider population (e.g., young children, seniors). In time, assistive technology advocates began to view some types of assistive technology as something that could be made available to all students in an inclusive classroom to support access and engagement of diverse learners; the perspective that assistive technologies had a role in the general classroom to help many students would become known as **inclusive technologies**.

## Policy Drivers of Technology Use in Special Education

The field of special education has routinely sought to implement large-scale change not through the application of research findings but by using federal education law as a tool for leveraging change (Edyburn, 2013a). Two examples provide evidence of how federal special education policy has influence in every local school.

The 1997 reauthorization of the Individuals with Disabilities Act (IDEA) included a requirement that students with special needs must have an **Individual Education Program (IEP),** or a written plan for how their needs will be addressed, and that **IEP teams** tasked with creating and carrying out the IEP must consider assistive technology in their planning. Advocacy for this mandate was based on the observation that the marketplace had produced many assistive technology solutions that had yet to find their way into schools and as a result, students were losing considerable opportunities for accessing and engaging in the curriculum. Hence, the assistive technology policy initiative sought to ensure that the potential of technology for students with disabilities was realized.

Edyburn (2013b) argued that this policy effectively expanded the notion of assistive technology as something more than an intervention for students with physical, sensory, and communication impairments. In essence, it added 3.8 million students with high incidence disabilities to the assistive technology caseload. High-incidence disabilities are learning disabilities, mild or moderate intellectual disabilities, communication disorders, and emotional or behavioral disorders. And, since inclusion had become the primary special education service delivery system, this altered the conversation by requiring IEP teams to consider what technology supports were needed in the general classroom to support the academic success of a student with a disability. As a result, schools today are still subject to the assistive technology consideration mandate and must work diligently to ensure that all students with special needs are adequately evaluated for appropriate assistive technology devices and services.

### Universal Design for Learning (UDL).
The second legislation, **Universal Design for Learning (UDL)**, which emerged in the early 2000s, provided a new way of thinking about technology as an embedded support that could be made available to all students (Edyburn, 2010). UDL is set of principles that underlie how to develop technology to give all individuals equal opportunities to learn. It is intended to offer students multiple ways to access, engage, and demonstrate their mastery of the learning outcomes. Whereas accessibility is one aspect of UDL, the allure of UDL promised to help not only students with disabilities (the primary beneficiary) but also to provide benefit to many other struggling students who could benefit from similar supports (secondary beneficiaries). UDL is best known for its three core principles of providing multiple means of representation, multiple means of expression, and multiple means of engagement. To learn more about UDL, visit the National Center on Universal Design for Learning.

The early 21st century provided the perfect convergence between the academic needs of students with disabilities, concern in general education about poor academic performance, and the potential of universal design to harness the power and potential of technology to engage and support diverse students. There is currently minimal research on UDL, but the National Education Technology Plan features UDL prominently and encourages school districts to adopt this intervention as a method of using technology to meet the needs of diverse learners (U.S. Department of Education, 2010). While at the present time the National Technology Plan has not been adopted, it provides a useful blueprint for planning for future directions of technology in education and illustrates how federal education policy seeks to influence the use of inclusive technologies.

Web accessibility.     In the last decade, there has been a concentrated effort by educational organizations to make websites more usable by people with various disabilities. This practice is referred to as **Web accessibility** and consists of designing websites with a set of criteria in mind, such as using text equivalents with screen readers, using large or enlargeable images for people with low vision, underlining links as well as coloring them for users with colorblindness, and making pages navigable using the keyboard only. Like UDL, the intention of Web accessibility is to provide greater access to information for all users by designing websites for accessibility from the ground up. Also see the Hot Topic Debate that addresses this issue.

## Educational Reform and Accountability in Special Education

Historically, students with disabilities have not performed as well as their peers. In 2002, President Bush signed the No Child Left Behind (NCLB) Act of 2001 (P.L. 107-110). This landmark federal education law created expectations for closing the achievement gap by holding schools, districts, and states accountable for annual achievement gains as measured and reported as Adequate Yearly Progress (AYP). Essentially each school, district, and state must report annually on the achievement of its students. Historically when test scores were reported for a school or district, the average of all children was reported. The problem with this approach is that low academic performance is lost in the process of averaging. Therefore, AYP had the impact of drawing attention to four groups of students who have demonstrated chronic low academic performance: (1) students of color, (2) students with disabilities, (3) students living in poverty, and (4) students whose first language is not English. Schools, districts, and states are required to disaggregate the scores of these four subgroups of students when reporting student performance on annual tests of academic achievement to ensure that their progress is not lost in the process of school reform. The requirements of NCLB placed intense pressure on schools to raise academic performance, as measured by annual high-stakes tests, and outlined a series of sanctions for schools that failed to meet their annual goals.

## Hot Topic Debate
### Does Online Learning Discriminate Against Students with Disabilities?

*Take a position for or against (based either on your own position or one assigned to you) on the following controversial statement. Discuss it in class or on an online discussion board, blog, or wiki, as assigned by your instructor. When the discussion is complete, write a summary of the main pros and cons that you and your classmates have stated, and put the summary document in your Teacher Portfolio.*

As online learning grows in importance in K–12 schools, Web accessibility issues are becoming increasingly critical. Educational

organizations are coming under fire if they do not provide students who have impairments with alternative ways of accessing written or video information. Though virtual school courses often enlarge text and provide text-to-sound reading capabilities, they are not able to provide devices that compensate for other impairments, leaving schools to provide these alternatives. In light of this, does online learning discriminate against students with certain disabilities? What evidence in research or practice can you cite to support or refute this position?

The rhetoric of inclusion is apparent in the context and accountability associated with school reform. The goal of including students with disabilities in the general classroom now means that the language of school reform also applies to these students. One of the key features of NCLB was the emphasis on standardized assessment as a method of accountability for closing achievement gaps. However, this law, now known as the Elementary and Secondary Education Act (ESEA), as of 2014 has yet to be reauthorized by Congress. So the Obama administration has been issuing waivers to grant states flexibility in meeting the legal requirements. To learn more about the flexibility guidelines and to review the documents concerning your state's waiver request, visit the U. S. Department of Education Flexibility Waivers.

Beginning in 2014–15 school year, states will need to administer tests to assess student performance on the CCSS in English language arts and mathematics, thereby replacing the state-specific accountability assessments that were required under NCLB. In anticipation of this transition, in September 2010, the U.S. Department of Education awarded approximately $400 million dollars of Race to the Top funding to two consortia, PARRC and Smarter Balanced, to develop a new generation of high-stakes tests that would allow states to implement a new accountability system. A month later, two additional awards were made, for approximately $67 million, to two consortia—the National Center and State Collaborative Partnership (NCSC) and the Dynamic Learning Maps Alternate Assessment System Consortium (DLM)—that would create a new generation of alternate assessments on alternate achievement standards, aligned to the CCSS for students with the most significant cognitive disabilities.

## Trends in the Prevalence of Autism Spectrum Disorders (ASD)

In the United States, annual special education enrollment data indicated that the number of children who received special education services under the autism reporting category increased by 1700% between 1992 and 2008 (Maenner & Durkin, 2010). At the present time, the Center for Disease Control and Prevention (2012b) estimates 1 in 88 children has been identified with an autism spectrum disorder (ASD), which has led to widespread public concern about a possible epidemic of autism. Technologies have proven to have special benefits for individuals with ASD. These are reviewed in the next section of this chapter.

**TECHNOLOGY LEARNING CHECK**

Complete TLC 15.2 to review what you have learned from this section about issues that affect technology uses to meet special needs.

# ◉ TECHNOLOGY INTEGRATION STRATEGIES TO MEET SPECIAL NEEDS

This section provides information about general approaches to using assistive and instructional technologies for students with special needs and describes specific products that are commonly integrated into curricula for helping achieve academic, behavioral, or social goals. Table 15.1 summarizes all these strategies. Also see the Top Ten Must-Have Apps for Special Education.

## Foundations of Integration Strategies for Special Education

Special educators must be concerned with two types of technology: assistive technology and instructional technology. Technology integration efforts must include both types of technology. Historically, the emphasis on technology for individuals with disabilities has been in the

## TABLE 15.1 Summary of Technology Integration Strategies for Special Education

| Target Groups | Sample Technology Integration Strategies |
|---|---|
| Students with mild and moderate to severe cognitive disabilities | **For individuals with mild cognitive disabilities:**<br>• Reading: Use reading skill software, text-to-speech products, and interactive storybooks.<br>• Writing: Use voice recognition software and word prediction software.<br>• Mathematics: Use graphing software, drills, games, and tutorials.<br><br>**For individuals with moderate to severe cognitive disabilities:**<br>• Software helps teach/reinforce functional skills (e.g., money management, daily living, employability).<br>• Videos enhance acquisition, maintenance, and transfer of functional and community-based behaviors. |
| Students with physical disabilities | • Provide alternative methods of accessing keyboard, mouse, and/or monitor like those available from Ablenet.<br>• Determine the best placement of adaptive technologies, and provide training to ensure the student is able to operate it independently.<br>• Monitor function to ensure maximum level of participation is obtained without undue physical demands. |
| Students with sensory disabilities | **For individuals who are blind:**<br>• Use canes and sensor technologies to assist movement.<br>• Use text-to-Braille converters.<br>• Use screen readers.<br><br>**For individuals who are visually impaired:**<br>• Use closed-circuit television (CCTV) magnification systems.<br>• Use built-in computer screen magnification control panels.<br><br>**For individuals who are hearing impaired:**<br>• Use FM amplification systems (assistive listening devices). |
| Students with special gifts and talents | • Use of word processing to improve quantity and quality of writing, especially for boys.<br>• Use of computer-based games and activities to assess higher-level skills such as strategic thinking and ability to focus and resist distractions.<br>• Use of online learning to offer access to learning opportunities and learning communities. |

area of assistive technology. Indeed, the legal definition of assistive technology is considerably broad:

> **Section 300.5 of IDEA: Assistive technology device.** As used in this part, assistive technology device means any item, piece of equipment, or product system, whether acquired commercially off the shelf, modified, or customized, that is used to increase, maintain, or improve the functional capabilities of a child with a disability. (Authority: 20 U.S.C. 1401(1))

### Assistive technology evaluation referral.

The value and significance of assistive technology can be best understood when a person with a disability encounters a task she is unable to complete and an appropriate assistive technology device allows the person to successfully complete the same task. Assistive technology devices and services enhance the performance of individuals with disabilities by enabling them to complete tasks more effectively, efficiently, and independently than otherwise possible.

The decision to qualify a student for special education services must be made by an IEP team, described earlier. Once a child is qualified for special education services, a team is developed and convened to create and oversee the child's IEP. An assistive technology team is not the same as the IEP team. Rather, an assistive technology team is established within a school district to provide building-based and cross-building services relative to two key functions. First is the need to assess students for assistive technology. Much like a referral for special education services, a referral must be initiated for an assistive technology evaluation. A second responsibility of assistive technology teams is to facilitate the implementation of assistive technology devices and services. The caseload of an assistive technology team member is often determined though the IEP meeting. Finally, assistive technology teams may be called upon to assist with significant school transitions between grades levels, new schools, and so forth. (Behnke & Bowser, 2010). The assistive technology team may include assistive technology specialists, occupational therapists, physical therapists, speech-language therapists, and others.

### Classifying solutions.

The assistive technology evaluation process generally seeks to identify solutions on a continuum involving no technology ("no tech"), low technology ("low tech"), and advanced technology ("high tech").

- No-tech solutions are strategies such as teaching a person to use his or her body in a different manner to minimize the impact of an impairment (e.g., one-handed typing). The obvious advantage to solutions involving no technology is that they are available in any environment at any time.

- Low-tech solutions are generally considered to be nonelectrical. Personal word lists, highlighting markers, and organizing systems are all examples of low-technology solutions that can provide a person with appropriate levels of support to be successful in specific tasks. These solutions tend to be relatively inexpensive but quite flexible for enhancing individual performance.

- High-tech solutions are complex electrical or hydraulic systems (e.g., stair lift, powered wheelchair, voice-activated environmental control). Clearly, high-tech solutions tend to be the most costly and have the greatest number of restrictions regarding their use (e.g., user skill level, limited portability).

Professional practice in special education calls for the evaluation of potential solutions beginning with no tech, continuing to low tech, and then going to high tech, as the needs dictate. For example, spelling words is most efficient when the words are committed to memory. However, if a person displays persistent difficulty in spelling from memory (no tech), low-tech options such as personal word lists or portable dictionaries may be helpful. High-tech solutions such as electronic spelling checkers should be considered only after other options have proved less satisfactory because of dependency on batteries, fragility, and so on.

### Multiple means of representation (MMR).

**Multiple means of representation (MMR)** is a core principle associated with UDL and involves providing students with alternatives to acquiring information beyond a textbook. Today's teachers have many choices when it comes to presenting instructional content to students: watch a YouTube video, listen to a podcast, read text on a website, look up a topic using Wikipedia, and more. These options permit them to break out of the one-size-fits-all model, which assumes that all students learn in the same way, and to encourage teachers to use a wider palette of information containers to reach diverse students.

When teachers seek to implement the UDL principle of MMR, they are valuing academic diversity by discarding the historical notion that an information source is the only one needed. In reality, providing students with a menu of information sources is thought to enhance access, engagement, and learning outcomes for both targeted students (primary beneficiaries), who we know will struggle with the content, and also a large number of other students (secondary beneficiaries), who we cannot identify in advance. Technology tools and resources are critical for ensuring that diverse students have access to appropriate curricular resources to achieve CCSS.

### Multiple means of expression (MME).

The UDL principle of **multiple means of expression (MME)** draws attention to the need to provide students with various methods of demonstrating what they know. Some teachers recognize the value of this principle as they allow students a choice of writing a paper, preparing a slideshow presentation, recording a video, and so on. The key notion is to provide students with choice in how they demonstrate what they have learned and the media they use to express themselves in. Twenty-first century educators will likely need to alter their instructional practices in order to place students in the role of Goldilocks; that is, allowing them to try multiple options to determine which option is "just right" for ensuring their performance meets increasingly high standards.

This UDL principle highlights the importance of providing students with choices on how they express what they have learned. In many classrooms, teachers expect students to make

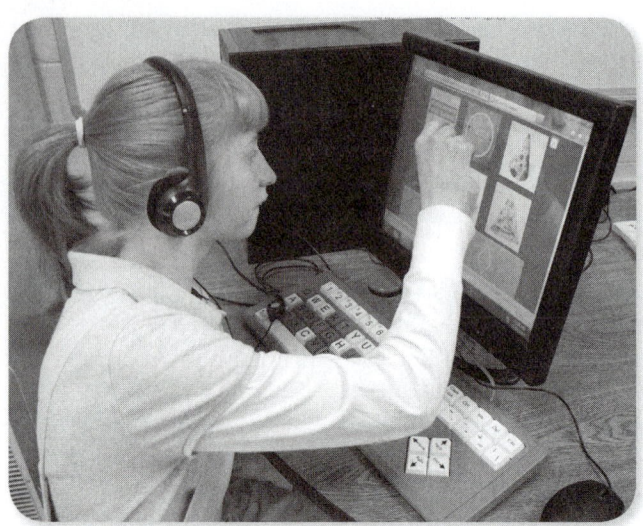

▲ Special software can allow students alternative ways of interacting with on-screen information. (Photo courtesy of W. Wiencke)

presentations to the class regarding a topic that they have studied. The MME principle means that the students are given a choice in the presentation tool; they can opt to learn a new tool or use one that they are familiar with or one that supports specific features (e.g., collaboration [Google Drive]; visualization [Prezi]; or cognitively simplified interface [Kid Pix 3D]) that they want to utilize in this particular context. Since the teacher may not be an expert in each of the products, students are directed to use each other as resources for learning about the tools as well as take advantage of online help and tutorials. This frees the teacher to devote more time and energy to helping the students learn about the content and performance standards. Once such a menu has been created, it may be reused frequently.

All of the technology integration strategies discussed in this book have important applications for students with disabilities. An essential consideration for all educators when planning for the needs of students with disabilities involves ensuring that the curriculum is accessible to all students, even those with visual or other impairments. When technology is used to make the curriculum accessible, students with disabilities have the same opportunities to learn as their peers (King-Sears, Swanson, & Mainzer, 2011; Seo & Woo, 2010).

Smith and Okolo (2010) argue that technology is underutilized for students with disabilities, yet these learners stand to benefit most from technological affordances. As technology continues to evolve, it holds great potential for the flexible instructional support necessary for meeting the evolving learning needs of students with disabilities. In fact, research conducted by Wehmeyer, Palmer, Williams-Diehm, Shogren, Davies, and Stock (2011) suggests that technology-supported curriculum in classrooms that have students with special needs may lead to increased student involvement and enhanced self-determination. Because some applications of technology in special education are commonly associated with specific disabilities, the following information will provide a brief overview of specific examples of technology used by people with disabilities.

## Strategies for Students with Cognitive Disabilities

A variety of conditions may impair an individual's cognitive abilities. Such disabilities are often referred to as cognitive disabilities, developmental disabilities, or intellectual disabilities (formerly referred to as mental retardation).

**FIGURE 15.1** Laureate's First Words App

book

**Strategies for students with mild cognitive disabilities.**
Mild disabilities are considered to be the most prevalent type of disability. They include learning disabilities, emotional disabilities, and intellectual disabilities. Lerner and Johns (2014) describes the following characteristics as being associated with mild disabilities: cognitive (i.e., intellectual ability, attention deficits, memory and thinking skills), academic (i.e., reading, language arts, mathematics), and social-emotional.

Typically, the important issue for these students is not physical access to the technology, but reading, writing, memory, and retention of information. While these students often have some learning difficulties (e.g., the inability to read at grade level), many have difficulty in learning in only one aspect of the curriculum. As a result, educators planning for the needs of students with mild disabilities often use productivity software as well as other software materials and online resources that can be used with many low-performing students (see Technology Integration Example 15.1). These may include materials for developing reading, writing, and mathematics skills. The key with all of these uses is to balance remediation of skill deficits with activities that help develop more creative, higher level thinking skills.

# TECHNOLOGY INTEGRATION

## Example 15.1

**TITLE:** Kurzweil 3000-firefly

**CONTENT AREA/TOPIC:** Language arts, reading

**GRADE LEVELS:** K–2

**ISTE STANDARDS•S:** Standard 3—Research and Information Fluency; Standard 4—Critical Thinking, Problem Solving, and Decision Making; Standard 6—Technology Operations and Concepts

**DESCRIPTION:** The Kurzweil 3000-firefly™ is a text reader with many built-in features, all of which are designed to support struggling readers. For example, words can be highlighted in context as they are read aloud for the student. Words that students are typing can also be read aloud, and the program supports reading in several languages. Language tools like a multilanguage dictionary, thesaurus, syllabification, and phonetic spelling provide additional support. Use this tool for students with learning disabilities to help them focus better on what they are reading and writing, and with students who have visual impairments to give them auditory access to reading and writing activities. Because Kurzweil allows students with special needs to work independently, it builds their confidence. Instead of investing time and effort on decoding words, students will put their energy on solving problems that require higher-order thinking.

*SOURCE: Based on concepts from Barbara Green and Joan Thormann's "Testing Kurzweil 3000" in the March/April, 2009 issue of Learning and Leading with Technology.*

---

**Reading skills for students with mild cognitive disabilities.** A characteristic associated with many disabilities is difficulty in learning how to read and in developing grade-level reading skills. As a result, special education teachers tend to devote a great deal of time and energy to the teaching of reading and are likely to use a variety of software products to remediate students' reading abilities. Software products such as MEville to WEville (Ablenet, Inc.), Simon Sounds It Out (Don Johnston, Inc.), and apps such as First Words (Laureate Learning, Inc., see Figure 15.1) are commonly used in classrooms where emergent readers are working on acquiring specific skills. Interactive storybooks are another commonly used resource. **Text-to-speech** products help students with poor decoding skills by reading the words aloud for the student with the aid of the computer's speech synthesizer. These products include NaturalReader (Natural Soft Ltd.), Snap and Read (Don Johnston Inc.), and Dragon Naturally Speaking (Nuance Inc.). If teachers provide all instructional text in a digital format, students with disabilities and other struggling readers will be able to copy and paste the information into talking word processors, apps, and other text-to-speech products so that they can listen to information they cannot read. Products such as Attainment's GoTalk (Figure 15.2) device add images to the text-to-speech capability so students can associate pictures of objects with printed and spoken words.

**FIGURE 15.2** Attainment's GoTalk

**Writing skills for students with mild cognitive disabilities.** Many tools have been developed to support students who struggle in various phases of the writing process. For students who are unable to write by hand, who have illegible handwriting, or who find handwriting extremely tedious, there is voice recognition software such as Nuances's Dragon Naturally Speaking and numerous mobile apps such as Dragon Dictation, Evernote for Android, and Voice Assistant. Some students who are slow typists or have difficulty spelling can benefit from word prediction software such as Co:Writer (Don Johnston, Inc.), which offers word choices to complete the first few letters the student types. Also, talking word processors, such as Don

## FIGURE 15.3 Don Johnston's Co:Writer

Co:Writer® by Don Johnston, Inc. Used with permission.

▲ Switches like the one this student is pressing (with his left hand) offer an alternative to the typical keyboard for controlling and getting input to the computer. Ablenet, Inc. Blue2™ Bluetooth Switch

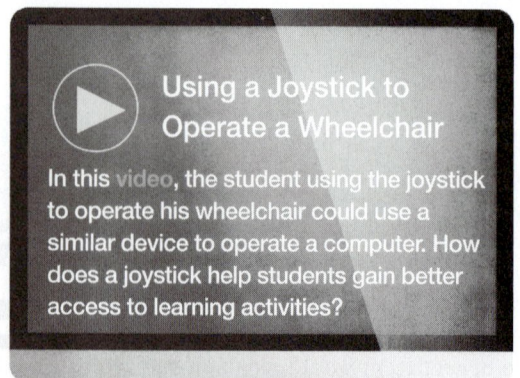

**Using a Joystick to Operate a Wheelchair**

In this video, the student using the joystick to operate his wheelchair could use a similar device to operate a computer. How does a joystick help students gain better access to learning activities?

Johnston's Write:OutLoud (see Figure 15.3), feature speech synthesis to allow students to hear what they have written.

### Math skills for students with mild cognitive disabilities.

Calculators are an important intervention for students with disabilities. A specialized calculator, the Coin-U-Lator® (PCI Education) was developed to assist students having difficulty counting coins and making change. Other strategies have been developed around simple graphing software materials, as well as drills, games, and tutorials. Again, there are numerous mobile apps that are available to assist learners with math skills. Apps such as eyeMath (fishdog.net) and Math Racer (i4software) allow learners to acquire math skills more easily through games that maximize visual depictions of math facts.

### Skills for students with moderate and severe cognitive disabilities.

For individuals with moderate and severe cognitive disabilities, considerable effort is devoted to ensuring that they acquire daily living skills such as personal hygiene, shopping, and use of public transportation. In addition, software is available to help teach important functional skills such as money and time management. For example, the Time, Money, & Fractions On-Track iPad app (School Zone Publishing) allows learners to acquire skills for managing money and time (see Technology Integration Example 15.2).

Teachers working with students with moderate and severe cognitive disabilities need to be familiar with an array of devices that provide an alternative means for accessing the computer or mobile device since the typical keyboard may be problematic for many students. To simplify the physical or cognitive demands of interacting with the computer, **alternative keyboards**, such as the Intellikeys keyboard (Intellitools), can be used to create customized keyboards. (See the photo here for an example.) For instance, keys can be enlarged to provide more space for the student to press a key; keys that are not relevant for a given software program can be removed; and multistep functions such as save, print, or quit can be programmed into a single key press. Companies such as AbleNet assist teachers in integrating the assistive technology into instruction.

## Strategies for Students with Physical Disabilities

Physical disabilities typically affect a person's mobility and agility. Difficulties with motor movements may involve gross- or fine-motor movement and frequently exist concurrently with other disabilities. Assistive technology for individuals with severe physical disabilities may take the form of a power wheelchair operated by a **joystick**, a device with a handle that moves in all directions. Joysticks can also control the movement of the cursor or pointer on a computer screen. To provide access to a computer, it is often necessary to offer an alternative to the typical keyboard. **Switches** are also commonly used for controlling and getting input to the computer as well as activating environmental control systems.

Assessing the need for assistive technology involves a team of specialists including occupational therapists, physical therapists, rehabilitation engineers, and assistive technology specialists. The goal is to identify appropriate tools for

# TECHNOLOGY INTEGRATION

## Example 15.2

access and control that will allow the individual to function across environments: home, school, community, and eventually work.

## Strategies for Students with Sensory Disabilities

**Sensory disabilities** involve impairments associated with the loss of hearing or vision. If there is a complete loss of vision, a person is considered blind. An individual is considered partially sighted if there is some visual acuity. Similarly, if there is a complete loss of hearing, a person is considered deaf. Hearing impaired is the term used to describe an individual with some hearing.

> **Using Adaptive Keyboards**
>
> The video illustrates a student with special needs using an alternative keyboard for computer input. What kinds of physical disabilities do adaptive keyboards accommodate?

**For students who are blind.** For an individual who is blind, three kinds of technology facilitate independence and access to environments and information:

- **Canes and sensor technology.** These are used to provide the person with mobility and orientation information when navigating various environments.
- **Tools to convert printed information.** Other essential tools convert printed information into audio so that a person who is blind can gain information by listening rather than reading. This is accomplished through the use of a scanner, **optical character recognition (OCR)** software to scan and translate print into a word-processed file, and speech synthesis. It works by placing text material on the scanner and scanning the material into the computer. The OCR software then converts the scanned information into text, and the speech synthesis tools read the material aloud.
- **Screen readers. Screen readers** work as utility software, operating in the background of the computer operating system and reading any text that appears on the screen—for example, menus, text, or Web pages. Examples of screen readers include SuperNova Screen Reader (Dolphin Computer Access) and JAWS for Windows (Freedom Scientific).

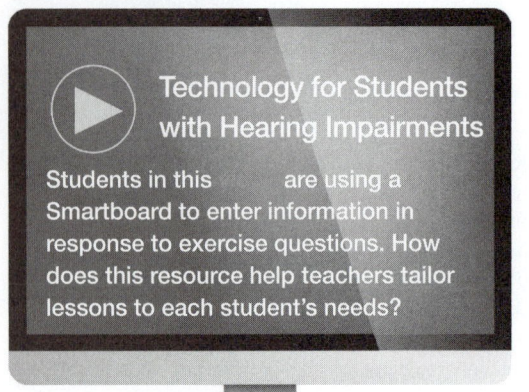

**Technology for Students with Hearing Impairments**

Students in this _____ are using a Smartboard to enter information in response to exercise questions. How does this resource help teachers tailor lessons to each student's needs?

**For students who have partial sight.** Partially sighted individuals must have text information enlarged, or the contrast altered, in order to perceive printed information. When information is in printed form (e.g., books, magazines, flyers) a **closed-circuit television (CCTV)** magnification system can be used. CCTV is a video camera mounted on a frame with a television monitor. Users place materials on the desktop below the camera, set the desired magnification level, and move the materials around as necessary such that the information appears on the monitor in a size that can be read comfortably. Many partially sighted individuals can see print on a computer screen by simply activating the built-in screen magnification control panel. This function allows users to select the desired magnification of everything appearing on the screen.

**For students who are deaf.** Individuals who are deaf often can use most technologies without significant modifications. However, two problematic areas involve the use of audio feedback (i.e., error messages) and the reliance on sound in multimedia software. When designers provide essential information only in audio form, this information is inaccessible to deaf individuals. As a result, advocacy and design initiatives encourage that all information be available in multiple formats (e.g., error messages that produce a message on screen as well as an auditory signal; multimedia software that includes closed captioning of audio tracks).

Individuals with hearing impairments need few modifications to be able to use computers. However, a technology that is being used in classrooms today is **FM amplification systems** (Lewis, 2010). These systems, also referred to as **assistive listening devices**, involve the teacher wearing a wireless microphone and those students with hearing impairments and those with learning disabilities that involve auditory processing difficulties wearing receivers that amplify the teacher's voice and serve to focus attention. Research suggests that sound amplification technology may benefit all students, not just those with diagnosed hearing impairments, by focusing their attention. In a study conducted by Millett and Purcell (2010) in which classrooms were equipped with sound-field amplification systems and the teacher wore a transmitter, teachers reported higher levels of student attentiveness, a decreased need for repetition, and fewer classroom management challenges. In active classrooms in which noise levels tend to rise, all students benefit from being able to listen and hear more effectively.

**Technology to teach American Sign Language (ASL).** Innovative strategies have been designed to teach ASL, the language most often used by American students with hearing impairments and educators who work with them. Snoddon (2010) described how students used video to tell stories in ASL, thus enhancing their ASL literacy. Andrei, Osbourne, and Smith (2013) described using a program that enabled a signing avatar, or on-screen presentation of a person, called Lamar University's Signing Avatar (LUSA). This software was designed in response to the problem of not having enough ASL interpreters available to support students with hearing deficits who wanted to take science, technology, engineering, and mathematics (STEM) courses. Usually, ASL interpreters require knowledge of technical concepts to do an effective job of supporting students in these courses. This software proved so effective that authors said its use would be expanded to other courses and to K–8 grades. Finally, there are numerous apps and YouTube tutorials available to help those who want to learn and/or use ASL. YouTube resources include those by Dr. Bill Vicars, himself a person with hearing deficits, and My Smart Hands. Apps include ASL Coach, ASL:Fingerspelling, and Marlee Signs.

## Strategies for Students with ASD

Technology has proven to have special benefits for children on the autism spectrum. Ploog, Scharf, Nelson, and Brooks (2013) reviewed research on these uses and found a treasure trove of successful uses that included:

- Remediation of deficits in expressive and receptive language (including reading skills)
- Enhancement of face processing and emotion recognition

▲ Research has shown good results for children with ASD who use video modeling to learn desired social behaviors. (Photo courtesy of Dr. Tom Buggey, the Siskin Children's Institute, Chattanooga, Tennessee)

- Teaching theory of mind (i.e., the ability to make inferences about others' intentions, thinking, reasoning, emotions, and motivation)
- Video modeling (i.e., using video "models" to show students how to do desired behaviors and asking them to imitate them)
- Virtual reality applications
- Teaching social skills: communication, play, and daily living skills, and related behaviors
- Teaching communications skills
- Teaching play skills
- Teaching daily living skills

Bailey (2011) also recommends touch screens and apps to support various types of learning for students with ASD. These applications have the advantage of making a more direct, hands-on connection between the students' actions and the software's response. For example, with touch screens, there is no mouse or keyboard needed that can disconnect the student's attention from the screen. Bailey also recommends the Autism Speaks.org website for a listing of these and other helpful resources. Finally, Herold (2014) said that a new virtual-reality headset called the Oculus Rift, currently in limited use with students who have ASD, has achieved results that teachers find most promising. Herold reports that this device has eliminated many of the problems with dizziness and nausea that characterized many previous virtual-reality systems.

## Strategies for Students with Gifts and Talents

The federal definition of gifted students was developed in the 1972 *Marland Report to Congress*, and has been modified several times since then. The current definition reads:

> Students, children, or youth who give evidence of high achievement capability in areas such as intellectual, creative, artistic, or leadership capacity, or in specific academic fields, and who need services and activities not ordinarily provided by the school in order to fully develop those capabilities (No Child Left Behind Act of 2001, Title IX, Part A, Section 9101(22); U.S. Department of Education, 2004).

In reviewing research and best practices for using technology to enhance gifted education, Periathiruvadi and Rinn (2012–2013) found that technologies can improve the quality of education for students with special gifts and talents in two primary ways: by providing differentiated instruction and a creative outlet for their works. Some of their key findings on technology in gifted education are briefly summarized here:

- **Attitudes toward technology uses.** Students in lower grades report higher levels of satisfaction with using technology than students in higher grades. Males express more confidence with their use of technology than females, but all had high interest in using technology for problem solving.

- **Impact on writing.** Research indicates that not only do gifted boys write more when they use word processing than they would otherwise, but the quality of their writing, which is usually less than that of girls, seems to increase to be equal with girls.

- **The role of technology in assessment.** The research shows that computer-based games and activities are effective at assessing the higher-level skills of gifted students. For examples, studies were reported that assessed strategic thinking and ability to focus and resist distractions. Also, online assessments were especially useful to help teachers track how much time gifted students were spending on various assignments in order to get an idea of difficulties they might be having.

- **Gifted students in online learning.** The greatest single benefit online learning offers gifted students is access to advances and elective courses they would like to take but do not have available to them locally. These courses also offer flexible learning environments that gifted students value.

Chen, Dai, and Zhou (2013) proposed a framework for how technology could be integrated into education for gifted students based on three kinds of strategies: enabling, enhancing, and transforming. Summarized briefly here, it echoes many of the best-practices findings reported by Periathiruvadi and Rinn:

- **Enabling strategies.** These include the kinds of online learning opportunities described in Periathiruvadi and Rinn's review, as well as technology tools for recruiting and managing online programs and for building online learning opportunities.

- **Enhancing strategies.** These include curriculum enrichment activities such as online explorations, group training activities, and individual and small-group problem solving. As Periathiruvadi and Rinn found, technology tools can also enhance assessment and allow teachers of gifted students better access to timely, helpful professional development.

- **Transforming strategies.** Technologies can also allow gifted programs to offer more tailored services to meet diverse needs among this population. Chen et al. (2013) said that technologies can radically alter the way we think of giftedness, changing the focus from individual knowledge to communities of learners working together. Like Periathiruvadi and Rinn, Chen et al. said that advanced technologies such as simulations and intelligent tutoring can transform methods used to teach and assess gifted students.

**TECHNOLOGY LEARNING CHECK**

Complete TLC 15.3 to review what you have learned from this section about technology integration strategies to meet special needs.

# TEACHING TEACHERS TO INTEGRATE TECHNOLOGY FOR STUDENTS WITH SPECIAL NEEDS

This section gives recommendations for how teachers can prepare to integrate technology effectively into instruction for students with IEPs. Teachers of special students have two kinds of challenges when it comes to matching technology solutions to each student need. The first is to become familiar with the array of resources available and the strategies that they enable. But the second challenge is how to get access to these resources, which may be expensive to purchase and implement. The latter requires teachers or those who support them to identify and keep in touch with state and federal agencies that help resolve these issues. For example, the U.S. Department of Education has a State Grants for Assistive Technology Program that supports providing assistive technology to individuals with disabilities.

## Rubric to Measure Teacher Growth in Special Education Technology Integration

Begin by reviewing the rubric in Figure 15.4 to measure teachers' progress in effectively integrating technology in special education. Part I of the rubric addresses knowledge of issues and challenges, and Part II addresses special education integration strategies.

## Learning the Issues and Applications

The first step in technology integration is to become acquainted with the issues and challenges discussed in this chapter and how they shape teachers' uses and applications of technologies. Then teachers can begin developing capabilities to address instructional standards and curriculum goals. The following is a suggested sequence of learning activities.

- **Issues and challenges in special education.** After reviewing the information in this chapter, go to the Council for Exceptional Children (CEC) website. Review the standards in the *What Every Special Educator Must Know* handbook and CEC's initial and advanced teacher preparation standards. See professional development resources the site offers, and

**FIGURE 15.4** Rubric to Measure Teacher Growth in Technology Integration for Teachers of Students with Special Needs

| Part I: Teacher Knowledge of Special Education Issues and Challenges | | | |
|---|---|---|---|
| | **Basic knowledge (1–2 points)** | **Intermediate knowledge (3–4 points)** | **Advanced knowledge (4–5 points)** |
| Special education and inclusion requirements | I can articulate the nature of the issue. | I can both articulate the nature of the issue and some of the possible ways to address it. | I can articulate my own plan for addressing the issue in my own teaching. |
| Policy drivers of technology use in special education | I can articulate the nature of the issue. | I can both articulate the nature of the issue and some of the possible ways to address it. | I can articulate my own plan for addressing the issue in my own teaching. |
| Educational reform and accountability in special education | I can articulate the nature of the issue. | I can both articulate the nature of the issue and some of the possible ways to address it. | I can articulate my own plan for addressing the issue in my own teaching. |
| Trends in the prevalence of autism spectrum disorders (ASD) | I can articulate the nature of the issue. | I can both articulate the nature of the issue and some of the possible ways to address it. | I can articulate my own plan for addressing the issue in my own teaching. |
| **Part II: Teachers' Technology Integration Strategies for Special Education** | | | |
| | **Basic knowledge (1–2 points)** | **Intermediate knowledge (3–4 points)** | **Advanced knowledge (4–5 points)** |
| Strategies for students with cognitive disabilities | I can describe the strategies and identify technologies to carry them out. | I have designed at least 1–2 activities based on these strategies to enhance my teaching and my students' learning. | I have designed plans for how I will integrate these strategies throughout my curriculum to enhance my teaching and my students' learning. |
| Strategies for students with physical disabilities | I can describe the strategies and identify technologies to carry them out. | I have designed at least 1–2 activities based on these strategies to enhance my teaching and my students' learning. | I have designed plans for how I will integrate these strategies throughout my curriculum to enhance my teaching and my students' learning. |
| Strategies for students with sensory disabilities | I can describe the strategies and identify technologies to carry them out. | I have designed at least 1–2 activities based on these strategies to enhance my teaching and my students' learning. | I have designed plans for how I will integrate these strategies throughout my curriculum to enhance my teaching and my students' learning. |
| Strategies for students with ASD | I can describe the strategies and identify technologies to carry them out. | I have designed at least 1–2 activities based on these strategies to enhance my teaching and my students' learning. | I have designed plans for how I will integrate these strategies throughout my curriculum to enhance my teaching and my students' learning. |
| Strategies for students with gifts and talents | I can describe the strategies and identify technologies to carry them out. | I have designed at least 1–2 activities based on these strategies to enhance my teaching and my students' learning. | I have designed plans for how I will integrate these strategies throughout my curriculum to enhance my teaching and my students' learning. |
| **Total points** | _____ **of 45 possible points** | | |

# OPEN SOURCE
## OPTIONS _for Special Education_

| | |
|---|---|
| **Assistive technologies** | **Free Assistive Technology Resources** (ucdenver.edu/academics/colleges/medicalschool/programs/atp/Resources/FreeATSoftware/Pages/FreeATSoftware.aspx)—Links to free specialized assistive technology software. |
| **Materials generators** | **Intervention Central** (interventioncentral.org)—A collection of tools for creating instructional materials and managing academic, behavioral, and social performance data.<br>**KidTools** (kidtools.org)—A collection of free tools designed for students with emotional and behavioral disabilities. |
| **Tools to assist reading** | **Text Compactor** (textcompactor.com)—A free online tool that enables users to paste a text passage and then interact with a slider to create a real-time summary of the most important information in the passage. Ideal for struggling readers.<br>**Natural Reader** (naturalreaders.com)—Free text-to-speech tool that is downloaded to your computer. Once it is installed, simply copy and paste text into the reader and listen to an individual word, sentence, or the complete passage. |

decide on which can help you gain insight into the issues and challenges outlined in this chapter. Discuss and reflect on the two questions under the Collaborate, Discuss, Reflect feature at the end of the chapter. Complete Part I of the rubric in Figure 15.4 before you begin this sequence and again at various points in your progress.

- **Special education technology integration strategies.** After reviewing the information in this chapter, review examples of the technologies suggested in the Open Source Options feature and the websites and projects described under each section, and do the lesson evaluation and lesson development activities outlined in the Technology Integration Workshop at the end of this chapter. Reflect on how you will plan for implementing these strategies in your own classroom using the TIP model. Complete Part I of the rubric in Figure 15.4 before you begin this sequence and again at various points in your progress.

### TECHNOLOGY LEARNING CHECK
Complete TLC 15.4 to review what you have learned from this section about how teachers of students with special needs can develop their knowledge and skills in technology integration.

Monkey Business/Fotolia

**The following questions may be used either for in-class, small-group discussions or may be used to initiate discussions in blogs or online discussion boards:**

1. If we begin with the premise that every classroom is composed of diverse learners and that teachers must support them before they have a chance to fail, we realize that every teacher must have a "technologies toolkit" to provide access, expand choice, and engage students in academic tasks at an appropriate challenge level. Some of these tools include alternatives to usual methods of input in order to exploit the full potential of technologies such as word processors, web browsers, email clients, and social media.. After reviewing one or more of the following types of technology integration professional development resources, decide what specific tools should be in your "technology toolkit." Search for these sites: EdTech Solutions: Teaching Every Student, I Teach Tech, and The Educator's PLN.

2. According to IDEA 2004, the federal law governing special education, school districts cannot deny special education services because the solutions—many of which are assistive technologies—are expensive. But there is often a tension between what parents want and what school districts believe they can afford. What is a good protocol or manner to address such situations before you encounter them?

**Chapter** **15** Summary

**The following is a summary of the main points covered in this chapter.**

1. **Introduction to Special Education.** The terms *impairment*, *disability*, and *handicap* are often used synonymously, differences among these concepts have important implications for the use of technology in classrooms.

2. **Issues and Challenges in Special Education.** These issues include special education and inclusion requirements, policy drivers of technology use in special education, educational reform and accountability in special education, and trends in the prevalence of autism.

3. **Technology integration strategies to meet special needs.** Concepts in this section include:
   - Foundations of integration strategies for special education include the definition of *assistive technology device*; how an assistive technology evaluation referral works; how solutions are classified; multiple means of representation (MMR), alternatives to acquiring information beyond a textbook; and multiple means of expression (MME), multiple methods of demonstrating what they know.
   - General requirements of integration strategies for all students include making curriculum accessible and offering flexible instructional support.
   - Integration strategies are specific to disabilities including those for cognitive, physical, and sensory disabilities.
   - Some technology integration strategies such as video modeling have proven especially beneficial for students with ASD.
   - Strategies for gifted and talented students are based on research on best practices, which has found that technology use is especially popular among boys and students at higher grade levels, though girls also like using it to solve problems. There is also positive impact on writing, especially for boys. Also, technology offers innovative and effective ways to assess student progress, and online learning offers unique access to learning opportunities and connectivity with learning communities. It offers capabilities to enable, enhance, and transform education for gifted students.

4. **Teaching Teachers to Integrate Technologies for Students with Special Needs.** Teachers can begin by consulting the rubric provided in this chapter to measure their own growth in special education technology integration. After that, they may review issues and challenges in special education and use chapter resources to learn technology integration strategies they can use to address the issues and challenges.

# TECHNOLOGY INTEGRATION **WORKSHOP**

## 1. APPLY WHAT YOU LEARNED

To apply the concepts and skills you've read about throughout this chapter, go to the Chapter 15 Technology Application Activity.

## 2. TECHNOLOGY INTEGRATION LESSON PLANNING: PART 1—EVALUATING AND CREATING LESSON PLANS

Complete the following exercise using the sample lesson plans found on any lesson planning site that you find on the Internet.

**a.** Locate lesson ideas—Identify three lesson plans that focus on any of the tools or strategies you learned about in this chapter. For example:
  - Using adaptive input devices for students with impairments
  - Using technologies to allow multiple means of representation
  - Using technologies to allow multiple means of expression
  - Using voice recognition and word prediction software
  - Engaging gifted students through problem-based learning environments

**b.** Evaluate the lessons—Use the Technology Lesson Plan Evaluation Checklist to evaluate each of the lessons you found.

**c.** Create your own lesson—After you have reviewed and evaluated some sample lessons, create one of your own using a lesson plan format of your choice (or one your instructor gives you). Be sure the lesson focuses on one of the technologies or strategies discussed in this chapter.

## 3. TECHNOLOGY INTEGRATION LESSON PLANNING: PART 2—IMPLEMENTING THE TIP MODEL

Review how to implement the TIP model in your classroom by doing the following activities with the lesson you created in the Technology Integration Lesson Planning exercise above.

**a.** Describe the Phase 1—Planning activities you would do to use this lesson in your classroom:
  - What is the relative advantage of using the technology(ies) in this lesson?
  - Do you have resources and skills you need to carry it out?

**b.** Describe the Phase 2—Implementation activities you would do to use this lesson in your classroom:
  - What are the objectives of the lesson plan?
  - How will you assess your students' accomplishment of the objectives?
  - What integration strategies are used in this lesson plan?
  - How would you prepare the learning environment?

**c.** Describe the Phase 3—Evaluation/Revision activities you would do to use this lesson in your classroom: What strategies and/or instruments would you use to evaluate the success of this lesson in your classroom in order to determine revision needs?

**d.** Add lesson descriptors—Create descriptors for your new lesson (e.g., grade level, content and topic areas, technologies used, ISTE standards, 21st Century Learning standards).

**e.** Save your new lesson—Save your lesson plan with all its descriptors and TIP model notes.

## 4. FOR YOUR TEACHING PORTFOLIO

Add the following to your Teaching Portfolio:
  - Reflections on Hot Topic Debates.
  - Summary notes from the Collaborate, Discuss, Reflect activity.
  - Lesson plan evaluations, lesson plans, and products you created above.
  - Your *Apply What You Learned* Product from Activity 1.

**accelerometer**—A device that assists with analyzing and monitoring physical fitness levels by counting calories.

**Acceptable Use Policy (AUP)**—An agreement created by a school or other educational organization that describes the risks involved in Internet use; outlines appropriate, safe student behavior on the Internet; asks students if they agree to use the Internet under these conditions; and asks what information about themselves, if any, may be posted on the school's website.

**accommodation**—Piagetian view of how children change their views of the world by incorporating new experiences.

**ActionScript**—In Adobe Flash, an advanced authoring environment for creating content for the Web, including mobile applications, or virtually any digital platform.

**Adequate Yearly Progress (AYP)**—(See No Child Left Behind (NCLB) Act of 2001.)

**adventure learning (AL)**—An approach that lets students learn through real-world experiences, either by taking actual trips themselves with mentors or by using distance tools to engage with the explorations of others.

**alternative keyboard**—Customized keyboards created for users with special needs (e.g., enlarging the keys to provide more space for the student to press a key; removing keys that are not relevant for a given software; programming multistep functions like save, print, and quit into a single key press).

**app**—Abbreviation for *application*; any software specifically designed to carry out a specific task. (See also universal app.)

**applications programs**—Computer software written to support tasks that are useful to a computer user (e.g., word processing) in contrast with systems software.

**aptitude-treatment interaction (ATI)**—Research finding that a treatment beneficial for one group has a negative impact on a group with the opposite characteristic.

**ARPAnet**—Network created in 1969 by the U.S. government–funded Advanced Research Projects Agency (ARPA) to enable communications among important defense sites in the event of a worldwide catastrophe such as a nuclear attack; later became the Internet.

**artificial intelligence (AI)**—Computer programs that try to emulate human decision-making capabilities.

**ASP.NET**—Scripting language that that generates HTML source code to create dynamic Web pages (See also PHP.)

**assimilation**—Piagetian view of how children learn by fitting new experiences into their existing view of the world.

**assistive listening devices**—A system in which a speaker wears a wireless microphone and persons with auditory impairments wear receivers that amplify the speaker's voice.

**assistive technology**—Devices that extend the abilities of an individual in ways that provide physical access (i.e., wheelchairs, braces) and sensory access (i.e., Braille, closed captioning).

**asynchronous**—Form of distance communications in which information and messages are left for the receiver to read later, rather than sent and received immediately. (See also synchronous.)

**audiobook**—Book stored on a medium such as a disc that allows texts to be read aloud to users.

**audio recording and editing program**—Software that allows users to select audio clips in a given recording and to manipulate elements such as pitch and tempo to achieve various effects.

**Audio Video Interleave (AVI) format**—One of several digital formats for video that are able to be used with video editing software.

**augmented reality**—Coined by a Boeing researcher in 1990, it refers to a computer-generated environment in which a real-life scene is overlaid with information that enhances our understanding and uses of it.

**autocorrect**—A built-in feature of word processing software that automatically detects and corrects misspelled words and incorrect capitalization.

**automaticity**—A level of skill that allows a person to respond immediately (i.e., automatically) with the correct answer to a problem.

**auto-tuning**—A unique vocal distortion technique made possible with vocal-editing software.

**avatar**—A graphic representation of a real person in cyberspace; a three-dimensional image that a person can choose to represent himself or herself in a virtual reality environment.

**avatar spaces**—Online environments in which users can interact through their graphic representations (i.e., avatars).

**blended intercultural collaborations**—In language learning, "international class-to-class partnerships in which projects and tasks are developed by the partner teachers in the collaborating institutions" (O'Dowd, 2011, p. 3); students work with students of other cultures to provide authentic writing and research experiences.

**blended learning**—In distance education, opportunities that allow students to blend online and face-to-face learning; also referred to as hybrid learning.

**blog**—Short for "Web log," a Web page that serves as a publicly accessible location for discussing a topic or issue; began as personal journals and expanded to become public discussion forums.

**blood pressure devices**—Devices that assist with analyzing and monitoring physical fitness levels by monitoring and reporting blood pressure.

**BMP**—Stands for "bitmapped," an image format used for drawn images, illustrations, clip art, or animations.

**body composition analyzer**—A device that assists with analyzing and monitoring physical fitness levels by determining the percent of body fat.

**bookmarks file**—In a browser, a set of Internet locations or URLs organized so that a user can return to them quickly. (See also favorites file.)

**Bring Your Own Device (BYOD, or Bring Your Own Technology, BYOT)**—A strategy that allows students to use their own personal handheld devices for learning.

**browser**—Also known as a Web browser; software designed to allow a computer user to go to Internet websites that are connected to each other via the World Wide Web (WWW).

**bulletin board (BB)**—A computer system set up to allow notices to be posted and viewed by anyone who has access to the network.

**calculator-based lab (CBL)**—Calculator with probes or sensors connected to it to allow gathering of numerical data.

**cell**—In a spreadsheet, a row–column location that may contain numerical values, words, or character data as well as formulas or calculation commands.

**charting/graphing tools**—Software tools that automatically draw and print desired charts or graphs from data entered by users.

**chatroom**—A location on the Internet set up to allow people to converse in real time by typing in messages or allowing their avatars to meet and "talk" to each other.

**classical conditioning**—Pavlovian view of learning as involuntary physical responses to outside stimuli (e.g., dogs salivate automatically at the sight of a dog food can).

**clickers**—(See student response systems or SRS).

**clip art**—One or more pieces of professionally prepared art work, stored as files and designed to be inserted into a document or Web page.

**closed circuit television (CCTV)**—A magnification system in which a video camera is mounted on a frame with a television monitor. Users place materials on the desktop below the camera, set the desired magnification level, move the materials around as necessary, and information appears on the monitor in a size that can be read comfortably by an individual with visual impairments.

**cloud computing**—The practice of storing software on servers that are accessed through the Internet.

**Cloze exercises**—Comprehension exercises with certain words removed to require students to fill in the blanks.

**cognitive load**—The amount of working memory that is available to a learner to process new information and that is taken up at a given time by a learning task.

**Common Core State Standards**—Statements of what students should learn, developed by the National Governors Association Center for Best Practices (NGA Center) and the Council of Chief State School Officers (CCSSO) and adopted by many U.S. states.

**Common Gateway Interface (CGI)**—An authoring specification on the Internet for how data will be collected at a website; CGI programs are written in a language such as PERL.

**computer adaptive testing (CAT)**—Computer software that continuously analyzes a student's test responses and presents more or less difficult questions based on the student's performance. (See also computer-assisted testing.)

**computer-aided design (CAD)**—Software used by architects and others to aid in the design of structures such as houses and cars.

**computer algebra system (CAS)**—Either software or devices with software that help carry out complex numeric calculations involved in higher-level math problems (e.g., Maple).

**computer-assisted instruction (CAI)**—Software designed to help teach information and/or skills related to a topic; also known as instructional software or courseware, computer-based instruction (CBI), computer-based learning (CBL), computer-assisted learning (CAL), or generically as software learning tools.

**computer-assisted language learning (CALL)**—For learners of English and foreign languages, activities in which they use computers in language testing, teaching, and learning in and out of class.

**computer-assisted testing (CAT)**—Using a computer system to administer and score assessment measures; also, computer adaptive testing, computer-based testing.

**computer-managed instruction (CMI)**—Computer software systems designed to keep track of student performance data, either as part of CAI programs or by themselves.

**computer platforms**—Types of computer systems identified by their operating systems (e.g., PCs with Windows operating systems or Macintoshes with Mac-OS operating systems).

**computer programs**—(See software.)

**concept-mapping software**—Tools designed to help people think through and explore ideas or topics by developing concept maps (i.e., visual outlines of ideas).

**constructivism**—The belief system that holds that humans construct all knowledge in their minds by participating in certain experiences; knowledge is the result of constructing both mechanisms for learning and one's own unique version of the knowledge, colored by background, experiences, and aptitudes.

**constructivist learning**—Teaching/learning model based on cognitive learning theory; holds that learners should generate their own knowledge through experience-based activities rather than being taught that knowledge by teachers. (See also directed instruction.)

**content management system (CMS)**—An online system of course design and delivery tools; Desire-to-Learn and Blackboard are examples.

**contingencies of reinforcement**—According to learning theorist B. F. Skinner, these are experiences (positive reinforcement, negative reinforcement, punishment) that shape desired behavioral responses.

**copyright laws**—Laws that give the creator of an original work exclusive rights to use and profit from it.

**cookie**—A small text file transferred to a Web browser through an Internet server for the purpose of tracking the Internet usage habits of the person using the browser.

**courseware**—(See computer-assisted instruction or CAI.)

**crowdsourcing**—A type of outsourcing in which many people are asked to give their input online to solve a problem that has proven resistant to efforts of single individuals or organizations.

**curation tool**—Software that allows users to collect and organize Internet-based information from various boards into a personal account.

**cyberbullying**—Harassing behaviors in online social networks.

**cybercheating**—In education, academic dishonesty in which someone uses another's work obtained from the Internet as his/her own, also known as online cheating.

**cyberporn**—General term for any pornographic Internet site.

**database**—A collection of information systematized by computer software to allow storage and easy retrieval through keyword searching; the program designed to accomplish these tasks.

**data dashboard**—A location in a CMS that summarizes course data in ways that allow instructors to track student participation and progress.

**data loggers**—Devices that use sensors to record data over time.

**data mining**—The practice of collecting data from all the information available and searching it to see relationships among the data elements.

**desktop publishing**—Term coined in 1984 by the president of the Aldus Corporation to refer to the activity of using software to produce documents with elaborate control of the form and appearance of individual pages.

**digital citizenship**—The use of technology resources in safe, responsible, and legal ways.

**digital dictionaries (a.k.a., word atlas)**—Electronic dictionaries and thesauruses that give pronunciations, definitions, and example uses for each word entry, and offer search and multimedia features similar to those of encyclopedias and atlases.

**digital divide**—A discrepancy in access to technology resources or technology-enabled opportunities among socioeconomic groups.

**digital literacy**—Originally, the ability to use computer devices and software to locate and use information; now often refers to skills in using the information that technological devices carry, in addition to skills in using the devices themselves.

**digital storytelling**—Using digitally produced images and audio to tell the stories of lives, events, or eras.

**directed instruction**—A teaching and learning model based on behavioral and cognitive theories; students receive information from teachers and do teacher-directed activities (See also constructivist learning.)

**disability**—Condition that occurs when an impairment limits an individual from performing an activity in a manner normally expected for human beings (communicating with others, hearing, movement, manipulating objects, etc.) (See also handicap and impairment.)

**discovery learning**—According to learning theorist Jerome Bruner, a more effective way of children learning concepts by discovering them during their interaction with the environment.

**disequilibrium**—Piagetian view of condition children experience when they confront new and unfamiliar features of their environment that do not fit with their current views of the world.

**distance education**—A form of education in which some means, electronic or otherwise, is used to connect people with instructors and/or resources that can help them acquire knowledge and skills. According to Holden & Westfall (2010), "structured learning that takes place without the physical presence of the instructor" (p. 3). Sometimes used as synonymous with "distance learning."

**distributed knowledge network**—Group of online users in which some individuals are more expert than others on certain skills/knowledge but all participants in the classroom use social media to maximize everyone's learning.

**domain designator**—Also referred to as a domain name, a required part of a Uniform Resource Locator (URL) on the Internet that indicates what kind of group owns the server; examples include ".edu," ".com," and ".org."

**domain name**—(See domain designator.)

**download**—To bring information (e.g., text files, images) to a computer from the Internet or other network or from a computer to a disc.

**drill and practice**—An instructional software function that presents items for students to work on (usually one at a time) and gives feedback on correctness; designed to help users remember isolated facts or concepts and recall them quickly.

**e-books (ebooks)**—Texts in digital form that may be read on a computer or e-book readers; becoming a popular alternative to printed texts.

**educational technology**—A combination of the processes and tools involved in addressing educational needs and problems, with an emphasis on applying the most current digital and information tools.

**electronic field trip**—(See virtual field trip.)

**electronic gradebook**—Software designed to maintain and calculate student grades.

**electronic outliner**—(See outlining tools.)

**electronic portfolio**—A collection of a person's work products over time, arranged so that he or she and others can see how skills have developed and progressed, and presented in an electronic format such as a website or multimedia product. (See also portfolio.)

**electronic publishing**—Activity when students submit their written or artistic products to a website.

**electronic slide shows**—Sequences of frames shown in a linear way with presentation software (e.g., PowerPoint).

**electronic storybooks**—Stories that can be read from a computer screen, on mobile devices, or as print books with interactive buttons; also known as interactive storybooks.

**enactive learning**—Proposed by learning theorist Albert Bandura as learning that occurs through actions, rather than by observation.

**English as a Second Language (ESL)**—Designates a type of learning of English that occurs after a student achieves some level of proficiency in another, native language; more commonly used term is now English Language Learning or ELL.

**English Language Learners (ELL)**—Individuals who are learning English as their majority language for everyday uses, employment, and educational purposes; ELL also stands for English Language Learning.

**epistemologies**—Beliefs about the nature of human knowledge as well as how to develop it.

**e-portfolio**—Websites created by students to showcase their work and organize, revise, and store digital assets that they have created inside and outside the classroom.

**EPS (Encapsulated PostScript)**—An image format designed to allow transfer of artwork between any software packages that use PostScript printing files; not usually seen in today's technology.

**exergaming**—"Video games that provide physical activity or exercise through interactive play" (Mears & Hansen, 2009, p. 29).

**EXtensible Mark-up Language**—(See XML.)

**fair use**—Limited rights to use brief excerpts of copyrighted material without the need for permission.

**favorites file**—In a browser, a set of Internet locations or URLs organized so that a user can return to them quickly. (See also bookmarks file.)

**field**—The smallest unit of information in a database.

**files**—The products created by a database program; any collection of data stored in a computer or on a computer medium.

**File Transfer Protocol (FTP)**—On the Internet, a way of transferring files from one computer to another using common settings and transmission procedures; also, to transfer files.

**filtering software**—Program stored on individual computers or on the school or district network in order to prevent access to Internet sites with inappropriate materials.

**firewall**—Software that protects a school's or company's entire computer system from attempts by others to gain unauthorized access to it and also prevents access by users to certain sites.

**firewall software**—Programs set up to prevent someone from going to certain locations on the Internet; prevention may be by keyword, by site name, or a combination of means.

**Flash**—A type of hypermedia authoring software from Adobe that has become commonly used to create interactive Web-based animations.

**flipped classroom**—Models in which students engage with concepts, for example via lectures stored as downloadable videos or vodcasts, before coming to class, then spend class time on other learning activities.

**FM amplification system**—Resource for students with hearing impairments in which the teacher wears a wireless microphone and students with auditory processing learning disabilities wear receivers that amplify the teacher's voice, which serves to focus attention.

**font**—Typeface used in word processing, desktop publishing, or other software that produces text.

**foreign language (FL)**—A target language, or language of study, when the language being studied is spoken mainly in countries other than the one where students reside.

**foreign language dictionaries**—Online sites that allow people to look up definitions for words and phrases in common usage by typing a word or phrase in one language and getting the meaning in another language.

**forms makers**—Software tools that create documents and Web pages with "fillable" forms.

**formula**—In a spreadsheet, a command inserted in a cell to do calculations on data.

**frame**—Sections programmed to display on a Web page; the contents of each frame are actually different Web pages displayed on one screen.

**full immersion systems**—Type of virtual reality (VR) system in which a user places a headset (e.g., goggles or a helmet) over the eyes to provide a channel through which the wearer "sees" (i.e., is immersed in) a computer-generated environment.

**gamification**—Incorporating the most motivational aspects of games (e.g., badges awarded for success) into nongame activities.

**geocaching**—An online activity in which students look at a database of caches listed at a geocaching website, decide on a cache to hunt for, use GPSs to help them locate it, and share their experiences with others.

**Geographic Information System (GIS)**—A computer system that stores and manipulates a database of information about geographic locations; users see data pertaining to a geographic location overlaid on a map of the area.

**geospatial technologies**—Systems that allow individuals to view and examine the world through multiple layering of geographic data overlaid on maps that are then used for visualization, analysis, and measurement of features and phenomena.

**gesture-recognition system**—System in which a camera or sensor reads body movements and communicates them to a computer, which processes the gestures as commands and uses them to control devices or displays.

**GIF (Graphics Interchange Format)**—An image format used for drawn images, illustrations, clip art, or animations.

**Global Positioning System (GPS)**—A worldwide radio-navigation system made possible by a bank of orbiting satellites and their ground stations to pinpoint exact geographic locations on earth; a device that cross-references a GPS signal with mapping software and shows the location to a user.

**Google Docs**—Tools offered through a special Google site that provide users access to online programs for word processing, spreadsheets, and presentations; the site offers storage of documents on a Google server and allows for sharing of documents among multiple users.

**graphic document makers**—Software tools that simplify the activity of making highly graphic materials such as awards certificates and greeting cards by offering sets of clip art and predesigned templates to which people add their own content.

**graphing calculators**—Advanced calculators that can graph equations and perform calculation functions involved in higher-level math and science problems; allows users to enter equations and shows graphs that result from those equations.

**hacker**—Computer user who engages in unauthorized use of a computer system.

**hacking**—Use of online systems to do malicious acts such as disabling a website or accessing personal data to accomplish identity theft.

**handheld technologies**—Small, multipurpose devices such as smartphones, e-books, and "smart" pens that make it easy to view, communicate, and share information, regardless of location. (See also mobile device.)

**handicap**—A condition that arises when an individual is unable to fulfill a role due to an impairment or disability. (See also impairment and disability.)

**hands-on/minds-on science**—A common term in science education reform, synonymous with immersing students in authentic learning experiences.

**haptic interface**—One of the devices (e.g., a data glove) that allows users to experience a full immersion virtual reality system by providing tactile or touch input.

**hardware**—The devices or equipment in a computer system (in contrast with software or computer programs).

**hash tag**—A term used on the Twitter system for a prefix to a message (Tweet) consisting of a pound sign (#) and a topic name (e.g., #ripstevejobs). Users begin a Tweet with a hash tag to allow others to identify posts and create their own messages on that topic.

**head-mounted display (HMD)**—In a full immersion virtual reality (VR) system, a headset that provides the sensory channel through which the wearer "sees" a computer-generated environment.

**heart rate monitor**—Device consisting of a transmitter that senses the heartbeat from the heart's electrical impulses and a wristwatch receiver that receives and records each beat through radio transmission from the transmitter.

**hits**—Pages or items listed as results of an Internet or database search.

**HTML**—(See Hypertext Markup Language.)

**HTML 5**—A revision of the HTML standard that provides many of the features of a Flash environment without using Flash. (See also Flash.)

**human performance technology**—A systematic approach to improving human productivity and competence by using strategies for solving problems.

**hybrid learning**—(See blended learning.)

**hypermedia**—Software that allows information stored in various media or various parts of media to be connected (often via the Internet).

**hypertext**—On the Internet, texts that contain links to other texts.

**Hypertext Markup Language (HTML)**—The primary authoring language used to develop Web pages.

**IEP generator**—Software that assists teachers in preparing individual educational plans (IEPs) required by law for students with special needs; automates the process by providing on-screen prompts that remind teachers of the required components in the plan.

**IEP team**—Individuals tasked with creating and carrying out the IEP.

**image editing programs**—Software tools used to enhance and format photos that are then imported into desktop publishing systems or Web page products.

**image formats**—Ways of storing digitized images for use in Web pages and multimedia products (e.g., GIF, JPEG).

**inclusive technologies**—The perspective that assistive technologies have a role in the general classroom to help many students other than those with special needs.

**impairment**—An abnormality or loss of function in a physical, anatomical, or psychological structure; may be congenital (present at birth) or acquired through accident or disease. (See also handicap and disability.)

**inclusion**—Activity in which students with disabilities are placed in general education classrooms; often used interchangeably with *mainstreaming*, though the terms originally had different meanings. (See also mainstreaming.)

**individualized educational program (IEP)**—The educational program required by law to be designed for each student with a disability.

**inert knowledge**—A term introduced by Whitehead in 1929 to mean skills that students learn in isolation but do not know how to transfer later to problems that require them.

**information and communication technology (ICT)**—Term for all technologies used in education and training, as well as strategies for using them; originally in more common use outside the United States, but becoming more popular worldwide due to UNESCO's ICT standards for education.

**information literacy**—According to the American Library Association (ALA), skills in knowing how to recognize when one needs information and knowing how to locate it, evaluate it, and be able to use it effectively.

**inquiry-based learning**—(See constructivist learning.)

**instant messaging (IM)**—A communications service that allows users to create a private chat room that only members of a mutually agreed-upon list may enter; the system alerts a user when someone from the IM list is online; IM also designates the act of instant messaging, as in "to IM."

**instructional game**—Type of software function designed to increase motivation by adding game rules to a learning activity.

**instructional software**—Applications software that is designed specifically to deliver or assist with student instruction on a topic. (See also courseware.)

**instructional technology**—The subset of educational technology that deals directly with teaching and learning applications (as opposed to educational administrative applications).

**integrated learning system (ILS)**—Networked or online system that provides both computer-based instruction and summary reports of student progress.

**integrated packages**—Software products (e.g., Microsoft Works and AppleWorks) that have several applications in a single package (e.g., word processing, spreadsheet, presentation functions, database programs).

**integrating educational technology**—The process of determining which digital tools and which methods for implementing them are the most appropriate responses to given educational needs and problems.

**intelligent tutoring systems**—Sophisticated kinds of branching tutorial software that adapt the sequence of instruction to the needs of each learner.

**interactive asynchronous online model**—Online course model in which students "meet" and interact with their instructor (and often with other students) in a course space enabled by a content management system.

**interactive or dynamic geometry software**—Programs that allow users to create and manipulate geometric constructions and provide environments for making discoveries and conjectures about geometry.

**interactive storybooks**—(See electronic storybooks.)

**interactive whiteboard**—A device that includes a display screen connected to a computer and digital projector; allows information projected on the screen to be manipulated with special pens or one's hands and also allows drawings or notes from a given session to be saved and brought back later; sometimes referred to as an electronic whiteboard.

**interactive whiteboard activity software**—Programs that allow teachers to author and display lessons for use with interactive whiteboard systems.

**Internet**—A worldwide collection of computer networks that can exchange information by using a common software standard; sometimes referred to (erroneously) as synonymous with the World Wide Web (WWW), which is actually a subset of the Internet.

**intranet**—An internal network or a subset of the Internet, usually available only to the members of the organization that set it up.

**ISTE Standards**—Benchmark technology skills created by the International Society for Technology in Education (ISTE) for teachers, students, and educational administrators.

**Java**—Originally called OAK, a high-level programming language developed by Sun Microsystems. An object-oriented language similar to C++, it has become popular for its ability to do interactive graphic and animation activities on Web pages; the latter are called Java applets.

**Javascript**—An object-oriented scripting language that, like Java, is used to create dynamic websites.

**joystick**—Input device, used primarily with games, that moves on-screen figures or a cursor with a handle that moves in all directions.

**JPEG (also JPG)**—Stands for "Joint Photographic Experts Group," an image format used for photographs.

**language translators (machine translation)**—Online sites that allow users to input sentences and paragraphs of text in one language and get a translation into another language.

**laptop computer**—Small, stand-alone, portable personal computer system.

**learning commons**—Areas in a school that integrate school media centers and ELA classrooms around knowledge sharing and can even involve parents, student peers, counselors, administrators, and other teachers.

**learning hierarchies**—According to learning theorist Robert Gagné, a sequenced set of building block skills a student must learn in order to learn a higher-order skill.

**Likert scale**—An assessment instrument consisting of a series of statements with which students indicate their degree of agreement or disagreement; created by psychologist Rensis Likert.

**link**—Also known as a hot link or hot spot. On the Internet, a piece of text or an image that has been programmed into a Web page to send the browser to another Internet location; in a multimedia product, a piece of text or an image that has been programmed to send the user to another location in the product.

**listserv (list)**—On the Internet, a program that stores and maintains mailing lists and allows a message to be sent simultaneously to everyone on the list.

**logic bomb**—A type of computer virus that is set to "go off" (i.e., carry out its program) at a certain time.

**Logo**—A high-level programming language originally designed as an artificial intelligence (AI) language but later popularized by Seymour Papert as an environment to allow children to learn problem-solving behaviors

**long-term memory (LTM)**—According to information-processing learning theorists, one of the three kinds of memory or "stores" the brain uses to process information, much like a computer; LTM can hold information indefinitely after it is linked to prior knowledge already in LTM.

**lurkers**—Students who sign on to and spend time in an online course space but never post anything.

**machine translation**—(See language translators.)

**mainframe**—Early designation for a large-scale computer that could support many users at one time who connected to it with terminals.

**mainstreaming**—An activity in which students with disabilities participate in one or more selected classes in general education; often used interchangeably with *inclusion*, though the terms originally had different meanings. (See also inclusion.)

**malware**—Short for malicious software, any software specifically designed to damage, destroy, disrupt operations, or spy on the operation of computers.

**mastery learning**—According to learning theorists Benjamin Bloom and B. F. Skinner, an instructional approach in which students learn a sequence of objectives that define mastery of the subject; students pass tests on each objective to demonstrate they have mastered a skill before proceeding to the next one.

**meta-analysis**—A statistical method designed by Gene V Glass (1976) to summarize results across studies and measure the size of the effect a "treatment" such as technology-based methods has over and above traditional methods.

**microcomputer**—Also called a personal computer; a stand-alone, desktop, or laptop computer that uses a microprocessor and is designed for use by an individual.

**microcomputer-based lab (MBL)**—A type of instructional software tool consisting of hardware devices.

**minicomputer**—An early designation for computer systems smaller than mainframes that could support fewer users at a time.

**mobile device**—General category of portable computer devices such as smartphones and tablets (e.g., iPads). (See also handhelds.)

**MOOC (Massive Open Online Courses)**—Originally, open-access university offerings that allowed anyone anywhere in the world to participate in college courses for free; now has evolved into large-scale courses offered by college and other organizations; some are fee-based.

**morphing**—Short for metamorphosing; refers to an animation technique in which one image gradually turns into another; also known as tweening.

**Mosaic**—One of the first browser programs designed to allow Internet resources to be displayed graphically rather than just in text.

**Motion Picture Experts Group (MPEG) format**—A file format for storing and sending video sequences on a network.

**MP3**—A file format for compressing a sound sequence into a file small enough to allow digital storage and transmission.

**multimedia**—Literally "multiple media" or "a combination of media"; a software product or system that incorporates combinations of graphics and photographs, sound, motion video, animation, and/or text items for the purpose of communicating information in multiple ways.

**multiple intelligences theory**—According to learning theorist Howard Gardner, nine different and relatively independent types of intelligence that may be fostered by differentiated instruction and assessment.

**multimedia learning stations**—On the IBM 1500, terminals capable of displaying animation and video.

**multiple means of expression (MME)**—The practice of providing students with various methods of demonstrating what they know.

**multiple means of representation (MMR)**—The practice of providing students with alternatives to acquiring information beyond a textbook.

**multitasking**—The practice of doing several (usually technology-enabled) activities at the same time.

**Multi-User-Virtual Environment (MUVE)**—Web-based VR in which users have their avatars meet in 3-D environments on a computer screen.

**Musical Educators National Conference (MENC)**—(See National Association for Music Education [NAfME].)

**Musical Instrument Digital Interface (MIDI)**—A standard adopted by the electronic music industry for controlling devices that play music.

**music editor**—Software that provides on-screen blank musical bars on which the user enters the musical key, time, and individual notes that constitute a piece of sheet music.

**music sequencer**—Can be either software that supports the on-screen creation of music scores with several parts or tracks, or a hardware component of a music synthesizer workstation. (See also sequencer.)

**music synthesizer**—Music-making equipment controlled by a Musical Instrument Digital Interface (MIDI) device.

**National Arts Education Association (NAEC)**—Professional association for arts educators.

**National Association for Music Education (NAfME)**—Formerly MENC, the professional association for music educators.

**National Association for Sport and Physical Education**—Formerly the American Alliance for Health Physical Education Recreation and

Dance (AAHPERD); the professional association for educators of health and physical education.

**netiquette**—A contraction of *Internet* and *etiquette*; refers to guidelines for posting messages to online services (e.g., email or discussion boards) to demonstrate courtesy and regard for other users.

**new literacies**—The new skills, strategies, and insights necessary to utilize the rapidly changing and emerging.

**Nine Events of Instruction**—Guidelines identified by Gagné that can help teachers arrange optimal "conditions for learning" for various types of knowledge and skills technologies in the world.

**No Child Left Behind (NCLB) Act of 2001**—Federal law that put in place accountability measures of all U.S. students, teachers, and schools; requires schools to demonstrate adequate yearly progress (AYP) toward target goals, as demonstrated by test scores, attendance, and other quality indicators.

**noninteractive online model**—Online course model consisting of content presentations with built-in assessments.

**notation software**—Computer programs that facilitate music making in the visual domain by allowing flexibility in music score and page setup, part extraction, text formatting, and other print-related issues.

**nutritional analysis program**—Software that analyzes calorie intake and monitors portions of required food groups.

**objectivism**—A belief system that views knowledge as objective truths that have been established by scientific observation and testing and have a real and separate existence outside human perception; instructional strategies based on objectivist learning theories (i.e., behavioral, cognitive-behavioral, and information processing theories) hold that these objective truths must be transmitted through teacher-directed instructional methods and that learners must demonstrate their knowledge of them.

**one-to-one computing**—The practice of a school or district allocating a school computer for each student.

**open source software**—Computer software available online in which the source code is made available in the public domain and permits users to use, change, and improve the software, and to redistribute it in modified or unmodified form.

**operant conditioning**—According to learning theorist B. F. Skinner, a way of shaping human behavior in which the consequences of people's past actions can act as stimuli to shape future behaviors.

**online plagiarism (cybercheating)**—Academic dishonesty in which someone uses another's work obtained from the Internet as his/her own.

**optical character recognition (OCR)**—Software that allows text to be scanned and placed in a word processing file.

**outlining tools**—Software designed to prompt writers as they develop outlines to structure documents they plan to write.

**pedometer**—Device that assists with analyzing and monitoring physical fitness levels by monitoring the number of steps one takes.

**personalized learning systems (PLSs)**—Computer-based management programs that (1) assess individual student learning needs using complex algorithms and collections of data across students, and (2) provide a customized instructional experience matched to each student.

**phishing**—Emails that falsely claim to be a legitimate business or user in order to glean private information to be used for identity theft.

**PICT**—Stands for "picture"; an image format developed originally for use on Macintosh computers

**plug-in**—A program that adds a specific feature or service to a computer system; many types of audio and video messages are played through plug-ins.

**podcast**—A term coined by British journalist Ben Hammersley in 2005 that combines *iPod* and *broadcast*; originally meant digitized audio files saved in a format that can be shared over the Internet for playback on the computer or personal media devices; now can also mean posting video on a site. (See also vodcast.)

**portable document format (PDF)**—Format that allows documents to be seen and sent with all the formatting and design elements (e.g., margins, graphics) of the original document without requiring the desktop publishing or word processing software used to create it.

**portfolio**—A collection of work products that demonstrate achievement of skills over time; for students, collection arranged so that they and others can see how their skills have developed and progressed. (See also electronic portfolio.)

**presentation software**—Type of software that allows a display of information organized as a set of slides. (See also electronic slide show.)

**probeware**—(See microcomputer-based laboratory or MBL.)

**problem-based learning (PBL)**—According to Sage (2000), learning organized around the investigation and resolution of an authentic, ill-structured problem.

**problem-solving software**—Instructional software function that either teaches specific steps for solving certain problems (e.g., math word problems) or helps the student learn general problem-solving behaviors for a class of problems.

**programmed instruction**—Techniques for training and instruction based on learning theorist B. F. Skinner's reinforcement principles.

**puzzle generator**—Software tool that automatically formats and creates crossword puzzles, word search puzzles, and similar game-like activities, based on content entered by a user.

**Quick Response (QR) code**—A two-dimensional, square-shaped code that may be scanned using a QR code-scanning app on a smartphone. When scanned, the code sends the user to a web site with information, materials, and/or data.

**QuickTime movie format (.mov)**—Video sequences that may be viewed on a computer screen by a program designed by Apple Computer Company (i.e., QuickTime).

**QWERTY keyboard**—Traditional typewriter-like keyboard, so named because of the first six letters in the first line of a typewriter keyboard.

**radio frequency identification (RFID)**—An electronic monitoring system that tracks the location of a person or object with an embedded computer chip and can update information on the chip; RFID devices are being field-tested to track student attendance, increase school security, and monitor the location of library resources.

**record**—In a database file, several related fields (e.g., all the information on one person).

**relative advantage**—Term coined by Everett Rogers to refer to the perception by potential adopters of how much better an innovative method or resource is than the old one; one of five factors that largely determines whether or not an innovation is adopted.

**relay writing (chain writing)**—Activity in which one student or group of students writes a part of a document and sends it on to the next student or group to add to.

**rubric**—An assessment instrument designed to measure complex behaviors such as writing; for each of several elements in the performance, it gives a set of descriptions of various levels of quality.

**sans serif typeface**—Typeface in which letters have no small curves (serifs or "hands and feet") at the ends of the lines that make them up; usually used for short titles rather than the main text of a document.

**scaffolding**—Term associated with learning theorist Vygotsky's belief that teachers can provide good instruction by finding out where each child is in his or her development and building on the child's experiences.

**screencasting**—Video captures of actions a user does with a cursor on a computer screen.

**screen reader**—Utility software that operates in the background of the computer operating system, reading aloud any text that appears on the screen (e.g., menus, text, Web pages).

**search engine**—A program designed to search documents, either on one's computer or on the Internet, for keywords and list the locations of documents where the keywords were found; often used to refer only to programs used for Internet searches such as Google.

**self-efficacy**—According to learning theorist Albert Bandura, students' belief in their abilities to accomplish the actions necessary to learn.

**semantic differential**—Type of assessment instrument in which students respond to a topic or question by checking a line between each of several sets of bipolar adjectives to indicate their level of feeling about the topic.

**sensory disabilities**—Impairments associated with the loss of hearing or vision.

**sensory registers**—According to information-processing learning theory, the parts of the brain that receive information a person senses through receptors (i.e., eyes, ears, nose, mouth, and/or hands) and, after a second or so, is either lost or transferred to short-term memory (STM) or working memory.

**sequencer**—A device that facilitates music making in the aural domain by allowing users to record, edit, and play back digital audio and MIDI data. (See also music sequencer.)

**serif typeface**—Typeface in which letters have small curves (serifs or "hands and feet") at the ends of the lines that make them up; usually used for the main text of a document.

**sexting**—The practice of sending explicit photos or text messages using cell phones or the Internet.

**short-term memory (STM)**—According to information-processing learning theory, one of the three kinds of memory or "stores" the brain uses to process information, much like a computer; STM is said to hold information for about 5–20 seconds, after which it is either transferred to long-term memory (LTM) or lost.

**simulation**—Type of software that allows users to work with a computerized model of a real or imagined system in order to learn how the system works.

**site map**—An at-a-glance guide to the contents of a website.

**situated cognition**—According to constructivist learning theorists, instruction anchored in experiences that learners considered authentic because they emulate the behavior of adults.

**slide sorter**—Presentation software option that allows frames to be placed in a desired sequence.

**SMART Table Interactive Learning Center**—An electronic device produced by the Prometheus company that consists of a table with a touch-screen surface and that allows several students to give input to it at the same time.

**social action project**—Web-based project in which students are responsible for learning about and addressing important global social, economic, political, or environmental conditions.

**social activism theory**—Characteristic agenda of renowned educator John Dewey that shaped his views about teaching and learning; resulted in the belief that social consciousness was the ultimate aim of all education and learning was useful only in the context of social experience.

**social networking site (SNS)**—Sites that focus on building communities; individually designed Web pages that allow users to upload their content, meet and connect with friends from around the world, and share media and interests in an online, easy-to-use website environment.

**social presence**—The perception of "connectedness" or actually being with someone in a virtual environment.

**social studies**—The integrated study of the social sciences and humanities to promote civic competence.

**software**—Contrasts with hardware, or equipment; computer programs written in a computer language to perform various functions.

**software or music piracy**—Illegally copying and using a copyrighted software package or a musical piece

**software suite**—A set of programs that perform different functions but are placed in the same package and designed to work well together (e.g., Microsoft Office). (See also integrated packages.)

**spam**—Any unsolicited email message or website posting, usually sent for the purpose of advertising products or services, soliciting funds, or phishing. (See also phishing.)

**spirometer**—A device that assists with analyzing and monitoring physical fitness levels by measuring lung volume.

**spreadsheet**—Software designed to store data (usually, but not always, numeric) by row–column positions known as cells; can also do calculations on the data.

**spyware**—Software placed on a computer without the user's knowledge for the purpose of gathering information about them (usually to sell to marketing firms).

**STEM**—Stands for "science, technology, engineering, and mathematics" and refers to skills and careers in these areas.

**statistical software packages**—Software tools that help with qualitative data collection and analysis of student performance on tests by performing the calculations involved in any of these kinds of procedures.

**storage media**—Materials such as flash drives, CDs, and DVDs that are used to store programs and data outside the computer's hardware.

**storyboard**—A frame that serves as part of a planning blueprint from which a multimedia product or Web page can be designed; also the process of producing these frames (a.k.a., wireframing).

**streaming (or streamed) video/audio**—A way of transmitting video or audio on the Internet so that it can be seen or heard as the file downloads.

**student information systems (SIS)**—Networked software systems that help educators keep track of student, class, and school data (e.g., attendance, test scores) in order to maintain records and support decision making.

**student response systems (SRS)**—Also referred to as personal response systems, classroom response systems, or clickers; a combination of handheld hardware and software that permits each student in the classroom to answer a question simultaneously and lets the teacher see and display a summary of results immediately.

**switches**—In a network, equipment to compress data in order for information to be transmitted at higher speeds (e.g., Asynchronous Transfer Mode [ATM] switches); in special education, devices that allow a person with a disability an alternative to the typical keyboard and thus permit easier input to the computer.

**synchronous**—Form of distance communications in which messages are sent and received immediately; contrasts with asynchronous communications, in which information and messages are left for the receiver to read later. (See also asynchronous.)

**systems approaches to instructional design**—Methods originated by educational psychologists such as Robert Gagné and Leslie Briggs, who applied principles from military and industrial training to developing curriculum and instruction for schools.

**talking word processor**—A software package that reads typed words aloud.

**Technological Pedagogical Content Knowledge (TPCK, TPACK, or Tech-PACK)**—A framework that identifies a combination of essential skills/knowledge in three areas (content, pedagogy, and technology) that are required if teachers are to integrate technology to greatest effect in their teaching; termed Tech-PACK in this textbook.

**technology education**—A view of technology in education that originated with industry trainers and vocational educators in the 1980s and is currently represented by the International Technology and Engineering Educators Association (ITEEA); holds that (1) school learning should prepare students for the world of work in which they will use technology, and (2) vocational training can help teach STEM areas.

**Technology Institute for Music Educators (TI:ME)**—Professional organization for music educators who use technology in their teaching.

**Tech-PACK**—(See Technological Pedagogical Content Knowledge.)

**teletandem (a.k.a., telecollaboration)**—Experiences in which students use videoconferencing or other collaborative technologies to work together to learn each other's native language.

**test generator**—Software designed to help teachers prepare and/or administer tests.

**test item bank**—Premade pools of questions that can be used by test generator software to create various versions of the same test.

**text messaging**—An instant form of communications carried out on cell phones or other handheld devices that allows sending images and short videos, as well as text.

**text-to-speech products**—Systems consisting of software and the computer's speech synthesizer to help students with poor decoding skills by reading the words aloud.

**3D printers**—Devices that can "print" models or actual products when a 2-D image is supplied. [query

**TIF (Tagged Image File)**—An image format designed to allow exchange of image files among various software applications and computers.

**track changes**—An editing command in word processing software that can be turned on from one of the program's drop-down menus to show changes as they are made to an original document; changes can either be accepted or rejected.

**transactional distance**—The potential gap in communications between instructors and learners that must be bridged for most students to learn successfully.

**Trojan horse**—A type of computer virus offered to users as a helpful program but which is actually destructive; named after the giant wooden horse, ostensibly given as a gift from the Greeks to the Trojans (during the Trojan War), in which Greek soldiers hid to enter the Trojan fortress under cover.

**tutorial**—Type of instructional software that offers a complete sequence of instruction on a given topic, including explanation, examples, embedded practice and feedback, and, usually, also assessment.

**tweening**—(See morphing.)

**universal app**—App that that work on all handheld platforms (e.g., on a Droid and iPhone). (See also app.)

**universal design**—Adjustments made to physical environments as a result of understanding the special needs of individuals with disabilities (e.g., curb cuts in sidewalks to allow wheelchair access).

**Universal Design for Learning (UDL)**—A set of principles that underlie how to develop technology to give all individuals equal opportunities to learn.

**URL (Uniform Resource Locator)**—A series of letters and/or symbols that acts as an address for a site on the Internet.

**vicarious learning**—Proposed by learning theorist Albert Bandura as learning that occurs through observation, rather than by actions.

**videoconferencing**—An online "meeting" between two or more participants at different sites using a computer or network with appropriate software; video cameras, microphone, and speakers; and telephone lines or other cabling to transmit audio and video signals.

**video editing software**—Programs that allow a user to make additions and changes to a selection of digital video (e.g., iMovie).

**video sharing**—(See vodcast.)

**virtual field trip**—Online "visits" students make to Internet sites to see places they could not easily go in real life or that can help them get more out of trips they are able to take; sometimes involves communicating with learners at those sites; also known as electronic field trip.

**virtual manipulative**—Software replicas of real objects often used in learning mathematics; accessed via the Internet and can be manipulated with a keyboard or other input device.

**virtual office hours**—Time period when instructor is available (usually via course space options such as chatrooms) to answer questions immediately.

**virtual reality (VR)**—A computer-generated environment designed to provide a lifelike simulation of actual settings; often uses a data glove and/or headgear that covers the eyes in order to immerse the user in the simulated environment; representation of real or imaginary worlds in which the user interacts through multiple senses.

**virtual reality modeling language (VRML)**—A programming language that allows the creation and display of three-dimensional objects on a computer screen and allows users to have the illusion of moving around the objects.

**virtual school**—The K–12 version of distance learning; a K–12 school with most or all learning activities online.

**virus**—A program written with the purpose of doing harm or mischief to programs, data, and/or hardware components of a computer system. (See logic bomb, Trojan Horse, worm.)

**virus protection software**—Software put into place to protect computers from hackers and virus attacks. (See hacker, virus.)

**vlog**—A combination of the terms *video* and *blogging*; a video version of the blog in which posts are video clips instead of text entries.

**vocal processing software**—Programs that are to voice audio what word processing software is to text; allows users to make changes to the pitch and create interesting vocal distortions with recorded voice tracks.

**vodcast**—A term that combines *iPod*, *video*, and *broadcast*; refers to digitized video files saved in a format that can be shared over the Internet on sites such as YouTube for playback on the computer or on a personal media device. (See also podcast.)

**VRML (Virtual Reality Modeling Language)**—An authoring specification for displaying three-dimensional objects on the Internet.

**web accessibility**—The level to which a website is designed following a set of criteria that make it usable by people with various disabilities.

**Web-based learning (or lessons)**—General terms for learning or learning activities that take place via the Internet.

**Web-based programs**—Completely online (on the Internet) courses and curriculum.

**Web browser**—(See browser.)

**webcam**—A video camera that is connected to a computer in order to gather local video for viewing at other locations.

**webcasts**—Live video broadcasts of an event sent over the Internet.

**Web page editors**—Authoring programs that allow creation of Web pages in the same way word processing is used to create to create documents.

**webquest**—A curriculum project in which students explore websites to find and analyze information on a topic.

**Web 2.0 authoring tools**—Authoring tools that enable Internet users to generate and share online content.

**wiki**—A collection of Web pages located in an online community that encourage collaboration and communication of ideas by having users contribute or modify content; contain the work of many authors.

**wireframing**—(See storyboarding.)

**word atlas**—(See digital dictionaries.)

**worksheet**—Another name besides "spreadsheet" for the product of a spreadsheet program.

**worksheet generator**—Software tool that helps teachers produce exercises for practice (rather than for assessment) by prompting them to enter questions of various kinds.

**World Wide Web (WWW)**—A subsystem of the Internet that connects sites through hypertext links; now often used (incorrectly) as synonym for Internet.

**worm**—A type of virus that makes copies of itself in order to use up a computer's resources and slow down or shut down the system.

**XML**—Acronym for Extensible Mark-up Language, a language that describes the geometry and behavior of a virtual world or scene.

**zone of proximal development (ZPD)**—Term coined by learning theorist Vygotsky to refer to the difference between two levels of cognitive functioning (i.e., adult or expert and child or novice) that can be bridged by supplying appropriate learning experiences known as "scaffolds."

Abreu-Ellis, C., Ellis, J., Carle, A., Blevens, J., Decker, A., Carvalho, L., & Macedo, P. (2013). Language learning: The merge of teletandem and Web 2.0 tools. *Journal of Interactive Learning Research, 24*(4), 353–369.

AbuSeileek, A. (2013). Using track changes and word processor to provide corrective feedback to learners in writing. *Journal of Computer Assisted Learning, 29*(4), 4, 319–333.

Adams, C. (2006). PowerPoint, habits of mind, and classroom culture. *Journal of Curriculum Studies, 38*(4), 389–411.

Adams, D. M., Mayer, R. E., MacNamara, A., Koenig, A., & Wainess, R. (2012). Narrative games for learning: Testing the discovery and narrative hypotheses. *Journal of Educational Psychology, 104*(1), 235–249.

Ak, S. (2011). The effects of computer supported problem based learning on students' approaches to learning. *Current Issues in Education, 14*(1). Retrieved from http://cie.asu.edu/ojs/index.php/cieatasu/article/view/712

Akpan, J., & Strayer, J. (2010). Which comes first: The use of computer simulation of frog dissection or conventional dissection as academic exercise? *Journal of Computers in Mathematics and Science Teaching, 29*(2), 113–138.

Alessi, S., & Trollip, S. (2001). *Multimedia for learning: Methods and development.* Needham Heights, MA: Allyn & Bacon.

Alfieri, L., Brooks, P., Aldrich, N., & Tenenbaum, H. (2011). Does discovery-based instruction enhance learning? *Journal of Educational Psychology, 103*(1), 1–18

Allen, I., & Seaman, J. (2013). *Changing course: Ten years of tracking online education in the United States.* New York: The Alfred P. Sloan Foundation. Retrieved from http://sloanconsortium.org/publications/survey/changing_course_2012

Alshare, K., Freeze, R., Lane, P., & Wen, H. (2011). The impacts of system and human factors on online learning systems use and learner satisfaction. *Decision Sciences Journal of Innovative Education, 9*(3), 437–961.

Alvermann, D. E., Hutchins, R. J., & McDevitt, R. (2012). Adolescents' engagement with web 2.0 and social media: Research, theory, and practice. *Research in the Schools, 19*(1), 33–44.

American Academy of Pediatrics. (2013). Policy statement: Children, adolescents, and the media. *Pediatrics, 132*(5), 958–961.

American Alliance for Health Physical Education Recreation and Dance. (2013). *National Standards and Grade-Level Outcomes for K-12 Physical Education.* Retrieved from http://www.aahperd.org/whatwedo/nationalStandards.cfm

American Chemical Society. (2008). *Computer simulations in academic laboratories. ACS position. Public Policy Statement 2008–2011.* Retrieved from http://portal.acs.org/portal/PublicWebSite/policy/publicpolicies/invest/computersimulations/WPCP_011381

American Heart Association. (2013). *Heart attack risk assessment.* Retrieved from http://www.heart.org/HEARTORG/Conditions/HeartAttack/HeartAttackToolsResources/Heart-Attack-Risk-Assessment_UCM_303944_Article.jsp#

An, S., Ma, T., & Capraro, M. M. (2011). Preservice teachers' beliefs and attitude about teaching and learning mathematics through music: An intervention study. *School Science and Mathematics, 111*(5), 236–248.

Andrei, S., Osborne, L., & Smith, Z. (2013). Designing an American sign language avatar for learning computer science concepts for deaf or hard-of-hearing students and deaf interpreters. *Journal of Educational Multimedia and Hypermedia, 22*(3), 229–242.

Aoun, J. (2011, May 8). Learning today: The lasting value of place. *The Chronicle of Higher Education.* Retrieved from http://chronicle.com

Artman, M., Frisicaro-Pawlowski, E., & Monge, R. (2010). Not just one shot: Extending the dialogue about information literacy in composition classes. *Composition Studies, 38*(2), 93–109.

Ash, K. (2011, March 17). Digital gaming goes academic. *Education Week, 30*(25), 22, 28.

Ash. K. (2014, February 19). States struggle to hash out funding formulas for virtual charter schools. *Education Week.* Retrieved from http://blogs.edweek.org/edweek/charterschoice/2014/02/states_struggle_to_hash_out_funding_formulas_for_virtual_charter_schools.html?intc=es

Association of Mathematics Teacher Educators. (2006). *Preparing teachers to use technology to enhance the learning of mathematics: A position of the association of mathematics teacher educators.* San Diego, CA: Authors. Retrieved from http://www.amte.net/publications

Atkinson, R., & Shiffrin, R. (1968). Human memory: A proposed system and its control processes. In K. Spence & J. Spence (Eds.), *The psychology of learning and motivation (Vol. 2).* New York: Academic Press.

Ausubel, D. (1968). *Educational psychology: A cognitive view.* New York: Holt, Rinehart & Winston.

Azvedo, A. (2012, September 26). In colleges' rush to try MOOC's, faculty are not always in the conversation. *The Chronicle of Higher Education.* Retrieved from http://chronicle.com

Bahrani, T. (2011). Speaking fluency: Technology in EFL context or social interaction in ESL context? *Studies in Literature and Language, 2*(2), 162–168.

Bai, H., Pan, W., Hirumi, A., & Kebritchi, M. (2013). Assessing the effectiveness of a 3-D instructional game on improving mathematics achievement and motivation of middle school students. *British Journal of Educational Technology, 43*(6), 993–1003.

Bailey, B. (2011, July 18). Using touch screens and apps to treat autism. *San Jose Mercury News.* Retrieved from http://www.mercurynews.com

Baker, W. M. (2013). Empirically assessing the importance of computer skills. *Journal of Education for Business, 88*(6), 345–351.

Bakia, M., Shear, L., Toyama, Y., & Lasseter, A. (2012, January). *Understanding the implications of online learning for educational productivity.* U.S. Department of Education, Office of Educational Technology. Retrieved from http://www.sri.com/work/publications/understanding-implications-online-learning-educational-productivity

Bangert-Drowns, R. (1993). The word processor as an instructional tool: A meta-analysis of word processing in writing instruction. *Review of Educational Research, 63*(1), 69–93.

Banville, D., & Polifko, M. (2009). Using digital video recorders in physical education *Journal of Physical Education, Recreation, & Dance, 80*(1), 17–21.

Barab, S., Pettyjohn, P., Gresalfi, M., Volk, C., & Soomou, M. (2012). Game-based curriculum and transformational play: Designing to meaningfully positioning person, content, and context. *Computers & Education, 58*(1), 518–533. doi:10.1016/j.compedu.2011.08.001

Bargerhuff, M., Cowan, H., Oliveira, F., Quek, F., & Fang, B. (2010). Haptic glove technology: Skill development through video game play. *Journal of Visual Impairment & Blindness, 104*(11), 688–699.

Barla, M., Bielikova, M., Ezzeddinne, A., Kramar, T., Simko, M., & Vozar, O. (2010). On the impact of adaptive test question selection for learning efficiency. *Computers & Education, 55*(2), 846–857.

Barmer, J. (2014, February 26). MOOCs go to high school. Retrieved from *eCampus News:* http://www.ecampusnews.com/top-news/school-moocs-388/

Barnett, C. (2013, May 8). Top 10 Crowdfunding sites for fundraising. *Forbes Magazine.* Retrieved from http://www.forbes.com/sites/chancebarnett/2013/05/08/top-10-crowdfunding-sites-for-fundraising/

Baroody, A., Eiland, M., Purpura, D., & Reid, E. (2013). Can computer-assisted discovery learning foster first graders' fluency with the most basic addition combinations? *American Educational Research Journal, 50*(3), 533–573.

Bartels, E., McCown, M., & Wilkie, T. (2013). Designing peace and conflict exercises: Level of analysis, scenario, and role specification. *Simulation & Gaming, 44*(1), 36–50.

Basu, S. (2013, April 15). *10 Amazing ways for teachers & tutors to use twitter in education.* [Web log post]. Retrieved from http://www.makeuseof.com/tag/10-ways-to-use-twitter-in-education/

Bauer, W. I. (2010). Technological, pedagogical, and content knowledge, music, and assessment. In T. S. Brophy (Ed.), *The practice of assessment in music education: Frameworks, models, and designs. Proceedings of the Florida Symposium on Assessment in Music Education 2009* (pp. 423–433). Chicago, IL: GIA Publications.

Bauer, W. I., Harris, J., & Hofer, M. (2012). "Grounded" technology integration using K–12 music learning activity types. *Learning and Leading with Technology, 40*(3), 30–32.

Bayer Corporation. (2010). *Facts of science education survey: Executive summary.* Retrieved from http://bayerfactsofscience.online-pressroom.com/#a

Beach, R. (2012). Uses of digital tools and literacies in the English language arts classroom. *Research in the Schools, 19*(1), 45–59.

Beach, R., & Swiss, T. (2011). Digital literacies, aesthetics, and pedagogies involved in digital video production. In P. Albers, & J. Sanders (Eds.), *Literacies, the arts, and multimodality.* (pp. 300–320). Urbana, IL: National Council of Teachers of English.

Beach, R., Anson, C., Breuch, L., & Swiss, T. (2008). *Teaching writing using blogs, wikis, and other digital tools.* Norwood, MA: Christopher-Gordon.

Beauchamp, G., & Kennewell, S. (2010). Interactivity in the classroom and its impact on learning. *Computers & Education, 54*(3), 759–766.

Bebell, D., & Kay, R. (2010). One to one computing: A summary of the quantitative results from the Berkshire wireless learning initiative. *Journal of Technology, Learning, and Assessment, 9*(2), 5–59. Retrieved from http://www.jtla.org

Bebell, D., & O'Dwyer, L. (2010). Educational outcomes and research from 1:1 computing settings. *The Journal of Technology, Learning, and Assessment, 9*(1), 5–15.

Bedrossian, M. (2010). From generation to generation: Oral histories of scientific innovations from the 20th century. *The Science Teacher, 77*(5), 39–42.

Behnke, K. D., & Bowser, G. (2010). Supporting transitions of assistive technology users. *Journal of Special Education Technology, 25*(1), 57–62.

Beigie, D. (2010). Probability experiments with shared spreadsheets. *Mathematics Teaching in the Middle School, 15*(8), 486–491, 494.

Benacka, J. (2010). Solution to projectile motion with quadratic drag and graphing the trajectory in spreadsheets. *International Journal of Mathematical Education in Science and Technology, 41*(3), 373–378.

Bennett, T., O'shaughnessy, D., & Bedford, A. (2011). Predicting a tennis match in progress for sports multimedia. *Insight, 24*(3), 190–204.

Bergmann, J., & Sams, A. (2014). Flipped learning: Maximizing face time. *T + D, 68*(2), 28–31.

Berkowicz, J., & Myers, A. (2014, February 4). Will we ever allow computers to grade students' writing? *Education Week.* Retrieved from http://www.edweek.org

Bernard, R. M., Abrami, P. C., Borokhovski, E., Wade, C. A., Tamim, R. M., Surkes, M. A., et al. (2009). A meta-analysis of three types of interaction treatments in distance education. *Review of Educational Research, 79*(3), 1243–1279.

Berrett, D. (2012). How "flipping" the classroom can improve the traditional lecture. *The Education Digest, 78*(1), 36–41.

Berson, I. R., & Berson, M. J. (2013). Getting to the core: Using digital resources to enhance content-based literacy in the social studies. *Social Education, 77*(2), 102–106.

Berson, I. R., Berson, M. J., & Manfra, M. (2012). Touch, type, and transform: IPads in the social studies classroom. *Social Education, 76*(2), 88–91.

Bhattacharjee, Y. (2009). A personal tutor for algebra. *Science, 323*(5910), 64–65.

Biddiss, E., & Irwin, J. (2010). Active video games to promote physical activity in children and youth: A systematic review. *Archives of Pediatrics & Adolescent Medicine, 164*(7), 664–672.

Biro, F., & Wien M. (2010). Childhood obesity and adult morbidities. *American Journal of Clinical Nutrition, 91*(5), 1499S–1505S.

Blanchard, M., Sharp, J., & Grable, L. (2009). Rev your engines! *The Science Teacher, 76*(2), 35–40.

Blood, E., & Neel, R. (2008). Using student response systems in lecture-based instruction: Does it change student engagement and learning? *Journal of Technology and Teacher Education, 16*(3), 375–383.

Bloom, B. (1986). Automaticity. *Educational Leadership, 43*(5), 70–77.

Blumenstyk, G. (2011, February 6). Fast-growing U. of Phoenix calculates a more careful course. *The Chronicle of Higher Education.* Retrieved from http://chronicle.com

Bradley, J., & Farland-Smith, D. (2010). 3-D teaching models for all. *The Science Teacher 77*(3), 33–37.

Breslow, L., Pritchard, D., DeBoer, J., Stump, G., Ho, A., & Seaton, D. (2013). Studying learning in the worldwide classroom: Research into edX's first MOOC. *Research and Practice in Assessment, 8*, 13–25.

Bromley, K. (2010). Picture a world without pens, pencils, and paper: The unanticipated future of reading and writing. *Journal of College Reading and Learning, 41*(1), 97–108.

Brown, E. (2013, January 15). Experts discuss use of tablet computers in schools. *Education Daily, 46*(9), 3–4.

Brown, V. (2010). Digital media learning supports individuals with cognitive disabilities. *Childhood Education, 87*(1), 61–64.

Brown, J. S., Collins, A., & Duguid, P. (1989). Situated cognition and the culture of learning. *Educational Researcher, 18*(1), 32–41.

Browning, C. A., & Garza-Kling, G. (2010). Graphing calculators as tools. *Mathematics Teaching in the Middle School, 15*(8), 480–485.

Bruce, B. (2000). Dewey and technology. *The Journal of Adolescent and Adult Literacy, 42*(3), 222–226.

Bruner, J. (1966). *Toward a theory of instruction.* Boston: Little, Brown.

Brunsell, E., & Horejsi, M. (2012). Science 2.0: Using web tools to support learning. *The Science Teacher, 79*(9), 8.

Bryant, C. (2010). A 21st century art room: The remix of creativity and technology. *Art Education, 63*(2), 43–48.

Bucher, C., & Edwards, M. (2011). Deepening understanding of transformation through proof. *The Mathematics Teacher, 104*(9), 716–722.

Buggey, T., & Ogle, L. (2013). The use of self-modeling to promote social interactions among young children. *Focus on Autism and Other Developmental Disabilities, 28*(4), 202–211.

Buhi, E., Daley, E., Fuhrmann, H., & Smith, S. (2009). An observational study of how young people search for online sexual health information. *Journal of American College Health, 58*(2), 101–110.

Bull, P. (2013). Cognitive constructivist theory of multimedia: Designing teacher-made interactive digital. *Creative Education, 4*(9), 614–619.

Burris, J. T. (2013). Virtual place value. *Teaching Children Mathematics, 20*(4), 228–236.

Byrne, R. (2011). OMG! Texting in class? *School Library Journal, 57*(3), 16.

Byrne, R. (2012). Making the most of video in the classroom. *School Library Journal, 58*(8), 15.

Byrne, R. (2012). Keep good searches from going bad. *School Library Journal, 58*(1), n/a. Retrieved from http://www.thedigitalshift.com/2012/01/ebooks/keep-good-searches-from-going-bad/

Candreva, C. (2010). Paving new pathways to literacy in the 21st century. *School Talk, 15*(2), 3–4.

Caldwell, J. (2007). Clickers in the large classroom: Current research and best-practice tips. *CBE-Life Sciences Education, 6*, 9–20.

Careless, J. (2012, January). Social media: It does have a place in the classroom. *Tech & Learning.* Retrieved from http://www.techlearning.com/features/0039/social-media-it-does-have-a-place-in-the-classroom/52186

Carr, N. (2011). *The shallows: What the Internet is doing to our brains.* New York, NY: Norton.

Casia, A. V., & Zubiaga, I. S. (2010). Paternity testing in a PBL environment. *Biochemistry and Molecular Biology Education, 38*(1), 37–42.

Castek, J. (2012). If you want students to evaluate online resources and other new media—teach them how. In D. Lapp & B. Moss (Eds.), *Exemplary instruction in the middle grades* (pp. 105–123). New York: Guilford.

Castleberry, G., & Evers, R. (2010). Twenty ways to incorporate technology into the modern language classroom. *Intervention in School and Clinic, 45*(3), 201–205.

Cause, L., & Chen, D. (2010). A tablet computer for young children? Exploring its viability for early childhood education. *Journal of Research on Technology in Education, 43*(1), 75–98.

Cavanaugh, S. (2013, June 11). "MOOC" provider Coursera jumps into K–12 and teacher ed. *Education Week: Digital Directions.* Retrieved from http://www.edweek.org/dd/articles/2013/06/12/03bits-mooc.h06.html

Center on Educational Policy. (2007). *Choices, changes and challenges: Curriculum and instruction in the NCLB era.* Washington, DC: Author.

Centers for Disease Control and Prevention. (2010a). *The association between school based physical activity, including physical education, and academic performance.* Atlanta, GA: U.S. Department of Health and Human Services.

Centers for Disease Control and Prevention. (2010b). Surveillance for certain health behaviors among states and selected local areas-United States, 2008. *Morbidity and Mortality Weekly Report, 59*(SS-10), 1–224.

Centers for Disease Control and Prevention. (2010c). Youth Risk Behavior Surveillance-United States, 2009. *Morbidity and Mortality Weekly Report, 59*(SS-5), 1–148.

Centers for Disease Control and Prevention. (2012a). Youth risk behavior surveillance -United States, 2011. *Morbidity and Mortality Weekly Report, 61*(4), 1--168.

Centers for Disease Control and Prevention. (2012b). *Press release: CDC estimates 1 in 88 children in United States has been identified as having an autism spectrum disorder.* Retrieved from http://www.cdc.gov/media/releases/2012/p0329_autism_disorder.html

Centers for Disease Control and Prevention. (2013). *BAM! Body and mind.* Retrieved from http://www.cdc.gov/bam/

Centers for Disease Control and Prevention. (2014a). *Characteristics of an effective health education curriculum.* Retrieved from http://www.cdc.gov/healthyyouth/sher/characteristics/index.htm

Centers for Disease Control and Prevention. (2014b). *Components of coordinated school health.* Retrieved from http://www.cdc.gov/healthyyouth/cshp/components.htm

Centers for Online Learning and Students with Disabilities. (2012). *The foundation of online learning for students with disabilities.* Lawrence, KS: author. Available from: http://centerononlinelearning.org/resources/vpat/.

Chairatchatakul, A., Jantaburom, P., Kanarkard, W. (2012). Using social media to improve a parent-school relationship. *International Journal of Information and Education Technology, 2*(4), 378–381.

Chen, J., Dai, D., & Zhou, Y. (2013). Enable, enhance, and transform: How technology use can improve gifted education. *The Roeper Review, 35,* 166–176.

Chin, A. (2013). Utilizing technology to enhance communication and collaboration. *Distance Learning, 10*(3), 13–20.

Chingos, M. (2013, April). Questioning the quality of virtual schools. *Education Next, 13*(2). Retrieved from http://educationnext.org/questioning-the-quality-of-virtual-schools/

Cingel, D., & Sundar, S. (2012). Texting, techspeak, and tweens: The relationship between text messaging and English grammar skills. *New Media & Society, 14*(8), 1304–1320.

Clark, R. (1983). Reconsidering research on learning from media. *Review of Educational Research, 53*(4), 445–459.

Clark, R. (1985). Evidence for confounding in computer-based instruction studies: Analyzing the meta-analyses. *Educational Communications and Technology Journal, 33*(4), 249–262.

Clark, R. (1991). When researchers swim upstream: Reflections on an unpopular argument about learning from media. *Educational Technology, 31*(2), 34–40.

Clark, R. E. (1982). Antagonism between achievement and enjoyment in ATI studies. *Educational Psychologist, 17*(2), 92–101.

Clark, R. E. (1994). Media will never influence learning. *Educational Technology Research and Development, 42*(2), 21–29.

Clark, R. E., Yates, K., Early, S., & Moulton, K. (2009). An analysis of the failure of electronic media and discovery-based learning: Evidence for the performance benefits of guided training methods. In Silber, K. H. & Foshay, R. (Eds.). *Handbook of training and improving workplace performance, volume I: Instructional design and training delivery* (pp. 263–297). New York: John Wiley and Sons.

Clayton, K., Blumberg, F., & Auld, D. P. (2010). The relationship between motivation, learning strategies and choice of environment whether traditional or including an online component. *British Journal of Educational Technology, 41*(3), 349–364.

Clements, A. (2010). *Alternative approaches in music education.* Lanham, MD: Rowman & Littlefield.

Cobb, P., & Yackel, E. (1996). Constructivist, emergent, and sociocultural perspectives in the context of developmental research. *Educational Psychologist, 31* (3/4), 175–190.

Cognition and Technology Group at Vanderbilt (CTGV). (1990). Anchored instruction and its relationship to situated cognition. *Educational Researcher, 19*(6), 2–10.

Colucci, W., & Koppel, N. (2010). Impact of the placement and quality of face-to-face meetings in a hybrid distance learning course. *American Journal of Business Education, 3*(2), 119–131.

Comas-Forgas, R., & Sureda-Negre, J. (2010). Academic plagiarism: Explanatory factors from students' perspective. *Journal of Academic Ethics, 8*(3), 217–232

Committee on Science, Engineering, and Public Policy (COSEPUP). (2011). *Rising above the Gathering Storm Five Years Later.* Retrieved from http://sites.nationalacademies.org/PGA/COSEPUP/PGA_049885

*Common core state standards for English language arts & literacy in history/social studies, science, and technical subjects.* (2010). National Governors Association. Retrieved from http://www.corestandards.org/

*Common Core State Standards Initiative. (2012). Implementing the common core state standards.* Retrieved from http://www.corestandards.org

Connell, C., Bayliss, L, & Farmer, W. (2012). Effects of ebook readers and tablet computers on reading comprehension. *International Journal of Instructional Media, 39*(2), 131–140.

Cooper, M. (2013). lol . . . OMG! What every student needs to know about online reputation management, digital citizenship and cyberbullying. *The Hispanic Outlook in Higher Education, 23*(7), 51.

Corbett, S. (2010, September 15). Learning by playing: Video games in the classroom. *The New York Times.* Retrieved from http://www.nytimes.com/2010/09/19/magazine/19video-t.html

Cordero, R. (2013). Does exergaming influence physical activity in third-grade physical education? *Journal of Physical Education, Recreation & Dance, 84*(4), 16.

Corey, M. (1944). The poor scholar's soliloquy. *Childhood Education, 33,* 219–220.

Council for Exceptional Children (CEC). (2009). *What every special educator must know: Ethics, standards, and guidelines.* Arlington, VA: Author.

Crary, A., & Wilson, W. S. (June 16, 2013). The faulty logic of the "math wars." *The New York Times.* Retrieved from http://opinionator.blogs.nytimes.com/2013/06/16/the-faulty-logic-of-the-math-wars/?_php=true&_type=blogs&_r=0

Crespo, C. J., Smith, E., Troiano, R. P., Bartlett, S. J., Macera, C. A., & Anderson, R. E. (2001). Television watching, energy intake and obesity in U.S. children: Results from the 3rd NHANES: 1988–1994. *Archives of Pediatric and Adolescent Medicine, 155,* 360–365.

Criswell, C. (2011). Now playing under the radar. *Teaching Music, 18*(4), 26–27.

Criswell, C. (2013). Going straight to video, online. *Teaching Music, 20*(4), 26–27.

Dalenius, K., Boreland, E., Smith, B., Polhamus, B., & Grummer-Strawn, L. (2012). *Pediatric nutrition surveillance, 2010 report.* Atlanta, GA: U.S. Department of Health and Human Services, Centers for Disease Control and Prevention.

Dalton, B., & Grisham, D. (2011). EVoc strategies: 10 ways to use technology to build vocabulary. *The Reading Teacher, 64*(5), 306–317.

Dalton, B. B., & Smith, B. E. (2012). Teachers as designers: Multimodal immersion and strategic reading on the Internet. *Research in the Schools, 19*(1), 12–25.

Damianov, D. S., Kupczynski, L., Calafiore, P., Damianova, E. P., Soydemir, G., & Gonzalez, E. (2009). Time spent online and student performance in online business courses: A multinomial logit analysis. *Journal of Economics and Finance Education, 8*(2), 11–22.

Dammers, R. (2010, September). *Technology-based music classes in high schools in the United States.* Presentation at the 2010 ATMI/CMS Conference, Minneapolis, Minnesota.

Dammers, R. J. (2012). Technology-based music classes in high schools in the United States, *Bulletin for the Council of Research in Music Education, 194,* 73–90.

Dania, A., Hatziharistos, D., Koutsouba, M., & Tyrovola, V. (2011). The use of technology in movement and dance: Recent practices and future perspectives. *Procedia Social and Behavioral Sciences, 15*, 3355–3361.

Dave, A., & Russell, D. (2010). Drafting and revision using word processing by undergraduate student writers: Changing conceptions and practices. *Research in the Teaching of English, 44*(4), 406–434.

Davenport, M. G., & Gunn, K. (2009). Collaboration in animation: Working together to empower indigenous youth. *Art Education, 62*(5), 6–12.

Davis, M. (2009). Simulated vs. hands-on lab experiments: New model is likely to require more actual lab work for those taking Advanced Placement modules online. *Digital Directions, 2*(4), 32–33.

Davis, M. (2011, January 12). Cyber students taught the value of social skills: Virtual schools are adding face-to-face experiences to the curriculum to satisfy concerns about potential isolation in the online world. *Education Week, 30*(15), 8–10.

Davis, M. (2012, October 24). Florida virtual school incorporates face-to-face learning. *Education Week, 32*(9), s16–s18.

Davydov, V. (1995). The influence of L. S. Vygotsky on education theory, research, and practice. *Educational Researcher, 24*(3), 12–21.

DeLuca, A., & Hoffman, B. (2003). Vamos a darles algo a discutir (Let's give 'em something to talk about). *Learning and Leading with Technology, 30*(5), 36–41.

Delacruz, E., & Bales, S. (2010). Creating history, telling stories, and making special: portfolios, scrapbooks, and sketchbooks. *Art Education, 63*(1), 33–39.

Demski, J. (2010). How music teachers got their groove back. *T.H.E. Journal, 37*(9), 27–31.

DeSorbo, A., Noble, J., Shaffer, M., Gerin, W., & Williams, O. (2012). The use of an audience response system in an elementary school-based health education program. *Health Education and Behavior, 40*(5), 531–535.

Devaney, L. (2010, July 26). Study reveals factors in ed-tech success. *eSchool News.* Retrieved from http://www.eschoolnews.com

Devaney, L. (2013, October 7). Augmented reality snags a coveted spot in classrooms. *eSchool News.* Retrieved from http://www.eschoolnews.com

Devaney, L. (2013, November 13). More educators turning to educational gaming. *eSchool News.* Retrieved from http://www.eschoolnews.com

Diem, R., & Berson, M. J. (Eds.). (2010). *Technology in retrospect: Social studies in the information age, 1984–2009.* Charlotte, NC: Information Age Publishing.

DiPietro, M. (2010). Virtual school pedagogy: The instructional practices of K–12 virtual school teachers. *Journal of Educational Computing Research, 42*(3), 327–354.

Doe, C. (2009). Mobile devices. *MultiMedia & Internet@Schools, 16*(2), 30–33.

Dolamic, L., & Savoy, J. (2010). Retrieval effectiveness of machine translated queries. *Journal of the American Society for Information Science and Technology, 61*(11), 2266–2273.

Dorfman, J. (2013). *Theory and practice of technology-based music instruction.* New York, NY: Oxford University Press.

Drayton, B., Falk, J.K., Stroud, R., Hobbs, K., & Hammerman, J. (2010). After installation: ubiquitous computing and high school science in three experienced, high-technology schools. *Journal of Technology, Learning, and Assessment, 9*(3). Retrieved from http://www.jtla.org

Dredger, K., Woods, D., Beach, C., & Sagstetter, V. (2010). Engage me: Using new literacies to create third space classrooms that engage student writers. *Journal of Media Literacy Education, 2*, 85–101.

Drew, S. V. (2012). Open up the ceiling on the Common Core state standards: Preparing students for 21st-century literacy—now. *Journal of Adolescent & Adult Literacy, 56*(4), 321–330. doi: 10.1002/jaal.00145

Druckman, D., & Ebner, N. (2008). Onstage or behind the scenes? Relative learning benefits of simulation role-play and design. *Simulation & Gaming, 39*(4), 465–497.

Duggan, M. (2013, October). *Photo and video sharing grow online.* Report of the Pew Research Center. Retrieved from http://pewinternet.org/Reports/2013/Photos-and-videos.aspx

Dunford, S., & Fink, L. (2011). Reviewing student papers electronically. *English Journal, 100, 5*, 71–74.

Duran, E., Duran, L., Haney, J., & Scheuermann, A. (2011). A learning cycle for all students. *The Science Teacher, 78*(3), 56–60.

Duxbury, D. (2000). Make sweet music with electronic portfolios. *Learning and Leading with Technology, 28*(3), 28–31, 41.

Edwards, P. (2010). Reconceptualizing literacy. *Reading Today, 27*(6), 22.

Edwards, M., & Phelps, S. (2008). Can you Fathom this? *The Mathematics Teacher, 102*(3), 210–216.

Edyburn, D. (2010). Would you recognize universal design for learning if you saw it? Ten propositions for new directions for the second decade of UDL. *Learning Disability Quarterly, 33*(1), 33–41.

Edyburn, D. (2013a). Critical issues in advancing the special education technology evidence-base. *Exceptional Children, 80*(1), 7–24.

Edyburn, D.L. (2013b). *Inclusive technologies: Tools for helping diverse learners achieve academic success.* San Diego, CA: Bridgepoint Education, Inc.

Edyburn, D., Higgins, K., & Boone, R. (2005). *Handbook of special education technology research and practice.* Whitefish Bay, WI: Knowledge by Design.

Eggen, P., & Kauchak, D. (2013). *Educational psychology: Windows on classrooms* (9th ed.). Columbus, OH: Pearson Education.

Ehrmann, S. (2011). Taking the long view: Ten recommendations about time, money, technology, and learning. *Planning for Higher Education, 39*(2), 34–40.

Elbro, C. (2010). Dyslexia as disability or handicap: When does vocabulary matter? *Journal of Learning Disabilities, 43*(5), 469–478.

Ellerson, N. M. (2010). *A cliff hanger: How America's public schools continue to feel the impact of the economic downturn.* Alexandria, VA. Retrieved from http://www.aasa.org/uploadedFiles/Policy_and_Advocacy/files/CliffHangerFINAL(1).pdf

Ellington, A. J., & Hardin, A. (2008). The use of video tutorials in a mathematical modeling course. *Mathematics and Computer Education, 42*(2), 109–117.

Elliott, S., & Gordon, M. (2006). Using PowerPoint to promote constructivist learning. *Educational Technology, 46*(4), 34–38.

Engineering in Massachusetts Collaborative (EMC). (2003). *Fueling the Pipeline: Attracting and Educating Math and Science Students.* Retrieved from http://media.umassp.edu/massedu/stem/science-and-engineering-pipeline.pdf

Eskrootchi, R., & Oskrochi. G. R. (2010). A study of the efficacy of project-based learning integrated with computer-based simulation—STELLA. *Educational Technology & Society, 13*(1), 236–245.

Evagoroua, K. Nicolaoub, C., & Constantinoub, C. (2010). An investigation of the potential of interactive simulations for developing system thinking skills in elementary school: a case study with fifth graders and sixth-graders. *International Journal of Science Education, 31*(5), 655–674.

Faure, C., & Orthober, C. (2011). Using text-messaging in the secondary classroom. *American Secondary Education, 39*(2), 55–76.

Fell, C. (2013, October 30). Flipped classroom courses create same results as traditional classes. *The Daily Nebraskan.* Retrieved from http://www.dailynebraskan.com/news/article_a9366aa8-411e-11e3-99ef-0019bb30f31a.html

Feurzeig, W. (2010). Toward a culture of creativity: A personal perspective on Logo's early years and ongoing potential. *International Journal of Computers in Math Learning, 15*, 257–265.

Fish, W., & Wickersham, L. (2009). Best practices for online instructors. *Quarterly Review of Distance Education, 10*(3), 279–284.

Fletcher, S. (2013). Machine learning. *Scientific American, 309*(2), 62–68.

Florida TaxWatch Center for Educational Performance and Accountability. (2007). *Final report: A comprehensive assessment of Florida Virtual School.* Retrieved from http://www.inacol.org/cms/wp-content/uploads/2013/04/FLVS_Final_Final_Report10-15-07.pdf

Foulds, R., Adamovich, S., Gordon, A. M., & Okita, S. Y. (2010). Augmenting pediatric constraint-induced movement therapy and bimanual training with video gaming technology. *Technology & Disability, 22*(4), 179–191.

Franklin, P. (2008). Elements project. *School Library Media Activities Monthly, 24*(7), 15–16.

Fritts, B., & Marszalek, J. (2010). Computerized adaptive testing, anxiety levels, and gender differences. *Social Psychology of Education, 13*(3), 441–458.

Fuller, B. (2010, July 11). The Spanish road to English. *The Los Angeles Times.* Retrieved from http://articles.latimes.com/2010/jul/11/opinion/la-oe-fuller-english-20100711

Gagné, R. (1982). Developments in learning psychology: Implications for instructional design. *Educational Technology, 22*(6), 11–15.

Gagné, R. (1985). *The conditions of learning* (4th ed.). New York: Holt, Rinehart and Winston.

Gagné, R., Briggs, L., & Wager, W. (1992). *Principles of instructional design.* Orlando, FL: Harcourt, Brace, Jovanovich.

Gagné, R., Wager, W., & Rojas, A. (1981). Planning and authoring computer-assisted instruction lessons. *Educational Technology, 21*(9), 17–26.

Garber, K., & Picking, D. (2010). Exploring algebra and geometry concepts with GeoGebra. *The Mathematics Teacher, 104*(3), 226–228.

Gardner, H. (1983). *Frames of mind.* New York: Basic Books.

Gardner, H., & Hatch, T. (1989). Multiple intelligences go to school: Educational implications of the theory of multiple intelligences. *Educational Researcher, 18*(8), 4–10.

Gargiulo, R. M. (2012). *Special education in contemporary society: An introduction to exceptionality* (4th ed.). Thousand Oaks, CA: Sage Publications.

Gasperetti, B., Milford, M., Blanchard, D., Yang, S. P., Lieberman, L., & Foley, J. T. (2010). Dance Dance Revolution and eyetoy kinetic modifications for youths with visual impairments. *The Journal of Physical Education, Recreation & Dance, 81*(4), 15–55.

Gauci, S., Dantas, A., Williams, D., & Kemm, R. (2009). Promoting student-centered active learning in lectures with a personal response system. *Advances in Physiology Education, 33*(1), 60–71.

Gay, L. R. (1992). *Educational research: Competencies for analysis and application* (4th ed.). New York: Merrill, Macmillan Publishing Company.

Gelbart, H., Brill, G., & Yarden, A. (2009). The impact of a web-based research simulation in bioinformatics on students' understanding of genetics. *Research in Science Education, 39*, 725–751.

Ghassib, H. B. (2010). Where does creativity fit into a productivist industrial model of knowledge production? *Gifted and Talented International, 25*(1), 13–19.

Gillin, P., & Gillin, D. (2010). *The joy of geocaching: How to find health, happiness and creative energy through a worldwide treasure hunt.* Fresno, CA: Quill Driver Books.

Glass, G. V (1976). Primary, secondary, and meta-analysis of research. *Educational Researcher, 5*, 3–8.

Glass, G. (2010). Potholes in the road to virtual schooling. *The School Administrator, 4*(67), 32–35. Retrieved from http://www.aasa.org/SchoolAdministratorArticle.aspx?id=12934

Glass, G. V. (2009). *The realities of K–12 virtual education.* Boulder, CO: Education and the Public Interest Center & Education Policy Research Unit. Retrieved from http://epicpolicy.org/files/PB-Glass-VIRTUAL.pdf

Glass, G. V., & Welner, K. (2011). *Online K–12 schooling in the U S.: Uncertain private ventures in need of public regulation.* National Education Policy Center, School of Education, University of Colorado-Boulder.

Glenberg, A., Goldberg, A., & Zhu, X. (2011) Improving early reading comprehension using embodied CAI. *Instructional Science, 39*(1), 27–39.

Goertler, S., Bollen, M., & Gaff, J. (2012). Students' readiness for and attitudes toward hybrid FL instruction. *CALICO Journal, 29*(2), 297–320.

Goldberg, A., Russell, M., & Cook, A. (2003). The effects of computers on student writing: A meta-analysis of studies from 1992–2002. *Journal of Technology, Learning, and Assessment, 2*(1), 1–51.

Goldsworthy, R., & Schwartz, N. (2008). Development and evaluation of a multimedia-enhanced STD/HIV curriculum for middle schools. *Journal of Educational Multimedia and Hypermedia, 17*(3), 413–444.

Goodman, B. (2011, March 28). Social networking may affect kids' health. *WebMD Health and Parenting.* Retrieved from http://www.webmd.com/parenting/news/20110328/social-networking-may- affect-kids-health

Goodwin, B., & Miller, K. (2013). Evidence on flipped classroom is still coming in. *Educational Leadership, 70*(6), 78–80.

Gortmaker, S. L., Must, A., Sobol, A. M., Peterson, K., Colditz, G. A., & Dietz, W. H. (1996). Television viewing as a cause of increasing obesity among children in the U.S., 1986–1990. *Archives of Pediatric and Adolescent Medicine, 150*, 356–362.

Graf, A. (2010). Think outside the polygon. *Mathematics Teaching in the Middle School, 16*(2), 82–87.

Graham, L., Bellert, A., Thomas, J., & Pegg, J. (2007). QuickSmart: A basic academic skills intervention for middle school students with learning difficulties. *Journal of Learning Disabilities, 40*(5), 410–419.

Graham, S., & Perin, D. (2007). A meta-analysis of writing instruction for adolescent students. *Journal of Educational Psychology, 99*(3), 445–476.

Gran, M. (2013). Camera phones for class. *School Arts, 112*(8), 26.

Greene, J. (2010, December 13). False claim on drill and kill. *EducationNext.* Retrieved from http://educationnext.org/false-claim-on-drill-and-kill/

Gubacs-Collins, K., & Juniu, S. (2009). The mobile gymnasium: Using tablet PCs in physical education. *Journal of Physical Education, Recreation, & Dance, 82*(2), 24–31.

Gulek, J. C. & Demirtas, H. (2005). Learning with technology: The impact of laptop use on student achievement. *Journal of Technology, Learning, and Assessment, 3*(2). Retrieved from http://www.jtla.org.

Halvorsen, A. (2012). "Don't know much about history": The New York Times 1943 survey of U.S. history and the controversy it generated. *Teachers College Press, 114*, 1–37.

Hamdan, N., McKnight, P., McKnight, K., & Arfstrom, K. (2013). *A review of flipped learning.* A report of the Flipped Learning Network's Research committee. Retrieved from http://researchnetwork.pearson.com/wp-content/uploads/LitReview_FlippedLearning1.pdf

Hammett, R. (2013). 'Tech FTW!!!' Ninth graders, Romeo and Juliet, and digital technologies. *Language and Literacy, 15*(1), 6–22.

Harouni, H. (2009). High school research and critical literacy: Social studies with and despite Wikipedia. *Harvard Educational Review, 79*(3), 473–493.

Harris, C., & Rooks, D. (2010). Managing inquiry-based science: Challenges in enacting complex science instruction in elementary and middle school classrooms. *Journal of Science Teacher Education, 21*, 227–240.

Harris, J., Grandgenett, N., & Hofer, M. (2010). Testing a TPACK-based technology integration assessment rubric. In C. D. Maddux, D. Gibson, & B. Dodge (Eds.), *Research highlights in technology and teacher education 2010* (pp. 323–331). Chesapeake, VA: Society for Information Technology & Teacher Education (SITE).

Hartley, J., Trueman, M., Betts, L., & Brodie, L. (2006). What price presentation? The effects of typographic variables on essay grades. *Assessment and Evaluation in Higher Education, 31*(5), 523–534.

Haury, D., & Rillero, P. (1994). *Perspectives of hands-on science teaching.* Retrieved from http://www.ncrel.org/sdrs/areas/issues/content/cntareas/science/eric/eric-1.htm

Hawisher, G. (1989). Research and recommendations for computers and compositions. In G. Hawisher, & C. Selfe (Eds.), *Critical perspectives on computers and composition instruction.* New York: Teachers College Press.

Hayes, S., & Desler, G. (2009). Change writers: Bridging gaps and divides. *Voices from the Middle, 17*(2), 49–51.

Healey, D., Hanson-Smith, E., Hubbard, P., Ioannou-Georgiou, S., Kessler, G. & Ware, P. (2011). *TESOL technology standards: Description, implementation, integration.* Alexandria, VA: TESOL

Healy, L., & Hoyles, C. (2001). Software tools for geometrical problem solving: Potentials and pitfalls. *International Journal of Computers for Mathematical Learning, 6*, 235–256.

Helms, A. (2013, January 7). Education and video games are no longer enemies. *Charlotte Observer Online.* Retrieved from http://www.charlotteobserver.com

Henson, K. (2008). It's a zoo out there! It's a zoo out there! *Science Teacher, 75*(2), 44–47.

Herold, B. (2013, July 10). Adaptive testing gains momentum, prompts worries: Bills in congress highlight debate. *Education Week, 32*(36), 18.

Herold, B. (2013, August 13). Video-game research delves into how children succeed. *Education Week.* Retrieved from http://www.educationweek.com

Herold, B. (2013, September 30). 1:X Computing aims to tailor digital tools to learning tasks. *Education Week, 33*(6), s2-s3, s6-s7.

Herold, B. (2014, August 26). Oculus Rift fueling new vision for virtual reality in K–12. *Education Week, 34*(2)10–11.

Hersey, J. C., & Jordan, A. (2007). *Reducing children's TV time to reduce the risk of childhood overweight: The children's media use study.* Retrieved from http://www.cdc.gov/obesity/downloads/TV_Time_Highligts.pdf

Hickey, M. (2012). *Music outside the lines: Ideas for composing in K–12 music classrooms.* New York, NY: Oxford University Press.

Hicks, L., & Higgins, J. (2010). Exergaming: Syncing physical activity and learning. *Strategies, 24*(1), 18–21.

Hilton, C., Cumpata, K., Klohr, C., Gaetke, S., Artner, A., et al. (2014). Effects of exergaming on executive function and motor skills in children with autism spectrum disorder: A pilot study. *The American Journal of Occupational Therapy, 68*(1), 57–65.

Hirsch, E. D. (2002). Classroom research and cargo cults. *Policy Review No.115*, Hoover Institution, Stanford University. Retrieved from http://www.hoover.org/publications/policy-review/article/7262

Holden, J., & Westfall, P. (2010). *An instructional media selection guide for distance education: Implications for blended learning.* Washington, DC: USDLA. Retrieved from http://www.usdla.org/assets/pdf_files/AIMSGDL%202nd%20Ed._styled_010311.pdf

Hong, D. (2013). A classroom note on exploring mathematical topics with free software. *Mathematics and Computer Education, 47*(1), 24–36.

Hong, J., Cheng, C., Hwang, M., Lee, C., & Change, H. (2009). Assessing the educational values of digital games. *Journal of Computer Assisted Learning, 25*(5), 423–437.

Hossain, M., & Wiest, L. (2013). Collaborative middle school geometry through blogs and other web 2.0 technologies. *The Journal of Computers in Mathematics and Science Teaching, 32*(3), 337–352.

Houssart, J., & Sams, C. (2008). Developing mathematical reasoning through games of strategy played against the computer. *International Journal for Technology in Mathematics Education, 15*(2), 59–71.

Hubbard, B., & Mitchell, N. (2011). Online K–12 schools failing students but keeping tax dollars. *I-News Network.* Retrieved from http://www.inewsnetwork.org/special-reports/online-k-12-schools

Hubbard, P. (2013). Making a case for learner training in technology enhanced language learning environments. *CALICO Journal, 30*(2), 163–178. Retrieved from https://www.cco.org/html/article_1082.pdf

Huerta, L., Rice, J., & Shafer, S. (2013). *Virtual schools in the U.S. 2013: Politics, performance, policy, and research evidence: Part 2.* National Education Policy Center, University of Colorado School of Education. Retrieved from http://nepc.colorado.edu/files/nepc-virtual-2013.pdf

Hughes, J. E. (2000). *Teaching English with technology: Exploring teacher learning and practice.* Unpublished doctoral dissertation, Michigan State University, East Lansing, MI.

Hung, M. L., Chou, C., Chen, C. H., & Own, Z. Y. (2010). Learner readiness for online learning: Scale development and student perceptions. *Computers & Education, 55*(3), 1080–1090.

Hutchison, A. (2012). Literacy teachers' perceptions of professional development that increases integration of technology into literacy instruction. *Technology, Pedagogy & Education, 21*(1), 37–56. doi: 10.1080/1475939X.2012.659894

Hutchison, A., & Reinking, D. (2011). Teachers' perceptions of integrating information and communication technologies into literacy instruction: A national survey in the United States. *Reading Research Quarterly, 46*(4), 312–333.

Iannou, A., Brown, S., Hannafin, R., & Boyer, M. (2009). Can multimedia make kids care about social studies? The GlobalEd problem-based learning simulation. *Computers in the Schools, 26*, 63–81.

Inman, D., Loge, K., Cram, A., & Peterson, M. (2011). Learning to drive a wheelchair in virtual reality. *Journal of Special Education Technology, 2*(3), 21–34.

International Reading Association. (2009). *New literacies and 21st century technologies.* Newark, DE: International Reading Association. Retrieved from http://www.reading.org/Libraries/Position_Statements_and_Resolutions/ps1067_NewLiteracies21stCentury.sflb.ashx

International Research Foundation (2013). *Mobile assisted language learning.* Retrieved from http://www.tirfonline.org/english-in-the-workforce/mobile-assisted-language-learning

Jaakkol, T., & Nurmi, S. (2008). Fostering elementary school students' understanding of simple electricity by combining simulation and laboratory activities. *Journal of Computer Assisted Learning, 24*, 271–283.

Jackson, N. (2013). MOOCs go to K12: Higher ed. trend expands to high schools. *District Administration: Solutions for School District Management.* Retrieved from http://www.districtadministration.com/article/moocs-go-k12-higher-ed-trend-expands-high-schools

Jamieson, J., & Chapelle, C. (2010). Evaluating CALL use across multiple contexts. *System, 38*, 357–369.

Jewett, P. (2011). Multiple literacies gone wild. *The Reading Teacher, 64*(5), 341–344.

Johnson, L., Levine, A., Smith, R., & Stone, S. (2010). *The 2010 horizon report.* Austin, Texas: The New Media Consortium.

Johnson, L., Smith, R., Willis, H., Levine, A., & Haywood, K., (2011). *The 2011 horizon report.* Austin, TX: The New Media Consortium.

Johnson, L., Adams Becker, S., Cummins, M., Estrada, V., Freeman, A., & Ludgate, H. (2013). *NMC horizon report: 2013 higher education edition.* Austin, Texas: The New Media Consortium.

Johnson, L., Adams Becker, S., Estrada, V., & Freeman, A. (2014). *NMC Horizon Report: 2014 Higher Education Edition.* Austin, Texas: The New Media Consortium.

Johnson, R. D., Gueutal, H., & Falbe, C. M. (2009). Technology, trainees, metacognitive activity, and e-learning effectiveness. *Journal of Managerial Psychology, 24*(6), 545–566.

Joint Committee on National Health Education Standards. (2007). *National health education standards: Achieving excellence* (2nd ed.). Atlanta, GA: American Cancer Society.

Jones, L., Mitchell, K., & Finkelhor, D. (2013). Trends in youth Internet victimization: Findings from three youth Internet safety surveys 2000–2010. *Journal of Adolescent Health, 50*, 179–186.

Jonker, T. (2011). Information power. *School Library Journal, 57*(4), 72.

Jordan, L., & Papp, R. (2013). PowerPoint®: It's not "yes" or "no"—it's "when" and "how." *Research in Higher Education Journal, 22*, 1–12.

Juvonen J., & Gross E. (2008). Extending the school grounds? Bullying experiences in cyberspace. *Journal of School Health, 78*, 496–505.

Kaplan, D., & Wu, E. (2006). Computer-based graphical displays for enhancing mental animation and improving reasoning in novice learning of probability. *Journal of Computing in Higher Education, 18*(1), 55–79.

Ke, F., & Im, T. (2013). Virtual-reality-based social interaction training for children with high-functioning autism. *The Journal of Educational Research, 106*, 441–461.

Kenwright, K. (2009). Clickers in the classroom. *TechTrends, 53*(1), 74–77.

Kerski, J., Demirci, A., & Milson, J. (2013). The global landscape of GIS in secondary education. *The Journal of Geography, 112*(6), 232–247.

Kim, P. (2006). Effects of 3D virtual reality of plate tectonics on fifth-grade students' achievement and attitude toward science. *Interactive Learning Environments, 14*(1), 25–34.

King-Sears, M. E., Swanson, C., & Mainzer, L. (2011). Technology and literacy for adolescents with disabilities. *Journal of Adolescent & Adult Literacy, 54*(8), 569–578.

Kirchen, D. (2013). Making and taking virtual field trips in pre-K and the primary grades. *YC Young Children, 66*(6), 22–26.

Kirschner, P. A., Sweller, J., & Clark, R. E. (2006). Why minimal guidance during instruction does not work: An analysis of the failure of constructivist, discovery, problem-based experiential, and inquiry-based teaching. *Educational Psychologist, 41*(2), 75–86.

Klemm, W. (2007). Computer slide shows: A trap for bad teaching. *College Teaching, 55*(3), 121–124.

Ko, S., & Rossen, S. (2010). *Teaching online: A practical guide* (3rd ed.). New York: Routledge.

Kozma, R. (1991). Learning with media. *Review of Educational Research, 61*(2), 179–211.

Kozma, R. (1994). Will media influence learning? Reframing the debate. *Educational Technology Research and Development, 42*(2), 5–17.

Krall, R. M. (2010). Cruising the climate with spreadsheets [Part of a special issue: Weather]. *Science and Children, 47*(8), 46–51.

Lach, C., Little, E., & Nazzaro, D. (2003). From all sides now—weaving technology and multiple intelligences into science and art. *Learning and Leading with Technology, 30*(6), 32–35, 59.

LaFee, S. (2013). Flipped learning. *The Education Digest, 79*(3), 13–18.

Lalley, J., Piotrowski, P., Battaglia, B., Brophy, K., & Chugh, K. (2010). A comparison of V-Frog© to physical frog dissection. *International Journal of Environmental & Science, 5*(2), 189–200.

Lanier, J. (2010, September 3). The end of human specialness. *The Chronicle of Higher Education*, B7. Available from: http://chronicle.com/

Lanius, R. (2013). Public history wars, the "one nation/one people" consensus, and the continuing search for a usable past. *OAH Magazine of History, 27*(1), 31–36.

Larson, L. (2010). Digital readers: The next chapter in e-book reading and response. *The Reading Teacher, 64*(1), 15–22.

Larson-Guenette, J. (2013). "It's just reflex now": German language learners' use of online resources. *Die Unterrichtspraxis/Teaching German, 46*(1), 62–74.

Lawrence, R., & Chang, C. (2012). Videoconferencing Using SCOPIA for teaching and learning English as an additional language—pedagogical and technological observations. *Proceedings of the Seventh Annual International Conference on e-Learning*, Hong Kong, pp. 244–250.

LeBlanc, L. (2010). Using video-based interventions with individuals with autism spectrum disorders: Introduction to the special issue. *Education & Treatment of Children, 33*(3), 333–337.

Lee, C., & Chen, M. (2010). Taiwanese junior high school students' mathematics attitudes and perceptions towards virtual manipulatives. *British Journal of Educational Technology, 41*(2), 17–21.

Lee, Y., & Choi, J. (2011). A review of online course dropout research: Implications for practice and future research. *Education Technology Research and Development, 59*, 593–618.

Lee, Y., & Guo, Y. (2008). Explore effective use of computer simulations for physics education. *Journal of Computers in Mathematics and Science Teaching, 27*(4), 443–466.

Legg, A. M., & Wilson, J. H. (2009). E-mail from professor enhances student motivation and attitude. *Teaching of Psychology, 36*(3), 205–211.

Lerner, J.W., & Johns, B. (2014). *Learning disabilities and related disabilities: Strategies for success* (14th ed.). Stamford, CT: Cengage Learning.

Leu, D. J., & Forzani, E. (2012). New literacies in a web 2.0, 3.0, 4.0, . . . [infinity] world. *Research in the Schools, 19*(1), 75–81.

Leu, D., Forzani, E., Rhoads, C., Maykel, C., Kennedy, C., & Timbrell, N. (2014). The new literacies of online research and comprehension: Rethinking the reading achievement gap. *Reading Research Quarterly*, (online preview), 1–23.

Leu, D. J., Kinzer, C. K., Coiro, J., Castek, J., & Henry, L. A. (2013). New literacies: A dual-level theory of the changing nature of literacy, instruction, and assessment. In D. E. Alvermann, N. J. Unrau & R. B. Ruddell (Eds.), *Theoretical models and processes of reading* (Vol. 6th, pp. 1150–1181). Newark, DE: International Reading Association.

Leu, D. J., McVerry, J. G., O'Byrne, W. I., Kiili, C., Zawilinski, L., Everett-Cacopardo, Kinnedy, C., Forzani, E. (2011). The new literacies of online reading comprehension: Expanding the literacy and learning curriculum. *Journal of Adolescent & Adult Literacy, 55*(1), 5–14. doi:10.1598/JAAL.55.1.1

Levy, A. (2010, June). Third of children have seen online porn by the time they are 10, shocking study reveals. *Daily Mail Online News*. Retrieved from http://www.dailymail.co.uk/news/article-1284425/THIRD-children-seen-online-porn-time-10-shocking-study-reveals.html

Lewis, D. (2010). Individual FM systems for children: Where are we now? *Perspectives on Hearing and Hearing Disorders in Childhood, 20*, 56–62.

Li, Q., & Ma, X. (2010). A meta-analysis of the effects of computer technology on school students' mathematics learning. *Educational Psychology Review, 22*, 215–243.

Lim, J., Pellett, H., & Pellett, T. (2009). Integrating digital video technology in the classroom. *Journal of Physical Education, Recreation, & Dance, 80*(6), 40–55.

Link, D. (2009). Commentary: Never trust your word processor. *Biochemistry and Molecular Biology Education, 37*(6), 377.

Livingstone, S., & Smith, P. K. (2014). Annual research review: Harms experienced by child users of online and mobile technologies: The nature, prevalence and management of sexual and aggressive risks in the digital age. *Journal of Child Psychology and Psychiatry*. doi: 10.1111/jcpp.12197

Long, C. (2013). Does cursive need to be taught in the digital age? *NEA Today, 3*, 3. Retrieved from: http://neatoday.org/2013/07/22/does-cursive-need-to-be-taught-in-the-digital-age/

Looney, M. (2008). Using an online survey tool to enhance teaching. *Measurement in Physical Education and Exercise Science, 12*, 113–121.

Lorenzi, N. (2012). Creating future filmmakers. *Instructor, 121*(6), 57–58.

Luik, P. (2011). Would boys and girls benefit from gender-specific educational software? *British Journal of Educational Technology, 42*(1), 128–144.

Lynch, S., Lynch, J., &Bolyard, J. (2013). I-THINK I can problem solve. *Mathematics Teaching in the Middle School, 19*(1), 10–14.

MacArthur, C. (2009). Reflections on research on writing and technology for struggling writers. *Learning Disabilities Research & Practice, 24*(2), 93–103.

Macfadyen, L., & Dawson, S. (2010). Mining LMS data to develop an "early warning system" for educators: A proof of concept. *Computers & Education, 54*(2), 588–599.

Madden, M., Lenhart, A., Cortesi, S., Gasser, U., Guggan, M., Smith, A., & Beaton, M. (2013, May 21). Teens, social media, and privacy. *Report of the Pew Research Center's Internet & American Life Project*. Retrieved from: http://pewinternet.org/Reports/2013/Teens-Social-Media-And-Privacy.aspx

Maenner, M. J., & Durkin, M. S. (2010). Trends in the prevalence of autism on the basis of special education data. *Pediatrics, 126*(5), 989–990.

Makice, K. (2012, April 13). Flipping the classroom requires more than video. *Wired*. Retrieved from http://www.wired.com/geekdad/2012/04/flipping-the-classroom/

Manca, S., & Ranierit, M. (2013). Is it a tool suitable for learning? A critical review of the literature on Facebook as a technology-enhanced learning environment. *Journal of Computer Assisted Learning, 29*, 487–504.

Manfra, M., & Lee, J. (2012). "You have to know the past to (blog) the present:" Using an educational blog to engage students in U.S. history. *Computers in the Schools, 29*, 118–134.

Marino, M., Tsurusaki, B., & Basham, J. (2011). Selecting software for students with learning and other disabilities. *The Science Teacher, 78*(3), 70–72.

Marovich, B. (2012, September 3). More than MOOC's. *The Chronicle of Higher Education*. Retrieved from http://chronicle.com

Martin, M. (2014, March 17). Virtual reality headsets are coming, and I'm not ready. *The State Press*. Retrieved from http://www.statepress.com/2014/03/17/virtual-reality-headsets-are-coming-and-im-not-ready/

Mayer, R. (1992). *Thinking, problem solving, cognition* (2nd ed.). New York: W.H. Freeman and Company.

Mayes, R. (1992). The effects of using software tools on mathematics problem solving in secondary school. *School Science and Mathematics, 92*(5), 243–248.

McBrien, J. L., Cheng, R., & Jones, P. (2009). Virtual spaces: Employing a synchronous online classroom to facilitate student engagement in online learning. International *Review of Research in Open and Distance Learning, 10*(3), 1–17. Retrieved from http://www.irrodl.org/index.php/irrodl/article/viewArticle/605

McDermott, J. (2010). Returns-based style analysis: An Excel-based classroom exercise. *Journal of Education for Business, 85*(2), 107–113.

McDevitt, T., & Ormrod, J. (2010). *Child development and education* (4th ed.) Columbus, OH: Pearson Education.

McLaughlin, J., Roth, M., Glatt, D., Gharkholonarehe, N., Davidson, C., Griffin, L., Esserman, D., & Mumper, R. (2014). The flipped classroom: A course redesign to foster learning and engagement in a health professions school. *Academic Medicine, 89*(2). Retrieved at http://journals.lww.com/academicmedicine/Abstract/publishahead/The_Flipped_Classroom___A_Course_Redesign_to.99241.aspx

McLeskey, J., Landers, E., Williams, P., & Hoppy, D. (2012). Are we moving toward educating students with disabilities in less restrictive settings? *Journal of Special Education, 46*(3), 131–140.

McLeskey, J., Rosenberg, M., & Westling, D. (2013). *Inclusion: Effective practices for all students* (2nd ed.). Boston: Pearson Education.

McLeskey, J., Waldron, N., & Redd, L. (2014). A case study of a highly effective, inclusive elementary school. *The Journal of Special Education, 48*(1), 59–70.

McVee, M., Bailey, N., Shanahan, L. (2008). Using digital media to interpret poetry: Spiderman meets Walt Whitman. *Research in the Teaching of English, 43*(2), 112–143.

Means, B., Toyama, Y., Murphy, R., Bakia, M., & Jones, K. (2010). *Evaluation of evidence-based practices in online learning: A meta-analysis and review of online learning studies*. Washington, DC: U.S. Department of Education,

Office of Planning, Evaluation, and Policy Development. Retrieved from http://www2.ed.gov/rschstat/eval/tech/evidence-based-practices/finalreport.pdf

Mears, D. (2012a). Physical activity monitoring devices: Types, policies guidelines and recommendations. In Steve Saunders & L. Witherspoon (Eds.), *Contemporary uses of technology in K–12 physical education: Policy, practice and advocacy.* Charlotte, NC: Information Age.

Mears, D. (2012b). Welcome to the "iGeneration": Implications of children's technology use on physical education and childhood obesity prevention. In S. Sanders & L. Witherspoon (Eds.), *Contemporary uses of technology in K–12 physical education: Policy, practice and advocacy.* Charlotte, NC: Information Age.

Mears, D., & Hansen, L. (2009). Active gaming: Definitions options and implementation. *Strategies: A Journal for Physical and Sport Educators, 23*(2), 26–29.

Mears, D., Hansen, L., Fine, P., Lawler, P., & Mason, K. (2009). *Appropriate use of instructional technology in physical education [Position Statement].* Reston, VA: National Association for Sport and Physical Education.

Merrill, D., & Salisbury, D. (1984). Research on drill and practice strategies. *Journal of Computer-Based Instruction, 11*(1), 19–21.

Michel, J., Shen, Y. K., Aiden, A. P., Veres, A., Gray, M. K., Brockman, W., The Google Books Team, Pickett, J. P., Hoiberg, D., Clancy, D., Norvig, P., Orwant, J., Pinker, S., Nowak, M. A., and Aiden, E. L. (2011). Quantitative analysis of culture using millions of digitized books. *Science, 331*(6014), 176–182.

Miller, M. (2009). *Basic writers using clickers: A case study.* Unpublished doctoral dissertation. University of Akron, Akron, OH.

Millett, P., & Purcell, N. (2010). Effect of sound field amplification on grade 1 reading outcomes. *Canadian Journal of Speech-Language Pathology and Audiology, 34*(1), 17–24.

Millstone, J. (2012, May 2). *Teacher attitudes about digital games in the classroom.* New York: The Joan Ganz Cooney Center at Sesame Workshop. Retrieved from http://www.joanganzcooneycenter.org/publication/national-survey-and-video-case-studies-teacher-attitudes-about-digital-games-in-the-classroom/

Milman, N. (2012). The flipped classroom strategy: What is it and how can it best be used? *Distance Learning, 9*(3), 85–87.

Mineer, S. (2014, March 28). Putting Google Glass into practice. *eSchoolNews.* Retrieved from http://www.eschoolnews.com/2014/03/28/google-glass-learning-204/2/

Miranda, T., Williams-Rossi, D., Johnson, K. A., & McKenzie, N. (2011). Reluctant readers in middle school: Successful engagement with text using the e-reader. *International Journal of Applied Science and Technology, 1*(6), 81–91.

Miron, G., Horwitz, B., & Gulosino, C. (2013). *Virtual schools in the U. S. 2013: Politics, performance, policy, and research evidence: Part 1.* National Education Policy Center, University of Colorado School of Education. Retrieved from http://nepc.colorado.edu/files/nepc-virtual-2013.pdf

Miron, G., & Urschel, J. (2012, July). *Understanding and improving fulltime virtual schools: A study of student characteristics, school finance, and school performance in schools operated by K12, Inc.* National Education Policy Center, University of Colorado School of Education. Retrieved from http://nepc.colorado.edu/publication/understanding-improving-virtual

Mishra, P., & Koehler, M. (2006). Technological pedagogical content knowledge: A framework for teacher knowledge. *Teachers College Record, 108*(6), 1017–1054.

Mishra, P., & Koehler, M. (2009). Too cool for school? No way! *Learning and Leading with Technology, 36*(7), 14–18.

Mogey, N., Paterson, J., Burk, J., & Purcell, M. (2010). Typing compared with handwriting for essay examinations at university: Letting the students choose. *ALT-Journal, Research in Learning Technology, 18*(1), 29–47.

Mohnsen, B. (2000). Vaughn, Nekomi, and Luis: What they were doing in middle school physical education. *Learning and Leading with Technology, 27*(5), 22–27.

Molnar, M. (2013, August 27). New sites aim to help pick best ed-tech tools. *Education Week.* Retrieved from http://www.edweek.org/ew/articles/2013/08/28/02reviews.h33.html

Moore, M. G. (1986). Three kinds of interaction. *American Journal of Distance Education, 3*(2), 1–6.

Morelli, T., Folmer, E., Foley, J. T., & Lieberman, L. (2011). Improving the lives of youth with visual impairments through exergames. *Insight: Research & Practice in Visual Impairment & Blindness, 4*(4), 160–170.

Moreno, N., & Erdmann, D. (2010). Addressing science teacher needs. *Science, 327*(5973), 1589–1590.

Morphy, P., & Graham, S. (2012). Word processing programs and weaker writers/readers: A meta-analysis of research findings. *Reading and Writing, 25,* 641–678.

Moss, K., & Crowley, M. (2011). Effective learning in science: The use of personal response systems with a wide range of audiences. *Computers in Education, 56*(1), 36–43.

Mouza, C., Karchmer-Klein, R., Nandakumar, R., Ozden, S., & Hu, L. (2014). Investigating the impact of an integrated approach to the development of preservice teachers' technological pedagogical content knowledge (TPACK). *Computers and Education, 71,* 201–221.

Muller, K. (2010). How technology can promote the learning of proof. *The Mathematics Teacher, 103*(6), 436–441.

Naisbitt, J. (1984). *MegaTrends.* New York: Warner Books.

National Art Education Association (NAEAa). (2009). *Standards for art teacher preparation.* Reston, VA: Author.

National Art Education Association (NAEAb). (2009). *Professional standards for visual arts educators.* Reston, VA: Author.

National Association for Sport and Physical Education. (2007). *Physical education teacher evaluation tool.* Reston, VA: Author.

National Association for Sport and Physical Education. (2008). *PE metrics: Assessing the national standards: Standard I: Elementary.* Reston, VA: Author.

National Association for Sport and Physical Education. (2009). *Appropriate instructional practice guidelines, K–12: A side by side comparison.* Reston, VA: Author.

National Association for Sport and Physical Education. (2010). *PE metrics: Assessing national standards 1-6 in secondary school.* Reston, VA: Author.

National Association for Sport and Physical Education, & American Heart Association. (2012). *Shape of the nation report: Status of physical education in the USA.* Reston, VA: American Alliance for Health Physical Education Recreation and Dance.

National Association of Schools of Music (NASM). (2013). *Handbook 2012-13.* Reston, VA: National Association of Schools of Music. Retrieved from http://nasm.arts-accredit.org/site/docs/Handbook/NASM_HANDBOOK_2012-13.pdf

National Conference of State Legislatures. (2013). *State policies on sex education in schools.* Retrieved from http://www.ncsl.org/research/health/state-policies-on-sex-education-in-schools.aspx

National Council for the Social Studies (NCSS). (2010). *National curriculum standards for social studies.* Silver Spring, MD: Author.

National Council for the Social Studies (NCSS). (2013). *College, career, and civic life (C3) framework for social studies.* Silver Spring, MD: Author.

National Council of Teachers of Mathematics (NCTM). (2000). *Principles and Standards for School Mathematics.* Reston, Virginia: Author.

National Council of Teachers of Mathematics. (2013). *Supporting the Common Core state standards for mathematics.* Reston, VA: Authors. Retrieved from http://www.nctm.org/ccssmposition/

National Forum on Education Statistics. (2006). *Forum guide to elementary/secondary virtual education* (NFES 2006–803). U.S. Department of Education. Washington, DC: National Center for Education Statistics.

National Governors Association Center for Best Practices & Council of Chief State School Officers. (2010). *Common Core state standards for mathematics.* Washington, DC: Authors.

National Research Council (NRC) (1996). *National science education standards.* Washington, DC: National Academies Press.

National Research Council. (2012). *A framework for k–12 science education: Practices, crosscutting concepts and core ideas.* Washington, DC: The National Academies Press.

National Science Teachers Association (NSTA). (2007). NSTA Position statement: The integral role of laboratory investigations in science instruction. Retrieved from http://www.nsta.org/about/positions/laboratory.aspx

National Science Teachers Association (2011, July). *Science & Children, 48*(9). Retrieved from http://www.nsta.org/elementaryschool

NCTE. (2013). *NCTE Framework for 21st century curriculum and assessment A statement on an education issue approved by the NCTE Board of Directors or the NCTE Executive Committee.* Retrieved from http://www.ncte.org/positions/statements/21stcentframework

New grant program seeks solutions to toughest classroom challenges. (2010, September 8). *eSchool News.* Retrieved fromhttp://www.eschoolnews.com/2010/09/08/new-grant-program-seeks-solutions-to-toughest-classroom-challenges/

New Lifestyles. (2013). *New-lifestyles nl-200i activity monitor.* Retrieved from http://www.thepedometercompany.com/nl2000.html

Nichols, A. (2012). Blogging across the curriculum: An action research project. *Journal of Educational Multimedia and Hypermedia, 21*(2), 165–174.

Nichols, R., Davis, K., McCord, T., Schmidt, D., & Slezak. A. (2009). The use of heart rate monitors in physical education. *Strategies, 22*(6), 19–23.

Nickel, J. (2012). Word clouds in math classrooms. *Mathematics Teaching in the Middle School, 17*(9), 564–566.

Nielsen Company. (2013). *U. S. music industry year-end review.* Retrieved from http://www.nielsen.com/content/dam/corporate/us/en/reports-downloads/2014%20Reports/nielsen-us-music-year-end-report-2013.pdf

Niess, M. L. (2012). Rethinking pre-service mathematics teachers' preparation: Technological, pedagogical and content knowledge (TPACK). In D. Polly, C. Mims, & K. Persichitte (Eds.), *Developing technology-rich, teacher education programs: Key issues* (pp. 316–336). Hershey, PA: IGI Global.

Niess M. L., van Zee, E., & Gillow-Wiles, H. (2010–2011). Knowledge growth in teaching mathematics/science with spreadsheets: Moving PCK to TPACK through online professional development. *Journal of Digital Learning in Teacher Education, 27*(2), 52–62.

Noar, S., Pierce, L., & Black, H. (2010). Can computer-mediated interventions change theoretical mediators of safer sex? A meta-analysis. *Human Communication Research, 36,* 261–297.

Nugent, G., Barker, B., Grandgenett, N., & Adamchuk, V. (2010). Impact of robotics and geospatial technology interventions on youth STEM learning and attitudes. *Journal of Research on Technology in Education, 42*(4), 391–408.

Nussbaum-Beach, S., & Hall, L. R. (2012). *The connected educator: Learning and leading in a digital age.* Bloomington, IN: Solution Tree Press.

Nye, S. (2010). Tablet PCs: A physical educator's new clipboard. *Strategies, 23*(4), 21–23.

Obaiduzzaman, K. (2010). *Five iPhone apps can help you for dance.* Retrieved from http://thetechjournal.com/electronics/iphone/5-iphone-apps-can-help-you-for-dance.xhtml

Obara, S. (2010a). Constructing spatial understanding. *Mathematics Teaching in the Middle School, 15*(8), 472–478.

Obara, S. (2010b). The role of technology in a geometry investigation. *Mathematics and Computer Education, 44*(3), 196–204.

O'Dowd, R. (2011). Online foreign language interaction: Moving from the periphery to the core of foreign language education? *Language Teaching, 44*(3), 368–470.

Offner, S., & Pohlman, R. (2010). Visualizing proteins and their evolution. *The American Biology Teacher, 72*(6), 373–376.

Ogden C., Carroll M., Curtin L., Lamb M., & Flegal K. (2010). Prevalence of high body mass index in US children and adolescents, 2007–2008. *Journal of the American Medical Association, 303*(3), 242–249.

O'Hara, S., & Pritchard, R. (2008). Hypermedia authoring as a vehicle for vocabulary development in middle school English as a second language classrooms. *The Clearing House, 82*(2), 60–65.

Oliver, K., Osborne, J., Patel, R., & Kleiman, G. (2009). Issues surrounding the deployment of a new statewide virtual public school. *The Quarterly Review of Distance Education, 10*(1), 37–49.

Olson, C. A. (2010). Making the tech connection. *Teaching Music, 17*(5), 30–35.

Ormrod, J. (2014). *Educational psychology: Developing learners* (8th ed.). Columbus, OH: Pearson Education.

Owston, R. (2009). Digital immersion, teacher learning, and games. *Educational Researcher, 38*(4), 270–273.

Pannell, F., & Hutchison, L. (2010). Podcasting for understanding. *Mathematics Teaching in the Middle School, 15*(8), 431–433.

Papert, S. (1980). *Mindstorms: Children, computers, and powerful ideas.* New York: Basic Books.

Paris, R. (n.d.). How to read critically. Retrieved from http://aix1.uottawa.ca/~rparis/critical.html

Park, J.-H., & Choi, H. J. (2009). Factors influencing adult learners' decision to drop out or persist in online learning. *Educational Technology & Society, 12*(4), 207–217.

Pashler, H., McDaniel, M., Rohrer, D., & Bjork, R. (2008). Learning styles concepts and evidence. *Psychological Science in the Public Interest, 9*(3), 105–119.

Passe, J., & Fitchett, P. (Eds.). (2013). *The status of social studies: Views from the field.* Charlotte, NC: Information Age Publishing

Patterson, B., & McFadden, C. (2009). Attrition in online and campus degree programs. *Online Journal of Distance Learning Administration, 12*(2). Retrieved from http://www.westga.edu/%7Edistance/ojdla/summer122/patterson112.pdf

Pearman, C., & Chang, C. (2010). Scaffolding or distracting: CD-ROM storybooks and young readers. *Tech Trends, 54*(4), 52–56.

PE Central. (2013). *Classroom teacher/Integrated lesson ideas.* Retrieved from http://www.pecentral.org/lessonideas/classroom/classroom.asp

Pedersen, S. (2003). Motivational orientation in a problem-based learning environment. *Journal of Interactive Learning Research, 14*(1), 41–77.

Peppler, K. (2010). Media arts: Arts education for a digital age. *Teachers College Record, 112*(8), 2118–2153.

Perez-Hernandez, D. (2014, May 5). Technology provides foreign-language immersion at a distance. *The Chronicle of Higher Education.* Retrieved from http://chronicle.com/article/Technology-Provides/146369/?cid=at&utm_source=at&utm_medium=en

Periathiruvadi, S., & Rinn, A. (2012–2013). Technology in gifted education: A review of best practices and empirical research. *Journal of Research on Technology in Education, 45*(2), 153–169.

Perry, L. (2012). Using word clouds to teach about speaking style. *Communication Teacher, 26*(4), 220–223.

Pierce, D. (2013, April 24). Common Core testing will require digital literacy skills. *eSchool News.* Available at: http://www.eschoolnews.com/2013/04/24/common-core-testing-will-require-digital-literacy-skills

Pinkstone, R. (2010). A great opportunity for student filmmakers. *Education, 91*(13), 12.

Ploog, B., Scharf, A., Nelson, D., & Brooks, P. (2013). Use of computer-assisted technologies (CAT) to enhance social, communicative, and language development in children with autism spectrum disorders. *Journal of Autism and Developmental Disorders, 43,* 301–322.

Pohl, J. (2014). *Dance choreography.* Retrieved from https://itunes.apple.com/us/app/dance-choreography/id443379839

Polly, D. (2011). Technology to develop algebraic reasoning. *Teaching Children Mathematics, 17*(8), 472–478.

Popelka, S. (2010). Now we're really clicking! *Mathematics Teacher, 104*(4), 290–295.

Proctor, C., August, D., Snow, C., & Barr, C. (2010). The interdependence continuum: A perspective on the nature of Spanish-English bilingual reading comprehension. *Bilingual Research Journal, 33*(1), 5–20.

Puentedura, R. (2009). *As we may teach: Educational technology, from theory into practice.* [Audio podcast]. Retrieved from https://itunes.apple.com/itunes-u/as-we-may-teach-educational/id380294705?mt=10

Purcell, K., Buchanan, J., & Friedrich, L. (2013). *The impact of digital tools on student writing and how writing is taught in schools.* Report of the Pew Research Center's Internet & American Life Project. Retrieved from: http://pewinternet.org/Reports/2013/Teachers-technology-and-writing

Queen, B., Lewis, L., & Coopersmith, J. (2011). *Distance education courses for public elementary and secondary school students: 2009–10.* NCES 2012-008. National Center for Education Statistics, Institute of Education Sciences, Washington, DC. Retrieved from http://nces.ed.gov/pubs2012/2012008.pdf

Quillen, I. (2011). Technology evolves to offer a clearer view of science. *Education Week, 30*(35), s2–s3.

Ratcliff, C., & Anderson, S. (2011). Reviving the Turtle: Exploring the use of Logo with students with mild disabilities. *Computers in the Schools, 28*(3), 241–255.

Raths, D. (2013, December 4). 9 video tips for a better flipped classroom. *THE Journal*. Retrieved from http://thejournal.com/articles/2013/11/18/9-video-tips-for-a-better-flipped-classroom.aspx#1y7ybk34ZYE7Ucrf.99

Ravenna, G., Foster, C., & Bishop, C. (2012). Increasing student interaction online: A review of the literature. *Journal of Technology and Teacher Education, 20*(2), 177–203.

Ray, D. (2013). Integrating math & computer skills in the biology classroom: An example using spreadsheet simulations to teach fundamental sampling concepts. *The American Biology Teacher, 75*(7), 455–460.

Rees, J. (2014, January 16). Do you really want to use a commercial learning-management system? *The Chronicle of Higher Education.* Retrieved from http://chronicle.com/

Reich, J., Murnane, R., & Willett, J. (2012). The state of wiki usage in U.S. K–12 schools: Leveraging web 2.0 data warehouses to assess quality and equity in online learning environments. *Educational Researcher, 41*(1), 7–15.

Rheingold, H. (n.d.) *Crap detection 101.* Retrieved from http://critical-thinking.iste.wikispaces.net/Crap+Detection+101

Rice, J. (2007). New media resistance: Barriers to implementation of computer video games in the classroom. *Journal of Educational Multimedia and Hypermedia, 16*(3), 249–261.

Richardson, W., Fox, J., & Lehman, J. (2012). Successful videoconferencing scenarios for teacher education programs. *Tech Trends, 56*(5), 17–24.

Rideout, V., Foehr, U. G., & Roberts, D. F. (2010). *Generation M2: Media in the lives of 8- to 18-year-olds.* Menlo Park, CA: Kaiser Family Foundation. Retrieved from http://kaiserfamilyfoundation.wordpress.com/uncategorized/report/generation-m2-media-in-the-lives-of-8-to-18-year-olds/

Risinger, C. F. (2010). Using online field trips and tours in social studies. *Social Education, 74*(3), 137–138.

Ritzhaupt, A., Liu, F, Dawson, K., Barron, A. (2013). Differences in student information and communication technology literacy based on socioeconomic status, ethnicity, and gender: Evidence of a digital divide in Florida schools. *Journal of Research on Technology in Education, 45*(4), 291–307.

Robinson, C., & Sebba, J. (2010). Personalising learning through the use of technology. *Computers & Education, 54*(3), 767–775.

Robinson, T. N. (1999). Reducing children's television viewing to prevent obesity: A randomized controlled trial. *Journal of the American Medical Association, 282*, 1561–1567.

Rodriguez, C. (Ed.). (2004). *Bridging the gap: Popular music and music education.* Reston, VA: MENC.

Rogers, E. (2003). *Diffusion of innovations* (5th Ed.). New York: The Free Press.

Roblyer, M. D., & Wiencke, W. (2004). Exploring the interaction equation: Validating a rubric to assess and encourage interaction in distance courses. *Journal of Asynchronous Learning Networks, 8*(4), 24–37.

Roblyer, M. D. (2015). *Introduction to systematic instructional design for traditional, online, and blended environments.* Columbus, OH: Pearson Education.

Rodchua, S., Yiadom-Boakye, G., & Woolsey, R. (2011). Student verification system for online assessments: Bolstering quality and integrity of distance learning. *Journal of Industrial Technology, 27*(3), 1–8.

Rosen, C. (2008). The myth of multitasking. *The New Atlantis, 20*, 105–110. Retrieved from http://www.thenewatlantis.com/publications/the-myth-of-multitasking

Rosen, D., & Hoffman, J. (2009). Integrating concrete and virtual manipulatives in early childhood mathematics. *YC Young Children, 64*(3), 26–32.

Rosen, L. D. (2010). *Rewired: Understanding the iGeneration and the way they learn.* New York: St. Martin's Press.

Rudd, D. P, II; Rudd, D. P. (2014). The value of video in online instruction. *Journal of Instructional Pedagogies, 13*, 1–7.

Ruthven, K., Deaney, R., & Hennessy, S. (2009). Using graphing software to teach about algebraic forms: A study of technology-supported practice in secondary-school mathematics. *Educational Studies in Mathematics, 71*(3), 279–297.

Saettler, P. (1990). *The evolution of American educational technology.* Englewood, CO: Libraries Unlimited.

Salden, R., Koedinger, K., Renkl, A., Alevnen, V., & McLaren, B. (2010). Accounting for beneficial effects of worked examples in tutored problem solving. *Educational Psychology Review, 22*(4), 379–392.

Salisbury, D. (1990). Cognitive psychology and its implications for designing drill and practice programs for computers. *Journal of Computer-Based Instruction, 17*(1), 23–30.

Salmerón, L., & García, V. (2011). Reading skills and children's navigation strategies in hypertext. *Computers in Human Behavior, 27*(3), 1143–1151. doi:10.1016/j.chb.2010.12.008

Samsonov, P., Pedersen, S., & Hill, C. (2006). Using problem-based learning software with at-risk students: A case study. *Computers in the Schools, 23*(1–2), 111–124.

Santos-Trigo, M., Cristobal-Escalante, C. (2008). Emerging high school students' problem solving trajectories based on the use of dynamic software. *Journal of Computers in Mathematics and Science Teaching, 27*(3), 325–340.

Sarama, J., & Clements, D. (2009). "Concrete" computer manipulatives in mathematics education. *Child Development Perspectives, 3*(3), 145–150.

Savin-Baden, M., Gourlay, L., Tombs, C., Steils, N., Tombs, G., & Mawer, M. (2010). Situating pedagogies, positions and practices in immersive virtual worlds. *Educational Research, 52*(2), 123–133.

Schoppek, W., & Tulis, M. (2010). Enhancing arithmetic and word-problem solving skills efficiently by individualized computer-assisted practice. *Journal of Educational Research, 103*(4), 239–252.

Schugar, J., & Schugar, H. (2014, April). *Reading in the post-PC era: Students' comprehension of interactive e-books.* Paper presentation at the AERA Annual Conference, Philadelphia, Pennsylvania.

Schugar, H., Smith, C., & Schugar, J. (2013). Teaching with interactive picture e-books in grades K– 6. *The Reading Teacher, 66*(8), 615–624.

Schul, J. (2011). Revisiting an old friend: The practice and promise of cooperative learning for the twenty-first century. *The Social Studies, 102*(2), 88–93.

Schunk, D. (2012). Learning *theories: An educational perspective* (6th ed.). Boston, MA: Pearson Education.

Schwebach, J. (2008). Science seminar: Science capstone research projects as a class in high school. *American Biology Teacher, 70*(8), 488–497.

Senning, D., & Post, A. (2013). *Emily Post's manners in a digital world: Living well online.* New York: Open Road Media.

Serafini, F. (2012). Expanding the four resources model: Reading visual and multimodal texts. Pedagogies: *An International Journal 7*(2), 150–164.

Sfard, A. (1998). One–two metaphors for learning and the dangers of choosing just one. *Educational Researcher, 27*(2), 4–13.

Shafer, K. (2010). Scrambling data with Fathom to simulate the null hypothesis. *The Mathematics Teacher, 103*(6), 453–457.

Shaffer, D., & Collura, M. (2009). Evaluating the effectiveness of a personal response system in the classroom. *Teaching of Psychology, 36*(4), 273–277.

Shaffer, S. (2012). Distance education assessment infrastructure and process design based on international standard 23988. *Online Journal of Distance Learning Administration, 15*(2). Retrieved from http://www.westga.edu/~distance/ojdla/summer152/shaffer152.html

Shayne, R., Fogel, V., Miltenberger, R., & Koehler, S. (2012). The effects of exergaming on physical activity in a third-grade physical education class. *Journal of Applied Behavior Analysis, 45*(1), 211–215.

Sheer, V. C., & Fung, T. K. (2009). Can email communication enhance professor-student relationship and student evaluation of professor? Some empirical evidence. *Journal of Educational Computing Research, 37*(3), 289–306.

Shulman, L. S. (1986). Those who understand: Knowledge growth in teaching. *Educational Researcher, 15*(2), 4–14.

Shumack, K., & Reilly, E. (2011). Video podcasting in physical education. *Journal of Physical Education, Recreation, & Dance, 82*(1), 39–43.

Simonson, M., Smaldino, S., Albright, M., & Zvacek, S. (2012). *Teaching and learning at a distance: Foundations of distance education* (5th ed.). Upper Saddle River, NJ: Merrill.

Seo, Y., & Bryant, D. (2012). Multimedia CAI program for students with mathematics difficulties. *Remedial and Special Education, 33*(1), 217–225.

Seo, Y., & Woo, H. (2010). The identification, implementation, and evaluation of critical user interface design features of computer-assisted instruction programs in mathematics for students with learning disabilities. *Computers & Education, 55*(1), 363–377.

Shapiro, J. (2013, July 9). Are kids who make their own video games better prepared for the digital future? *Forbes Magazine*. Retrieved from http://www.forbes.com

Shapley, K.S., Sheehan, D., Maloney, C., & Caranikas-Walker, F. (2010). Evaluating the implementation fidelity of technology immersion and its relationship with student achievement. *Journal of Technology, Learning, and Assessment, 9*(4). Retrieved from http://www.jtla.org

Shea, V. (2004). *Netiquette.* San Francisco: Albion Books.

Shihadeh-Shald, E. (2010, August 25). Formative assessment that 'clicks' with students. *eSchoolNews Online*. Retrieved from http://www.eschoolnews.com/2010/08/25/formative-assessment-that-clicks-with-students/

Shirkey, C. (2010, June 18). The souls of the machine. *The Chronicle of Higher Education*, B7. Available from: http://chronicle.com/

Sileo, J.M., & van Garderen, D. (2010). Creating optimal opportunities to learn mathematics: Blending co-teaching structures with research-based practices. *Teaching Exceptional Children, 42*(3), 14–21.

Skinner, B. F. (1968). *The technology of teaching.* New York: Appleton-Century-Crofts.

Slater, T., & Beaudrie, B. (2000). Far out measurements: Bringing the planets closer to home using image-processing techniques. *Learning and Leading with Technology, 27*(5), 36–41.

Smith, G. D. (2013). *I drum, therefore I am.* London, UK: Ashgate.

Smith, K. H. (2010). Using Audacity and one classroom computer to experiment with timbre. *General Music Today, 24*(3), 23–27.

Smith, S. J., & Okolo, C. (2010). Response to intervention and evidence-based practices: Where does technology fit? *Learning Disability Quarterly, 33*(4), 257–272.

Snape, P., & Fox-Turnbull, W. (2013). Perspectives of authenticity: Implementation in technology education. *International Journal of Technology and Design Education, 23*, 51–68.

Snoddon, K. (2010). Technology as a learning tool for ASL literacy. *Sign Language Studies, 10*(2), 197–213, 293.

Snyder, I. (1993). Writing with word processors: A research overview. *Educational Research, 35*(1), 49–68.

Sory, T., Willard, T., & Kim, B. (2010). Create your own digital thermometer! *The Science Teacher, 77*(3), 56–60.

Southern Regional Educational Board (SREB). (2013). *Trends in state-run virtual schools in educational technology the SREB region.* Retrieved from the SREB website: http://publications.sreb.org/2013/13T01_Trends_State-Run.pdf

SPARKPE. (2014a). *SPARK alignment to the Common Core: Making the connections—meeting the standards: SPARK elementary physical education (Grades K-5): English language arts and literacy in technical subjects.* Retrieved from http://www.sparkpe.org/wp-content/uploads/4-13-Common-Core-K-5-Alignments-to-Literacy.pdf

SPARKPE. (2014b). *SPARK alignment to the Common Core: Making the connections—meeting the standards; SPARK middle school and high school physical education (Grades 6-12): English language arts and literacy in technical subjects.* Retrieved from http://www.sparkpe.org/wp-content/uploads/4-13-Common-Core-6-12-Alignments-to-Literacy.pdf

Sparks, S. (2010). Early-grade math programs go head-to-head in study; ongoing federal research shows an edge for some widely used curricula. *Education Week, 30*(11), 11.

Spinello, E. F., & Fischbach, R. (2008). Using a web-based simulation as a problem-based learning experience: Perceived and actual performance of undergraduate public health students. *Public Health Report, 123*(2), 78–84.

Stagg, A., Kimmins, L., & Pavlovski, N. (2013). Academic style with substance: A collaborative screencasting project to support referencing skills. *The Electronic Library, 31*(4), pp. 452–464.

Staker, H., & Horn, M. (2012). *Classifying k–12 blended learning.* San Mateo, CA: Innosight Institute. Retrieved from http://www.innosightinstitute.org/media-room/publications/education-publications/classifying-k-12-blended-learning

Stansbury, M. (2010, August 11). Ten of the best virtual field trips. *eSchool News*. Retrieved from: http://www.eschoolnews.com/2010/08/11/coming-soon-to-a-classroom-near-you-robot-teachers/

Stansbury, M. (2012, April 6). Ten education blogs worth following. *eSchool News*. Retrieved from: http://www.eschoolnews.com/2012/04/06/ten-education-blogs-worth-following/

Stansbury, M. (2013, April 3). Coming soon to a classroom near you: Robot teachers? *eSchool News*. Retrieved from: http://www.eschoolnews.com/2013/04/07/ten-of-the-best-virtual-field-trips/2/

Stansbury, M. (2014, January 10). 5 best practices in online learning. *eSchool News*. Retrieved from: http://www.eschoolnews.com/2014/01/10/practices-online-learning-407/

Steding, S. (2009). Machine translation in the German classroom: Detection, reaction, prevention. *Unterrichtspraxis, 42*(2), 178–189.

Steenbergen-Hu, S., & Cooper, H. (2013). A meta-analysis of the effectiveness of intelligent tutoring systems on K–12 students' mathematical learning. *Journal of Educational Psychology, 105*(4), 970–987.

Steinbach, L. (2011). 3D or not 3D? Is that a question? *Curator: The Museum Journal, 54*(1), 41–54.

Stetter, M., & Hughes, M. (2010). Computer-assisted instruction to enhance the reading comprehension of struggling readers: A review of the literature. *Journal of Special Education Technology, 25*(4), 1–16.

Stoddard, J. (2009). Toward a virtual field trip model for the social studies. *Contemporary Issues in Technology and Teacher Education, 9*(4). Retrieved from http://www.citejournal.org/vol9/iss4/socialstudies/article1.cfm

Stowell, J., Oldham, T., & Bennett, D. (2010). Using student response systems ("clickers") to combat conformity and shyness. *Teaching of Psychology, 37*(2), 135–140.

Stripling, B. (2010. Teaching students to think in the digital environment: Digital literacy and digital inquiry. *School Library Monthly, 26*(8), 16–19.

Stubbs, R. (2012). *Public funding for the arts: 2012 update.* Seattle, WA: Grantmakers in the Arts.

Subrahmaniyan, N., Krishnaswamy, S., Chowriappa, A., Bisantz, A., Shriber, L., & Kesavadas, T. (2012). A visual haptic system for children with learning disabilities: Software and hardware design considerations. *Journal of Interactive Learning Research, 23*(2), 113–141.

Suhr, K.A., Hernandez, D.A., Grimes, D., & Warschauer, M. (2010). Laptops and fourth-grade literacy: Assisting the jump over the fourth-grade slump. *Journal of Technology, Learning, and Assessment, 9*(5). Retrieved from http://www.jtla.org

Sun, K., Lin, C., & Wang, S. (2010). A 3-D virtual reality model of the sun and the moon for e-learning at elementary schools. *International Journal of Science and Mathematics Education, 8*(4), 689–710.

Supon, V. (2009). Cursive writing: Are its last days approaching? *Journal of Instructional Psychology, 36*(4), 357–359.

Tao, J., Ramsey, C., & Watson. (2011). Using blended learning to prepare future distance learning: A technology perspective. *International Journal of Instructional Technology & Distance Learning, 8*(1), 37–46.

Taylor, M. J. D., McCormick, D., Shawis, T., Impson, R., & Griffin, M. (2011). Activity-promoting gaming systems in exercise and rehabilitation. *Journal of Rehabilitation Research & Development, 48*(10), 1171–1186.

Taylor, R. (1980). *The computer in the school: Tutor, tool, tutee.* New York: Teachers College Press.

TESOL. (2008). *TESOL technology standards framework.* Alexandria, Virginia: Author.

Thesen, A., & Kira-Soteriou, J. (2011). Using digital storytelling to unlock student potential. *New England Reading Association Journal, 46*(2), 93–102.

Tichon, J., Hall, R., Hilgers, M., Leu, M., & Agarwal, S. (2003). Education and training in virtual environments for disaster management. In D. Lassner, & C. McNaught (Eds.), *Proceedings of World Conference on Educational Multimedia, Hypermedia and Telecommunications 2003* (pp. 1191–1194). Chesapeake, VA: AACE.

Tobias, S., & Fletcher, J. (2012). Reflections on "A review of trends in serious gaming." *Review of Educational Research, 82*(12), 233–237.

Todd, P., & Wiechmann, J. (2008). Problem solving in calculus with symbolic geometry and CAS. *Australian Senior Mathematics Journal, 22*(2), 49–56.

Tomei, L. (2013). Top 10 technologies for designing 21st century instruction. *International Journal of Information and Communication Technology Education, 9*(3), 80–93.

Tomlinson, C.A. (2013). Teachers who stare down poverty. *Educational Leadership, 70*(8), 88–89.

Tremblay, E. (2010). Educating the mobile generation-using personal cell phones as audience response systems in postsecondary science teaching. *Journal of Computers in Mathematics and Science Teaching, 29*(2), 217–227.

Trost, S. G., & Van Der Mars, H. (2009). Why we should not cut P.E. *Educational Leadership, 67*(4), 60–65.

Tsai, C., & Chiang, Y. (2013). Research trends in problem-based learning (PBL) research in e-learning and online education environments: A review of publications in SSCI-indexed journals from 2004 to 2012. *British Journal of Educational Technology, 44*(6), E185–E190.

Tuckman, B. (1965). Developmental sequence in small groups. *Psychological Bulletin, 63*(6), 384–389.

Tufte, E. (2003). Power corrupts. PowerPoint corrupts absolutely. *Wired Magazine, 11*(9). Retrieved from http://www.wired.com/wired/ archive/11.09/ ppt2.html

Ullman, E. (2013). The whole world in your hands. *Tech & Learning, 34*(2), 57,59–61.

United Health Foundation & American Public Health Association and Partnership for Prevention. (2009). *America's Health Rankings–2009 edition.* Minnetonka, MN: Author.

Urban-Woldron, H. (2009). Interactive simulations for the effective learning of physics. *Journal of Computers in Mathematics and Science Teaching, 28*(2), 163–176.

U.S. Department of Agriculture. (2013). *SuperTracker and other tools.* Retrieved from http://myplate.gov/supertracker-tools.html

U.S. Department of Education, Institute of Education Sciences. (2008, August). *Accelerated Reader: What Works Clearinghouse intervention report.* Retrieved from http://www.eric.ed.gov/PDFS/ED502922.pdf

U.S. Department of Education, Institute of Education Sciences. (2009, December). *Accelerated Reader: What Works Clearinghouse intervention report.* Retrieved from http://www.eric.ed.gov/PDFS/ED507570.pdf

U.S. Department of Education. (2010). *National education technology plan.* Washington, DC: Author. Retrieved from http://www.ed.gov/technology/netp-2010/

U.S. Department of Education. (2011–2012). *Schools and Staffing Survey (SASS) Public School Teacher Data File.* National Center for Education Statistics, Institute of Education Sciences.

U.S. Department of Education, Institute of Education Sciences. (2010, August). *Carnegie Learning Curricula and Cognitive Tutor[R] Software: What Works Clearinghouse intervention report.* Retrieved from http://www .eric.ed.gov/PDFS/ED511596.pdf

U.S. Department of Health and Human Services. (2013a). *Stopbullying.gov-Kids.* Retrieved from http://www.stopbullying.gov/what-you-can-do/teens/ index.html

U.S. Department of Health and Human Services. (2013b). *What you can do: Teens.* Retrieved from http://www.stopbullying.gov/what-you-can-do/ teens/index.html

Vacek, H., & Fuhrhop, B. (2013, September 9). Debate it: Do kids need to learn cursive? *Scholastic News, Edition 5/682.2,* 7.

Vasquez, E., & Straub, C. (2012). Online instruction for K-12 special education: A review of the empirical literature. *Journal of Special Education Technology, 27*(3), 31–40.

Veletsianos, G., & Doering, A. (2010). Long-term student experiences in a hybrid, open-ended and problem based Adventure Learning program. *Australasian Journal of Educational Technology, 26*(2), 280–296.

Vandewaetere, M., & Clarebout, G. (2011). Can instruction as such affect learning? The case of learner control. *Computers & Education, 57,* 2322–2332.

van 't Hooft, M. (2013). Taking it to the street: using QR codes to tell student-created (hi)stories on location. *Social Education, 77*(2), 99–101.

Vardi, M. (2012). Will MOOCs destroy academia? *Communications of the ACM, 55,* 11, 5.

Vargas, M. (2013). PBL and technology: A perfect match. *Distance Learning, 10*(4), 9–14.

Vigdor, J., & Ladd, H. (2010, June). *Scaling the digital divide: Home computer technology and student achievement. Working paper No. 48.* Washington, DC: The National Center for Analysis of Longitudinal Data in Education Research (CALDER), the Urban Institute. Retrieved from http://www .caldercenter.org/upload/CALDERWorkingPaper_48.pdf

Voogt, J., Fisser, P., Roblin, N., Tondeur, J., & van Braak, J. (2012). Technological pedagogical content knowledge – a review of the literature. *Journal of Computer Assisted Learning, 29,* 109–121.

Vurdien, R. (2013). Enhancing writing skills through blogging in an advanced English as a foreign language class in Spain. *Computer Assisted Language Learning, 26*(2), 126–143.

Walgren, J. (2011). Innovative use of a classroom response system during physics lab. *Physics Teacher, 49*(1), 30–32.

Walker-Dalhouse, D., & Risko, V. (2008). Learning from literacy successes in high-achieving urban schools. *The Reading Teacher, 61*(5), 422–424.

Wang, Y., Beydoun, M. A., Laiang, L., Caballero, B., & Kumanyika, S. K. (2008). Estimating the progression and cost of the U.S. obesity epidemic. *Obesity, 16*(10), 2323–2330.

Wang, F., Kenzie, M., McGuire, P., & Pan, E. (2010). Applying technology to inquiry-based learning in early childhood education. *Early Childhood Education, 37,* 381

Ware, J., & Stein, S. (2013). From "mentor" to "role model": Scaling the involvement of STEM professionals through role model videos. *Journal of Educational Multimedia and Hypermedia, 22*(2), 209–223.

Watson, T., Murin, A., Vashaw, L., Gemin, B., & Rapp, C. (2013). *Keeping pace with K-12 online and blended Learning: An annual review of policy and practice.* Retrieved from http://kpk12.com/

Webster, P. (2002). Computer-based technology and music teaching and learning. In R. Colwell & C. Richardson (Eds.), *The new handbook of research on music teaching and learning* (pp. 416–439). New York: Oxford University Press.

Weeden, S., Cooke, B., & McVey, M. (2013). Underage children and social networking. *Journal of Research on Technology in Education, 45*(3), 249–262.

Wehmeyer, M., Palmer, S., Williams-Diehm, K., Shogren, K., Davies, Daniel K., & Stock. (2011). Technology and self-determination in transition planning: The impact of technology use in transition planning on student self-determination. *Journal of Special Education Technology, 26*(1), 13–24.

Wei, K., Teo, H., Chan, H. C., & Tan, B. C. Y. (2011). Conceptualizing and testing a social cognitive model of the digital divide. *Information Systems Research, 22*(1), 170–187.

West, J.E., & Whitby, P.J. (2008). Federal policy and education of students with disabilities: Progress and the path forward. *Focus on Exceptional Children, 41*(3), 1–16.

Weston, M.E. & Bain, A. (2010). The end of techno-critique: The naked truth about 1:1 laptop initiatives and educational change. *Journal of Technology, Learning, and Assessment, 9*(6). Retrieved from http://www.jtla.org

White House Task Force on Childhood Obesity. (2010). *Solving the problem of childhood obesity within a generation: White House task force on childhood obesity report to the president.* Retrieved from http://www.letsmove.gov/ sites/letsmove.gov/files/TaskForce_on_Childhood_Obesity_May2010 _FullReport.pdf

Wieman, C., & Perkins, K. (2005). *Transforming physics education. Physics Today, 58*(11), 36–41.

Wijekumar, K., Hitchcock, J., Turner, H., Lei, P., & Peck, K. (2009). *A multisite cluster randomized trial of the effects of CompassLearning Odyssey® Math on the math achievement of selected grade 4 students in the Mid-Atlantic region.* Report of the U. S. Department of Education, Institute of Education Sciences (No. NCEE 2009–4068).

Williamson, P., McLeskey, J., Hoppey, D., & Rentz, T. (2006). Educating students with mental retardation in general education classrooms. *Exceptional Children, 72*(3), 347–361.

Wilson, C., Trautmann, N., MaKinster, J., & Barker, B. (2010). A world of data at your fingertips: Exploring biodiversity with online visualization and analysis tools. *Science Teacher, 77*(7), 34–39.

Wilson, G., Michaels, C., & Margolis, H. (2005). Form versus function: Using technology to develop individualized education programs for students with disabilities. *Journal of Special Education Technology, 20*(2), 37–46.

Wilson, K. (2013). Incorporating video modeling into a school-based intervention for students with autism spectrum disorders. *Language, Speech, and Hearing Services in Schools, 44,* 105–117.

Wilson, L., & Wilson, A. (2013). Seed storage proteins as a system for teaching protein identification by mass spectrometry in biochemistry laboratory. *Biochemistry and Molecular Biology Education, 41*(2), 79–86.

Winzer, M. A. (2009). *From integration to inclusion: A history of special education in the 20th century.* Washington, DC: Gallaudet University Press.

Wirth, A. (2013). Getting real-world ready. *Leadership for Student Activities, NASC Edition, 41*(8), 12–14.

Witherspoon, L. (2012). Active gaming. In Steve Saunders & L. Witherspoon (Eds.), *Contemporary uses of technology in K-12 physical education.* Charlotte, NC: Information Age.

Wohlwend, K. (2010). A Is for avatar: Young children in literacy 2.0 worlds and literacy 1.0 schools. *Language Arts, 88*(2), 144–152.

Wong, T. (2013). Meeting needs: Are you connected? *School Library Monthly, 29*(8), 33–34.

Wu, Y. (2007). Impact of a spreadsheet exploration on secondary school students' understanding of statistical graphs. *Journal of Computers in Mathematics and Science Teaching, 26*(4), 355–385.

Xu, D., & Jaggers, S. (2013, February). *Adaptability to online learning: Differences across types of students and academic subject areas. Community College Research Center.* (CCRC) Working Paper No. 54. Teachers College, Columbia University. Retrieved from http://ccrc.tc.columbia.edu/publications/adaptability-to-online-learning.html

Yenner, B. (2011). Top 10 ways to use interactive whiteboards in elementary classrooms. *TeacherNet Gazette, 8*(2). Retrieved from http://gazette.teachers.net/gazette/wordpress/barbara-yenner/interactive-smart-board-in-the-elementary-classroom/

Young, J. (2008, June 6). Journals find many images in research are faked. *The Chronicle of Higher Education.* Retrieved from http://chronicle.com

Young, M., Slota, S., Cutter, A., Jalette, G., Mullin, G., Lai, B., Simeoni, Z., Tran, M., & Yukhymento, M. (2012). Our princess is in another castle: A review of trends in serious gaming. *Review of Educational Research, 82*(1), 61–89.

Youngman, O. (2013, December 9). To measure a MOOC's value, just ask students. *The Chronicle of Higher Education.* Retrieved from http://chronicle.com

Gargiulo, R. M., 403
Garza-Kling, G., 166, 314
Gasperetti, B., 388
Gauci, S., 154
Gay, L. R., 151
Gelbart, H., 88
Gemin, B., 27, 245
Gerin, W., 154
Ghassib, H. B., 365
Gibson, W., 251
Gillin, D., 346
Gillin, P., 346
Gillow-Wiles, H., 316–317
Glass, G. V., 22, 208, 228
Glaser, R. 40
Glenberg, A., 271
Goertler, S., 299
Goldberg, A., 271
Goldsworthy, R., 393
Goodman, B., 14
Goodwin, B., 213
Gordon, A. M., 388
Gordon, M., 129
Gortmaker, S. L., 383
Gourlay, L., 208
Grable, L., 165
Graf, A., 314
Graham, L., 80
Graham, S., 115, 135
Gran, M., 157
Grandgenett, N., 20, 326
Green, B., 410
Greene, J., 103
Gresalfi, M., 275–276
Griffin, M., 388
Grisham, D., 272
Gross E., 14
Grummer-Strawn, L., 382
Gubacs-Collins, K., 388–389
Gueutal, H., 210
Gulek, J. C., 22
Gulosino, C., 248, 250
Gunn, K., 370
Guo, Y., 92

Hall, L. R., 268
Hall, R., 90
Halvorsen, A., 339
Hamdan, N., 213
Hammersley, B., 215
Hammett, R., 190
Haney, J., 321
Hannafin, R., 88
Hansen, L., 383, 386, 387
Hardin, A., 84
Harris, C., 319
Harris, J., 20, 359
Hatch, T., 44–46, 47
Hatziharistos, D., 390
Haury, D., 320–321
Hawisher, G., 115
Hayes, S., 192
Helms, A., 95
Hennessy, S., 158
Henry, L. A., 261
Henson, K., 132
Herold, B., 8, 94, 95, 156, 415
Hersey, J. C., 382, 384
Heumann, J., 404
Hicks, L., 388
Higgins, J., 388
Higgins, K., 404
Hildebrand, A., 360
Hilgers, M., 90
Hill, C., 98
Hilton, C., 388
Hirsch, E. D., 40
Hirumi, A., 94
Hitchcock, A., 197
Hitchcock, J., 102
Hofer, M., 20, 359

Hoffman, B., 286
Hoffman, J., 313
Holden, J., 206
Hong, J., 93
Hoppey, D., 404
Horejsi, M., 88, 165
Horn, M., 212
Horvitz, B., 248, 250
Hossain, M., 186
Hu, L., 35
Hubbard, B., 248
Hubbard, P., 299
Huerta, L., 249
Hughes, J. E., 19
Hughes, M., 272
Hung, M. L., 210
Hutchings, C., 347
Hutchins, R. J., 265
Hutchison, A., 268
Hutchison, L., 217
Hwang, M., 93

Iannou, A., 88, 89
Im, T., 254
Impson, R., 388
Inman, D., 254
Irwin, J., 388

Jaakkol, T., 88
Jackson, L., 275
Jackson, N., 236
Jacobson, S., 265
Jacoby, M., 361
Jaggers, S., 207
Jamieson, J., 287
Jantaburom, P., 190
Jewett, P., 24
Jobs, S., 187
Johns, B., 411
Johnson, K. A., 266
Johnson, L., 25
Johnson, R. D., 210
Jones, K., 235
Jones, L., 66
Jones, P., 210
Jonker, T., 265
Jordan, A., 382, 384
Jordan, L., 128
Juniu, S., 388–389
Juvonen J., 14

Kanarkard, W., 190
Karchmer-Klein, R., 35
Kauchak, D., 37, 44, 46, 47
Ke, F., 254
Kebritchi, M., 94
Kemm, R., 154
Kennewell, S., 209
Kenzie, M., 252
Kerski, J., 166
Kim, B., 316
Kim, P., 87
Kimmins, L., 86
King-Sears, M. E., 410
Kinzer, C. K., 261
Kira-Soteriou, J., 132, 278, 279
Kirschner, P. A., 81
Kleiman, G., 251
Klemm, W., 129
Ko, S., 210, 239
Koedinger, K., 98
Koehler, M., 19–20, 164
Koehler, S., 388
Koenig, A., 35, 40
Koppel, N., 209–210
Koutsouba, M., 390
Kozma, R., 22
Krall, R. M., 121
Kumanyika, S. K., 382
Kurzweil, R., 27, 410

Lach, C., 157
Ladd, H., 16

LaFee, S., 213, 228
Laiang, L., 382
Lalley, J., 88
Landers, E., 404
Lane, P., 210
Lanier, J., 14
Lanius, R., 339
Larson, L., 272
Larson-Guenette, J., 290
Lasseter, A., 211
Lawler, P., 383
Lawrence, R., 185
Lee, C., 93, 313
Lee, Y., 92, 208
Legg, A. M., 184
Lehman, J., 185
Lei, P., 102
Lerner, J. W., 411
Leu, D. J., 207, 261, 263, 272
Leu, M., 90
Levy, A., 16
Lewis, D., 414
Lewis, L., 208, 250
Li, Q., 252, 313
Lieberman, L., 388
Lim, J., 389
Lin, C., 253
Lincoln, A., 92
Link, D., 117
Lipscomb, S., 361
Little, E., 157
Liu, F., 207
Livingstone, S., 66
Loge, K., 254
London, J., 272, 277
Looney, M., 152
Lorenzi, N., 218
Luehrmann, A., 6–7
Luik, P., 80
Lynch, J., 54
Lynch, S., 54

Ma, T., 365
Ma, X., 252, 313
MacArthur, C., 160
Macaulay, D., 265
Macfadyen, L., 238
MacNamara, A., 35, 40
Madden, M., 187, 190
Maenner, M. J., 407
Mager, R., 40
Mainzer, L., 410
Makice, K., 27, 212
MaKinster, J., 150
Manca, S., 190
Manfra, M., 186, 340
Margolis, H., 148
Marino, M., 315
Marovich, B., 235
Marszalek, J., 156
Martin, M., 252
Mason, K., 383
Mawer, M., 208
Mayer, R. E., 35, 40
Mayes, R., 97
McBrien, J. L., 210
McCord, T., 387
McCormick, D., 388
McCown, M., 88
McDaniel, M., 200
McDermott, J., 121
McDevitt, R., 265
McDevitt, T., 47
McFadden, C., 210
McGuire, P., 252
McKenzie, N., 266
McKnight, K., 213
McKnight, P., 213
McLaren, B., 98
McLaughlin, J., 214
McLeskey, J., 404

McPherson, J., 412
McVee, M., 132
McVey, M., 190
Means, B., 212, 235, 250
Mears, D., 382, 383, 384, 386, 387, 391, 394
Merrill, D., 40
Michaels, C., 148
Michel, J., 278
Miller, K., 213
Miller, M., 154
Millett, P., 414
Millstone, J., 95
Milman, N., 27, 212
Milson, J., 166
Miltenberger, R., 388
Mineer, S., 26
Miranda, T., 266
Miron, G., 208, 248, 249, 250, 251
Mishra, P., 19–20, 164
Mitchell, K., 66
Mitchell, N., 248
Mogey, N., 116
Mohnsen, B., 380, 386
Mokros, J., 150
Molnar, M., 77
Monge, R., 265
Moore, M.G, 239
Morelli, T., 388
Moreno, N., 320
Morphy, P., 115
Moss, K., 154
Moulton, K., 35, 40
Mouza, C., 35
Muller, K., 314
Murin, A., 27, 245
Murnane, R., 188
Murphy, R., 235
Murray, B., 290
Myers, A., 281

Naisbitt, J., 10
Nandakumar, R., 35
Nazzaro, D., 157
Neel, R., 154
Nelson, D., 414
Nichols, A., 186
Nichols, R., 387
Nickel, J., 160
Nicolaoub, C., 88
Niess, M. L., 313, 316–317
Noar, S., 393
Noble, J., 154
Nugent, G., 326
Nurmi, S., 88
Nussbaum-Beach, S., 268
Nye, S., 389

Obaiduzzaman, K., 391
Obama, M., 382
Obara, S., 314
O'Dowd, R., 288, 294
O'Dwyer, L., 22
Offner, S., 84
Ogle, L., 216
O'Hara, S., 132
Okita, S. Y., 388
Okolo, C., 410
Oldham, T., 154
Oliveira, F., 27
Oliver, K., 251
Olson, C. A., 365
Ormrod, J., 44, 45, 46, 47
Orthober, C., 185
Osborne, J., 251
Osborne, L., 414
O'shaughnessy, D., 121
Oskrochi. G. R., 88
Own, Z. Y., 210
Owston, R., 319
Ozden, S., 35

Palmer, S., 410
Pan, E, 252
Pan, W., 94
Pannell, F., 217
Papert, S., 7, 43–44, 75
Papp, R., 128
Paris, R., 265
Park, J.-H., 208
Parris, C., 296
Pashler, H., 200
Passe, J., 338
Patel, R., 251
Paterson, J., 116
Patterson, B., 210
Pavlovski, N., 86
Pearman, C., 164
Peck, K., 102
Pedersen, S., 98
Pegg, J., 80
Pellett, H., 389
Pellett, T., 389
Peppler, K., 355
Perez-Hernandez, D., 296
Periathiruvadi, S., 415, 416
Perin, D., 115
Perkins, K., 89
Perry, L., 159
Peterson, M., 254
Peterson, R., 222
Pettyjohn, P., 275–276
Phelps, S., 317
Phillip, G., 206, 214
Piaget, J., 43, 44, 45
Picking, D., 315
Pierce, D., 24
Pierce, L., 393
Pinkstone, R., 218
Pinzás, J., 296
Piotrowski, P., 88
Ploog, B., 414
Poe, E. A., 277, 278
Pohl, J., 391
Pohlman, R., 84
Polhamus, B., 382
Polifko, M., 389
Polly, D., 321
Popelka, S., 154
Post, A., 179
Pritchard, R., 132
Proctor, C., 289
Puentedura, R., 68, 69
Purcell, K., 265
Purcell, M., 116
Purcell, N., 414
Purpura, D., 35–36

Queen, B., 208, 250
Quek, F., 27
Quillen, I., 293, 324, 325

Ramsey, C., 208
Ranierit, M., 190
Rapp, C., 27, 245
Ratcliff, C., 75
Raths, D., 214
Ravenna, G., 209
Ray, D., 121
Redd, L., 404
Rees, J., 236
Reich, J., 188
Reid, E., 35–36
Reigeluth, C., 40
Reilly, E., 216, 394
Reinking, D., 268
Renkl, A., 98
Rentz, T., 404
Rheingold, H., 265
Rice, J., 95, 249
Richardson, W., 185
Rideout, V., 266
Rillero, P., 320–321

Rinn, A., 415, 416
Risinger, C. F., 370
Risko, V., 157
Ritzhaupt, A., 207
Roberts, D. F., 266
Robinson, C., 209, 210
Robinson, T. N., 383
Roblin, N., 19–20
Roblyer, M. D., 40, 179, 212, 234, 235, 238, 239, 244, 245, 246–247
Rodchua, S., 238
Rodriguez, C., 357
Rogers, E., 56
Rohrer, D., 200
Rojas, A., 39, 79
Rooks, D., 319
Rosen, D., 313
Rosen, L. D., 382, 383, 384
Rosenberg, M., 404
Rossen, S., 210, 239
Rudd, D. P., 215
Rudd, D. P, II, 215
Russell, D., 115–116
Ruthven, K., 158

Saettler, P., 3–4, 28, 40
Sagstetter, V., 267
Salden, R., 98
Salisbury, D., 80
Salmerón, L., 265
Sams, A., 27, 212, 214
Samsonov, P., 98
Sarama, J., 313
Savin-Baden, M., 208
Savoy, J., 289
Scharf, A., 414
Scheuermann, A., 321
Schmidt, D., 387
Schoppek, W., 80
Schrock, K., 132, 199, 245
Schugar, H., 263, 272
Schugar, J., 263, 272
Schul, J., 54
Schunk, D., 38, 43, 46
Schwartz, N., 393
Schwebach, J., 132
Scieszka, J., 259–260
Scriven, M., 40
Seaman, J., 208
Sebba, J., 209, 210
Senning, D., 179
Seo, Y., 97, 410
Serafini, F., 263
Sfard, A., 35
Shafer, K., 317
Shafer, S., 249
Shaffer, D., 154
Shaffer, M., 154
Shaffer, S., 238
Shanahan, L., 132
Sharp, J., 165
Shawis, T., 388
Shayne, R., 388
Shea, V., 179
Shear, L., 211
Sheer, V. C., 184
Shiffrin, R., 37, 38
Shogren, K., 410
Shulman, L. S., 19–20
Shumack, K., 216, 394
Sileo, J.M., 402
Silverstein, S., 139
Simonson, M., 206
Skinner, B. F., 37
Slater, T., 158
Slezak. A., 387
Smaldino, S., 206
Smith, B., 382
Smith, B. E., 265
Smith, C., 263
Smith, G. D., 358

Smith, K. H., 362
Smith, P. K., 66
Smith, R., 150
Smith, S., 393
Smith, S. J., 410
Smith, Z., 414
Snape, P., 35
Snodden, K., 414
Snow, C., 289
Snyder, I., 115
Soomou, M., 275–276
Sory, T., 316
Southcott, J., 363
Southworth, M., 150
Sparks, S., 311
Spielberg, S., 197
Spinello, E. F., 221
Spooner, F., 404
Stagg, A., 86
Staker, H., 212
Stansberry, M., 187, 220, 243, 244
Starr, B., 222
Steding, S., 167
Steenbergen-Hu, S., 85
Steils, N., 208
Stein, S., 217
Steinbach, L., 370
Stetter, M., 272
Stock, S., 410
Stoddard, J., 220
Stowell, J., 154
Straub, C., 195
Strayer, J., 321
Stripling, B., 24
Subrahmaniyan, N., 253
Sun, K., 253
Sundar, S., 185, 200
Supon, V., 116
Suppes, P., 7
Sureda-Negre, J., 28
Swanson, C., 410
Sweller, J., 81
Swiss, T., 24

Tan, B. C. Y., 207
Tao, J., 208
Taylor, M. J. D., 388
Taylor, R., 34
Taylor, S., 358
Teo, H., 207
Thesen, A., 278, 279
Thomas, J., 80
Thormann, J., 410
Tichon, J., 90
Tierney, J., 135
Tobias, S., 92
Tombs, C., 208
Tombs, G., 208
Tomei, L., 154
Tomlinson, C. A., 404
Tondeur, J., 19–20
Toyama, Y., 211, 235
Trautmann, N., 150
Tremblay, E., 325
Trollip, S., 83, 87, 88
Trost, S. G., 382
Tsai, C., 220
Tsurusaki, B., 315
Tuckman, B., 244
Tufte, E., 128, 129
Tulis, M., 80
Turner, H., 102
Tyrovola, V., 390

Ullman, E., 115
Urban-Woldron, H., 88
Urschel, J., 208, 250, 251

Vacek, H., 116
van Braak, J., 19–20
Van Der Mars, H., 382
Vandewaetere, M., 210

van Garderen, D., 402
Van Lue, E., 324
van 't Hooft, M., 346
van Zee, E., 316–317
Vargas, M., 54
Vashaw, L., 27, 245
Vasquez, E., 195
Veletsianos, G., 344
Vicars, B., 414
Vigdor, J., 16
Volk, C., 275–276
Voogt, J., 19–20
Vurdien, R., 186
Vygotsky, L. S., 43, 44

Wager, W., 39, 79
Wainess, R., 35, 40
Waldron, N., 404
Walgren, J., 154
Walker-Dalhouse, D., 157
Wang, F., 252
Wang, S., 253
Wang, Y., 382
Ward, R., 159
Ware, J., 217
Watson, M., 208
Watson, T., 27, 245, 248, 249
Webster, P., 358
Weeden, S., 190
Wehmeyer, M., 410
Wei, K., 207
Welner, K., 208, 228
Wen, H., 210
West, J. E., 404
Westfall, P., 206
Westling, D., 404
Whitby, P. J., 404
Wickersham, L., 210–211
Wieman, C., 89, 214
Wien, M., 381
Wiencke, W. R., 239, 245, 246–247
Wiest, L., 186
Wijekumar, K., 102
Wilkie, T., 88
Willard, T., 316
Willett, J., 188
Williams, D., 154
Williams, O., 154
Williams, P., 404
Williams-Diehm, K., 410
Williamson, P., 404
Williams-Rossi, D., 266
Wilson, A., 84
Wilson, C., 150
Wilson, G., 148
Wilson, J. H., 184
Wilson, K., 216
Wilson, L., 84
Wilson, W.S., 311
Winzer, M. A., 404
Wirth, A., 54
Witherspoon, L., 386
Wohlwend, K., 268
Wong, T., 268
Woods, D., 267
Woolsey, R., 238
Woo, H., 410
Worth, K., 320–321
Wu, Y., 122

Xu, D., 207

Yackel, E., 311
Yarden, A., 88
Yates, K., 35, 40
Yiadom-Boakye, G., 238
Young, M., 92, 93, 94
Youngman, O., 235

Zhou, Y., 416
Zhu, X., 271
Zubiaga, I. S., 220
Zvacek, S., 206

Computer-assisted testing, 156
Computer-based instruction (CBI), 76, 77
Computer-based learning (CBL), 76, 77
Computer Curriculum Corporation (CCC), 7
Computer literacy movement, 7
Computer-managed instruction (CMI), 7, 153
Computer platforms, 112
Computers. *See also* Hardware
  in classrooms, arrangement of, 11–12
  laboratories of networked, 11
Computer systems, educational technology as, 4, 5
Computer viruses, 175, 176
Concept mapping, 160, 273
Concrete operational stage, 45
Cone of Experience, Dale's, 206
Consortium programs, 248
Constructivist instruction, 34–36, 311
Constructivist integration models, 41–54
  child development theory, 43, 44, 45
  discovery learning, 44, 46
  inquiry-based approach, 46, 48
  integrating with directed models, 48–54
  multiple intelligences theory, 44, 45, 46, 47
  scaffolding theories, 43, 44
  social activism theory, 42
  social cognitive theory, 42, 43
Content-area problem-solving skills, 97
Content-area tools, 141, 142, 163–67
  animation software systems, 163, 164
  calculator-based-labs, 166
  calculators, 165
  computer-assisted design, 163, 164
  foreign language dictionaries, 166
  Geographic Information System, 166
  Global Positioning System, 166
  graphing calculators, 165, 166
  language translators, 166–67
  microcomputer-based lab, 165
  MIDI tools, 164
  music editor, 164
  music sequencers, 164
  overview of, 141, 142, 163
  reading tools, 164–65
  software sites, 143
  3-D modeling, 164
Content-free problem-solving skills, 97
Content management system (CMS), 188, 226, 236
Contingencies of reinforcement, 37
Copyright laws, 17
Council of Chief State School Officers (CCSSO), 17
Course outcomes, resources to monitor, 237, 238
Course support tools, 237
Courseware, 76
Creativity in web development, 192
Crowdfunding sites, 189

Crowdsourcing, 6, 186, 188-189
Cultural issues in educational technology, 15–16
Curation tools, 262, 274
Curriculum support, in technology integration, 65
Cursive writing controversy, 269
Cyberbullying, 14, 175, 177
Cybercheating, 17, 176–77
Cyberporn, 16
Cyberschools, 245. *See also* Virtual schools

Dance, supporting students' work in, 390–91
Data analysis, 221
Database software, 109, 110, 149, 150–51
  current database integration strategies, 151
  shift in database uses and instruction, 150–51
Data collection and analysis tools, 149–54
  database software, 149, 150–51
  online survey tools, 151–53
  overview of, 141, 142, 150
  software sites, 143
  statistical software packages, 151
  student information systems, 153
  student response systems, 153–54
Data dashboard, 237, 238
Data mining, 151
Deaf, 414
Desktop publishing, 144–46
  classroom applications, example of, 144–45
  effective, criteria for, 145–46
  *vs.* word processing, 144
Digital atlases, 162
Digital citizenship, 15, 24, 177
Digital dictionaries (word atlases), 163
Digital divide, 15, 16, 207–8, 251
Digital footprint, 176, 177
Digital Library for Earth System Education (DLESE), 324
Digital literacy, 15, 24, 191
Digital media, creating from imported files, 215
Digital portfolios, 20
Digital publishing, 278
Digital storybooks, 164
Digital storytelling, 278, 344–45
Digital technologies in education
  timeline of, 6 (*See also* History of educational technology)
  tools in, 10–12 (*See also* Hardware; Software)
Digitized images, 367, 368–69
Diigo, 262
Directed instruction, 34–35, 311
Directed integration models, 36–41, 48–54
  behaviorist theories, 37
  cognitive-behaviorist theory, 38, 39
  information-processing theories, 37, 38
  instructional design models, 39–40
  integrating with constructivist models, 48–54
  objectivist theory foundations for, 40, 41

Disabilities, students with. *See* Students with disabilities/ special needs
Disabilities Education Act (IDEA), 404
Disability, 403
Discovery learning, 44, 46
Disequilibrium, 45
Display technologies, 10–11
Distance education, 27, 206–27. *See also* Blended environments
  classification system for, 207
  cost-effectiveness of, 211
  developmental issues, 208
  digital divide, 207–8
  education reform and, 208
  face-to-face courses compared with, 208, 209
  issues in, 207–8
  models, 206–7
  overview of, 206–11
  research, 208–11
  self-paced, 53
  successful distance instructors, 210–11
  successful distance learners, 210
  success of, characteristics that affect, 209, 210
  virtual schools, 8, 15
Distance instructors, successful, 210–11
Distance learners, successful, 210
Distributed knowledge network, 261
Domain designator, 180
Domain name, 199
Downloaded, defined, 195
Downloading music illegally, 357
Draw/paint programs, 157
Drill-and-practice software, 34, 53, 78, 77–83
  benefits of, 80–81
  brief overview of, 82
  limitations and problems related to, 81
  selecting, 80
  types of, 79–80
  using, strategies and guidelines for, 82, 83

E-books/e-texts, 8, 25
Editing tools, 276–77
Educational applications, emerging trends in, 26–27
Educational technology
  "big picture" on, 3
  as communications media, 4
  as computer systems, 4, 5
  digital technology tools, 10
  educational applications, 26–27
  educational issues in, 15
  emerging trends in, 25–27
  framework for viewing, 5
  hardware, software, and system development, 25–26
  history of (*See* History of educational technology)
  as instructional design, 4
  as instructional systems, 4
  instructional technology as subset of, 5
  integrating, 5
  issues (*See* Educational technology issues)
  organizations with perspectives on, 4

perspectives that define, 3–5
  for problem-solving, 22–24
  processes in, 5
  for research, 22
  resources in, 10–12
  skills (*See* Educational technology skills)
  software applications in schools, 12
  technology facilities, 10–12
  today's uses for, 21–24
  tools in, 5
  as vocational training, 4–5
Educational technology issues, 12–17
  cultural and equity, 15–16
  educational, 15
  legal and ethical, 16–17
  social, 12, 13–15
Educational technology skills, 17–21
  Common Core State Standards, 17
  information and communication technology (ICT) framework, 18–19
  National Educational Technology Standards, 18
  Partnership for 21st Century Skills, 18, 34
  Tech-PACK framework, 19–21
Education management organizations (EMOs), 248
Education reform, distance education and, 208
Electronic gradebooks, 155
Electronic mentoring, 219
Electronic outlining, 274
Electronic pen pals or "key pals," 219
Electronic portfolios, 20, 21
Electronic publishing, 220
Electronic slide shows, 129
Electronic storybooks, 164
Elementary and Secondary Education Act (ESEA), 407
Email, 184
Email attachments with viruses, 175
Enactive learning, 43
Enactive stage, 46
English and language arts, 261–81
  Common Core State Standards for, 263, 264
  cursive writing controversy, 269
  diverse learners, challenges of working with, 266
  instructional strategies to address new needs, 263–66
  issues and challenges in, 261–69
  motivating students to read and write, challenges of, 266–67
  QWERTY keyboarding, 268, 269
  technology integration strategies for, 269–79
English and language arts teachers, 279–81
  changing responsibilities for new literacies, 261–63
  growth as literacy professionals and leaders, 267–68
  integration strategies, 281
  issues and challenges, 281
  rubric to measure teacher growth, 279–81
  teaching to integrate technology effectively, 279–81

English as a second language (ESL), 287. *See also* Foreign and second language learning
English language learners (ELLs), 287–89. *See also* Foreign and second language learning
Epistemologies, 35
Equity issues in educational technology, 15–16, 66
Essential conditions, 33–34
Ethical issues. *See* Legal and ethical issues
Evaluation checklist for a Technology Integrated Lesson, 227
Events of Instruction, 39
Exergaming, 387–88
Extensive feedback activities, 80
External storage, 11

Face-to-face (FTF) courses, 208, 209
Facilities, setting up and maintaining, 66
Fair use, 17
Favorites, 181
Favorites file, 181
Field, 150
Field-test, 199
File-exchange compatibility, 112
Files, 112
File Transfer Protocol (FTP), 194
Filtering software, 174
Financial assistance, 66
Firewalls, 16
Firewall software, 174, 182
Fitness plans and portfolios, 387
Flash, Adobe, 193, 194
Flash card activity, 79
Flipped classroom models, 27, 86, 189, 212–14
   to address social interaction, 266
   background and research on, 213–14
   defined, 212
   implementation tips, 214
Flipped Learning Network (FLN), 213, 214
FM amplification systems, 414
Fonts, 145, 158, 159
Foreign and second language learning, 287–302
   issues in, 287–91
   technology integration strategies for, 291–99
Foreign and second language learning teachers, 300–302
   issues and applications, learning, 300
   rubric to measure teacher growth, 300, 301–2
Foreign language dictionaries, 166
Foreign language (FL) learning, 287, 290–91. *See also* Foreign and second language learning
Formal operations stage, 45
Forms makers, 148, 149
Formulas, 121
Frames, 197
Fraud, 176
Full immersion systems, 252
Funding, 15, 66, 67, 249, 365

Games, 26, 293
Gamification, 26
Gender equity, 16

Geocaching, 346
Geographic Information System (GIS), 166, 346, 348
Geospatial technologies, 345–47
Gesture-recognition systems, 26
GIF, 195
Gifted students, 415–16
Global Learning and Observations to Benefit the Environment (GLOBE) Program, 323
Global Positioning System (GPS), 142–143, 163, 165–166, 346–347
Google Drive, 10
Google Glass, 13, 25–26
GPS technologies, 12
Grading tools. *See* Testing and grading tools
Graphic design, 192, 369–70
Graphic document makers, 148
Graphics tools, 156–60
   animations, 158, 159
   charting/graphing tools, 158
   clip art, 158, 159
   draw/paint programs, 157
   font collections, 158, 159
   image editing tools, 157
   overview of, 141, 142, 157
   photos, 158, 159
   software sites, 143
   sounds, 158, 159
   video, 158, 159
   word cloud generators, 159–60
Graphing calculators, 165, 166, 314
Graphing tools, 158
Group cooperation skills, 54
Group product development, 220

Hackers/hacking, 14–16, 175–176
Handheld technologies, 10
Handheld translation devices, 294
Handicap, 403
Hands-on/minds-on science, 321
Hands-on opportunities, 68
Handwriting, word processing and, 116
Haptic interfaces, 252
Hardware, 10–12
   display technologies, 10–11
   emerging trends in, 25–26
   external storage, 11
   handheld technologies, 10
   imaging technologies, 11
   microcomputers, 10
   peripherals, 11, 58
   in technology integration, 66
Hash tag, 187
Head-mounted display (HMD), 252
Health behaviors, influencing, 393
Health education. *See* Physical and health education instruction
Health-related concerns in educational technology, 14
History, for navigating the Internet, 181
History of educational technology, 6–10
   Internet era, 8
   lessons learned from the past, 9–10
   microcomputer era, 6, 7–8
   mobile technologies, social media, and open access era, 6, 8
   pre-microcomputer era, 6, 7
Hot links/hot spots, 129–130, 180

Hot topic debate
   "best practices" in technology integration, 35
   calculators and memorizing math facts, 311
   cyberbullying, social networking and, 175
   electronic music ensemble *vs.* traditional one, 356
   exergaming in physical education programs, 388
   interactive whiteboards, 147
   learning online *vs.* face-to-face, 210
   multitasking with social networking as distraction, 14
   online learning and students with disabilities, 406
   online translators for learning foreign language, 290
   PowerPoint, 129
   video games in school, 95
   virtual schools and digital divide, 251
   Wikipedia in social studies research, 342
   word processing replacing cursive writing, 269
Human performance technology, 4
Hypermedia resources for web page and website development, 192–95
Hypertext, 174
HTML, 112, 146, 186, 191–194
   HTML editors, 191
HTML, 5, 192

IBM 1500, 6–7
Iconic stage, 46
ICT framework. *See* Educational technology skills
IEP teams, 405
Illegal downloads/software piracy, 17
Image editing programs, 157
Image formats, 195
Images, downloading, 195
Imaging technologies, 11
Impairment, 403
Incentives, 66
Inclusion, 404
Inclusive technologies, 405
Individual Education Program (IEP), 405
Individualized educational program (IEP) generators, 147, 148
Inert knowledge, 46
Information and communication technologies (ICTs), 18–19, 267–68
Information literacy, 24, 51–52, 177, 223, 262
Information-processing theories, 37, 38
Information visualization strategies, 343
Inquiry-based learning, 34–35, 46, 47, 48
Instant messaging (IM), 184–85
Instructional design. *See also* Systematic instructional design
   educational technology as, 4
   models, 39–40
Instructional environment, 62
Instructional game software, 78, 92–96

benefits of, 94
brief overview of, 94
limitations and problems related to, 94, 95
selecting, 93–94
using, strategies and guidelines for, 95–96
Instructional models, 27
Instructional software, 12, 72–102
   adapting for special needs, 77
   drill-and-practice, 34, 53, 79–83
   instructional game, 92–96
   overview of, 77–79
   personalized learning systems, 101–2
   problem-solving, 97–100
   programming languages as, 75–76
   simulation, 87–92
   sites, 76
   sources, 77
   terms, 76, 77
   tutorial, 34, 83–87
Instructional systems, educational technology as, 4
Instructional technology, 5
Integrated Learning System (ILS), 7, 101. *See also* Personalized learning systems (PLSs)
Integrating educational technology, 5
Integration framework, design of, 58–62
Intelligent tutoring systems, 84
Interaction in course spaces, types of
   learner-content interaction, 239
   learner-instructor interaction, 239–40
   learner-learner interaction, 240
Interactive asynchronous online model, 234–35
Interactive online model with synchronous events, 235
Interactive or dynamic geometry software, 314
Interactive storybooks, 131, 164, 293
Interactive whiteboard, 146
Interactive whiteboard activity software, 146–47
Interdisciplinary thinking, 75
International Reading Association (IRA), 262, 263, 281
International Society for Performance Improvement (ISPI), 4
International Society for Technology in Education (ISTE), 4, 18, 33, 64
International Technology and Engineering Educators Association (ITEEA), 4
International Technology Education Association (ITEA), 326
Internet
   apps in education, 191
   digital citizenship concepts, 177
   era, 6, 8
   ethical and legal issues, 176–77
   history of, 173–74
   inappropriate materials, sites with, 174
   legal and ethical issues, 176–77
   navigation options, 179–82
   netiquette concepts, 178–79

Internet (*continued*)
online communications, 184–85
Rules for Online Learning
Etiquette, 179
safety and security issues, 174–76
searching options, 182–84
social networking, 185–90
trouble shooting, 181–82
Internet Corporation for Assigned
Names and Numbers
(ICANN), 180
Interpersonal intelligence, 47
Intrapersonal intelligence, 47
Inverted classroom, 212
Iterative simulations, 87

Java, 193
Java applets, 193
Javascript, 193
Joystick, 413
JPEG, 195
Just-in-time training, 68

Keyboarding skills, 116. *See also*
QWERTY keyboarding
Keyword searches, 183, 265
Knowledge transfer, 54
Kurzweil reader-*firefly*, 410

Laboratories of networked
computers, 11
Language arts, cloud generators
and, 159
Language labs, 293
Language subskills, practice in,
296–97
Laptop, 22
Learning, approaches to
constructivist strategies, 34–36
directed instruction, 34–35
inquiry-based, 34–35, 46, 47
objectivist strategies, 35–36, 40,
41
origin of, 34–36
Learning analytics, 26
Learning at a distance. *See* Distance
education
Learning commons, 266
Learning environments, 27
Learning hierarchy, 39
Learning Management System
(LMS), 226
Learning needs, analysis of, 55–58
Learning objects, 212
Learning theory foundations, 33
Legal and ethical issues
in educational technology, 16–17
online, 176–77
piracy, 177
plagiarism, 176–77
Lesson planning software, 160, 161
Likert scale, 61
Linear tutorial, 83
Linguistic intelligence, 47
Links, navigation, 180, 197
Listservs, 184
Literacy development. *See* Reading
comprehension and literacy
development
Literature learning, 277–78
background information on
authors, accessing, 277
online copies of published works,
accessing, 277
support for literary analysis,
accessing, 277–78

Logical-mathematical intelligence,
47
Logic bombs, 14
Logo, 75
Logo movement, 7–8
Long-term memory (LTM), 38
Lurkers, 238

Machine translation, 166–67, 289
Mainframe, 7
Malware, 14
Mapping tools, 162
Massive Open Online Courses
(MOOCs), 8, 25, 235–36
Mastery learning, 40
Materials generators, 143–49
desktop publishing software,
144–46
graphic document makers, 148
individualized educational
program generators, 147, 148
interactive whiteboard activity
software, 146–47
overview of, 141, 142
PDF and forms makers, 148, 149
puzzle generators, 147
software sites, 143
Web design software, 146
worksheet generators, 147
Mathematics instruction, 308–18
accountability for standards in,
308–10
Common Core State Standards
for, 308–10
directed *vs.* social-constructivist
teaching strategies, 311
issues and challenges in, 308–11
problem solving, 97, 98
spreadsheets and, 121, 124
for students with mild cognitive
disabilities, 412
teaching teachers to integrate
technology, 327–29
technology integration strategies
for, 311–18
word cloud generators and, 160
Mathematics teachers
issues and applications, learning,
327
rubric to measure teacher
growth, 327, 328–29
teaching to integrate technology,
327–29
Media with screen-capture
software, creating, 215
MENC, 357
Mentoring, 68
Meta-analysis, 22
Metacognition, 53
Metacrawlers, 183
Meta-level reflection, 76
Metaphors, 35
Microblogs, 187–88, 262
Microcomputer-based lab (MBL),
165
Microcomputer era, 6, 7–8
Microcomputers, 10
Minicomputer, 7
Misuses of technology, 14
Mobile access, 8
Mobile apps, 111, 112
Mobile computing, 26
Mobile devices, 141
Mobile technologies, 6, 8, 10, 25
Modeling, 68
Models for online courses, 234–36

interactive asynchronous online
model, 234–35
interactive online model with
synchronous events, 235
Massive Open Online Course
model, 235–36
noninteractive online model, 234
selecting, 238
Models of technology integration,
36–64
constructivist, 41–54
directed, 36–41
as essential condition for
technology integration, 68–69
merging directed with
constructivist model, future
directions for, 48–50
SAMR, 68, 69
strategies based on constructivist
models, 53–54
strategies based on directed
models, 52–53
strategies useful for either model,
50–52
Technology Integration Planning,
33, 54–64
Monitoring systems, 238
Moodle, 188
Morphing, 164
Movie player plug-ins, 196
Movies, creating as art form,
370–71
Moving Picture Experts Group
(MPEG) format, 215
Multicultural immersion, 224
Multidistrict fully online schools,
248
Multimedia authoring software, 20
Multimedia learning stations, 7
Multimedia software, 293
Multimodal communication, 278
Multimodal texts, 278
Multiple intelligences theory, 44, 45,
46, 47
Multiple means of expression
(MME), 409–10
Multiple means of representation
(MMR), 409
Multitasking, 14
Multi-user virtual environments
(MUVE), 252
Music
cloud generators and, 160
composition and production,
support for, 360–62
history, support for, 364–65
illegally downloading, 357
literacy, 356
performance, support for, 362–63
web development skills and, 192
Musical Instrument Digital
Interface (MIDI), 164, 353,
360–62
Musical intelligence, 47
Music editor, 164
Music instruction
downloading music illegally, 357
issues and challenges in, 356–58
music director as small business
administrator, 358
music literacy, changing
definition for, 356
popular music, technology, and
music instruction, 357–58
technology integration strategies
for, 358–65

Music piracy, 17
Music sequencers, 164, 356
Music synthesizers, 164
Music teachers
issues and applications, learning,
374
rubric to measure teacher
growth, 371–74
teaching teachers to integrate
technology, 371–74
training to meet standards,
356–57

NAEC, 366
NAfME, 357–58
National Art Education Association
(NAEA), 366
National Association for Music
Education (NAfME), 357–58
National Coalition for Core Arts
Standards (NCCAS), 371
National Council for the Social
Studies (NCSS), 336–38
National Council of Teachers of
English (NCTE), 262, 263, 281
National Council of Teachers of
Mathematics (NCTM),
308–10, 327
National Educational Technology
Standards (NETS), 18
National Education Policy Center
(NEPC), 249
National Governors Association
Center for Best Practices
(NGA Center), 17
National Research Council (NRC),
318
National Science Digital Library
(NSDL), 324
National Science Education
Standards (NSES), 318
National Science Foundation (NSF),
324
National Science Teachers
Association (NSTA), 318, 327
National Standards for Arts
Education, 366
Naturalist intelligence, 47
Navigation buttons, 180
Navigation links, 180, 197
Navigation options, 179–82
bookmarks, 181
buttons, 180
favorites, 181
history, 181
links, 180
online organizers, 181
quick response codes, 181
trouble shooting, 181–82
uniform resource locators,
179–80
NCTE/IRA Standards for the
English Language Arts, 262,
263, 281
Negative reinforcement, 37
Netiquette, 178–79
NETS for Students, 18
NETS for Teachers, 18
New literacies, 261–63
defining competencies and focus
for 21st-century literacies, 262
materials to develop literacy, 262
materials to organize
information, 262–63
New Media Consortium's (NMC)
Horizon Project, 25

Safety issues
  computer viruses and hacking, 175, 176
  in educational technology, 16
  fraud and phishing, 176
  Internet, 174–76
  online identity and reputation issues, 176
  social networking sites, 174–75
Sales pitches aimed at children, 175
SAMR model, 68, 69
Sans serif typeface, 145
Scaffolding theories, 43, 44
Scheduling tools, 161, 162
Science, technology, engineering, and mathematics (STEM), 75–76, 308, 318, 319–20
Science instruction, 318–29
  accountability for standards in, 318–19
  cloud generators and, 159
  Common Core State Standards for, 318
  issues and challenges in, 318–21
  K-8 science, 320
  scientific literacy, 320
  scientific talent, narrowing, 319–20
  teaching teachers to integrate technology, 327–29
  technology integration strategies for, 321–26
  virtual science labs, 320–21
Science teachers
  issues and applications, learning, 327
  rubric to measure teacher growth, 327, 328–29
  teaching teachers to integrate technology, 327–29
Scientific and Engineering Practices (S& EP), 318–19
Screen-capture software, 215
Screencasting, 86, 276
Screen readers, 413
Search engines, 183
Search tools and strategies, 183–84
  advanced searches, 183, 184
  keyword searches, 183
  subject index searches, 183
Security issues, Internet, 174–76
Segments, 197
Self-efficacy, 43
Selfie, 176
Self-paced distance learning, 53
Semantic differential, 61
Sensorimotor stage, 45
Sensor technology, 413
Sensory disabilities, 413–14
  American Sign Language, 414
  blind, 413
  deaf, 414
  partially sighted, 414
Sensory registers, 38
Serif typeface, 145
Sexting, 14
Short-term memory (STM), 38
Simulated activities, 221
Simulations, 340
Simulation software, 78, 87–92
  benefits of, 88, 89–90
  brief overview of, 89
  iterative simulations, 87
  limitations and problems related to, 90–91
  physical simulations, 87

procedural simulations, 88
selecting, 88
situational simulations, 88
using, strategies and guidelines for, 91–92
Single-district programs, 248
Site connection failures, 181–82
Situated cognition, 46
Situational simulations, 88
Skype, 185
Slide sorter, 135
SMART Table Interactive Learning Center, 146
Snail mail, 206
Social action projects, 221–22
Social activism theory, 42
Social issues in educational technology, 12, 13–15
  hacking, 14–15
  health-related concerns, 14
  malware, 14
  online behaviors, 14
  privacy issues, 12, 13
  spam, 14
  technology misuses, 14
  viruses, 14
Social media era, 6, 8
Social networking, 185–90
  blogs, 186–87
  chatrooms, 188
  microblogs, 187–88
  multitasking with, 14
  tools, 185–86
  video- and photo-sharing communities, 189
  wikis for classroom use, 188–89
Social networking sites (SNSs), 190
  integration strategies for, 190
  research on, 190
  safety and privacy issues for students, 174–75
Social presence, 296
Social studies instruction, 336–49
  cloud generators and, 159
  content and focus of, 339
  definition of social studies, 336
  information explosion, 339
  issues and challenges in, 336–39
  standards, 336–38
  technology integration strategies for, 340–47
Social studies teachers
  challenges for, 338
  issues and applications, learning, 348
  rubric to measure teacher growth, 348, 349
  teaching teachers to integrate technology, 348–49
Society of Health and Physical Educators (SHAPE), 383
Software, 12. See also Instructional software
  administrative, 12
  computer-aided design, 5
  computer algebra system, 314, 315
  emerging trends in, 25–26
  emerging trends in, 25–26
  FTP, 194
  instructional, 12
  interactive or dynamic geometry, 314
  multimedia authoring, 20
  for portfolios, 20
  productivity, 12

screen-capture, 215
  for technology integration, 66
  video editing, 215
  web development, 194
Software piracy, 17
Software suites, 109, 112, 142
Software support tools, 141–67. See also Software tools
  adapting for special needs, 149
  content-area tools, 141, 142, 163–67
  data collection and analysis tools, 141, 142, 149–54
  graphics tools, 141, 142, 156–60
  materials generators, 141, 142, 143, 144–49
  planning and organizing tools, 141, 142, 160–62
  recent developments in, 141, 142
  research and reference tools, 141, 142, 162–63
  software sites, 143
  testing and grading tools, 141, 142, 155–56
  types, overview of, 141, 142
Software tools, 109–35. See also Software support tools
  database software, 109, 110
  developments in, 111, 112
  file-exchange compatibility, 112
  mobile apps, 111, 112
  open-source software, 111
  overview of uses for, 109–11
  presentation software, 109, 110, 125–35
  reasons for using, 109
  software sites, 111
  software suites, 109, 112
  spreadsheet software, 109, 110, 121–25
  web-based collaboration tools, 111
  web-enabled features, 112
  word processing software, 109, 110, 112–20
Sounds, 158, 159
Southern Regional Education Board, 248
Spam, 14
Spatial intelligence, 47
Special education instruction, 403–18. See also Students with disabilities/special needs
  autism spectrum disorders, 407, 414–15
  educational reform and accountability, 406–7
  inclusion requirements, 404–5
  introduction to, 403
  issues and problems in, 403–7
  policy drivers of technology use in, 405–6
  technology integration strategies to meet special needs, 407–16
  Universal Design for Learning, 405–6
  web accessibility, 406
Special education teachers
  issues and applications, learning, 416, 418
  rubric to measure teacher growth, 416, 417
  teaching teachers to integrate technology, 416–18
Specialist language, 76

Special needs, adapting for. See Adapting for special needs
Special needs students. See Students with disabilities/special needs
Spell-check, 276
Spirometers, 387
Spreadsheet software, 121–25
  features, summary of, 122
  impact of, in education, 121–24
  instructional integration strategies, 124
  issues in using, 123
  overview of uses for, 109, 110–11
  productivity strategies, 123–24
  reasons for using, 121, 122
  research on impact of, 121, 122
  teaching spreadsheet skills, 125, 126
Spyware, 14
Stages of cognitive development, Bruner's, 46
Stages of cognitive development, Piaget's, 45
Standards
  art instruction, 366–67
  music instruction, 356–57
  physical and health education instruction, 383
  science instruction, 318–19
  in technology integration, 65
State-supported supplemental options, 248
Statistical software packages, 151
Storage media, 10
Storyboarding, 197
Streamed video and audio, 196
Student information systems (SISs), 153
Student research, 222
Student response systems (SRS), 10–11, 153–54
  integration strategies for, 154
  research on, 154
Students
  motivating and engaging, 22–23, 24
  preparing for the future, 24
  supporting learning needs, 23, 24
Students with disabilities/special needs. See also Adapting for special needs; Special education instruction
  access to technology resources, discrepancy in, 16, 62
  assistive technologies for, 16
  developing online courses, support for, 237
  educational options for, 27
  English and language arts, 266
  exercise and sport opportunities for, 388
  individualized educational program, 147, 148
  reading and writing tools, 267
  universal design for learning, 16
Subject index searches, 183
Switches, 413
Symbolic stage, 46
Symbols, 119
Systematic instructional design, 40
System development, emerging trends in, 25–26
Systems approaches to instructional design, 36, 40
Systems-thinking, 75